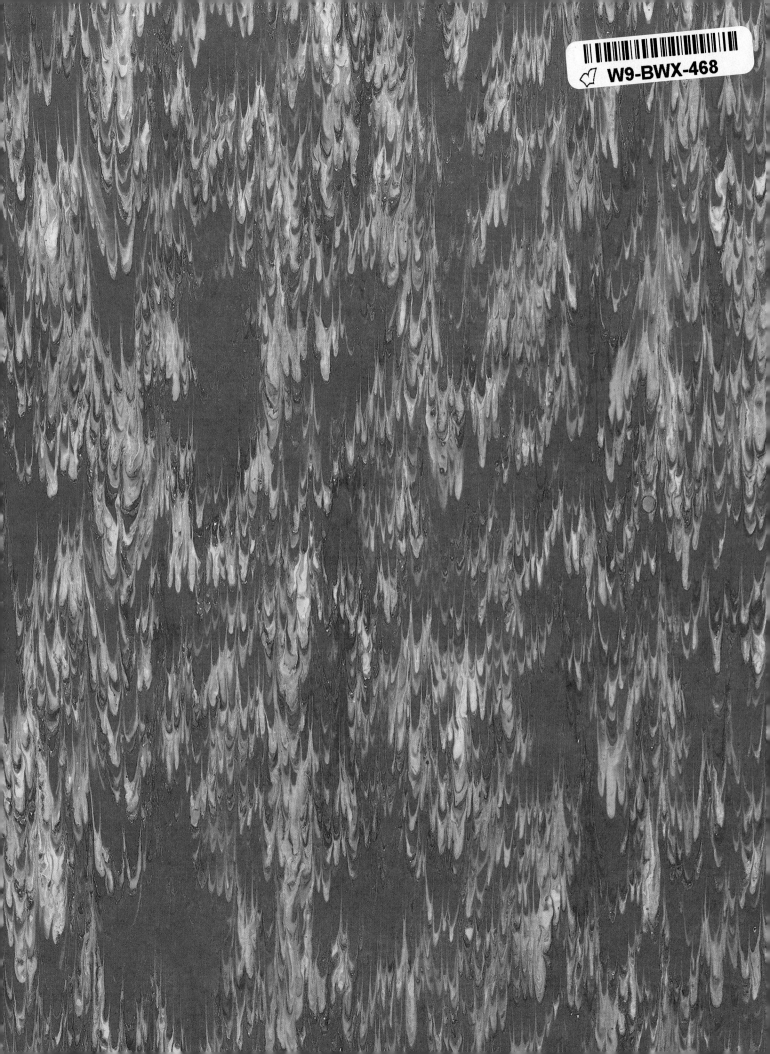

International Encyclopedia of Communications

THE UNIVERSITY OF PENNSYLVANIA

The *International Encyclopedia of Communications*
was conceived, developed, and edited at
The Annenberg School of Communications,
University of Pennsylvania.

International Encyclopedia of Communications

ERIK BARNOUW
Editor in Chief

GEORGE GERBNER
Chair, Editorial Board

WILBUR SCHRAMM
Consulting Editor

TOBIA L. WORTH
Editorial Director

LARRY GROSS
Associate Editor

Volume 1

Published jointly with
THE ANNENBERG SCHOOL OF COMMUNICATIONS,
University of Pennsylvania

OXFORD UNIVERSITY PRESS
New York   Oxford

Oxford University Press

Oxford   New York   Toronto
Delhi   Bombay   Calcutta   Madras   Karachi
Petaling Jaya   Singapore   Hong Kong   Tokyo
Nairobi   Dar es Salaam   Cape Town
Melbourne   Auckland

and associated companies in
Berlin   Ibadan

Copyright © 1989 by the Trustees of the University of Pennsylvania

Published jointly by
The Annenberg School of Communications,
University of Pennsylvania,
and Oxford University Press, Inc.,
200 Madison Avenue, New York, New York 10016

Oxford is a registered trademark of Oxford University Press

Library of Congress Cataloging-in-Publication Data

International encyclopedia of communications / Erik Barnouw, editor-in-chief . . . [et al.].
p.   cm.
Bibliography: p.
Includes index.
1. Communication—Dictionaries.   I. Barnouw, Erik, 1908–
P87.5.I5 1989   001.51′0321—dc19   88-18132   CIP
ISBN 0-19-504994-2 (set)
ISBN 0-19-505802-X (vol. 1)
ISBN 0-19-505803-8 (vol. 2)
ISBN 0-19-505804-6 (vol. 3)
ISBN 0-19-505805-4 (vol. 4)

2 4 6 8 9 7 5 3 1

Printed in the United States of America
on acid-free paper

Editorial Board

Editorial and Production Staff

AT THE UNIVERSITY OF PENNSYLVANIA

Editorial Director
Tobia L. Worth

Assistant Editors
Harold Branam   Lee Ann Draud   Pedro F. Hernández-Ramos
Catherine E. Kirkland   Deborah Rohr   John Ziff

Editing Coordinator
Lee Ann Draud

Art Editor
Gillian M. L. Speeth

Bibliographic Researcher
Michele A. Belluomini

Indexers
Cheryl Cutrona, *Director*
Michele A. Belluomini
Pedro F. Hernández-Ramos
Deborah Rohr

Project Manager
Robinette M. Dasher-Alston

Executive Assistant
Carol Welty Faris

Assistant to the Project Manager
Debra D. Williams

*Administrative Staff and
Computer Operations*
Lessie V. Boyd   Sharon Cothran
Rebekah A. Hendricks

AT OXFORD UNIVERSITY PRESS, NEW YORK

Executive Editor
William Mitchell

Senior Project Editor
Marion E. Britt

Managing Editor
Ellen B. Fuchs

Copyeditor
Wendy Warren Keebler

Permissions Assistants
Allan E. Bulley   Sydney G. Recht

Production Coordinator
Sarah Flanagan

Book Designer
Victoria Wong

Graphic Artist
Jeanyee Wong

Layout Artists
Woods End Studio, Yonkers, N.Y.

Contents

International Encyclopedia of Communications

Section Editors

Editorial Advisers

MURIEL G. CANTOR
Professor of Sociology, American
University, Washington, D.C.

JAMES W. CAREY
Dean, College of Communications,
University of Illinois at Urbana-
Champaign

THOMAS F. CARNEY
Professor of Communication Studies,
University of Windsor

STEVEN H. CHAFFEE
Janet M. Peck Professor of
International Communication and
Chair, Department of Communication,
Stanford University

JACK CHEN (CHEN I-WAN)
President, The Pear Garden in the West,
San Francisco; former Consultant
Editor, *Peking Review,* Beijing

NOAM CHOMSKY
Institute Professor, Department of
Linguistics and Philosophy,
Massachusetts Institute of Technology

ARTHUR C. CLARKE
Chancellor, University of Moratuwa,
Sri Lanka

THOMAS C. COCHRAN
Benjamin Franklin Professor Emeritus
of History, University of Pennsylvania

HERMAN COHEN JEHORAM
Professor of Intellectual Property,
Media, and Information Law,
Universiteit van Amsterdam

MICHAEL COLE
Professor of Communications and
Psychology and Director, Laboratory of
Comparative Human Cognition,
University of California, San Diego

PETER COWIE
Film historian, London and Helsinki

RITA CRUISE O'BRIEN
Fellow, London School of Economics
and Political Science, University of
London

DAVID CRYSTAL
Honorary Professor of Linguistics,
University College of North Wales

JONATHAN CULLER
Professor of English and Comparative
Literature, Cornell University

NABIL H. DAJANI
Assistant Dean, Faculty of Arts and
Sciences, American University of Beirut

CHIDANANDA DAS GUPTA
Arts Editor, *The Telegraph,* Calcutta

HAROLD DE BOCK
Director, Burke Inter/View B.V.,
Instituut voor Marktinformatie,
Amsterdam

BRENDA L. DERVIN
Professor and Chair, Department of
Communication, Ohio State University

JUAN E. DÍAZ BORDENAVE
International consultant in
communication and education, Rio de
Janeiro

HENRI GEORGES DIEUZEIDE
Director, Division of Structures,
Content, Methods, and Techniques of
Education, UNESCO, Paris

WIMAL DISSANAYAKE
Research Associate and Assistant
Director, Institute of Culture and
Communication, East-West Center,
Honolulu

WILSON P. DIZARD
Senior Fellow, Center for Strategic and
International Studies, Washington, D.C.

ARIEL DORFMAN
Chilean essayist and novelist; Visiting
Professor of Literature and Latin
American Studies, Duke University

SERGEI V. DROBASCHENKO
Professor of Film Studies and Deputy
Director, Cinema Art Institute, Moscow

UMBERTO ECO
Professor of Semiotics, Università degli
Studi, Bologna

ELIZABETH L. EISENSTEIN
Alice Freeman Palmer Professor of
History, University of Michigan, Ann
Arbor

PHOEBE C. ELLSWORTH
Professor of Psychology and Professor
of Law, University of Michigan, Ann
Arbor

HAROLD EVANS
Editor in Chief, *Condé-Nast's Traveler,*
New York

ITAMAR EVEN-ZOHAR
Professor of Poetics and Comparative
Literature, Porter Institute for Poetics
and Semiotics, Tel-Aviv University

CECILIA VON FEILITZEN
Senior Researcher, Centrum för
Masskommunikationsforskning,
Stockholms Universitet; Publik- och
programforskningsavdelningen, Sveriges
Radio

GLORIA D. FELICIANO
Professor of Communication, University
of the Philippines; President and
Chairman of the Board, International
Social Research and Development
Foundation, Inc., Quezon City

WILLIAM F. FORE
Assistant General Secretary for
Communication, National Council of
Churches in the U.S.A., New York

JAN FREESE
President and Director-General,
Datainspektionen, Stockholm

OSCAR H. GANDY, JR.
Associate Professor of Communications,
The Annenberg School of
Communications, University of
Pennsylvania

HERBERT J. GANS
Robert S. Lynd Professor of Sociology,
Columbia University

Preface

The ways in which members of the human species perceive and influence one another and envision their own roles in the scheme of things have been changed by a series of momentous innovations, which we now call a communications revolution. The revolution is clearly far from over.

But when did it begin? The revolution may be said to have begun when our ancestors started adding word-language to age-old repertoires of gesture, glance, body signal, touch, grunt, growl, moan, rhythm, intonation, melody. With the growth of word-language, humanity diverged increasingly from fellow species and acquired an oral tradition, tribal memory, and the beginnings of a history.

The revolution may be said to have moved through further phases as humans began to record on cave wall, stone tablet, bone, wood, bark, pottery, skin, and plant fibers messages that others might note. As such messages began to use symbol systems for conveying word-language, links with past and future were strengthened. The sense of community widened and deepened. Segments of humanity acquired their special recorded histories bolstered by artifacts, rituals, and sacred records. All this favored the complex evolution of societies and their hierarchies.

A further phase came with the devising of mechanisms for the mass production and distribution of words, images, and symbols through printing and paper and all their associated technologies. The reverberating effects have only gradually been perceived. The wider diffusion of information and ideas, sometimes circumventing those in power, could upset old orthodoxies and bring schisms and shifts in the social order. But it could also be used to consolidate power and extend hegemony. A growing deluge of messages embedded in multiplying languages, literary media, and works of art created larger social linkages as well as divisions.

Each of these phases brought great changes to the human experience. Most were spread over eons or centuries, so that few people felt they were living through anything that might be called a revolution. With the phases that followed, the situation has been different. The technologies of the past century, catapulting us from photography, film, telegraphy, telephone, and the broadcast media via video, cable, computer, satellite, and the laser beam into a telecommunications era, have set in motion such startling changes in our institutions and lives that the term *communications revolution* has become an ever-present reality to people everywhere. The resulting ferment has also generated a new and rapidly spreading field of academic study under the name *communications,* which takes as its domain the entire revolution, its social effects, and its meaning for the future.

The developments constituting the revolution, shaped largely by the human species itself, have at the same time reshaped it. Modern society is to an astonishing extent the constantly evolving product of this revolution. The centrality of communication in human history has become clear, explaining why such varied disciplines as anthropology, arts, education, ethology, history, journalism, law, linguistics, philosophy, political science, psychology, and sociology have all gravitated toward the study of communication processes and have collaborated in the creation of the new discipline.

The present work, a first effort to define the field in a comprehensive way, got its start in 1982 with a feasibility study under the leadership of George Gerbner of The Annenberg School of Communications, University of Pennsylvania. Within months Oxford University Press had joined the University of Pennsylvania as co-publisher. By the fall of 1983 a full-time staff was in place; supported by an international structure of editorial advisers and consultants, it began working its way toward an *International Encyclopedia of Communications*.

We include in communications all ways in which information, ideas, and attitudes pass among individuals, groups, nations, and generations. We offer entries on the histories and social roles of media from cuneiform tablets to communication satellites, from the genres of Nineveh to the genres of Hollywood. Other entries examine communication processes from psychological, sociological, anthropological, and other perspectives. Individuals who have enriched our understanding of these processes or who have made pioneering contributions to the evolution of media are discussed throughout the work, in some cases in separate "name entries." The role and influence of the arts, education, religion, commerce, journalism, politics, and other social activities in the diffusion of ideas are examined, as are the institutions that have grown up around them: libraries, museums, universities, broadcasting systems, advertising agencies, data banks, and telecommunications networks. Roadblocks to communication, psychological and societal, are analyzed. The historic communications impact of such developments as exploration, colonization, migration, revolution, and war is considered. A number of entries focus on forms of nonverbal communication—emphasizing that although each stage in communications history has added new ways of communicating, all have remained with us, in patterns of ever-growing complexity. Numerous types of animal communication, and the light they throw on human communication, are also examined. Special communications phenomena and problems in various parts of the world are analyzed, and the challenging tasks of intercultural communication form a pervasive theme in the work.

A communication system, like the human nervous system, sorts and distributes data and provides for their storage and retrieval. Its signals can evoke memories, rouse emotion, and trigger action. As in a nervous system, aberrations can cause deep disturbances in the organism. Communications scholars concern themselves with everything that may block, disrupt, poison, or distort communication. They strive to understand such aberrations and to further the quest for remedies.

In almost all our articles you will find cross-references to others, throwing light on related topics that may in turn lead you to still other topics, a process that should reflect and illuminate the fascinating ramifications of all communication. Following the trails of cross-references, we hope and trust that you will find what you are looking for, and more besides.

ERIK BARNOUW
Editor in Chief

Foreword

Creating the *International Encyclopedia of Communications* has been a six-year journey of discovery, of worldwide recruitment and mobilization of talent, of many serendipitous finds and some misses—and, in general, a great intellectual adventure.

It began on a day in 1982 in my office as Dean of The Annenberg School of Communications, University of Pennsylvania, as I sat talking with Tobia Worth of our staff. She had long publishing experience, specializing in encyclopedias, and now wondered whether our field might be ready for an important new initiative. She did not have to say it twice.

Soon afterward I had an opportunity to mention the idea to Walter H. Annenberg, the founder of the Annenberg Schools of Communications. I did not have to say it twice either. Ambassador Annenberg replied instantly. I remember his words: "This is a big-league idea."

A feasibility study was launched. Its task was to probe every aspect of the proposed venture to make certain that, if undertaken, it would be on a sound intellectual foundation. A steering committee, consulting a diversity of scholars, began drafting a conceptual framework that might serve to generate ideas for topics and titles. This framework recognized three ways of approaching the study of communication. Although the reader would not guess it from reading the articles in these volumes, the feasibility study began with this three-phased survey of the field:

1. Communication *systems* and *organizations*. The history of communications; its institutions from library and school to data base and television network; public policy and technology related to communications and culture; the structure, regulation, and social functions of the mass media; theories of social communication systems.
2. Communication *modes, media,* and *codes*. Theories of communication content, information, semiotics, signs, symbols, and the strategies we use in the articulation and interpretation of meaning across modes, media, and codes. *Modes* comprises such systems as the visual-pictorial, the verbal-lexical, the musical, and the socio-gestural. *Media* refers to specific means of articulating within modes—such as film and video, painting and drawing, speaking and writing, piano and violin. *Codes* has to do with specific conventions by which messages are framed in specific media or their genres. These modes, media, and codes can be studied within and across aesthetic, social, cultural, political, and ideological contexts.
3. Communication *behavior* and *effects*. Study of the ways in which people learn and develop the ability to articulate and interpret symbolic behavior; how beliefs, attitudes, and public opinions are formed and maintained or changed by a variety of symbolic means ranging from interpersonal interaction to enculturation and socialization through the mass media. Research methods used in such studies.

During the fall and winter of 1982–1983 three gatherings of noted communication scholars were convened, each focusing on one of the above approaches. How well could its needs be satisfied in an encyclopedia format? Each gathering also debated the general feasibility of the proposed encyclopedia, how it might serve the field, what form it should take (alphabetical or thematic), what its scope should be, what users it might seek to serve.

In each of these gatherings, the intense discussion was dominated by the following concerns: (1) to build a work of enduring value, (2) to make this work international in scope by virtue of both its contributors and its coverage, (3) to draw on the work of leading scholars and practitioners in their special areas of knowledge, (4) to draw from the arts and social sciences those interests that could best be seen, or reinterpreted, in the context of communications, and (5) to use the dimension of history, through both direct narrative and biography, to convey the solidity of the field at a time when technology is soaring and reintegration of knowledge seems vital.

Early in each of the meetings, words of caution were heard. Was this the time? In view of the momentous growth of the field, was the project practical—or quixotic? Was it premature? But during the hours and days of discussion, skepticism vanished and a broad consensus developed. Creation of an encyclopedia of communications was considered both feasible and timely.

By great good fortune, the leadership of our choice became enthusiastically committed to the project. Joining us as editor in chief was media historian Erik Barnouw; as consulting editor, the late Wilbur Schramm, a founder of the field of communications study; as associate editor, Larry Gross, whose truly encyclopedic scholarship has infused many aspects of this work; and as editorial director, Tobia L. Worth, originator of the idea and manager of the project.

It was decided that concentrating on basic long-range trends and processes would be the best way to avoid early obsolescence in a rapidly changing, technology-driven field. It was also determined that the work should be addressed to college students, scholars, professionals, and educated laypersons. Physically it would be a four-volume set, printed in two colors, of about 1.2 million words, with approximately twelve hundred illustrations. A tentative schedule envisioned a five-year timetable culminating in a 1988–1989 publication date. The work is being published on schedule.

The *International Encyclopedia of Communications* is an attempt to define, reflect, summarize, and explain the field in an accessible, comprehensive, and authoritative way. It signals a new stage in the development of the field of communications as an area of knowledge, study, practice, technique, and research, and as an academic discipline.

On behalf of the Editorial Board, I want to thank for their contributions and support Ambassadors Walter Annenberg and Lee Annenberg, the other Trustees and officers of The Annenberg School and the University of Pennsylvania, a very able editorial staff, our publishing partners at Oxford University Press, and the dedicated members of the feasibility study groups, almost all of whom subsequently participated as contributors, editors, or advisers, appearing in lists elsewhere in these volumes.

GEORGE GERBNER
Chair, Editorial Board

Introduction

A new encyclopedia is one of the most daring of publishing ventures. A new encyclopedia that is also the first in its field carries an even greater burden. It was our task to make all the elements of this work—formal and pictorial as well as textual—reflect our commitment to the field of communications, to explicating it, and to honoring its international scope.

Under the following headings the reader will find our decisions about handling the formal elements of this encyclopedic reference work.

Organization. The *International Encyclopedia of Communications (IEC)* is structured alphabetically, on the word-by-word principle. Hence, "New Wave Film," in this system, precedes "News, Television." Each alphabetic section is announced by a letterbreak page, which displays a letter of the alphabet accompanied by a text fragment drawn from *The Oxford English Dictionary* (Oxford: Clarendon Press, 1933, 1961). Each fragment is the introductory etymological description of the particular letter.

Article Titles. The words *communication* and *communications* are used sparingly in titles because it is implicit in this encyclopedia that every article marks the subject as germane to an understanding of the field. When *communication* does appear in an article title (as in "Group Communication"), it is because lucidity would suffer from its absence.

Composite Entries. We have often clustered articles on related topics, written by individual authors, under a common heading, to reinforce their relation to one another. Such composites are signaled by a brief headnote to indicate the scope of the subject, followed by a list of the constituent sections. Thus, such subjects as newspaper trends come into sharper focus when developments in different areas of the world are presented in a sequence rather than located under a geographical title. The first section of a composite entry is often an overview, offering the reader a broad introduction to the topic that relates its parts.

Name Entries. Biographical entries in the *IEC* are career biographies only. We have called them name entries because they make no pretense of presenting the full range of information found in a standard biographical reference book. As such, these articles are in most cases shorter than other entries, ranging between five hundred and one thousand words. In planning them, an arbitrary birth date of December 31, 1919, was established as qualification for inclusion of living persons among the *IEC*'s name entries, thereby avoiding the difficulties associated with writing about the accomplishments of people who are currently engaged in shaping the field.

Name-entry subjects were selected with a view to their unique relationships to significant communications issues. In many cases, their repeated mention in different articles attests to the need for a more in-depth discussion of their work. The focus of the name entries is on those aspects of the subject's life and achievements most relevant to the study of communications. The entry on Charles S. Peirce, for example, emphasizes his theory of signs and his contribution to the study of meaning rather than his research on mathematics and logic.

Cross-references. Three types of cross-reference have been used, all indicated by the typographical distinction of being set in even small capitals (e.g., ANIMAL SIGNALS). The first type occurs naturally in running text to signal the existence of an entry in the identical form of the article title itself. There is one exception to this rule: because of the clumsiness and redundancy engendered by inverting names to indicate biographical entries in their precise form, we have elected to indicate them in natural order. Hence, "the U.S. linguist EDWARD SAPIR" instead of "the U.S. linguist Edward Sapir (*see* SAPIR, EDWARD)." For the same reason birth and death dates, although part of the article title proper, are not used in cross-references.

The second type of cross-reference is the *see* or *see also* reference. These are used to enlarge and enrich the reader's understanding of a subject by announcing the presence of other, related articles that might not be obvious from the text itself.

The third type is the blind reference, also known as a reference entry or a main reference. Blind references appear in alphabetical order in article-title position. They can direct the reader to an article alphabetized under an equivalent term (e.g., from FILM to MOTION PICTURES) or to an article alphabetized under an alternate form of its title (e.g., from MUSICAL, FILM to FILM, MUSICAL). The blind reference can also, in annotated form, direct the reader from a single term to multiple articles that will provide complete coverage of an important concept (e.g., from AUDIENCE to a great variety of relevant articles).

Bibliographies. Most articles are followed by brief bibliographies. The citations were selected by the author with some emendations made by the various Section Editors. These suggestions for further reading include basic texts and landmark journal literature as well as texts embodying a more general review of the literature on the subject. Writings in languages other than English have been included when appropriate. The bibliographies reflect the interdisciplinary nature of the evolving field of communications.

The Research Bibliographer has verified the accuracy of each entry using standard references, such as the National Union Catalog of the United States, Online Computer Library Center (OCLC) records, the national bibliographies of various countries, and the Cumulative Book Index. With few exceptions works are listed alphabetically by author, with information concerning additional series titles or conference proceedings also provided as needed within the citation. The exceptions are bibliographies that cite the works of one author only. In those cases, the works are listed in chronological order of publication so as to present the reader with a conceptual development of the author's ideas. Works cited that were in press at the time the *IEC* was printed have been listed as such.

Art. There are more than eleven hundred illustrations in the *International Encyclopedia of Communications,* halftone and line art, as well as maps, charts, and tables. Some illustrative material has been provided by authors, but in most cases it has been chosen by the Art Editor. Most often, when a figure illustrates an example from the text, there is a specific textual reference to it; elsewhere art is used to reflect generic ideas and often to enlarge the scope of the text. Although the overall look of the volumes has been a basic concern, each illustration has been selected for its value to the article; long sequences of articles may carry no art, whereas certain articles may be heavily illustrated. The art, in accordance with the principles governing text, has been chosen with an eye to emphasizing the international perspective of this work.

Topical Guide. In the back matter of volume 4 will be found a topical guide, or synoptic outline of contents, organized into large sections containing article titles that relate to the general heading. Every entry in the *IEC* appears in at least one of these sections. The Topical Guide is a valuable tool for students and librarians seeking a structure for studying the field of communications.

Articles are grouped under the following headings: Advertising and Public Relations, Ancient World, Animal Communication, Area Studies, Arts, Communications Research, Computer Era, Education, Folklore, Government

Regulation, Institutions, International Communication, Journalism, Language and Linguistics, Literature, Media, Middle Ages, Motion Pictures, Music, Nonverbal Communication, Photography, Political Communication, Print Media, Radio, Religion, Speech, Television, Theater, Theories of Communication, and Theorists.

Index. The index for the *IEC* is an analytical, or complex topical, index containing more than fifteen thousand entries. Every article appears as a main entry and may also appear as a subentry. Our concern has been to reach an international audience of specialists in communications as well as readers with a general interest in the field. Because communications research is done all over the world and also because it often includes work from other disciplines, there is not always agreement among scholars in the use and meaning of terminology. Accordingly, terms used in index entries have been chosen with the aim both of representing the field using its own terminology and of accommodating the needs and interests of nonspecialists. We have therefore included blind index entries for many words and concepts that will direct readers to the word or phrase we have chosen for the actual entry. This concern for adequate coverage of the variations in communications terminology, heightened by our sense of responsibility for being the first encyclopedia in the field, has resulted in an index of unusual depth.

Acknowledgments. The contributions of many people are visible from the presence of their names in one section or another in the front matter of volume 1: Section Editors, Editorial Advisers, and editorial and production staffs at both the University of Pennsylvania and Oxford University Press. The excellence of their work, and the close and rewarding relationships that sprang from our association, has infused every page of these volumes.

The women and men of the editorial and administrative staff of the *IEC* deserve special recognition for their exceptional achievement in realizing the dream of this work. Their expertise and fierce devotion to our common aim cannot be overstated.

I must single out here the contribution of a few of the people who made valuable contributions as consultants in the initial, conceptual stages of our encyclopedia, especially during the feasibility study preceding formal staff work: David I. Eggenberger, former Director of Publications, National Archives, Washington, D.C.; David L. Sills, Editor, *International Encyclopedia of the Social Sciences*, and Executive Associate, Social Science Research Council, New York; Barbara A. Chernow, Chernow Editorial Services, Inc., New York; and Marsha Siefert, Editor, *Journal of Communication*. We thank them all.

We also thank Elvira Fitzgerald, Assistant Dean, and Mary Brennan, Business Manager, of The Annenberg School of Communications, University of Pennsylvania, for their unfailing and sympathetic support in all matters relating to the physical comfort and financial sanity of the project.

Working with our colleagues at Oxford University Press has been an especially happy experience. At Editorial Board meetings Sheldon Meyer, David Attwooll, and William Mitchell lent us strong intellectual support, as well as a feeling of camaraderie. Marion Britt was our principal and almost daily liaison for four years; we thank her for her devotion to us and to the project. Claude Conyers arrived at a late but critical moment in the life of the *IEC*, taking over supervision of its final production stages with great skill and exceptional grace.

I would also like to express the inexpressible: my thanks to and appreciation of the role played by Carol Welty Faris, who, in addition to doing invaluable backup research, supported us with unflagging patience.

TOBIA L. WORTH
Editorial Director

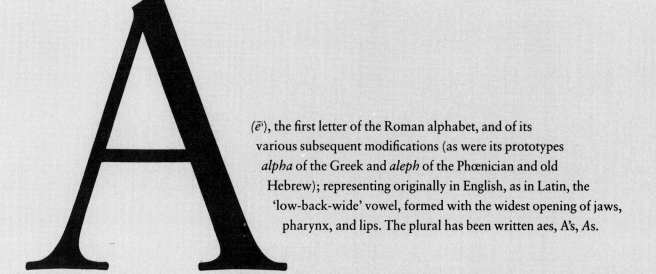

A ($\bar{e}^1$), the first letter of the Roman alphabet, and of its various subsequent modifications (as were its prototypes *alpha* of the Greek and *aleph* of the Phœnician and old Hebrew); representing originally in English, as in Latin, the 'low-back-wide' vowel, formed with the widest opening of jaws, pharynx, and lips. The plural has been written aes, A's, As.

ACTING

Acting style pertains to a general theory of communication as a vague but powerful language, a CODE of substituted behaviors, and a phenomenon of social intercourse. As a language it includes the actor's formation of images, gestures, intonations, rhythms, postures, silences, and facial expressions governed by a general grammar of theatrical convention (see FACIAL EXPRESSION). To characterize acting style as NONVERBAL COMMUNICATION frames the issue too narrowly. Acting embodies the expressive delivery of the spoken word as well as BODY MOVEMENT and GESTURE. It also entails the actor's use of costumes, settings, and properties to shape the MEANING of his or her actions by placing them in an appropriate physical context. George Henry Lewes, the Victorian DRAMA critic and psychologist, called all these diverse expressive elements the "actor's symbols." They seem to signify the world directly, without the interpolation of arbitrary signs (see SIGN). With the speed of gesture they can locate a PERFORMANCE in the correct social milieu and the appropriate theatrical GENRE—COMEDY (high or low), TRAGEDY, travesty. Style may be in part unique to the individual actor, as in CHARLES CHAPLIN's style, but it more often identifies a tradition or a school, as in the style of Balinese PUPPETRY.

Issues in the Analysis of Acting Style

Style by definition is somewhat removed from reality, but it also constitutes the actor's principal means of intensifying the truths he or she has imaginatively discovered. Style is a highly selective representation of human action, continually mediating between the public's various preconceptions about the natural order of life and the THEATER's aesthetic embodiment of it. As Michel Saint-Denis said in *Theatre: The Rediscovery of Style,* "Style does not lie. It is the expression of real understanding, of deep communication with the world and its secrets."

Though we might assume initially that style in acting is opposed to REALISM (thinking of the Japanese No or Kabuki actor, say, as rigidly stylized and of the Method actor trained in the United States as living the role), deeper reflection reveals that realism is itself a pronounced theatrical style. U.S. actor Marlon Brando's celebrated gutturalisms represent a rigorously circumscribed shorthand of the human experience. Conversely, the great Japanese Kabuki actor Sakatu Tojuro, quoted in *The Actors' Analects* (ca. 1700), remarked on his own style: "In acting, I think that everyday life should be the model." Historians know that conventions remain unrecognized until they are nearly outgrown. Performances once thought to be the epitome of naturalness and realistic

detail eventually seem dated and even risible, as old movies often reveal. Viewed in broad terms, then, all acting is stylized behavior, continuously developing from period to period or even from audience to audience. The relation of style to reality is always relative. At once social and aesthetic, it rests on the readiness of the community to accept the essential paradox of the actor, the actor's double being.

Theatrical conventions, like the rituals in which some of them originated, might also be interpreted as a code (see RITUAL). The rules of operation of this code are largely preestablished, but they can be modified spontaneously in performance, as anthropologist Victor Turner noted in *From Ritual to Theatre*: "The rules may 'frame' the performance, but the 'flow' of action and interaction within that frame may conduce to hitherto unprecedented insights and even generate new symbols and meanings, which may be incorporated into subsequent performances." The successful operation of the code, however, depends on the mutual assent of the celebrants (performers and spectators) to a specific agenda of substitutions. What René Girard has said about sacrificial substitution in *Violence and the Sacred* applies by extension to the stylized relationship of the actor to the reality he or she represents. Sacrificial substitution partially conceals the displacement, the surrogation of the victim, on which the rite is based, yet at the same time it retains its awareness that the original object of the sacrifice has been replaced by another. As a "monstrous double," the actor stands in for the king who must die. In a more expansive sense the actor may double the audience itself. As the Polish director Jerzy Grotowski has said, the actor is there not *for* us but *instead* of us.

Acting style grows from the elaboration of these codified substitutions. Like ritual expectancy among initiates, style regulates the transfer of behavior from the originals to the surrogates. It establishes the propriety of some behaviors and the indecorum of others. It authorizes certain actions, gestures, intonations, and expressions in relation to the originals they double. As in the performance of a ritual, one false substitution in the theater may ruin the efficacy of the rite. In ritual and in drama the final arbiter is nature. This principle of regulated substitution underlies the most famous of all pronouncements on acting style, Hamlet's advice to the Players: "o'erstep not the modesty of nature," he urges, for to substitute falsely "out-Herods Herod" as if "Nature's journeymen had made men, and not made them well."

History of Theatrical Style

The history of theatrical style demonstrates that nature has been variously understood at different times and places. The ancient theatrical gesture of grasping

Figure 1. *(Acting)* Nikolai Cherkasov in Sergei Eisenstein's *Ivan Grozny, Part 1*, 1944. The Museum of Modern Art/Film Stills Archive.

or striking the knees to express grief over the loss of a child, for instance, seems arbitrary unless we realize that a popular belief in antiquity was that the locus of sperm production was in the kneecaps. The *Natyasastra*, the ancient Sanskrit "Science of Dramaturgy," systematically catalogs twenty-four movements of one hand alone and thirty-six of the EYES, but these stylized signs stand in for complex correspondences, moods, and states of mind, universalized in the direct experience of the competent Sanskrit audience. Even the substitution that we take to be the clearest evidence of high stylization in ancient and oriental acting—MASK wearing—seems somewhat less radical when we reckon with a concept of personality (from *persona*, "mask") at once more public and more stable than our modern one. The importance that the classical theater attached to the public setting of dramatic action (confirmed by the continuous presence of the chorus) in contrast to the pervasiveness of the private settings in the modern theater highlights an important stylistic distinction. This distinction is between *presentational* acting style, which

Figure 2. *(Acting)* Katsukawa Shunko, *Kabuki Actors in Dance*, 1781. Honolulu Academy of Arts, James A. Michener Collection.

explicitly acknowledges the presence of the audience, and *representational* acting style, which explicitly denies it. Theater practitioners commonly speak of various levels of stylization existing between the presentational "theater theatrical" at one extreme and the representational theater of illusions and slices of life at the other. In the twentieth century these styles may coexist side by side, even in the same artist's work. André Antoine, the father of French theatrical naturalism, who once arranged sofas facing upstage from the curtain line to perfect the realistic impression of a four-sided room and whose Théâtre Libre shortly became known as "the theatre of Antoine's back," finally discovered "true reality in acting" on the completely bare stage of Jacques Copeau's Théâtre du Vieux-Colombier. Russian actor-director Vsevolod Meyerhold first mastered the naturalistic style of his mentor, Konstantin Stanislavsky, then broke away to found the radically theatrical Biomechanical school. German playwright and theorist Bertolt Brecht urged the stylization of the oriental theater on his actors concurrently with the art of *gestus*, the commonly intelligible social gesture. Brecht and Stanislavsky, seemingly irreconcilable on the question of style, both regarded the acting of Chinese female impersonator Mei Lan-fang as exemplary. But in broad historical terms acting in the modern theater has generally evolved away from the presentational style of the classical past, a trend reinforced by the development of cinema and television.

Until the eighteenth century the close connection between acting and ORATORY, as described in such rhetorics as the *Institutio oratoria* of the Roman rhetorician Quintilian, established the physical orientation of the actor toward the public. Early prints show the actors opened up to the audience and lined up along the apron of the stage. This style was based on the idea that orators physically stirred the passions of their auditors through eye-to-eye contact (the same power accounts for love at first sight and the "evil eye"). Spectators actually occupied seats onstage in European theaters until around 1750, an unambiguous testimony to the public occasion of the actor's art and a considerable obstacle to making an entrance in a hooped skirt. Although rules of oratorical declamation circumscribed the actor's vocal delivery and gesture, particularly in tragedy, these too were founded on nature. Classical RHETORIC, following ancient medical superstition, forbade gesturing with the left hand alone. An eyewitness account of the great English tragedian Thomas Betterton shows the persistence of these doctrines as the source of natural style around 1700: "His Left Hand frequently lodg'd in his Breast, between his Coat and his Waistcoat, while with his Right, he prepared his Speech." This style eventually devolved into the "teapot school," so called on account of the characteristic silhouette of its practitioners. As late as 1815 English critic Leigh Hunt deprecated "the puttings forth of the old oratorical right hand," but by that time the system of nature that had rendered such gestures intelligible and acceptable as substitutions for natural behavior had passed into oblivion.

During the eighteenth century acting style changed markedly under the influence of new doctrines of natural law. Acting of this period, as described in the many manuals and commentaries that replaced old rhetorics, classified the human passions into well-defined mechanical poses, or "points," that climaxed a sequence of preparatory actions. Acting style shared with history painting the doctrine of the "fruitful moment," a stillness in time charged with pathos. English actor David Garrick was the supreme master of eighteenth-century style, but his audiences believed that he had rediscovered nature by "breaking the tones" of chanted declamation and by incorporating elements of comedy into tragic acting. In France the philosophe DENIS DIDEROT set forth a theory in *The Paradox of Acting* (1773) that accommodated the actor's divided self within the emerging representational style. At midcentury Garrick and Voltaire banished the spectators from the stage. Writing against the presentational style, Diderot articulated for the first time the "theory of the fourth wall," urging actors to play scenes wholly absorbed within the frame of the proscenium arch as if the curtain had not yet risen. He idolized the tragedienne Mlle. Clairon for her intense powers of absorption, her ability to generate a complete illusion of character without any acknowledgment of the presence of the audience: "She is the informing soul of a huge figure, which is her outward casing, and in which her efforts had enclosed her."

This kind of self-absorption points the way toward the subsequent development of modern acting style. The romantic acting of Edmund Kean in England and Pavel Mochalov in Russia, for instance, emphasized the explosive revelation of deep interior motives. As romantic interest in the prior biography of dramatic character intensified (there were even studies of the girlhoods of Shakespeare's heroines), more elaborate renderings of inverted psychological states took the stage. Many of the great stars of the nineteenth-century theater (who had distinctive personal and national styles), including Rachel (Élisa Félix) in France, William Charles Macready in England, Edwin Booth in the United States, and Eleonora Duse in Italy, were celebrated for their ability to evoke the inner subtleties of complex behavior. They excelled particularly at making exquisitely wrought transitions between powerful states of contradictory emotion. Concurrently the development of the private setting of the modern domestic interior severed the actors from the public and altered their style of playing to the representational MODE. The way was prepared for the development of Stanislavsky's psychological realism and ultimately for the absorptive interiority of film-acting styles.

See also MIME; MUSIC THEATER.

Bibliography. William Archer, *Masks or Faces: A Study in the Psychology of Acting,* London, 1888; Toby Cole and Helen Krich Chinoy, eds., *Actors on Acting* (1949), rev. ed., New York, 1970; Edwin Duerr, *The Length and Depth of Acting,* New York, 1962; René Girard, *Violence and the Sacred* (La violence et le sacré), trans. by Patrick Gregory, Baltimore, Md., 1977; Michael Goldman, *The Actor's Freedom: Toward a Theory of Drama,* New York, 1975; Alois M. Nagler, *Sources of Theatrical History,* New York, 1952; Joseph R. Roach, *The Player's Passion: Studies in the Science of Acting,* Newark, Del., 1985; Michel Saint-Denis, *Theatre: The Rediscovery of Style,* New York, 1960; Victor Turner, *From Ritual to Theatre: The Human Seriousness of Play,* New York, 1982.

JOSEPH R. ROACH

ADORNO, THEODOR (1903–1969)

German philosopher and music critic. Born in Frankfurt, Theodor Adorno studied philosophy, sociology, psychology, and music at the University of Frankfurt. He moved in 1925 to Vienna, where he studied composition for three years with Alban Berg and participated in the musical discussions of the Schoenberg circle. In 1931 he became a privatdocent (instructor) at the University of Frankfurt and began an informal association with the Institute of Social Research (the institutional basis of the later Frankfurt school of critical theory). After the Nazis seized power he emigrated to Britain and continued his studies in Oxford before moving to New York and becoming a full member of the institute in 1938. In the United States Adorno continued his philosophical writings and studies of music. He also participated in a research project on prejudice and authoritarianism that resulted in an influential collective work, *The Authoritarian Personality* (1950). When the institute returned to Frankfurt in 1950, Adorno became assistant director and, in 1959, director.

All of Adorno's work was concerned with communication—with the creation, diffusion, and deformations of CULTURE in its diverse forms. One of his earlier works (in collaboration with Max Horkheimer), *Dialektic der Aufklärung* (Dialectic of Enlightenment, 1947), includes an essay on "the culture industry," which argues that modern mass culture is "depraved" as a consequence of the "fusion of culture and entertainment" and, further, that the merging of the culture industry with ADVERTISING makes both simply "a procedure for manipulating men." The critique of culture as IDEOLOGY became one of the distinguishing features of critical theory, in the writings of Horkheimer and Herbert Marcuse as well as Adorno, and it has persisted in the more recent work of Jürgen Habermas, in his studies of legitimacy in modern societies and of the meaning of cultural modernity.

Against mass culture as a system of DECEPTION and manipulation and against positivist science, which aims at the domination of nature and thereby contributes to political domination, Adorno counterposed the critical and liberating function of "genuinely modern art," which he represented in his last, unfinished work, *Ästhetische Theorie* (Aesthetic Theory), as having the capacity to negate existing reality and provide intimations of what human society could become (*see* ART). Rejecting what he regarded as the narrow and misleading conceptions of classical Marxism (including the Hegelian Marxism of his own earlier work) and of "scientism" in all its forms (positivism, empiricism, critical rationalism), Adorno ultimately formulated a social and aesthetic theory that was almost wholly negative and critical—a theory that became influential in the radical movements of the 1960s but has been strongly criticized by some later writers as expressing in extremely vague terms only an unacknowledged skepticism and despair.

See also COMMUNICATIONS RESEARCH: ORIGINS AND DEVELOPMENT; MARX, KARL; MARXIST THEORIES OF COMMUNICATION.

Bibliography. Martin Jay, *Adorno*, London and Cambridge, Mass., 1984; Leszek Kolakowski, *Main Currents of Marxism* (Główne nurty marksizmu), Vol. 3, chap. 10, trans. by P. S. Falla, Oxford, 1978.

TOM BOTTOMORE

ADVERTISING

This entry consists of four articles:
1. Overview
2. History of Advertising
3. Advertising Agency
4. Advertising Economics

1. OVERVIEW

Since ancient times advertising has been communication designed to attract favorable attention to goods or services (see section 2, below). In modern societies it generally refers to the use of mass media to carry paid messages, whether for a commercial purpose or to advance a cause, an institution, or a political candidate.

Advertising has become a ubiquitous and powerful element in many contemporary societies. It is also a major factor in the shaping and operation of the whole mass communication system, for which it provides the primary economic support in most countries. At one extreme, advertising as a form of sales promotion borders on such activities as pricing, packaging, store design, display, the offering of sales incentives, product sampling, and personal selling. At the other end of the spectrum, it fuses with publicity, PUBLIC RELATIONS, PROPAGANDA, and politics.

A basic function of advertising is to establish a presence, to create awareness, as in the case of the large gilded effigy of a shoe over the medieval shoemaker's door. But advertising also seeks to reinforce that awareness by reminders when the product and the point of sale are remote. Advertising is informative even when it provides only the price of merchandise and the address of the seller. It can be directly persuasive when it proclaims the merits of what is for sale. And advertising, especially when carried out through time in a consistent style, provides the advertiser with a reputation derived from the messages' form, content, and context.

Advertising encompasses the use of an extraordinarily heterogeneous assortment of communications media: package and label design; signs of paint and neon; show windows and in-store displays; billboards and posters (outdoors and in public vehicles); skywriting and aerial streamers; balloons; leaflets and flyers; catalogs; announcements; letters and postcards; coupon offers; matchbook covers; calendars; books and book jackets; magazines, newspapers, and other publications (distributed free or paid for by readers); telephone directory listings; lantern slides; and MOTION PICTURES, RADIO, television, teletext, and VIDEOTEX.

The proportion of all advertising represented by these various media has changed over time with the emergence of new media, and it varies from country to country depending not only on the stage of development but on the restrictions in force. In the United States the major media—daily newspapers, television, direct mail, magazines, and radio—generally account for well over half of all advertising investments, with newspapers and television generally winning the largest shares. In a number of other countries (the Federal Republic of Germany, Sweden, Norway, and Belgium, for example) advertising on television has been restricted by law in an effort to safeguard the financial health of the print media.

Relation to Consumption

The growth of advertising has been linked to that of the market economy and to a productive manufacturing capacity adequate to satisfy consumer demand. But advertising is also highly visible in less advanced countries like those of Latin America and South Asia, where a consuming elite coexists with a predominantly subsistence economy. Advertising has also found a small but growing niche in socialist countries, in spite of the long-standing Marxist contempt for it as the epitome of capitalism's wasteful competitive spirit.

Fundamental to the critique of advertising, which many non-Marxists share, is the thesis that it results in a misallocation of economic resources by encouraging the consumption of products and services that are socially undesirable or unnecessary. Advertising

Figure 1. *(Advertising—Overview)* Side street in Tokyo. Courtesy of Japan Air Lines.

can successfully introduce new products and create a market for them. It can also be used ingeniously to increase a particular competitor's market position. There is little solid indication, however, that advertising can in itself build the consumption of an established product that has remained unchanged in its attributes.

Consumer surveys find that objections to advertising generally mask objections to the advertised products or services themselves. So long as a society permits these to be sold in a free and competitive market, restrictions on advertising would merely channel sales pressures into alternative forms of promotion.

The percentage of gross national product spent on advertising varies greatly from country to country, just as advertising's percentage of sales revenues varies within each country for different types of industries. The advertising-to-sales ratio is generally lowest for expensive products and for those sold to limited numbers of industrial users rather than to the general public. The ratio is highest for consumer products characterized by small differences between competing market entries. For such "parity products," advertising must depart farthest from its primary informational function in order to create a symbolic aura of special identity for a particular company, brand, or store. In this process, whatever is advertised is endowed with meanings and values extraneous to its essential function. The consumer may be lured with nonverbal intimations of health, wealth, romance, and esteem (*see* MOTIVATION RESEARCH).

Advertising styles. Since parity products are widely used and frequently purchased, consumers make purchase decisions over and over with considerable turnover in their selection of brands. Thus each brand requires a continuing reminder of its existence, if only on the premise that familiarity leads to approval. As a result, advertising for packaged goods such as soap, instant coffee, hand lotion, beer, and deodorants has a prominence out of all proportion to their actual places in the consumer economy. This type of advertising attracts the greatest visibility and comment and is notable for its stylistic trendiness.

Styles in advertising come and go, reflecting its fast, competitive pace, the mobility of personnel, and a penchant for emulating innovators. From its origins, advertising has used humor gently, brashly, tongue-in-cheek, to gain attention or approval. It has exploited fears and fantasies. It has used personal testimonials by authorities, by nonauthoritative but well-known personalities, by company spokespersons, and by ordinary consumers captured in a pseudodocumentary "slice of life." It has featured beautiful women, cuddly animals, and engaging children. It has been dryly informative and irrationally emotional. It has knocked the competition head on. It has screamed and whispered.

Figure 2. *(Advertising—Overview)*
Kiosk and subway entrance, Paris.
Courtesy of the French Government
Tourist Office.

Brilliant advertising is generally considered the kind that is most memorable, whose phrases and images enter the popular culture through imitation and parody. The memorability of ads and COMMERCIALS is measured routinely, and throughout the world a wide array of awards is bestowed by copywriters and art directors upon one another. However, the advertising that is best remembered or most admired is not necessarily the most convincing or the most effective in selling the advertised product. Advertising textbooks abound with the rules and principles of good advertising, generally based on the findings of copy research. Most of these relate well to communication theory, stressing, for instance, the importance of focusing attention, of minimizing visual distraction, of avoiding incongruity between the visual and aural components of a message. But, as with any art, mastery of basic principles is only a foundation for creative achievement.

Effects on sales. Advertising idealizes and articulates the goals of competing business enterprises and thus energizes their constant struggle for advantage and improvement. While most firms consider advertising a current expense against which an immediate sales return may be credited, advertising may be treated as an investment with a long-term payout. For any advertiser who communicates on a continuing basis, the effects of a single advertisement are notoriously difficult to measure because they interact with the residue of all the previous messages and leave a trace on future sales. The effects of an ad are difficult to extricate from the concurrent effects of distribution, pricing, merchandising, and the inherent appeal of the product itself. Moreover, a message from one source is perceived amid a cacophony of competing messages, which may totally obscure its impact.

Much advertising cannot be evaluated on the basis of its direct sales effect, since its purpose is to build, over time, a "brand image" or "personality" that dovetails with the psychological profile or product usage motives of a definable segment of the buying

Figure 3. *(Advertising—Overview)*   Promotional billboard that appeared during a world badminton championship, Hangchow, China. UPI/Bettmann Newsphotos.

public. When the products themselves are of low interest, advertisers generally assume that their messages must be "intrusive," to break through the barriers of inattention. First radio and then television advertising have been deemed especially appropriate for this purpose. In the United States television is used for over half of all national consumer advertising and nine-tenths of all advertising for certain major types of packaged goods.

In most television advertising campaigns, advertisers repeat the same messages, not only to heighten the effect on the individuals exposed to them initially, but to increase their cumulative exposure to additional people—a tactic made possible by the continual turnover of media audiences. Repeated exposure of a given individual to the same message eventually provokes disinterest or even revulsion. While this can be overcome by varying the form and content of the message, most advertisers recoil from the expense required to do this. Repetition, required by the considerable expense of television commercial production, has shaped the public's perceptions of advertising as an institution as well as the communications environment of advertising itself. Commercials have become progressively shorter as pressure has grown

to expand the total number of advertising positions within a limited amount of broadcast time.

Retail promotion. Image building has been extended from the arena of advertising for branded goods and services to the field of retail advertising, in which merchants have traditionally looked for immediate and direct returns on their investments. A store's image or reputation is created not only by those ads that are produced expressly for this purpose but also by the layout, copy, art style, models, and merchandise selections in its routine daily advertisements for specific items. Chain retailers have steadily expanded in most Western countries. Store brands or "private labels" represent a growing proportion of their business, and they have turned to advertising agencies to produce campaigns that emphasize the merits of the store itself rather than individual items of merchandise. But most retail advertising continues to stress information about specific merchandise items and prices and is produced either by the store's own advertising staff or by the medium. Although merchandise sales can be directly attributed to a particular ad, retail advertising also serves the more important purpose of generating traffic that results in sales of unadvertised items.

As marketing precepts have increasingly penetrated retailing, there has been a heightened concern with "targeting" specific segments of the public through the use of selective saturation distribution methods (direct mail, zoned editions of daily newspapers, free and paid weeklies, hand-distributed circulars) in the limited geographic areas from which customers are drawn (*see* CONSUMER RESEARCH). Advertising has made possible the growth of direct retailing by mail or telephone. This rapidly growing field of direct marketing will be stimulated further with the development of home communications systems that permit merchandise to be displayed or even demonstrated and ordered through a personal computer (*see* DIRECT RESPONSE MARKETING).

Retail and other local advertising account for about 60 percent of U.S. consumer advertising but for a smaller share in most other countries, especially those where retailing is fractioned among a myriad of small businesses serving neighborhoods rather than an entire community. Classified newspaper advertising and telephone directory advertising similarly represent highly informative and utilitarian communications that are generally immune from the questions, comment, and criticism that envelop the subject of national brand advertising (*see* CLASSIFIED ADVERTISING).

Also utilitarian but generally invisible to the general public is the vast field of business, trade, and professional advertising directed through special media to small but influential audiences. In the United States alone, business-to-business advertising involves expenditures of billions of dollars annually. This sustains a considerable variety of publications, mostly distributed free, that often account for the principal flow of communication in an occupational group and thus for its sense of community and cohesion (*see* MAGAZINE).

Cultural Effects

Whatever the economic functions of advertising may be for the individual firm or for the market system as a whole, advertising has a cumulative effect on the culture that runs far deeper than the slogans and images it renders familiar or even popular. Advertising is the good news that offsets the predominantly disquieting bulletins of the real news. It depicts a world of unbounded pleasure and abundance, inhabited by remarkably comely, good-humored, and articulate people who exist in a single dimension, that of consumers.

The advent of television has made this opulent, imaginary world universally familiar and has fostered the illusion that its possessions and values are normal as well as desirable. The endless representation and glorification of consumer goods can act either as a stimulant or as an irritant to those who lack them. Advertising heightens the awareness of consumption and thus of property as an indicator of social status. By constantly massaging the public's acquisitive instincts, it adds emphasis to the material aspects of human life and presents consumption as the goal of work. Thus advertising raises not merely hopes but the sense of entitlement, and it fosters not merely expectations but frustrations.

Most mature adults can distinguish between this fantasy world and the realities of their economic power, just as they can distinguish between the hyperbole of claims in individual ads and the reality of the products' merits. Young children, however, do take advertisements literally and must be acculturated into recognition of their metaphors and exaggerations (*see* CHILDREN—MEDIA EFFECTS).

Exaggerated claims are held in check by advertisers' realization that they can be counterproductive if they fail to jibe with consumer experience. They are further restrained by the vigilance of competitors, by

Figure 4. (*Advertising—Overview*) Sandwich sign carrier. The Bettmann Archive, Inc.

acceptability standards set by the major media, by self-policing systems set in place within the advertising industry itself, and by the regulatory practices of government agencies with a more comprehensive mission of consumer protection (*see* GOVERNMENT REGULATION).

U.S. influence. The United States, with slightly less than a quarter of the world's income, has accounted for over half of all advertising investments. The preeminent position of U.S. advertising has given its techniques and procedures a disproportionate influence elsewhere. This has been bolstered by the spreading power of multinational corporations based in the United States, which have adapted U.S. marketing methods to other countries. It has been spurred also by the growth of internationally familiar brands and by the multiplication of overseas branches and affiliations on the part of U.S. advertising agencies. The much-deplored "Coca-Colonization" of the world is visible primarily as a phenomenon of advertising, not of manufacturing. However, the world's largest advertising company, Saatchi and Saatchi, is British, and the growth of international marketing has made the exchange of personnel and ideas a reciprocal process.

Advertising agencies. Most national advertising is channeled through advertising agencies. These agencies are basically organized to translate the advertiser's requirements into advertisements, but with the evolution of modern marketing these requirements are no longer limited to the narrow goal of selling a product. A large, diversified agency employs a corps of account executives with responsibilities for the affairs of their respective clients. Its creative department includes copywriters, art directors, jingle writers, video producers, and production specialists. Its media department, lately transformed by the availability of vast quantities of computerized data on audiences and rates, prepares media schedules and negotiates contracts for space and time. Other departments cover market research, market planning, sales promotion, and public relations (see section 3, below).

As a hired advocate for its clients, the agency has nothing more to offer than the array of talent it has assembled, talent that must be nurtured and well compensated to meet both the frequently intense pressures of the workplace (which make advertising an occupation with below-average life expectancy) and the constant lure of competition.

In the United States the proportion of national advertising placed by the one hundred leading national advertisers has generally, since World War II, represented about half the national total and has at the same time shown an upward trend. A similar trend has occurred among advertising agencies. In part, concentration came through mergers and ac-

quisitions, which have made it possible to handle competitive accounts through different entities of the same corporation. This tendency jibes with the general trend toward corporate mergers and diversification.

In some instances, large advertisers circumvent agencies by setting up their own "house agencies" or by using outside organizations to provide creative work, buy broadcast time, or perform other special services. However, an agency is of value to its clients precisely because it fosters a cross-fertilization of ideas. As the major agencies have become multinational, this cross-fertilization occurs across an ever broader range of cultures, economies, and market conditions. Although the nature of the agency-client relationship varies greatly from case to case, agencies have often had a profound effect on their clients' businesses, suggesting and developing plans for new products and activities and encouraging changes in operations. A successful advertising campaign leads to a change in corporate self-image and affects the evaluation of the company by investors.

Marketing concepts. Advertising agencies fostered the rise of marketing concepts, with their emphasis on the satisfaction of latent consumer demand and heavy reliance on research data. The marketing task begins with the assessment of opportunities for market entry through analysis of sales and consumption patterns even before the product exists. Agencies are commonly involved in product development and marketing strategy as well as in the creation and placement of ads.

Although all agencies pride themselves principally on their ability to generate convincing and striking advertisements, they have increasingly had to relate those advertisements to overall marketing plans in which consumers' characteristics, predilections, and media habits have been carefully identified. There has been a growing appetite for data, both for guidance in the preparation of plans and as evidence of the wisdom of those plans. Large agencies routinely conduct research of their own to test alternative creative approaches in designing ads; in some instances they have also conducted or sponsored innovative studies on basic problems of persuasive communication (for example, on the effect of positioning a commercial message at different places in a series).

Of even greater significance has been the pressure agencies have exerted on advertising media to provide information about their audiences. For different media, as for individual publications or broadcast programs, audience size has been related to advertising charges to produce comparisons of yield by the criterion of cost-per-thousand. But since both marketing theory and common sense recognize that different marketing objectives require different targets, more and more emphasis has been placed on matching product consumption and media audience characteristics (*see* PRINT-AUDIENCE MEASUREMENT; RATING SYSTEMS: RADIO and TELEVISION).

Research trends. The growing use of common data bases (*see* DATA BASE) provided by syndicated media research services has encouraged the concentration of advertising budgets against those elements of the public that represent the most rewarding targets as potential consumers. Advertisers, through whatever combination of media they use, generally seek to concentrate their impact on "upscale" and youthful consumers and are willing to ignore the rest. Thus advertising research has not only speeded up the process of media specialization but has also altered the rate at which commercial communication flows to different sectors of the public.

Apart from general reliance on survey research, the practice of advertising has been influenced by the social sciences, especially in the areas of communication, motivation, and PERSUASION. There is little evidence that they have had an impact in the aggregate, but specific advertisements and campaigns and even specific new products have in many instances been successfully developed with the help of consumer research.

The techniques and media of advertising have long been employed for purposes other than the sale of goods and services. Advertising has been used as a tool of corporate public relations to plead a company's case when it faces a problem with labor, government, or independent critics. Institutional advertising is widely used to influence public officials on specific issues or to improve the general climate of favorable recognition in which every business likes to operate. Similar advertising is widely done by nonbusiness organizations defending particular interests and viewpoints. Public service advertising, much of it using volunteer professional talent and space and time donated by media, pleads for godliness, kindliness, adherence to safety rules, and support for charity.

Involvement in government. In many countries government is itself a major advertiser on behalf of state-owned industries or such general services as the post office and the military. This may create temptations and opportunities for direct pressure on the media by public officials. A town's mayor may withdraw official legal announcements from the local newspaper; a national government may expand commercial hours on the state-run television channel in order to weaken and punish an opposition press.

While advertising is coopted into the propaganda apparatus of an authoritarian regime, it has a distinctive political role in many democratic countries through its involvement in the electoral process. This

Figure 5. *(Advertising—Overview)* Southern California landscape. The Bettmann Archive, Inc.

has become most critical with the ascendancy of television. Press advertisements have long appeared on behalf of political candidates and parties to make their names well known and to describe their qualifications and platforms. Since the early 1950s, U.S. television has been used by advertising professionals to project the image of candidates for major office, and the same techniques have been widely adopted in other countries with free elections and unrestricted television advertising. See ELECTION.

Although there is no evidence that political ads in themselves make the difference between election victory and defeat, the entrance of advertising agencies into politics has had another consequence. Agencies and agency-originated "political consultants" have become essential to the planning of primary and general election campaigns (see POLITICAL COMMUNICATION). Just as the product marketer conducts consumer surveys to identify the copy appeals to which likely customers are most susceptible, so the political marketer uses research to identify the points in a candidate's platform that should be stressed, soft-pedaled, or even eliminated in order to maximize vote-getting appeal. Fund-raising campaigns are conducted with the computerized skill of the direct mail marketer. The candidate's public and television appearances are planned and modeled by the same experts and to the same specifications that govern the preparation of commercials. Advertising practitioners have become a major political force, just as advertising has become an integral element in free-market economies.

Impact on communications. Among countries at a common level of technical development, those that permit advertising enjoy a much greater number of media choices than those that discourage or limit it. Free-market countries that restrict advertising on their state-operated broadcast systems generally provide fewer hours and channels than comparable countries with advertiser-supported radio and television. Although the ratio of advertising to circulation revenues for the periodical press varies widely from country to country, advertising is almost everywhere essential to the survival of an unsubsidized mass press.

In a mass communication system dependent on advertising income, the main influence of advertisers is not in the occasional outrageous instance of CENSORSHIP, bias, or blatant puffery in ostensibly non-advertising content. The interests of advertisers determine whether publications and programs are started up, whether they survive and flourish, whether they struggle and die.

As with any other product, media ventures are initiated in the expectation that there is a market for them, and these markets are defined by the desires of advertisers rather than those of the public. Those

desires may coincide, inasmuch as advertisers look for cost efficiency and thus for audiences of maximum size, or inasmuch as they aim for people with a distinctive set of interests that a medium can serve and define. But a conflict arises when advertisers following their herd instincts desert a medium that still satisfies an audience of many thousands or millions of people.

Advertisers, not individually but through their collective institutions, can be held responsible for the disappearance of great magazines, the waning of press competition, and the continual turnover of television programs in the course of the endless ratings war. Advertising's greatest communications impact is therefore felt in its shaping of the media on which people in advanced societies and elites in all societies depend for information and entertainment.

Bibliography. Leo Bogart, *Strategy in Advertising,* 2d ed., Chicago, 1985; John Caples, *Tested Advertising Methods,* Englewood Cliffs, N.J., 1974; Bart A. Cummings, *Benevolent Dictators,* Chicago, 1984; Claude Hopkins, *Scientific Advertising,* New York, 1966; Otto Kleppner and Thomas Russell, *Otto Kleppner's Advertising Procedure,* 8th ed., Englewood Cliffs, N.J., 1983; Martin Mayer, *Madison Avenue USA,* New York, 1958; David Ogilvy, *Confessions of an Advertising Man,* New York, 1963; Frank S. Presbrey, *The History and Development of Advertising,* New York, 1929, reprint Westport, Conn., 1968; Rosser Reeves, *Reality in Advertising,* New York, 1961.

LEO BOGART

2. HISTORY OF ADVERTISING

The global scope and pervasive presence of contemporary advertising make it difficult to imagine a world without it. The emphasis on consumer advertising is mainly a product of the era of industrial capitalism. Yet the roots of advertising go back much farther.

Early Advertisers

Even before the advent of the printing press in the fifteenth century (see PRINTING—HISTORY OF PRINTING) there was advertising. The craft economies of Europe and Asia gave rise to colorful carved shop signs announcing that a particular kind of good or service might be acquired at a given establishment. These signs were directed at a largely nonliterate population, and they drew upon a visual vernacular of commonly understood symbols. As early forms of trademarks, they developed in rich variety. A particularly artful tradition of shop signs, known as *Kanban,* developed in Japan during the Tokugawa and Meiji periods (Figure 1). See also SIGNAGE.

Early printed advertising consisted largely of crudely illustrated handbills distributed by tradesmen. By the sixteenth century the modern world market system was beginning to develop. With the European explorations and an expanding network of international mercantile trade, economic life was moving beyond subsistence farming, home production, and small-workshop activity toward an international world of commercial enterprise (*see* COLONIZATION; EXPLORATION). As trade routes created commercial links between strangers—sellers and buyers across broad expanses of land and sea—advertising emerged as an important tool of commercial communications. By the early eighteenth century in England and by the mid-eighteenth century in its North American colonies, many newspapers came to be known as "Advertisers" and carried large classified advertisements (often on the front page) aimed at small but affluent readerships. In England, where the growth of an urban mercantile population gave rise to a significant middle class of consumers, some ads offered items for personal consumption. For the most part, however, these newspaper advertisements were communications between people of business, for the purpose of carrying out business. Wholesale advertising an-

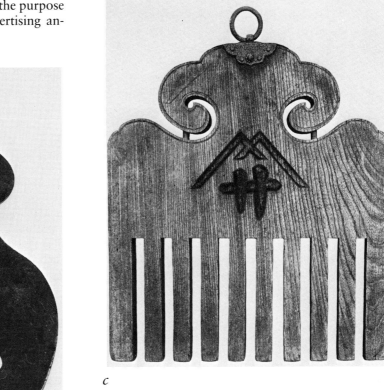

a

b

c

Figure 1. *(Advertising—History of Advertising)* *Kanban* (signboards) of Japan: *(a)* miso shop, Edo Period; *(b)* bucket shop, Meiji Period; *(c)* comb shop, Edo Period. From Dana Levy, Lea Sneider, and Frank B. Gibney, *Kanban: Shop Signs of Japan,* New York and Tokyo: Weatherhill, 1983, pp. 35, 55, 79.

nounced the arrival of shipments of coffee, tea, gingham, sailcloth, and so on, for purchase by dealers in grocery or dry goods. Other ads announced the availability of urban properties.

The development of a mobile economy involved not only the transporting of goods and money but also the transporting of labor forces. Some ads announced the availability of labor for sale or hire. Slavery was the cash-crop labor system by which both England and the United States amassed much of their wealth, and it is not surprising that a considerable amount of eighteenth- and early nineteenth-century advertising space was devoted to the sale of slaves or to offering rewards for the capture and return of runaways (see Figure 2).

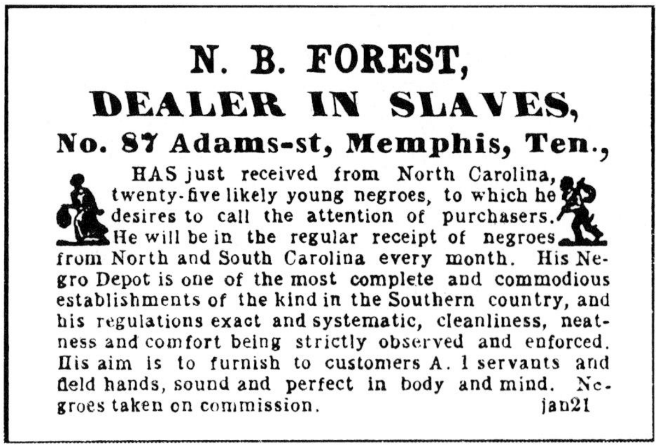

The classified listings that comprised most advertising into the latter half of the nineteenth century were not products of an advertising industry (*see* CLASSIFIED ADVERTISING). For the most part the business of advertising was handled by printers and publishers of newspapers who sold advertising space to help finance their publications. If we were to look for the leading figures in eighteenth-century American advertising, we would find them among the ranks of JOHN PETER ZENGER, publisher of the *New York Journal*, and Benjamin Franklin, publisher of the *Pennsylvania Gazette*. Classifieds were laid out in simple agate columns of print. While some printers added small illustrations (woodcuts) to break up the typography, the primary role of advertising was to provide unembellished, useful information to an interested commercial readership.

As newspapers developed in the nineteenth century, advertising continued to be mainly classified business information. Yet, at the same time, newspapers were changing in ways that would prove important to later developments in advertising. Both in Europe and in America the early nineteenth century saw the appearance of newspapers that reached beyond a traditional merchant readership. Called the "Penny Press" in England and later in the United States, such papers were affordable to many and tended toward a sensational style of journalism. They continued to be vehicles of commercial intelligence but also had large, literate working-class readerships. These papers were the beginnings of vernacular commercial media, read by popular audiences. While advertising still utilized the classified format, these papers inaugurated the mass media environment in which modern forms of consumer advertising would flourish by the late nineteenth and early twentieth centuries. *See* NEWSPAPER: HISTORY.

Industrialism

The shift from utilitarian classified advertising to a kind of advertising that situated consumer goods

N. B. FOREST, DEALER IN SLAVES,
No. 87 Adams-st, Memphis, Ten.,

HAS just received from North Carolina, twenty-five likely young negroes, to which he desires to call the attention of purchasers. He will be in the regular receipt of negroes from North and South Carolina every month. His Negro Depot is one of the most complete and commodious establishments of the kind in the Southern country, and his regulations exact and systematic, cleanliness, neatness and comfort being strictly observed and enforced. His aim is to furnish to customers A. 1 servants and field hands, sound and perfect in body and mind. Negroes taken on commission. jan21

Figure 2. *(Advertising—History of Advertising)* A classified advertisement in a Tennessee newspaper of the 1850s. The Bettmann Archive, Inc.

within provocative contexts of visual display cannot be explained purely on the level of a growing sophistication of advertising technique. At the heart of the shift lay great changes in the way goods were being produced, distributed, and consumed. The rise of industrialism in the nineteenth century drew an ever-increasing number of people into its expanding orbit of influence. Goods previously made by hand were now being produced and standardized on a mass scale. The prodigious capacity of industrial production required the development of markets far beyond traditional locales, and alongside industrial production there developed modern national and international networks of transport (railroads, shipping, canals) and communication (TELEGRAPHY, improved POSTAL SERVICE) to facilitate distribution. The structure of daily life was changing as well. People whose work lives had once been defined by the home production of goods for personal and localized consumption now increasingly worked in factories or commercial enterprises that left little time or energy for customary productive activities. As industrialism magnified the scale of goods production, and as an exchange economy and wage labor began to displace traditional subsistence living, the potential for vast consumer markets began to emerge. While low wages severely limited many people's ability to consume, it was within this late-nineteenth-century milieu that the modern institution of consumer advertising began to take hold.

Agency beginnings. Prior to the 1840s, advertising generally involved direct negotiations between publishers and advertisers. The subsequent appearance of the advertising agency (see section 3, below) as intermediary received special impetus in the expanding United States, where an agency could help manufacturers reach out to new markets via newspapers springing up in widely scattered communities. The first agency in the United States was the Country Newspaper Advertising Agency founded in the 1840s by Volney B. Palmer of Philadelphia, and it was soon followed by others. They served at first mainly as space brokers, buying large amounts of advertising space from numerous rural papers, then selling the space, inch by inch, to advertisers. Among pioneer agencies worthy of note were those of George P. Rowell (Boston, 1865) and N. W. Ayer and Son, founded by Francis Wayland Ayer (Philadelphia, 1869). A commission fee, generally 15 percent of space transactions, gradually became the standard form of agency compensation.

These early agencies were important on a number of counts. First, they represented the beginnings of a systematic, consolidated approach to advertising. Second, because they placed ads primarily in rural papers, they represented a channel by which urban industrial manufacturers made their way into the countryside. Third, while these agents began as adjuncts to the newspaper business, by the 1870s the advertising industry had become a relatively independent arena of entrepreneurship. Fourth, by the late 1870s Ayer was providing advertisers with marketing surveys and media strategies that moved agencies beyond the simple role of space brokerage. Such market analysis marked the emergence of the modern service agency. By 1890 Lord and Thomas, Pettengill and Co., and J. Walter Thompson had followed Ayer's lead. With the development of circulation listings and marketing surveys, media audiences were becoming commodities, to be estimated in value and sold to advertisers interested in attracting their attention.

These early agencies were not involved in the creative side of advertising. Creative innovations and techniques occurred more haphazardly. One important arena of creativity in many countries was patent medicine advertising, which often demonstrated the seductive power and potential of advertising copy and illustration. Similarly, the activities of showmen like PHINEAS T. BARNUM demonstrated the power of puffery and promotion to excite the public's imagination.

Several institutional and technical developments contributed to the scope and appearance of advertising in the late nineteenth century. The halftone printing process aided in the ability to publish a realistic pictorial display. The development of chromolithography, especially in Germany, made possible the mass production of brilliant color images. The technique allowed an advertiser's products to be represented in sensuous and imaginative tableaux. Even poor people who could not afford the goods collected advertising chromos, decorating their homes with these readily available examples of mass-produced "art."

Figure 3. *(Advertising—History of Advertising)* Advertisement for ready-made clothing. Courtesy of Levi Strauss and Co.

Age of the consumer. The burgeoning of the large-circulation MAGAZINE in many countries in the late nineteenth and early twentieth centuries facilitated advertising's growth, and vice versa. Magazines provided excellent vehicles for the advertising of soaps and cleansers, packaged and canned foods, toothpastes and shaving products. Another important consumer item promoted by late-nineteenth-century advertising was ready-made clothing (see Figure 3). Previously most homemakers had sewn their own families' clothes, but industrial life both expanded the production of textiles and diminished people's ability to carry on the home production of garments. Ready-to-wear became a feature of industrial life. In many U.S. cities, by the mid-nineteenth century, department stores made steady use of advertising copy and display to sell clothes and other goods. Another development, introducing ready-to-wear and other new consumer products to rural areas, was the mail-order catalog, such as those of Montgomery Ward and Sears Roebuck and Company. Densely illustrated with a previously unimaginable variety of items, they engaged the fantasies of people who had been schooled by scarcity.

The expanding consumer industries and the growing need for markets continually added new impetus to the advertising industry. By the late 1870s adver-

Figure 4. *(Advertising—History of Advertising)* "The Orphan Asylum": Life insurance advertisement. From *The Literary Digest*, October 16, 1926. Courtesy of The Prudential Insurance Company of America.

tising was a significant independent business, particularly in the United States.

Twentieth-Century Changes

The period between 1890 and the 1920s marked dramatic changes in the ad industry and its social impact. Before 1890 agencies focused on selling space, analyzing media markets, and trying to convince businesses that they should advertise; after 1890 advertising represented an increasing range of creative and business functions. Through the use of jingles, artwork, typeface, and layout, advertising became an avenue of multifaceted PERSUASION, attempting to appeal aesthetically, to draw attention to products, and to embed the message in people's memories. Trademarks and trade characters were developed to enhance and establish corporate identities.

An important figure in U.S. advertising during this period was ALBERT LASKER. Beginning in 1898 as a janitor and then as an ad salesman at the Chicago

firm of Lord and Thomas, he eventually came to be recognized as the dean of the U.S. advertising world. Under his leadership at Lord and Thomas, perceptive copywriters John E. Kennedy and Claude Hopkins refined a simple style of persuasive logic, embellished with drama.

Internal expansion of the ad industry was mirrored throughout the society. As assembly-line production was applied to a growing number of consumer industries, the need to generate competitive national markets magnified the utility of advertising. Modern consumer advertising—in newspapers, magazines, and door-to-door-distributed chromos and on rural and urban signboards—was becoming part of the landscape. Writing as early as 1914, WALTER LIPPMANN complained about advertising's growing presence. It had become a feature of daily life.

Expanding social role. As advertising became a profession between 1900 and World War I (1914), it shared certain features with many other new professions arising in the business world. The period witnessed great industrial development but also social turmoil and widespread opposition to many of the miseries of industrial life. Numerous business professions developed that were concerned not only with increasing productivity and profit but also with managing the social environment. Scientific management experts, such as F. W. Taylor and Frank and Lillian Gilbreth, and industrial psychologists were committed to furthering enhanced output by habituating new industrial populations to the rhythms of mass industrial work. This impulse toward social engineering became manifest in advertising as well.

Advertising as a device of social engineering and opinion molding moved into the political realm during World War I. The Committee for Public Information, directed by George Creel, employed advertising people and techniques to build support for the war, not only in the United States but abroad. *How We Advertised America* was the title Creel gave to his report, published in 1920. His committee, in consolidating the largest-ever advertising campaign, fueled the national ad industry. Between 1918 and 1920 the volume of advertising doubled, reaching $3 billion annually.

In the 1920s the U.S. ad industry employed social scientists and psychologists in an attempt to perfect methods of opinion and behavior management. Walter Dill Scott, who had begun as an industrial psychologist, was a prominent figure in the new field of advertising psychology. J. Walter Thompson employed Johns Hopkins University psychologist John B. Watson to aid in the delineation of advertising strategies. Edward L. Bernays consulted SIGMUND FREUD's disciple E. E. Brill in developing a promotional campaign for Lucky Strikes cigarettes. They all sought to define a universally applicable catalog of human instinct, in order to develop effective and predictable appeals. Advertising by the 1920s spoke less about the product being advertised and more to the hopes, fears, insecurities, and desires of the people at whom the message was being directed (see Figure 4). In their classic study *Middletown* (1929), Robert and Helen Lynd found that advertising along with movies had helped to recast people's understanding of dissatisfaction and desire. Advertising copy, they reported, functioned to make "the reader emotionally uneasy, to bludgeon him with the fact that decent people don't live the way he does." Others, however, saw the process as socially beneficial. To Calvin Coolidge, advertising was a method by which "the desire is created for better things." To a large extent, the debate over modern advertising has revolved around these two general perspectives ever since the 1920s. *See* MOTIVATION RESEARCH.

A crucial development of the 1920s was RADIO broadcasting. When it began its boom period in 1920 radio was not thought of as a vehicle for advertising, but within two years station WEAF in New York began to sell radio time commercially. Many people deplored what they considered a commercial intrusion into the home. Even the advertising trade journal *Printer's Ink*, speaking for a then print-oriented industry, said that radio advertising would prove "positively offensive" to many people. In Britain and other countries such concerns led at first to the establishment of noncommercial radio, but in the United States advertiser-sponsored programs became the norm for radio by the mid-1920s and for television later. Both media became major channels for advertising, sparking the evolution of a powerful U.S. broadcast industry. *See* SPONSOR.

Following the stock-market crash of 1929 and during the worldwide depression of the 1930s, advertising as a business experienced a decline, but advertising as a phenomenon persevered. Within a shrinking consumer market, ads adopted a zealously competitive approach. Sexual themes and nudity became more pervasive in many countries. Against the grim realities of the depression, some advertisers drew on modern art forms, adopting a futuristic depiction of commodities. Amid the struggle for commercial survival, the hard-sell approach became common.

One of the few agencies in the United States to flourish during the 1930s was Young and Rubicam, under the direction of Raymond Rubicam. He bolstered creative know-how with intensive market research, bringing Northwestern University professor GEORGE GALLUP into the service of advertising to conduct advertising research and opinion polls (*see* POLL).

Impact of World War II. To a large extent it was World War II that lifted the U.S. economy out of the depression. Yet, if the productive apparatus was once again moving, the shift to war production cut significantly into the availability of many consumer products. Within this context advertising functioned as a tool for keeping corporate and brand-name identities alive in the public mind (see Figure 5). Using techniques of institutional advertising developed in the 1920s, and especially associated with Bruce Barton of the Batten, Barton, Durstine and Osborn advertising agency, some ads informed audiences of cor-

Figure 5. *(Advertising—History of Advertising)* "Remember this wrapper": a World War II advertising campaign reminded consumers of the Wrigley brand name at a time when the company's products were removed from the U.S. market. Courtesy of Wm. Wrigley Jr. Co.

porate contributions to the war effort. Many ads displayed consumer items that would be available after the war (see Figure 6). Conspicuous among these projected spoils of victory was a household appliance that would have a revolutionary impact in the postwar era: television (*see* TELEVISION HISTORY).

As promised, the period following the war was one of economic boom for the United States. Consumer industries, feeding a massive suburban migration, increasingly used the services of advertising to sell their products (see Figure 7).

The war had stimulated an interest in PROPAGANDA research. By the end of the war, research for the purpose of influencing PUBLIC OPINION had gained a new legitimacy in academic, business, and government circles. Bernays argued in 1947 that "the engineering of consent" had become a necessary activity in a democracy. Noting that the "media provide open doors to the public mind," Bernays saw an implied "right of persuasion" in the Bill of Rights. In the area of consumer advertising such ideas held a great deal of sway in the 1950s.

Drawing on such ideas, Marion Harper, Jr., built the McCann-Erickson agency into an advertising colossus during the 1950s. McCann and other leading agencies expanded internationally as a part of the massive exportation of consumer goods and con-

△

Figure 6. *(Advertising—History of Advertising)* "U plan for V day": Potential newlyweds were encouraged to deposit money into war bonds designated for the purchase of Universal appliances "after Victory." Courtesy of Stuart Ewen.

Figure 7. *(Advertising—History of Advertising)* Oldsmobile advertisement from the 1950s. From *Life*, August 27, 1956, p. 62. Courtesy of Oldsmobile Division, General Motors.

sumer culture that marked U.S. world power in the postwar years.

Postwar era. The greatest influence on advertising in the 1950s and after was the international rise of television. There was also a reverse influence. With television having begun in the United States as a medium underwritten by advertising, television programming and advertising went hand in hand during the following decades, promoting the material and psychic values of a consumer way of life. In industrial societies advertising had become generalized as a way of presenting information on a mass scale, on almost any conceivable subject. As the U.S. advertising industry internationalized, European and Japanese advertising agencies likewise flourished. No corner of the earth was now beyond the reach of advertising. These developments contributed to what the historian E. J. Hobsbawm termed "the international and interlinguistic standardization of culture" characterizing much of twentieth-century life (see Figure 8).

The primary public arena of advertising continued to be consumer goods and services, yet advertising principles were applied in a growing number of other areas. ENTERTAINMENT, information, and even education became subject to market testing and packaging. Another area in which advertising techniques became prevalent was politics. In the United States, from the 1950s on, it became common for politicians and political policies to be promoted like commodities. Presidential advisers were increasingly drawn from the advertising and public relations industries (*see* POLITICAL COMMUNICATION). Whether the "engineering of consent" is consistent with the effective practice of democracy is a question that deserves ongoing attention.

Bibliography. Stuart Ewen, *Captains of Consciousness: Advertising and the Social Roots of the Consumer Culture,* New York, 1976; Stuart Ewen and Elizabeth Ewen, *Channels of Desire: Mass Images and the Shaping of American Consciousness,* New York, 1982; Stephen Fox, *The Mirror Makers: A History of American Advertising and Its Creators,* New York, 1984; Ralph Hower, *The History of an Advertising Agency,* rev. ed., Cambridge, Mass., 1949; Otis A. Pease, *The Responsibilities of American Advertising,* New Haven, Conn., 1958; Richard W. Pollay, ed., *Information Sources in Advertising History,* Westport, Conn., 1979; Daniel Pope, *The Making of Modern Advertising,* New York, 1983; Henry Sampson, *A History of Advertising from the Earliest Times,* London, 1874, reprint Detroit, 1974; Roy Sheldon and Egmont Arens, *Consumer Engineering: A New Technique for Prosperity,* New York and London, 1932; John W. Wright, ed., *The Commercial Connection: Advertising and the American Mass Media,* New York, 1979.

STUART B. EWEN

Figure 8. *(Advertising—History of Advertising)* Austrian billboard, 1980. Photograph by Lee Ann Draud.

3. ADVERTISING AGENCY

An organization retained by an advertiser to prepare advertising messages and place them in advertising media. An advertiser does not usually turn over the entire advertising function to an advertising agency. More typically the advertiser divides the advertising function into components, assigning some to one or more advertising agencies while handling others within the advertiser's organization. The advertiser almost always determines how much money will be spent and how effectiveness is to be measured. Advertising strategy and research are jointly determined. Advertisers marketing a large range of products are likely to divide them among several advertising agencies.

Role and Structure

The advertising agency is expected to analyze the marketing situation that characterizes products or services and to identify the advertising implications. Once the major strategy decisions have been made, it plans and executes individual advertisements, always subject to the approval of the advertiser, and places the finished advertisements in the selected advertising media. Finally, the agency ascertains that advertisements have been run by the media as agreed and oversees the processing of media bills and payments.

Agencies are generally organized into four basic groupings or departments: account service, creative, media, and business affairs. Each of these groups provides a basic advertising agency service.

- *Account service.* Maintains agency liaison with the advertiser. Determines agency services needed by the advertiser and transmits the information to the relevant departments. Makes sure that the work is finished on time and in accordance with client specifications and agency standards. Continuously monitors the marketing situation facing the client's products and services, analyzing the implications and making recommendations.
- *Creative department.* Develops and recommends advertising ideas to carry out agreed strategies. Oversees production of these advertising ideas into final form by personnel within the agency and/or by such outside services as recording studios and animation firms.
- *Media department.* Evaluates and analyzes the audiences and advertising environments provided by all media that offer time and space for advertising. Recommends the media to be used and related placement strategies. Upon client approval, contracts for specific units of time and space.
- *Business affairs department.* Arranges for actual placement of advertisements in the contracted time and space. Bills clients for the time and space provided by the media, confirms the actual appearance of advertisements in this time and space, and remits payments to the media.

Types of Agencies

Many advertising agencies characterize themselves as full-service agencies. There is no commonly accepted definition of just what such "full" service comprises. Most advertising agencies, in addition to providing the four basic services, offer one or more peripheral services. These may include advertising and marketing research, sales promotion planning, PUBLIC RELATIONS and publicity, yellow pages advertising service, DIRECT RESPONSE MARKETING, sales meeting arrangements, merchandising, package design, design and development of annual reports and other non-advertising corporate communications, and speech writing for client executives.

Advertising agencies rarely maintain peripheral service capabilities that are not in active use by current clients. Thus the particular assortment of peripheral services maintained by an advertising agency depends on the service requirements of its clients. National advertising accounts require very different services, especially media services, from accounts that are primarily local or regional.

Specialist advertising agencies. The largest advertising agencies are generally able to serve the needs of any advertiser, regardless of the nature of the

products or services to be advertised. They can deal with consumer goods, business-to-business, direct response, retail, and institutional advertisers with equal facility. It is not uncommon, however, for a smaller advertising agency to develop a specialization that makes it particularly well suited to handle the needs of a particular kind of advertiser. This may be a particular type of business activity, such as retail advertising, or it may represent a particular kind of content, such as medical, theatrical, investment, or travel advertising.

Limited service agencies. Some advertising-related organizations offer some but not all of the basic advertising agency services. Creative "boutiques," for example, specialize in the creation and execution of advertising ideas. Media buying services plan and execute media programs and handle the business affairs activities implicit in such programs. Advertising strategy specialists concern themselves with marketing situation analyses and advertising strategy development. In addition, a great deal of creative work and media placement is done in organizations that do not conceive of themselves as advertising agencies and make no attempt to provide the basic agency services. Foremost among these are the media themselves, which offer production facilities and in some cases, particularly in local situations, will assist in the creation of advertising copy. Also, much advertising is produced by printing shops for those advertisers whose total budgets are too small to justify the involvement of a full-fledged advertising agency.

Another variant of limited service advertising agencies is the "in-house" advertising agency. In this case the advertiser creates an advertising agency within the advertiser's own organization, thereby becoming its own provider of advertising agency services. The in-house agency has never gained widespread popularity, apparently because advertisers welcome an objective outside view and the broad service capabilities that cannot easily be achieved when employees attempt to provide agencylike services.

Compensation Arrangements

The traditional method of advertising agency compensation is a commission system. The agency receives, from each medium used, a commission on the gross value of the space or time purchased, usually 15 percent. In practice, the agency bills the advertiser for the gross value but remits only 85 percent to the medium, retaining the brokerage fee. The 15 percent fee is a widespread standard, but in some countries rates may vary from as low as 10 percent to 20 percent or higher and may vary from one medium to another.

When large space or time purchases are involved,

the commission fee may be considered adequate compensation for such other services as an advertiser may require. But with the growing complexity of advertising and the rise of new media and services, the shortcomings of the system have become clear. When required service includes, for example, advertising agency supervision of the on-location production of a series of commercials, an additional fee is obviously needed—and in this case is paid by the client. This may be on a cost-plus or negotiated basis. Negotiated fees may thus be used to supplement the traditional commission system, but they may also replace it entirely.

Advertisers who decide to compensate their agencies by a negotiated-fee system tend to define the amount and kinds of agency services needed more rigorously than do those advertisers who depend on the commission method of compensation.

Extended Roles

Advertising agencies have long been involved in politics. The nature of the involvement has varied widely from country to country. In some countries advertising agencies align themselves openly with particular political parties and share unabashedly in the division of government advertising appropriations and campaigns, such as those promoting bond sales and military recruitment.

Another aspect of the advertising agency role in politics, particularly since World War II, involves ELECTION campaigns. In some countries, notably the United States, it has become common for political parties and candidates running for major offices to retain advertising agencies to handle media purchases and to prepare campaign "commercials." The trend has been widely criticized. Most countries have banned the sale of broadcast time for political appeals.

With the burgeoning of international trade, advertising agencies in many countries have faced marketing and advertising problems on an international scale, involving an array of new relationships. It is generally recognized that most advertising campaigns cannot be implemented universally because of sociocultural differences among individual countries. Yet in many instances agencies have successfully adapted their expertise to the solution of cross-cultural marketing problems.

After World War II a strong trend toward the internationalization of advertising agencies developed, particularly among U.S. advertising agencies. The trend reflected the world expansion of U.S. business. As many corporations turned multinational, their advertising agencies opened new offices to provide the needed services. By the 1970s a number of U.S. agencies had more offices and personnel abroad, and were earning more there, than in the United States. The advertising agency proliferation involved various kinds of affiliation—including mergers—with agencies of other countries. These developments gave U.S. advertising practices increasing influence over advertising elsewhere, in a wide variety of countries.

See also COMMERCIALS.

Bibliography. Leo Bogart, *Strategy in Advertising*, 2d ed., Chicago, 1985; James P. Neelankavil, *Agency Remuneration: Practices and Prospects around the World*, New York, 1982; William M. Weilbacher, *Auditing Productivity: Advertiser-Agency Relationships Can Be Improved*, New York, 1981; idem, *Choosing an Advertising Agency*, Chicago, 1983.

WILLIAM M. WEILBACHER

4. ADVERTISING ECONOMICS

Narrowly viewed, advertising is important to society for the information it puts into circulation. More broadly viewed, it is important for how it affects the whole system of buyer and seller interactions by which market economies organize the production and distribution of goods. Advertising affects economic performance not only according to how well it communicates information but also according to how it affects the efficiency with which the economic system provides goods to buyers.

Information, the Media, and Public Goods

Under certain conditions, the market system provides private goods efficiently without advertising. Private goods are goods like tomatoes and toothpaste that, when consumed by one person, become unavailable for anyone else's consumption. Efficiency requires sellers to expand their provision of such goods up to the point at which the price that buyers are willing to pay for one unit just equals the cost of providing it. Ideally, the profit motive induces sellers to expand their provision of private goods up to this point. If, say, there is too little production of toothpaste, then price will exceed the cost of producing one more unit (that is, it will exceed marginal cost), and toothpaste producers will be able to make a profit equal to the difference by expanding production. They will expand production until they have exhausted every opportunity to make such additional profits. Price will tend to equal marginal cost without sellers' wishing or needing to advertise.

For the profit motive to lead to efficiency in this way, buyers must know what goods are available and sellers must know the goods for which buyers are willing to pay prices high enough to cover production and distribution costs. If information about goods were a private good, then, ideally, sellers would provide just the right amount of it. Production and distribution would expand until price equaled marginal cost. But information is a public good: the consumption of a unit by one person does not prevent another person from consuming the same unit. Once a firm communicates information about, say, the development of a new product to one consumer, the information becomes cheaply available to other consumers through word of mouth and other sources. Firms thus find it difficult to charge consumers for information about new products.

The communications media themselves exhibit varying degrees of this public character. Once a publisher has placed a copy of a MAGAZINE or newspaper in the hands of one reader, the same copy or another copy becomes available, at comparatively little cost, to another reader. Once a broadcaster has transmitted a RADIO or television signal to one receiver, it can transmit the same signal at little or no cost to another. Publishers and broadcasters thus find it difficult to charge for their services without some mechanism for selling time and space.

Advertising provides such a mechanism. In commercial systems media time and space are private goods, and their providers can induce advertisers to pay for them. Because advertising reduces the cost to buyers of receiving advertising messages to nearly zero, buyers are expected to absorb and respond to these messages with sufficient predictability to make it worthwhile for sellers to pay for placing them. Advertising therefore serves to correct for the underprovision of product information and of media services that would characterize economic activity in its absence.

Competition and Monopoly

In an ideally working market economy, competition is "perfect": buyers are fully informed about goods, and there are so many sellers that no one seller is important enough to be able to affect price. Sellers have no reason to advertise because competition makes them "price takers," able to sell all they want at the market-determined price but unable to sell any amount at any higher price. When competition is imperfect, however, sellers discover that they cannot expand sales without either persuading buyers to buy more of their goods or reducing price. Imperfectly competitive sellers have monopoly power; they are "price searchers."

Monopoly power reduces the efficiency with which the market system provides goods. Because price falls as production expands, sellers having monopoly power find that, as they provide more of a product, the additional revenue yielded by providing one more unit is less than price. Hence, they find that it pays to produce some amount less than the amount that equates price and marginal cost.

Anticompetitive effects of advertising. A seller might use advertising as a method for exploiting its monopoly power over buyers. The seller might increase its advertising at the same time that it raises price, attempting thereby to get a higher price for its product without reducing the quantity that buyers are willing to buy. If the increase in revenue captured by raising price more than offsets the cost of the additional advertising, profits will rise. A seller using this method to increase profits will continue to raise price until the increase in revenue brought about by raising price is just equal to the cost of the additional advertising that is needed to keep quantity sold from falling.

A seller might also use advertising to expand its monopoly power and thus its ability to increase profits through further increases in price. If, by advertising, the seller is able to make buyers less sensitive to price, it will be able to reduce the amount by which quantity sold falls as it raises price. Less additional advertising will be needed to offset the negative effect of raising the price on the quantity sold, and the positive effect on revenue will rise. Buyers are, then, twice damned: once by the diminution of their price sensitivity and again by the rise in price that by virtue of this diminution becomes all the more advantageous a method for raising sellers' profits.

Buyers also suffer from advertising by which sellers aim to exploit buyer ignorance about goods. In the absence of legal or ethical deterrents, sellers sometimes use deceptive advertising to expand sales of products that are poor buys. The incentive to conduct deceptive advertising is especially great when there is initially little prospect of a seller's enjoying repeat sales and when rivals are not likely to offer and advertise products that are better buys than a deceptively advertised product. Advertising that is anticompetitive (permitting sellers to exploit or expand their monopoly power over buyers or to exploit buyer ignorance) reduces economic efficiency.

Procompetitive effects of advertising. Advertising can also be procompetitive. Suppose that sellers of some product A have monopoly power and that buyers are unaware of the fact that some other product B represents a better buy. Sellers of B might advertise to increase buyer awareness of the advantages of B over A. This will raise efficiency by leading buyers to substitute B for A and by subjecting sellers of A to increased competition. Buyers of A will become more price sensitive, and the monopoly power commanded by sellers of A will fall.

Sellers in both centrally planned and market-oriented economic systems use advertising to inform buyers of the availability of unsold goods. Under central planning, producers have relatively little incentive to advertise, owing to their hegemony over distributors and their inclination to avoid product innovation in favor of meeting production targets. Distributors (and producers prodded by distributors) will, however, advertise from time to time to bring new but unsold products to the attentions of buyers.

Economies of Scale in Advertising

Whether advertising improves economic performance depends largely on whether its procompetitive effects outweigh its anticompetitive effects. The weight of its procompetitive effects relative to its anticompetitive effects depends, in turn, on the behavior of advertising costs.

There are economies of scale in advertising if a given percentage rise in a seller's outlays on advertising produces a greater percentage rise in sales revenue. Economies of scale reduce the cost to established sellers of expanding sales and increase the cost to newcomers of capturing sales revenues from established sellers. By exploiting any economies of scale in advertising to which they might have access, established sellers thus tend to increase concentration (the fraction of sales accounted for by leading established sellers) and monopoly power. The possible adverse consequences for economic performance posed by these considerations have led to a number of policies and proposals to limit advertising, especially by manufacturers of consumer goods.

Economies of scale in advertising stem from any quantity discounts that the media offer to advertisers and from any slowness by consumers to respond to less than some threshold amount of advertising. It is not clear from the evidence whether media discounts and advertising thresholds exist or, if they do, whether they offer a substantial advantage to established sellers over newcomers.

The ability of a seller to expand monopoly power by exploiting any economies of scale to which it might have access depends in part on the accessibility of economies of scale to its rivals. Sellers expand their access to economies of scale by expanding the number of product groups within which they offer brands and by expanding the number of brands that they offer within given product groups. An established seller in product group A might, for example, take advantage of media discounts by entering product group B. Established sellers in product group B will find that their ability to expand monopoly power by taking advantage of media discounts has correspondingly diminished.

The ability of rival sellers to introduce new brands into existing product groups or to promote old ones similarly diminishes the monopoly power that sellers of heavily advertised established brands are able to exercise. A seller might attempt to expand its monopoly power over a given product group by raising buyer awareness of its brand above a threshold at which advertising cost per dollar of sales begins to fall. Insofar as the same product group will accommodate other brands, however, other sellers will attempt to exploit the same economies by promoting existing brands or introducing new ones. The more brands that sellers try, in this way, to crowd into a given product group, the less monopoly power any one seller can exercise over any one brand.

Advertising and Product Information

There is evidence that advertising increases profits in the manufacture of consumer goods, particularly low-priced, frequently purchased convenience goods. There is also evidence of a positive relationship between advertising and concentration. The implications of this evidence for economic performance depend not only on any monopoly power that manufacturers are able to exercise over buyers, but also on how buyers seek product information.

Buyers tend to seek product information from whatever source makes the cost of obtaining it as low as possible. For consumer goods there are usually two sellers—the manufacturer and the distributor—to which the consumers (final buyers) can turn for information. For some consumer goods, especially little-advertised, high-priced, infrequently purchased nonconvenience goods, distributors offer the cheaper source of information. Because time and household budgets limit the number of distributors that consumers can identify and compare, distributors can exercise monopoly power over consumers whose patronage they build through advertising and personal selling.

Manufacturers' advertising limits the ability of distributors to exercise this power. When a manufacturer uses advertising to increase consumer familiarity with a product, it shifts accountability for product quality from the distributor to itself. In centrally planned economies the authorities sometimes require branding of consumer durables in order to shift accountability in this way. In market-oriented economies manufacturers of consumer goods advertise, in part to shift monopoly power over consumers from distributors to themselves. Hence manufacturers' advertising can be anticompetitive for its effect on manufacturers' prices but procompetitive for its effect on distributors' prices.

Advertising and Consumer Goods

Controversy about the effects of advertising on economic performance centers on manufacturers' advertising of consumer goods. Other advertising is less controversial, either because it is less important than other methods of sales promotion or because it offers less potential for causing harm.

Advertising causes harm when sellers use it to exploit monopoly power or consumer ignorance. Advertising used for this purpose reduces economic efficiency by causing prices to rise and by inducing consumers to purchase brands that offer poor buys. Advertising can also increase economic efficiency, however. Advertising used to increase the number of products and brands that are available and familiar to consumers causes prices to fall and induces consumers to purchase brands that offer good buys.

Manufacturers ordinarily aim their advertising at expanding the market share—the fraction of the total sales of a given product group—that they are able to capture for their own brands. The problem of assessing the economic effects of advertising therefore depends largely on how manufacturers' brand advertising affects brand qualities and prices. Is advertising of this kind likely to result in better buys or in worse buys for consumers? The answer depends on whether advertising is, on balance, anticompetitive. Although there is evidence of economies of scale in advertising and of positive effects of advertising on profits and concentration, this evidence does not appear strong enough to support the conclusion that advertising generally results in worse buys for consumers.

A different problem arises over the possibility that advertising can expand not just market share but also the total sales of some product groups and even the size and variability of total consumer expenditures. The possibility that advertising expands total sales of dangerous products like cigarettes and alcoholic beverages has led to policies and proposals to require warning labels or to impose outright bans on advertising.

The extent to which measures of this kind protect consumers rests on the effect of advertising on total sales and on producer accountability. The evidence concerning total sales is mixed, suggesting that the effect of advertising is weak and greatly outweighed by other factors such as fashion, demographics, and income. The ability of advertising to increase producers' accountability argues against banning the advertising of dangerous products. The uncertain quality of illegal and, hence, unadvertised drugs results largely from the nonexistence of brand name familiarity of the kind that induces sellers of advertised products to maintain high levels of product quality.

Concerns about the effects of advertising on consumer expenditures arise also from the supposed propensity of advertising to magnify swings in business activity and to encourage consumption at the cost of saving. Neither argument can claim substantial support from the facts. Advertising appears to follow, not lead, swings in consumer expenditures. This is consistent with the hypothesis that advertising is a form of investment, the demand for which is derived from the demand for consumer goods. According to this hypothesis, sellers can be expected to gear their advertising to their expected sales, adjusting to swings in consumer expenditures in such a way as to keep the ratio of advertising to sales roughly constant.

Conclusions

Advertising is probably best understood as a method by which economic systems correct, albeit imperfectly, for deficiencies to which they are vulnerable in its absence. These deficiencies are, for market-oriented systems, a propensity to provide too little product information and too few media services, and, for centrally planned systems, a propensity to discourage product innovation and producer accountability.

Proponents of regulations to limit manufacturer's advertising of consumer goods argue that such advertising encourages the exploitation of manufacturer's monopoly power, promotes the use of products that represent poor or dangerous buys, and leads to economic instability. Opponents argue that manufacturers' advertising reduces the ability of both manufacturers and distributors to exercise monopoly power over consumers and that it increases producer accountability at little sacrifice in economic stability. The ability of market-oriented systems that exhibit high levels of consumer-good advertising to provide consumers with good buys argues against the idea that limiting such advertising promotes consumer welfare.

See also CONSUMER RESEARCH; GOVERNMENT REGULATION.

Bibliography. Mark S. Albion, *Advertising's Hidden Effects: Manufacturers' Advertising and Retail Pricing*, Boston, 1983; Mark S. Albion and Paul W. Farris, *The Advertising Controversy: Evidence on the Economic Effects of Advertising*, Boston, 1981; William S. Comanor and Thomas A. Wilson, *Advertising and Market Power*, Cambridge, Mass., 1974; James M. Ferguson, *Advertising and Competition: Theory, Measurement, Fact*, Cambridge, Mass., 1974; Philip Hanson, *Advertising and Socialism*, White Plains, N.Y., 1974; Michael E. Porter, *Interbrand Choice, Strategy, and Bilateral Market Power*, Cambridge, Mass., 1976; W. Duncan Reekie, *The Economics of Advertising*, London, 1981; Julian L. Simon, *Issues in the Economics of Advertising*, Urbana, Ill., 1970; Robert L. Steiner, "A Dual Stage Approach to the Effects of Brand Advertising on Competition and Price," in *Marketing and the Public Interest*, ed. by John F. Cady, Cambridge, Mass., 1978; David G. Tuerck, ed., *Issues in Advertising: The Economics of Persuasion*, Washington, D.C., 1978.

DAVID G. TUERCK

ADVERTISING, CLASSIFIED. See CLASSIFIED ADVERTISING.

AESTHETICS

Widely defined as the philosophical analysis of ART and art works. Aesthetics is particularly concerned with the ontology of art, addressing such topics as the relation between physical nature and human CULTURE, and with the methodology and epistemology of criticism and appreciation, meaning the descriptive, interpretive, and evaluative aspects of discourse about the arts.

Modern aesthetics is usually said to have begun more or less formally in the eighteenth century with the appearance in Germany of Alexander Gottlieb Baumgarten's *Reflections on Poetry* and the unfinished *Aesthetica Acroamatica* and of Gotthold Ephraim Lessing's *Laokoon,* and to have achieved a compendious, enormously influential orientation in Immanuel Kant's *Critique of Judgment.* Kant viewed the field largely in terms of the logical peculiarities of aesthetic judgments, their claim to universal validity despite being grounded in subjective taste and feeling, their extension to the beautiful and sublime in nature as well as in art, genius as the source of "aesthetical ideas," the autonomy of the aesthetic and the moral, and the function of the aesthetic as enabling humanity to appreciate the moral order of things. Since Kant's time aesthetics has focused rather more narrowly on the theory of art and on the theory of criticism in the arts, although Kant's own formulations continue to be vigorously debated. As a well-defined discipline in the Western world, aesthetics is markedly insulated from the ways of theorizing about the arts and criticism characteristic of Asia and other non-Western cultures.

Origins. Pre-Kantian aesthetics is usually understood to include certain classical pronouncements regarding the arts from ancient Greece and Rome, early and medieval Christian authorities, and the High Renaissance (*see* RENAISSANCE). Perhaps the most important and systematic of these are ARISTOTLE's *Poetics,* Horace's *Ars poetica,* and Longinus's *On the Sublime.* The *Poetics* is viewed as an exemplar of a certain essential way of working in aesthetics. Its extant first part presents a brilliant account of the generic features of ancient Greek TRAGEDY, a model that substantially influenced Longinus. But, encouraged by the Aristotelian model, there has always been a tendency in aesthetics and allied disciplines (e.g., STRUCTURALISM, SEMIOTICS, and POETICS) to view aesthetic theories as primarily favoring an analysis of the poetic use of LANGUAGE (or the creative use of other media in a way analogized to the use of poetic language or in a way that features the communicative and infectious function of the arts). This tendency has encouraged a strong sense of contemporaneity bridging current analyses and the works of the ancients. For example, mimesis, the doctrine that art imitates nature—in effect the

first grand theory of the arts and developed in rather different ways by PLATO, Aristotle, and Longinus—is expressly treated in instructional, didactic, or morally infectious terms. Mimetic theories appear to emphasize the communicative effectiveness of the arts in terms that are not confined to or centered explicitly in linguistic communication even when they are specifically literary. The reality said to be imitated—ultimately the creative power of nature—is usually linked closely to human interests and dispositions. Art itself is said to function communicatively because it fashions in some sense a representation of such reality, and its communicative effectiveness is characteristically exhibited in its influence on the conduct and affective responses of those who attend the arts. The study of the logical structures of representation (*see* REPRESENTATION, PICTORIAL AND PHOTOGRAPHIC), expression, SIGN and symbol (*see* SYMBOLISM), METAPHOR, FICTION, and the rhetorical process in general (*see* RHETORIC) has largely collected the threads of such early theory.

In the MIDDLE AGES the communicative emphasis is, if anything, strengthened. For example, according to the English philosopher Roger Bacon, the arts (notably painting) have in their representational power the ability to instruct the faithful in an accurate and easy way. According to the Italian philosopher Thomas Aquinas, the arts, like the natural world itself, instruct by producing beautiful things. The artist produces what is good (pleasing when contemplated or seen, congruent with what all creatures are said naturally to desire), and the work thus produced, in being good or beautiful, pointedly draws our attention to what in accord with God's creation may be predicated of all beings. In this sense art communicates or at least tacitly conveys the import of the entire created order and of the relationship between creator and creation.

Perhaps the most influential modern theories of art and art production derive from the romantic movement (*see* ROMANTICISM) of the eighteenth and early nineteenth centuries. The key idea of romanticism is that through their creative powers artists express themselves, their inner lives, their "intentions," even their eras. Audiences must be able to grasp or be appropriately affected by what is conveyed in an effective artwork. The expressive function is not thought to be subsumable under the mimetic and is distinctly associated with notions of the novel, the personal, and the creative. In the view of the French poet Alfred de Musset, for instance, POETRY becomes a sob overheard or a personal sentiment made public. This is the egoistic, perhaps even egotistic, communicative idea of art that the Russian novelist Leo Tolstoy inveighed against in *What Is Art?* (1898), but his own theory, which was devoted to the redemptive role of the Russian peasant, simply favors another expressive preference.

Hermeneutics. The most important and explicit modern version of the communicative theme of art is memorably adumbrated in the early nineteenth-century speculations of the German philosopher Friedrich Schleiermacher. In Schleiermacher's so-called romantic hermeneutics the interpretive complexities of the communicative function of art are first explored in terms close to contemporary aesthetic interests. Hermeneutics, generally construed as the theory of INTERPRETATION or of interpreting texts, is focused on the problem of how to understand what authors of a previous age must have meant in producing the texts bequeathed to us. Hence interpretation and expression are, historically, quite closely linked conceptions. The hermeneutic question, whether formulated in romantic or other terms, restricted to literary texts or enlarged to include the productions of the other arts, centered on our sense of increasing historical distance or addressed to contemporary texts, has become one of the focal issues in theorizing about the arts.

Generally speaking, the hermeneutic tradition construes art works or texts as artifacts (*see* ARTIFACT) intended to be communicatively rich and significant. Their importance is usually said to lie with their content, but their ability to communicate requires the skill on our part to recover that original intent or to achieve some suitable alternative objective. Hermeneutics in this sense is a relatively autonomous discipline that since the eighteenth century has become increasingly intertwined with aesthetic theory. Because communicative and interpretive themes are of paramount importance in contemporary aesthetic analysis, the convergence of the two disciplines is quite natural. Yet the dominance of interpretive rather than specifically hermeneutic puzzles needs to be emphasized for two reasons. First, the term *hermeneutic* usually pertains fairly specifically to the contributions of theorists such as Schleiermacher, Emilio Betti, Hans-Georg Gadamer, E. D. Hirsch, Jr., Wolfgang Iser, and Hans Robert Jauss, who address a distinctly circumscribed tradition. Second, twentieth-century theorists of interpretation as different as the U.S. philosopher and New Critic Monroe C. Beardsley, the French belletrist ROLAND BARTHES, the literary critic Stanley Fish, the so-called Yale deconstructionists (Geoffrey Hartman, Hillis Miller, Paul de Man, Harold Bloom), Marxist theorists such as Fredric Jameson and Terry Eagleton, and many others representing Anglo-American analytic philosophy, phenomenology, Prague semiotics, and Freudian analysis are not concerned primarily with bringing their theories of interpretation into line with the distinctive claims and idiom of the hermeneutic school. Also opposed to this orientation but partly inter-

twined with it are numerous versions of structuralism analyzing the semiotic, symbolic, signifying, or communicative functions of the arts (indeed of all human culture) in terms that distinctly avoid or subordinate their semantic, pragmatic, referential, representational, and expressive functions and favor instead the syntactic, formal, grammatical, and generative rules by which MEANING is said to be constrained. Nevertheless, the contest between hermeneutic and structuralist themes attests to the abiding emphasis of communicative concerns in the history of aesthetics. In twentieth-century U.S. aesthetics, for instance, Nelson Goodman featured the syntactic structures of art at the expense of semantic content, and Arthur Danto displayed the intentional complexities of representation and related rhetorical functions. Characteristically the second is profoundly historicized, and the first is relatively indifferent to historical change.

Art works, intention, and history. Theories of these sorts are not confined to questions of criticism and appreciation; they invariably color our theories of the nature of art works. For it is the ontology of art that generates the puzzles of interpretation, and it is the importance of interpretive questions that obliges us to characterize the peculiar nature of art in some suitably congruent way. The result, by and large, is that contemporary theories of the nature of art are focused on the difference between natural (or physical) objects and culturally generated objects (works of art, texts, words and sentences, institutions). There is therefore a characteristically double theme in nineteenth- and twentieth-century aesthetics stressing the conceptual linkage between the properties of critical discourse addressed to the arts (largely interpretive) and the properties of art works (examined both descriptively and interpretively). This is quite apparent in romantic theories of the arts.

Romantic theories hold that there is an original, individual, authorial intent that generates the art work and that, once correctly recovered, fixes the meaning or communicative import of the work (*see* AUTHORSHIP). Such theories hold that the original intent is fixed once and for all in historical time and is recoverable in principle, despite the "distance" between author and reader, by virtue of either the constancies of human nature or those of interpretive techniques or methods. Very early on it became clear that the author's intent could not be taken to be an actual, deliberate, or observable event but must be reconstructed in terms of a grasp of the prevailing practices, traditions, and genres (*see* GENRE) that a responsive artist may reasonably be supposed to have internalized in producing a work of a particular kind. Since the eighteenth and early nineteenth centuries the complexities of this reconstructive effort of interpretation have come under the influence of an increasingly radicalized sense of history—ranging, say, from the French Revolution and the reflections of the nineteenth-century German philosopher G. W. F. Hegel to the theories of history and HISTORIOGRAPHY favored by the influential twentieth-century German philosophers Gadamer and Martin Heidegger. Schleiermacher seems to have emphasized the effectiveness of hermeneutic method and therefore to have accommodated (but not fully grasped the implications of) the idea of discerning distinctly individual intention. More recent "romantics," notably Hirsch, are aware that the recovery of particular styles and genres within which individual variability may be located argues for the existence of even more fundamental human uniformities themselves capable of encompassing or accounting for such large historical diversities.

The key change in theory from Schleiermacher to Gadamer is as follows. For Schleiermacher history poses the problem of interpretation but does not in principle disallow the recovery of the meaningful past and does not disable the full recovery of a particular author's original intent or, through that, the original meaning of what the author intended by the text. For Heidegger and Gadamer the very process of interpretation has a radically historical nature because human nature is radically historicized. It is therefore no longer possible or even meaningful to speak of simply recovering the separate past in terms of its own sense of meaning. For these theorists historical time precludes ahistorical constancies of meaning, which affects the separate careers of both texts and efforts to interpret them. Neither texts nor their interpreters have constant natures. The meaning of the past is a construction projected from a present historically linked with the authors of the past. There is literally nothing to be recovered from a frozen and separate past, although there is indeed a fair sense in which we may still be in touch with the authors of the past.

Contemporary aesthetics, both Anglo-American and western European, focuses increasingly on the problem of artistic communication in terms of the paradoxes of history and historical meaning and the paradoxes of intentionality, both personal and societal. In this regard it has obviously converged and intersected with hermeneutics. But hermeneutics itself has had to accommodate other theories addressed to the dynamics of human history—from Freudian, Marxist, Frankfurt school, and Nietzschean sources, for instance—and these have directly influenced the course of aesthetics. The hermeneutic tradition, in fact, has no distinctive theory of the social processes that determine significant social movements affecting representational and expressive content. It has no particular ideological orientation (see IDEOLOGY) to be compared with those of critical theorists such as THEODOR ADORNO and WALTER BENJAMIN, who have had distinct views about the content of interpretive discourse; of more orthodox Marxists such as György Lukács; or of SIGMUND FREUD himself or the structuralist Freudian Jacques Lacan.

Nevertheless, because of the growing importance of interpretive and communicative questions to the aesthetic tradition and, perhaps even more important, because of the dawning difficulty of defining the nature of art works under the conditions of historicizing interpretation, modern puzzles about the ontology of art have implicitly if not actually paralleled the central puzzles of the hermeneutic tradition. In the context of strong currents stressing historicism, intentionality, and poststructuralist doubts, hermeneutic, phenomenological, structuralist, and deconstructive themes have inevitably become prominent.

Implications. The importance of this eddy of theory and criticism rests with the fact that it preserves the essential theme that art works may be construed as texts, cultural deposits of some sort that have no function other than inviting efforts to fathom their meaning. In so doing, art works utterly defeat every effort at an orderly or professionalized practice of determining their actual meaning. The French scholar MICHEL FOUCAULT, for example, sees the process as yielding forms of "normalization," habits of mind that congeal into traditions and are eventually overturned by subterranean forces that yield still other formative traditions. And Barthes construes reading as a game of free interpretation disciplined only in the sense that the players play best when they are as remarkably informed about the possibilities of the tradition as is Barthes himself. A particularly notable flowering of the optimistic advantage of this loss of objective discipline appears in the theory of Fish, who asserts that the meaning of a text is a function of specific, interpretive communities that arrive at their own consensual interpretations or conceptualizations of the text's communicative import (see READING THEORY).

In the process of absorbing these developments, the standard concern of aestheticians to analyze and define art works ontologically has been either stalemated or distinctly radicalized. The stalemate results from the view that defining art is an impossible undertaking based on the pretense that there is an essence assignable to art or that art is cognitively transparent. The radicalization of aesthetics stems from the view that art works, as with all texts, are themselves indivisible parts of the seamless matrix of human culture or are repeatedly reconstituted heuristically in the process of human attempts at self-understanding. The first development is largely Nietzschean; the second is largely the work of post-Heideggerean hermeneutics.

There is now before us—in aesthetics, poetics, and allied disciplines—the threat of interpretive anarchy, of a drift toward extreme relativism on the one hand or the opportunistic imposition of meanings by fiat on the other. This threat attests to the growing difficulty of collecting reliable, orderly efforts at interpretation and at fixing the ontology of art. Yet similar conceptual difficulties have emerged with respect to theory in the physical sciences and concerning the very enterprise of philosophy itself. Viewed optimistically, the disruption of aesthetics may be no more than an invitation to a fresh conception of the arts and human culture, one both larger and freer than previously envisioned.

See also LITERARY CRITICISM.

a

Bibliography. Monroe C. Beardsley, *Aesthetics from Classical Greece to the Present: A Short History,* New York, 1966; idem, *The Possibility of Criticism,* Detroit, Mich., 1970; Arthur C. Danto, *The Transfiguration of the Commonplace,* Cambridge, Mass., 1981; Jacques Derrida, *Of Grammatology* (De la grammatologie), trans. by Gayatri Chakravorty Spivak, Baltimore, Md., 1977; Hans-Georg Gadamer, *Truth and Method* (Wahrheit und Methode), trans. from 2d ed. by Garrett Barden and John Cumming, New York, 1975, reprint 1986; Nelson Goodman, *Languages of Art,* 2d ed., Indianapolis, Ind., 1976; E. D. Hirsch, Jr., *Validity in Interpretation,* New Haven, Conn., 1967; Joseph Margolis, *Art and Philosophy,* Atlantic Highlands, N.J., 1980; idem, ed., *Philosophy Looks at the Arts,* 3d ed., Philadelphia, 1986; F. D. E. Schleiermacher, *Hermeneutics: The Handwritten Manuscripts* (Hermeneutik), ed. by Heinz Kimmerle, trans. by James Duke and Jack Forstman, Missoula, Mont., 1977.

JOSEPH MARGOLIS

AFRICA, PRECOLONIAL

Communication across regions of precolonial sub-Saharan Africa was restricted to a greater degree than elsewhere in the world by geographical and historical factors and by the cultural and linguistic differences among African societies. Although WRITING was introduced into various portions of the African continent during ancient and medieval times, the primary medium of communication remained the spoken word. Furthermore, African languages varied to an extent unknown in any other contiguous land mass of similar size and population density. Nonetheless, precolonial African communities did not live in anything like total isolation from one another. Instead they managed to maintain a number of large-scale political systems and even more extensive trad-

b

Figure 1. *(Africa, Precolonial)* African rock art: *(a)* Petroglyph, Tassili. Photograph by Jürgen Kunz. *(b)* Painting of bowmen, Masange, Central Tanzania. After H. Sassoon. From A. R. Willcox, *The Rock Art of Africa,* New York: Holmes & Meier Publishers, 1984, opposite p. 64, and p. 115.

ing networks, and they also shared important elements of social and cultural identity.

Geographical Obstacles

Geography is the most serious barrier to the operation of communications systems within Africa, in terms of the shape of the African continent, its physical relationship to other populated areas, and its ecological conditions. As a physical entity the African continent seems designed to separate rather than integrate human communities. The formation of the vast Sahara Desert some five thousand years ago cut off the major part of Africa from easy contact with the Mediterranean, one of the most active and influential regions in the entire early world. Navigation on any regular basis was impossible from the Mediterranean or the Atlantic Ocean until the era of the Portuguese discoveries in the fifteenth century. African, Arab, Chinese, Indian, and Persian navigators did maintain sea traffic between Asia and East Africa from the second century on, and Arab-Berber camel caravans crossed the Sahara by the eighth century. However, all these contacts were limited by the coastline and the Sahel, the semidesert area at the south of the Sahara, both remarkable for their lack of major indentations. This left most inland inhabitants far from points of direct communication with outsiders. Unlike the pre-Columbian Americas (*see* AMERICAS, PRE-COLUMBIAN) and the South Seas, Af-

rica was always part of the Old World of Asia and Europe—but links with the Old World were limited to specific places.

Another geographical constraint on outside contact was the nature of soil and climate conditions in the supposedly lush tropics. African soil is generally limited in nutritive value and subject to marked, often irregular seasonal shifts between heavy rain and intense sunlight. Early African populations maintained maximum agricultural productivity by shifting cultivation sites at varied intervals. There was thus little concentration of human settlement, a major requisite for the development of complex communications systems.

The contours of the continent and its rainfall patterns have also severely limited the transportation role of African rivers, thus cutting off one more traditional means for regular contact with distant peoples. Because the tropical African environment is particularly hospitable to insects and microorganisms of various kinds, human demography is further restrained by disease, and large beasts of burden—the other major preindustrial means of transport—cannot survive in many parts of the continent.

Although great expanses of space tended to separate small African communities, there were nonetheless motives for overcoming these barriers. The most common was trade, both domestic and foreign. Certain African commodities such as gold and ivory were in particularly high demand in Asia and Europe.

Figure 2. *(Africa, Precolonial)* Abraham Cresques, map of West Africa, 1375: the first European depiction of the area, based on reports from North African Muslim traders. The detail shows the Muslim ruler of Mali, Mansa Musa *(right)* and the Atlas Mountains represented as a stone wall. Phot. Bibl. Nat., Paris.

Figure 3. *(Africa, Precolonial)* Helmet mask *(hemba)*, Bayaka, southwest Zaire. These masks are worn while displaying important charms to young Suku boys at initiation camps and again when they return to their villages. The University Museum, Philadelphia. Neg. 805.

Along with eastern Europe and central Asia, Africa also served as a major source of slaves in the medieval Islamic world. European plantations in the New World relied entirely on Africans for their labor supply *(see* SLAVE TRADE, AFRICAN). Trade routes for the export of African goods extended over great distances. Large African population centers were established at various key entrepôts.

Given the absence of writing and the range of different African languages, how did communication take place within these enlarged systems? The gravity of the problem is illustrated by a long-standing belief that African trade was conducted through dumb barter, an exchange limited to the display of goods and signals or gestures *(see* GESTURE) indicating assent when a bargain was struck. There is no documentary evidence for any such trading practice in Africa. At every marketing point there were always people who spoke at least a rudimentary common LANGUAGE, a lingua franca shared by long-distance

travelers such as the Swahili speakers of East Africa, the Juula Manding and Hausa of West Africa, or the Lingala speakers of the Congo basin. In the Juula and Hausa cases merchant groups did not simply adopt a second language for limited trade purposes but actually took on the full ethnic identity of the core Manding and Hausa speakers. Thus involvement in trade contacts could extend cultural boundaries to varying degrees. *See also* LANGUAGE VARIETIES.

Restricted literacy. African Swahili, Juula, and Hausa merchants were also Muslims and were exposed to LITERACY through their own religious education as well as through interaction with foreign trading partners at international entrepôts. There is some historical dispute about the extent to which these trading communities kept written commercial records, but in any case the practice did not help the DIFFUSION of literacy into the larger CULTURE. Precolonial Africa constitutes a prime example of what has been called restricted literacy, that is, the con-

guages, thus increasing the scope of literacy in areas such as commerce and creating the potential for the extension of literacy into much wider realms of indigenous African culture. Because of the subsequent European COLONIZATION we will never know how these uses of writing would have affected the development of African communication systems, but they at least demonstrate the possible range of internally generated change. *See* AFRICA, TWENTIETH CENTURY.

Talking drums. In the absence of widespread literacy Africans developed alternative methods of communicating across distances. The most famous of these, the talking drums found in western Africa from Guinea to Zaire, has, like dumb barter, been the subject of exotic myth. Much African drum communication does not actually translate SPEECH but consists of coded signals not unlike the bugle calls and drum signals of Western culture. In order to translate words into beats, using either the membrane of a true drum or a slitted wooden cylinder gong, words are broken into constituent units and then are reaggregated into standardized phrases. The first part of the operation is not possible using anything like Morse CODE, because there is no ALPHABET representing consonants and vowels to which the equivalents of dots and dashes can refer. Rather, the constituent verbal units are syllables, and the drummers represent words by imitating their patterns of rhythm and tone. Almost all African languages are rhythmically more complex than European ones, and many African peoples, including most of those who employ talking drums, use varying tones as speech markers. Each word in these languages is thus characterized by a particular, if not unique, pattern of syllabic rhythm and tone. These patterns can in turn be reproduced in drumming by the immediate rhythm of the beats and the manipulation or choice of the surfaces on which they are produced (tone). Within any African language many words have the same rhythm or tone pattern. Ambiguous messages are avoided by placing words within set phrases so that the receiver of the message can associate word patterns with one another.

In practical terms talking drums constitute a very complex but also technically limited medium for long-distance communication. Under optimal conditions a single drum can be heard clearly only at a maximum distance of perhaps five miles. Sending messages over greater distances thus involves highly coordinated relays of drummers. In addition, the vocabulary translated into drum language remains limited, even with all the devices of rhythm, tone, and phrasing. J. H. K. Nketia, one of the leading scholars of the subject, has calculated the Akan (Ghanaian) drumming vocabulary at about five hundred words. Finally, the ability to transmit and understand a drum message is limited to the speakers

Figure 4. *(Africa, Precolonial)* Helmet mask, Bembe, Zaire. The Metropolitan Museum of Art, New York, The Michael C. Rockefeller Memorial Collection, bequest of Nelson A. Rockefeller, 1979. (1979.206.243)

finement of READING and writing to foreign communities (including African merchants scattered along international trade routes), sacred purposes, or foreign or liturgical languages (mainly Arabic). Even Muslim rulers of African states apparently did not use writing for any state business other than communication with other Mediterranean rulers. *See* ISLAM, CLASSICAL AND MEDIEVAL ERAS.

This restriction of literacy illustrates the fact that communication systems not only shape culture but also are shaped by culture and the larger conditions to which it responds. It should be kept in mind that, given the ecological constraints to which precolonial Africans were subject, they had only limited needs for communication across long distances that were adequately served by the existing trade networks. During the eighteenth and nineteenth centuries, when external and internal trade had intensified to a point at which large numbers of ethnically diverse people were concentrated in or around urban settlements, major Muslim uprisings occurred in West Africa. These movements replaced many existing states with larger, more Islamized ones and also generated widespread religious EDUCATION in local vernacular lan-

Figure 5. *(Africa, Precolonial)* Queen Mother's head, Benin, Nigeria, ca. fourteenth to sixteenth century C.E. Bronze, life-size. Reproduced by courtesy of the Trustees of The British Museum.

Figure 6. *(Africa, Precolonial)* Bambara dance head-dress, which is worn attached to a wickerwork cap. Mali. The antelope with young represents the spirit *chi wara*, who introduced agriculture to the Bambara. Reproduced by courtesy of the Trustees of The British Museum.

of a given African language and even within this group requires a corps of highly skilled specialists.

Talking drums were thus never a means for maintaining very wide or frequent communication in precolonial Africa. Their use tended to be restricted to major events such as an important RITUAL or the arrival of European explorers (who then exaggerated the role of the practice) or just to play—to display skill or to insult rivals.

Oral Tradition

It has been argued that writing is essential to the preservation of ideas over time and that without literacy precolonial Africa had no history. Africanist scholars often respond to this contention by pointing out that Africans possess the functional equivalent of written historical records in their highly developed oral traditions. The ability to recite detailed accounts of past events from memory is indeed more fully cultivated among nonliterate peoples in general, and among Africans in particular, than in societies that have come to rely on the written word. Furthermore, for the recording of events with broad public significance African communities often relied on specialist bards who made use of various poetic and musical devices to formalize their accounts of the past. *See* ORAL CULTURE; ORAL POETRY.

The arguments against treating oral tradition as history rest on two bases: first, that the traditions only touch on a highlighted set of events, essentially the "kings and battles" of political NARRATIVE rather than the underlying social, economic, and cultural transformations; and second, and more important, that these traditions are not reliable records of the past but rather are mythical reconstructions designed to meet contemporary ideological needs (*see* IDEOLOGY). Both criticisms are largely valid and account for the retreat among professional historians from the enthusiastic embrace of oral tradition that characterized the period of African decolonization in the early 1960s. Nonetheless, oral tradition represents an important African medium for addressing the past and should be taken seriously both as myth and as history. *See* HISTORIOGRAPHY; ORAL HISTORY.

With regard to the categories of events on which it focuses—royal genealogies and deeds, natural disasters such as droughts, and encounters with other groups and peoples—oral tradition has a distinct and even self-critical sense of the past. However distorted, these events are viewed as taking place outside the present and are often associated with one another so as to convey a real sense of an earlier but connected time, the essence of historical consciousness. Moreover, at least some of the ideological tendencies in such accounts were not shared by the entire cultural community to which they were addressed and, as in the genealogies of rival lineages or the tales of battles told by competing or hostile groups, may be compared with variant versions.

Written history conventionally bases accounts of the past on documents actually recorded at the time of the events described. The existence of written texts makes it possible to compare one account with another and thus to defend any given version of the past in explicit, rational terms. British anthropologist Jack Goody has contended that it is this critical self-consciousness along with its attendant mode of dialectical discourse that forms the great cultural divide between traditional African societies and those of the West. Whether or not one fully accepts this view, it is relevant to any consideration of African oral traditions. An excellent example of the role of literacy in changing precolonial African historical consciousness can be seen in the writings of the nineteenth-century northern Nigerian Islamic reformist Muhammad Bello, whose accounts of the past are highly ideological but present and explicitly dispute the versions found in earlier Muslim writings.

Communication among African Cultures

The division of precolonial Africa into literally hundreds of language groups was a major obstacle to communication throughout the sub-Saharan regions of the continent. Nonetheless, observers frequently refer to "culture zones," large areas in which peoples speaking different languages still share a

Figure 7. *(Africa, Precolonial)* Funerary figure, Bakota, Congo. These figures, which were placed on top of baskets containing the skulls and bones of ancestors, were supposed to guard the relics from noninitiates and evil forces that might weaken their power. The University Museum, Philadelphia. Neg. 70291.

wide range of practices, beliefs, and artifacts (*see* ARTIFACT). What factors account for such cultural diffusion?

One answer may be none. Shared culture may be a result of residual rather than active common experience. Peoples living in similar circumstances develop similar institutions even when they have no contact with one another. In African cases when the contours of certain cultural elements are too closely related to be explained by some universal "primitive" life-style, it is possible that the groups themselves may have diffused through out-MIGRATION from a common historical core. The Bantu-speaking peoples who dominate entire regions of equatorial, East, and southern Africa probably originated in various migrations from a single West African cradle. However, their languages, although similar, are mutually unintelligible, and there is no reason to assume that other shared cultural traits are the result of sustained contact. *See* INTERCULTURAL COMMUNICATION.

Other cultural artifacts obviously passed along

Figure 8. *(Africa, Precolonial)* Wooden chair used only by a chief or by nobility, BaMileke, Cameroon. Reproduced by courtesy of the Trustees of The British Museum.

Figure 9. *(Africa, Precolonial)* Village chief's house in Pô, near the Ghana border, illustrating traditional design and building materials. 1983. United Nations photo 152872/Kay Muldoon.

Figure 10. *(Africa, Precolonial)* View of traditional house architectural style and building materials in the Dogon village of Sangha, Mali, 1971. United Nations photo 120924/J. Laure/PAS.

long-distance trade routes or are the result of political conquest and centralization. The fact that these events did not produce a major common language suggests that the broad economic and political systems of precolonial Africa did not penetrate very deeply into the lives of most people. Even in the very recent history of western Europe it is the modern state that has imposed linguistic unity on the citizenry as much as it was the ethnic "nation" that gave rise to the state.

Precolonial Africa is thus a good example of how nonverbal cultural elements can be communicated across ethnic boundaries without an accompanying integration of the resulting culture zones. There is ample evidence of technology, rituals, artistic styles, and aural signals circulating over extensive and linguistically diverse areas. Some of these items are associated with the real or imagined power of larger institutions, such as distant rulers or trade in exotic goods or luxury items. Thus elements of Islam were incorporated into the culture of people who did not read the Qur'an and did not abandon any of their traditional religious identity. Communities that were not linguistically or politically integrated into any centralized state often adopted the symbolic names and drumming codes of African kings, as well as such famed royal regalia as masks (see MASK) and wood carvings. At a more basic level, agricultural methods, medicines, and rituals for dealing with all kinds of afflictions have spread across many regions of Africa.

Among the most widely diffused African cultural items are cults for the defense against witchcraft. These provide a key to the relationship between general African historical experience and the pattern of precolonial African communication. Antiwitchcraft cults spread because they were a tested means of dealing with common dangers, but these dangers were also identified with the very sources of regional integration: ambitious rulers, foreign influence, and the possibility of personal enrichment through trade. What the cults communicated was the danger of intimate contact with systems that seemed to threaten the precarious welfare of Africa. The posture of precolonial Africans toward communication with the outside world was conservative, but it was a conservatism tragically vindicated by later African experience.

Bibliography. E. Arnett, *The Rise of the Sokoto Fulani, Being a Paraphrase and in Some Part a Trans. of the Infaku'l Maisuri of Sultan Muhammad Bello*, London, 1922; Ralph A. Austen, *African Economic History: Internal Development and External Dependency*, London, 1987; René A. Bravmann, *Open Frontiers: The Mobility of Art in Black Africa*, Seattle, Wash., 1973; David Dalby, ed., *Language and History in Africa*, London, 1970; Jack Goody, *The Domestication of the Savage Mind*, Cambridge, 1977; idem, ed., *Literacy in Traditional Societies*, Cambridge, 1968, reprint Cambridge and New York, 1975; John Middleton and E. H. Winter, eds., *Witchcraft and Sorcery in East Africa*, New York, 1963; Thomas A. Sebeok and Donna Jean Umiker-Sebeok, eds., *Speech Surrogates: Drum and Whistle Systems*, The Hague, 1976; Jan Vansina, *Oral Tradition as History*, Madison, Wis., 1985.

RALPH A. AUSTEN

AFRICA, TWENTIETH CENTURY

In terms of mass communication facilities Africa is the poorest-served region in the world. This is the result of Africa's generally low level of economic development, which in turn has consequences for the infrastructure required for media development and the ability to acquire communications hardware and software. Advances in media technology have had a limited impact on Africa; in fact, the gap between the industrialized nations and the developing nations of Africa has widened rather than narrowed. *See* DEVELOPMENT COMMUNICATION.

The vital role of communication in the promotion of national integration and development in Africa has led to the allocation of large resources for communication facilities, but rapidly changing technology and the need to keep up-to-date has tended to neutralize such efforts. Among the factors accounting for the slow development of mass communication in Africa are the lack of an adequate telecommunications infrastructure, low levels of LITERACY and individual income affecting mass media consumption, and severe economic problems limiting countries' abilities to acquire the necessary plant, machinery, and supplies and to train a work force in the operation and maintenance of equipment.

Despite these formidable constraints, modern mass communication has become an integral part of the modern social system in Africa. Efforts have been made at the continental level to pool resources in order to find solutions to problems best handled on a regional rather than a national basis.

Development of the Press

The newspaper made an early appearance in West Africa in the second decade of the nineteenth century with the publication of official newsletters by the British colonial authorities (see COLONIZATION; NEWSLETTER). It did not take long for the indigenous people to start small newspapers with more nationalistic zeal than either capital or professional training. Missionary efforts also helped with the development of the press, especially in Nigeria. However, progress was slow and sporadic, and not until the period between the two world wars was there a systematic growth of newspapers in West Africa produced and managed by the indigenous people. These papers were highly political in content and were used by their proprietors as instruments of political education and mobilization (*see* POLITICAL COMMUNICATION).

While the press was being developed in the English-speaking colonies of West Africa, progress was very slow in French-speaking West and equatorial Africa, where the colonial administration opposed the establishment of newspapers by Africans. The very small papers that had appeared at the end of the nineteenth century were published by French nationals for the French settlers and administrators. The first newspaper managed and edited by an African was started in the Ivory Coast in 1935. In the 1930s the de Breteuil group established a chain of newspapers in West Africa meant to serve the French and the small group of African *évolués* in colonies such as Senegal and the Ivory Coast. The activities of the publishing group were extended to other colonies such as Guinea and Cameroon after World War II.

In East Africa the beginning of the twentieth century saw the establishment of the *African Standard* in Nairobi, Kenya, which served the East African region until a paper specifically serving Tanganyika was established in 1930. The Standard group of newspapers represented the interest of the white settlers, supported the colonial administration, and took positions against the nationalist aspirations of the Africans.

The most significant strides in the development of the newspaper press were made in the immediate postwar period, when the London Daily Mirror group established important dailies in three British West African colonies: the *Daily Times* in Nigeria (1947), the *Daily Graphic* in Ghana (1950), and the *Daily Mail* in Sierra Leone (1952). The Mirror group invested considerable technical and financial resources in these papers, which became the best-produced papers on the western coast. Their efficient management and prestige helped to attract talented journalists. A few whites occupied management positions on these papers, but their editorial staffs were entirely African. The papers tried to remain neutral between the colonial administration and the nationalistic leaders and maintained a professional detachment that pleased neither of the contending factions. They changed ownership in the postindependence period and were acquired either by the state, as in Ghana, or by local entrepreneurs, as in Nigeria.

A tradition of private ownership of newspapers had been established in Africa in the colonial period. The government was generally not involved with the establishment or production of newspapers except for official government bulletins and gazettes. With the rise of an indigenous press most newspapers were used as instruments for mobilizing the people for independence. They were clearly partisan, made few concessions to impartiality or balance in the presentation of views, and were more concerned with advocacy than with the detached reporting of news. When political parties were formed, these newspapers became party papers opposing the colonial government. With independence, when the party became the government, these newspapers became mouthpieces of the ruling party (*see* GOVERNMENT-MEDIA RELATIONS). In this way government ownership of newspapers became established in Africa. Dissenting views are generally not allowed an audience in one-party states (*see* CENSORSHIP—GOVERNMENT CENSORSHIP). In a few countries private, independent publications are tolerated, but these face daily crises of survival. Unless they are supported by some political or religious group, their mortality rate is high.

Economic factors directly affect the production and distribution of newspapers. Stagnant economies do not provide the competitiveness that makes ADVERTISING, an indispensable source of revenue, feasible for businesses. The result is that even when there are no political restrictions, economic realities do not encourage investment in newspapers. In addition, high levels of illiteracy keep circulation and readership low. There are a few countries in Africa in which a diversity of information sources exists, as in Senegal or Nigeria, but these are exceptions in a continent where the press has been aptly described as "gagged," "besieged," or "shrinking." *See* NEWSPAPER: TRENDS—TRENDS IN AFRICA.

Radio and Television

RADIO can be considered the only true mass medium in Africa. It reaches an estimated 85 percent of Africans, a much larger percentage than any other medium. Although from its introduction into Africa in the 1920s radio was largely restricted to urban centers, the transistor revolution of the late 1950s and early 1960s helped to spread it to the more remote areas.

Radio was at first seen primarily as a means for European settlers and colonial civil servants to keep in touch with political, social, and cultural developments in the metropolitan areas. It also served the interests of the small educated African elite. Radio was first introduced in South Africa in 1920 and seven years later in Kenya. On the west coast it was introduced into Sierra Leone in 1934, the Gold Coast (now Ghana) in 1935, and Nigeria in 1936. The French followed the British and introduced radio into their colonies of Senegal and Congo in 1939. Outlying stations were treated as relay or rediffusion services of the metropolitan stations.

During World War II Africans were recruited into the colonial armies fighting on the side of the Allies. In order to mobilize people to help in the war effort and to keep them informed of the progress of the war, it became necessary to broadcast in local languages. Radio was used as a rallying point for the Free French Forces, particularly in the French colonies of West and Central Africa, and this led to the expansion and strengthening of transmission facilities to counter pro-Vichy broadcasts from Dakar, Senegal. These powerful transmitters installed for PROPAGANDA purposes proved helpful in the postwar development of African radio.

With very few exceptions the ownership and control of radio in Africa is vested in the state (see GOVERNMENT REGULATION). The exceptions are small stations run by private companies, such as Radio Syd in The Gambia, or by religious organizations, such as Radio ELWA in Liberia (see RELIGIOUS BROADCASTING). Because radio is the most effective medium for reaching the vast majority of the people, African leaders see it as a useful tool for educating and mobilizing them for development.

Broadcasting systems in Africa can be divided into two broad categories. In some cases they are operated as government departments or agencies directly under the supervision of a ministry of information. In other cases they have been established as statutory corporations with autonomous governing boards. However, in actual practice there is not much difference between the two arrangements because even in the case of the statutory corporations the president or the minister exercises such wide discretionary powers as to undermine the theoretical independence of the governing board.

The government grip on broadcasting is strengthened because in most cases the government is the sole or major source of funds. In a few countries license fees are charged on receivers either at the time of purchase or on a yearly basis. Such license fees contribute a negligible percentage of the total expenditure on broadcasting. Another source of revenue in some countries is radio and television COMMERCIALS, but hardly any broadcasting station derives more than 10 percent of its total income from advertising.

Broadcasting is seen as an instrument for building or maintaining national integration and is therefore highly centralized. Despite the multiplicity of languages there is a reluctance to decentralize the system for fear that it may cause fragmentation and encourage regionalism. The major exception is Nigeria, where the vast territory and the federal structure have resulted in each of the nineteen states owning and operating its own radio and television stations alongside the operations of the Federal Radio Corporation of Nigeria and the Nigerian Television Authority.

Most African radio stations operate shortwave and medium-wave transmitters. Although shortwave broadcasting has the advantage of covering longer distances, it is also subject to severe atmospheric interference in the tropics. Since the mid-1970s a number of countries have shifted to medium-wave and FM transmission, but progress has been slow because of the expense involved. Sometimes the transmitters are not powerful enough to enable the signals to reach the whole country, and with the absence of booster stations, in some countries the penetration of radio signals does not exceed 80 percent. *See also* RADIO, INTERNATIONAL.

Television was introduced into Africa in the post-independence period of the 1960s, although Nigeria had established the first television station in its western region in 1959 (see TELEVISION HISTORY). Because the installation and operation of a television station is very capital-intensive, not all African countries can afford television. In most of the countries in which it exists, television constitutes an elitist, urban medium out of the reach of the vast majority of people living in the rural areas.

Like radio, television is part of the government's broadcasting system coming directly under a ministry of information or run by a statutory corporation. It depends mainly on government subvention supplemented in some cases by revenue from advertising or income from fees levied on television receivers. Because Nigeria operates both federal and state stations, it has the best broadcasting coverage of both land area and population. In many other countries the transmitters cannot cover more than 60 percent of the land area. In some cases only about 10 percent of the land area is covered, and the population reached is about 25 percent. Even then good reception is limited to the zones reasonably close to the transmission center.

In terms of television-set ownership, only about half a dozen countries in sub-Saharan Africa (excluding South Africa) have reached the UN minimum of twenty receivers per thousand people. About half the total number of television stations and receivers in the region are to be found in Nigeria, which has seven television receivers for every hundred people. To make television available to a larger number of people, community receivers were provided in some countries, but supervision and maintenance problems arose and the experiment was largely suspended.

There is no uniform pattern of television programming in Africa. Whereas in countries such as Nigeria and Ghana about 75 percent of programs are locally produced, particularly in the countries of southern Africa up to 75 percent of programs aired on television are imported, mainly from the United States and western Europe. This is an issue of great concern to many African governments that are aware of television's potential for portraying national CUL-

TURE. In some cases the large percentage of imported programs can be accounted for by the fact that it costs far less to import an old foreign series than it does to produce programs locally. In other cases, even when there are no serious financial constraints there is a lack of trained technical and production talent.

Other communication technologies. As is the case for television, cinema is very underdeveloped in Africa. The motion picture industry is embryonic, and local film activity is scarce. Documentaries (*see* DOCUMENTARY), short instructional films, and newsreels (*see* NEWSREEL) are produced by film units attached to information ministries, but full-length feature films for commercial exhibition are very limited in number, although a few have attracted wide attention (*see* MOTION PICTURES). Most features are the result of coproduction efforts. The reasons for the underdevelopment of the film industry include the high cost of film equipment and materials and the expense of processing, which makes heavy demands on limited foreign exchange resources. For this reason almost all the films exhibited are imported from the United States and western Europe, and—in eastern Africa—from India (*see* MUSICAL, FILM).

What has been called the VIDEO revolution has come to Africa, but it has had very little impact. The videocassette recorder (VCR) is increasingly used by religious groups for evangelistic and social work. In a few countries video is used for teaching literacy and for training and educating women about child care, nutrition, health, and income-generating activities (*see* AUDIOVISUAL EDUCATION). These are examples of the development uses to which the new video technology can be put, but so far in Africa most video recording and production equipment is used in the home or in small groups for entertainment.

The VCR has become the newest status symbol in Africa after color television. VCRs are generally owned by the more affluent urbanites, and their prohibitive cost limits ownership to a small circle of privileged people. However, the technology has had an impact on film and television similar to that found in other parts of the world. Single-channel television stations are increasingly deserted as far as entertainment programs are concerned, and movie theaters are losing their customers to the video theaters that are springing up in many African cities.

The application of SATELLITE communication technology in Africa is quite recent and has been used mainly for TELEPHONE and telex communication. Occasionally its use has been extended to broadcast-program distribution, but this is very limited because of the high costs involved. Some countries covering a large landmass have domestic satellite systems with transponders leased from INTELSAT, but the capital and operational costs are very high. It is this high cost that has made it difficult for African countries to take full advantage of the satellite facilities available for broadcasting, although a small number of countries have domestic systems for receiving foreign news via satellite. A direct satellite broadcasting system can be cost-effective only when it covers a large territory. For this reason considerable interest has been shown in the establishment of an African regional satellite system for common-carrier communication and for broadcasting, but the major deterrent has been the high initial investment and projected annual costs.

Inter-African cooperation. There is increasing evidence of cooperation in the development of media in Africa, a result of the recognition that the communication problems facing the continent can be best solved on a continentwide basis rather than by individual states. In the field of broadcasting the Union of National Radio and Television Organisations in Africa (URTNA) was set up in 1962 to promote the development of radio and television at an inter-African level. URTNA's Technical Committee keeps in touch with the technical services of national broadcasting systems, and it has been active in the work of the Pan-African Telecommunications Network (PANAFTEL) project, whose main objective is to provide common-carrier telecommunications systems by terrestrial and satellite interconnections (*see* TELECOMMUNICATIONS NETWORKS).

After years of experimentation a center for the exchange of broadcast programming was set up in Nairobi in 1977. About thirty member organizations are actively engaged in the exchange, intended to reduce the dependence of African countries on non-African programming. Despite the increase in the number of countries participating in the URTNA exchange program, URTNA exchange material accounts for less than 0.5 percent of the total; U.S. and European programming still dominates television fare. URTNA has experienced severe resource limitations in the areas of finance, telecommunications facilities, technical equipment, and personnel. On occasion satellite facilities have been used for inter-African SPORTS events, but regular news and program exchange takes place via air transport. Appreciable outside assistance has been obtained from UNESCO and the Federal Republic of Germany's Agency for Technical Cooperation, but URTNA still faces many problems.

In order to reduce dependence on the transnational NEWS AGENCIES for foreign news, especially for news concerning other African countries, the Pan-African News Agency (PANA) was established by an Organization of African Unity (OAU) convention in 1979 and began operating in May 1983. PANA serves mainly as a pool of more than forty African news agencies, which transmit national news either directly to its headquarters in Dakar or through five regional offices. These regional pool offices are Lagos (Nigeria) for western Africa, Tripoli (Libya) for northern Africa, Khartoum (Sudan) for eastern Africa, Kinshasa (Zaire) for central Africa, and Lusaka (Zambia) for southern Africa. Materials received at the headquarters are processed and retransmitted by shortwave radio or telex to member countries.

The mode of transmission does not always ensure speed, fidelity, or economy, and a number of African countries continue to depend on the transnational news agencies even for news about Africa. These older agencies have satellite facilities that speed the transmission of dispatches. Like URTNA, PANA also faces formidable problems in carrying out the functions for which it was established. The largest problem is that of a very weak telecommunications infrastructure in Africa. Efforts are under way to solve it by establishment of the Pan-African Telecommunications network (PANAFTEL). In addition, PANA has financial problems severely limiting its ability to acquire up-to-date transmission and reception equipment and computer facilities for the processing, storage, retrieval, and distribution of information. Yet PANA has helped to reduce dependence on the transnational news agencies for information about Africa.

Outlook. In deciding on priorities for communication development, Africa faces a series of dilemmas. Africa depends on the industrialized countries for increasingly sophisticated communications technology. But the communications infrastructure in most countries is so rudimentary that road construction, rural electrification, the extension of telephone facilities to rural areas, the provision of television sets for communal viewing, and the development of the rural press appear to have much stronger claims on resources than do the introduction of color television, computers, microwave links, and satellites.

There can be no simple choices; the construction of an infrastructure has to be pursued simultaneously with equipment modernization. The large investments demanded by both must contend with the financial difficulties facing Africa and other developing countries (*see* LATIN AMERICA, TWENTIETH CENTURY). The development of communication in Africa will not make spectacular strides before the end of the twentieth century. African countries must first cope with the more basic problems of building an infrastructure, training personnel, and providing the rural majority with access to modern communication facilities.

See also AFRICA, PRECOLONIAL; INTERNATIONAL ORGANIZATIONS; NEW INTERNATIONAL INFORMATION ORDER; TELECOMMUNICATIONS POLICY.

Bibliography. Rosalynde Ainslie, *The Press in Africa: Communications Past and Present*, New York, 1966; Frank Barton, *The Press of Africa*, New York and London, 1979; William A. Hachten, *Muffled Drums: The News Media in Africa*, Ames, Iowa, 1971; Sydney W. Head, *Broadcasting in Africa: A Continental Survey of Radio and Television*, Philadelphia, 1974; Elihu Katz and George Wedell, *Broadcasting in the Third World*, Cambridge, Mass., 1977; Graham Mytton, *Mass Communication in Africa*, Baltimore, Md., and London, 1983; George Wedell, ed., *Making Broadcasting Useful: The Development of Radio and Television in Africa in the 1980s*, Manchester, Eng., 1986.

PAUL A. V. ANSAH

AGENDA-SETTING

Term used for the hypothesis that editors and broadcasters—the mass media in general—play an important part in shaping social reality as they go about their daily task of selecting and displaying news. A link between media and what WALTER LIPPMANN called "the pictures in our heads" has long been assumed; empirical studies since World War II have sought a more precise definition of the relationship, which many felt had been overstated in early assessments. J. S. M. Trenaman, Denis McQuail, Bernard Cohen, and others suggested that the mass media are not always successful in telling us what to think but are stunningly successful in telling us what to think *about*. In 1972 Maxwell McCombs and Donald Shaw posited an "agenda-setting" role for mass communications. The phrase and the views it implies have won wide currency.

Editorial judgments, including those relating to the placement and length of news items, reflect the relative journalistic salience ascribed to topics by media personnel. Audiences absorb these saliences from the news media, incorporating similar priorities into their personal agendas. Even though these saliences are largely a by-product of journalistic practice, here may lie the most important effect of mass communication: its ability to order and organize our world.

Agenda-setting is not limited to the correspondence between salience of topics for the media and the audience, but it also subsumes such concepts as status conferral, stereotyping, and image making. All deal with the salience of objects or their attributes. In each instance we are dealing with a generic question of agenda-setting research: How does press coverage influence our perception of objects and their attributes? Early mass communications research focused on immediate effects on ATTITUDES and found minimal media influence. Agenda-setting research redirected attention to longer-term cognitive effects of exposure to mass communications.

Media and public. That much of the world we deal with is a media-inspired secondhand reality is a truism. Two decades of studies have developed specific assertions about the role of the news media in highlighting and emphasizing certain elements—to the exclusion of others—in our pictures of the world.

Initial investigations compared public concern over the most important issues of the day with the array of issues presented in the press. Substantial correlations were found between these agendas of press and public, especially when there were controls for appropriate contingent conditions, such as heavy exposure to the media and high need for orientation.

Need for orientation is defined by level of interest in and perceived uncertainty about a topic. This idea provides a key conceptual bridge between the effects tradition of MASS COMMUNICATIONS RESEARCH and the uses-and-gratifications tradition with its emphasis on audience motivation. *See* MASS MEDIA EFFECTS.

Increased attention to each individual's experience with the issues of the day and the distinction between immediate experience and media dependency have brought agenda-setting studies down to the individual level of analysis. As a result, four different notions of agenda-setting defined by a two-by-two typology can be identified in the research literature. Along one dimension is the distinction between aggregate population versus individual analysis (e.g., POLL marginals versus individual measures). The second dimension distinguishes sets of issues from the prominence of a single issue. In terms of personal experience each issue can be arrayed along a continuum whose anchors are labeled obtrusive (extensive personal contact) and unobtrusive (lack of any personal contact). Unobtrusive issues follow the rise and fall of the news agenda, while obtrusive issues are independent of media attention. Studies by Chaim Eyal, James Winter, and Warwick Blood utilizing the conceptual distinction between obtrusive and unobtrusive issues have moved across this typology, shifting away from aggregate analysis of sets of issues to focus on changes in the salience of specific issues among populations and individuals over time.

Broadening the focus. Agenda-setting research began and grew in the long tradition of presidential ELECTION studies in the United States. Within this tradition, agenda-setting united survey research among voters and CONTENT ANALYSIS of the news media. Continuing interest in agenda-setting took researchers beyond campaign settings. It also led to experimental tests of the agenda-setting hypothesis to, supplement the causal evidence supplied by major longitudinal studies in 1972 and 1976. Owing to the variety of measurement procedures and operational definitions of agenda-setting relationships, the accumulating evidence generated by multiple methodologies provides a fruitful foundation for continuing explorations.

Almost all agenda-setting research to date has been concerned with the impact of media agendas on the public agenda. But agenda-setting as a theoretical concept about the transmission of salience is not limited to mass communications and PUBLIC OPINION. This concept also can be used to analyze earlier stages in the mass communications process.

The second decade of agenda-setting research has revived and redirected the gatekeeper theme in journalism research, documenting the impact of news organizations on one another, such as wire service influence on local media agendas. Attention also has been directed to the nature and origins of the news agenda per se and to the social implications of this specialized genre of writing and communication. For example, coverage in the national media of environmental pollution, a topic and a condition that have been present for a very long time, more than doubled after its emphasis in Richard Nixon's 1970 State of the Union address. Since most news stories can be framed (i.e., presented) from a number of perspectives, Wenmouth Williams and his colleagues have examined the implications of framing for agenda-setting. Analysis of the 1980 U.S. presidential campaign yielded strong correlations between the public agenda and the media agenda of issues specifically framed as campaign issues. However, the match was substantially weaker with the media agenda of issues in noncampaign frames.

This expanding look at a series of agenda-setting steps in the mass communication process has been labeled the agenda-building process by Kurt and Gladys Lang. Understanding how the national agenda is formed is central to our civic and theoretical concerns in POLITICAL COMMUNICATION.

Bibliography. Bernard Cohen, *The Press and Foreign Policy*, Princeton, N.J., 1963, reprint Westport, Conn., 1983; Maxwell E. McCombs, "The Agenda-Setting Approach," in *Handbook of Political Communication*, ed. by Dan Nimmo and Keith Sanders, Beverly Hills, Calif., 1981; Donald L. Shaw and Maxwell E. McCombs, eds., *The Emergence of American Political Issues*, St. Paul, Minn., 1977; David Weaver, Doris Graber, Maxwell E. McCombs, and Chaim Eyal, *Media Agenda-Setting in a Presidential Election*, New York, 1981.

MAXWELL E. MCCOMBS

ALPHABET

A system of WRITING, in which each sign represents a single phonetic value, as opposed to systems in which signs represent syllables or complete words. First developed in Palestine about 1700 B.C.E., alphabetic writing made it possible for languages to be expressed by means of relatively few characters, in contrast to word-based writing systems (such as modern Chinese and Japanese), which employ hundreds and even thousands of symbols. The modern languages that can be represented with only twenty-six signs are the descendants of the first alphabetic writing system.

Origins. The common ancestor of all alphabetic writing systems currently in use—Latin, Greek, Cyrillic, Arabic, Hebrew, and others—is the so-called Proto-Canaanite script, which was introduced by the Canaanites in the first half of the second millennium B.C.E. (see Figures 1 and 2). By that time other scripts, each of which included hundreds of signs, were already flourishing in the ancient world. None of them were alphabetic systems, however, because their signs represented whole words or syllables rather than single phonetic units. In Mesopotamia and its vicinity various peoples, such as the Babylonians, Assyrians, Elamites, Hurrians, and Hittites, used CUNEIFORM writing, in which wedge-shaped signs were impressed on wet clay. In the cuneiform systems, which evolved from the originally pictographic Sumerian writing, the various signs sometimes represented words but usually stood for syllables, like *ba* or *bi*, each of which contained a vowel and one or two consonants. Pictographic scripts were invented by the Hittites in Anatolia (although they wrote in cuneiform as well), by the Minoans in Crete (whose script was the ancestor of Linear A and Linear B), and by the Egyptians (*see* EGYPTIAN HIEROGLYPHS). In the Egyptian script, signs were triconsonantal, biconsonantal, or uniconsonantal. Had the Egyptians used only the uniconsonantal signs, their writing would have resembled the alphabetic system developed by the Canaanites. However, they maintained their traditional script by preserving the bi- and triconsonantal pictographs, and the total number of signs remained large. Presumably under the inspiration of the Egyptian uniconsonantal hieroglyphic signs, the Canaanites invented the alphabet about 1700 B.C.E. Their revolutionary innovation was to discard the bi- and triconsonantal signs and assign a single uniconsonantal sign to each consonantal phoneme in their LANGUAGE.

The Proto-Canaanite script consisted of twenty-seven pictographic signs of acrophonic values; that is, each picture represented the first consonant of its name. For example, the sign for a house, ⌐▭ in Canaanite *bet,* stood for *b;* the sign for water, ∿∿∿, in Canaanite *mem,* designated *m.* By the thirteenth century B.C.E., after five consonants fell into disuse in the language of the Canaanites, the number of signs was reduced to twenty-two. At the same time, the pictographic origins of the letters were still sufficiently evident to permit flexibility of the stances (symbols could face left or right) and writing in any direction: from left to right, from right to left, in boustrophedon (from left to right and from right to left in alternate lines), or even—before about 1100 B.C.E.—in vertical columns. By the middle of the eleventh century B.C.E., all the letters were linear (without pictographic characteristics), the stances had become fixed, and writing was only from right to left. The scholarly term for the script after about

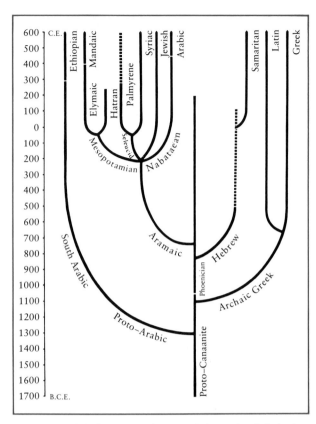

Figure 1. *(Alphabet)* Family tree of the early alphabetic scripts. Redrawn after Joseph Naveh, *Early History of the Alphabet,* Jerusalem: The Magnes Press, The Hebrew University, 1982, p. 10.

1050 B.C.E. is now no longer Proto-Canaanite (or Canaanite), but Phoenician; *Phoenician* is the Greek name for the Canaanite descendants living in the city-states of the Syria littoral in the first millennium B.C.E.

Transmission to the Greeks. In the second millennium B.C.E., the Minoans in Crete and the Mycenaeans in Greece wrote in pictographic and linear scripts, of which only Linear B—a syllabic writing system used by the Greek-speaking Mycenaeans—has been deciphered (in 1953). Whereas the Cypriots of Mycenaean descent continued to use a syllabic script until the later part of the first millennium B.C.E., Linear B died out in Greece with the Mycenaean civilization, which was destroyed by the Doric invasion about 1100 B.C.E.

There is general consensus that the Greeks learned alphabetic writing from the West Semites, who developed the Proto-Canaanite (later Phoenician) script. This conclusion is based on the following evidence:

1. According to Greek tradition, the alphabetic characters, which the Greeks called "Phoenician letters" or "letters of Kadmos," were introduced by the Phoenicians, who came to Greece with a person named Kadmos.

#	Late Proto–Canaanite variation 1200–1050 B.C.E.	Archaic Greek variation	Classical Greek	Latin
1			A	
2			B	
3			Γ	C
4			Δ	D
5			E	
6			-	F
7			Z	- G[1]
8			H	
9			Θ	-
10			I	J
11			K	
12			Λ	L
13			M	
14			N	
15			Ξ	-
16			O	
17			Π	P
18			-	
19			-	Q
20			P	R
21			Σ	S
22			T	
			Y	U,V,W
			Φ	- X[2]
			X	Y
			Ψ	Z
			Ω	

1 G is variation of C   2 X from Greek Ξ

Figure 2. *(Alphabet)* The Proto-Canaanite script, ancestor of archaic and classical Greek and Latin scripts. Redrawn after Joseph Naveh, *Early History of the Alphabet*, Jerusalem: The Magnes Press, The Hebrew University, 1982, p. 180.

2. The names of the letters, such as *alpha, beta, gamma,* and *delta,* have no meaning in Greek, but most of their Semitic equivalents, such as *alef, bet, gimel,* and *dalet,* are Semitic words.
3. The sequence of the Greek letters is basically identical to the Phoenician or Hebrew alphabetic order.
4. The earliest Greek letter forms are very similar to, and some are even identical to, the equivalent West Semitic letters.

The archaic Greek alphabet used the twenty-two Semitic letters, although not all of them served as consonants. *A, E, I,* and *O* were systematically used as vowels, which was a most important innovation (see below). The Greeks also added five supplementary letters: Υ, Φ, X, Ψ, and Ω. The archaic Greeks wrote in horizontal lines from left to right, from right to left, or in horizontal boustrophedon. The archaic Greek script had many local variations. Only in the fourth century B.C.E., when the Ionian version of the script was generally accepted, did the uniform classical Greek script emerge.

There is much controversy about the date when the alphabet was introduced to the Greeks. Scholars have generally placed it in the eighth century B.C.E. However, based on various kinds of evidence, including the similarity of many of the letter forms in archaic Greek inscriptions to Canaanite script of much earlier date, some have suggested that the alphabet may have come to Greece—or at least to some Greek islands, such as Crete or Thera—as early as 1100 B.C.E. The question remains a subject of scholarly debate.

Significance for the history of writing. As stated above, the Proto-Canaanite script, by using only twenty-seven uniconsonantal pictographic signs, streamlined the system of Egyptian hieroglyphic script, which had a very large number of tri-, bi-, and uniconsonantal signs. There are scholars who minimize the importance of this development and contend instead that real alphabetic writing was invented only by the Greeks. This is based on the fact that each "letter" of the Semitic writing system stood for a fixed consonant plus any vowel, leading scholars to conclude that the West Semitic writing was syllabic rather than alphabetic. According to this point of view, only Greek writing, expressing single sounds by means of separate signs for consonants and vowels, marks the final step in the history of writing and can be called alphabetic. This interpretation emphasizes that from the Greek period to the present no comparable innovation has occurred in the inner structural development of writing because, generally speaking, consonants and vowels are written in the same way as in ancient Greek.

While there is no doubt that the Greek alphabet and its descendants are more developed than the Semitic alphabets, there was a Canaanite attempt to notate vowels in the alphabetic cuneiform texts from Ugarit as early as the fourteenth century B.C.E., and in the eleventh century B.C.E. the Aramaeans introduced vowel signs at the ends of words. Furthermore, some scholars maintain the view that the systematic notation of vowels is, relatively speaking, a minor change in the history of writing. They contend that the real revolution took place when a reduced set of signs made LITERACY a much more widely accessible skill.

Semitic and European descendants. The relationships between descendants of the early Canaanite-Phoenician script are illustrated in Figure 1. Proto-Arabic script branched off from the Proto-Canaanite about 1300 B.C.E. It is the ancestor of the scripts used in the ancient South Arabian kingdoms of Saba, Maʿin, Hadramaut, and others. The modern descendant of this branch is the Ethiopian script, which consists of seven series of twenty-six letters and is written from left to right. The seven series are formed by slight modifications of the basic character, indicating whether a certain consonant is to be vocalized by a particular vowel or is to remain unvocalized.

The next important departures from the Canaanite-Phoenician roots were Hebrew and Aramaic. The Hebrews adopted the Canaanite script in the twelfth century B.C.E. and used it until the ninth century B.C.E., when they began to develop a script of their own. The Aramaeans borrowed the Phoenician script in the eleventh century. The Aramaic script began its independent development in the eighth century B.C.E., after which Aramaic was spoken and written by peoples other than the Aramaeans, because the Assyrians introduced it as an official means of communication among the various nations living in the Assyrian Empire. Moreover, it became the lingua franca for diplomatic and commercial transactions among many nations. As a result, abbreviated letter forms were introduced to produce a quick and efficient version of the script. Meanwhile, the Phoenician script continued to flourish, both on the Phoenician mainland and in the Phoenician settlements along the shores of the Mediterranean Sea, until the second century C.E.

Aramaic continued to be used as an official language for many centuries over a wide geographical area. For example, Aramaic inscriptions from the Persian period (ca. 530–330 B.C.E.) have been found in a region extending from Asia Minor as far as Egypt and Afghanistan, but the Aramaic script remained uniform, and no local traditions of writing developed even in the most remote provinces. The various derivatives of the Aramaic script emerged only a century or two after the fall of the Persian Empire. At this time Greek replaced Aramaic as an official language, but Aramaic was too well established to be completely replaced. Thus, during the third and second centuries B.C.E., distinctive versions of the Aramaic scripts were developed by various national, cultural, and geographic units. In the East, local scripts such as Palmyrene, Syriac, and Mandaic developed as well as scripts for Middle Iranian languages and possibly the earliest Indic scripts, from which the modern Indian (Devanagari) and derived South Asian scripts are descended. In the West two offshoots emerged: the Nabataean and Jewish (square Hebrew) scripts.

The Nabataean script—the ancestor of Arabic writing—developed very cursive letter forms, and, therefore, the original Aramaic is not discernible in Arabic. However, the Jewish script, which is currently used by the Jews and is called (square) Hebrew, preserved most of the shapes of fourth-century B.C.E. Aramaic letters.

The original Hebrew script (Palaeo-Hebrew), which developed in Israel and Judah in the First Temple Period (950–586 B.C.E.), was increasingly neglected by the Jews. In the time of the Second Temple (515 B.C.E.–70 C.E.), both scripts—the original Hebrew and the Jewish (square Hebrew)—existed side by side. However, the use of the Palaeo-Hebrew was restricted mainly to coin legends and sacred texts, whereas the Jewish script eventually became the only script of the Jews. Only the Samaritans have continued to use the original Hebrew script into modern times.

The archaic Greek local scripts were used by mainland, island, and colonial Greeks as well as by peoples who did not speak Greek at all. These included, in Asia Minor, the Phrygians, Lydians, Lycians, and Carians; and, on the Italian peninsula, the Etruscans, Umbrians, Oscians, and Romans. When different peoples adopted the script, they accepted or rejected certain letters according to the requirements of their particular languages. Classical Greek, the local script of Ionia, which was universally accepted from the fourth century B.C.E. on, omitted three letters from the archaic Greek alphabet. The Latin (or Roman) alphabet adopted the archaic Greek local script that was used by the Etruscans, who had learned it in turn from the Chalcidian Greek colonies in Italy. First the Etruscans and then the Romans made various alterations in the alphabet to serve their own languages. After the Romans conquered Greece, and the Latin language began to borrow Greek words, more alterations were made, such as the addition of the letters Y and Z. In the MIDDLE AGES, in order to distinguish between consonantal and vowel signs, the letters *J, U,* and *W*—as variations of *I* and *V*—were added to the Latin alphabet of twenty-three letters. Thus, the Latin alphabet employed today for most European languages has twenty-six letters.

The other modern derivative of the Greek alphabet is the Cyrillic script. In the ninth century C.E., it is said, two Salonican Greek brothers, St. Cyril and St. Methodius, who journeyed to convert the Southern Slavs to Christianity, adapted the Greek alphabet for writing texts in the Old Slavonic language. Since the phonetic system of Slavonic languages was richer than that of Greek, new letters were invented. It is maintained that Cyril knew Hebrew and that he took two letters, *sade* (צ) and *shin* (ש), from the Hebrew alphabet and transformed them into three Slavonic letters for the sounds *ts* (Ц), *tsh* (Ч), and *sh* (III). The Cyrillic script is used in the USSR, Bulgaria, and Yugoslavia.

See also AMERICAS, PRE-COLUMBIAN—WRITING SYSTEMS; CLAY TOKENS; INDUS SCRIPT; WRITING MATERIALS.

Bibliography. David Diringer, *The Alphabet: A Key to the History of Mankind*, 3d ed., New York and London, 1968; idem, *Writing*, New York and London, 1962; G. R. Driver, *Semitic Writing: From Pictograph to Alphabet*, 3d ed., New York and London, 1976; I. J. Gelb, *A Study of Writing*, rev. ed., Chicago, 1963; Lilian H. Jeffery, *The Local Scripts of Archaic Greece*, Oxford, 1961; P. Kyle McCarter, Jr., *The Antiquity of the Greek Alphabet and the Early Phoenician Scripts*, Missoula, Mont., 1975; Joseph Naveh, *Early History of the Alphabet: An Introduction to West Semitic Paleography*, Jerusalem and Leiden, 1982; idem, *Origins of the Alphabet*, London, 1975.

JOSEPH NAVEH

ALTERNATIVE MEDIA. *See* CITIZEN ACCESS; VIDEO.

AMERICAS, PRE-COLUMBIAN

This topic is discussed in two sections:
1. Communications
2. Writing Systems

1. COMMUNICATIONS

There is still considerable debate about the origins of the pre-Columbian cultures of the Americas. It is assumed that the original inhabitants of the New World migrated there from somewhere in the Old World, where they had evolved and had acquired sufficient cultural skills to enable them to survive in cold climates. No fossils of primitive humans or their apelike precursors or even any of the great apes have been discovered anywhere in the Americas.

Migration

MIGRATION in prehistoric times must be inferred by the distribution of Paleo-Indian artifacts and languages. From about 40,000 B.C.E. until quite recently an unknown number of groups entered the American continent from northeastern Asia, crossing the Bering Strait, which formed a land bridge several times during the maxima of glaciation and a chain of islands during interglacials. These groups are ancestral to the LANGUAGE groups of prehistoric America. They had already acquired a limited number of technical skills, especially those for big-game hunting, protection against cold (CLOTHING, housing), and traveling by water and on snow. Although undoubtedly of Asian origins, these groups cannot yet be traced to their precise cultures of origin in Asia.

Historically documented migrations. Migrations of large groups over long distances occurred continuously, even after the continent had been completely occupied by humans by about 20,000 B.C.E. Many Indian tribes preserved memories of such migrations (Leni-Lenape in North America and Pipil groups in Central America). Pipil migrations (from 900 to 1300 C.E.) are among the best attested through many independent sources and linguistic studies. Similarly, Tupi migrations in the South American lowlands have been reconstructed by studying their myths and cultural as well as linguistic relations with other tribes.

Transatlantic migrations. Vikings from Greenland visited and settled the east coast of North America from 1000 to 1300, as attested by their oral traditions and excavations in Newfoundland (Anse aux Meadows). They had no lasting impact on Indian cultures. Other transatlantic contacts before Columbus have been proposed repeatedly (Egyptians, Phoenicians, Romans, Irish) but have never been proved by undisputable archaeological or documentary evidence.

Transpacific migrations. Contacts of fishermen from the Jomon culture in prehistoric Japan with Valdivia people in coastal Ecuador have been proposed for the introduction of ceramic technology in South America. However, these claims have been challenged for stratigraphic and chronological reasons. Belief systems, temple-pyramid ARCHITECTURE, the art of manuscript painting, and other cultural complexes of Classic Mesoamerica are said to have had their origins in India, China, Indonesia, or Cambodia and to have been transferred through transpacific shipwrecks and/or purposeful EXPLORATION. Formal and conceptual similarities and purported loan words in contact languages are put forward as arguments. This issue is not yet settled. It has also been proposed that contacts by boat between Andean civilizations (Inca) and eastern Polynesia (Easter Island) in both directions were responsible for shared useful plants (e.g., sweet potato, gourd, and cotton) and similarities in concepts of deities (tiger/jaguar complexes) and social structure on the basis of rather weak documentary hints and the well-known navigation skills of the Polynesians. Other migrations and/or sporadic contacts resulting in important communication have been proposed, such as Austronesian immigration via Antarctica and extraterrestrial astronauts leaving traces in Palenque, Nazca, and other sites. These claims are impossible to prove and in any case are unlikely.

Language

As with all human groups, spoken language was the prevalent means of communication among pre-

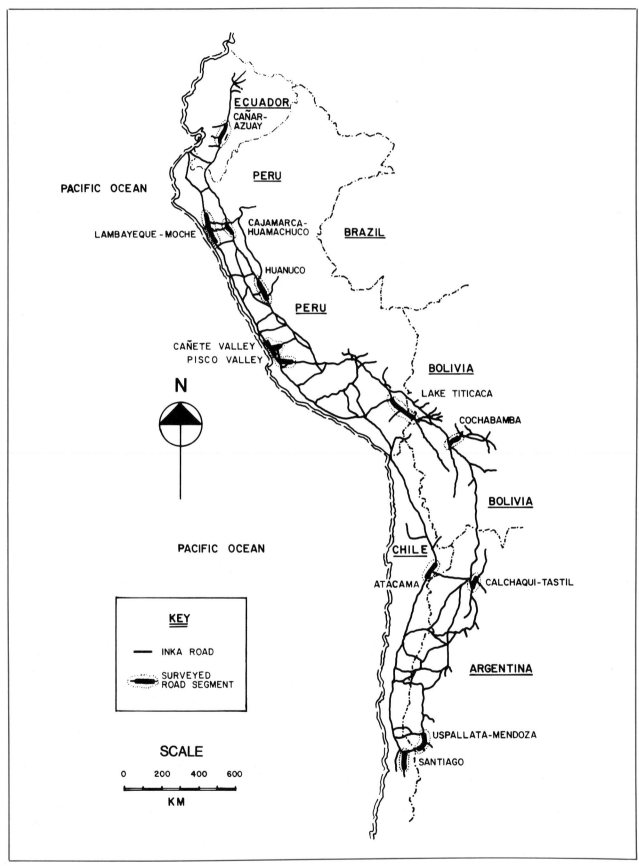

Figure 1. *(Americas, Pre-Columbian—Communications)* Surveyed segments of the Inca road system.
From John Hyslop, *The Inka Road System,* Orlando, Fla.: Academic Press, 1984, p. 4.

48

Columbian people in the Americas. Approximately fifteen hundred distinct languages were spoken in aboriginal America. They are grouped into twenty genetic families (some of them more like residual categories than attested genetic classes) implying common ancestry. Some languages still remain unclassified.

History. Studies of the history of American Indian languages are revealing for the reconstruction of migrations (through glottochronology), contact with other languages (through loan-word studies), and political, economic, and social dominance (through cultural vocabulary studies). These kinds of analysis are fairly advanced for Mesoamerican and Uto-Aztecan languages. Archaeologically attested cultures can now be matched with languages. For example, the Olmec CULTURE is now associated with the Proto-Mixe-Zoque language, and this language has been found to be the mother language for basic cultural vocabulary in Mesoamerica. Proto-Mixe-Zoque *kakawa* means "cocoa" and is the source for Aztec *cacahuatl* and Maya *cacaw*. Interestingly enough, historical relations between North American and South American language families cannot as yet be firmly established.

Varieties. Some internal variations reflecting social structure as well as differential geographical contacts are well attested. Dialect fragmentation is much more pronounced in mountainous environments, such as the state of Oaxaca in Mexico and the Bolivian and Peruvian Montaña, than in settings easily traveled, such as the North American Arctic, Subarctic, and Plains, and the South American Patagonia. For several languages in the Caribbean, distinct forms of SPEECH exist for males and females. Differentiation according to social rank developed among some of the more populous and complex societies (Aztec), and these societies also show the beginnings of occupationally specialized vocabulary. On a more general level, specific forms of speaking (metaphorical speech, secret language) were confined to religious specialists (shamans, priests, day keepers) and to the political elite (Zuyua language of the Yucatec Maya).

Mazatec Indians of Mexico developed a whistle language, using the phonemic tonal pattern of spoken utterances and reproducing them through whistling. Whistle language can be used for communication across valley floors or canyons.

From Alaska to California and in the Columbia River drainage area the Chinook jargon was in use. In the southern Plains, Comanche developed into a trade language; along the coast of Louisiana and Florida, Mobilian (Chickasaw) was generally used. The Aztec in Mexico and the Inca in Peru imposed their languages onto regions that they dominated economically, politically, and militarily. For example, Quechua, the language spoken in the Cuzco

region of Peru, became a lingua franca for the Inca Empire as Inca armies extended their control over surrounding areas. It was taught to the newly conquered populations and was the medium of communication between them and the Inca rulers. In lowland South America migration was the prime factor in establishing Tupi-Guaraní as a generally accepted trade language.

Sizable portions of a population living in a linguistically segmented environment with strong social, commercial, or ceremonial intercourse can be expected to utilize two or more languages. This situation prevailed in parts of Mesoamerica, the Andes, and parts of Amazonia (Northwest and Xingu); yet the extent of pre-Columbian multilingualism is not known. *See also* LANGUAGE VARIETIES.

Oral literature. Formal speech used in specific social and RITUAL contexts was highly developed in many language groups in ancient America. Some examples are verbal dueling (Eskimo), individually owned ceremonial songs (Northwest Coast), historical narrations (Leni-Lenape), jokes (Shoshone), prayers and incantations (Aztec), lyrical songs and poems (Quechua), and colorful myths (Araucanian). The extent and process of dispersal of themes and forms of oral literature is not yet known. *See also* ETHNOPOETICS; FOLKLORE; ORAL CULTURE; ORAL POETRY; SPEAKING, ETHNOGRAPHY OF.

Writing

Systems of signs fixed (written) on a permanent medium to serve interpersonal and diachronic communication are classified here into two groups according to their ability to reproduce the spoken language. Systems that are capable of reproducing language completely are called full WRITING systems. Others that use signs not exclusively to represent sounds, that do not have signs for all sounds (or syllables, morphemes, etc.) of a specific language, and that do not render language completely or unequivocally are called partial writing systems. *See also* SIGN; SIGN SYSTEM.

Full writing systems. Full writing systems are second only to the spoken word in their ability to transmit messages, and they are more durable if written on an appropriate medium and stored. In pre-Columbian America only the Lowland Maya developed a full writing system (see section 2, below). It was used to convey data on dynastic history, calendrical and astronomical matters, and divination.

Partial writing systems. In the Americas partial writing systems are found exclusively in Mesoamerica. They emerged around 500 B.C.E. in Olmec culture of the Gulf Coast of Mexico and developed into two distinct branches: the Isthmian (Tres Zapotes, Izapa, Abaj Takalik, Kaminaljuyu) and the Oaxacan/

Figure 2. *(Americas, Pre-Columbian—Communications)* Mayan stela: Piedras Negras number 14. Mexico. The University Museum, Philadelphia. Neg. 23059.

Central Mexican (Zapotec, Xochicalco, Mixtec, Aztec). The Mesoamerican partial writing systems were used to convey data on dynastic history, territorial and political organization, economics (tribute specified with regard to merchandise, quantity, and provenience), ritual, and divination. Writing was done on stone monuments, in books of bark fiber or leather whose pages were connected like sections of a folding screen, on large cotton cloths (called *lienzo*), and on jewelry. Many such documents survived the general destruction by the Spaniards. *See also* WRITING MATERIALS.

Postcontact developments. Mesoamerican partial writing systems and the controversial Peruvian *tocapu* system survived in part until around 1600, when they were completely replaced by the Latin ALPHABET. In subsequent centuries and even before, many new systems (partial and full) emerged through stimulus DIFFUSION from European models. The more remarkable are Alaska-Neck, Cherokee-Sequoyah, Apache-Silas-John in North America; Cuna in Central America; and Aymara in South America. Others originate from direct invention and introduction by European missionaries. The best known of those is the Mesoamerican Testerian writing system, employed largely by missionaries in propagating the Christian faith. Study of postconquest inventions and developments is important for clarification of the process of invention, adaptation to specific languages, communicative purposes, and social acceptance or rejection.

Sign Systems

Gestures used in nonlinguistic communication and as an adjunct to speech in specific situations (e.g., greeting, trade) are important means of communication and hence ubiquitous. They are also highly individual with regard to tribe and social group. Gestures intended as a surrogate for linguistic communication were developed into sign systems for communication between partners, one of whom at least was deaf or mute (e.g., Tapiete of the South American Chaco). A wider use of such sign systems was made in North America (Plains) when persons speaking mutually unintelligible languages met. Signs are preponderantly of a representational nature. They are formed mostly with arms, hands, and fingers, less frequently with other body parts or extrasomatic objects. *See also* GESTURE; SIGN LANGUAGE.

Messages were sent on pieces of birchbark (*Betula papyrifera*) by Indians of the Great Lakes region. They were delivered by messengers or posted on trees along trails and water routes. Their content could be strictly personal (letters) or could contain information on hunting and potential danger. The sign system used consisted of self-explanatory pictures scratched into the bark. These birchbark messages could be comprehended only by someone who had good background knowledge of the local conditions.

MUSICAL INSTRUMENTS, especially drums, flutes, and trumpets, were used by several Indian groups to transmit messages over considerable distances. In addition to general news transmittal (Plains) they were employed in warfare to coordinate movements of bodies of warriors (Aztec, Maya, Inca). For bridging even larger distances, smoke signals during the day and fires at night were used, especially on the plains, on seacoasts, and in mountainous areas where visual contact could be established over long distances. In addition, maps drawn in the sand are reported from many North American Indian tribes.

In what is now the eastern United States, wampum belts, formed of strings of shell disks (later glass pearls), might have been exchanged ceremonially as tokens of important (political) agreements. The design would allude to the event commemorated but would be intelligible only to the parties involved. The Navajo Indians of the North American Southwest fashioned intricate geometrical and pictorial designs of highly symbolic content during shamanic healing ceremonies. A much more ambitious ritualistic sign system possibly underlies the designs found in the Pampa de Nazca in southern Peru. Some investigators have interpreted them as mythological and/or astronomical designs.

Especially in Mesoamerica, where a dense population and intensive agriculture made arable land a valuable and scarce resource, territorial boundaries were often marked off. Stone walls, cactus hedges, heaps of stones, and preexisting trees served this purpose.

For counting days or quantities of goods, carved or painted sticks and boards were in general use (e.g., Iroquois, Plains Indians, Chamulas). A special and more elaborate means of numerical notation was developed by ancient Andean cultures (pre-Inca and Inca) in the form of the quipu. To a main cord smaller single cords were attached, which represented quantities in a decimal system of counting. Quipus were used by merchants and stewards (*quipucamayoc*) in charge of state storehouses. Similar but much more simple quipus are still used today by herdsmen in the Andes to keep track of their flocks.

Routes of Communication

The most elaborate and sophisticated route systems in pre-Columbian America were the Inca highways, built to a great extent on smaller, pre-Inca roads. They extended in two main highways (mountain and coastal) from northern Ecuador to central Chile and northern Argentina. The two main highways were connected by transverse roads. Retaining walls, bridges (stone, wooden, and suspension bridges), and stairways cut into hills and slopes were the major con-

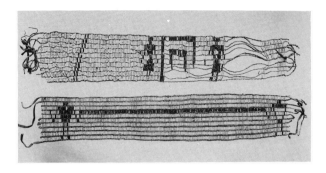

Figure 3. *(Americas, Pre-Columbian—Communications)* Wampum belt: First Penn Treaty Belt. The University Museum, Philadelphia. Neg. 12964.

struction features of these highways. Rest houses served the organized traffic of goods, messages, and military movements. The roads could also be used by private travelers.

Similar systems of lesser extent and sophistication existed in the northern Maya Lowlands and in the Aztec state, centering in the island capital Tenochtitlán (now Mexico City). Where population was less dense and where there was no territorial political structure and little traffic in goods, Indian trails and buffalo trails (North America) served the limited needs. These trails were often quite extensive.

Cleared plazas in the village centers that connected paths between houses and walkways from the village to, for example, water sources were standard forms of local roads. Remarkable exceptions were the paved roads and huge plazas with stairways connecting them at different levels, found in Maya, Aztec, Zapotec, and Inca cities, as well as the walled roads in pre-Inca cities of the Peruvian north coast (Chan-Chan).

The American continents have vast systems of navigable streams and lakes, such as the Columbia, Yukon-Mackenzie, Great Lakes-St. Lawrence, Mississippi-Missouri, Cauca-Magdalena, Orinoco-Amazon, and Paraguay-Paraná. These were used extensively for transportation by boat, such as birchbark and buffalo-hide boats in North America, dugout canoes in most other regions, and, more rarely, bark canoes and rafts. Some river systems pass so close to each other that portages were installed, and virtually all of North and South America, excluding the western cordilleras, could be traveled by boat.

Sea traffic along the coasts was especially important in the Arctic for hunting sea mammals, and the boats used for such hunting were kayaks and umiaks. On the Atlantic coast of Middle America, centering on the Yucatán peninsula, among the Caribbean islands, and off the Pacific coast of South America sea traffic served trade purposes. Apart from dugout canoes and balsawood rafts, big rafts were used for transporting merchandise.

Merchants were not the only people to play important roles in the transfer of news and information over great distances. Another special group were the *chasquis*, the messengers of the Inca state, who were stationed in pairs several miles apart along the main roads. As a messenger approached, the waiting runner began to run alongside him and to listen to the message to be memorized and passed on and/or to receive any written material to carry, after which he began his run to the next relay station. This system was incredibly speedy, given the good road system with rest houses. In addition to memorized messages, quipus could be used to fix and deliver the messages.

Ad hoc messengers were also employed by other groups as the need arose, and they also occasionally carried written messages (Aztecs with picture writing, Algonkians with wampum or birchbark messages). Among the communication specialists were spies known to have been employed by Plains Indians and Aztecs on a rather regular scale in preparation for war. Pathfinders for hunting were used by groups making their living from big game, such as the Aleut, Eskimo, Arctic Indians, and Plains Indians.

Arts

ART communicates indirectly, emotionally, and therefore often unconsciously. Its general scope and its aesthetic appeal make it a powerful means of communication. Highly complex and stratified societies have a tendency to control or to co-opt the visual arts and to use them to propagate state RELIGION (Chavín), prestige, and legitimacy of rulership (Classic Maya) and to create tribal or state identities (Aztec).

Visual arts. Visual arts closely associated with the human body were often part of a symbolic system communicating role, social status, and religious belief. The most direct form—scarification and body painting—prevailed in the tropics and subtropics (*see* BODY DECORATION). Age and kinship groups were thus indicated but never rank. Clothing and adornment were extremely sophisticated among the Northwest Coast Indians and the Aztec, Maya, Muisca, and Andean high civilizations. Here rank (general and military), occupational specialization, and tribal group were often represented. Especially impressive is the Indian tradition of masks (*see* MASK) worn during winter ceremonies (Northwest Coast), rituals of secret societies (Iroquois), and DANCE dramas (Mesoamerica). However, European influence on the use of masks in dance dramas is difficult to measure. *See also* ARTIFACT; VISUAL IMAGE.

Decoration of buildings (Northwest Coast facade painting, Plains Indians winter counts painted on tipis, temple decoration and MURAL painting of Mesoamerican and Andean civilizations) and associated monuments (Northwest Coast totem poles, stelae and altars of Classic Maya culture) often inform us directly about the social group, kinship organization, individual deeds, and occupations of the person or group using the building. Grave monuments (San Agustín) and grave furniture (Maya, Peruvian Coast) provide visible evidence of such things as social rank. They have helped modern archaeologists to distinguish stratified from egalitarian societies and to trace intragroup ranking and development. *See also* ART, FUNERARY.

Dance and music. Dance was often incorporated into rituals and combined with speech, chants, and instrumental music. Elaborate dances, often of an imitating nature, are known from the Pueblo and Plains Indians (animal imitations) as well as the Aztec (imitation of idiosyncrasies of foreign people). Full-fledged Indian dance dramas are reported from Mesoamerica (Aztec, Quiche "Rabinal-Achi") and from the Inca, although for the Inca no undisputably pre-European DRAMA is preserved with good description or reliable text.

Belief and Religious Systems

In the absence of rational scientific thought, belief systems and religion are the main vehicles to process knowledge and to stabilize or revolutionize human attitudes. Religion and beliefs are communicated mainly through language (myth, prayer, etc.) but also to some extent through emotional outbursts (trance, ecstasies), dramatic performance (gesture, dancing, self-mutilation), ritual, and art and its associated SYMBOLISM.

Sacred places, which were often respected by otherwise hostile groups and were therefore ideal meeting and trading places as well as places of pilgrimage, played a major role in general communication among

Figure 4. *(Americas, Pre-Columbian—Communications)* Quipu from Peru. The University Museum, Philadelphia. Neg. 134153.

Figure 5. *(Americas, Pre-Columbian— Communications)* Chippewa wooden feather box with a pictographic song record of the *Midéwiwin* ceremonies on the cover. Courtesy Museum of the American Indian, Heye Foundation, New York. Photograph by Carmelo Guadagno.

Indians. The most important and long-lasting were Pipestone Quarries in southwestern Minnesota, Teotihuacán and Cholula in central Mexico, Chichén Itzá and Cozumel in Yucatán, and Pachacamac on the Peruvian coast.

Social Networks

Among sedentary groups the extended family, including lineal and collateral kin beyond the nuclear family, was the basic sphere of interaction. Further extensions based on lineage (Iroquois) or moieties (Bororo) were common.

Education. The EDUCATION of CHILDREN is the most important means of intergenerational transfer of knowledge and values. In pre-Columbian America it was mostly the responsibility of the parents. Mothers exclusively cared for babies, but as children grew older education became the responsibility of both parents or close relatives (e.g., matrilateral uncles) according to GENDER. Playmates often played an important role within the same family or residential unit. Learning was partly through imitation, backed by practical instruction. Thus specialized crafts were taught in the familiar social settings, especially by the parents (California basketry, Aztec metalworking). Instruction could be individual and even abstract, as with the Eskimo, who devised practical problems (canoeing, hunting) for children to solve and resorted even to the discussion of hypothetical problems. A common educational task was the replication of adult instruments (weapons for hunting, ritual puppets) to be used by children to reenact rituals (Pueblo) or everyday life (Karaja). Clay figu-

rines, especially abundant in formative Mesoamerica, may have served similar ritual, educational, or even recreational purposes.

Corporate education, supposing that children were educated in nonfamilial contexts, was also known. It was highly formalized with the Aztecs, who offered two different careers: the priesthood, by way of the temple or monastery SCHOOL (*calmecac*), and the military, by way of the military school (*telpochcalli*). Formal education is well expressed in educational speeches of the Aztec called *huehuetlatolli* (precepts of the elders).

At certain ages children were introduced collectively or individually into new roles through rites of passage (spirit seeking in North America), often accompanied or followed by formal introduction into secret societies (Plains), medical societies (*Midéwiwin* of the Woodlands), and religious societies (kachina of the North American Southwest). Sometimes separate places or buildings (kiva) existed for the introductory ceremonies.

Social cooperation. Most economic activities made use of some social interaction. Among Amazonian hunters and gatherers small groups of males hunted jointly, forming a cooperating and closely knit group, and women also worked together collecting seeds and plants. Where agriculture played a primary role, harvest time was an opportunity to cooperate. In addition military organizations were counted among the more important coercive and communicative units in many Indian societies.

Feasts were opportunities for personal contact, exchange of news, and economic transfer. Their main purpose, of course, was the demonstration of social

Figure 6. *(Americas, Pre-Columbian—Communications)* Ruins of the ancient Zapotec city of Monte Albán, Mexico. Giraudon/Art Resource, New York.

solidarity, transcending class and rank (as in the potlatches of the Northwest Coast). They also could serve as indoctrination and training opportunities for state IDEOLOGY and religion (Aztec feast cycles) and to give frame to communal labors (Inca seasonal feasts), especially those connected with agriculture (harvest festivals).

In some regions formal declarations of war were symbolized by special markings at the border of the territories of the warring parties (painted arrows). Warfare itself could be formalized (Plains Indians coup), as could treatment of prisoners of war, even if they were destined to lose their lives as sacrificial victims (Aztec). Ambassadors and special emissaries were also involved in matters of foreign politics, at least in states and chiefdoms with political institutions.

Forced resettlement. Resettlement of whole populations was undertaken by the Inca as a means to control conquered people. Potentially hostile groups were transferred by their Inca conquerors to other locations, where they would be easier to control, and their lands were occupied by people whose loyalty was more certain. This probably was a major factor contributing to the spread of the Quechua language and the Inca way of life, as well as to the rapid disappearance of pre-Inca cultural traditions of the Central Andes.

Commerce

Commerce as communication is highlighted by three different processes: (1) Direct contact between peoples leads to exchanges of information; (2) Agreement on values and exchange items tends to standardize economic activities; and (3) Commodities exchanged are by themselves channels of technical, artistic, and natural resource information.

Forms of local trade. Direct individual exchange was the prevalent form of local trade during pre-

Columbian times. Sometimes silent barter was used, especially among hostile groups in South America (e.g., between the Guaitaca and Tupinamba Indians). Market trade was generally important among advanced tribes, chiefdoms, and states. Local markets were well developed almost everywhere in agricultural regions. Especially active ones have been reported for the contact period in Nicaragua. Markets were often situated at religious shrines, near navigable water courses (Cauca Valley), and intermediary between different sources of important raw materials (e.g., Tikal). International or state-controlled markets are reported for the Aztec, Mixtec, Uraba, Inca, and the Cauca Valley.

Redistribution. Besides market exchange, redistribution of collected taxes was an important form of commercial exchange in the Inca and Aztec states. This system was probably responsible for the rapid standardization of cultures and societies in the central Andes under Inca rule.

Long-distance trade. Long-distance trade had developed everywhere on the American continents, stimulated by unavailable local resources, such as metals (copper), useful and precious minerals (soapstone, volcanic tuff and basalt, obsidian, turquoise, jadeite, rock crystal), seashells, salt, and feathers (parrot, quetzal). The linking of state politics with trade in Aztec society is noteworthy. Traders were often military spies, and trade relations prepared the terrain for later military conquest and full economic exploitation through the exaction of tribute. So-called ports of trade were an important feature of long-distance trade, serving as safe places for traders from different countries. These were especially important in Mesoamerica (Cimatan, Xicalango, Xoconochco, Naco) but might have existed elsewhere as well, for example, in ritually and religiously important places like the soapstone quarries in North America.

Currency. Standardized and widely accepted values were not highly developed in aboriginal America. In North America different kinds of shell money, sometimes called wampum, were in use on the Pacific and Atlantic coasts. Copper was the raw material for other forms of currency—copper plates in the Northwest Coast, copper bells and axes in Mesoamerica and the central Andes. In Mesoamerica other currencies were cocoa beans, woven cotton blankets, and gold dust. Slaves had standardized values in some parts of South America.

Transportation. The American Indian is remarkable for never having developed mechanical transportation machinery, such as wheeled carts. The Indians' bodies were the ubiquitous means of transportation. Tumplines (Mesoamerica), in addition to small carriers like bags (Mataco) and baskets (North American Southwest, California, and Gran Chaco),

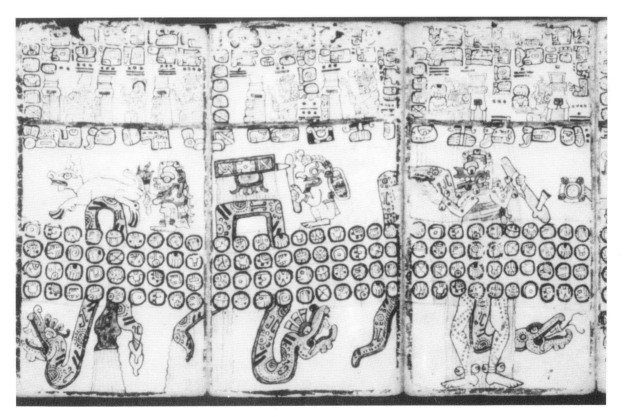

Figure 7. *(Americas, Pre-Columbian—Communications)* Detail from the Madrid Codex. Mayan. Scala/Art Resource, New York.

were used to ease the burden of carrying. Boats were important on rivers and in coastal waters, but, again, they were technically undeveloped, as exemplified by the almost complete lack of large plank boats and sailing techniques. The only animals employed in transportation were dogs, pulling sledges in Arctic North America above 40 degrees northern latitude and pulling racks (travois) on the Plains. In the Andes llamas were used for back loads.

Pre-Columbian communication routes were essential in the rapid expansion and conquest of America by Europeans. When the Europeans arrived with their wheeled vehicles and their horses, the elaborate system of roads and trails that already existed saved them time and backbreaking labor and allowed them to find and conquer the Indian civilizations more quickly. Many of these roads traveled first by the pre-Columbian Indians and then by the Europeans are still in use today.

Bibliography. Lyle R. Campbell and M. Mithun, eds., *The Languages of Native America: Historical and Comparative Assessment*, Austin, Tex., and London, 1979; W. P. Clarke, *The Indian Sign Language*, Philadelphia, 1885; Gordon F. Ekholm, *A Possible Focus of Asiatic Influence in the Late Classic Cultures of Mesoamerica* (Memoirs of the Society for American Archaeology, Vol. 9), Washington, D.C., 1953; Georg Friederici, *Die Schiffahrt der Indianer*, Stuttgart, 1907; John B. Glass, "A Survey and Census of Native American Pictorial Manuscripts," *Handbook of Middle American Indians*, Vol. 14, ed. by Howard F. Cline, Robert Wauchope, gen. ed., Austin, Tex., 1975; Thor Heyerdahl, *American Indians in the Pacific*, London, 1952; John Hyslop, *The Inka Road System*, Orlando, Fla., 1984; Helge M. Ingstad, *Die erste Entdeckung Amerikas*, Berlin, 1966; Garrick Mallery, "Picture Writing of the American Indians," in *10th Annual Report of the [U.S.] Bureau of American Ethnology, 1888–1889*, Washington, D.C., 1893; Wolfgang Marschall, *Transpazifische Kulturbeziehungen*, Munich, 1972; Erland Nordenskjöld, *Calculations with Years and Months in the Peruvian Quipus* (Comparative Ethnographical Studies, Vol. 6, pt. 2), Göteborg, 1925; Timothy Smith, "Wampum as Primitive Valuables," *Research in Economic Anthropology* 5 (1983): 225–246; Gordon Randolph Willy, *An Introduction to American Archaeology*, 2 vols., Englewood Cliffs, N.J., 1966.

BERTHOLD RIESE

2. WRITING SYSTEMS

Mesoamerica is the only New World CULTURE area in which WRITING originated independently rather than through contact with literate cultures. Thus the

◁ **Figure 8.** *(Americas, Pre-Columbian—Communications)* Haida totem pole. Northwest coast of North America. The University Museum, Philadelphia. Neg. 101708.

history of Mesoamerican hieroglyphic systems is important for theories concerning the evolution of writing generally. There are two main traditions. The western, Oaxacan branch "devolved" from a fully textual script to a nontextual system of iconographic captions for the accompanying scenes; it never developed more than rudimentary phonetic principles or grammatical representation. The eastern, Mayan branch, exhibiting the more typical pattern of expanding phonetic and grammatical representation in a textual tradition, provides evidence of the processes causing and the contexts promoting these developments.

Origins

Mesoamerican writing emerged sometime between 1100 and 600 B.C.E. as the confluence of two originally separate notational systems: numeral tallies and Olmec-style representational ART (Figure 1). Comprising probably the first state society in Mesoamerica, the Olmec were then its most powerful and prestigious group. Outside the Olmec heartland the objects bearing the precursors of writing were evidently used in public rituals, with RITUAL paraphernalia bearing Olmec ICONOGRAPHY manifesting an Olmec alliance. Linguistic coding may have been introduced into graphic communication through the juxtaposition of numeral tallies (see below) with depictions of animals and plants for which the days of the 260-day ritual CALENDAR (the *tzolkin* or *tonalamatl*) were named. *See also* CLAY TOKENS; EGYPTIAN HIEROGLYPHS.

Archaic Mesoamerican writing parallels other early scripts in its columnar (rather than row) format, left-to-right and top-to-bottom reading order, depictive signs, and in facing its signs against the order of reading. The meanings of signs shared among early Mesoamerican scripts (Figure 2), plus other shared content among them, suggest that the ancestral script included numerals from 1 to 19 or 20, day names, and personal and place names (often as captions in scenes), with emphasis on sacrificial rites, accession, and ritual prerogatives of rulership.

Two descendant script traditions flanked the Olmec heartland by around 600 to 400 B.C.E. Earliest documentation is fuller in the Oaxacan branch, originating with the Zapotec; the Southeastern branch, descended from Olmec, yields fewer but generally lengthier texts dating mostly from around 300 B.C.E. to 250 C.E. (see Figures 3 and 4). In both branches early written forms are found on monuments and portable art that served to legitimize and/or glorify secular rulers, perpetuating the functional and social context of the inchoate script that had developed from Olmec-style art.

The earliest Oaxacan and Southeastern scripts were adopted fairly faithfully by neighbors and spread quickly throughout Mesoamerica. Descendants of ancestral Zapotec writing, such as Mixtec and Zapotec, eventually stopped representing words in a textual format, passing this reduced script on to the Aztec. Both the Isthmian and Izapan subgroups of the Southeastern branch maintained the textual tradition. Mayan writing was a form or offshoot of Izapan. The first Maya using it were probably Cholan

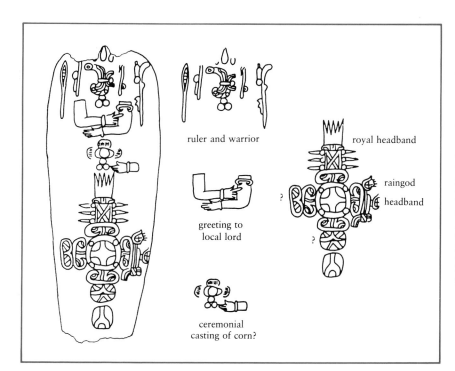

ruler and warrior

greeting to
local lord

ceremonial
casting of corn?

royal headband

raingod
headband

Figure 1. *(Americas, Pre-Columbian—Writing Systems)* Iconographic precursors of writing often used iconographic elements outside the pictorial context in which they normally derived their meanings. The Humboldt Celt (ca. 1100–900 B.C.E.) depicts several elements from a traditional representation of an Olmec dignitary but eliminates depiction of his body: his symbols of power and office, normally worn on or held alongside the head; a gesture of greeting to a lord whom he is visiting; and a casting ritual that was the prerogative of rulers, usually involving corn or incense. The less depictive elements composing the lower register are also found in normal iconographic context; their function here is obscure.

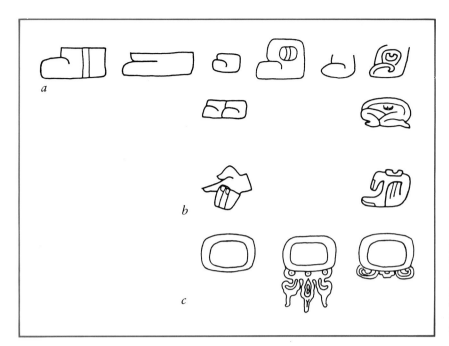

Figure 2. *(Americas, Pre-Columbian—Writing Systems)* Signs shared among early Mesoamerican scripts: *(a)* signs for seating in office; *(b)* signs for the casting ritual; and *(c)* a cartouche sign surrounding the day names (and marking them as such).

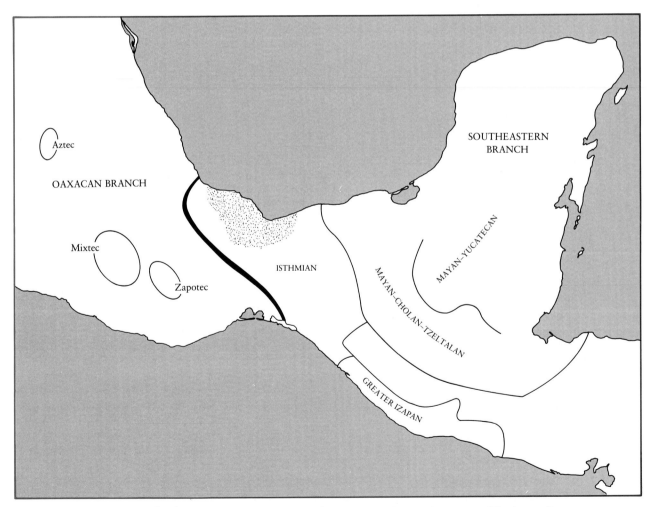

Figure 3. *(Americas, Pre-Columbian—Writing Systems)* Major Mesoamerican script groups. The heavy line separates the Oaxacan from the Southeastern branch. Boundaries are imprecise and are based in part on noncontemporaneous data. Some would put the boundary within Mayan farther north.

speakers, perhaps coparticipants with Mixe-Zoque people in Izapan civilization. They passed it to Yucatecan speakers in the Maya Lowlands.

Numeration and the Calendar

Calendrical recording and historical NARRATIVE are mutually reinforcing forms of graphic communication. Calendric records thus remained the basic framework of most Mesoamerican texts and affected the subsequent development of writing in all areas. Because of the high level of interregional integration and communication in Mesoamerica, structurally similar calendar systems combining 260-day and 365-day cycles were used throughout the area, and for a similar range of functions.

Numeral systems. All Mesoamerican languages express numerals in a vigesimal (base 20) system, structurally similar to decimal except that units were expressed as a sum of multiples of powers of 20 (Figure 5a). The quinary-vigesimal structure of numerals in Mesoamerican languages was reflected in written numerals. All areas used the tallylike bar-and-dot system (Figure 5b) to represent these digits. Bars represented 5, dots represented 1, and a given numeral represented the sum of the referents of its parts; for example, two bars and three dots represented 13. Higher numerals were expressed in pictographic systems by repeating each sign for 20^n the appropriate number of times. The Preclassic Southeastern scripts represented numerals by a positional or place-value notation (Figure 6a, b); place values were ordered from the highest to the lowest power of 20. Probably no sign for zero was present in the original place-value system (nor is such a word found in Mesoamerican languages); rather, the zero was a late development fostered by the system.

Calendrical systems and historical records. The most basic calendar in Mesoamerica was the tzolkin, a ritual calendar of 260 days. It was used in all cultures for divination concerning the scheduling of important events. It consisted of two separate cycles: one (the *trecena*) of consecutive numbers 1 through 13, the other (the *veintena*) of 20 consecutive named days. Recording a tzolkin date "13 Snake" (not equivalent to "13 snakes") therefore required a record of the numeral 13 and of the veintena name Snake. Veintena names were all plants, animals, and natural forces, which could be depicted in representational art.

The calendar priests in charge of ritual were also the scribes responsible for the development of this recording system. They faced a problem in presenting historical narrative. Almost all calendars in Mesoamerica were cyclical. Although the 260-day and 365-day calendars were useful for the short spans involved in scheduling imminent events, reference to dates within a ruler's life or reign required a means

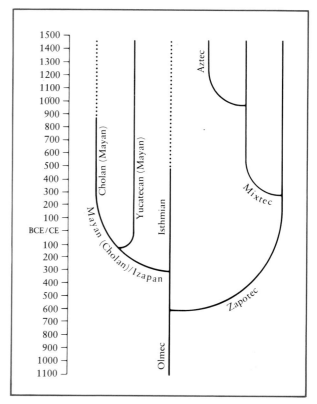

Figure 4. *(Americas, Pre-Columbian—Writing Systems)* Phylogenetic chart of script traditions.

of fixing dates in a longer historical span. Two types of solution were adopted in both the Oaxacan and the Southeastern traditions.

One solution was suggested by the pairing of two cycles in the tzolkin, a combination of two cycles producing a much longer one. The trecena position repeats every 13 days, the veintena position every 20 days; their combined positions repeat together only after 260 days, because 260 is the least common multiple of 13 and 20. All of Mesoamerica used a civil calendar or vague year of 365 days. The combination of the civil and ritual calendars produces a longer historical cycle; because $260 = 5 \cdot 52$, but $365 = 5 \cdot 73$, a position in the vague year is paired again with the same position in the ritual calendar only after $5 \cdot 52 \cdot 73$ days, or 52 civil years. Therefore, recorded dates could be referred to a 52-year cycle, rather than one of only 260 days, by recording the day in the tzolkin along with either (1) its position in the vague year (e.g., 2 Flower 18 Hawk) or (2) the name of the year bearer (e.g., 1 Flower, year 6 Earthquake).

The other method of fixing dates was to specify the number of days between two successive dates. In Oaxaca this was done using a count of units whose length is controversial, probably 20 or 13 days long.

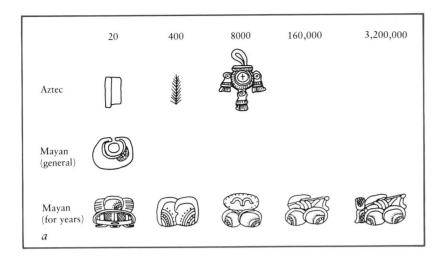

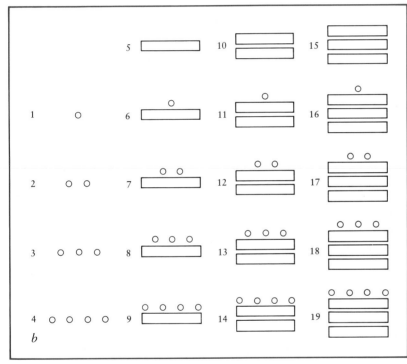

Figure 5. *(Americas, Pre-Columbian—Writing Systems)* Numeral signs. *(a)* Signs for powers of 20. The Aztec numeral signs are by rebus for number words or concepts; for example, *pan-* is the root for "400" and "hair, feather barbs," and *šikil-* is the root for "bag" and "8,000." The Maya sign for the word *k'al* ("20") could be used in enumerations of various items, such as the bar-and-dot numerals; otherwise signs for powers of 20 are known only for days and years, shown here in early forms. Among the latter, the compound for 20 years is numerical (the upper element represents the word *may* for "20 [of years]"); it is not clear whether the other compounds contain numerical significance or are simply names for time spans; none is securely read, and all are formed by placing modifying logograms before the compound for the 400-year period. *(b)* Bar-and-dot numerals 1–19.

In the Maya area arbitrarily long spans were indicated in (quasi-) positional notation.

History of Mesoamerican Writing Systems

Ancestral Mesoamerican scripts were almost purely logographic (each sign representing a word or root). Grammatical variations were not indicated; thus "He was seated" was written simply as "Sit." This did not permit complex relational information to be given, and it can be difficult to recognize how to separate distinct statements in a lengthy sign sequence. Perhaps because the tradition of writing evolved out of calendrical recording of events, longer texts emerged by giving a *series* of dates, each followed by a record of one or more events occurring on that date. Fairly long narratives could therefore be developed through short text segments, the beginning and end of each recognized by the occurrence of a tzolkin date. Relational information was recoverable to the extent that it was associated with sequence information or was reflected in an accompanying scene.

Most early nonnumerical signs were depictive. Phonetic spelling occurred initially only by rebus (the use of one sign for different words having the same pronunciation); hence MEANING was represented along with SOUND. It was by rebus that grammatical words and affixes added to words came to be represented in the Southeastern scripts and in Aztec writing. Because meanings of grammatical elements are notoriously difficult to pin down, these were the first signs extended in Mayan writing to phonetic use without conveying meaning—to be purely phonetic signs.

Some grammatical elements could not be spelled by rebus; they were not pronounced like separate roots or words preceding the actual root but were mutations in the pronunciation of the root itself through a change in a consonant or vowel already present (e.g., br*eath*/br*eathe; l*ife/l*ive-s, l*ife/l*ive; r*u*n/ra*n; m*ou*se/m*ice; old, *eld*-er) or through the insertion of a consonant or vowel infix within the root. Because many such elements affected most nouns and verbs in the original languages of the Oaxacan branch (Zapotec and Mixtec), grammatical representation was at best quite limited, and purely phonetic sign use was nonexistent. Text segments were necessarily simple in structure and content, and relational information was conveyed by iconographic associations. Much less affected by grammatical mutation or infixing, the languages of the Southeastern scripts (Mayan and Mixe-Zoque) and of the Aztec were more susceptible to grammatical representation. Aztec scribes expanded the Oaxacan script they had adopted, representing some grammatical affixes and perhaps just beginning to extend them to purely phonetic usage. All Southeastern scripts represented grammatical suffixes and produced lengthy text segments, and at least the Mayan developed simple phonetic spelling.

In each script rebus phonetic spelling was first used for forms that were difficult to indicate depictively (Figure 7*a*, *b*). The grammatical particles and affixes represented by rebus were seemingly those that helped to differentiate meanings (Figure 7*c*, *d*). Extended in Mayan to purely phonetic use, once-grammatical signs served the same purpose as phonetic complements (phonetic signs added to logograms). For example (Figure 7*e*), *tu·n* ("a [specific] year") and *ha?b'* ("a year [interval]") were both represented by the same sign, YEAR; a following phonetic sign *ni* showed that YEAR was for the word *tu·n*, ending in *n*, and a preceding sign, possibly for *h*, showed that it was for *ha?b'*. As grammatical extensions, signs for suffixes appeared mainly after the logogram and represented the final parts of words; signs for prefixes preceded the logogram and represented the initial parts of words.

Subsequent Mayan spelling conventions developed, like phonetic complements, by analogical extension, through interaction between existing spelling conventions and word structure or grammatical rules in Lowland Mayan languages. For example, two-syllable roots were treated as if they were a one-syllable root plus a suffix, the latter spelled as usual (Figure 7*f*); thus signs for grammatical suffixes began to indicate the closing parts of words that were not

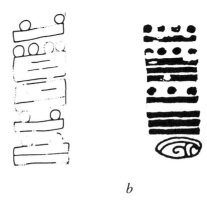

a   *b*

Figure 6. *(Americas, Pre-Columbian—Writing Systems)* Place-value notation. *(a)* El Baúl Stela 1, one of the earliest surviving examples of place-value notation, recorded the numeral 7 19 15 7 12. *(b)* The numeral 9 19 8 15 0, from the Dresden Codex, a place-value record using what is evidently a genuine numerical 0.

otherwise spelled, and logograms for roots served as signs for simple syllables. Because most roots by far were of one syllable, the latter extension affected the logograms only in reinforcing rebus usage. It also led to the establishment of phonetic sign sequences for spelling words with no logographic usage being involved. Once established, the pattern of use of these phonetic signs in purely phonetic spelling would also follow grammatical rules and analogies.

Nonrebus phonetic spelling is first attested around 380 C.E. It gradually increased thereafter both in frequency and in the range of words affected, most extensively in northern Yucatán and least extensively in the central Peten. The increase came about partly by exploitation of the existing resources of the script to render novel and contextually ambiguous material and partly because of the weakness of social conditions that had inhibited phonetic spelling: the decline of traditional central Peten influence, which supported a conservative orthography; the probable decline of interlingual LITERACY along the western and southern periphery with the breakdown of intersite political integration after around 700 C.E.; and the minimal display of writing as art in the northern lowlands. *See also* GRAMMAR; LANGUAGE; PHONOLOGY.

Diffusion among Mesoamerican scripts. Written forms and formats diffused among the early Southeastern scripts. Later, especially after 800 C.E. but with earlier traces, Isthmian writing influenced Mayan along the western river routes in visually apparent ways, reflecting and perhaps intentionally signaling great power or prestige of these northerners among the Maya elite. This impact is paralleled by linguistic and iconographic DIFFUSION from groups occupying the southern Gulf Coast.

There was scant early diffusion between the Oaxa-

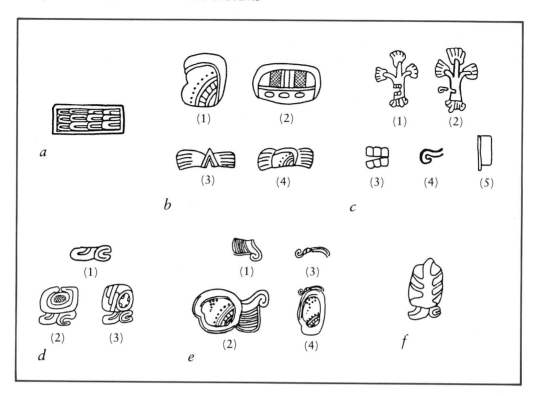

Figure 7. *(Americas, Pre-Columbian—Writing Systems)* Early forms of phonetic representation. *(a)* In Mixtec writing a bundle of feathers *(yodzo)* indicated the word "plain, valley" *(yodzo)* in place names. *(b)* (1) The Lowland Mayan word *tu·n* came to mean both "stone" and "year," so a sign for stone also meant year; (2) probably somewhat earlier, a sign for a hollow-log drum had come to represent the word *tu·n* ("year") because it had the same pronunciation; (3) a sign originally pronounced *mah* ("great") in the Mayan/Izapan script represented the word *may* "20 (of years)"; (4) the stone/year sign was infixed into it to indicate which interpretation of the sign was pertinent. *(c)* Many Aztec town names, such as (1) Cuauhtitlan ("Place of Trees") and (2) Cuauhnauhac ("By the Trees"), were identical except for locative suffixes. Most of these suffixes began to be represented by rebus, as in (3) *-tlan/titlan* ("place of") by teeth *(tlan-,* "tooth"), (4) *-nahua-k* ("adjacent to") by a speech scroll *(nahua-,* "fine speech"), (5) *-pan* ("on, upon") by a banner *(pan-,* "banner"). *(d)* The (1) sign for *-ab'/Vw/wa* derived (2), a word meaning the passage of *n* days from a numeral *n*, and (3), a word for an instrument from a verb for the action it performs, here *k'an xal-ab'* ("yellow shuttle"), with *xal-ab'* from *xal* ("to weave"). *(e)* (1) The sign *ni* suffixed to the stone/year sign (2) indicates the final *n* of the word *tu·n* ("year"); (3) the sign *h* prefixed to the stone/year sign (4) indicates the initial *h* of the word *ha?b'* ("year"). *(f)* The word **o·ne·w* was a simple root for a month name but was spelled as if it were a root *o·n* ("avocado [tree]") plus a suffix *ew.*

can and Southeastern script groups. Later, Isthmian writing was influenced by Mixteca-Puebla style variants of the Oaxacan tradition, for example, in the "dots only" numeral system and the style of glyphic elements. Increasing Mexican iconographic and linguistic influence is found in Postclassic Maya murals and manuscripts accompanied by hieroglyphic writing in recognizably Maya script. Mayan conventions and signs were unaffected, apart from possible stylistic impact.

The most persistent and pervasive case of diffusion was among the Maya, between Cholan and Yucatecan scribes. Spelling practices and sign values passed back and forth between them; phonetic spelling was inhibited, scribes avoiding those specific to either group.

Social functions and correlates of the use of writing. Occupationally, scribes were often painters; writing was painted primarily with fine brush on bark paper or deer hide, and it always maintained a close connection to the visual arts *(see* WRITING MATERIALS). The scribes used writing in manuscripts to aid them in prognostication concerning the timing of matters of civic significance, such as agriculture and warfare, and to record historical data pertinent to the legitimacy of rulers and potential rulers; minor economic use is found only in late pictographic systems. They also treated writing as a form of and/or adjunct to representational public art; where monumental and architectural art makes scant reference to rulers and other actual people, as in the greater part of the northernmost Maya Lowlands, at Teotihuacán, and among the Mixtec, writing is also seldom to be found. In the Southeastern script group the traditional use of logographic spelling featured the use of multiple signs for the same logographic or phonetic value(s) and inhibited the reduction of the script to a simple phonetic system. The terse textual tradition of the Oaxacan branch, which had relied on accompanying art for clarification, became increasingly an iconographic adjunct to that art; one-word captions to scenes or to figures in them expressed personal names, place names, and day names in the ritual calendar (some functioning as personal names, a Mesoamerican custom), but nothing corresponded to a sentence or a phrase.

See also VISUAL IMAGE.

Bibliography. *Codex Mendoza: Aztec Manuscript,* commentaries by Kurt Ross, ed., Fribourg, Switzerland, 1978; Linda Schele, George Stuart, and David Stuart, *Ancient Maya Writing,* Austin, Tex., forthcoming; Mary Elizabeth Smith, *Picture Writing from Ancient Southern Mexico: Mixtec Place Signs and Maps,* Norman, Okla., 1973.

JOHN S. JUSTESON

ANIMAL COMMUNICATION

Humans have a marvelously powerful tool in SPEECH. Yet we evolved from primate ancestors who already had rich communication that was not speech, and we continue to have abundant means of communicating in addition to speech (*see* NONVERBAL COMMUNICATION). Indeed, some of our signaling is still homologous with that of our extant primate relatives, and all of it shares basic features with a great range of other species. Rich communication is not peculiar to primates but is a common attribute of animals of diverse evolutionary lineages. Nonhuman communication shares with human both fundamental characteristics—repertoires of more than one kind of signaling, context-dependent meaning—and surprising specializations—bird songs of many species have dialects, singing sequences can be grammatical, social insects have a form of mass communication (*see* INSECTS, SOCIAL), diverse animals make signposts, and others make stages from which to signal.

Capacities for communicating evolved as means by which animals could profit from interacting with one another. All kinds of animals have some social encounters, and many species have richly complex social lives. The orderliness of their social behavior depends to a considerable extent on the ability of individuals to communicate—to share information with one another, making public what otherwise would be private.

Central to the efficient sharing of information are repertoires of specialized signaling behavior and other specializations such as color patterns, wattles, crests, and scents (*see* ANIMAL SIGNALS; ANIMAL SONG; ETHOLOGY). This article explores the kinds of information in which animals traffic as they communicate,

how recipients of such information respond, and issues involved with the biological functioning (and hence evolution) of their communicative specializations.

Kinds of Information

Various kinds of information are made available by the presentation of a signal. These are *referents* of animal signaling.

Identity and location. Signals provide information identifying the signaler (Figure 1). Wherever many species are likely to be present simultaneously, identification of species is usually essential if individuals

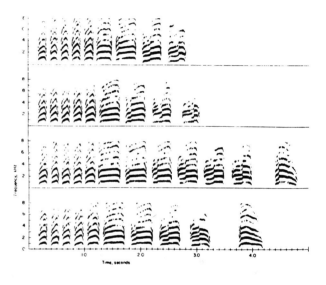

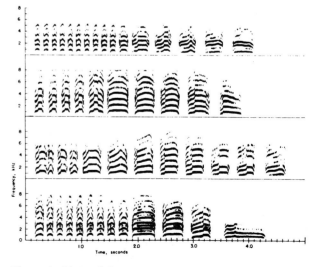

Figure 1. *(Animal Communication)* Sonagrams of long-calls of Laughing Gulls: *(top)* four calls by the same gull; *(bottom)* calls of four other gulls. Individual gulls can be identified by characteristics of these calls. From Colin G. Beer, "Individual Recognition of Voice and Its Development in Birds," *Proceedings of the XVth International Ornithological Congress,* Leiden: E. J. Brill, 1972, p. 344.

are to know what perceived signals are the most pertinent for them to attend. It is also necessary for animals to identify their species (and often their gender, age, and breeding condition—i.e., physiological state) when mating. Some animal signals do not provide information that identifies the species of the signaler, however. Occasionally signals of different species converge in mutual intelligibility if the species form multispecific social groups, or if one species deceptively copies signals of another as, say, a defense against predators. More often, however, specificity extends even to discriminations among individual signalers, at least in vertebrate animals.

The forms of vocal signals also contain information that makes it possible for recipients to determine a signaler's direction from them. Recipients do this by binaural comparisons of temporal differences in physical features as the sound reaches each ear in turn. Decreasing the complexity of a sound's form can decrease but not eliminate such information. Some vocalizations, such as those small birds utter when alarmed by hawks, have evolved toward this simplicity. However, most vocalizations do render signalers readily localizable.

Behavior. Signal acts correlate conditionally and probabilistically with the performance of other behavior. As a result they provide reliable information about these other actions.

In spite of numerous differences in phylogenetic history, social organization, and ecology, the kinds of behavioral referents of the basic signals called *displays* are remarkably similar among most of the species of at least vertebrate animals studied to date. All species appear to provide information about attacking or fleeing, for instance, often combining prediction of both with that of a third possibility in a single signal. The bill-downward, neck-upright signal posture of an Inca tern (*Larosterna inca*), for instance, predicts that the signaler is more likely to attack than to withdraw but is even more likely to hesitate and vacillate while committing to neither (Figure 2). Most species also appear to have one or more signals that provide information about the possibility of copulating (or other procedures for insemination). Many species have displays indicating that a signaler is interrupting other behavior to monitor some stimulus.

Few such behavioral referents are as narrowly predictive, however. Many displays provide information about the probability of the signaler interacting but give no indication of the kind of interaction the signaler will attempt, facilitate, or accept. The range can be considerable, from attack to copulation, including noncontact association and other relatively innocuous possibilities. Locomotory behavior is another common referent, with no specification of the function of the locomotion. Many displays even provide the information that the signaler may do some-

Figure 2. *(Animal Communication)*   Aggressive upright postures of the Inca tern *(Larosterna inca)*. From M. Moynihan, "Hostile and Sexual Behavior Patterns of South American and Pacific *Laridae*," *Behaviour,* Supplement VIII, Leiden: E. J. Brill, 1962, p. 262.

thing incompatible with another behavioral referent. For example, the signaler may interact or instead do something that precludes interacting, although the nature of the alternative—fleeing, foraging, or something else—is not predictable from the display.

Although the usefulness of such broadly predictive information might seem questionable, considerable predictability is engendered when a display is considered in the context of any given performance. Why animals should traffic in such information seems to be a matter of economy. No species has more than forty or fifty display units at its disposal, so the more situations in which each can be used, the more functions a signaler can get from communicating. That diverse species appear to have diverged little may imply that few behavioral options are as valuable as referents as the dozen or so now thought to be widespread.

There are exceptional behavioral referents, probably many when all species are considered. Nonetheless, most displays of most species may be involved only with the common referents discussed above. Other referents are now being found in signaling repertoires in addition to the basic display repertoire of each species. These repertoires are only just beginning to be explored systematically by ethologists, but they appear to contribute significantly to the richness and flexibility of animal communication.

In addition to information about the kinds of behavior that may be selected by a signaler, information is also made available about the conditional probability of that behavior being performed, the intensity of its performance, sometimes the direction it will take, or yet other issues that add to the predictions of classes of activities.

Making information available about behavior necessarily provides clues to some aspects of the signaler's internal motivational and emotional states that underlie behaving. These states were in fact the focus of most early ethological attempts to analyze signaling, which were concerned more with immediate causes of signaling than with the information it made available. How important information about motivational states is to interacting animals is unclear. Behavior is what each participant in an interaction must predict from moment to moment as it strives to cope with and manage the social event. The participants need information about behavior, but information about one another's internal states might also affect their expectations.

Stimuli to which a signaler is responding. Some signal acts correlate not just with behavior but also with particular classes of stimuli to which an individual is responding when it signals. For instance, California ground squirrels (*Spermophilus beechyi*) utter different forms of a chattering alarm call when they see predators from classes that have different hunting tactics. These chatterings also predict different behavior that the caller will show in response to the predators. Some monkeys (e.g., vervets, *Cercopithecus aethiops*) also utter different calls, or forms of a call, as they respond to predators of different classes. Rhesus monkeys (*Macaca mulatta*) utter screams during disputes with one another; different forms of screams provide information about whether the event involves physical contact and whether the opponent is dominant or subordinate to the screamer. Toque monkeys (*M. sinica*) utter a "whee" vocalization when they forgo traveling with their troop in order to use an important localized resource—usually food, although sometimes water or a place to sunbathe. Honey bees also communicate about flights they make to resources, again usually food.

All of these cases have in common the fact that the signaler or the referent is not near appropriate recipients. The recipients are being enlisted to interact with or respond to some important entity or situation that they may not otherwise notice. Referents of this sort may be relatively uncommon, and signals having them may always have behavioral referents also.

Ethology lacks appropriate terms with which to distinguish different categories of referents of signals,

and the literature can be misleading if not read carefully. For instance, ethologists have often referred to predators, resources, or other such stimuli as "external referents." The term arises in conceiving of information predictive of behavior as private (until made public by signaling). Yet so is information about perception of a predator or resource. And the term *external,* implying a contrast with *internal,* invites further preoccupation with motivational states—a perspective that slowed ethology's recognition of most of the various kinds of information about behavior that are made available by signaling. Some workers have also arbitrarily restricted the term *semantic* to signaling about predators and the like, as if all relations between signals and referents were not semantic. Sometimes such signals are called *representational* or *referential* instead of semantic—terms that may be only slightly preferable even though there is precedent for the latter in LINGUISTICS.

Responding to Signals

Communication does not occur simply when one individual presents a signal. Some other individual must perceive the signal and respond in some way, even if only by briefly storing the information. Responding is complexly determined, however. It is rarely possible for the recipient of a signal to choose an appropriate response solely on the basis of the information provided by that signal. Even though that information may be highly pertinent, it is not itself finely tuned to the features of any momentary event.

A recipient also attends to and uses information from sources contextual to the signal. These sources can be other signals, even repetitions of the same signal, and other behavior or attributes of the signaler. Some possibilities are the signaler's size, age class, gender, and much nonformalized behavior, such as its approach or withdrawal, the speed and continuity of its movements, its stance, and the like. Still other sources of information are brought to any event by the responding individual itself, such as genetic predispositions (e.g., to recognize the signals of its species) and memories (e.g., a categorization of the signaler as familiar or strange, the location with respect to territorial boundary conventions, the social situation with respect to its current progress through phases of, say, the breeding season). Much pertinent information also comes from events immediately preceding the perception of a signal, those more or less simultaneous with it, and any that follow before a recipient has committed itself fully to a particular response. No signal ever occurs in the absence of contextual sources of information, and no recipient responds to a signal without integrating the information from at least some of them.

Preoccupation with innate causes of behavior led

early ethologists to conceive of communication as primarily a matter of signals "releasing" predetermined patterns of response from recipient individuals. The relevance of stimuli contextual to signaling was sometimes recognized in detailed studies, but the enormous importance of context to communication was not realized in early work. Circumstances do exist in which information from sources contextual to a signal is minimally important in eliciting responses. For example, experiments with neonatal animals often show strong biases toward particular signals, almost to the exclusion of attention to contextual stimuli. But these naive response predispositions are quickly modified by learning, and older infants demand richer arrays of clues contextual to the key signals.

All responsiveness is selective, and organized perceptions require that some stimuli be taken as especially salient. Nonetheless, these focal stimuli are perceived in context; for each figure there is some sort of relevant ground that determines responses to it. In the process of formalization signals become specialized to be accepted by appropriate recipients as highly salient. (The evolution actually involves both the signals and the perceptual mechanisms, of course.) This is the basis of what impressed the early ethologists. But responding to signals requires attention to stimuli of lesser rank also. The latter are not simply discarded but are crucial to the fine-tuning of response behavior in each unique event.

This context dependency of responding has made it difficult to investigate relations between signals and responses through controlled experiments. Naturalistic observations suggest the kinds of responses that are usual but rarely provide conditions in which only the signal or some one contextual source of information changes while all other sources remain constant. (Such conditions, when approximated, provide the "natural experiments" that Niko Tinbergen and others have used as especially strong evidence of responses.) Ethological experiments in natural circumstances range from broadcasting selected vocalizations to presenting models or stuffed animals—sometimes with limited, remote-controlled movements—in signal postures. At least the initial responses to such stimuli are often revealing, particularly about animals' abilities to obtain species-specific and even individually specific identifying information from the signals.

Their behavioral responses are often more difficult to interpret, especially after responders begin to try to interact and then encounter events (e.g., continued repetition of a vocal signal from a stolidly posed model) that violate their expectations of the usual range of behavior accompanying a signal in real interaction. Initial responses of approach (e.g., toward what sounds like a territorial intruder) or fleeing (in responses to playback of an "alarm call") can be significant, but there is considerable elaboration and individual variation. British ornithologist David Lack, for instance, found that he could elicit postural signaling from some male European robins (*Erithacus rubecula*) by placing a stuffed robin near their nests (Figure 3). In real events the various postures were used to threaten intruders, and some responding robins did attack the decoy. A stuffed immature robin, with its brown rather than reddish-orange breast, was ineffective. In some tests headless or tailless decoys—even just an adult breast alone— were effective. Yet, as Lack cautioned, the red breast per se does not cause the response. Each robin had a mate, and the sexes have identical plumage, but in spite of their red breasts the mates were not attacked and could use the territories freely. Mates provided appropriate clues contextually to the red signal. The experimental decoys provided the signal in the absence of expected contextual clues, which was enough to lead some males to respond as if adopting a worst-case scenario: in the absence of sufficient information, threaten an object that has a key signal in common with a real intruder. (One male adopted a different scenario, accepting the decoy as a receptive female, who would be motionless, and he mounted instead of threatening.) Decoys left for long ceased to be accepted even as possible intruders and were often used as inanimate perches.

Both the usefulness and the limitations of such techniques are revealed by these experiments. Animals can be brought into laboratories for even greater control of contextual variables, yet further problems can emerge as the subjects' expectations are more

Figure 3. *(Animal Communication)* The stuffed juvenile robin *(left)* and the stuffed adult dyed brown *(right)* were both less effective in eliciting threat posturing when placed near a robin's nest than was just the red breast and white belly plumage *(center)*, even though this bit of feathers lacked all other features of a robin. The red breast is a highly significant signal to European robins, although even it elicits different responses as contextual circumstances change. From David Lack, *The Life of the Robin*, London: Penguin Books, 1953, p. 158.

thoroughly violated by the oversimplified, confining circumstances. However, laboratory conditions can be sufficient and often are for invertebrate subjects in particular. For example, biologist Edward O. Wilson has studied the chemical signaling of ants by removing their scent-producing Dufour's glands and using them to lay trails that other individuals will follow. Field experiments by Karl von Frisch, James Gould, and others have shown analogous responses to directional information in honey bee dances. These researchers have also shown that some responses to signals occur promptly, whereas others are more a "priming" of a recipient individual that can influence its behavior in later events. This, too, complicates research on responses.

Functions of Communicating

There are various consequences when a recipient responds to a signal. A mate may be attracted or a territorial intruder repelled when a bird sings. Or a hawk may notice and then kill the singer. The first two consequences are adaptive for the singer: they yield advantages that drive the evolution of this signaling. Getting killed is a nonadaptive consequence that works against the evolution of singing. Advantages must exceed costs, or singing will not be fostered and maintained by natural selection. To biologists the advantageous consequences are the functions of communicating.

Not just signalers but also responders must, on average, profit in order for communication to evolve. Benefits need not be equal. An individual whose threats give it access to a resource gains more than a responder who defers, yet both avoid an outright fight. If the deferent responder does better by continuing to search for resources than by expending energy and risking injury in fighting, then its response to the threat is appropriate. An individual who vocally alerts its companions when it detects a predator may save them from danger but increase its own vulnerability by drawing attention to itself. Yet such signaling can still pay off in many different ways. For example, the saved companions may alert it in subsequent events; they may be its offspring or other close relatives carrying many of its genes, and hence evolutionarily they are worth some risk (a "kin effect"); their responses when alerted may be to scatter in ways that distract and confuse the predator to the signaler's benefit.

Much communication is effectively cooperative. It functions to establish or maintain the social fabric on which individuals depend for regular interactions with one another. Thus individuals cooperate to form a pair bond and raise offspring, to form territorial boundaries, or to maintain a status hierarchy or a social group. This does not mean that each individual is not competitive, even in interactions with its mate and offspring, but that it competes within a social framework that must be maintained and kept more or less orderly (for each member's own evolutionary "fitness") through cooperation. Thus, although various members of a baboon troop may try to have some control over the speed and direction of group movement during foraging behavior, each also needs to stay with its group. When the group is moving through dense vegetation each member will provide information about its location and movements to others and will respond to information the others provide so that the troop remains coherent. As in this intraspecific case, members of species that regularly flock, herd, or school interspecifically will signal cooperatively to make their movements obvious and the detection of predators widely known. The same species may signal to maintain interspecific dominance orders, keeping their competitive encounters orderly.

Communication between species with opposing needs, such as predators and prey, is also sometimes cooperative. Prey may signal to a predator that it has detected the predator's approach, thus saving both individuals the costs of a pursuit in which the prey would escape. But there is always strong competition. Both prey and predator can profit greatly from misinforming each other in their life-and-death encounters, and this has led to the evolution of deceptive signaling. For instance, edible prey may mimic poisonous species or inedible backgrounds (rocks, twigs, leaves); predators may mimic innocuous species, becoming "wolves in sheep's clothing." Both procedures lead to counteradaptations, however. They are evolutionarily unstable.

Even within a species, individuals have many divergent needs. In principle they should attempt any potentially profitable behavior that is not ultimately self-defeating. There are thus pressures to evolve or to learn to perform at least some unreliable signaling. Yet manipulative social behavior endangers the continuing interdependence of individuals and hence the maintenance of their organized social groups. Thus the extent to which unreliable intraspecific communicating can evolve must be limited.

Among the limitations is that the evolution of communicative behavior involves coadaptation of signaling and responding. When signals misinform they provide selection for responders to be skeptical—and skeptical responding provides selection for reliable signaling. Unreliable signalers are put at a disadvantage if skeptical recipients of signals seek further information from sources contextual to a signal to check it or act to test the signaler before committing themselves. One evolutionary result is signaling with forms that cannot be deceptive and thus certify the honesty of the signaler. One example of such self-certification is a threat so energetically taxing that only a powerful signaler can perform it in sustained bouts, as is apparently the case with the bellowing of red deer stags (*Cervus elaphus*).

A basic limitation to the evolution of misinforming is that it yields its benefits for a signaler by parasitizing responses recipients make to what are normally reliable sources of information. It is thus based on mimicry. Like all mimicry, it requires the prior and continued existence of reliable models. It cannot become excessively common relative to these reliable models and will not succeed as the predominant form of signaling.

Ethologists have obtained little evidence for misinforming among individuals of the same species and considerable evidence for reliable informing. Subtle and relatively infrequent misinforming may be hard for us to detect, of course, just as it is hard for the animals themselves.

Bibliography. Charles Darwin, *The Expression of the Emotions in Man and Animals*, London, 1872; Robert A. Hinde, "The Concept of Function," in *Function and Evolution in Behaviour*, ed. by Gerard Baerends, Colin Beer, and Aubrey Manning, Oxford, 1975; Donald E. Kroodsma and Edward H. Miller, eds., *Acoustic Communication in Birds*, 2 vols., New York, 1982–1983; W. John Smith, *The Behavior of Communicating: An Ethological Approach*, Cambridge, Mass., 1977; idem, "An Informational Perspective on Manipulation," in *Deception: Perspectives on Human and Nonhuman Deceit*, ed. by Robert W. Mitchell and Nicholas S. Thompson, Albany, N.Y., 1986; Edward O. Wilson, *The Insect Societies*, Cambridge, Mass., 1971; idem, *Sociobiology*, Cambridge, Mass., 1975.

W. JOHN SMITH

ANIMAL-HUMAN COMMUNICATION. *See* HUMAN-ANIMAL COMMUNICATION.

ANIMAL SIGNALS

This entry consists of four articles:
1. Overview
2. Audible Signals
3. Chemical Signals
4. Visible Signals

1. OVERVIEW

All species of animals communicate. That is, individuals of each species share information with one another; often they also share it with other species. There are many means by which they make information available. Anything an animal does and any attribute it has that can be perceived by any other individual is necessarily informative. But some actions and attributes are highly relevant to communication because they have undergone specialization to be informative, much as others have been specialized to be locomotory or to serve in foraging or in the evasion of predators. Specialization to be informative can arise during genetic evolution, in the development and cultural modification of learned traditions, or in both and is broadly termed *formalization*. (Most of the study of ANIMAL COMMUNICATION is done by biologists in the subdiscipline of ETHOLOGY. Ethologists use primarily the term *ritualization* but almost always with a predominant connotation of genetic evolution; the term is subsumed here under formalization.)

Formalized actions and attributes (collectively termed simply *signals* here) lead indirectly to consequences that are functional for a signaler. When one individual attacks another and pushes it away forcefully from some contested resource, it gains access to that resource by direct action on its competitor. The same access may be obtained, however, if the first individual signaled a high probability of attack and the second individual responded by departing. The physical withdrawal is accomplished in this case solely through actions taken by the recipient individual; hence the signal achieves its functions for the signaler indirectly.

The direct/indirect distinction is important to ethological research on communication, most of which has focused primarily on indirectly functional (hence formalized) behavior and attributes. Formalizations are often strikingly conspicuous, even bizarre—particularly those employed in courtship—and ethologists have been much concerned with attempts to explain their evolution, proximate causation, and function. In fact, the historical roots of ethology are deeply involved with investigations of signaling, for instance CHARLES DARWIN's of FACIAL EXPRESSION, Oskar Heinroth's of courting ducks, Julian Huxley's of grebes, Niko Tinbergen's of gulls, and Karl von Frisch's of honey bee dances (*see* INSECTS, SOCIAL).

Communication is not simply a matter of providing and responding to signals, however. The information made available by a signal is insufficient to enable a recipient to select an appropriate response. Responding is instead based on a process of integrating information from a signal with information from sources contextual to the signal.

Formalization of Signal Receptors

Ethological accounts often divide animal signals according to the different sensory modalities by which they are received. Largely a classification of convenience, this does emphasize the existence of formalization for all available receptors, suggesting both that signaling is important to animals and that it is often adaptive to signal redundantly: an obstacle to one sense need not be an obstacle to another. Thus in the social din of a seabird colony visible signaling may accomplish what cannot be trusted to vocal signaling, whereas vocal signaling will often function even when a recipient is facing away from a signaler or is obscured from seeing it by line-of-sight obstacles.

Visible and audible signaling are both highly developed in the behavior of many species of animals (see sections 2 and 4, below). Tactile communication is somewhat less well understood, at least partly because it is relatively hard to study when observer and subject are not close. But animals are seen to make careful contact with each other using at least their noses, lips, teeth, tongues, necks, hands, arms, feet, flanks, tails, and genitalia, touching, embracing, neck rubbing, bumping, or pressing (see Figure 1). Male birds may tread the back of a female during copulation. A parrot may nibble its partner's toes to get it to move along a branch. Fish nudge with their noses and grasp with their mouths, and much of their fin- and body-movement signaling is both visible and received as pressure waves impinging on a recipient's lateral-line organs. All colonial insects use tactile signals, and during their famous dances honey bees make sounds that they feel rather than hear (bees have no ears). Substrate-borne vibrational signaling, effectively tactile, is also known in web-building spiders and in leeches, and surface waves are propagated in special signaling patterns by insects known as water striders (Gerridae). Much touching is involved in chemical communication (see section 3, below), as insects taste each other's surfaces with their antennae and mammals thrust noses against each other's axillary, anal, or genital glands. When elephants touch each other with their trunks it is difficult for an observer to know whether the signaling is tactile, olfactory, or both.

Release of chemical products, known as pheromones, is an important sort of signaling for many animals. Male moths are led to receptive females along wind-borne odor trails; ants are led to food at sites from which other foragers have laid down scent trails as they returned to the colony (see Figure 2). Snakes, snails, and even some bees also deposit pheromonal trails. Mammals use scent marks in communicating about individual and group identity, dominance rank, and important sites. Highly volatile pheromones are released by alarmed ants, deer, woodchucks, and countless other species. Mating is regulated or facilitated by pheromonal signaling in species from bees to humans.

Even electrical discharges have been developed for signaling in species with receptors specialized for their detection, especially some kinds of fishes that

Figure 1. *(Animal Signals—Overview)* Tail twining in the titi monkey *(Callicebus moloch)*, a tactile signal. From M. Moynihan, "Communication in the Titi Monkey, *Callicebus,*" *Journal of Zoology* (London) 150 (1966): 83.

live in muddy tropical waters. Every sensory modality (except possibly thermoreception) that detects external events has been involved. One result is enormous diversity: the signals of animal communication have been elaborated in many and often unimagined ways, and the vast majority will always remain unknown to us.

Further, animals have formalized many nonbehavioral sources of information. Some of these amount to "badges": visible color patches or marking patterns; elaborations of the shapes of feathers, scales, or fur; the horns and antlers of ungulates; the dewlaps of lizards; and the enlarged claws of male fiddler crabs. Badges may be kept visible or concealed until useful. Some are permanently or seasonally fixed and others behaviorally alterable through inflation, chromatophore change, and the like. Evolution has even produced analogues of badges in plants whose flowers or other features elicit responses from animals, after which the animals effect pollination or seed dispersal.

Other formalized sources are constructions that animals make as stages or backgrounds for signaling: nests, nestlike structures, shelters, and stages decorated by bowerbirds (Ptilonorhynchidae or Paradisaeidae) with colored fruits, flowers, and pebbles (see

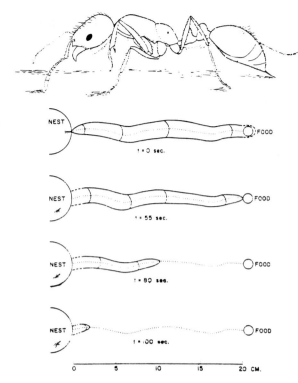

Figure 2. *(Animal Signals—Overview)* The form of the odor trail of *Solenopsis saevissima* laid on glass. As the trail substance diffuses from its line of application on the surface, it forms a semiellipsoidal active space within which the pheromone is at or above threshold concentration. This space, and therefore the entire signal, fades after about one hundred seconds. The worker ant pictured above is laying a trail from right to left. From Edward O. Wilson, *The Insect Societies*, Cambridge, Mass.: Harvard University Press, 1971, p. 252. Reprinted by permission.

Figure 3). Mammals may make conspicuous scent posts by removing bark from trees or depositing their feces in piles, then applying pheromones from special glands.

Signal Repertoires

More than one repertoire of signaling behavior is available to the animals of any species. These repertoires are distinguished not by specialization for different sensory modalities (each repertoire has arrays of signals for whatever sensory reception is appropriate) but by more fundamental features of their signal units and by the diverse ways in which they contribute to communication.

Display repertoire. The basic signal units of animal communication are acts ethologists call *displays*. Although the term was initially applied to visible signals, it has been generalized to include sounds and acts specialized for reception by other senses.

Displays are the signals with which we are most familiar in our casual relations with other species—the songs of birds, for instance, as well as their chirps, twitters, trills, caws, and quacks. (With only casual familiarity we underestimate considerably the number of vocal displays in the repertoire of each species.) Our mammalian pets bark and growl, hiss and mew, raise and wag their tails, ruffle tracts of fur, arch their backs, flatten back their ears, and sometimes deposit urine repeatedly at sites special to them. Fish court with spread fins and changing colors, frogs croak, crickets chirp, fireflies flash, and we read or hear recordings of the singing of whales, the roaring of lions, the bellowing of bison, and the chest beating of gorillas. Other examples are mentioned above in discussing signaling for various sensory modalities, but the true diversity of such signals cannot begin to be listed. We perhaps recognize too that many of our groans and giggles, gasps and laughs, smiles, frowns, eyebrow raisings, and blushes are comparable forms of signaling (*see* BODY MOVEMENT; EYES; FACE; KINESICS). Students of human NONVERBAL COMMUNICATION, however, typically use terms such as *expression* and *posture* instead of *display*.

These are the most obvious signal units, and every species has a repertoire ranging from a few (e.g., a relatively asocial frog) to a maximum of about forty or fifty (in some birds and mammals). Ethologists have cataloged them (or at least those most readily recognizable by humans) in diverse species. However, the cataloging has often raised problems of criteria. Just what constitutes a unit of display behavior has caused considerable concern. Variation in form, compounding of separable actions, and elaborate cooperative ceremonies of two or more participants have all confused the issue. These complexities also occur in human signaling, in which familiarity born of daily use makes it somewhat easier to distinguish words (for instance) from ways of altering their sounds or of compounding them. We accept words as the basic meaningful signal units of SPEECH. In effect, just as we have repertoires of both words and other kinds of signaling specializations, so too do members of other species. It is necessary to recognize the differences among kinds of signals, as each repertoire has its own properties and makes its own distinctive contribution to communication.

Repertoire of classes of form variation. Diverse procedures for altering the forms of basic signal acts are also formalized and comprise units of signaling behavior in their own right, just as they do in human speech. For instance, changes in duration, pitch, intonation contours, loudness, harshness, quavering, and other features add information to that carried by the words of a LANGUAGE. Taken together such procedures make up a repertoire of ways of varying the characteristics of speech sounds. Many of these formalized procedures are also employed in altering nonspeech utterances, by both humans and nonhu-

Figure 3. *(Animal Signals—Overview)* Bower of *Amblyornis flavifrons*. Male (with flared crest and holding fruit) is displaying to female (on sapling in background). The male has placed the sticks piled up around the tree fern, constructed the moss platform at the base, and placed the blue, yellow, and green mounds of fruit on the platform. From J. M. Diamond, "Rediscovery of the Yellow-fronted Gardener Bowerbird," *Science* 216 (1982): 433.

man species. Further analogous modifications are imposed on features such as the duration, smoothness, and amplitude of visible, tactile, and other displays. Every species has a repertoire of ways of varying display form.

Form variants are of two functionally disparate sorts, however. Some variation is manifested only at certain ontogenetic stages, after which forms become fixed. This is the source of differences among groups that ethologists recognize as dialects of bird songs, group-specific pulsed calls of killer whales, and the like (*see* ANIMAL SONG). It is also the source of many of the differences that make the signaling of individuals distinctive. The variation in such cases is temporary—characteristic only of a stage—and leads to stable differences among individual signalers that appear to function primarily in providing identifying information.

Other procedures remain available to individuals throughout their lives as means to modify the forms of their displays. These add richly to communication and can permit subtle shifts of information over very short intervals. For example, many birds can quaver the sound of their vocalizations, superimposing a frequency modulation on the basic display forms. In a North American flycatcher called the eastern kingbird (*Tyrannus tyrannus*) quavering has been shown to modify at least two different kinds of vocal display that are often uttered in flight. It alters the form of the first as a signaler veers from an attack on, say, a predator and detours around its target. Kingbirds also sometimes quaver the second kind of vocal display (a different unit in the species' repertoire,

with its own distinctive informative contribution) when suddenly breaking off attack. In addition, however, they may quaver this second vocalization when abruptly terminating social interaction with a mate in instances when attack is never at issue. The quavering adds information about the likelihood of quitting some current activity to the information already being provided by these two different displays. Further, individuals of many other species of birds, both flycatchers and species from other evolutionary lineages, add quavering to vocalizations when approaching mates, rivals, or groups as they veer away or stop short. That the information quavering adds to vocalizations may be similar among diverse species suggests that this is a signaling procedure with a long evolutionary history, largely independent of the evolution of units of display repertoires.

Ethologists have only begun to make detailed studies of members of the repertoire of procedures for varying display form. There are suggestions of other widespread commonalities. Harshening a vocal display, for instance, may provide the information that attack behavior is becoming probable; making that vocalization higher and shrill may shift the prediction toward escape. Such possible generalizations need much more thorough investigation. Even if few procedures are found to be widespread among species, however, the existence of repertoires of this kind is certainly widespread.

The repertoires include more than procedures for modifying vocalizations. Displays involving movement or posture are also varied in many ways, as are displays suited to yet other sensory modalities. Some classes of variation, such as changing duration or amplitude, are recognizable whatever the modality. Others are peculiar to particular sets of displays. For example, vervet monkeys (*Cercopithecus aethiops*) signal about approach and withdrawal by holding their tails in a continuously graded array of different positions. The probability of withdrawal increases as the tail droops backward from the vertical. The probability of attack is highest when the tip of the tail points forward and decreases as the tip dangles downward toward a signaler's back. With the tail in the latter position a vervet is likely to approach or pass by others without making any attempt to control them or some resource they might contest. As another example, the more a gull (*Larus* species) angles its bill downward from the horizontal, the more the probability of attack increases relative to that of escape; the more it lifts its bill upward above the horizontal, the more the probability of fleeing increases relative to an otherwise unspecified alternative.

Units of the repertoire of procedures for varying the forms of signals offer two sorts of enrichment to communication. They can either add to or modify the information made available by units of the display repertoire. And they can do this with fine gradations, through series of continuous variations in display form.

Repertoire of classes of combinations. Display units can become components in higher-order formalized signaling patterns. The displays are then combined according to rules that generate different classes of patterns. These rule-bound classes are the units of the third repertoire of signaling behavior.

Bouts in which a display unit is repeated at regular intervals are the simplest case of rule-bound sequences. The control of interval duration produces a readily recognizable pattern providing information about the stability of predictions engendered by the display units. In the barking of black-tailed prairie dogs (*Cynomys ludovicianus*) a signaler maintaining a steady interval continues to interrupt its other activities to monitor a predator or other bothersome stimulus. With a shortening interval its relative probability of fleeing increases; with a lengthening inter-

Figure 4. *(Animal Signals—Overview)* Male hawfinch *(Coccothraustes coccothraustes)* approaching female for bill-touching ceremony. From Guy Mountfort, "Some Observations on the Hawfinch *Coccothraustes coccothraustes,*" *Proceedings of the XIth International Ornithological Congress,* 1954, p. 606.

val the probabilities of continued monitoring and fleeing decrease.

Other rules generate markedly nonrandom sequential combinations of display units. In the singing of eastern pewees (*Contopus virens*) and eastern phoebes (*Sayornis phoebe*) one display unit is repeated in strings, each terminated by an utterance of a different display. The probability that a singer will act to facilitate interaction with other birds is highest for short strings and declines as string length increases. Yet other species (e.g., the yellow-throated vireo, *Vireo flavifrons*) sing larger numbers of different display units in patterned sequences and provide more detailed information about their interactional and other behavior. The extent to which such patterning rules are found among diverse species is largely unexplored, however. Rules may be common in some kinds of birds, and they appear to occur in at least some primates (e.g., *Callicebus moloch*) and whales (e.g., *Megaptera novaeangliae* and *Balaenoptera physalis*), but they may not be important in the communication of most animal species.

Not all commonly repeated sequences imply the existence of the performance rules that are fundamental to this repertoire. Some sequences arise frequently because their component displays are uttered in correlation with recurrent patterns in the flow of events rather than having their order imposed by processes strictly internal to that signaler. Similarly most simultaneous combinations of displays (as in human facial expressions or vocalizations birds utter while raising their crests) are probably concatenations fit to the event rather than to an internal rule structure. Thus none of these reflects membership in this repertoire. By employing display units contextually to each other the repertoire of classes of combinations of displays both gives signalers control of key contextual relations and reveals the proportional contributions of each component to recipients efficiently. And a few combinatorial rules plus a few display units can generate relatively large numbers of signaling patterns.

Repertoires of formalized interactions. Unlike those in the first three repertoires, many signal patterns cannot be performed by a single individual. A human handshake is a simple example of cooperative performance of a signal unit. Nonhuman animals have many comparable signals. Bills are struck together as individuals meet, for instance, by storks, herons, woodpeckers, and various finches. And both handshaking and bill touching (see Figure 4) are commonly embedded in longer cooperative sequences—sometimes of many steps—that are formal units of greeting behavior.

This sort of signaling is common when animals come together to greet, challenge, court, or accomplish any social task that is easily derailed. Formalized interactions provide the frameworks for negotiation. Humans find special use for them in managing conversational interactions and in all the little smoothings of encounters that ERVING GOFFMAN recognized as the "everyday rituals" or "supportive and remedial interchanges" of social life (*see* CONVERSATION; INTERACTION, FACE-TO-FACE).

Every formalized interaction provides parts for its participants to play. Each part defines behavior (as in a handshake) or at least a range of actions with certain characteristics and limits (e.g., dominating and deferent behavior or initiating and responding behavior). If the formalization extends for more than a single move it entails a program that meshes the playing of parts into prescribed routines and optional subroutines. A routine may require participants to behave alike (as when two courting gulls or grebes walk or swim in parallel, stop in parallel, and display alike and simultaneously; Figure 5) or in a complementary fashion (as when one courting cockroach attends while the other engages in monologuelike repetitive behavior or one conversing human speaks and gestures while another listens and watches, making slight feedback signals). Routines thus delimit the ways in which participants in a formalized interaction combine sequences of the behavior required by their respective parts. The formalization is seen both in particular acts and in features of the framework

that flexibly constrain and direct the interaction.

Because the units are interactional—joint products of more than one signaling participant—formalized interactions are usually relatively complex signals. Many have been described by ethologists, but few complex ones are known in enough detail to permit the rules of their programs to be written with much precision.

That there is more than one repertoire of formalized interactions is evident from the range extending from simple performances that are jointly performed analogues of display units to complex cooperative routines that involve sequencing rules, and from the flexibility of many sorts, much of it involving formally patterned variations. This suggests a dichotomy: several repertoires of signal units that individuals can perform alone on the one hand, and repertoires of jointly performed signal acts on the other.

The special contributions of formalized interactions are to organize and limit signaling exchanges at crucial times that involve either change or at least management of potentially disruptive disparities in the contributions of participants. Difficulties and instabilities often arise when interacting can be costly or hazardous—as it readily can when individuals begin an encounter or try to develop an event in ways for which they are unequally prepared. Partic-

Figure 5. *(Animal Signals—Overview)* Part of a weed rush by horned grebes. "The birds, coming together, turn and Rush side by side for a few to perhaps 30 ft. Then they move apart, move together and Rush, move apart, and so on. . . . As the birds separate at the end of each Rush, they subside into the Upright Posture and often swim about briefly before coming together for another Rush. . . . The ceremony ends when one or both birds drop the weeds." From Robert W. Storer, "The Behavior of the Horned Grebe in Spring," *Condor* 71 (1969): 197.

ipants use formalized interactional signaling to negotiate.

Such signaling achieves its functions first by enabling individuals to provide and elicit information about adherence to an expectable routine or about the imminence and nature of change by an associate. Second, the signals provide means by which each participant can share in control of the event and can attempt to influence another's course within the security offered by formal constraints on behavior.

No animal has an unlimited number of signals available for communicating. Each of its various repertoires probably has fewer than forty or fifty units, often many fewer. And at least the units of the display repertoire—at present the one most studied—appear to provide information about a limited number of referents, perhaps fewer than twenty. Nonetheless, units from at least two and sometimes several repertoires, each with different characteristics and making distinctive informative contributions, are brought to bear in each event of signaling. This diversity of kinds of signals greatly enriches both animal communication and the nonspeech communication of humans.

Bibliography. Charles Darwin, *The Expression of the Emotions in Man and Animals,* London, 1872; W. John Smith, *The Behavior of Communicating: An Ethological Approach,* Cambridge, Mass., 1977; idem, "Consistency and Change in Communication," in *The Development of Expressive Behavior: Biology-Environment Interactions,* ed. by Gail Zivin, New York, 1985; idem, "Signaling Behavior: Contributions of Different Repertoires," in *Dolphin Cognition and Behavior: A Comparative Approach,* ed. by R. J. Schusterman, J. A. Thomas, and F. G. Wood, Hillsdale, N.J., 1986; Edward O. Wilson, *The Insect Societies,* Cambridge, Mass., 1971.

W. JOHN SMITH

2. AUDIBLE SIGNALS

Animals make sounds for communication by means of an astonishing variety of anatomical and physiological mechanisms. These sounds encompass acoustical patterns from wideband noise to pure tones, and they range in frequency in different species from under ten cycles per second (below the limit of human audition) to over one hundred kilocycles per second (far above the limit of human audition). The detection and analysis of sounds by animals is likewise complex. In spite of these adaptations, though, acoustic communication by animals is ultimately limited by distortions of sounds while traveling through the environment (propagation).

Production of Sound

Production of sound requires the forced vibration of some anatomical structure. For the most effective emission of sound power, a source must produce sounds with wavelengths no greater than the dimensions of the source. For longer wavelengths, the emitted power drops steeply with increasing wavelength. Consequently, for animals with similar anatomical structures for producing sound, larger species often produce sounds of lower frequencies (longer wavelengths).

Among terrestrial vertebrates other than birds, many communicatory sounds result from vibrations of the vocal cords. These two flexible membranes in the larynx at the anterior end of the trachea are driven by the expulsion of air from the lungs. In some species, adjustment of the tension on the vocal cords alters the fundamental frequency of the sound. The amplitude of these sounds can be altered either by movement of the arytenoid cartilages in the larynx, as in certain toads, or by modulation of the force with which air is expelled from the lungs. Certain frequencies are made weaker or emphasized by resonances of the air spaces in the pharynx, mouth, and nasal passages, which produce a band-pass filtering of the vocal sounds. In humans this mechanism is highly developed to produce the formants of SPEECH. Mammals also produce important nonvocal communicatory sounds—for instance, by stamping their feet, by expelling air forcibly through the nostrils in a snort or whistle, and even in a few species by rattling stiff spines.

Birds do not use the larynx for producing sounds. Instead, an anatomically distinct structure—the syrinx—incorporating the distal ends of the bronchi and adjoining trachea serves this purpose. In the true songbirds (Oscines, Passeriformes) the syrinx consists of a thin membrane in the wall of each bronchus along with five to seven pairs of intrinsic and two pairs of extrinsic muscles (Figure 1). In other birds the syrinx includes two additional thin membranes, either in the walls of the trachea or in the bronchi, but in no case so many intrinsic muscles. Sound is produced by expulsion of air from the lungs past the membranes. In some species the vibration of the membranes determines the fundamental frequency of the sound produced; in others, including doves, constriction of the membranes produces a whistle as a result of turbulence in the downstream air column. Amplitude is controlled by the force with which air is expelled from the lungs or perhaps by constriction of the glottis in the larynx, which has an elaborate bony and muscular structure in Oscines. Frequency modulation in the true songbirds results from adjustments in the tension of the syringeal membranes. As an extraordinary consequence of this mechanism, in many species of songbirds a bird can sing a duet with itself by independently adjusting the membranes in its two bronchi.

In many species of birds, special elongations or enlargements of the trachea or esophagus, often in conjunction with the respiratory air sacs, produce resonant cavities that could amplify the emitted sounds at particular frequencies, although these effects still require experimental verification. Some birds also produce communicatory sounds by scraping together stiff feathers, by means of specialized feathers that vibrate in flight or when fanned vigorously, by clapping together the upper and lower parts of the beak, or by drumming their beaks on trees.

Among invertebrates, terrestrial forms that produce communicatory sounds include a variety of spiders and scorpions, but the most numerous are insects. Unusual mechanisms include knocking the head on another surface (certain beetles and termites) and whistling by brief expulsions of air from the tracheoles (queen honey bees). The two major groups of sound-producing insects are the Orthoptera (grasshoppers and crickets) and Cicadidae (Homoptera, cicadas). The former produce shrill creaking noises (stridulations) by scraping a stiff plectrum across a filelike structure, a series of ridges or protuberances. Acridoid crickets and grasshoppers scrape their hind legs against their closed forewings; grylloid and tettigonioid crickets and grasshoppers scrape their two forewings together. The wings themselves serve as sounding boards to improve the impedance match with the ambient air. In some species the wings have specialized thin membranes for this purpose. Cicadas produce a rapid series of clicks by buckling, inward and outward, curved tymbals formed by the exoskeleton on the sides of the first abdominal segment. *See also* INSECTS, SOCIAL.

Aquatic animals produce as much if not more noise than terrestrial ones. Many crustaceans, for instance, produce clicks or stridulations with specialized portions of their exoskeletons. The snapping shrimp has a tiny plunger that works when the major cheliped (pincer) is opened and closed; in many coastal areas of the world these shrimp are so abundant and active that the water sizzles continuously with their sounds. The action of the plunger ejects a stream of water during foraging, and the sound apparently serves no role in communication. It was, however, the cause of much speculation and consternation among naval acoustics experts during World War II before its source had been identified. In contrast, it has been known since antiquity that spiny lobsters produce rasping sounds by scraping the bases of their antennae against ridges on their heads.

Bony fish also produce many communicatory sounds. Some appear to result from bones snapping against each other. In other species, bones of the pharyngeal arches, which support the gills, scrape against each other or across special bony protuberances in the floor of the pharynx to produce rasping noises. Thrumming sounds often result from vibrations of the air sac, induced by muscles in the walls or medial septum of the sac. In some species, sound-

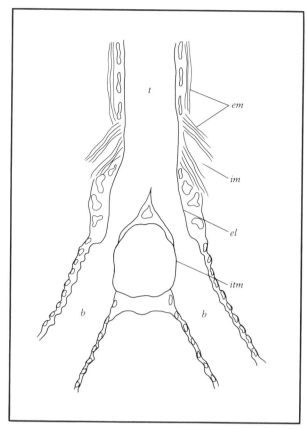

Figure 1. *(Animal Signals—Audible Signals)* Syrinx of an oscine songbird, schematic diagram of a longitudinal section: *(t)* trachea; *(b)* bronchus; *(itm)* internal tympaniform membrane; *(el)* external labium; *(em)* extrinsic muscles; *(im)* portion of the intrinsic muscles of the syrinx. The intraclavicular air sac lies against the external surfaces of the syrinx, including the extraluminal surfaces of the tympaniform membranes. Redrawn after F. Nottebohm.

producing portions of the pharyngeal arches lie against the air sac, which could then act as a resonating chamber.

Perhaps the most versatile of all animals in the range of sounds produced are the cetaceans: whales, porpoises, and dolphins. These animals produce sounds underwater without expelling air, by shifting air from one compartment to another within the head. The highly modified larynx includes an expandable chamber, which is filled by blocking the nasal passages at a point beyond the larynx while expelling air from the lungs. The air from the laryngeal chamber is then expelled through constrictions in the nasal passages controlled by muscular sphincters into diverticula located between the skull and the tightly closed blowhole. The air passing the nasal constrictions produces a startling variety of whistles, squeals, and flatulences.

Diversity of Communicatory Sounds

Most animals produce sounds well within the range of human hearing, but some, especially whales and certain birds, include some exceptionally low-frequency sounds near the lower limit for human hearing. Such frequencies have advantages for long-range communication (see below).

Ultrasonic sounds, greater than twenty kilocycles per second (the upper limit of human hearing), have evolved for special purposes. Because of their short wavelengths and high rate of absorption, they are ideal signals for echolocation of small objects at relatively close range. Bats, many of which rely on echolocation for capturing insects at night, produce intense ultrasonic chirps. Other animals that employ echolocation, including several birds and dolphins, make use of clicks or whistles at ultrasonic frequencies as well as frequencies audible to humans. These species only approximate the bats' extraordinary powers of discrimination.

Some rodents produce simple ultrasonic sounds, including distress cries of isolated young and certain male vocalizations during mating. In both cases the high rate of attenuation of these sounds effectively restricts them to nearby receivers and thus minimizes the chances of attracting predators or rivals.

Most birds have a surprisingly large repertoire of different types of vocalizations, in some species more than twenty. Most of these vocalizations are brief notes—some tonal, others harsh—used for close-range communication and alarm calls. Most species also have complex stereotyped vocalizations as well. Songbirds (Oscines) that defend relatively large territories usually have elaborate songs of complex, largely tonal patterns. In some species each individual masters a repertoire of these stereotyped patterns. Full development of these patterns usually requires experience with normal adult songs, a learning process that in some species is restricted to a sensitive period early in life. Interacting with adult birds in addition to hearing their songs can also enhance this learning.

Mammalian vocalizations are notable for their variability even within the repertoires of single individuals. The different calls in an individual's repertoire often merge with each other through a series of intermediate forms. Some of this variation, particularly though not exclusively in primates, is now known to be associated with different social contexts or external referents. As a general pattern in mammalian vocalizations, though, calls indicating aggressive threat tend to have low fundamental frequencies and wide spectra, while calls indicating submission or fear have the opposite features: high fundamental frequencies and tonal structure.

An important issue in research on animal sounds is the specificity of the information they encode about the signaling animal. For some mammalian and avian species, particularly primates, evidence now indicates that even subtle variation in the structure of calls correlates with differences in the signaler's social situations, relationships to the receiver, or external referents such as the type of predator detected or food discovered. In some cases, playbacks of tape recordings have verified that members of the same species can make these distinctions and respond appropriately on the basis of the sounds alone. Experiments with vocalizations of birds and mammals have also demonstrated capabilities for recognition of particular individuals, such as parents, offspring, mates, or territorial neighbors, on the basis of individual differences in vocalizations. Some birds' songs also vary geographically, in some cases in the form of distinct dialects. In these species, individuals tend to respond most readily to songs of their local dialect, a discrimination that applies both to females responding with solicitations for copulation and to males responding to a territorial threat. *See also* ANIMAL SONG.

At least one fish is also known to recognize individual differences in the sounds of territorial neighbors. In contrast, the sounds produced by amphibians and invertebrates, so far as is known, only convey information about species and sexual status to potential receivers. Unlike the vocalizations of many birds and mammals, there are no consistent, individual differences in sounds.

Detection and Perception of Sound

Of the diversity of mechanisms for detecting and analyzing sound, all involve the coupling of mechanical transduction with neural analysis. In mechanical transduction the incident sound wave produces movements in some anatomical structure. The mechanism can respond to two features of the incident sound: either the pressure wave or the accompanying local displacements of the molecules in the medium. In the near field of a source of sound (roughly within a distance corresponding to the wavelength of the sound or the maximum dimensions of the source), the medium undergoes substantial displacement. Farther from the source, in the far field, most of the energy in a sound field is present in a pressure wave. The propagation of the pressure wave is accompanied by slight displacements of the molecules of the medium backward and forward in the direction of propagation. Since sound travels more than four times as fast in water as in air, the wavelength of a sound of a given frequency is more than four times longer, and the near field of the source extends more than four times as far.

The simplest mechanical transducer for detecting

sound is a fine hair. Such a structure resonates, like a tine of a tuning fork, at a particular frequency, corresponding to its natural period of oscillation as determined by its mass and compliance. Movement occurs in response to the local displacement of molecules in the medium as a sound wave passes.

For transducing the pressure variations in sound waves rather than the molecular movements, terrestrial vertebrates and many insects have evolved specialized organs. These structures all include a thin membrane, or tympanum, which vibrates in response to fluctuations in the pressures applied to its two faces. There are two types of membranous detectors: pressure and pressure-gradient detectors. In the first type, found in the ears of humans and many other mammals, one side of each tympanum is exposed to a reference pressure in an essentially closed, rigid cavity. Fluctuations in external pressure create differences in pressure across the membrane and set it in motion.

In the second type of detector each tympanum is exposed to the fluctuations of external pressure on both its faces. The tympanal organs of some acridoid Orthoptera, for instance, consist of two tympana in pockets on either side of the first abdominal segment. Large tracheal air sacs with thin walls fill the space between the inside surfaces of the tympana (Figure 2) so that changes of pressure are transmitted through the thorax from one membrane to the other, at least for frequencies less than about eight kilocycles per second. At any instant, depending on the orientation of the body, the phase of the sound wave differs at the two tympana. Fluctuations in this pressure gradient as the wave passes set the membranes in motion. A fundamentally similar mechanism appears in some frogs, reptiles, and birds.

Both of the mechanisms for detecting the pressure waves of sound in air offer advantages over a vibrating hair. The greater surface of the thin membrane offers higher sensitivity and thus reduces the need for narrow selectivity of frequencies; tympanal detectors respond to wide ranges of frequencies. The two tympanal mechanisms, on the other hand, differ in one fundamental way: directionality. As the response of a pressure-gradient receptor depends on the phase difference of the wave at two locations, the response varies dramatically as the animal changes its orientation with respect to the direction of the sound wave. When the two tympana are equidistant from the source, so that the line between them is transverse to the direction of propagation, the phase difference drops to zero, and a null occurs in the response.

In contrast, the pressure detector, which makes use of a reference pressure, lacks inherent directionality. Fluctuations of pressure from passing sound waves, regardless of their direction of travel, induce move-

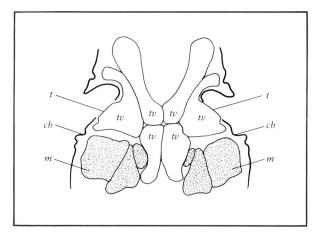

Figure 2. *(Animal Signals—Audible Signals)* Tympanal organs of a locust (Orthoptera: Acridoidea), schematic diagram of a cross-section through the first abdominal segment: *(t)* tympanum; *(tv)* tracheal vesicles (air spaces with thin walls); *(cb)* cuticular body at the site of attachment of sensory cells; *(m)* muscle. Note that air-filled tracheal vesicles bridge the space between the two tympana. Redrawn after H. Autrum.

ments of the tympanum, because the internal reference pressure remains constant. In actual cases, such ears have some directionality for wavelengths shorter than the distance between the ears because of sound shadows cast by the animal's head. To determine the direction of sound, these animals can use neural mechanisms to compare the responses of the two ears. Humans, for instance, can compare differences in the times of arrival, phases (for wavelengths greater than the width of the head), or amplitudes (for wavelengths shorter than the width of the head) of the incident sound on opposite sides of the head.

Discrimination of frequencies presents additional problems. All receptors, as emphasized above, have some selectivity in the frequencies to which they respond, although the narrowness of tuning varies considerably. Thus male mosquitoes' antennal hairs respond, as does the animal itself, to a narrow band of frequencies. Such a receptor—and the animal—cannot discriminate among different frequencies.

Frogs also have receptors in their inner ears tuned to certain frequencies. In this case the animals have two or more sets of receptors, each tuned to different bands of frequencies. Usually one or more sets of cells are tuned to frequencies in the males' mating calls; a separate set is tuned to low frequencies and perhaps is used to detect approaching predators.

Acridoid orthopteran insects discriminate among frequencies by another mechanical means. The membrane of the tympanal organ is divided into two portions, which differ in thickness and consequently resonate at different frequencies. Four separate attachments for sensory neurons differ in their response to the vibrations of these portions of the tympanum so that the animal has several distinct populations of neurons tuned to different frequencies.

Frequency discrimination reaches its greatest sophistication in the cochlea. These organs have evolved separately in birds and mammals from reptilian ears, yet in both cases they depend on apparently similar mechanical means for separating frequencies. The changes in width and thickness of the basilar membrane in the cochlear duct result in corresponding changes in the response to the imposed force of a traveling wave along the membrane. The ability of a bird's ear to discriminate frequencies is comparable to that in mammals. Birds generally have less sensitivity than mammals at high frequencies, but some at least have greater sensitivity at low, subsonic frequencies.

Detection of sound underwater poses a different set of problems. The largely aqueous bodies of marine organisms are essentially transparent to sound; there is little differential movement of anatomical structures, on which transduction of pressure waves depends. Consequently, air-filled spaces or solid structures in marine organisms help in the detection of fluctuating pressures. The swim bladders of some fish serve this purpose. In cetaceans the mandible— the long bone of the lower jaw—transmits vibrations to the inner ear. No external passage for the ear is required.

Neural specializations for analyzing sounds begin at the level of the sensory cells themselves. Poorly understood interactions among auditory neurons in the mammalian cochlea, for instance, improve discrimination of frequencies. Even sharper tuning occurs in higher-order neurons in the brain stem.

Animals with special capabilities in hearing tend to have special neural mechanisms at early stages in the analysis of sound. For instance, bats use abrupt sweeps of ultrasonic frequencies in detecting small targets by echolocation. The barn owl, which specializes in catching its prey by sound, incorporates in its auditory cortex a complete representation of auditory space, analogous to the representation of visual space in the visual cortex of most vertebrates. In the owl, neurons at lower centers analyze the direction of a source of sound in three dimensions; this information is then organized in the auditory cortex, where the cells at each point respond selectively to sounds from a particular direction.

Many other animals have perceptual or sensory mechanisms specialized for recognizing species-specific acoustic signals. Some insects and lower vertebrates, as already noted, have receptors selectively tuned to the frequencies in species-specific calls. In orthopteran insects central neurons respond selectively to timing differences in the pulses of species-specific calls, differences that turn out to be the critical parameters for recognition of species.

More complex specializations in auditory processing occur in some mammals. Rhesus macaques, for instance, can discriminate among variants of sounds within their species' repertoire more easily than they can discriminate among similar sounds from related species. This result recalls the differences in human ability to discriminate among sounds from one's native language and those from an unfamiliar language. *See also* PERCEPTION—SPEECH.

One special capability that has received much recent attention is categorical perception. Humans asked to discriminate phonemes tend to perceive them in discrete categories. As the acoustic characteristics of a phoneme are transformed experimentally in a continuous sequence into those of a similar phoneme, a person tends to categorize the variants as belonging to one of the phonemes until some threshold is passed. Similar capabilities are reported for other animals. In these cases the subject is first trained to discriminate between two different acoustic signals or between two variants of vocalizations in its species' repertoire. To which kinds of stimuli or task this sort of categorical generalization, as opposed to the more usual progressive generalization, applies is not yet clear. Perhaps any well-learned task generalizes categorically.

Propagation of Sounds through the Environment

The listener or receiver must deal with acoustic signals not as they originate from the source but after they have propagated through an environment. Two difficulties arise as a consequence: the signal mixes with irrelevant sounds in the background, and the signal itself degrades and attenuates.

Background sounds can mask a signal by having the same or similar effects on the receptor organs of the listener. All natural acoustic communication encounters irrelevant background sounds. Most terrestrial environments have low-frequency sounds from human sources. Automobiles and airplanes produce low frequencies that travel for miles, pass through vegetation, and diffract over hills. Rain and vegetation rustling in the wind produce noise with a wide spectrum of frequencies. These sources of background sound can often be minimized by choosing the best time of day for signaling. In fact, dawn offers advantages in this respect. The most serious background sounds for communication, however, are often vocalizations of other animals. Birds that live in colonies confront this problem in its worst form. Each bird trying to communicate with its mate or young must do so over a din of other birds using very similar vocalizations for the same purpose. These birds minimize the difficulties by using sounds that make localization by the listener as easy as possible: complex temporal patterns in which elements have abrupt onsets and terminations and wide spectra. By being able to focus attention on a portion of its auditory space a listener can effectively increase the signal-to-noise ratio.

The masking of acoustic signals by background sound also depends on the listener's selectivity for different frequencies. One advantage of narrow tuning of receptors or discrimination of frequencies is the exclusion of much background sound. This basic consideration explains why animals always have either narrowly tuned receptors or sophisticated mechanisms for discriminating frequencies.

During propagation through the atmosphere acoustic signals suffer attenuation and degradation that reduce a listener's ability to detect or recognize them. Attenuation results in the first place from the nearly spherical spread of sound from the source.

In addition to attenuation from spherical spreading, molecular relaxation in the atmosphere absorbs acoustic energy. This form of attenuation increases with frequency and also depends to a lesser extent on temperature and humidity. In general, higher frequencies attenuate more for propagation over a given distance than do lower ones. The ultrasonic cries of bats used for echolocation attenuate so rapidly with distance that they can hardly serve to detect even large targets at ranges of more than ten meters. Animals that use vocalizations for long-range communication often produce sounds with low frequencies, such as the hooting of owls. However, there are three limitations on the use of low frequencies: (1) the reduced sensitivity of the listener's ears at low frequencies, (2) the higher levels of background sound of low frequencies, and (3) in many cases the limitations imposed by small size of the animal on the possibility of producing low frequencies efficiently.

Sound also attenuates as a result of scattering from objects in the environment, particularly the leaves of trees. *Scattering* is a general term for multiple reflections and diffraction of waves. To produce scattering effectively, objects must have dimensions as large as or larger than the wavelengths of sound. Longer wavelengths (lower frequencies) scatter only from correspondingly larger objects. Attenuation in broad-leaved forests increases noticeably above three kilocycles per second in comparison to open environments. Bunches of needles on needle-leaved trees only appreciably scatter frequencies above eight to ten kilocycles per second at the upper range of the frequencies used by birds for territorial songs. Although atmospheric attenuation always makes lower frequencies more advantageous than higher ones for long-range communication, the additional attenuation of high frequencies by scattering in forests could lower the upper limit of frequencies acceptable for communication. Indeed, several studies have found evidence that birds in forests use lower frequencies than similar birds in more open environments.

A final source of attenuation results from effects

of the ground. When acoustic signals propagate close to the ground, the signal at the receiver is subject to interference between the direct wave from the source and the wave reflected from the ground. For transmission within a fraction of a meter of the ground, sound propagates as a ground wave, the result of an interaction between the air near the surface and the air within pores of the soil. This mode of propagation has a sharp cutoff frequency, so the effect is like a low-pass filter: all frequencies above a critical frequency are severely attenuated. With few exceptions, birds avoid this problem by singing from perches at least one meter above ground and often much higher, or by singing in flight well above the ground. This behavior is particularly striking in species that otherwise feed and spend most of their time on or near the ground. Those that do produce sounds near the ground use exceptionally low frequencies, such as the booming sounds of several species of grouse. Insects and frogs that communicate over distances of at least ten meters and are too small to produce low frequencies efficiently likewise crawl or fly to perches in vegetation well above the ground.

In addition to attenuation, degradation of acoustic structure by amplitude fluctuations and reverberation affects sounds during propagation. Amplitude fluctuations result from transitory heterogeneities in the atmosphere, particularly eddies and pockets of warm air rising from the ground. These variations in the density of air refract sound passing through them and can produce drastic variations in the amplitude of sound. These effects are more pronounced in open environments, where winds are often stronger and thermals more likely. Amplitude fluctuations thus produce effects like dropouts on a tape recording. In such environments long-range acoustic signals with complex, prolonged, stereotyped patterns with lots of specific detail in short intervals of time would be favored so that a listener could recognize the signal from hearing short snatches of it at irregular intervals. In fact, birds of prairies and other open environments often have territorial songs that sound like prolonged tinkling, an indication of the rich, stereotyped detail.

Reverberations result from multiple reflections of sound from objects in the medium. Consequently the sound arriving at the receiver comes by paths of different lengths and thus with different delays. A sound that terminates abruptly at the source wanes gradually at the receiver, with the consequence that temporal patterns are obscured (Figure 3). This problem arises especially in forests, where the foliage and tree trunks provide reflecting surfaces for sounds above roughly one kilocycle per second. Long-range sounds in this environment should differ diametrically from those just discussed for open habitats: they should avoid rapid repetitions of notes at any one frequency. In fact, the territorial songs of birds

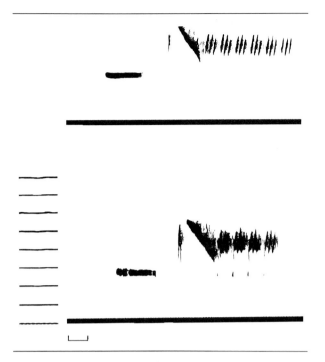

Figure 3. *(Animal Signals—Audible Signals)* Reverberation of a bird's song. *Upper,* spectrograph of the song of a rufous-sided towhee *(Pipilo erythrophthalmus)* recorded from five meters away; *lower,* spectrograph of the same song recorded from fifty meters away. Vertical scale, frequency in units of one kilocycle; horizontal scale, 0.2 second. Note the reverberations obscuring much of the acoustic pattern at a distance from the source. Reproduced by permission of D. G. Richards.

in forests lack rapid repetitions of this sort much more often than do those of birds in open areas. The songs of birds in forests often sound to our ears more melodious than those of birds of open habitats, because reverberation and attenuation by scattering from foliage create advantages for lower frequencies, more sustained tones, and a more measured tempo.

Reverberation also makes the task of locating acoustic signals more difficult. The onsets and terminations of sounds are diffused, and the directionality of the arriving sound is reduced. Notes sustained for longer than usual or repeated at regular but not too frequent intervals might permit more accurate localization of the source by the receiver. It is also possible that animals in forests might have evolved to use reverberation to obscure their locations in order to mislead rivals and predators.

Experiments with clean and degraded tape recordings of songs have demonstrated that at least some birds do have this ability to judge the distance to a source. If a listening animal had experience with the prevailing conditions for reverberation and frequency-dependent attenuation, and if it knew in a general way the characteristics of the signal at the source, it could judge the distance to the source.

Acoustic communication in water encounters the same problems of attenuation and degradation. The primary differences in comparison with communication in the atmosphere arise from the much greater speed of sound in water (approximately 1450–1550 meters per second in sea water) and the much lower rate of attenuation (approximately one hundred times less than in air). The higher speed of sound means that for a given frequency sound has a wavelength over four times as great as in air. It is significant that most echolocating bats eat small insects, whereas most echolocating cetaceans eat fish. Even though both use comparable ultrasonic frequencies, the dolphins achieve substantially less resolution.

One consequence of the lower attenuation of sound in water is the much higher background noise from human machinery. The sounds of ship propellers and engines create an underwater din far from their sources.

Attenuation of sound in the sea is further spectacularly reduced at a depth of about fifteen hundred meters. At this depth the speed of sound is at a minimum. The speed of sound in water increases with increasing temperature and increasing pressure. With increasing depth in the sea, temperature drops and pressure rises. As a consequence the speed of sound first drops with depth, but then, as pressure continues to increase and temperature stabilizes, it rises. A sound produced at the depth of the minimum speed is refracted downward from the layers above and upward from the layers below. In effect it is trapped in a waveguide and consequently spreads, not in three dimensions but in two. In combination with the lower attenuation by molecular absorption in water, intense sounds sometimes produced by whales in this layer could conceivably propagate throughout an ocean basin. Considerable distortion would occur, though, as in propagation through any waveguide. It remains to be demonstrated that whales actually use this channel for such long-range communication.

In any environment, background sounds, attenuation, and degradation increase the chances for error on the part of receivers, either because receivers fail to detect or to classify an acoustic signal correctly or because they respond in the absence of a signal. These errors can also occur during the central processing of auditory information. Regardless of their origin, these errors constitute noise in communication, as defined by communications engineers, and this noise in turn defines the channel for communication. The mechanical and neural processes by which sounds are produced, propagated, and detected are thus fundamental to an analysis of acoustic communication.

See also ANIMAL COMMUNICATION.

Bibliography. René-Guy Busnel, ed., *Acoustic Behaviour of Animals*, Amsterdam and New York, 1963; Donald R. Griffin, *Listening in the Dark*, New Haven, Conn., 1958; Klaus Kalmring and Norbert Elsner, eds., *Acoustic and Vibrational Communication in Insects*, New York, 1985; Donald E. Kroodsma and Edward H. Miller, eds., *Acoustic Communication in Birds*, 2 vols., New York and London, 1982–1983; Brian Lewis, ed., *Bioacoustics: A Comparative Approach*, London, 1983; P. E. Purves and G. E. Pilleri, *Echolocation in Whales and Dolphins*, London, 1983; Charles T. Snowdon, Charles H. Brown, and Michael R. Petersen, eds., *Primate Communication*, Cambridge, 1982.

R. HAVEN WILEY

3. CHEMICAL SIGNALS

Chemical signals are probably the most ancient means of communication among living organisms. Existing single-cell organisms communicate in this manner, and it is likely that the first living organisms did also. Among primitive organisms chemical communication between individuals could have been a simple extension of the mechanisms that had evolved for coordination of functions within the organism. It continues to be essential in the life of many species. In 1959 the term *pheromone* was coined to refer to chemical signals between individuals of the same species. At that time such signals were thought to be analogous to hormones in that they (1) were single chemical substances, (2) were secreted by specialized glands, and (3) had specific behavioral or physiological effects on the receiver. It has become clear that most chemical signals are both chemically and functionally more complex than this original concept implied.

Characteristics. Chemical signals differ greatly from visual and auditory signals. The most important difference is that chemical signals persist in time. Even the briefest odor can still be detected in the atmosphere for tens of seconds or even several minutes, and scent that is deposited on a surface may last for months. The most obvious advantage of this characteristic is that chemical signals will remain in an environment and be effective in the absence of the sender. Many animals use scent marks for such purposes as defining territorial boundaries, identifying a home burrow, or indicating a trail to a productive food source. A less obvious but more fascinating consequence of this persistence is that scent marks may provide information about the passage of time. The odor quality of scent marks containing numerous chemical compounds changes with time as the more volatile components evaporate. Experiments with both insects and mammals have shown that individuals detect these changes and may respond differently to scent deposits of different ages. Infor-

mation about the age of a scent can be useful for a variety of purposes, because it tells one individual how recently another individual has been in the vicinity. Perfumists, for example, recognize the problem of changing odor quality and have spent millions of research dollars on chemical additives that will bind volatiles and release them at a relatively slow and constant rate so that the perfume lasts and the scent does not change. Animals too have dealt with this problem over the course of evolution, and most of the so-called fixatives used originally by perfume chemists were extracted from animal scent glands—civetone from civets, muskone from musk deer.

Sources. Any animal products that are secreted or excreted into the environment may be used as a source of chemical signals. Many animals use urine, feces, or saliva as carriers for scents, the most common example being the urine-marking of dogs and wolves. Most species have also evolved specialized scent glands that produce secretions specifically for the purpose of communication. Scent glands can occur on any part of the body. Common sites in mammals include the anogenital region (most species), the corner of the mouth (cats, ground squirrels), in front of the eye (antelope and deer), on the bottom of the feet (deer), in or near the armpits (humans and some other primates), and on the flank, back, or ventral midline (rodents). Many mammalian species have an array of such glands, sometimes with quite different functions. In species that use urine or feces as a carrier for scent, specialized glands often produce the primary components of the signal and add them to the excretory product. Such glands may be under the animal's control, so that an individual may produce either scented, signal-bearing feces or unscented, noncommunicative feces, depending on the situation (e.g., European rabbits).

Chemical nature. Scent glands usually produce a mixture of chemical compounds. The number of compounds ranges from just a few into the hundreds. A major task for research is to determine the effective components, those responsible for the communicative functions of the gland.

In some cases the effective signal consists of a single chemical compound with a relatively limited and specific effect on the receiver (e.g., sex attractant in the gypsy moth, *Porthetria dispar*). In other cases, especially well studied in insects, the chemical signal consists of several compounds. The overall effect of the signal and the degree to which it is species-specific may depend on the ratios of the individual components. For example, the sex attractant of the female oriental fruit moth (*Grapholitha molesta*) is maximally effective when the ratio of its three major components is 100:6:3; even slight deviations in these ratios make it much less effective in attracting males. In yet other cases, especially evident among vertebrates, the scent secretion consists of a large number of chemical compounds. It is not clear to what extent all of these components are functional. In a number of mammalian species single components have been identified that can account for a significant percentage of a particular effect (such as the magnitude of sexual attraction), but such isolated components do not account for the full level of activity obtained when the complete scent is used. For some functions, such as individual, group, or kin recognition, many components are important in contributing to the "odor image," much as many components of a human FACE contribute to its individual distinctiveness. Both examples suggest that the complexity of many vertebrate scent signals, the richness and distinctiveness of their odor, is important for their function and that behavioral or physiological responses depend at least in part on the entire complex, not just a few components.

In some cases the chemical nature of the signal may have evolved to suit the function it serves. Alarm signals tend to be highly volatile substances that spread quickly but are short-lived in their action; sexual attractants also tend to be relatively volatile in order to attract partners from a distance but not so volatile that the scent disappears too quickly. At the other end of the continuum territorial marks are relatively nonvolatile and persist for a long time.

Deployment. Chemical signals may be emitted directly into the surrounding medium (air, water) or deposited onto objects in the environment (twigs, branches, rocks, or other prominent features). Signals released into the air or water will necessarily have a shorter effective lifetime than those deposited on an object, and the former tend to be for short-term functions such as signaling alarm, attracting a sexual partner, or repelling a predator. Indeed some of the most spectacular uses of chemical signals are for defense, the most well known being the obnoxious spray of skunks. Even more dramatic is the defensive spray of the bombardier beetle (*Brachinus sp.*), a mixture of irritating quinones that is emitted at approximately one hundred degrees centigrade. The beetle accomplishes this by mixing secretions from two glands, which react explosively and release heat.

Most species that employ scent signals have specialized behavior patterns for depositing scent in the environment, usually referred to as scent-marking behaviors. Such behaviors generally bring the scent gland into direct contact with an object in the environment, although some (such as the dog's raised-leg urination posture) allow the animal to aim at the appropriate object. Scent deposited in the environment generally persists for a considerable time and may have a variety of personal or group advertisement functions. Scent-marking behavior is usually distinctive and stereotyped in form, often appearing as an exaggeration of normal movement. For humans, with our relatively limited olfactory abilities, such visible behavior often provides the most obvious indication that animals are doing something important. It also gives scientists a means to study this elusive mode of communication.

Perception. Perception of chemical signals is mediated either by the olfactory system, specialized for reception of chemicals released into the air (or into the water in the case of aquatic species), or by taste or other contact chemical senses. In reptiles and mammals an important sensory system for reception of chemical signals is the vomeronasal (or Jacobson's) organ, a tubular structure located either in the roof of the mouth (snakes and a few mammals) or in the nasal cavity (most mammals).

The neural mechanisms mediating chemical communication are reasonably well understood among insects but not in other complex organisms. In simple systems, in which one or just a few chemical compounds constitute the signal, there are often sensory nerve cells that are highly specialized for sensitivity to a single chemical component of the signal. The function of such cells is primarily to indicate the presence or absence of this one chemical compound. Behavioral or physiological responses to a chemical signal thus depend on activity in this class of sensory neurons. In general, however, sensory nerve cells in the chemical senses tend to be generalists; they respond to a range of chemical compounds. Sensory processing is thus based on comparisons among the responses of many sensory cells that differ in their patterns of sensitivity. Although the details of the mechanisms are unknown, this kind of system allows subtle discriminations among complex odorants to be made with a relatively small number of sensory nerve cells.

Behavioral functions. When chemical signals from one individual influence the behavior of other individuals they are said to have behavioral functions. These include sexual attraction and excitation; trail following; alarm; threat; individual, kin, or group recognition; offspring or parent identification; and elicitation of nipple attachment and nursing. In some cases behavioral responses are immediate and highly predictable, but in other cases changes in behavior may be extremely subtle and/or greatly delayed.

Among the signals that have immediate effects on behavior are sexual attractants, known to occur in a wide range of animals. Such signals cause perceivers of the opposite sex to attempt to find the source of the scent, which may involve moving upwind or upcurrent or searching within the active space of the scent. Once the recipient of the signal is in the vicinity of the sexual partner, further courtship and mating activities are usually coordinated by other signals, some of which may be chemical.

Considerable speculation surrounds the question of whether humans also have sexual attractant or aphrodisiac scents. The existence of the controversy no doubt indicates that if we do, the effects are likely to be extremely subtle. It is known, however, that in many women regular changes do occur in the composition of vaginal secretions that correlate with the menstrual cycle, indicating some basic biochemical changes that could be used as signals. However, the nature of the changes varies among women, suggesting that this is not a highly elaborated signaling system. *See also* SMELL.

Among signals that do not necessarily elicit immediate behavioral responses are those that provide various kinds of categorical information—signals that allow recognition of individuals, kin, age classes, social status classes, or one's own versus a neighboring or unfamiliar group. Individual recognition, for example, is crucial for individual vertebrate animals that interact regularly with particular other members of their own species. This function is often entirely or partly dependent on chemical signals. All mammals that have been tested show the ability to discriminate individuals on the basis of odors. Such abilities indicate the presence of highly developed perceptual capacities for discrimination of subtle differences in odor quality and for memory of these qualities. Although human infants recognize the odor of their own mother versus another mother, and many adults can recognize at least a few other individuals by odor, nonhuman species rely much more heavily on chemical communication for this kind of information, and their abilities are accordingly much greater.

Physiological functions. When chemical signals influence the physiological state of a recipient they are said to have physiological or primer functions (and are often called primer pheromones). Among mammals chemical signals are known to accelerate or delay reproductive maturation, accelerate or retard reproductive cycles of females, cause abortion of fetuses or failure of implantation of the fertilized egg in the uterus, and cause rapid, short-term changes in circulating hormone levels. For example, in many species of rodents exposure of young females to the odors of unfamiliar adult males will result in the acceleration of sexual maturity. In humans it is known that women who associate closely tend to synchronize their menstrual cycles, an effect similar to that seen in other mammals; in both humans and nonhumans this effect is caused at least in part by chemical signals. Among other taxonomic groups a variety of similar effects have been discovered, such as suppression or acceleration of reproductive development in fish and insects and reproductive suppression leading to caste development in insects. *See also* INSECTS, SOCIAL.

Conclusions. Despite considerable information about chemical communication our knowledge of this kind (or class) of communication lags far behind that of signals for other sensory modalities. In part this may be because humans have relatively poorly developed olfactory capabilities and scent signaling systems and therefore lack intuitive insight into and/or interest in this mode of communication. Only since about 1960 have chemical techniques become sensitive enough to measure the small quantities of compounds used in chemical signals. In addition chemical senses have proved to be more difficult to investigate and understand than other senses. In the future we are bound to discover many new and intriguing ways in which animals use chemicals to communicate, possibly ways that we have not yet imagined.

See also ANIMAL COMMUNICATION.

Bibliography. Eric S. Albone, *Mammalian Semiochemistry,* Chichester, Eng., and New York, 1984; William J. Bell and Ring T. Carde, eds., *Chemical Ecology of Insects,* Sunderland, Mass., 1984; Martin C. Birch, *Pheromones,* The Hague, 1974; Richard L. Doty, ed., *Mammalian Olfaction: Reproductive Processes and Behavior,* New York, 1976; Dietland Müller-Schwarze and Maxwell M. Mozell, eds., *Chemical Signals in Vertebrates,* New York, 1977; Dietland Müller-Schwarze and Robert M. Silverstein, eds., *Chemical Signals in Vertebrates 3,* New York, 1983; John G. Vandenbergh, ed., *Pheromones and Reproduction in Mammals,* New York, 1983.

ROBERT E. JOHNSTON

4. VISIBLE SIGNALS

Used in communication by almost all freely moving, diurnal animals, including humans. The major classes of animals using visible signals are crustaceans (e.g., crabs), insects, spiders, cephalopod mollusks (e.g., octopuses), cartilaginous fishes (e.g., sharks), bony fishes, amphibians, reptiles, birds, and mammals. Most visible signals have evolved for intraspecific social communication, as in schooling and flocking, dominance and territoriality, courtship and sexual behavior, and parent-offspring relations. However, interspecific signaling is also important, as in predator-prey interactions, and most flowers are visible signals to pollinators such as insects (*see also* INSECTS, SOCIAL).

Forms

Visible signals of animals are mainly intrinsic, which is to say they are part of the signaler's body (e.g., color patches) or are created by the body (e.g., signal postures). Humans use many extrinsic signals—those having a physical existence separate from the signaler—such as writing, painting, road signs, and traffic lights (*see also* SIGN; SIGN SYSTEM). Extrinsic signals are rare among animals, however, being restricted to fecal deposits (scat), scratching on trees, earth piles made by digging animals, nests and marked nesting areas, and other such general signals that serve primarily to denote ownership of places in the environment (see also sections 1 and 3, above). The more common intrinsic signals are made visible either through the signaler itself generating light or through its body reflecting ambient illumination, usually sunlight.

Bioluminescent signals. A few animal species generate light, including certain nocturnal insects, some nocturnal squids, and a number of deep-sea fishes living in the lightless depths. The shrimp and the squid are known to secrete luminescent clouds into the water to hide their escape from predators. A few animals secrete a luminescent slime over their bodies, the communicative function of which has not been well studied. Most bioluminescence, however, is emitted from special cells collected into photic organs (photophores) with complex structures of reflectors, shields, and filters. In the firefly a pigmentlike molecule of low molecular weight (luciferin) emits light upon being oxidized, which process is mediated by an enzymatic protein (luciferase). Signals emitted by photophores can be regulated to produce flashing patterns and can be made various colors by means of filters. Probably best studied among bioluminescent signals are the flashing patterns of male fireflies searching for females (Figure 1). The female perched in the vegetation answers with a simpler reply, which guides males to her location. The female of one predatory species, nicknamed the "femme fatale," mimics the reply of other species' females, then catches and eats approaching males.

Behavioral signals. Reflected-light communication depends mainly on behavior, in which the orientation, shape, and movement of the body or bodily parts create the signal. These signaling acts are often enhanced by morphological elements, discussed below. Orientation with respect to the intended receiver or an environmental locus is often an important signal in aggressive and sexual interactions (Figure 2). Shapes of entire animals are often altered for communicative purposes. Some fishes can puff up by inflating themselves with air. Animals having bodily coverings such as mammalian fur and avian feathers can change shape by erecting or compressing the covering, called pilomotor responses (Figure 3). Most animal shapes, however, are created by positioning extremities through the action of skeletal muscles to

SPECIES	SIGNALS
Photinus consanguineus	
Photinus greeni	
Photinus macdermotti	
Photinus ardens	
Photinus obscurellus	
Kalm's photuris	
Photuris pennsylvanica	
Big Black Luciola	
Little Black Luciola	
Luciola peculiaris	
Luciola huonensis	
Luciola obsoleta	

Figure 1. *(Animal Signals—Visible Signals)* Morse-code-like flashing patterns of male fireflies, which signals are differently patterned in each species. Courtesy of Jack P. Hailman.

Figure 2. *(Animal Signals—Visible Signals)* Facing away in the black-headed gull, a typical orientational signal, communicates absence of aggressive intent. Courtesy of Jack P. Hailman.

form signal postures (Figure 4). Another element of behavioral signals is movement, as when a bird flies directly at another, supplanting it from a perch.

The elements of orientation, shape, and movement also are used with parts of the body to create signals. Eye contact and looking away, for example, can be behavioral signals involving only eye movements. CHARLES DARWIN pointed out that facial expressions in humans and other animals can be signals in which the shape of the mouth, EYES, and other parts convey different meanings. Similarly, movement of isolated

Figure 3. *(Animal Signals—Visible Signals)* The house cat's defensive shape, typical of pilomotor responses in which animals look large by erecting body covering in aggressive signals or otherwise alter their shapes. Redrawn from Charles Darwin, *The Expression of the Emotions in Man and Animals*, London, 1872.

Figure 4. *(Animal Signals—Visible Signals)* As Charles Darwin noted, an aggressive dog stands erect, whereas an appeasing dog lowers its forelegs and tail, typical signal shapes created by positioning extremities. Redrawn from Charles Darwin, *The Expression of the Emotions in Man and Animals*, London, 1872.

bodily parts is often communicative, as in human gestures with hands and arms. *See also* FACE; FACIAL EXPRESSION; GESTURE.

These elements of orientation, shape, and movement of the body and its parts often occur together as a coordinated signal, or *display*. Displays also can employ morphological elements, discussed below. Visible displays may be relatively simple postures or complex performances like the courtship display of the Anna's hummingbird (Figure 5). The term display is no longer restricted to visible communication but is used to refer to any signal specializations, even though, for example, "vocal display" seems almost a contradiction in terms.

Morphological features. Visible signaling is often enhanced by structural features and coloration. Display structures include modification of horns and antlers in ungulates, ear tufts and tail adornments in other mammals, extendable throat flaps (dewlaps) in some lizards, modified fins in many fishes, inflatable

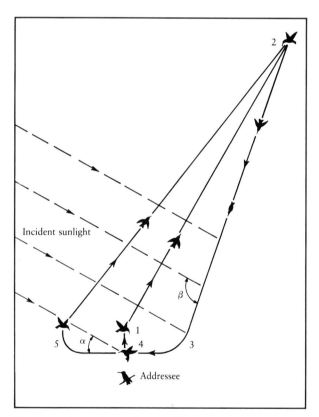

Figure 5. *(Animal Signals—Visible Signals)* The courting male Anna's hummingbird ascends above the female, hovers, power dives in an orientation to reflect sunlight from its iridescent plumage, hovers directly above the female, and then repeats the entire process time and again in a complex display involving orientation, shape, and movement as signal elements. Courtesy of Jack P. Hailman.

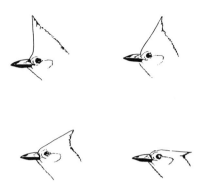

Figure 6. *(Animal Signals—Visible Signals)* The degree of aggressiveness of the Steller's jay is signaled by the angle of its crest, a typical morphological signal involving shape and movement. Courtesy of Jack P. Hailman.

throat pouches in some birds, streamer tails, erectable crests, and a huge variety of other adornments. These structural features can sometimes be controlled with respect to orientation, shape, and movement (Figure 6).

Most communicative coloration probably enhances behavioral signals and draws attention to display structure, but some color patches are signals in their own right (Figure 7). Color changes increase communicative possibilities. Some birds cover display plumage with more drab feathers: flocking signals for flight may consist of brightly colored rumps that are covered when the bird is at rest, for example; the red-winged blackbird covers its red epaulets with black feathers when fearful but displays the red when aggressive. Many animals can change color by means of cellular mechanisms that transport pigment to the

Figure 7. *(Animal Signals—Visible Signals)* The red spot on the herring gull's mandible is signal coloration that elicits pecking by the chicks, a form of begging that induces the parent to regurgitate food. Courtesy of Jack P. Hailman.

surface or retract it deeper (even covering it from view). Chameleons are well known for color changes but are outdone by many fishes and cephalopods (octopus, squid, etc.) in terms of speed of change. In these animals changes may be nearly instantaneous, and some cephalopods have "waterfall" displays in which lines of color sweep continuously along the body.

Evolution

Comparative evidence reveals factors favoring the evolution of visible signals, two of which are diurnal (daytime) habits and a reasonably open habitat. Nocturnal animals and those living in the deep sea or in caves can communicate visually only by generating their own signal light. Crepuscular species (those active at dawn and dusk) use black-and-white coloration because ambient light is insufficient for color vision; examples include whippoorwills and many mammals. Not all diurnal animals rely primarily on visible signaling, however, for birds living in dense vegetation often employ vocal communication more extensively. The answers to other evolutionary questions are less obvious and still actively under study.

Origins and ritualization. Every specialization in morphology, physiology, and behavior evolved from some less specialized precursor. Visible signals are no exception. It seems likely that pigmentation served a variety of functions in addition to social communication, and much animal coloration still serves these noncommunicative purposes. Black color (due to melanin), for example, is used to absorb infrared and visible radiation for thermal balance and to shield organs from damaging ultraviolet radiation. Both melanin and carotenoids (colored pigments) contribute to a feather's resistance to physical damage by abrasion. Physical adornments, such as antlers, crests, and so on, are elaborations of preexisting structures serving noncommunicative functions.

The origins of behavioral signals are harder to trace. Modern concepts have been elaborated by the Dutch zoologist Niko Tinbergen, along with investigators in the same tradition (*see also* ETHOLOGY). Display acts evolved from incipient movements of nonritualized precursors (Figure 8). It was originally believed that such displays could be evolved from "irrelevant" behavioral patterns occurring during times of high conflict. However, today it is generally believed that most or all behavioral signals originated from otherwise appropriate actions; for example, threat evolved from fighting acts. Almost anything an animal does may evolve into a display in some species, and signals have been traced to all these noncommunicative origins: agonistic behavior (fighting, fleeing, protective measures), reproductive behavior (mounting, copulation, nest building, parental care), maintenance activities (wallowing, scratching, bill wiping, preening, and grooming), and other skeletal actions (locomotion, foraging and feeding, antipredator responses). Autonomic responses are further sources of signals: pilomotor acts (sleeking, fluffing, and ruffling), respiratory responses (yawning), vaso-responses (flushing, blanching), and ocular responses (eye movements, pupillary actions).

The changes that take place during the evolution of a signal from precursor acts with other functions are termed *ritualization*. These changes commonly

Figure 8. *(Animal Signals—Visible Signals)* The upright threat posture of the herring gull evolved from actions preparatory to fighting, such as the head held in readiness to peck down on the opponent and the wings held out slightly at the wrists in preparation for striking the other bird. Courtesy of Jack P. Hailman.

Figure 9. *(Animal Signals—Visible Signals)* A signal dark-eyed juncos use in flocking is ritualized from incipient flight movements in which the spreading of the feathers in the tail flick is exaggerated and standardized and the outer feathers of the dark tail have become white so that they flash during the movement. Courtesy of Jack P. Hailman.

involve "freezing" an incipient movement to create a posture, suppressing variation to create stereotypy, exaggerating movement and shape to create distinctiveness, and adding coloration to emphasize movement or shape (Figure 9).

Selection for signal quality. Perhaps the least understood aspect of visible signals is their precise form, which is often a compromise resulting from conflicting pressures of natural selection. One important aspect is the visibility of signals, which is enhanced by orientations differing from background (e.g., longitudinal stripes on fishes living in aquatic vegetation having vertical striation), by colors contrasting with the background (e.g., red against the complementary green color of leaves), and by other similar factors. Physiological processes also affect the form of a signal. For example, yellow is an intrinsically bright and therefore conspicuous color because most eyes are maximally sensitive to the part of the visible spectrum reflected by yellow surfaces. True green pigmentation is rare among birds partly because green-reflecting pigments are rare, some of the few being undesirably water soluble; the green of parrots is due to a combination of yellow pigment and blue structural color created by a scattering phenomenon similar to that which renders the sky blue. Another constraint on signal features is imposed by visual-system mechanisms of the central nervous system, which perceptually fuse movement that is too rapid.

Darwin pointed out that displays are selected to be distinct from one another. He framed this general notion under his more specific "principle of antithesis" in which opposite emotions were supposed to give rise to opposite expressions, as in the distinctive difference between threat and appeasement displays in a variety of animals (Figure 10). Finally, many

Figure 10. *(Animal Signals—Visible Signals)* The threat and appeasement displays of the fox sparrow are nearly opposite in shape, illustrating Darwin's principle of antithesis in which displays having different meanings are selected to be visually distinct. Courtesy of Jack P. Hailman.

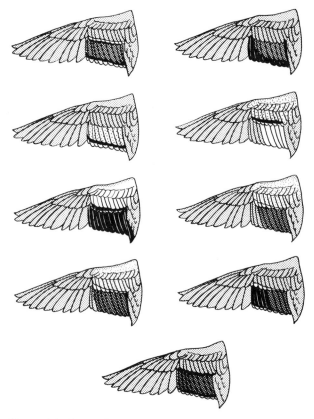

Figure 11. *(Animal Signals—Visible Signals)* Species-specific signals include the wing patches (specula) of ducks that promote grouping in flight.

displays appear to be selected for species specificity. As noted in Figure 1, the courtship flashing patterns of male fireflies are species specific, as are displays of other species (Figure 11).

See also ANIMAL COMMUNICATION.

Bibliography. Edward H. Burtt, Jr., ed., *The Behavioral Significance of Color* (proceedings, Animal Behavior Society Symposium, 1977), New York, 1979; Charles Darwin, *The Expression of the Emotions in Man and Animals*, London, 1872; Jack P. Hailman, *Optical Signals: Animal Communication and Light*, Bloomington, Ind., and London, 1977; Thomas A. Sebeok, ed., *How Animals Communicate*, Bloomington, Ind., and London, 1977; W. John Smith, *The Behavior of Communicating: An Ethological Approach*, Cambridge, Mass., 1977; Niko Tinbergen, *The Study of Instinct*, Oxford, 1951.

JACK P. HAILMAN

ANIMAL SONG

Animals such as grasshoppers and cicadas, frogs and toads, birds, and certain whales produce loud, sustained, or rhythmically patterned sounds that are customarily called songs. Animal sounds do not follow any universal features of rhythm or frequency relationships. They have developed largely in males and are used as long-range signals to attract sexually active females or to defend a territory that the female needs to raise her young. *See also* ANIMAL SIGNALS.

Insects

Among insects, the crickets, grasshoppers, locusts, and cicadas are the most well-known songsters. These instrumentalists produce and hear their sounds in different ways. The crickets, including katydids, rub the bases of their front wings together, and portions of the wings vibrate to produce the sounds; the sounds are heard by tympanal organs just below the knee joint on the front legs. Grasshoppers rub their hind legs against their front pair of wings; their hearing organs are on the abdomen near the base of the hind legs. The males sing to attract breeding females, and adjacent males often sing alternately or simultaneously in loud choruses. Male snowy tree crickets (*Oecanthus fultoni*) have synchronized their chorusing so well that the entire tree seems to pulsate with their songs. *See also* INSECTS, SOCIAL.

Amphibians

Frogs and toads produce their songs with a true larynx, or voice box. The vocal cords are vibrated with a burst of air from the lungs to the buccal cavity, and the sound is often intensified by resonating air sacs in the throat region. Again, it is the males who sing to defend a site and to attract a female for breeding. One tree frog from Puerto Rico (*Eleutherodactylus coqui*) even sings a two-noted song, "ko-kee," the first syllable directed to males and the second to females. Furthermore, the male's ear is selectively tuned to the "ko" and the female's to the "kee." By tuning only to the pertinent songs or parts of songs, frogs of each species can make sense of what, to us, is a cacophony of amphibian arias consisting of songs from as many as fifteen species in some tropical rain forests.

The songs of insects and amphibians are encoded in the genetic material; no learning or experience is required in order to produce or recognize the proper songs of the species. Hybrid species even produce and prefer songs that are intermediate to the two parental species, or in some cases they inherit the song from one of the two parents.

Birds

The songs of insects and amphibians may be functionally equivalent to the songs of birds and certain mammals, but one exciting achievement in these latter two groups has promoted the evolution of sounds that are especially long, complex, and aesthetically pleasing to the human ear. This achievement is vocal learning, which is simply the ability to learn and imitate sounds of others. In the parrots (Order Psittaciformes) and in the songbirds (the suborder with the more structurally complex vocal apparatus in the Order Passeriformes), this learning has been well documented by research conducted both in the laboratory and in nature. Here, then, is the beginning of a new form of communication: the communication of cultural vocal traditions from one generation to the next.

This song learning in songbirds can be demonstrated clearly in the laboratory. If a nestling songbird, such as a white-crowned sparrow (*Zonotrichia leucophrys*), northern cardinal (*Richmondena cardinalis*), chaffinch (*Fringilla coelebs*), or marsh wren (*Cistothorus palustris*), is taken from the nest and isolated from songs of adults, it will produce odd songs that are very unlike those of its wild relatives. If that young bird is tutored over loudspeakers with songs of its own species, however, it imitates the details of those sounds. Most species have a "sensitive" or "impressionable" phase during the first few months of life when learning ability is maximal. Songs are usually "memorized" during this stage, but only several months later, when a male is preparing for his first breeding season, does he actually learn to vocalize what he has memorized months before. While practicing his singing (a stage called subsong or plastic song), the male produces a variety of sounds that will later be reduced to a select few for use as an adult breeding bird. Though some species, such as the northern mockingbird (*Mimus polyglottos*), have made a habit of mimicking the sounds of other species, individuals of most species are highly selective and learn only the songs of their own species.

Song dialects. As with humans, one consequence of vocal learning and a limited dispersal from the site of learning is the formation of stable vocal dialects. These dialects have been studied most in the white-crowned sparrow in the coastal chaparral of California. Careful listening and spectrographic analysis of songs from these populations have revealed the existence of dialect areas that contain on average a little more than one hundred pairs of birds. Dialect boundaries are often abrupt and striking, with birds on opposite sides of the boundary singing unique and clearly recognizable variants of songs typical of the species. The dialect areas may not be delineated so easily in other songbirds, but in most songbirds neighboring males share nearly identical songs—songs that are noticeably different from birds of the same species at other nearby locations.

The exact function of song dialects remains a mystery. They could be a functionless by-product of vocal learning or simply a consequence of birds striving to match the songs of neighboring adults. A more exciting possibility is that dialect boundaries regulate the dispersal of young birds, thereby allowing the evolution of populations that are especially well adapted to local environmental conditions. In some populations of the rufous-naped sparrow (*Zonotrichia capensis*) of South America, the boundaries of different dialects and different habitats coincide, suggesting some support for this hypothesis. This system would work if young birds irreversibly learned the songs of either their father or other adults near the home territory before dispersing. Upon gaining independence, young birds would disperse from the home territory but be repelled by the strange songs of adjacent dialects. A crucial test of this hypothesis will require a careful study of exactly when, where, and how young birds learn their songs in nature; how they react to dialect boundaries during dispersal; and how successful they are at breeding within the home dialect or in other, "foreign" dialects. Proving this hypothesis would be especially exciting, for it would demonstrate a causal link among vocal learning, cultural traditions, and the rate of genetic evolution in this exceptionally successful songbird group.

Song repertoires. Learning of songs has also permitted the evolution of large signal repertoires. While individuals of many species, such as the white-crowned sparrow, may have a single song, individuals of other species may have ten (e.g., song sparrow, *Melospiza melodia*) or even hundreds of songs (e.g., marsh wren). The brown thrasher (*Toxostoma rufum*) has an enormous vocabulary; well over two thousand different songs have been documented from a single individual.

Song is used largely by males to defend territories and attract females, so a greater variety of songs might allow the job to be done even more effectively. Some evidence indicates this is true. Male canaries (*Serinus canaria*) may sing up to forty or fifty different sounds in their long and continuous songs. Female canaries that hear complex canary songs build nests faster than do females hearing simpler ones. Because male canaries increase their repertoire size each year, the female could actually count, by some physiological process, the number of male songs in order to obtain an accurate estimate of the male's age. Older males are usually better mates and parents, and the repertoire size could then be an honest indicator of the potential quality of a mate.

Larger song repertoires may also be helpful in defending territories. Male great tits (*Parus major*) or red-winged blackbirds (*Agelaius phoeniceus*) sing up to eight different songs each. If a male is removed from his territory and replaced with a system of loudspeakers, those territories from which large song repertoires are broadcast remain vacant from intruders longer than do territories "occupied" by smaller song repertoires. Other playback experiments on territories have demonstrated that the resident male maintains an interest longer if a simulated intruder has a large variety of songs. In many species with repertoires, males often countersing (i.e., sing alternately) with the same learned song variant, as if they were addressing each other in their territorial warnings. The number and kind of songs with which a male can reply may in some way indicate his overall quality, for learning of songs does demand a considerable investment of time and energy.

Gender difference. In most animal groups it is only the male that sings, but females of some bird species also sing. This female song occurs especially in tropical regions where birds are relatively long-lived and where they may remain paired on the same territory throughout the year or even for life. The male and female of a pair usually sing simultaneously, often in a synchronized duet. Such duetting may enable members of a pair to communicate more efficiently with each other; in addition, the female's song enables her to participate more effectively in defense of the territory in which she also has a considerable investment.

Research results. Some of the most notable discoveries about bird vocalizations have been made in studies of how the behavior of communicating by song is controlled in the brain. These discoveries include (1) neural lateralization for song control, similar to the way in which one-half of the human brain dominates in control of language; (2) discrete, identifiable groups of cells—"song-control nuclei"—in the forebrain that are involved in both hearing and producing sounds; (3) large sexual differences in brain anatomy correlated with sexual differences in vocal behavior; (4) correlations between the volume of the song-control nuclei in the brain and the total song repertoire size of an individual; (5) growth of new cells in the brains of adults that have learned additional songs; and (6) in some species an annual fluctuation in the volume of song-control nuclei as singing waxes and wanes. These spectacular findings make the songbird an important model system for assessing the relationship between brain structure and behavior.

Whales

Although the songs of many songbirds are exceedingly complex (e.g., the winter wren, *Troglodytes troglodytes*) or especially beautiful to our ears, the songs of whales have a quality that transcends description. Songs of humpback whales (*Megaptera novaeangliae*), for example, are long and complex, sounding somewhat like a bird song that has been slowed to many times its normal speed. The male humpbacks in different oceans sing different songs, but all humpback whales in the same area at a given time have identical songs. All whales in broad areas of an ocean, perhaps even an entire ocean, slowly change their songs, in unison, over time. The whales thus abandon old songs, introduce new variations, and continuously evolve new songs; they are constantly listening to each other and readjusting the latest version for the population. Knowing that there is a change in signal form does not, unfortunately, betray the function of this remarkable form of cultural evolution. Given the logistical problems of studying whales, a satisfying understanding of what these majestic oceanic denizens are doing is likely to remain elusive.

Animal Songs and Sounds

We are intrigued by animal songs because their duration, intensity, rhythm, and—not infrequently—beauty closely match features of our own songs; but we should be aware that the distinction between what is and what is not song among animals is anthropocentric and therefore arbitrary. Few animals are silent, and the simpler sounds of other animals, such as a spider plucking its web, a fruit fly "humming" with its wings, or a lobster rasping in the ocean, are functionally equivalent to the more noticeable sounds of animals such as grasshoppers, frogs, and birds. The currency of natural selection and evolution is offspring, and clearly a wide variety of animals use sounds, either instrumental or vocal or both, during crucial phases of territorial defense and courtship. The sounds of each animal match its own perceptual world, not ours, and they are all really animal songs.

See also ANIMAL COMMUNICATION; SONG.

Bibliography. Michael Bright, *Animal Language*, Ithaca, N.Y., 1985; Flora Davis, *Eloquent Animals: A Study in Animal Communication*, New York, 1978; Robert A. Hinde, ed., *Bird Vocalizations, Essays Presented to W. H. Thorpe*, London, 1969; Rosemary Jellis, *Bird Sounds and Their Meaning*, Ithaca, N.Y., 1984; Donald E. Kroodsma and Edward H. Miller, eds., *Acoustic Communication in Birds*, 2 vols., New York and London, 1982–1983; Roger Payne, ed., *Communication and Behavior of Whales*, Boulder, Colo., 1983; W. John Smith, *The Behavior of Communicating*, Cambridge, Mass., 1977.

DONALD E. KROODSMA

ANIMATION

In MOTION PICTURES, any technique using art materials and processes to produce an illusion of motion, as distinguished from live-action production, which uses PHOTOGRAPHY to record actions that actors and objects have performed. Animation depicts actions that did not previously exist: Mickey Mouse never waved hello except on film. Although originally applied to film, the term is now also used to describe imagery produced with videotape and computers. These technologies have enabled artists to create a wide range of synthetic illusions, usually designated as computer GRAPHICS.

In most animated films, two-dimensional artwork is used to create the illusion of motion, but three-dimensional sculptures and objects of almost any sort may also be used. Like live-action film, animated films are projected at twenty-four frames per second. Each frame of film represents a slightly different moment in the movement depicted. For the highest-quality animation, each frame must be photographed separately, with the artwork being changed or adjusted between exposures. As each minute of screen time requires 1,440 frames, good animation is highly labor-intensive and time-consuming.

The photography for two-dimensional animation is usually done on an animation stand, in which a camera is mounted vertically and pointed down toward the artwork, which lies flat on a table. Modern stands provide for complex computerized movements of the camera in relation to the art and for minutely calculated movements of each segment of artwork, sometimes on several levels. Three-dimensional animation, such as puppet animation, may require quite different procedures.

Origins

Animation may be said to have existed before film. Its basic principles were embodied in the flip-book and other nineteenth-century toys and diversions based on "persistence of vision." Such devices offered many artists experience with animated imagery and helped pave the way for the animated film, which also attracted experimenters from other fields.

Among the earliest animators was J. Stuart Blackton, a former vaudeville chalk-talk artist and cofounder of the Vitagraph studio. In 1900 Blackton made *The Enchanted Drawing*, an example of a trick film that involved substituting objects for drawings. As Blackton reaches for the hat, cigar, or wine bottle he has drawn on a large tablet, the real thing "miraculously" appears in his hand. In 1906 he produced *Humorous Phases of Funny Faces*, generally considered to be the first animated film. Faces drawn in chalk lines on a blackboard change expressions and

disappear; jointed cutouts of a clown and a poodle perform a balancing act.

In 1908 Émile Cohl, a French caricaturist who had entered the service of Léon Gaumont, began an animation career with *Fantasmagorie*, a film of cheerful grotesqueries. Its success was such that Gaumont soon had Cohl turning out a cartoon film every two weeks, a schedule that helped spur Cohl to explore the diverse possibilities of animation. At about the same time in the United States, Billy Bitzer, who had previously pursued a career in magic, was experimenting with clay animation. A sequence in *The Sculptor's Nightmare* (1908) shows a large lump of clay gradually changing into an image of Theodore Roosevelt. Hundreds of manipulations of the clay were made in the intervals of frame-by-frame photography.

In 1911 the American comic strip artist Winsor McCay used characters from his popular strip "Little Nemo in Slumberland" for his first film, *Little Nemo*. Three years later, he created *Gertie the Dinosaur*, the first example of character animation and one of the seminal films in the history of the medium (Figure 1). McCay used *Gertie* in his vaudeville act: whip in hand, he stood beside the screen and spoke orders that the animated dinosaur seemed to obey. McCay's draftsmanship and fluid animation set a standard of excellence that has rarely been surpassed.

Studios

The popularity of such experiments led to the establishment of animation studios. In 1913 Canadian-born Raoul Barré, who had studied and experimented in Paris and had devised the use of pegs to keep drawings in register to each other, opened a studio in New York. In the United States, John R. Bray fol-

Figure 1. *(Animation)* Winsor McCay, *Gertie the Dinosaur*, 1914. The Museum of Modern Art/Film Stills Archive.

lowed shortly, launching a cartoon series about the adventures of Colonel Heeza Liar. In 1914 Bray joined Earl Hurd to form the Bray-Hurd Process Company, which developed numerous innovations and improvements in animation technology. Hurd was credited with introducing the use of cels, clear sheets of celluloid that became basic materials of large-scale studio production of animation. Cels enabled animators to do their artwork in layers. A sequence of a man careening in a balloon might be photographed in three layers. For the bottom layer—the background landscape—the same artwork might be used throughout the sequence, though shifted for each frame. Over this would be placed the balloon, painted on a transparent cel with opaque colors. It might also serve for the entire sequence, but its position in relation to the landscape background would have to be changed for each frame. The third layer would be for the man in the balloon, gesticulating wildly to those below. His gestures would require a new drawing for each frame of film. Owing to the cel system, this meticulous work would be confined to a small portion of the frame.

Among the talents emerging from the Bray-Hurd studio were Max Fleischer and his brother David, who in 1919 completed the first of their "Out of the Inkwell" cartoons, which propelled them into a successful independent career. That same year saw the appearance of the most famous silent cartoon character, Felix the Cat, who debuted in *Feline Follies*, drawn by Otto Messmer at the Pat Sullivan studio (Figure 2). Working on principles explored by McCay—and CHARLES CHAPLIN—Messmer gave Felix a character delineated by an individual style of movement. Three years later, in Kansas City, WALT DISNEY entered the animation industry with the first of his "Laugh-O-Grams."

The United States dominated international animation during the late 1910s and the 1920s, with some important exceptions. In 1917, in Argentina, Quirino Cristiani created *El apostol*, the first animated feature (now lost), using jointed cutouts. During the 1920s Berlin became the center of the first experiments in abstract animation, with the work of Walther Ruttman, Viking Eggeling, Oskar Fischinger, and others (*see* AVANT-GARDE FILM). In 1919 Lotte Reiniger made her first silhouette film, *Das Ornament des verliebten Herzens* (The Ornament of the Lovestruck Heart), which she followed in 1926 with *Die Abenteuer des Prinzen Achmed* (The Adventures of Prince Achmed), the oldest extant animated feature.

Sound Era

A number of artists experimented with synchronization of animation and sound, but in 1928 Disney

Figure 2. *(Animation)* Otto Messmer, *Felix the Cat,* 1926. The Museum of Modern Art/Film Stills Archive.

released the first commercially successful sync-sound cartoon, *Steamboat Willie,* which premiered on November 18, 1928, at the Colony Theater in New York. The film also provided an introduction for Mickey Mouse, who became the world's most celebrated cartoon character. The Disney organization expanded dramatically during the following years, with an unparalleled emphasis on training and experimentation. The "Silly Symphony" shorts and the features *Snow White and the Seven Dwarfs* (1937), *Pinocchio* (1940), and *Fantasia* (1940) gave the Disney studio unquestioned artistic leadership in the medium (Figure 3). Its only serious rival in the United States was the Fleischer studio, creator of the highly successful Betty Boop, Popeye, and Superman shorts. During this period animated films were a regular part of the entertainment supplied by the HOLLYWOOD majors to theaters throughout the world.

In the United States animation generally meant cartoon films. In Europe other avenues were explored. In France the Czech artist Berthold Bartosch caused an uproar with his propagandistic film *L'idée* (The Idea, 1934), based on woodcuts by Frans Masereel, with music by Arthur Honegger. Also in France, the Russian-born Alexander Alexeieff and his American wife and collaborator, Claire Parker, devised the pinscreen, a metal grid filled with headless pins (its surface resembled velvet). When the pins were pushed in at differing heights, they cast tiny shadows of differing lengths. The patterns of shadows produced striking pointillist images. Parker and Alexeieff introduced the technique in *Une nuit sur le Mont Chauve* (A Night on Bald Mountain, 1933), a dark, moody film synchronized to the music of Modest Mussorgsky. In England, New Zealander Len Lye did the first paint-on-film animation in *Colour Box* (1935); the Scotsman Norman McLaren, who had been experimenting with similar techniques independently, drew directly onto film in *Love on the Wing* (1938). The first Soviet work in animation, *Sovetskie igrushi* (Soviet Toys), had been made in 1923 by Alexander Bushkin, Alexander Ivanov, and Ivan Beliakov for DZIGA VERTOV's *Kinopravda* NEWSREEL series. But screenings of several Disney shorts in 1933 led the government to establish the Soyuzmultfilm

Figure 3. *(Animation)* Walt Disney, *Snow White and the Seven Dwarfs*, 1937. The Museum of Modern Art/Film Stills Archive.

studio for more extensive work in animation. In Germany the Nazi hostility to nonobjective art ended the explorations and experiments of earlier years.

Wartime animation. During World War II animation was used extensively for training and PROPAGANDA films. Japanese experiments with animation had begun during the 1910s, but their first animated features were made for war purposes and included children's films about a boy called Momotaro, a figure derived from Japanese FOLKTALE tradition. Revived for World War II, he is shown leading troops of Disneyesque mice and other animals into victorious battle. In England the early work of John Halas and Joy Batchelor was largely war-related and included the feature-length training film *Handling Ships* (1946). In the United States Disney, the other Hollywood studios, and the U.S. Air Force First Motion Picture Unit (FMPU) produced enormous amounts of animation for the armed forces and various civilian organizations.

New directions. After the war, the initiative in cartoon shorts passed to the Warner Brothers and MGM (Metro-Goldwyn-Mayer) studios, where directors like Friz Freleng, Chuck Jones, Robert McKimson, Bill Hanna, and Joe Barbera developed the brash, fast-paced style of comedy pioneered by Tex Avery. Their short films featuring Bugs Bunny, Daffy Duck, the Road Runner, and Wile E. Coyote (Warners) and Tom and Jerry (MGM) have remained popular (Figure 4). Disney continued to dominate the animated feature with films like *Cinderella* (1950), *Peter Pan* (1953), and *Sleeping Beauty* (1959). These lavish productions, based on popular fairy tales and children's stories, featured highly realistic animation of human and animal motions.

Figure 4. *(Animation)* Tex Avery, *Tom and Jerry*. National Film Archive, London.

In 1943 three Disney alumni, David Hilberman, Zachary Schwartz, and Stephen Bosustow, founded the UPA (United Productions of America) studio. There, artists like John Hubley and Bobe Cannon explored limited animation, a new technique that used simple, highly stylized artwork, bold color schemes, and less realistic movements to suggest the activities of characters like Gerald McBoing-Boing and Mr. Magoo (Figure 5). The approach was sparked by the work of artists like Pablo Picasso, Henri Matisse, Joan Miró, and Paul Klee, while the Disney style was derived from nineteenth-century academic draftsmanship. The bold, clean look of UPA was less

Figure 5. *(Animation)* UPA (United Productions of America), *Mr. Magoo*. The Museum of Modern Art/Films Stills Archive.

expensive to produce and became extremely influential worldwide.

Inspired by the films of UPA, a group of Yugoslavian artists founded the Zagreb Animation studio in 1954, producing shorts with even more stylized graphics and more limited animation. As UPA declined during the late 1950s and early 1960s, Zagreb became the center for aesthetic experimentation in animation (Figure 6). In 1960 Dušan Vukotić became the first non-American to win the Oscar in the Animated Short Film category, with his *Ersatz*.

The socialist governments of eastern Europe established animation studios during the 1950s, including the Sofia studio in Bulgaria, VEB DEFA in the German Democratic Republic, Pannonia in Hungary, and Se-Ma-Four, Miniatur, and Kracow Short Film in Poland. In Czechoslovakia the puppeteer Jiří Trnka began animating in 1946, creating such puppet films as the feature-length *Sen noci svatojánské* (A Midsummer Night's Dream, 1959) and a short parable on tyranny, *Ruka* (The Hand, 1965).

During the 1950s the major U.S. studios, pressed by financial and legal problems, gradually dismantled their animation divisions. Many animation artists and producers turned to the new medium of television, working on commercials and programs—mainly children's series. Quality animation became the preserve of Disney, some commercial studios, and a scattering of independent filmmakers.

Animation flourished in postwar Europe. In Italy, Bruno Bozzetto made his first short, *Tapum! La storia delle armi* (Tapum, the History of Weapons), in 1958; two years later Emanuele Luzzati and Giulio

Figure 6. *(Animation)* Dušan Vukotić, *Piccolo*, 1959. Zagreb school. The Museum of Modern Art/Film Stills Archive.

Gianini made their first cutout film, *I paladini di Francia* (Paladins of France). Halas and Batchelor completed the first British entertainment feature in 1954, an adaptation of George Orwell's *Animal Farm*.

European animators used the medium as a vehicle for personal expression, stressing innovative styles and subjects. Artists like Raoul Servais (Belgium), Walerian Borowczyk (Poland and France), Paul Driessen (the Netherlands), Marcell Jankovics (Hungary), Paul Grimault (France), and Jannick Hastrup and Li Vilstrup (Denmark) offered a vision of animation as an artistic medium as flexible and protean as painting or opera.

During the late 1960s the National Film Board of Canada replaced Zagreb as the creative forum of world animation. Founded in 1941 by Norman McLaren (Figures 7 and 8), who had left England for Canada, the animation units of the NFB offered artists from all over the world—Ishu Patel, Co Hoedeman, Caroline Leaf, Derek Lamb, Zlatko Grgic, and John and Faith Hubley—a chance to explore not only unusual styles and subjects but also such new media as paint on glass and sand animation.

In Japan an animation industry arose that rivaled even the United States in volume of production. Since the early 1960s its studios have produced dozens of television shows and feature films in limited animation, mainly for domestic consumption. China, after the turmoil of the Cultural Revolution had subsided, began to emerge as a force in world animation. The films of the Shanghai studio, founded in 1957, offered a striking combination of traditional graphic styles and themes.

During the mid-1970s animation became the object of renewed interest in the United States, sparked

Figure 8. *(Animation)*   Norman McLaren, *Le merle* (The Blackbird), 1958. National Film Board of Canada.

by nostalgia for the shorts of the 1930s and the popularity of British director George Dunning's *Yellow Submarine* (1968) and Ralph Bakshi's *Fritz the Cat* (1972). This revival led to the production of a record number of animated features, including Disney's *The Rescuers* (1977), Don Bluth's *The Secret of NIMH* (1982), and Bakshi's *Fire and Ice* (1983).

The most significant technical innovation in animation in recent decades has been the advent of the computer. Used during the 1950s to visualize experiments in science and engineering, computer graphics became a medium employed by artists such as John Whitney, Sr., Larry Cuba, and Ed Emshwiller to realize highly personal graphic creations. Because of the cost, such use has not been widespread, and most computer animation in the United States has been done for television commercials and logos, and for SPECIAL EFFECTS in science-fiction films such as *Star Wars* and *Tron* (Figure 9). But these films stimulated intensive research in animation hardware and software; what effects these developments will have on conventional animation techniques remains uncertain.

See also VIDEO.

Bibliography. John Canemaker, *The Animated Raggedy Ann & Andy*, Indianapolis, Ind., 1977; Donald Crafton, *Before Mickey: The Animated Film, 1898–1928*, Cambridge, Mass., 1982; Bruno Edera, *Full Length Animated Feature Films*, ed. by John Halas, New York, 1977; Leonard Maltin, *Of Mice and Magic*, New York, 1980; Robert Russett and Cecile Starr, *Experimental Animation: An Illustrated Anthology*, New York, 1976; Charles Solomon, *Enchanted Drawings: A History of Animation in America*, New York, 1987; Charles Solomon and Ron Stark, *The*

Figure 7. *(Animation)*   Norman McLaren, *La poulette grise* (The Gray Pullet), 1947. National Film Board of Canada.

Figure 9. *(Animation)* Walt Disney Productions, *Tron*, 1982. National Film Archive, London. © 1982 The Walt Disney Company.

Complete Kodak Animation Book, Rochester, N.Y., 1983; Frank Thomas and Ollie Johnston, *Disney Animation: The Illusion of Life,* New York, 1981.

CHARLES SOLOMON

ARCHITECTURE

Unlike pictures or written statements, buildings do not transmit any message, and yet they do express something beyond their physical solidity and utilitarian purpose. The first known architectural theorist, the Roman Vitruvius, distinguished in the first century B.C.E. three basic qualities that the work of architecture must possess: *soliditas* (solidity), *utilitas* (utility), and *venustas.* According to Vitruvius, *venustas* is realized when the building appears pleasing and elegant, and when the constituent parts are adapted to one another in such a way that symmetry results. That is, a building ought to express a kind of general harmony that, in terms of systematic symmetry and simple numerical relations, reflects the harmony of the world. The Greek word *harmonikos* denotes the musical property of harmony, and the numerical ratios characteristic of musical consonances were in fact considered a proof of the hidden cosmic harmony. Cosmic harmony is also manifest in the position and movement of the celestial bodies; human music was therefore understood as an image of the "music of the spheres," and architecture as a kind of "mute" or "frozen" music. Vitruvius's *venustas* was therefore not limited to the qualities of order and symmetry as such, but also implied their symbolic value. *See* HELLENIC WORLD; ROMAN EMPIRE.

Figure 1. *(Architecture)* The Doric order. The Propylaea, Athens, 437 B.C.E. Courtesy of Christian Norberg-Schulz.

The expressive content of a building, however, is revealed not only in a harmonious organization of space but also in its embodiment, by means of an articulate built form, of a certain nature or "character." In one of his best-known passages, for example, Vitruvius says that the simple and mighty Doric style should be chosen for temples dedicated to male gods such as Mars and Hercules, whereas goddesses such as Venus and Flora ought to be represented by the gentle and ornate Corinthian style. Gods and goddesses who possess a "middle quality" should have temples in the Ionic style, which avoids both the severe manner of the Doric and the softer Corinthian. This implies that things have an identity corresponding to a certain form or gestalt and that architecture serves to make this property manifest.

Architectural Communication in History

From the beginning architectural theory has considered the building an *imago mundi*, or image of the world, that by means of its spatial organization

and concrete, plastic form communicates to the environment an INTERPRETATION of how things "are." Thus architecture is one of the modes of human understanding, helping humanity to gain an existential foothold.

In Western antiquity, however, we encounter two different versions of the architectural image. To the pre-Socratic philosophers the qualities of the world were immanent, as is implied in Thales' famous statement, "All things are full of gods." An image of immanent properties reveals the world as it is, rather than reflecting an ideal concept, and itself becomes an active force within the world, in accordance with the nature of myth and magic. The grand Pythagorean image of universal harmony was also conceived in concrete (musical) terms and in general implies that the world is understood as a kind of building. The image was the primary fact, and it was used as a model to illuminate the complex and opaque environment. It did not represent something already given but rather brought into the open hidden aspects of the cosmos, in accordance with the Greek concept

Figure 2. *(Architecture)*   Court of the Lions, the Alhambra, Granada, Spain, 1354–1391. Alinari/Art Resource, New York.

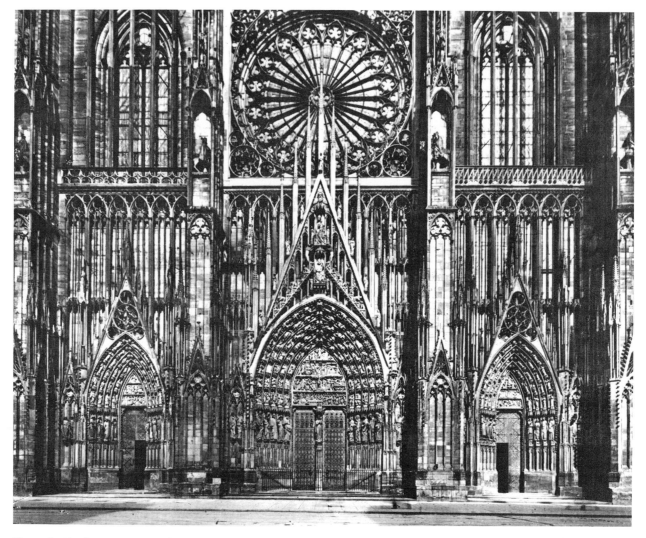

Figure 3. *(Architecture)*   Strasbourg Cathedral, west front. Courtesy of Christian Norberg-Schulz.

of *alétheia,* which understood truth as simultaneous revelation and concealment. A parallel may be found in the ancient Germanic image of the world as a house, which implies that the environment follows an order analogous to that of a dwelling.

An important change occurred in the notion of image when Platonic idealism superseded pre-Socratic immanence. PLATO's understanding of phenomena as mere shadows of transcendent ideas transformed the image into a reflection of the ideal cosmos. Hence the image was reduced to a kind of tool, which served to bridge the gap between the two parts of the divided world, between subject and object. As a consequence of the idealization of the image, its reference to everyday life was weakened. An example is the "ideal city" of the RENAISSANCE, whose geometrically regular layout was determined by Neoplatonic ideas of perfection, rather than the demands of daily life. We could also say that the image was transformed into a symbol, which represents something else by association, resemblance, or convention.

It is important to emphasize that the original function of architecture was not to symbolize but to make the world appear as what it "is." The difference is between the constitutive role of the image and the representational role of the symbol. A work of ART is primarily an image that brings a new being out of what is hidden. Art thereby resists the flux of phenomena and makes visible a stable world of things. This is the meaning of German poet Friedrich Hölderlin's famous phrase, "But that which remains, is founded by the poets."

Although the symbol has been given precedence by post-Platonic philosophers, in fact the history of architecture illustrates how image and symbol together account for architectural communication. The symbol represents the human concept of the world; the image reveals its qualities more directly. Both may be integral to a valid work of architecture. A mere symbol remains an abstraction, without reference to what is immediately given, whereas the image runs the risk of missing the general insight offered by conceptualization. The Gothic cathedral, for example, is at the same time a mirror of the world in a very direct sense, a symbol of theological concepts, and an image of the interaction of mundane qualities such as light and matter, horizontal and vertical (*see* MIDDLE AGES). The classical or Vitruvian tradition also embraces both modes of expression (*see* CLASSICISM). Whereas the early Renaissance architecture of the Italian quattrocento emphasized a relatively abstract, geometrical symbolism, the mannerist experiments of the cinquecento revived the image as an immediate revelation of concrete, natural qualities. Baroque architecture gained its powerful expression from a synthesis of revelation and symbolization; the revealed qualities were in fact considered representations of the world beyond (and often were connected with secular power). In particular, the expression of character through the use of the classical Doric, Ionic, and Corinthian orders was of primary concern in Renaissance and baroque architecture. For centuries architectural expression consisted of a language of meaningful forms or styles handed down from generation to generation.

A meaningful *imago mundi* for any CULTURE is constituted of SPATIAL ORGANIZATION and plastic embodiment, the basic formal aspects. An example is Islamic architecture, in which the world to be visualized is the dialectic whole of desert and oasis. As an artificial oasis, the interior complements the forbidding environment and makes human dwelling possible in a physical as well as a psychological sense. At the same time the Islamic building reveals how light transforms earthly matter into abstract patterns, thus negating the very idea of incarnation. *See* ISLAM, CLASSICAL AND MEDIEVAL ERAS.

The Crisis of Architectural Communication

During the nineteenth century a process took place that Swiss architectural historian Sigfried Giedion called the "devaluation of symbols." Forms that had been meaningful expressions of properties of the world or of human existence were now treated as mere status symbols to give the self-made man characteristic of the century a cultural alibi. The resulting confusion of styles interrupted the continuity of the Western architectural tradition, a tradition that could no longer satisfy the demands of a modern industrial society. A new, "open" world had come into being, and artists as well as theorists demanded new forms. The search for a new architecture culminated after World War I. One of the most important protagonists of the modern movement, Swiss architect Le

Figure 4. *(Architecture)* "Between earth and sky." Prague. Courtesy of Christian Norberg-Schulz.

Corbusier, stated the new aims clearly in the early 1920s. Asserting that a new epoch had begun and that the styles of the past were "lies," he demanded that the new spirit of the times find its own expression.

The answer offered by the pioneers of modern architecture was a new conception of space implied by the word *simultaneity*. Thanks to the mass media and increased mobility, in the modern world we may be in several places simultaneously. Physically, of course, we are only in one place at a time, but existentially we experience a simultaneity of places. How, then, does architecture make this state of affairs manifest? Le Corbusier's solution was to abolish all closed and static rooms in favor of a new, dynamic openness, which he called the *plan libre*, or "free plan." As a type of spatial organization that corresponds to a new understanding of the world, the free plan may be considered an *imago mundi*, a further development of certain traits of the Western tradition. However, it lacked the concrete figural quality of past architecture, and, furthermore, it neglected the embodiment of character, with a weakened sense

Figure 5. *(Architecture)* The "ideal" form of the Renaissance. S. Maria della Consolazione, Todi, Italy, ca. 1500. Courtesy of Christian Norberg-Schulz.

of presence as the result. The implicit anticommunicative tendencies culminated in the doctrine of functionalism, which defined architecture as a mere practical aid having no symbolic pretensions. The attitude was formulated in 1928 by Swiss architect Hannes Meyer, who stated that the only determinants are "function" and "economy" and that works of art are therefore useless.

Quite soon, however, a reaction against radical functionalism arose within the modern movement itself. In 1944 Giedion pointed out that something was lacking in modern architecture. Although the buildings executed may be functional, somehow they do not satisfy the need for "monumentality." Giedion used this term to amalgamate those symbolic forms that represent cultural values such as religious beliefs and social conventions. Thus a new quest for MEANING was initiated that has characterized archi-

tectural development since World War II. To satisfy the need for meaning, however, one could not simply return to the styles of the past; a new theoretical basis became necessary. Two approaches may be singled out: the semiological and the phenomenological.

Architectural semiology. The basic point of departure of semiology, according to its foremost theorist, Umberto Eco, is the tenet that "all cultural phenomena are systems of signs" (*see* SIGN SYSTEM). Semiology thus substitutes for notions of image and symbol the more general concept of SIGN. Although signs are by definition arbitrarily chosen, Eco aims at giving architectural semiology a functional-empirical basis, and as an example points out that a stair or ramp denotes the possibility of going up. In general, the content communicated by an ARTIFACT is the function it fulfills. Eco thus goes beyond functionalism in demanding that the forms denote the functions rather than just follow from them. He also recognizes that meanings other than utilitarian purpose come into play, such as different conceptions of inhabitation and use. As conceptions become routine, the artifacts usually constitute systems of signs, or codes (*see* CODE). The user has to know the code to be able to understand the content of the communication. As codes are temporal, local, and personal, any sign may connote diverse things, and Eco accordingly concludes that architecture is a "system of rhetorical formulas." *See* SEMIOTICS.

What is presented here is a thoroughly relativistic understanding of architectural communication. Although certain empirical relationships may be pointed out, their interpretation, according to Eco, varies in such a way that it is meaningless to talk about expressive values inherent in the forms themselves. Since forms undoubtedly possess expressive values, however, other semiologists have expanded the concept of sign to include various kinds. Charles Jencks thus revives CHARLES S. PEIRCE's distinction among indexical, iconic, and symbolic signs, but leaves out the architectural image. This lack is evidently felt by Jencks himself, who asserts that "most architectural signs are compound."

In general, semiology may be considered an offspring of Platonic thinking. Although it negates the existence of absolute ideas, it stems from the split of subject and object. In contrast to older philosophies, however, it concentrates its attention on the relation between the two aspects of the world, that is, on semiosis. What was formerly considered a mere tool is hence given precedence, whereas the real world of things fades away. What is left is a phantom world of signs, which by themselves mean nothing.

Architectural phenomenology. Phenomenology approaches the problem of meaning by taking the architectural phenomena themselves as its point of departure. It is therefore less formalized than semiology and comprises different varieties, which on closer scrutiny have certain things in common. Three surprisingly similar statements concerning the nature of architectural expression illustrate this point.

In his essay *Von deutscher Baukunst* (1772), the German poet Johann Wolfgang von Goethe describes his first visit to the cathedral of Strasbourg and his anticipation of the "lack of order" and "unnaturalness" of the Gothic. However, the experience was unexpectedly overwhelming. Goethe provides a vivid picture of the impression of a harmonious whole that unifies a thousand different details. Although he felt a strong sense of enjoyment, he could not understand or explain what he perceived. The nearest he could come to a general characterization was the phrase "earthly-heavenly delight." This is how many of us experience architecture: the building moves us in a

Figure 6. *(Architecture)* Cinquecento architecture. Palladio, La Basilica, Padua, Italy, 1549. Courtesy of Christian Norberg-Schulz.

profound sense, but we cannot really understand the complex nature of our PERCEPTION. Goethe suggests what it is all about when he describes how the firmly founded, enormous building rises up in the air, offering a sense of permanence although it is all "perforated." The work of architecture does not impress us because it transmits a particular message, because it denotes or connotes; rather, its expression consists in its standing firmly on the ground, in its rising up toward the sky, and in its opening up the environment. The way this happens makes a certain stability manifest, so that the building seems to resist the flux of time.

In his seminal book, *Vers une architecture* (1923), Le Corbusier included a definition of architecture that has been frequently cited to show that he was not a mere functionalist but a true artist who wanted to "move man's heart" with his buildings. In fact, Le Corbusier clearly states that the utilitarian purpose is only a point of departure, whereas the true meaning of the work of architecture resides in its expressive power. Again we encounter the idea that

Figure 7. *(Architecture)* Osaka castle, Japan, 1587. Courtesy of Japan National Tourist Organization.

architecture is expressive because the building rises in a certain way toward heaven, and furthermore that the way of rising is related to certain "moods," such as "gentleness," "brutality," "nobility," and "charm."

Martin Heidegger offers an explanation for the problem posed by Goethe and Le Corbusier. In his essay *The Origin of the Work of Art* (1935), he uses a description of a Greek temple to tell what any work of architecture expresses. A building does not portray anything, he says, but in its standing in a certain place, it shows us what that place really is. Thus it reveals the nature of the supporting ground, the quality of light, and the vicissitudes of weather. It even makes visible the invisible air. In general, a building "gives to things their look" and in so doing opens up a world and thereby reveals what shapes our own destiny. This is achieved simply by its "resting" and "towering," that is, by its "standing there."

A building may stand in many different ways and also in many different places, and expression will vary accordingly. But it always shows *where* and *how* we are. The building is not a sign; it does not portray anything, but rather brings a world into view. The phenomenological approach to architectural meaning therefore implies a return to the *image*, in the original sense of the word.

The differences among sign, symbol, and image are explained by Hans-Georg Gadamer, a major figure in modern hermeneutics, in his magnum opus, *Truth and Method* (1960). A sign has a mere indicative function, while a symbol represents by making perceptible something that is absent. An image, however, does not represent something else; it brings about an "increase in meaning"—that is, it opens up a world by combining various and scattered elements into a unitary vision. Thus the work of art "adds" to the "content" of the world. This idea is shared by the German poet Rainer Maria Rilke, who states that we are here to say certain things, "but to say them, understand me, *so* to say them as the things themselves never thought to be." As a work of art, the architectural image speaks by showing the things.

The Language of Architecture

The work of architecture gathers together qualities of earth and sky in relation to human life in a certain place, as well as the beliefs and values on which that life is based. Its relation to human life implies that a building always stands forth, exists, *as* something— as a house, a church, a school. These functions, however, have in common the basic relationship of earth and sky. Human life thus does not occur in an isotropic Euclidean space but in a concrete environment distinguished by qualitative differences between up and down, north and south, here and there. Such a concrete space is better called a place, and the content that is given form by architecture is a place where life takes place. The place is primarily a given landscape, with which we have come to terms in order to be able to dwell in it. To do that, we build, not only for shelter, but to gather the qualities of the landscape into an image that offers a sense of understanding and belonging. The primary purpose of architecture is thus to make a world visible.

The basic constituent images of the language of architecture are spatial patterns and built forms possessing a distinct figural quality because of their modes of extending, opening, standing, and rising. Some of these, such as the piazza and the street, the rotunda and the nave, the column, arch, gable, and dome, may be considered archetypes because they

Figure 8. *(Architecture)* Nicholas Hawksmoor, St. Mary Woolnoth, London, 1717–1727. Courtesy of Christian Norberg-Schulz.

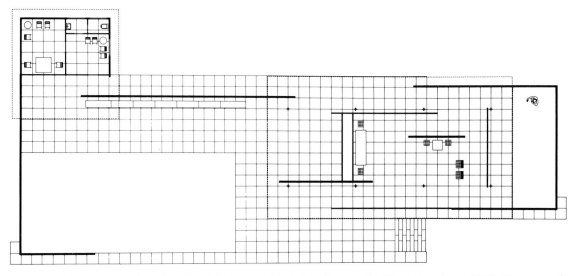

Figure 9. *(Architecture)* The "free plan." Mies van der Rohe, German Pavilion, Barcelona, 1929. Courtesy of Christian Norberg-Schulz.

Figure 10. *(Architecture)* "Mute architecture." New York. Courtesy of Christian Norberg-Schulz.

reveal basic structures of the world. Other figures are temporal and local, circumstantial variations on the archetype. While the archetypes constitute the language of architecture, the variations make up more particular styles and traditions.

In a certain sense, the archetypes themselves do not exist, only the individual variations. A type is a generalization, which cannot as such be physically realized. However, architecture needs such generalizations to make possible a more comprehensive gathering of meanings. In the city, for example, multifarious meanings are brought together, meanings that originally were discovered in other places. Thus the Greeks brought the temple from its holy place in nature into the polis. With translocation the image loses its orig-

inal function and becomes a symbol or *monumentum*, something that reminds. The Greeks regarded the goddess Mnemosyne (memory) as the mother of the Muses. Mnemosyne was herself the daughter of the earth and the sky, which suggests that the memories giving rise to art center on our understanding of their relationship. Architecture keeps and visualizes the most basic properties of earth and sky and therefore becomes the "mother of the arts."

Further, the word *mother* (related to the Latin *mater*) is related to *material*, which reflects the tenet that the architectural image is primarily a built form. It is basically technological, in the original Greek sense of *technē*, meaning a MODE of revealing or bringing into view. This does not mean that an

Figure 11. *(Architecture)* Michael Graves, "Rome 1981." From *Michael Graves: Buildings and Projects 1966–1981,* New York: Rizzoli, 1982, p. 9.

architectural form is necessarily built the way it looks. The important point is that the form appears as if it were constructed in a certain way. The language of forms thus has a technological origin, in accordance with the Vitruvian concept of *soliditas.* It is therefore deeply meaningful to define architecture as the "art of building," or *Baukunst.*

The recovery of the language of architecture has to be based on a study of memories, that is, of architectural history. The quest for meaning thus goes together with a renewed interest in the past. The aim is not a nostalgic flight from the new, "open" world, but the development of a figurative language adaptable to any expressive possibility. Only in this way may architecture restore its original communicative purpose and reestablish itself as an art.

See also AESTHETICS; DESIGN; SCULPTURE; VISUAL IMAGE.

Bibliography. Gaston Bachelard, *Poetics of Space,* Boston, 1969; Sigfried Giedion, *Architecture, You and Me* (Architektur und Gemeinschaft), Cambridge, Mass., 1958; Martin Heidegger, *Poetry, Language, Thought,* trans. by Albert Hofstadter, New York, 1971; Charles Jencks and George Baird, eds., *Meaning in Architecture,* London, 1969; Christian Norberg-Schulz, *The Concept of Dwelling,* New York, 1985; idem, *Meaning in Western Architecture,* New York, 1975; Vincent J. Scully, *The Earth, the Temple, and the Gods,* rev. ed., New Haven, Conn., 1979; Rudolf Wittkower, *Architectural Principles in the Age of Humanism,* 3d ed., rev., New York, 1971.

CHRISTIAN NORBERG-SCHULZ

ARCHIVES

The records of an institution or organization that are no longer needed to conduct current business but that are preserved because they document the activities of the institution or because of the reference and research value of the information they contain. The term *archive* (or *record office*) is also used to refer to the organizational unit responsible for administering such records, as well as to the building or part of a building in which such records are maintained.

Historical Development

WRITING initially developed to facilitate business transactions, and the oldest known archives are the financial and other records of institutions created by kings, priests, and merchants during the third millennium B.C.E. The recordkeeping practices developed by the Sumerians, Hittites, and Egyptians were inherited and improved upon by the Greeks and particularly by the Romans. With the collapse of Roman authority, the Catholic church kept these practices alive. They were then adopted and perfected in the national states that developed in western Europe. The advantages of concentrating the archives of individual offices in a centralized repository were first recognized by the Spanish in 1543, but it was not until the end of the eighteenth century that the French, during the course of their Revolution, created a national system of public archival administration directed by a central service agency. Other countries with unitary forms of government created similar systems in the nineteenth century. The British, reflecting their governmental structure, created a Public Record Office in 1838 for the national government.

Following World War I the USSR and the countries of eastern Europe established nationwide archival systems, and in 1934 the United States finally established a National Archives. It was the last major nation to do so. The decolonization movement that followed World War II ushered in a period of renewed archival activity, with newly independent countries creating national archival agencies they considered essential to their national identities and the writing of their national histories. In international law relating to the succession of states, government archives are regarded as an attribute of the basic sovereignty of the state and, therefore, as imprescriptible and inalienable.

Historically the basic rationale for the preservation of archives has been to establish the legitimacy and to protect the rights and interests of the sovereign and, by extension, of any institution. Archives have thus traditionally been retained in the custody of the institution for its own use. The records that are the tools of administration are also products of the administrative process; they document the policies and procedures as well as the functions and activities of the institution, serving as its corporate memory. They not only ensure continuity and consistency in operations but also constitute the most comprehensive and authentic sources of information regarding the institutions that produce and preserve them. Archives have therefore increasingly attracted the attention of historians. The widespread use of archives for historical research since the eighteenth century has consequently added to the "arsenals of law" function of archival repositories the additional function of serving as "arsenals of history." This development was accelerated by the French Revolution, out of which emerged the concept of a public right of access to government archives. Government archives thus continue to establish and protect the rights and interests of the citizens of constitutional governments based on popular sovereignty.

The right of public access to government archives is necessarily a limited right. The demands of national defense and security, the desirability of protecting personal PRIVACY and business information, and the need for a degree of administrative confidentiality if government is to operate efficiently and effectively—all require limitations on access to government archives. These requirements historically have been met by restricting access for a specified time, usually seventy-five or one hundred years. In the 1960s a movement was initiated by the International Council on Archives, a professional nongovernmental organization created in 1950 with the assistance of UNESCO, to liberalize access to archives. During the past three decades most governments have adopted a thirty-year restriction policy, with important exceptions for diplomatic, military, and personnel records and information. This basic conflict between the right to know and the need to govern has led to both freedom-of-information and privacy statutes in the Western democracies, and the issues have been further complicated by the pervasiveness of computer technology in information gathering, processing, and dissemination (see COMPUTER: IMPACT).

In the Soviet Union an important dimension to the uses of archives was added by V. I. Lenin in a decree of June 1, 1918. This decree asserted for archives an active and continuing role in support of Marxist-Leninist IDEOLOGY and in the development of the socialist state and society in the USSR. There have always been instances of political and ideological uses of archives, but this was the first declaration and justification for such use as a continuing public policy. The use of archives as a political weapon of the state and in support of official history written along ideological lines has been adopted by a number of socialist countries following World War II.

Archives in Transition

The basic functions of archival repositories throughout history have been to preserve and, on request, to provide access to archival material. Following World War I there were important and increasingly rapid changes in and expansion of these basic functions. Rather than accepting all noncurrent agency records, government archival repositories have been forced, because of the tremendous volume of generally routine documentation generated and accumulated by modern governments, to develop appraisal and selection criteria. As the range of government programs and information-gathering activities continues to expand, these criteria continue to be revised to ensure that basic documentation and information of significant reference or research value are not destroyed.

To assist agencies in better managing their records and to create fewer but more useful records, the U.S. National Archives during World War II developed the theory and practice of records management, which controls the entire life cycle of records from their creation or receipt through their maintenance and use to their disposition. An integral part of this control program is the creation of purpose-built intermediate repositories, or records centers, for the economical storage and servicing of semicurrent records pending their transfer to an archival repository or their destruction. Control over recurring series of records is exercised by means of schedules, which identify each series or class, specify where each is to be retained and for how long, and authorize for each, on a continuing basis, a particular type of disposition. Records-management techniques have been widely adopted by archival agencies in countries around the world.

Equally significant have been the changing media of archives. The remarkably durable clay tablets, the predominant record medium during more than half of recorded history, were eventually succeeded by much less durable papyrus and parchment (see WRITING MATERIALS). The advantages and particularly the convenience of paper, however, ensured its ascendancy as a record medium from the fifteenth century on. The development of PHOTOGRAPHY and SOUND RECORDING during the last half of the nineteenth century and, more recently, the development of magnetic media to record sound, images, text, and data are challenging paper. The documentary, reference, and research value of these new media justifies their selective archival retention, and archival repositories are developing new policies and procedures to accommodate their particular characteristics and requirements.

Particularly challenging is the task of preserving fragile films and tapes, as well as modern paper. The use of wood pulp and chemicals in the manufacture of paper, for example, combined with increased atmospheric pollution chiefly from the combustion of hydrocarbons, has greatly increased the cost of archival preservation. Most of the new media are non-archival in terms of longevity, and until technology produces more durable media the content of many records can be preserved only by microfilming or otherwise copying them.

The use of archives forms another area of significant development. Forced to compete for increasingly limited financial resources with other agencies, particularly in the cultural and educational fields, archival agencies, both public and private, have expanded old services and added new ones. Descriptions of holdings in the form of general and subject guides, inventories and detailed lists of particular groups of records, and other types of finding aids have been published to inform potential users of available sources and to facilitate their use. Traditional printed documentary editions are being supplemented and in numerous instances replaced by microfilm publications, which, at a fraction of the cost of printed texts, make exact copies of original documents conveniently available to academic researchers, a rapidly growing genealogical clientele, and other users. Facsimiles of laws, treaties, correspondence, maps, and photographs have been assembled into kits on a variety of historical subjects, usually with the advice and assistance of education specialists, and courses are offered to train primary- and secondary-school teachers in their use in the teaching and study of history and government. Courses have been organized to familiarize graduate students, genealogists, and other potential patrons with the nature and uses of archives and with research methods. Popular and other publications, scholarly journals, editions of conference proceedings, film festivals, and multimedia institutional and traveling exhibits all contribute to this new outreach initiative. The traditional and narrow concept of making archives available upon request has become what a 1984 international dictionary of archival terminology refers to as "communication," which it defines as the basic archival function of not only making archives available but also promoting their wider use.

An important element in each of these broad developments, and of great significance in its own right, has been the introduction of modern information-handling technology. In the life cycle of records, technology is revolutionizing the way data and information are created and received, stored and retrieved, and used and transmitted by government agencies and other institutions. New policies and procedures are being developed for the archival appraisal and disposition of electronic records as well as for their preservation and archival use. Electronic technology is also being used to establish more effective administrative and intellectual controls for traditional records, to assist in their preservation, and to promote their more effective utilization.

One final development worthy of note has been the extension of the term *archives* and of archival principles and techniques, principally in North America, to personal papers, literary and other types of historical manuscripts, and the collected archives of private institutions and organizations. Business, labor, church, and college and UNIVERSITY archives have multiplied since the 1960s; the great majority collect related personal papers and other manuscripts as well as the archives of other than their parent institutions. Discipline and special-interest archives have also been created to ensure preservation of documents in various fields of science, the performing arts, and causes and movements. State and regional networks of repositories have been created, and projects are under way to share information on appraisal decisions as well as on holdings. Like libraries—that other long-established, institution-based information system—archival repositories are undergoing fundamental changes as they seek to remain relevant to the needs and desires of modern society.

See also ARCHIVES, FILM; BOOK; DATA BASE; LIBRARY.

Bibliography. Adolf Brenneke, *Archivkunde: Ein Beitrag zur Theorie und Geschichte des europäischen Archivwesens*, ed. by Wolfgang Leesch, Leipzig, 1953; Frank B. Evans, François-Jean Himly, and Peter Walne, compls., *Dictionary of Archival Terminology*, ed. by Peter Walne, Munich, 1984; Hilary Jenkinson, *A Manual of Archive Administration*, Oxford, 1922, reprint (rev. ed., ed. by Roger H. Ellis) London, 1965; Ernst Posner, *Archives and the Public Interest: Selected Essays*, ed. by Kenneth W. Munden, Washington, D.C., 1967; idem, *Archives in the Ancient World*, Cambridge, Mass., 1972; James B. Rhoads, *The Role of Archives and Records Management in National Information Systems: A RAMP Study*, Paris, 1983; Theodore R. Schellenberg, *The Management of Archives*, New York, 1965; idem, *Modern Archives: Principles and Techniques*, Chicago, 1956; Peter Walne, ed., *Modern Archives and Records Management: A RAMP Reader*, Paris, 1985.

FRANK B. EVANS

ARCHIVES, FILM

Film, television, and VIDEO productions are among the most fragile of all the records of communication and imaginative expression produced since the 1890s. Often created for short-term gain or effects, they are frequently destroyed or neglected once the purposes of their creation have been achieved. Unless they are properly stored, regularly inspected, and copied, they are subject to accidental and intentional damage or erasure, to the perils of mechanical deformation, physical wear, chemical deterioration, and image fading. And yet they are some of the most valuable resources for historical research and for the production of new compilation films. In 1980 the General UNESCO Conference approved a recommendation on the protection of moving images and declared that "moving images constitute one of the most characteristic features of present day cultural creation and contemporary communication." *See* MOTION PICTURES.

In 1898 Bolesław Matuszewski, an early film exhibitor in Warsaw (1895) and a photographer for the czar of Russia (1897), noted the importance of films as historical documents. He promoted their collection and conservation in his short book, *A New Source of History*, published in Paris in 1898. Interested in films as "slices of public and national life," he called for the creation of a MUSEUM or depository for films of DOCUMENTARY interest and for supporting research and publications.

Although film libraries and collections began as early as the first copyrighted moving-picture deposit in the U.S. Library of Congress (1894), only in Stockholm in 1933 was a film archive established for the preservation of all types of films (*see* ARCHIVES; COPYRIGHT; LIBRARY). The 1930s were years of rapid growth. Collections with archival potential were begun in London, New York, Milan, Berlin, Moscow, Brussels, Paris, and elsewhere. In 1938 Iris Barry and John Abbot of the Museum of Modern Art in New York, Henri Langlois of the Cinémathèque Française in Paris, Olwen Vaughn and Ernest Lindgren of the British Film Institute, and Frank Hensel of the Reichsfilmarchiv in Berlin formed the International Federation of Film Archives. Known by its French acronym, FIAF, the members of this worldwide organization of nearly eighty archives hold films, film stills, scripts, unpublished documents about films, books and periodicals on film subjects, film music scores, music cue sheets, and, increasingly, the records of the creators and producers of all types of motion pictures.

The principal aims of FIAF are to promote the preservation of the film as ART and historical document and to bring together all organizations devoted to this end, to encourage the formation and development of film archives in all countries, to facilitate the collection and international exchange of films and documents, to develop cooperation among its members, and to promote the development of cinema art and culture. FIAF's place of incorporation is Paris, but its administrative site is Brussels, a choice made as the result of internal disputes during the 1960s. The organization sponsors annual meetings, conferences, technical publications, and a film-preservation summer school supported by the Staatliches Filmarchiv der DDR. It encourages the development of archives in Third World nations. Its research functions are performed by separate commissions on film preservation, cataloging, and documentation.

Film preservation requires controlled storage conditions and sophisticated copying and processing to maintain the quality and to prolong the life of film supports and the photographic, magnetic, or digital images bound to them. Ideally, for maximum life, each type of support (e.g., nitrate, acetate, polyester, video disk, and the various ways they hold their images) requires different environmental storage conditions. Practical considerations like humidity and temperature control, fire protection, operating practices, and operating costs make less-than-ideal storage conditions acceptable. Sophisticated copying and processing are required because of shrinkage, physical deterioration, and image fading.

The access, rediscovery, recycling, and reinterpretation of forgotten or never-used footage are preceded by cataloging activities describing the physical materials in an archive and by subject cataloging done in as complete a system as can be afforded. The collection and preservation of documents that describe and illuminate the writing, production, distribution, and marketing of films are also undertaken by film archives. In full-service archives these documentation materials are cataloged or indexed.

The use, exhibition, and distribution of moving images are often subject to legal and administrative restraints different from those applicable to printed materials. Along with the legal responsibility to obtain the right to use them, the use of archival images in new productions involves the possibility of historical distortion and falsification. Film archives diffuse a knowledge of film culture and cultural heritage through projections, individual study, distribution, archival loans, the controlled use of archival printing materials, publications, symposia, lectures, film courses, and historical research. Video plays an important role in the distribution of historical film footage for teaching, study, and research by making copies available that have a relatively long life, are easy to use, and do not wear out the originals from which they were made. When sensitively produced and not distorted, video copies of dramatic and documentary films make the classics of screen art and communication available for individual study.

See also NEWSREEL.

Bibliography. Raymond Borde, *Les cinémathèques,* Toulouse, France, 1983; Eileen Bowser and John Kuiper, *A Handbook for Film Archives,* Brussels, 1980; FIAF, *Preservation and Restoration of Moving Images,* Brussels, 1986; Paul L. Gordon, ed., *The Book of Film Care,* Rochester, N.Y., 1983; Bolesław Matuszewski, *Une nouvelle source de l'histoire,* Paris, 1898, reprint Warsaw, 1955.

JOHN B. KUIPER

ARISTOTLE (384–322 B.C.E.)

Greek philosopher and scientist, the inventor of formal logic, and the greatest biologist of antiquity. Aristotle's contributions to the history of communication are extensive. Coming after two centuries of Greek philosophical and scientific achievement (after the pre-Socratics, Socrates, and PLATO), Aristotle's universal genius fitted him for the task of systematizing existing knowledge and organizing future research. His treatises provided the framework for Western thought and expression for many centuries thereafter and also exercised a profound influence on Islamic learning (*see* ISLAM, CLASSICAL AND MEDIEVAL ERAS). His analyses, definitions, and systems of CLASSIFICATION are still integral to many fields—including some directly concerned with communication, such as logic (*see* SYMBOLIC LOGIC), RHETORIC, and DRAMA—long after most of his specific theories have been modified or rejected.

Aristotle's father was court physician to the king of Macedon, grandfather of Alexander the Great, and Aristotle was himself later tutor to Alexander. At the age of seventeen Aristotle came to Athens, where he spent twenty years in Plato's Academy. He wrote dialogues, now lost, that were admired by CICERO for their style. What we have are only the "esoteric" works designed for research and TEACHING, not for the general public. After years of travel Aristotle returned to Athens in 335 B.C.E. and began teaching in the public gymnasium known as the Lyceum; after his death his pupil Theophrastus established a regular school known as the Peripatos (named after a covered walk or arcade).

Aristotle's writings cover an astounding range of subjects, from metaphysics to biology and comparative government, from logic to LITERARY CRITICISM. The largest single group of works in the corpus is concerned with natural philosophy, including biology. The first work in this group, the *Physics,* discusses the theory of nature, the principles and causes of change, and the nature of motion, time, and place. Other physical treatises deal with the structure of the heavens, the four elements, and the phenomena of earth and atmosphere. Then come a series of treatises in biology preceded by the *De anima,* a study in comparative psychology focused on the theory of sense perception and conceptual thought (*see* COGNITION). Aristotle was a pioneer in comparative anatomy and also in embryology. Besides these works in natural science, the corpus includes four other main groups:

1. The *Metaphysics* consists of a dozen books or essays only loosely tied together. The title *Metaphysics* is late; Aristotle called this subject First Philosophy and thought of it as dealing with the most fundamental causes or explanatory principles of all reality. These principles include substance and its attributes (the attributes divided into eight or ten categories), matter and form as the basic components of all natural substances, potentiality and actuality as the two modes of reality, and the Unmoved Mover as the divine First Cause of all motion and change.

2. The *Nicomachean Ethics* (with a shorter, probably earlier version known as the *Eudemian Ethics*) contains the theory of the good life or happiness, including an analysis of the moral and intellectual virtues. The *Politics* sketches the social structure and educational scheme of an ideal city in the tradition of Plato's *Republic,* but it also contains a massive comparative study of citizenship, political structure, and political change throughout the Greek world.

3. The *Organon,* or "tool" of philosophical inquiry, consists of five quite different treatises collected together under this title many centuries later. The *Categories* gives a brief analysis of basic entities (substances) and modes of predication or types of attributes. The *De interpretatione* analyzes the struc-

ture of simple propositions. The *Prior Analytics* contains Aristotle's discovery of formal logic in the theory of syllogistic reasoning. The *Posterior Analytics* develops the theory of demonstrative science as an axiomatic deductive system based on the syllogism. The *Topics* expounds a system of dialectic: rules for constructing informal arguments for and against proposed theses, using premises accepted by all, by most people, or by the wise.

4. Most important for the study of communication are Aristotle's two works on ORATORY and literary criticism, respectively, the *Rhetoric* and the *Poetics*. The latter contains the classical theory of Greek TRAGEDY as "the imitation of an action that is serious, complete, and of a certain magnitude"; its influence on the history of criticism has been incalculable. The *Rhetoric* is less well known today, but its analysis of audience emotions and the devices by which the orator can appeal to them played an important role in early psychological theory—for example, in that of seventeenth-century British philosopher Thomas Hobbes. The *Rhetoric* also discusses the kinds of reasoning used to persuade an audience and the appropriate style and structure of a successful speech (*see also* PERSUASION; PUBLIC SPEAKING).

Because Aristotle's corpus consists of something like lecture notes, never revised for publication, the elliptical style creates innumerable difficulties for the reader. Scholars have responded by a long tradition of commentaries—first in Greek, then in Arabic, then in Latin. Commentary on Aristotle's text was a central function of the medieval UNIVERSITY. In the MIDDLE AGES Aristotle was known simply as "the philosopher." Thomas Aquinas and others regarded him as the spokesman for nature and reason; Dante refers to him as "the master of those who know." Modern science and philosophy began as a revolt against the Aristotelianism of the schools. More recently his thought has served as an inspiration for contemporary work, above all in moral philosophy, theory of action, and philosophy of mind.

Bibliography. Jonathan Barnes, Malcolm Schofield, and Richard Sorabji, eds., *Articles on Aristotle*, 4 vols., London and New York, 1975–1979; Werner Jaeger, *Aristotle: Fundamentals of the History of His Development* (Aristoteles: Grundlegung einer Geschichte seiner Entwicklung), trans. by Richard Robinson, Oxford, 1934; William David Ross, *Aristotle: A Complete Exposition of His Works and Thought* (1923), 5th ed., rev., London, 1960.

CHARLES H. KAHN

ARMSTRONG, EDWIN H. (1890–1954)

Pioneer U.S. RADIO engineer, best known for his invention of frequency modulation (FM). Along with

LEE DE FOREST, Edwin Howard Armstrong may be said to have created radio. He was an early amateur experimenter at his home in Yonkers, New York. He studied electrical engineering at Columbia University and in 1912, while a student, demonstrated his first major innovation, the regenerative circuit, which freed radio from dependence on earphones. In 1918 he invented the superheterodyne circuit, which—by transforming the carrier signal to an intermediate frequency that could be amplified far more clearly—made a basic contribution to modern radio, television, and radar systems. These first two achievements helped resolve one of the worst problems of early radio: even with enormous antennas, early receivers could not pick up signals and amplify them enough to drive speakers. Through Armstrong's designs these faint signals could be captured with the twirl of a dial and amplified enough to fill amphitheaters.

But Armstrong's greatest achievement was FM. Perfected in 1933 after years of work, it offered static-free reception and a range of frequencies not previously heard by radio listeners. Unfortunately this breakthrough brought him into conflict with formidable antagonists, including the dynamic DAVID SARNOFF of the Radio Corporation of America (RCA), which dominated the industry. Sarnoff and Armstrong had long known each other, and Sarnoff had once urged Armstrong to invent something to eliminate static. When he finally observed the result in a visit to Armstrong's laboratory, Sarnoff was astounded but also alarmed. It was not just an invention, he noted, but a revolution, an entirely new transmitting and receiving system. Sarnoff saw its introduction as certain to disrupt the hugely profitable AM radio system that RCA relied on to finance the final development and early introduction of electronic television (*see* TELEVISION HISTORY—EARLY PERIOD). Another problem was that both FM and television required wide new SPECTRUM allocations, which brought them into conflict before the Federal Communications Commission (FCC). The FCC commissioners were largely attuned to Sarnoff's television plans and schedule and were inclined to hold FM back. Armstrong, finding himself blocked (the FCC would grant him only an experimental license), resolved to fight for his system with all his resources. In 1937, at a cost of about three hundred thousand dollars, he built an FM station at Alpine, New Jersey, and began demonstrating FM's capabilities. Before long his gamble seemed to pay off. General Electric (GE) became an FM proponent. In 1940 the FCC decreed that U.S. television should have an FM sound system—a decision whose consequences would be felt after World War II. Also in the postwar period FM radio began to build a following, especially among music lovers.

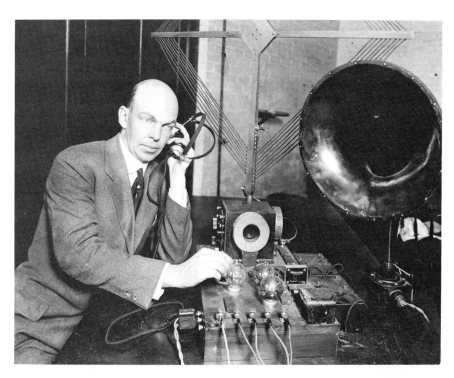

Figure 1. *(Armstrong, Edwin H.)* Edwin H. Armstrong. The Bettmann Archive, Inc.

But as his fortunes brightened, Armstrong faced a new struggle. Although GE, Westinghouse, Stromberg-Carlson, and Zenith were paying royalties for their use of FM in both radio and television receivers, RCA declined. It offered to pay a lump-sum settlement but not royalties (alleging an RCA role in the evolution of the invention). A few companies manufacturing under RCA license followed the RCA example. In 1948 Armstrong brought suit against the RCA group. For the next several years he faced batteries of renowned lawyers in agonizing, dragged-out litigation. In 1954, on the verge of bankruptcy and physical breakdown, he committed suicide. Years later the decisions in all suits went to Armstrong posthumously. By 1980 FM was the dominant radio medium.

Bibliography. Lawrence Lessing, *Man of High Fidelity: Edwin Howard Armstrong*, Philadelphia, 1956.

HARTLEY S. SPATT

ART

A term used in too many ways and applied to too many phenomena to have a simple or consistent meaning. However, common patterns can be discerned. The traditional definition of a communicative event involves a *source* who *encodes* a *message* that is *decoded* by a *receiver* (*see* MODELS OF COMMUNICATION). If one adapts this definition to the case of the arts, each term takes on a special property: an *artist creates* a *work of art* that is *appreciated* by an *audience*.

Not all messages are considered art, and not everyone who produces a message is an artist. Art is the product of human creative skill. But as not all manufactured products are given this honorific title, other criteria must be involved in the designation. In its modern use the term is applied primarily to the products of a particular set of activities known collectively as the fine arts. Some were presided over by the Muses of the ancient Greeks: music, POETRY, DANCE, TRAGEDY; others (e.g., painting, SCULPTURE, ARCHITECTURE) were joined to the concept of fine arts through a long process that culminated in the eighteenth century and was codified in DENIS DIDEROT's *Encyclopédie* and the newly emerging philosophy of AESTHETICS. More recently the practitioners of new media—PHOTOGRAPHY, MOTION PICTURES, VIDEO—have aspired to be included in this grouping of the fine arts.

The Western designation of the *fine* arts expresses a distinction between these exalted domains of cultural production and others disqualified on various grounds. Most notably excluded are those performers and products whose appeal may be too broad (the "popular" arts) or too utilitarian (crafts). It has often been noted that these exclusions follow and reinforce lines of class and GENDER privilege. In other periods and cultures such distinctions have not been made or have derived from different social and ideological formations.

Although we know little about the origins of prehistoric art such as the Paleolithic cave paintings of Lascaux, it is generally believed that their creation was intended to further through the magic of the VISUAL IMAGE the practical goal of hunting the animals depicted (*see* MURAL; Figure 1). Throughout history and across cultures, objects and performances on which we would bestow the label *art* have been created and used in ways that underscore the compatibility of their utilitarian and aesthetic functions.

Originally the term *art* (as in the Latin *ars*, meaning "skill" or "trade") was applied primarily to skillful performance according to definite rules; its modern meaning (as in the German *Kunst*) typically refers to the products of artists who are assumed to be free from such constraints and, moreover, are usually unhampered by pragmatic considerations of utility. These two definitional poles still coexist, although the balance remains tilted toward the latter. Art is generally assumed to result from the extraordinary technical abilities and personal qualities of its makers. Wide disparities exist among cultures and periods in their concepts of who can and should be seen as an artist and in the recruitment, training, and treatment of these individuals. In some instances artists are selected by clan, lineage, or gender; in others it is assumed that unique individual attributes—generally called talent—mark those eligible for the role of artist.

Figure 1. *(Art) Bison with Superposed Arrows*, Niaux, ca. 15,000–13,000 B.C.E. Ariège, France. From Paolo Graziozi, *Die Kunst der Altsteinzeit*, Florence: Sansoni, 1956, p. 201.

Concept of the Artist

In some contexts and cultures artists are valued for their virtuosity in exercising conventional skills (with the greatest accolades going to performances that approach the ideal realization of the conventional form); in others, aesthetic norms emphasize innovativeness and creative individuality (with an implicit expectation of radical novelty as the badge of genius). Each of these positions carries implications for the communicative role of the arts in society. The focus on skill is characteristic of most societies and periods, whereas the emphasis on originality is a peculiarly Western and modern perspective. Chinese art, for example, reveals a large measure of continuity over many centuries as traditional principles and practices were reworked to meet later needs. Thus a nineteenth-century critic wrote of the seventeenth-century Ch'ing painter Shih-t'ao, "How could he have attained such deep merit and strength if he had not absorbed the masters of T'ang and Sung in his heart and spirit?"

European cultures in the fifteenth and sixteenth centuries underwent a series of radical transformations with profound consequences. These upheavals, including the RENAISSANCE, originating in southern Europe, and the Protestant Reformation, originating in northern Europe, are seen as resulting in part from the political and economic developments associated with the decline of feudalism and the stirrings of bourgeois capitalism and in part from the technological revolution embodied in the invention of PRINTING. Among the legacies of this period is the Western preoccupation with the individual as the focus of theological, moral, political, economic, and social concern. Protestantism emphasizes the inescapably individual relation of each person to the deity, and the political and social philosophies of modern Western societies locate in individual citizens fundamental rights and obligations that define their relationships with the state and with their fellow citizens.

In the realm of the arts these shifts are reflected in the increasing focus on the individuality of the artist and of artistic creation. A great work of art comes to be defined as the product of creative genius transcending tradition and convention in the fulfillment of its inspiration. Thus achievement in art almost inevitably comes to be identified with innovation, as the artist's genius is manifested in the originality of style and execution. Coincidentally, the cults of genius and originality create an additional motivation and expanded market for forgery as they privilege works that can be attributed to canonical figures (*see* FORGERY, ART).

In the past several centuries artists in Western cultures have been expected and even encouraged, in keeping with the spirit of ROMANTICISM, to prove their worth by expressing a personal and unique vision. The resulting pattern of constant innovation in the arts undermines their ability to embody the common experiences and meanings of the society, to serve the central communicative functions of socialization and integration—roles now assigned to the domain of the popular arts and the mass media. Artists came to see themselves as the AVANT-GARDE, the "frontier scouts" of CULTURE moving away from their contemporaries into uncharted territories. This peculiarly romantic model of the artist as quintessential outsider both justifies and maintains the alienation of art from "real life" and the ambivalence that often characterizes the relationship between artists and their audiences.

Changing Concepts of Art

Most people in modern industrial societies do not view the arts as central, essential institutions in any personal, individual fashion. The activities and products associated with the arts are generally outside the mainstream of our daily lives and important concerns. Historically the term *art,* or *the arts,* came into currency in Europe as the common rubric for a diverse class of activities and products, partially in response to their increasing irrelevance to the lives of most people. As these various objects and events moved to the periphery of Western culture, their common characteristics became more visible, their differences less noteworthy, hence their ability to shelter comfortably under a common umbrella. In other words, a process of cultural realignment resulted in the banishment of the arts to a reservation on the psychological periphery of Western culture.

The image of a reservation is used here in the sense that the arts tend to be viewed as institutions that exist at the fringe of society. These are cultural "spaces" that real people may *visit* in their spare, fringe time but that only spare, fringe people inhabit in their *real* time. The territory of the arts is foreign to most of the population, is visited briefly by some as a LEISURE-time tourist attraction, and is lived in by a very few special people.

A second reservation is adjacent to that on which the arts reside and contains another institution, RELIGION, which has moved to the periphery of modern Western culture. As with the arts, those called or chosen for full-time participation are singled out by special qualifications of soul or temperament. In both cases there is a common tendency to view such cultural specialists—artists and clerics—with a mixture of respect and contempt. They are granted a degree of respect because of their unique abilities and their somewhat mysterious status as dwellers in an exotic realm. But the very quality of being removed from real life may also make them objects of disdain. As Clive Bell wrote:

The artist and the saint do what they do, not to make a living, but in obedience to some mysterious necessity. They do not produce to live—they live to produce. There is no place for them in a social system based on the theory that what men desire is prolonged and pleasant existence. You cannot fit them into the machine, you must make them extraneous to it. You must make pariahs of them, since they are not a part of society but the salt of the earth.

However, throughout most of Western history and in most non-Western societies even today it would be inaccurate to say that religion and the arts (the rubric itself would be inappropriate) occupy positions at the fringe of real life. Certainly many of their practitioners may have been viewed as special in a variety of ways, but the activities and products we designate as artistic and religious can generally be seen at the center of life and consciousness, and often joined together. Both are carriers and articulators of basic cultural beliefs about the nature of things and about the moral order.

Religion is a nonbeliever's way of labeling a set of beliefs about what exists in the world, about how these things came into being and how they are related to one another, about what is important and what is right. In most cultures and periods other than the modern West such commonly held beliefs and values are articulated, preserved, and communicated in a variety of symbolic modes (*see* MODE). These beliefs are conveyed through oft-told stories (what nonbelievers may call myths) and proverbs (*see* PROVERB); they are depicted in paintings, statues, stained-glass windows, and other visual forms; they are danced and sung (*see* SONG) and chanted; they are embodied in the architecture of churches, temples, monuments, mausoleums (*see* ART, FUNERARY), palaces, and public squares; they are even manifested in the role-reversing revelry of carnival (*see* FESTIVAL; MASK). All of these are means by which humans have been able to articulate their understandings of how the world works and how we should behave in it. From the outside we may view them primarily as "art" because we do not comprehend or accept their intended messages, but we do understand that their articulation is governed by a concern for form and beauty.

Communicative Functions of Art

Although in many instances the artist is producing images and objects that mimic the appearance of portions of the visible world—and is therefore often seen as a creator, even as a rival to the creator-deity—art is rarely held to be merely a representation of outward appearances (*see* REPRESENTATION, PICTORIAL AND PHOTOGRAPHIC). The choice of elements and their manipulation and form, as well as the content of the work, will generally be taken to articulate meanings that lie beyond the visible surface of the objects and events depicted. Often the formal properties of the work of art are intended to be metaphoric representations of nonvisible truths that cannot be apprehended directly (*see* METAPHOR).

The Japanese monk Kukai, who introduced Shingon Buddhism to Japan in the ninth century, saw the role of art as essential to the teaching of religious truth:

The law [dharma] has no speech, but without speech it cannot be expressed. Eternal truth [*tathata*] transcends color, but only by means of color can it be understood. . . . In truth, the esoteric doctrines are so profound as to defy their enunciation in writing. With the help of painting, however, their obscurities may be understood. The various attitudes and mudras of the holy images all have their source in Buddha's love, and one may attain Buddhahood at the sight of them. . . . Art is what reveals to us the state of perfection.

The sculptors of classical Greece were not presenting copies of particular individuals but rather were constructing on the basis of natural appearances geometrically perfected surfaces and shapes that the beholder's eyes would contemplate with enjoyment and the beholder's mind would intuitively recognize as representing the true form and ideal essence of humanity (*see* HELLENIC WORLD; Figure 2). In the Italian Renaissance the Greek conceptualization of the world in mathematical terms was revived and applied to painting, sculpture, and buildings. The architecture of sacred buildings is at all times a matter of great importance, as these edifices are the embodiment of the divine spirit. The goal of Renaissance architects was to unite the mathematical perfection of geometry, which they learned from the Greek classical sources, with the spirit of Christian theology (*see* CLASSICISM). One solution came from combining a classical aesthetic dictum—Vitruvius's assertion that a well-built man fits with extended hands and feet exactly into the most perfect geometric figures, the circle and square (Figure 3)—with the Christian belief, derived from Genesis, that man was created in the image of God. The resulting characteristic Renaissance church plan, based on the circle and the square and their three-dimensional expressions, the sphere and the cube, was thus a microcosmic echo of the mathematical perfection of God's macrocosmic creation (Figure 4). In the words of the sixteenth-century architect Palladio, "We cannot doubt that the little temples we make ought to resemble this very great one, which, by His immense goodness, was perfectly completed with one word of His." This is strikingly similar to the ancient Indian belief quoted from the Sanskrit by Ananda Coomaraswamy: "Our scriptures teach that the architecture of our temples is all made after the heavenly pattern, that is of forms prevailing in Heaven."

In the seventeenth century the artist and architect

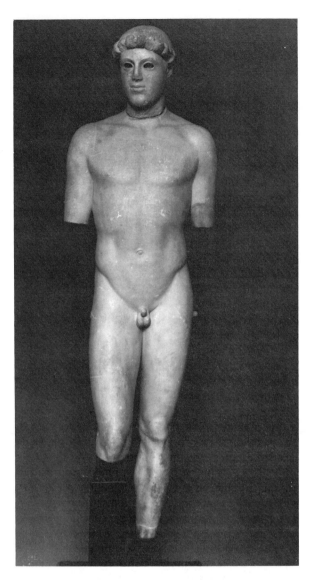

Figure 2. *(Art)* *Kritios Boy,* ca. 480 B.C.E. Acropolis Museum, Athens. Marburg/Art Resource, New York.

Giovanni Lorenzo Bernini designed the final form of St. Peter's in Rome, adding to the magnificent edifice an enormous oval square surrounded by a colonnade (Figure 5). This was not merely an aesthetic decision, as Bernini's words reveal: "For, since the church of St. Peter's is the mother of nearly all the others, it had to have colonnades, which would show it as if stretching out its arms maternally to receive Catholics, so as to confirm them in their faith, heretics, to reunite them to the Church, and infidels, to enlighten them in the true faith."

The evocative power of images has not been universally embraced by the world's religions, as can be seen in the prohibitions against images in orthodox JUDAISM and Islam (*see* ISLAM, CLASSICAL AND ME-

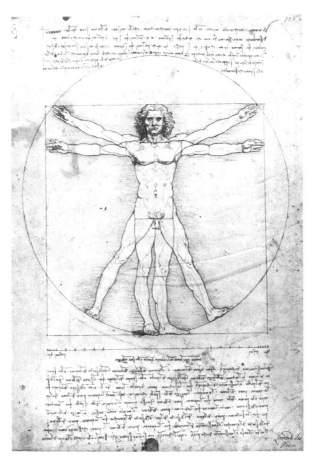

Figure 3. *(Art)* Leonardo da Vinci, *Vitruvian Man* ca. 1490. Gallerie dell'Accademia, Venice. Alinari/Art Resource.

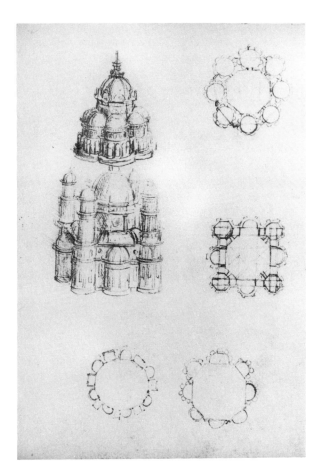

Figure 4. *(Art)* Leonardo da Vinci, designs of churches, Ms.B25b. Bulloz/Bibliothèque de l'Institut de France, Paris.

Figure 5. *(Art)* Aerial view of St. Peter's, Rome. Alinari/Art Resource, New York.

DIEVAL ERAS) and the violent disputes over icons in the early Christian church. However, in most societies images have been created for the purpose of focusing devotional attentions (e.g., figures of deities and saints; Figure 6), encouraging and celebrating civic virtues (allegorical figures; Figure 7), and manifesting power and authority (figures of rulers and military leaders; Figure 8).

The possibility of reproducing the features of particular individuals leads to the peculiarly though not exclusively Western practice of PORTRAITURE. Portraits preserve for posterity the memory of loved ones and glorify important and powerful persons; they also identify the physical image of rulers with the authority of the state (e.g., as on COINS). Departures from the goal of honorific representation can lead to the moral and political criticism often found in CARICATURE and to portraits that seem to reveal psychological characterization manifested in the physiognomy of the subject (Figure 9).

Works of art also serve to present and interpret social experience. NARRATIVE works such as drama often present social roles and relationships and instruct members of a culture in the norms of society and the price for transgression. The stories societies tell one another through the arts, both "fine" and "popular," are prime vehicles for the cultivation of images of human motivations and personalities and thus provide individuals with the basis on which they understand (or misunderstand) one another. Consequently societies often feel the need to monitor and control the content of art works to ensure that they support and do not subvert the established order. Creative works, wrote English critic Leslie Stephen in 1875, are both the producer and the product of society and should therefore "stimulate the healthy, not the morbid emotions."

Artistic Creation

Artistic communication is a form of symbolic behavior in which an artist creates or arranges objects and/or events so as to imply meanings and evoke emotions according to the conventions of a CODE, and these objects or events elicit inferences and emotions in the artist and in others who possess competence in the same code. For artistic communication to occur it is not necessary for the artist and the audience to coexist in either time or space; however, it is

Figure 6. *(Art)* Crucifix of Archbishop Gero, ca. 969–976 C.E. Cathedral of Cologne, FRG. Marburg/Art Resource, New York.

Figure 7. *(Art)* Frédéric-Auguste Bartholdi, *Statue of Liberty* ("Liberty Enlightening the World"), 1886. The Bettmann Archive, Inc.

necessary that they share to a significant extent a common symbolic code.

The process of artistic creation occurs within the boundaries of specific modes of symbolic thought and action, and in terms of the conventions of specific stylistic codes. A poetic style in English employs a limited set of SOUND elements and orders them according to principles that differ from other LANGUAGE usages. A style can be defined as a set of rules that influences the choices made by an artist operating within a specific code. Some of these rules are culturally determined and may constitute what is considered at that time and in that culture the only possible style in art. Other rules are more individual and tend to be identified with the particular artist and his or her followers.

Successful communication in a symbolic mode re-

quires at a minimum that communicator and audience share the basic rules of implication and inference in the appropriate code. The artist, in a crucial sense, is the initial member of the audience. As Leonard Meyer has noted, "It is because the composer is also a listener that he is able to control his inspiration with reference to the listener." This does not mean, however, that the audience experiences whatever emotions were felt by the artist either before or during the act of creation. The artist's creative experience is rarely equivalent to the felt experience of any emotions that are conveyed by the work of art, despite a romantic faith in the false assumption that an artist can only convey emotions and experiences that he or she has lived through personally.

There are important differences between the artist's experiences and the process of appreciation by

Figure 8. *(Art)* *Constantine the Great,* ca. 330 C.E. Alinari/Art Resource.

even the most sophisticated audience. First, the artist is actually making choices and the audience is at best anticipating and enjoying them. Moreover, in the vast majority of media, acts of creation are different in time, space, and pace from acts of appreciation. The artist interacts with a work of art in the process of creation in ways that can never be repeated by the artist or by anyone else. Audiences encounter a finished work of art or witness the articulation of a rehearsed performance. The process will always be in some sense closed and determined by the actions of the artist. For the artist, in contrast, the process is to some degree always open; whether within or beyond the bounds of convention, the artist always has a potential to succeed—or fail—in the realization of artistic goals.

The actions of the artist in creating a work of art can be schematically characterized as the *selection* of elements (subject, media, materials, etc.), the *manipulation* and transformation of selected elements, and the organization of an overall *structure*. This is not typically a chronological sequence; in fact, it might

be more accurately seen as a constant dialectic of actions and responses on the part of the artist and, in the case of performances, the audience, which shapes the emerging work. These choices can, however, be seen as foci of aesthetic attention and evaluation in the response to the work of art. They are always made and are generally responded to within the framework of conventions and standards of artistic legitimacy and skill that obtain in the particular art world. Works of art, like all symbolic creations, are produced and perceived as figures set against the ground of the conventional forms of the particular medium, style, and context. The challenge to the artist is to reveal sufficient mastery of conventional skills and forms to provide the audience with a basis for understanding and appreciation, and at the same time to demonstrate an individuality that distinguishes his or her work from that conventional ground.

The artist's selections of elements, manipulations, and structures are governed by a sense of their fittingness to the present task, which often results in modifications or violations of the conventions embodied in previous works. The artist may follow intuition across the borders of convention, guided by personal standards of taste. For the audience, which has not shared in the choices and decisions through which the work was shaped, an important judgment to be made is that of legitimacy: is it art? Unless and until they are satisfied that the work in question is indeed a work of art, audiences typically will not invoke the response strategies considered appropriate to art. For many audiences, in many cases, the setting of the encounter with the work (e.g., hanging in an art gallery or MUSEUM, played by a symphony orchestra, published in a poetry magazine) suffices to ensure its legitimacy; for other audiences, in other cases, this judgment depends on the degree to which the work conforms to conventions of selection, manipulation, and structure.

The loudest controversies often center on unconventional choices made by artists and attacked as illegitimate by other artists, by critics, by patrons, and by audiences. In times and cultures in which aesthetic conventions are considered absolute and even divinely sanctioned, artists have been punished for violating them. In the modern world, owing in part perhaps to the diminishing role of orthodox religions and to the technological availability of vast realms of past and present art, rigid standards of legitimacy have been largely abandoned. The expectation that artistic achievement is marked by radical individuality, and therefore radical innovation, has guaranteed that conventions will be continually violated and legitimacy constantly in doubt.

The quickest road to recognition, if not acceptance, of a new style is by extending or contracting the bounds of legitimacy through changes in the distinctive features of a code or style. Audiences may be shocked by the inclusion of subjects or elements hitherto considered at best irrelevant and at worst taboo in works of art. In the nineteenth century, U.S. poet Walt Whitman was accused of figuratively bringing the slop pail into the parlor; in the twentieth century, French artist Marcel Duchamp did so literally by exhibiting a urinal as a work of art (Figure 10). Some of the clearest ways in which standards of legitimacy are debated and enforced are conventions governing the use of erotic images in art and disputes over whether particular works are art or PORNOGRAPHY (i.e., not exculpated by the status of art). An example that is less dramatic because there is no longer dissension about it is the introduction of working-class characters and concerns into nineteenth-century FICTION (e.g., in the work of Charles Dickens or Émile Zola), which violated conventions of proper subject matter for an essentially bourgeois art form (see REALISM).

Judgments of legitimacy also operate in response to manipulations and orderings used by artists. A new verse form may be attacked as barbaric and unpoetic. The musical innovations of twentieth-century Austrian composers Arnold Schoenberg, Alban Berg, and Anton Webern aroused vocal condemnation from critics and audiences. The original performances of Russian composer Igor Stravinsky's *Le sacre du printemps* (The Rite of Spring) in Paris in 1913 provoked such vociferous debate between supporters and attackers that the music itself was drowned out. A style becomes accepted when its originators are granted the legitimacy of their actions and their intentions. Its characteristic patterns of choice and organization may now be used as the ground against which particular works can be appreciated.

Appreciation of Art

An important part of the process of appreciation is the perception and evaluation of the competence displayed by the artist. The fundamental criterion for the evaluation of artistic competence is the degree of skill that can be attributed to the acts of selecting, transforming, and ordering the elements constituting the work of art. Skill is attributed to the artist to the extent that these actions reveal both intention and ability: did the artist intend particular outcomes, and were these intentions realized?

Art works that follow conventional lines may highlight failures to achieve artistic intentions. A poet who is clearly stretching the meaning of a line to achieve a rhyme, a singer who reaches for but cannot attain a high note, a filmmaker who cannot edit a sequence coherently—all these reveal inadequacies of ability. Conversely, artists working in familiar forms are rewarded with appreciation when they succeed

Figure 9. *(Art)* Vincent van Gogh, *Self-Portrait*, 1889–1890. Louvre, Paris. Giraudon/Art Resource, New York.

in meeting the challenges of their craft. The line of poetry that perfectly fits the meaning and feeling of the poem, the singer who seems to effortlessly traverse a coloratura passage, the filmmaker whose pacing of images and action leaves audiences gasping—all these reveal the successful realization of artistic intention.

Artists who make unconventional choices evoke somewhat different responses: are their actions the successful realization of an unconventional intention or the failure to achieve a conventional one? Are they departing from the familiar territory of the conventional because they cannot meet its demands, and seeking the ambiguity of novel terrain? Not surprisingly, critics faced with unconventional works from an established artist often comfort their audiences with the assurance that the artist has earned the right to be taken seriously through previous conventional performances.

The appreciation of aspiration as well as achievement requires a knowledgeable audience capable of perceiving the artist's choices and the manner in which they are carried out and comparing them to the choices and skill embodied in other works and performances. Appreciative competence evolves through constant involvement with works of art in which the audience learns to distinguish the conventional from the idiosyncratic, the difficult from the flashy, the controlled from the random. Many of the

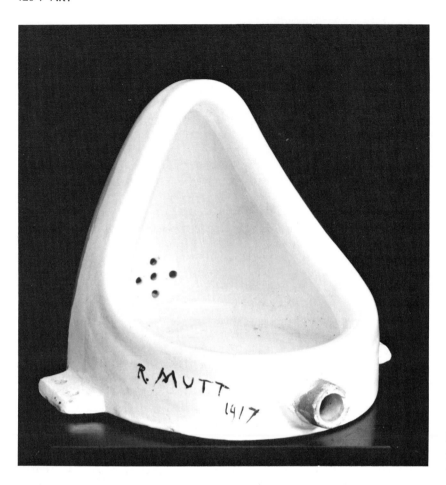

Figure 10. *(Art)* Marcel Duchamp, *Fountain*, 1917. Courtesy Sidney Janis Gallery, New York.

elements of skill in art tend to be invisible; creative performance often appears effortless precisely when it achieves the highest levels of competence. Sophisticated appreciation may require an understanding of the structural conventions that give weight and meaning to elements and operations purposively excluded as well as to those that are included. The high level of appreciative skill labeled connoisseurship thus involves the evaluation of creative products and performances as figures set off against a rich array of grounds provided by extensive exposure to and recall of artists and their works.

This description of the appreciative process need not be limited to the audiences for those works and performances that fall within the boundaries of the "fine arts." The audiences for most of the "popular arts," as well as such nonartistic domains as SPORTS, cooking, and even politics, can readily be seen as acquiring and exercising similar competence in the PERCEPTION, evaluation, and enjoyment of skillful performance by both professional and amateur practitioners. Any activity that requires skill can afford the aesthetic pleasures of competent performance and appreciation.

See also ARTIST AND SOCIETY; CHILD ART; ICONOGRAPHY; TASTE CULTURES.

Bibliography. Clive Bell, *Art,* London, 1914, reprint New York, 1958; Daniel P. Biebuyck, ed., *Tradition and Creativity in Tribal Art,* Berkeley, Calif., 1969; Georges Charbonnier, *Conversations with Claude Lévi-Strauss* (Entretiens avec Claude Lévi-Strauss), trans. by John Weightman and Doreen Weightman, London, 1969; Ananda K. Coomaraswamy, *The Transformation of Nature in Art,* Cambridge, Mass., 1934; Arnold Hauser, *The Sociology of Art* (Soziologie der Kunst), trans. by Kenneth J. Northcott, Chicago, 1982; Eugen Herrigel, *Zen in the Art of Archery* (Zen in der Kunst des Bogenschiessens), trans. by R. F. C. Hull, New York, 1971; Leonard B. Meyer, *Emotion and Meaning in Music,* Chicago, 1956; Charlotte M. Otten, ed., *Anthropology and Art,* New York, 1971; Osvald Siren, *The Chinese on the Art of Painting: Translations and Comments,* New York, 1963; Barbara Herrnstein Smith, *Poetic Closure: A Study of How Poems End,* Chicago, 1968; Janet Wolff, *The Social Production of Art,* New York and London, 1981.

LARRY GROSS

ART, FUNERARY

Historically, few religious systems have seen death as a natural event; rather, it has been surrounded with fear and superstition. The dead were often regarded as a threat to the living, and had to be appeased to keep them at bay. Different cultures supplied their dead with elaborate housing, prepared them for long journeys, and gave them gifts, and these concepts helped to create funerary ART and ARCHITECTURE.

Concepts of Death

While a desire to protect human sensibilities from the physical facts of decomposition has played some part in the practice of burying or entombing the dead, a consideration of duty toward the dead has also had a role. Even early burials had ritualistic aspects, some designed to propitiate the dead and to ensure that the living would not be disturbed by uneasy or maleficent spirits. For example, inhumations where bound corpses have been found in a crouching position may have been intended to prevent the dead from escaping to threaten the living. Fear of contamination led to the development of elaborate rites of purification involving washing, the burning of incense, and the airing of premises. Similarly, corpses themselves were washed, dressed in special clothes, anointed, and otherwise prepared for disposal, not only to protect them from demons but also to shield the living from the displeasure of the deceased. Gifts for the dead, the creation of a permanent abode of the dead and its proper equipment, libations and ceremonies on anniversaries and other significant dates, and the performing of rites of remembrance as a token of respect for antecedents all point to a desire to please the dead in order to keep them benign.

The finality of death has often been rationalized as a moment of transition from one aspect of existence to another, less obvious, plane. The concept of the dead setting off on a voyage seems to have been widespread and involved crossing mysterious rivers, bridges, valleys, and other obstacles to reach some distant place. Such passages involved payment of fares, and money was often placed in the mouth to settle the bills of ferrymen and to bribe guards, tollkeepers, and the like.

A remarkable number of civilizations have regarded burial rites as preparation for a new existence in which food, drink, companions, weapons, jewelry, furniture, vessels, and servants would be as necessary as during life. In ancient Mesopotamia, for example,

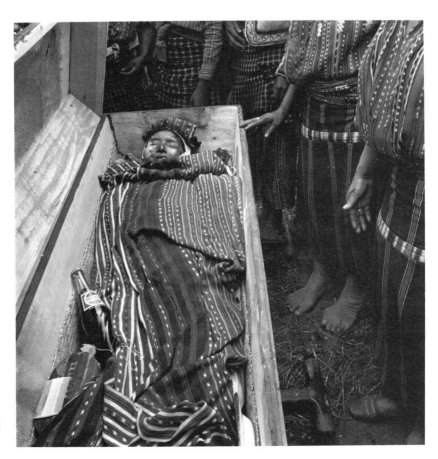

Figure 1. *(Art, Funerary)* Burial, Guatemala, 1976. © 1986 Rosalind Solomon.

the burial of important personages involved killing and entombing people and animals so that they could accompany the deceased to a new life beyond death. The slaying of large numbers of dependents seems to have been an Indo-European custom from the Neolithic period, and the Hindu practice of suttee was a survival of this RITUAL.

Just as objects and people were sometimes entombed with the dead, they were also burned with the corpse at cremation so that they could accompany the dead. The effect of such practices on primitive economies was considerable. It is significant that the more developed a culture, the less luxurious was the furnishing of tombs. Predynastic tombs in Egypt already contained models, statuettes, and substitute offerings instead of real objects and human beings—a practice that was cheaper and less of a temptation to grave robbers. In several cultures, pottery and other artifacts were "slaughtered" by being broken so that their "souls" would go with the dead. Some Chinese royal tombs have been discovered to contain whole armies of terra-cotta statues representing foot soldiers and cavalry. Remnants of ancient customs can be found in the modern world, as when mourners place rings or COINS in coffins or when a riderless horse follows the coffin in a state funeral.

Many religions make the important distinction between the soul, which is immortal, and the body, which quite clearly is not. One concept is that the soul exists before the body is formed and continues to exist after the body is destroyed; incarnation, therefore, is only a phase and may even be punishment for wrongs committed, while after the death of the body the soul's future is determined by the quality of the life lived during incarnation. This cyclical idea of destiny is found in Hinduism and Buddhism and was common among some cults of the Greco-Roman world. Enlightenment, the Buddhist nirvana, can be achieved only when the material world recedes and the personality is no longer slave to fleshly desires. This spiritual notion is far removed from the crude materialism of cultures that stressed the burial of valuable objects with the corpse.

It was a belief of the ancient Hebrews, Mesopotamians, and Greeks that the dead person became a wraithlike creature enduring a wretched existence in some miserable abode of the dead. Inhumation suggested that the abode of the dead was somewhere in

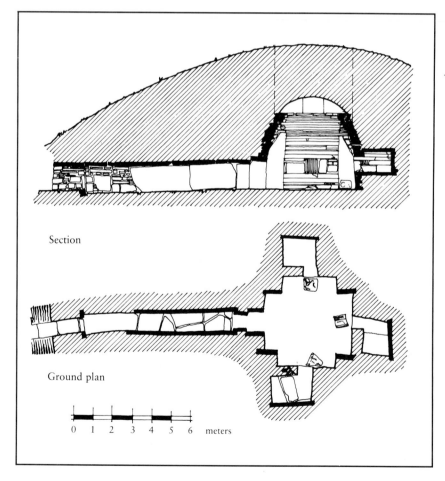

Figure 2. *(Art, Funerary)* Megalithic chamber tomb, Maes Howe, Orkney, Scotland. Section and ground plan. Courtesy of Dr. James Stevens Curl.

Section

Ground plan

0 1 2 3 4 5 6   meters

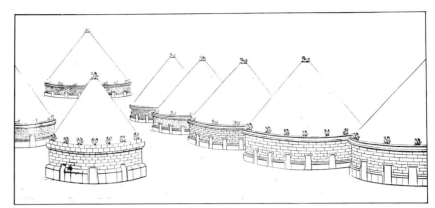

Figure 3. (*Art, Funerary*) Restoration of the Etruscan necropolis, Tarquinia, Italy, ca. seventh to fifth century B.C.E. From Mrs. Hamilton Gray, *Tour to the Sepulchres of Etruria in 1839*, London, 1841. Courtesy of Dr. James Stevens Curl.

the bowels of the earth in a gloomy underworld. Significantly, the religions of ancient Egypt, as well as those of JUDAISM, Zoroastrianism, Christianity, and Islam, all incorporated the notion of the preservation of the personality as an essential part of "survival" after death. The resurrection of the body became an important belief, especially to ancient Egyptians and Christians, sometimes even involving elaborate practices to prevent physical decay. *See* ISLAM, CLASSICAL AND MEDIEVAL ERAS; RELIGION.

Types of Funerary Structure

The Egyptians' tombs were their permanent dwellings and were thus superior in architectural quality to the houses of the living. Elaborately decorated burial chambers had chapels attached to them where ceremonies would take place, and in this respect they were not unlike the chantry chapels associated with tombs in medieval Christian churches. Tombs were endowed to ensure that they were kept in good repair, and priests were paid to perform rituals.

Significance has been given to burial places by the erection of structures, mounds, or symbolic markings over them. Several tomb types resemble burial mounds, while formal planning is a feature of tombs found in China, Egypt, Europe, and other civilizations. Burial chambers, often of imposing architecture and with long passages leading to them, are features of Orcadian, Irish, Mycenaean, and other tombs, all covered by mounds of earth. The Etruscan necropolis at Tarquinia contained many lavishly decorated burial chambers covered with conical mounds surrounded at the base with walls of masonry. These Etruscan tombs were models for the vast imperial mausoleums of the Roman emperors Hadrian and Augustus, and indeed Egyptian pyramids may be viewed as huge, regularized masonry mounds with elements symbolic of steps to the heavens and the rays of the sun. In Rome large underground sepulchers known as hypogea were created for families, groups, or sects; the even larger underground public cemeteries were known

as catacombs. Roman funerary customs also demanded large columbaria for the reception of the ash-chests of extended family groups. Individual house-tombs built along the roads to Rome often were surrounded with gardens, the produce of which helped to pay for upkeep. They were pleasant places for commemorative family gatherings. The interiors of such tombs were plastered and painted or finished in more permanent materials.

In the classical world places of cremation or entombment were outside city walls. Early Roman tombs were simply marked holes in the ground. The rectangular house-tombs of the Via Appia or Pompeii were more elaborate, and larger tombs often resembled temples. Ambitious tombs were constructed for the reception of cremated remains as well as for whole bodies; several cultures in antiquity preserved the ashes instead of scattering them. Where the ashes were cast into rivers or otherwise dispersed (as in Hindu custom), permanent memorials seem to have been eschewed. When bodies could not be found—often regarded as a disaster in the ancient world—cenotaphs (literally, "empty tombs") were erected both as memorials and as gifts to appease the dead. *See* HELLENIC WORLD; ROMAN EMPIRE.

Modern Funerary Art

With the ascendancy of Christianity in the Western world, the dead were buried in churches or in churchyards. Cults of saints contributed to a lessening of fear of the dead; relics were sought after, and it became desirable to be buried as near the holy shrines as possible. The building of tombs in churches and the custom of saying masses for the repose of the souls of the dead (chantries) were responsible for a great flowering of funerary art in Europe that included the creation of sarcophagi, ledger stones, altar tombs, canopied tombs, effigies, and chantry chapels of exquisite design (as in Winchester Cathedral in Hampshire, England). The Christian rituals of preparation for death, the burial or entombment of the

Figure 4. *(Art, Funerary)* Rock-cut tomb, "el-Khazneh" ("The Treasury"), Petra, Jordan (Eastern Roman Empire), first to second century C.E. Collection of A. F. Kersting.

Figure 5. *(Art, Funerary)* Medieval funerary monument of Edward, the Black Prince, Canterbury Cathedral, 1377–1380. Drawn and engraved by Edward Blore. Courtesy of Dr. James Stevens Curl.

dead, and the practices designed to assuage purgatorial existence played a major role in financing the church and in sponsoring funerary art. For example, the dispersal of parts of the body by burying the heart in one church, the bowels in a second, and the shell of the body in a third meant that three monuments would be erected (heart monuments are among the most interesting of medieval sculptures to have survived), while the clergy benefited from the endowments given to each church for burial privileges.

Toward the end of the MIDDLE AGES the physical facts of death were commonly represented in funerary art, and the memento mori or *gisant* admonitory figure of the decomposing corpse often was placed under or near the effigy of the deceased. These representations of mortality derive from the *danse macabre,* or "dance of death," recounted in a thirteenth-century poem about three young men who saw their own decomposing bodies. Illustrations of this occur at the Campo Santo in Pisa, Italy, and in other cloisters of ecclesiastical establishments throughout Europe. Admonitory skeletal figures oc-

Figure 6. *(Art, Funerary)* Hans Holbein the Younger. *The Peddler,* from *The Dance of Death,* 1523–1526. Bibliothèque Nationale, Paris. Giraudon/Art Resource, New York.

Figure 7. *(Art, Funerary)* Neoclassical tombs, Père-Lachaise Cemetery, Paris, early nineteenth century. Courtesy of Dr. James Stevens Curl.

curred in the decor of Pompeian dining rooms and on Roman drinking vessels, to remind revelers of the transient nature of life; they were the precursors of the gleeful skeletons of the *danse macabre*. Medieval "dooms," or representations of the Last Judgment, often decorated chancel arches or even portals of churches, and conveyed in startling imagery the torments of the damned.

Burial grounds attached to churches filled up rapidly, and it became usual to disinter the bones and store them in charnel houses. One of the largest of such urban cemeteries was that of the Innocents in Paris, which was surrounded by arcaded cloisters above which were the charnels for the storage of bones. This type of walled, arcaded enclosure developed from medieval cloisters and is exemplified by the celebrated Campo Santo, begun in 1270.

While canopied tombs, effigies, and elaborate memorials were made during the RENAISSANCE period, figures became more animated and were shown sitting up, resting on an elbow, or kneeling; the architectural detail changed with prevailing style. The *gisant* figure, often a mere skeleton, was also found as late as the seventeenth century, but with the baroque style the skeleton became an animated, threatening figure, as in Giovanni Bernini's tombs for the popes or the Nightingale monument in Westminster Abbey. With Bernini, too, came the pyramidal form

of the sculptured group, often set against a squat obelisk—a type of funerary monument common throughout Europe.

Modern cemeteries. Gross overcrowding of churchyards and the problems of intramural interment in the eighteenth century led to an essentially secular movement to bury the dead in new cemeteries laid out on hygienic principles and set apart from places of worship and away from the living. Among the first were the Surat Cemetery in India, dating from the seventeenth century, and the South Park Street Cemetery in Calcutta, founded in 1767, both featuring spacious layouts in magnificent classical tombs. Although small burial grounds outside towns had been established by various Dissenting sects in the eighteenth century, the first large modern metropolitan European cemetery, carefully designed as a landscape in which tombs could be erected, was that of Père-Lachaise in Paris, dating from 1804. It was admired by many contemporaries and became the model for the great nineteenth-century cemeteries of Britain, the United States, and elsewhere. Most of these cemeteries contain tombs of considerable architectural quality, mortuary buildings of distinction, and layouts important in the history of landscape DESIGN.

Mausoleums, above-ground structures with the character of a roofed building set aside for the en-

Figure 8. *(Art, Funerary)* Wax crayon rubbing of a New England gravestone, West Woodstock, Connecticut, eighteenth century. From Edmund Vincent Gillon, Jr., *Early New England Gravestone Rubbings*, New York: Dover Publications, Inc., 1966, plate 68.

tombment of the dead, were built in large numbers in Europe from the eighteenth century on (although they had been common in antiquity, notably in Greco-Roman civilizations). Great mausoleums based on formal plans had been built by the Islamic civilizations of Persia and Mogul India, and they astounded Europeans who saw them. The Taj Mahal at Agra, with its formal gardens, and the tomb of the Mogul emperor Humāyūn at Delhi are two serene and splendid examples that were the inspiration for European tombs at Surat and elsewhere. Mausoleums of special significance, such as the tomb of Muhammad at Medina or V. I. Lenin's neoclassical mausoleum in Moscow, are themselves places of pilgrimage. Other buildings, like the "towers of silence" of the Parsis in which the dead were laid out in trays to be devoured by carrion birds, have their own characteristic and unique forms reflecting the religious ethic of giving back to nature something in return for life.

Modern memorials. The nineteenth and twentieth centuries saw an unprecedented increase both in the technological means of waging warfare and in the

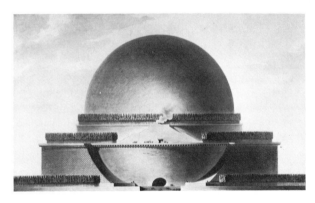

a

b

Figure 9. *(Art, Funerary)* Étienne-Louis Boullée, project for a cenotaph to Sir Isaac Newton, 1784: *(a)* exterior; *(b)* sectional view, with lighting to resemble day and a blazing globe in the center. Phot. Bibl. Nat., Paris.

Figure 10. *(Art, Funerary)* Ossip Zadkine, *The Destroyed City*, 1953, Rotterdam. Giraudon/Art Resource, New York.

casualties inflicted by war. Vast, formally designed military cemeteries—for example, those at Arlington in the United States and Verdun in France—reflect a need to commemorate death on a scale unknown in the past. Such monuments as Edwin Landseer Lutyens's Cenotaph at Whitehall in London, the Thiepval Memorial on the Somme River in France, and the many tombs of unknown soldiers around the world serve as national shrines for the remembrance of human sacrifice in war. Yet even the language of art is inadequate to express the outrage and profound loss suggested by such horrors as the extermination camps at Auschwitz or Sobibor. Only the remarkable Deportation Memorial in Paris seems to rise to the occasion with its controlled geometry and severe economy of means.

Public memorials to individuals, usually representations of those commemorated, have their place as civic art. Portrait memorials, including coins, medals, paintings, and SCULPTURE, have a long history. Mummy portraits of the Ptolemaic and Roman periods in Egypt are startlingly realistic, while Greco-Roman funerary busts, statuary, and reliefs attempted to capture the appearance of the deceased. Death masks, fashionable in the eighteenth and nineteenth centuries, not only provide accurate records of the faces of the dead but were themselves models for funerary sculpture and PORTRAITURE. *See* MASK.

Art and architecture celebrate death by transcending the ordinary. It is paradoxical that as death becomes more hidden from daily experience and the dead are disposed of discreetly, fear of the dead and of death is more apparent than in societies in which funerary art is a valuable and functional part of life.

Bibliography. Philippe Ariès, *The Hour of Our Death* (L'homme devant la mort), trans. by Helen Weaver, New York, 1981; T. S. R. Boase, *Death in the Middle Ages: Mortality, Judgement, and Remembrance*, New York and London, 1972; James Stevens Curl, *A Celebration of Death: An Introduction to Some of the Buildings, Monuments, and Settings of Funerary Architecture in the Western European Tradition*, London and New York, 1980; Leslie V. Grinsell, *Barrow, Pyramid, and Tomb: Ancient Burial Customs in Egypt, the Mediterranean, and the British Isles*, Boulder, Colo., and London, 1975; Donna C. Kurtz and John Boardman, *Greek Burial Customs*, Ithaca, N.Y., and London, 1971; J. M. C. Toynbee, *Death and Burial in the Roman World*, Ithaca, N.Y., and London, 1971; F. Parkes Weber, *Aspects of Death and Correlated Aspects of Life in Art, Epigram, and Poetry*, 3d ed., New York, 1918.

JAMES STEVENS CURL

ARTIFACT

The word (*arte* + *factum*) literally means "something made by skill or craft" and may refer to any artificial product. In common usage, artifact denotes an object manufactured or modified by human hands. Most dictionary definitions and representative examples not only confer simplicity and primitiveness upon artifacts, but are themselves deceptively simple, concealing both the tangled connotations of the term and the overwhelming diversity and complexity of human makings as well as the uses, meanings, and valuations thereof. The domain of artifacts (otherwise known as material CULTURE) has been endlessly subdivided and variously modified: implements, tools, weapons, ornaments, domestic utensils, religious objects, antiquities, primitive artifacts, folk materials, vintage clothing, and so on. The primary division, however, is into practical or utilitarian versus aesthetic or expressive things, with "artifact" or "craft" usually denoting the former and "art" or "art object" the latter. This distinction is problematic and confusing and is best discarded because the idea of ART as a separate category of things "beyond necessity" is alien to most of the world's cultures. All artifacts have an aesthetic dimension, and aesthetic valuation is extremely relative. Artifacts are perhaps best and most broadly understood in German sociologist GEORG SIMMEL's terms as "objective culture"—the world of cultural forms and their material artifacts that define and shape human life and that, however simple and mundane, are essential elements in the production and reproduction of cultural persons and social relations.

Artifacts are distinguished among cultural forms by their tangible substantiality and relative imperishability. Frequently used interchangeably with "remains" or "survivals," artifacts imply both residue and surplus, those products of human work that have been used but not consumed in the business of living and that survive as witnesses (sometimes the only ones we have) to what once was. Artifacts are uniquely detachable from their contexts of production and use and are thus eminently collectible. In Western cultures artifacts are associated, both literally and figuratively, with museums and collections—accumulations of exotic things appropriated from peoples who are temporally, spatially, or culturally remote. *See* MUSEUM.

Implicit in the conception and the collection of artifacts is the assumption that cultures not only create, represent, and re-create their distinctive patterns through what they say and do, but through articulations of the material world, and that the former not only can be but, in many cases, can only be reconstructed and "read" through the latter. The making and using of objects (*homo faber*) coexist with LANGUAGE, thinking, and symbol-using (*homo sapiens*) in all definitions of humanity. Clearly, we would not have collected, arranged, and displayed millions of artifacts if we did not believe that the

Figure 1. *(Artifact)* Navajo Two Gray Hills rug, 1947–1948. Woven by Daisy Touglechee, New Mexico and Arizona. © 1981 Denver Art Museum.

Figure 2.

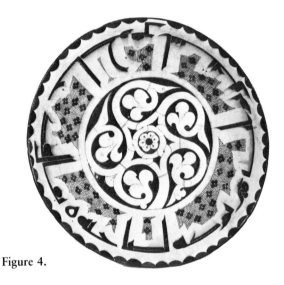

Figure 4.

Figure 3.

Figure 2. *(Artifact)* Karok twined basket with lid, 1890. Karok, Salmon Mountain Area. © 1985 Denver Art Museum.

Figure 3. *(Artifact)* Wooden comb, Uganda. Collected in 1946. Neg./Trans. No. 2A 10444 (Photo by Logan). Courtesy Department Library Services, American Museum of Natural History, New York.

Figure 4. *(Artifact)* Persian pottery bowl, tenth century. Samanid period. Courtesy of the Freer Gallery of Art, Smithsonian Institution, Washington, D.C. (Acc. no. 57.24)

things people have shaped to their use and pleasure are informed with significance, and that artifactual communication is constitutive of the human condition. Nonetheless, social scientists have been far more concerned with the meanings of words and actions and patterns of relationship than with the meanings of things. With a few notable exceptions, such as Petr Bogatyrev's analysis of folk costume and anthropologist Nancy Munn's analysis of Walbiri iconography, even structural and semiotic studies analyzing culture as a system of signs have neglected objectual sign systems (*see* SEMIOTICS; STRUCTURALISM). Fortunately, some of the more insightful social scientists, such as anthropologists Marcel Mauss, FRANZ BOAS, and Bronislaw Malinowski, have resisted the widely shared assumption that things, especially primitive things, are simple and self-evident.

The study of artifacts has shifted since the mid-1960s from things themselves to their producers and the processes and contexts of production and use. Psychologists, sociologists, and symbolic anthropologists as well as folklorists and archaeologists are reviewing the things with which we fill our lives and demonstrating that they *are* "interpretations," "objectifications," or "materializations" of experience; that artifacts are indeed repositories of significance, both embodying and collecting cultural meanings; and that "objects speak" and are vehicles as well as vestiges of human communication and interaction.

Artifacts as Signs

If, as Mauss and others have argued, nearly all phenomena of collective life are capable of expression

Figure 5. *(Artifact)* Susa "A" painted goblet, Persia, ca. 4000 B.C.E. By courtesy of the Visitors of the Ashmolean Museum, Oxford. Long-term loan from the Louvre, Paris.

Figure 7. *(Artifact)* Urn from Prunay, France, late La Tène culture. Fourth century B.C.E. Reddish ware painted with brown pigment. Reproduced by courtesy of the Trustees of The British Museum.

Figure 6. *(Artifact)* Animal (coyote?) effigy vessel, "plumbate" earthenware. Early postclassical period, 900–1200 C.E. Toltec, Mesoamerica, location unknown (Maya area?). The Saint Louis Art Museum, Anonymous Loan.

in objects, the problem of interpreting artifacts and how and what they communicate is much more complex and demanding than is commonly assumed. Existing studies of objects as signs and as sign systems reveal at least five distinctive and problematic aspects of artifactual communication. *See also* SIGN; SIGN SYSTEM.

Multifunctionality and polysemy. In contrast to verbal signs, most objectual signs are not used only or primarily as signs. Like written rather than spoken discourse, artifactual messages can be produced as well as received (appreciated, interpreted) in isolation and are easily and frequently desituated. Since all artifacts are not intended as signs but any artifact may be used or interpreted as a sign, we need to distinguish between what U.S. folklorist Henry Glassie terms "intentional and interpretative signifying" as well as to determine a thing's manifest and latent functions. For example, even though it may signify a great deal about Pueblo culture and worldview or personal and village identity, a traditional pottery jar, or olla, was shaped primarily to carry and store water. This practical, manifest, and necessary function determined both its form and its painted designs, for the latter frequently incorporated motifs "to call the rain," such as rain clouds, lightning, and water serpents. Without reducing meaning entirely to function, it should be noted that significance and use are inextricably connected and that few if any artifacts have but one function and one meaning. In their respective contexts, such typical handmade objects as Anglo-American quilts and Mesoamerican huipils (one-piece blouselike garments) have multiple functions and meanings in addition to the obvious utilitarian *and* aesthetic functions of warmth or covering and decoration. Bogatyrev suggests that artifacts have bundles of hierarchically arranged functions, ascribes no less than six functions to Moravian holiday dress alone, and demonstrates that how and what an artifact communicates is intimately related to how, where, when, and by whom it is used.

Figure 8. *(Artifact)* Massimo and Adriano Lagostina, Stockpot, 1955. Stainless steel, 7¾ in. high. Collection, The Museum of Modern Art, New York. Phyllis B. Lambert Fund.

Figure 9. *(Artifact)* Wilhelm Wagenfeld, Teapot, 1932. Heat-resistant glass, 4½ in. high, 6 in. diameter. Collection, The Museum of Modern Art, New York. Gift of Fraser's, Inc.

Multiple frames and contextual determinants. The use and meaning of an artifact can change radically depending on the context in which it is placed and the perspective from which it is viewed. For example, in its indigenous context, the carved and painted wooden figure of a Zuni Pueblo war god is a powerful religious being; in the National Museum of Natural History's Pueblo collection, it is an ethnological artifact; and in New York's Museum of Modern Art's "Primitivism in Modern Art" show (1984), it is an art object. Context can alter an artifact's shape and substance as well as its meanings and functions. Studies of the arts of acculturation have demonstrated that the presence of an alien art market that changes an indigenous object's context of destination and use produces marked changes in form, size, materials, and technique. Pueblo potters, for example, began making nontraditional forms such as ashtrays and candlesticks for tourists at the turn of the century, and although they have continued to produce traditional utilitarian shapes as well, most of these are smaller and less finely made, many are painted with commercial paints, and none of them can hold water or cook food.

Multiple channels and multivocality. The analysis of artifacts as signs is also complicated by the fact that objects speak in many voices, for all artifacts have more than one signifying dimension—shape, material(s), size, technique, color, design elements, and structure, for example. Changes in any one of these aspects may radically alter function and meaning as well as signify a shift in context. A dress made in gold brocade says something very different from a similar dress made in homespun; a miniature bow and arrow may be a native child's toy, a tourist item, a funerary object, or a ceremonial prop; a Navajo sand painter making a "Holy Person" on a board for sale to tourists will desacralize the figure by changing or omitting at least one element in the design, the color symbolism, or the composition; the defunctionalizing modifications made by a Mexican-American turn a Detroit assembly-line vehicle into an art object and self-advertising status symbol, a "lowrider."

Recycling and bricolage. The multivocality of popular artifacts, as exemplified by the lowrider, is further complicated by the widespread practice of recycling and transforming industrial objects. Like collage in fine art and INTERTEXTUALITY in verbal art, the bricolage of handmade things such as patchwork quilts involves the construction of a significant object out of the bits and pieces of one's life, the fragments of other signs and sign systems. Tires become flower planters; horseshoes are fashioned into mailbox stands and countless other functional/decorative farm and ranch items; the handlebars of a bicycle are turned into the horns of a roping dummy; beer cans are a primary material in the construction of Sonoran tin *retablos* (religious pictures) and countless other tourist items. The list is endless, but as the French anthropologist CLAUDE LÉVI-STRAUSS and others have demonstrated, the practice of recycling is by no means limited to modern industrial debris. For centuries, Pueblo potters have been using cracked and broken "potteries" to make chimneys and grinding up sherds for temper.

Ephemerality. Many artifacts leave no residue, even in recycled form. One of the major difficulties in studying objectual sign systems such as Navajo sand paintings is that a great many highly significant cultural products are ephemeral, are meant to be used and used up, and can never be collected. Ice sculptures, sand castles, arrangements of food, floral displays, and Tournament of Roses floats are as evanescent as the events of which they are a part. Many ephemeral forms such as Mbari houses and sculptures, Navajo sand paintings, or Pueblo prayer sticks that collectors have contrived either to preserve in controlled environments or to record in drawings, photographs, and other less perishable media were never meant to be fixed and, if not consumed or allowed to disintegrate, were deliberately destroyed. The practice of burning masks, costumes, and other ritual paraphernalia, for example, is widespread (*see* MASK). Ephemeral forms demonstrate that the study of material culture cannot and should not rely only on the products and remains of cultural processes and events. The extent to which perishability and process are central to the semantics and aesthetics of many cultural things should be considered as well. What does it mean to invest months of creative energy in the production of something that will be erased, eaten, or burned in minutes?

Approaches to Artifacts

Numerous methods have been devised (some already implied) for studying artifacts and their meanings and uses. The principal approaches are grouped according to focus and arranged more or less chronologically following the development of material culture studies in the last century.

Description and classification. Confronted with a chaotic collection of things, the curator's first job was to describe and define the objects themselves; to divide and catalog them according to type and material, date, and place; and then to classify them into typologies and sequences on the basis of formal and morphological features.

Stylistic analyses. Nineteenth-century theories of evolutionism and diffusionism produced two primary arrangements of formal features that are still used in both archaeological and art-historical approaches to artifacts: vertical or chronological and horizontal or spatial. Recent stylistic analyses have become much more elaborate and refined, frequently using structural linguistic models, but they are still focused on the patterning of formal features and the spatial and temporal configurations thereof.

Technique and technology. Attention to things in themselves and to the evolution of forms and designs inevitably included an interest in the processes by which they were constructed. But, more than simply investigating specific techniques of, for example, basketry, early students of material culture and evolutionists such as the U.S. ethnologist Otis T. Mason were concerned more generally with human/environment adaptations, with the development of primitive technologies, and with the changes in modes of production and social organization made possible by material inventions.

Social uses and cultural meanings. As anthropologists moved out of the museum and into the field, they began to examine the social uses as well as technologies of artifacts and the relationship of things to larger, less tangible sociocultural patterns and

Figure 10. *(Artifact)* Vanity bag *(istrajal).* Baluchi tribes, Nimroz (Chakhansur), Afghanistan. Reproduced by courtesy of the Trustees of The British Museum.

Figure 11. *(Artifact)* Woman painting a Kwakiutl chief's hat. From Edward Curtis, *The North American Indian*, vol. 10, plate 329. The University Museum, Philadelphia.

structures. More specifically, Boas's study of the potlatch of Northwest Coast tribes, Malinowski's analysis of the Melanesian kula, and Mauss's cross-cultural analysis of gifts focused attention on the circulation of things in society and the political and economic as well as symbolic role of objects in engendering, maintaining, and controlling social relationships. These early studies are still exemplary in their attention to the interrelationships of technological, social, and symbolic/linguistic systems.

Communication and interaction. All studies of this sort are stylistically based, but in contrast to many formal analyses of style that are virtually a-cultural, these are concerned with what and how a system of forms communicates within and between human groups—with what anthropologist Victor Turner has described as "operational meanings." Since the mid-

1960s the emphasis has shifted from what artifacts reflect of sociocultural matrix to how objects communicate and what they actually do in RITUAL or exchange systems, to the influence of interactional patterns—social, economic, residential, kinship—on both the consistency and the variability of stylistic features.

Structural or semiotic. In contrast to operational meanings, these studies have been more concerned with iconographic and "positional meanings." Exemplary analyses by Glassie, Nancy Munn, and RO-LAND BARTHES show the structures and SEMANTICS of artifacts in relation to the total configuration or structure of the sign system of which they are a part and in the relation of that sign system to other cultural subsystems. Such analogies frequently delineate homologies between artifactual structures and, for example, social, religious, cognitive, narrative, or ideological patterns. Those artifactual interpretations influenced by the work of the U.S. anthropologist Clifford Geertz are somewhat less structured and diagrammatic but no less concerned with art "as a cultural system."

Ethnosemantic or ethnoaesthetic. These studies focus on "exegetical meanings," aesthetic categories and valuations, and artifact classification "from the native point of view." Despite the value of such studies in material culture since the mid-1970s, the native too often disappears behind "his" categories and the analyst's formal models. Such, however, is not the case in older, less "scientific" ethnoaesthetic work, such as U.S. anthropologist Ruth Bunzel's classic 1929 study of Pueblo potters.

Producer- or artist-centered. Such studies have overturned both the product-centered bias and the myth of the anonymous primitive or folk artist that have dominated material culture scholarship. Despite Boas's dictum that "we have to turn our attention first of all to the artist himself," few artifact studies did so until the mid-1960s. Since then an increasing number of folklorists and anthropologists have followed Warren d'Azevedo's lead in contributing significantly to our understanding of meaning from the maker's point of view without reducing art to biography or psychology.

Acculturation. Acculturation has wrought changes in the lives of producers and in all aspects of artifact production and consumption. Traditional items of everyday use such as Navajo blankets and Pueblo water jars are still made but are now made differently and have acquired new value as items of economic exchange and statements of ethnic identity. Since 1970 several important studies have examined the extent to which artifacts reflect and participate in intercultural communication, cultural change, and cultural survival.

Politics of the production and reproduction of things. Influenced both by French neo-Marxism (in particular the work of Pierre Bourdieu) and by feminist theory, post-1975 material culture studies have gravitated toward a truly materialist approach. Their focus has been the relation of things to cultural, symbolic, and economic power, and the social and sexual division of labor in the production and manipulation of material signs. In studies such as Annette Weiner's reanalysis of the kula, artifacts are analyzed in terms of both use-value and representative-value—what Bourdieu calls "symbolic capital"—in expressing, maintaining, and subverting power relations. *See also* FEMINIST THEORIES OF COMMUNICATION.

Performance- or event-centered. In this approach of the 1970s and 1980s, material as well as verbal art is conceived as PERFORMANCE and is studied in the context of the public performances in which it appears. Several important museum exhibits have revivified and recontextualized previously collected artifacts by presenting them to the public in multimedia reconstructions of the events in which they once participated.

Ideally, our readings of objective culture should combine all the preceding approaches, for they are all relevant to how artifacts exist, function, and communicate in society. Ironically, one study that comes especially close to that synthetic vision, *Zuni Breadstuff* (1920), by U.S. ethnologist Frank Hamilton Cushing, is often absent from material culture bibliographies. This unique account of the role of corn, the mother food, in all aspects of Zuni life is a telling demonstration that much of a people's artistry and finest artifacts is associated with subsistence activities and the necessities of life, that material objects do indeed signify a whole context of meaning in the life of a people, that human beings create "a mirror of their ways" in the things they make as well as in the stories they tell and the ceremonies they perform, and that attention to the material world can yield invaluable and in some cases otherwise unattainable insights into cultural life.

See also FOLKLORE.

Bibliography. Roland Barthes, *The Fashion System*, New York, 1983; Franz Boas, *Primitive Art*, New York, 1955; Petr Bogatyrev, *The Functions of Folk Costume in Moravian Slovakia*, The Hague, 1971; Ruth Bunzel, *The Pueblo Potter*, New York, 1929, reprint 1972; Mihalyi Csikszentmihalyi and Eugene Rochberg-Halton, *The Meaning of Things: Domestic Symbols and the Self*, 2d ed., Cambridge and New York, 1981; Frank Hamilton Cushing, *Zuni Breadstuff*, New York, 1920; Warren L. d'Azevedo, ed., *The Traditional Artist in African Societies*, Bloomington, Ind., 1973; Nelson Graburn, ed., *Ethnic and Tourist Arts*, Berkeley, Calif., 1976; Ian Hodder, *Symbols in Action: Ethnoarchaeological Studies of Material Culture*, Cambridge and New York, 1982; Bronislaw Malinowski, *Argonauts of the Western Pacific*, New York, 1922; Marcel Mauss, *The Gift: Forms and Functions of Exchange in Archaic Societies*, New York, 1967; Nancy Munn, *Walbiri Iconography*, Ithaca, N.Y., 1973; Victor W. Turner, ed., *Celebration: Studies in Festivity and Ritual*, Washington, D.C., 1982; Annette B. Weiner, *Women of Value, Men of Renown*, Austin, Tex., 1976.

BARBARA A. BABCOCK

ARTIFICIAL INTELLIGENCE

A discipline concerned with simulating intelligent behavior on the computer so that computers can perform tasks more intelligently. In addition artificial intelligence (AI) is the study of general principles of intelligent behavior, regardless of physical embodiment. It suggests the computer METAPHOR for mind, the effort to understand human COGNITION by analogy with computation. Artificial intelligence is therefore one of the principal elements in cognitive science, and it has had a deep influence in recent years on psychology, LINGUISTICS, and the philosophy of mind.

The principal branches of artificial intelligence are PERCEPTION, expert systems, robotics, reasoning, and natural LANGUAGE processing.

Perception. Most research in perception has been concerned with vision, although some AI work has dealt with SPEECH recognition and other sensory modalities as well. Research on vision has concentrated on the problem of how to use viewer expectations about what will be in a scene to identify patterns in the sensory information from an image that correspond to semantically important objects. In particular the effort has been to reconstruct three-dimensional scenes from two-dimensional images. Some problems that have been worked on extensively have been edge detection, texture and shading analysis, extracting shape information from these low-level features, determining corresponding elements in images slightly displaced spatially or temporally (for stereopsis and motion detection), and using all of this information to identify the objects in a scene.

Expert systems. An expert system is a computer program intended to capture the specialized knowledge of an expert in some field. The major examples of expert systems implemented so far have been for medical diagnosis, financial advice, evaluation of geological sites, and determination of computer configurations. Expert systems are intended to make the expertise widely available. They typically work by applying a large number of general rules to specific data in order to draw conclusions about the situation described. A programmer building an expert system tries to reduce the expert's knowledge to a set of such rules. In addition weights are often attached to the rules to allow for uncertainty and to encode heuristics (procedures that give the correct answer almost always but not always).

Robotics. Much research in robotics has dealt with industrial automation. As such it is concerned with perceiving and manipulating objects of particular shapes and sizes with a robot arm equipped with a television camera or other sensing device. Other research has focused on individual robots and autonomous vehicles. This research is directed largely toward the perception, planning, and motion problems involved in moving across various sorts of terrains and through environments with various kinds of obstacles. Recently researchers have begun to investigate the problem of individual robots communicating with one another, on the model of communication described below.

Reasoning. Research in reasoning lies at the heart of artificial intelligence, in that virtually every AI project involves problems of reasoning. Reasoning must be *about* some knowledge, and this knowledge must be represented in a form that is accessible to a computer. Thus much research has centered on the representation of knowledge. Three of the most common representational schemes have been semantic nets, frames, and expressions in formal logic. They are very similar, but they emphasize different aspects of the knowledge. Semantic nets encode subset, superset, instance, and other relations among concepts in a way that lends itself to determining associations among concepts. Frames encode highly structured knowledge about complex objects by associating properties and values for these properties with each object. Formal logic allows one to state both general and specific knowledge about implication and other logical relations among predications made about individual entities. The relations among these representational systems and the advantages and disadvantages of each are controversial issues in the field.

Some of the earliest research on reasoning with this knowledge was in the domain of theorem proving. In theorem proving one expresses knowledge in formal logic and attempts to draw conclusions from it using deductive rules, in particular *modus ponens* and universal instantiation (inferring specific instances from general laws). Work on theorem proving began as an attempt to simulate what mathematicians do when they prove mathematical theorems. Later, however, it was recognized that many, if not all, kinds of computation could be viewed as deduction and that theorem proving was therefore perhaps the central problem in AI. On the other hand, many researchers feel that deduction is a poor model of human reasoning and are investigating other modes. One such mode is nonmonotonic logic, or logic in which, unlike classical logic, acquiring new information can make previously true conclusions false. Another mode is reasoning with uncertain information, frequently according to probabilistic models.

A particularly important kind of reasoning is *planning*, that is, reasoning about what to do. In planning one begins with a goal to be achieved or maintained and then tries to determine a sequence of actions that will bring about that goal. This is done by decomposing the goal into subgoals and these subgoals into further subgoals until one has a sequence of executable actions. Among the research issues in planning are how to optimize the outcome when there are conflicting goals and how to modify plans in response to failure or to new information from the environment.

Central to virtually every effort in AI is the problem of *search*. Most AI tasks can be formulated in terms of successively applying rules to a current state of knowledge to transform it into a new state of knowledge until a solution is discovered. For example, drawing inferences in a deductive system and decomposing a goal into subgoals can both be seen as transformations of this sort. However, for most tasks there are so many rules and therefore so many possible transformations that the set of possibilities is far too large to be examined exhaustively. The problem, therefore, is how to search through a subset of these possibilities efficiently and in a manner that will always or almost always guarantee the right, or at least a good, solution. The search problem is seen in its purest form in programs for playing chess and other games. Because of the large number of possible moves at each turn and the number of turns per game, it is estimated that there are 10^{120} possible chess games, a more than astronomical number. It is impossible to search through all of these exhaustively, so a chess-playing program must use knowledge of chess strategies to select only the most plausible moves at each turn and must use some kind of evaluation function to estimate the goodness of intermediate positions in the game. This process is known as *heuristic search* because the evaluation function is not exact; analogous processes are required in most other AI programs.

Natural language processing. The field of natural language processing is the effort to use AI techniques in the comprehension and production of natural language texts. It is typically divided into syntax, SEMANTICS, and pragmatics. Syntax is the study of the logical structure of sentences, including the predicate-argument relations among elements in the sentence. The formalisms for specifying the syntax of natural language sentences generally have two parts: a phrase-structure rule that specifies the structure of a grammatical construction in terms of the classes of its constituent words or phrases, such as a sentence being composed of a noun phrase followed by a verb phrase; and a set of constraints on the application of the phrase-structure rules, expressed in terms of the agreement of features associated with the constituent phrases, such as a noun phrase and a verb phrase having to agree in number. These rules are used by parsing algorithms to analyze sentences into "parse trees" representing their syntactic structure. Syntactic processing, in the absence of semantic and pragmatic processing, reveals most sentences to be highly ambiguous. The sentence "I saw the man in the park with the telescope," for example, has six different interpretations, depending on what the prepositional phrases are taken to modify.

Semantics is the study of the meanings of words and how they compose into the meanings of sentences. Rules are specified for translating parse trees of sentences into logical expressions encoding the MEANING of the sentences. Beyond this two principal emphases in research in semantics should be noted. First of all, in natural language systems operating in the context of some limited domain, or microworld, there has been work on determining what entities and actions in the microworld are being referred to by phrases and sentences in a text. This requires reasoning with knowledge about the microworld and about the language in the text. Second, there has been work on drawing the appropriate inferences from the information conveyed in the text for the purpose of paraphrasing the text, generating expectations about the portion of the text to follow, or solving INTERPRETATION problems posed by the text itself, such as the problems of resolving syntactic ambiguities and resolving the reference of pronouns and definite noun phrases.

Pragmatics is the study of the ways sentences and larger texts are used by speakers. It differs from semantics because many utterances are indirect. For example, we often ask someone if he or she knows the time as a way of requesting that person to tell us the time. The most common approach in this area combines insights from speech-act theory in the philosophy of language with AI research on planning. Utterances are seen as actions in some plan by the speaker to realize some goal or goals. Research on the production of texts has therefore followed the planning paradigm. A goal is broken into a sequence of subgoals and these into further subgoals until a sequence of utterances results. A speaker can appeal to the rich resources of language to achieve the best possible outcome when there are conflicting goals, and he or she can modify or elaborate the original plan "on the fly" in response to failures to communicate and to unexpected contributions from other participants in a CONVERSATION. In this paradigm the principal problem for comprehension becomes the recognition of the speaker's intention. The hearer must determine what the goals of the utterance could be. These goals are often unclear, but because the speaker and the hearer are attempting to communicate with each other, the speaker presumably has constructed the utterance in such a way that, given their common knowledge, the hearer will be able to interpret it unambiguously. Researchers in pragmatics hope that this fact will constrain the search for correct interpretations.

The major applications of natural language processing so far have been in programs that allow a user to request information from a data base and in machine translation, generally of scientific or technical documents. These efforts have had moderate, but only moderate, success.

Future prospects. The prospects for the success of artificial intelligence have been hotly debated. Some critics of AI argue that the achievements so far have been meager because intelligent thought is much more than can be modeled by formal computation. They argue that AI will never have anything to say about such human capabilities as creativity and, indeed, ordinary common sense. Defenders of AI reply that if the achievements of AI have been meager it is because the field is young and that research in AI reveals more productive lines of inquiry than dead ends. To the extent that AI does succeed, there is still the question of whether it tells us anything specific about *human* intelligence. It may be that the intelligent computer would be to the human mind as the airplane is to the bird. Against this, many defenders of AI argue that it will reveal general principles of intelligent behavior, independent of the particular embodiment of that intelligence, and that these principles will delimit the possibilities for the mechanisms of human intelligence. Finally, there has been much debate about the social consequences of having intelligent computers. Some believe that they would be no more than tools in the service of humanity, no different in kind from the other tools developed by technology over the centuries. Others feel there is a real danger of losing control of the tools.

Bibliography. Dana H. Ballard and Christopher M. Brown, *Computer Vision*, Englewood Cliffs, N.J., 1982; Margaret A. Boden, *Artificial Intelligence and Natural Man*, New York, 1977; Ronald J. Brachman and Hector J. Levesque, eds., *Readings in Knowledge Representation*, Los Altos, Calif., 1985; Eugene Charniak and Drew McDermott, *Introduction to Artificial Intelligence*, Reading, Mass., 1985; John J. Craig, *Introduction to Robotics: Mechanics and Control*, Reading, Mass., 1986; Barbara Grosz, Karen Sparck-Jones, and Bonnie Lynn Webber, *Readings in Natural Language Processing*, Los Altos, Calif., 1986; Frederick Hayes-Roth, Donald A. Waterman, and Douglas B. Lenat, eds., *Building Expert Systems*, Reading, Mass., 1983; Wendy G. Lehnert and Martin H. Ringle, eds., *Strategies for Natural Language Processing*, Hillsdale, N.J., 1982; Nils Nilsson, *Principles of Artificial Intelligence*, Palo Alto, Calif., 1980.

JERRY R. HOBBS

ARTIST AND SOCIETY

The antithesis of artist and society is a commonplace in discussions of ART. A widespread romantic vision sees artists as creative individualists who, as they produce works of art, are in perpetual conflict with a constraining and repressive society (*see* ROMANTICISM). It is perhaps more realistic to see artists and art works simply as one aspect of the elaborate networks of cooperative activity which any society consists of and in which artists and their work are embedded.

A work of art requires the coordination of a number of activities. In such fully developed arts as contemporary literature, music, or the visual arts, the list of relevant activities is very long. Someone must have a conception of what the work should or could be. Someone must have created the conventional forms and practices used to make the work and the artistic tradition against which it will make sense. Someone must provide the materials and tools to execute that conception. Then someone must actually make the object or perform the work. Someone must provide the space in which all this will take place. Someone must provide some form of financing so that materials and tools will be available and so that the people who do the work will have the time to do it. Someone must distribute the work so that an audience can experience it, and someone must preserve it so that people not immediately present can experience it at other times. People must then experience the work. Critics must discuss and evaluate it, and aestheticians must produce the arguments underlying their critical principles. *See* AESTHETICS.

These activities can be done in a variety of ways, simple or complex, elaborated or truncated. The work can exist even if they are not all done, but then it will be different from what it would have been had all these activities occurred. The activities can be divided among a large or small number of people. We can imagine a limiting case in which one person would do everything, including experiencing the work, but then we would not be talking about art as a living social institution but as some sort of private activity. More realistically, the necessary work is usually divided among a number (sometimes a large number) of people, often organized into named, specialized occupations routinely responsible for particular portions of it. The combined efforts of these specialists produce the art work.

To be specific, a HOLLYWOOD film may be conceived by a writer, director, producer, or other studio executive. Actors, camera operators, editors, designers, composers, musicians, electricians, and a host of other highly specialized craftsworkers execute the conception, using film, cameras, lights, and other equipment on sound stages or at real-life locations (each creating special problems handled by still other specialized occupations), all of this financed with money raised by financial specialists. The films are distributed through organized networks of theaters to be seen by audiences recruited by ADVERTISING campaigns, the opinions of critics, and the informal circulation of opinion in existing social networks ("word of mouth").

Even art forms that appear on the surface to be

Figure 1. *(Artist and Society)* Robert Rauschenberg watching the printers moving one of the lithographic stones for the Stoned Moon project, Gemini workshop, 1969. Photograph by Malcolm Lubliner. Courtesy of Gemini G.E.L., Los Angeles.

Figure 2. *(Artist and Society)* H. Ramberg and P. S. Martini, *The Exhibition of the Royal Academy, 1787.* Reproduced by courtesy of the Trustees of The British Museum.

Figure 3. *(Artist and Society)* Interior view of Solomon R. Guggenheim Museum, New York. Photograph by Robert E. Mates. Collection, Solomon R. Guggenheim Museum, New York.

done by one person involve similar networks of cooperative activity carried out by specialists. Poetry requires the work of editors, publishers, printers, critics, bookstore employees, and readers. Painting requires the work of makers of paints and canvasses, curators and critics, museum guards, art historians, art dealers, collectors (sometimes patrons), and viewers. The network of social relations embodied in the cooperative activities of all these people can be called an *art world*. Art worlds, themselves small societies, are linked through the other social relationships of their members to other institutions. This is the chief sense in which art is a part of society rather than standing in opposition to it.

Since so many specialists contribute to the art work, which of them is the artist? Every society in which art exists as a specialized activity has some method, usually employed by specialists, for choosing who is to receive that honorific title. This involves defining some of the specialized activities that go into

an art work as requiring a special gift that only a rare few have, and defining the people who have it as artists. The people who do other work, thought to require only ordinary abilities, are defined as support personnel. Different media and forms in different societies make the choices differently. Nothing in the nature of any medium makes any particular choice more reasonable than any other. In contemporary Western music, for instance, the symphonic classical tradition defines composition and performance as separate artistic activities requiring different artistic gifts. Rock music defines the two as inseparable, and jazz ignores formal composition in favor of improvised performance (*see* MUSIC COMPOSITION AND IMPROVISATION). Who the artist is is decided by convention, custom, and tradition, as those are invoked in specific situations characterized by differential distributions of cultural, economic, and political resources.

The resulting art work shows the marks of the

organizations in which this cooperative activity takes place. Every *cooperative link*, where some of the work is done by someone else, serves both as an opportunity for artists to devote more of their time and resources to what they regard as key artistic tasks, and as a constraint, since the way these specialized professionals are accustomed to do things may not be the way the artist wants them done. A composer may want a passage played in a way that violates the craft standards of players; a painter may want a MUSEUM to display a work that is too large, too sexually explicit, or in some other way outside the limits museums ordinarily observe in choosing works for display. If the people defined as artists do not accept the customary limits imposed in these cooperative links, they must recruit or train new people and organizations who will do it in some other way, or they must do it themselves. Since artists who divert time or other resources to such support work produce less art work, most artists will prefer to accept the constraints of cooperation in return for its advantages. The opportunities for cooperation on what might be called art-world terms thus act as a conservative force, influencing artists to produce conventional work.

The editors and publishers who helped produce the classic novels of Charles Dickens, George Eliot, William Makepeace Thackeray, and Thomas Hardy, for instance, were in a position to (and often did) suggest or require that authors produce works in a particular style, sometimes influencing the smallest details of the novels we attribute to those writers. Art patrons like Pope Urban VIII played a direct role in the DESIGN and ICONOGRAPHY of the works of such artists as Giovanni Bernini. Specialized occupations develop special professional interest, and most art forms embody chronic conflicts between those groups over control of the work's final form, appropriate aesthetic standards, and patterns of deference and hierarchy.

Many art forms develop conventional organizational solutions to these problems, often reflected in such mundane documents as a union contract, but in others the issues remain undecided, theoretically if not practically. The Hollywood film is a classic example: while ultimate control (the right to the "final cut" of the film, for instance) is usually exercised by the banks and other investors involved, theoreticians cannot agree about whether film is primarily a director's, an actor's, or a writer's medium. Such occupational groups as editors argue, in addition, that the ultimate shape of the film results from *their* work.

Art worlds may as a result be conservative, but that does not mean that innovation and creativity are stifled. On the contrary, though patterns of cooperation constrain much of what goes into an art work, they also increase the available resources, allowing artists to do things they could not do themselves (e.g., composers can write music they cannot themselves play). In addition, artists can (and often do) decide to pay the price of doing it themselves, whenever they think the constraints imposed by the involvement of others unduly limit their aesthetic options. Photographers who wish to make prints on platinum paper, which the manufacturers of photographic materials no longer make, can produce it themselves. The process is difficult, expensive, and time-consuming, and many photographers prefer to do without the added artistic resources rather than make their own paper.

The resources an art world provides for artists come in connected packages, so that rejecting any of them may lead to an enormous amount of extra work. Suppose a composer rejects the system of twelve equidistant tones conventional in Western music, as the twentieth-century U.S. composer Harry Partch did in favor of a system of forty-two tones. Forty-two-tone scores cannot be played on conventional instruments, and what can be played on the appropriate instruments cannot be conveniently written in the conventional notation. As a result, a composer with such a conception must invent and build new instruments and create a new notational system, as Partch did. But then conventionally trained musicians cannot read the resulting scores or play the new instruments, so such a composer must recruit and train instrumentalists whenever the music is to be played (*see* MUSIC THEORIES—NOTATIONS AND LITERACY). Partch's example shows that the existence of the networks of cooperation characteristic of art worlds does not make innovation impossible, but at the same time the cost of innovation is so high that few people can or will make the extensive investment required.

Figure 4. (*Artist and Society*)   U.S. jazz musicians. The Bettmann Archive, Inc.

Figure 5. *(Artist and Society)* Filming on the set of *Blue Thunder,* 1983. National Film Archive, London/ Columbia Pictures.

Artists often view audiences as troublesome and extraneous participants, but audiences play an important role in the cooperative networks in which art is made. The art of contemporary societies is seen and heard by a multitude of audience members. Art works come into existence anew each time someone experiences them. The character of the art work thus created results not only from the work itself as a physical and conceptual object but also from the way audience members interpret it. What members know how to respond to sets the limits for what they can make of an art work.

Italian painters of the RENAISSANCE, for instance, routinely used iconographic references whose effect depended on viewers having a detailed knowledge of biblical events now available only to people who have studied art history. The typical Renaissance viewer knew from the attitude of the Virgin in a painting what stage of the Annunciation was being portrayed. The painters expected many of their patrons to know how to interpret the arcane geometric jokes they embedded in their paintings. Contemporary ballet relies for some of its effects on audiences recognizing duets as abstract versions of a familiar boy-meets-girl story, and music requires listeners to recognize the conventional tones, scales, harmonies, and cadences through which it achieves its effects. In all these instances, the audience's contribution is as necessary as the contributions of the professionals who collaborate to produce the art work.

Art results, then, from the activities of highly organized art worlds, themselves part of the larger network of organized activities that makes up society. Artists are those people, out of everyone involved in the production of art, who have been so defined by people empowered to make the definition.

Bibliography. Michael Baxandall, *Painting and Experience in Fifteenth Century Italy,* Oxford, 1972; Howard S. Becker, *Art Worlds,* Berkeley, Calif., 1982; Aljean Harmetz, *The Making of the Wizard of Oz,* New York, 1977; Francis Haskell, *Patrons and Painters: A Study in the Relations between Italian Art and Society in the Age of the Baroque,* 2d ed., rev. and enl., New Haven, Conn., 1980; Raymonde Moulin, *Le marché de la peinture en France,* Paris, 1967; Harry Partch, *Genesis of a Music,* 2d ed., enl., New York, 1974; J. A. Sutherland, *Victorian Novelists and Publishers,* Chicago, 1976.

HOWARD S. BECKER

ASIA, TWENTIETH CENTURY

Communication patterns and communications institutions in twentieth-century Asia have been shaped by three fundamental processes: (1) Western domination, (2) the success and consequences of modernization by Japan, and (3) national integration and development, or nation building.

Asia, as defined here, encompasses the territory from Iran to Japan, excluding the USSR. This territory is the world's largest continent and holds over three-fifths of its population. The majority of Asia's peoples live in rural, predominantly agricultural villages; only about 15 percent live in the fast-growing cities, yet the total Asian urban population is huge. Some research has suggested that one of the primary causes of urbanization and modernization is the growth and use of modern mass media.

The geographical boundaries of modern Asian states tend to conform to traditional and cultural boundaries that in most cases are more than a thousand years old. The predominant cultural traditions affecting the content and form of communications remain the Hindu-Buddhist tradition originating in India, the Confucian-Taoist from China, and the Islamic from Arabia. They should be recognized as major factors in the process of conflict and/or accommodation between tradition and modernization in Asian developments in this century, particularly in the postindependence period. In addition, there are many ethnic minorities, languages, religious sects, and cults mostly indigenous to the region but more recently also of external origin. The other main sources of traditional communication have been the various political systems, from the nomadic empire of the Mongols to the centralized bureaucracies of China, Japan, Vietnam, and Korea to the decentralized kingdoms of India, Tibet, and most of Southeast Asia. See EAST ASIA, ANCIENT; SOUTH ASIA, ANCIENT.

Asian communication must also be considered at three levels: within societies (usually equivalent to the modern state), within the regions (a function of both commercial and religious interests as well as political movements), and between Asia and the West (primarily commercial).

Western Dominance

The dominance of Asia by European powers, in which the United States joined in the mid-nineteenth century, was at first motivated primarily by a desire to reach India for luxury commodities and spices and to circumvent Muslim control of land routes to India, across areas bordering the eastern Mediterranean. Aided by superior military organizations and weapons, the development of rapid transportation (steamship), communications (telegraph wires, submarine cables), and the practice of a skillful "divide and rule" policy, Western powers achieved control of most of Asia (except for Japan, Thailand, and parts of China) by the beginning of World War I (see COLONIZATION). That control was not only military, economic, and political, but also cultural, especially in urban areas. Western education and modern mass media (newspapers, radio, movies) were introduced in the cities. Films were first imported from Europe and the United States and later were produced locally. They continue to be the most popular form of entertainment in all of Asia, especially in India. Pictures in motion were nothing new to Asian audiences, who were familiar with various types of shadow plays in their traditional THEATER. Combinations of the heroic, the fantastic, the tragic, and the romantic, as well as goodness and evil in modern movie themes, were hardly different from themes of Indian and Chinese classics. See MUSICAL, FILM—BOMBAY GENRE; MOTION PICTURES; MYTHOLOGICAL FILM, ASIAN; PHALKE, DHUNDIRAJ GOVIND; PUPPETRY.

Modernization Strategy

The adoption by Asian nationalists of modernization as a strategy for national independence, particularly before World War I, was localized and sporadic. Asians who attended colonial schools began to recognize the need for an objective look at the strength of the "white masters"—their machines, their institutions, and their ideas—while still refusing to accept the cultural superiority of Europeans. This painful recognition of European superiority in military, transportation, and telecommunications technologies as well as economic and political organizations created among sensitive Asian intellectuals a deep feeling of humiliation. This feeling led to a search for a way to "use the master's stick to beat the master's back" and a model to follow. The solution was modernization, and the model was Japan.

In 1858 Japan was forced by American warships to open its doors to trade with the United States and Europe (see TOKUGAWA ERA: SECLUSION POLICY). From these contacts with the West, Japan learned the art and weapons of modern warfare, the economic and political systems, and the communications technologies. The beginning of the Meiji Restoration (1868) marked the beginning of Japan's path to modernization. Sakuma Shōzan (1811–1864), a samurai (feudal warrior) and counselor to a powerful lord, summed up the Japanese modernization strategy in a simple slogan: "Eastern ethics, Western science." He recommended the adoption of techniques of modern mass education and improved means of communications from the West. "Eastern ethics, Western science" has become the strategy of modernization for independence and the subject of debates in all Asian countries. The debate continues and is made even more relevant with China's "four modernizations" (agriculture, industry, science, defense) in the 1980s and the Chinese fear of capitalist "cultural pollution."

The Japanese success at modernization was demonstrated dramatically to a dispirited Asia in the early years of the twentieth century by the 1904–1905 victory of the Japanese navy over Russia (considered then a European power). Nationalists from Asia flocked to Tokyo to learn Japanese "secrets." Obsessed by the evils of colonialism, they forgot that it was the same modernized Japan that had attacked China in 1894–1895. Soon the imperialist policies of westernized Japan, which joined the European powers for the conquest and dismemberment of Asia, awakened Asian patriots to a new reality: a successful imitation of Western science and technology could also lead to the adoption of the then-prevailing European political IDEOLOGY—imperialism. Asian nationalists who wanted to understand the Japanese "betrayal" and the root causes of imperialism in general left Japan and went to the metropolitan capitals of Europe and the United States to learn firsthand about imperialism and the lives of the colonizers in their homelands. They studied and communicated with those who shared their opposition to colonialism, including fellow nationals from Asia and Africa as well as "progressive" citizens of the imperialist powers.

With the outbreak of World War I, the conflicts among Western powers over spheres of influence in Asia and Africa were exposed (see AFRICA, TWENTIETH CENTURY). In addition, many of the colonies were forced to contribute soldiers and laborers to the war effort in Europe. India alone provided eight hundred thousand soldiers and over four hundred thousand laborers for the western front and the Mesopotamian campaign. Nearly two hundred thousand Chinese and more than one hundred thousand Indo-Chinese (mostly Vietnamese) served in labor battalions behind the French lines. Asians living and working in the metropolises watched the spectacle of Europeans slaughtering one another. Asian peasants drafted for wartime service witnessed the decadence of European societies: poverty, unemployment, crime, and prostitution. Whatever respect, admiration, or fear they had had for the colonial masters was drained away.

Wartime demands for soldiers and laborers had other consequences for the colonials in addition to exposure to the problems in Europe. Many Europeans who were officials in the colonial governments or businesses were recalled to Europe at the outbreak of World War I, and their positions had to be filled by the local inhabitants. For the first time colonial subjects were eligible for jobs with authority and responsibility. They became more involved in economic activities and could see how dependent Europeans were on the colonies for raw materials and labor to meet production, manufacturing, and other war-related needs in Europe. The colonies were meeting these needs so successfully that there began to be talk of postwar economic development by which the colonies' economic assets could be further exploited in order to speed up recovery in Europe.

A growing anticolonial consciousness was spreading, not only because of contacts with the social, political, and economic realities of wartime Europe, but also because of ideological positions taken by two Western powers on the periphery of the conflict. In the United States, President Woodrow Wilson's Fourteen Points plan for peace and especially the principle of national self-determination (the fifth of the Fourteen Points) endeared the United States to the Asian nationalists. In Russia the 1917 victory of the Bolsheviks, V. I. Lenin's thesis that imperialism is a stage of capitalism, and the official anti-imperialist policy of the new USSR attracted Asian nationalists to Moscow. Directed by Lenin and the Third International, an Anti-Imperialist League was founded in 1924, and Communist parties were formed in several Asian countries during the 1920s. Under the league's sponsorship, the Association of Oppressed Peoples was organized, which in turn organized the Congress of Oppressed Nationalities in Belgium in 1927. Future Communist leaders like Ho Chi Minh of Vietnam and Socialist-oriented nationalists like Jawaharlal Nehru of India met at this congress to discuss strategies of modernization and tactics for anticolonial agitation.

The new international solidarity was, however, short-lived because of the subordination of the nationalist line to Soviet policies and interests. By 1935 the entire nationalist line had been discarded in favor of the "united front against fascism," which allied Soviet policies with those of non-Fascist European powers. The Japanese annexed Manchuria in 1935, and by 1938 Japan had joined the Fascist Axis with Nazi Germany and Italy. The stage was set for World War II.

World War II ended with the defeat of Japan, the weakening of Europe, and the emergence of the United States as a leading power in competition with the USSR. That competition, also known as the cold war, created both opportunities and dangers for the independence movements of Asian countries and sowed the seeds of internal ideological divisions and civil war in some, such as Korea and Vietnam.

Independence movements in Asia followed two different forms—violent and nonviolent—depending mostly on the reactions of the specific colonial power. MOHANDAS GANDHI led India to independence through a successful nonviolent struggle against Great Britain.

Vietnam, under the direction of Ho Chi Minh and the Vietnam Communist party, defeated the French in 1954 after an eight-year war. After battling the Japanese during World War II and the rival Kuo Min Tang party at home, Mao Zedong brought his Communist party into power in China in 1949. In both China and Vietnam, the "people's armies" were organized first as armed PROPAGANDA units, stressing communication and politics as basic military achievements. Both violent and nonviolent independence movements in Asia were sustained by a new pattern of communication based on the political education of the masses (the peasantry) and the extension and establishment of international and regional communication. While exploiting all available Western media (posters, pamphlets, newspapers, radio, films), Gandhi, Mao Zedong, and Ho Chi Minh did not ignore the traditional forms of communication (religious, political, social, and ethnic groups), using popular themes, languages, and symbols to explain unfamiliar situations, emphasizing all the time the importance of simplicity, personal example, collective morality, sacrifices, and optimism. But the most important development within independence movements was the participation of women in the national struggle. The decisive commitment of women, who represent over half the population of Asia, to community and national issues has transformed communication patterns. Also important were the rising political consciousness and demands for autonomy by national minorities. *See also* NEWSPAPER: TRENDS; PAMPHLET; POSTER; RADIO.

Modernization for Nation Building

By the end of the 1950s all Asian countries except Hong Kong (to be returned to the People's Republic of China in 1997) and Macao had regained their independence. Before independence, modernization was essentially a formula to get rid of colonialism; after independence, modernization became the framework for nation building. Such a task required both the mobilization of national resources and the existence of a favorable international and regional environment. Once independent, Asian countries joined the United Nations and organized new regional arrangements and international structures with other Third World nations. In 1955 at Bandung (Indonesia), an Asian-African conference met to lay the foundations for the Non-Aligned Movement, formed in 1961. The Association of Southeast Asian Nations (ASEAN) is the most recent regional organization. *See also* INTERNATIONAL ORGANIZATIONS.

Discussions at the United Nations and the Non-Aligned Movement meetings generally concentrated on the maintenance of world peace, the establishment of a New International Economic Order, and a New World Communication and Information Order (*see* NEW INTERNATIONAL INFORMATION ORDER). The aim of a conference on communication policies in Asia and Oceania, sponsored by the United Nations Educational, Scientific and Cultural Organization (UNESCO) in 1979, was "to provide an opportunity for the exchange of experience of communication systems in relation to economic and social development, and to consider the establishment of administrative, technical, research and training infrastructures on the national and regional levels, for the formulation, implementation and evaluation of communication policies." The agenda of the conference demonstrated the following major concerns and expectations of the communication policymakers of Asia: the problem of imbalance in the field of information and the means by which the communication gap between the north and the south and between the industrialized and the developing countries could be reduced; international cooperation among countries of Asia and Oceania to increase information flow and develop mutual understanding; the role of the media in an integrated approach toward development, especially in education, science, and culture; communication as a means of affirming and preserving cultural identity and as an instrument for national integration; public participation in communication; traditional media and transfer of technology; development of endogenous production and distribution capabilities; media structures; social responsibilities of media; responsibilities and protection of communication professionals; nature, place, and composition of the most appropriate structures for the formulation of communication policies; planning of communication development; data collection, research, and evaluation; and problems of professional communication training.

Outlook

If the end of colonialism in Asia was marked by the French defeat at Dien Bien Phu in 1954, then the futility of outside intervention by proxy was demonstrated by the collapse of the U.S.-supported regime in South Vietnam in 1975, the successful fundamentalist REVOLUTION in Iran in 1979, and the Soviet quagmire in Afghanistan beginning the same year. Regional interventions such as the Indo-Pakistan wars of 1948 and 1965, the India-China war of 1962, the Chinese attack against Vietnam in 1979, and the Vietnamese invasion of Kampuchea beginning in 1978 were failures. All of these events demonstrated that problems in Asia can no longer be solved by military means.

In an environment of international peace and regional cooperation, and as demonstrated by the economic progress and technological advances in China,

India, and especially among members of ASEAN, Asian countries—individually and collectively—can find the best paths and methods for modernization, combining "Eastern ethics and Western science."

See also DEVELOPMENT COMMUNICATION; MARX-IST THEORIES OF COMMUNICATION—THIRD WORLD APPROACHES; POLITICAL COMMUNICATION—IMPACT OF NEW MEDIA.

Bibliography. Raymond F. Betts, *Uncertain Dimensions: Western Overseas Empires in the Twentieth-Century,* Minneapolis, Minn., 1985; John A. Lent, ed., *Newspapers in Asia: Contemporary Trends and Problems,* Hong Kong, 1982; Lin Yut'ang, ed., *The Wisdom of India,* New York, 1942; J. Saxon Mills, *The Press and Communications of the Empire,* London, 1924; Joseph Needham, *Science and Civilization in China,* Vol. 1, New York and Cambridge, 1954; Robert T. Oliver, *Communication and Culture in Ancient India and China,* Syracuse, N.Y., 1971; K. M. Panikkar, *Asia and Western Dominance,* London, 1953; Carlos Pena Romulo, *The Meaning of Bandung,* Chapel Hill, N.C., 1956; Donald Eugene Smith, *South Asian Politics and Religion,* Princeton, N.J., 1966; Tran Van Dinh, *Independence, Liberation, Revolution: An Approach to the Understanding of the Third World,* Norwood, N.J., 1986; UNESCO, *Intergovernmental Conference on Communication Policies in Asia and Oceania* (Kuala Lumpur, Malaysia, Feb. 5–14, 1979, Final Report), Paris, 1979.

TRAN VAN DINH

AŚOKA (d. 232 B.C.E.)

Indian emperor. For most of his thirty-seven-year rule over the bulk of present-day India, Pakistan, and Afghanistan, Aśoka kept his vast empire together through a highly developed administrative system and an active advocacy of *Dhamma,* the Buddhist concept of virtuous conduct. From his capital city of Pataliputra (modern Patna), he presented his spiritual experiences and religious faith in the form of edicts to his diverse peoples—Indians, Greeks, Iranians, Afghans—through a large number of clearly dated inscriptions on rocks, pillars, and caves spread throughout his dominions. Inscriptions at nearly forty places have been found, most of them in Brahmi, from which most of modern India's scripts have been derived.

One major rock edict refers to the emperor's conquest of Kalinga (modern Orissa) and the killing of hundreds of thousands of people, and to Aśoka's consequent remorse and increasing devotion to the Buddhist creed of nonviolence:

When an independent country is conquered, the slaughter, death and deportation of the people is grievous to the Beloved of the Gods [Aśoka] and weighs on his mind. . . . The Beloved of the Gods considers victory by *Dhamma* to be the foremost victory. . . . This inscription

of *Dhamma* has been engraved so that any sons or grandsons that I may have should not think of gaining new conquests.

Some of Aśoka's edicts preach the Buddhist principles of good conduct; others instruct the officials of the state to behave in prescribed ways of righteousness. The cave inscriptions are behests to the monks. All were used as a durable means of conveying the king's thoughts, beliefs, and instructions to a vast empire and its far-flung administration. His thinking was to be engraved "wherever there are stone pillars or stone slabs so that it may last long." One of the major edicts refers to the conversion to Buddhism of several leaders from Syria, Egypt, Macedonia, and elsewhere by missionaries sent out by Aśoka. Aśoka's awareness of the importance of communication expressed itself further in the well-planned roads he laid out across his empire, with banyan trees planted alongside "which will give shade to men and beasts . . . and I have had wells dug and rest-houses built. . . . I have done many things that my people might conform to *Dhamma.*"

Some scholars have challenged the conventional view of Aśoka's benevolence, asserting that his conversion to Buddhism was not a sudden step occasioned by the Kalinga war but a gradual movement toward a subtle and deliberate policy of promoting central control over a vast and highly centralized empire. However, Aśoka is regarded, particularly in Buddhist countries, as a model ruler for his tolerance and his nonviolence. Modern India invoked his revered image when it adopted as its national emblem the four back-to-back lions of the Sarnath pillar.

Bibliography. D. R. Bhandarkar, *Aśoka,* 4th ed., Calcutta, 1925, reprint 1969; S. Bhattacharya, *Select Aśokan Epigraphs,* 2d ed., Calcutta, 1960; Romila Thapar, *Aśoka and the Decline of the Mauryas,* London, 1961.

CHIDANANDA DAS GUPTA

ATTENTION. *See* CHILDREN; COGNITIVE CONSISTENCY THEORIES.

ATTITUDES

The concept of attitude is frequently used in efforts to explain and/or predict human behavior. It is generally defined as a mental predisposition toward persons (including oneself), objects, and events that guides or influences one's behavior toward those objects. The concept has played a central role in social psychology, in the history of communications research (*see* COMMUNICATIONS RESEARCH: ORIGINS AND DEVELOPMENT), and is a factor in many forms of social communication such as EDUCATION, PERSUASION, and INTERPERSONAL COMMUNICATION.

Sometimes communication tactics are aimed specifically at creating, accounting for, or changing attitudes—as when employers attempt to improve employee job satisfaction, politicians try to sway PUBLIC OPINION, or advertisers seek to create a brand image (see ADVERTISING). Attitudes are seen as a means to change people's behavior. Thus, for example, antismoking campaigns focus on the consequences of smoking, consumer promotions emphasize product attributes, and fund-raising drives appeal to moral and social beliefs in order to get people to act in desired ways.

A very large body of literature is devoted to the study and analysis of attitudes, much of it coming from the disciplines of psychology, social psychology, and MASS COMMUNICATIONS RESEARCH. In the 1930s Gordon W. Allport published an influential review of the already large number of studies, and his definition of attitude as "a mental or neural state of readiness, organized through experience, exerting a directive or dynamic influence on the individual's response to all objects and situations with which it is related" became widely though not unanimously accepted. In the 1950s the research team led by CARL HOVLAND at Yale University conducted a series of experiments investigating different factors influencing processes of attitude formation and change, and its findings influenced a generation or more of social psychologists and communication researchers.

Two directions characterize contemporary attitude research. Most studies concentrate on the mediating psychological *processes* occurring between communication cues (e.g., messages) and attitude change. The goal of this research is to discover which psychological reactions govern ultimate attitudinal responses to particular communication cues. Attitude in these studies typically has been construed as a unidimensional *affective* or *evaluative* outcome of information processing. Rather than examining the nature of effects of attitudes per se, studies in this tradition stress the conditions under which attitudes arise or change.

The second stream of research is *structural*. Inquiry here looks at the content and form of attitudinal responses. In contrast to process theories, structural theories place more emphasis on the *formation* of attitudes and their cognitive representation and on the influence that attitudes have in decision making and on behavior. Attitude in this tradition has been modeled as both unidimensional and multidimensional constructs.

Process Theories

Two major approaches have emerged under this general framework. One argues that attitude change is a consequence of people's superficial processing of external (peripheral) cues; the other maintains that people process information deeply, paying close attention to everything from message claims and structure to an evaluation of their goals in relation to the attitude object. The former is called the *peripheral* route to attitude change, and the latter the *central* route.

Peripheral routes. Research into the external conditions (e.g., rewards and punishments) producing attitude change has a long tradition and has taken many directions. One particularly influential framework for investigating the antecedents of attitude change is HAROLD D. LASSWELL's categorization of contextual forces into *source, message, media* (channel), and *receiver* factors. Whereas early research tended to be stimulus-centered (focusing on the design of message content, message structure, media, and other input variables), research since at least the early 1980s has been more response-centered.

An important approach in this regard is the heuristic model of persuasion. In this model people are assumed to process certain structural characteristics of communications in order to ascertain their validity or meaningfulness. Structural characteristics refer to particular features of the communicator (e.g., attractiveness), the message (e.g., use of promises versus threats), the media (e.g., visual versus verbal modes), and/or the receiver (e.g., self-esteem). The heuristic model hypothesizes that exposure to a communication leads to an interpretation of it in terms of *decision rules* (abstract, stored cognitive relations that often have policy or evaluative overtones). A cue such as "Many positive arguments," for example, might be interpreted as activating a decision rule such as "The more of a good thing, the better." An attractive spokesperson might engender the implicit response "Likable people tend to tell the truth," and a person about to begin reading a long article might be influenced in his or her prejudgments by a "Length implies importance" rule.

The heuristic model asserts that such rule-based responses are more or less automatic and involve only a surface assessment of any communication. Rather than deeply processing the semantic content and implications of a message, say, people are assumed to make a relatively superficial assessment of the structural cues surrounding the message. This is apt to occur especially when a receiver lacks the ability or motivation to process a message. In sum, under the heuristic model simple cognitive rules are assumed to mediate the impact of communications on attitude change.

A number of other theories also presume information processing of peripheral communication cues but, unlike the heuristic and similar models, provide no formal explanation of cognitive processes per se. Rather, attitude change is represented as a function of attributions or inferences one makes about one's own behavior or psychological state, the behavior or psychological state of another person, and/or the context of the communication.

Self-perception theory hypothesizes that people form their attitudes on the basis of an awareness of how they performed in the past and an assessment of why they performed that way. For example, as illustrated by the "foot-in-the-door" tactic, people are more likely to comply with a costly request after they have acquiesced to a significantly less costly request than if they had been asked to comply with the costly request only. The rationale is that the person asked to comply with a costly request after complying with a less costly one infers that, because he or she complied with the less costly request, he or she must have had a personal reason for doing so (e.g., "I am the type of person who does this sort of thing"). Therefore, when the person is asked to comply with a more costly request, the self-perception attitude so formed leads to a greater chance of compliance with the more costly request. The person confronted only with the costly request lacks the same internal information and therefore sees himself or herself as a relatively less compliant individual.

Still another peripheral processing model of attitude change is attribution theory. In one version of the theory people are hypothesized to make inferences about the cause of a communicator's behavior. The causes might be personal characteristics of the source and/or forces in the situation. In either case a message recipient is believed to compare the actual position taken by the source of a persuasive communication with the position inferred from the source's personal characteristics and/or the situation. When the inferred position conforms to the actual one, a discounting of the believability of the message position results because, with many possible causes of the actual position, attribution to any particular one is less likely, thus inhibiting attitude change. On the other hand, when the actual position goes *against* the one inferred from source characteristics or the situation, an augmentation of the believability of a message advocacy ensues because the position was taken (from the receiver's point of view) in the face of counteracting personal and/or situational determinants. Hence attitude change should be enhanced.

Attribution theory can also be applied to the nature of a message's advocacy and the content of its delivery. To the extent that a particular advocacy achieves consensus across communicators, consistency over time and media, and distinctiveness in its content, form, and relevance to an audience, it will be perceived as valid and attitude change will occur.

Central routes. Attitude change resulting from peripheral cues does not entail extensive information processing of these cues and does not involve much thought about message content or structure. People,

of course, do respond deeply and complexly to messages: they concentrate attention on claims made in messages; they attempt to comprehend arguments; they organize, store, and retrieve information in coherent ways; and they evaluate data in relation to their needs, decisions, and goals. This more complete processing of communications is largely cognitive and has been termed the central route to attitude change.

The most thoroughly researched framework in the central-route tradition is known as the *cognitive response* approach. Here it is assumed that people react to information (e.g., a persuasive communication) with unique, self-generated thoughts in an effort to relate the information to their existing knowledge and attitudes. Any communication is believed to stimulate one or more of three broad cognitive responses: favorable thoughts, unfavorable thoughts, or irrelevant thoughts with respect to an actual or anticipated message. Whether a person agrees or disagrees with a message, or whether or not it changes the person's attitude, is hypothesized to depend on the net polarity of all thoughts. If favorable thoughts outweigh negative ones a person will change or form an attitude in agreement with the message advocacy; otherwise no attitude change will occur. In sum, cognitive responses mediate the effect of information on attitudes.

In addition to counterargumentation and support argumentation (i.e., mentally upholding, corroborating, or backing a point made in a message with additional favorable arguments) a receiver might react to a spokesperson with self-generated elaborations of disparagements or negative evaluations (i.e., source derogations) or, alternatively, positive evaluations and respect (i.e., source bolsterings). On occasion cognitive responses relate to neither the message nor the source. Rather, they entail tangential or random thoughts or feelings stimulated by the communication that are loosely associated with a person's deeper needs and values, recent exigencies, or situational distractions. These "irrelevant" responses interfere with the processing of a message or, alternatively, lead to greater agreement or disagreement with a message depending on the polarity and strength of the particular mental associations.

Cognitive response analyses provide insights into the effects of peripheral cues and help to resolve ambiguities not handled well by classic approaches such as the source-message-media-receiver framework or the attention-comprehension-acceptance model of Hovland and his colleagues. For example, contrary to early thinking, it has been found that sources with low credibility sometimes induce more attitude change than sources with high credibility. A cognitive response interpretation helps account for this finding: high ego involvement or considerable prior knowledge about an issue tends to lead to increased attention to the message and extensive cognitive response to the topic at hand (because it is more personally relevant). However, when involvement is low or knowledge is lacking, a person is relatively more vulnerable to the augmenting or weakening effects of such peripheral cues as source credibility. Under these latter conditions a person exposed to a proattitudinal communication delivered by a source *high* in credibility will think *less* about the message than one exposed to a source low in credibility. Therefore, high source credibility will lead to fewer support arguments and counterarguments than low source credibility. Because receivers will initially respond favorably to the message (because it is proattitudinal to begin with), more support arguments than counterarguments are expected to occur. Thus persons exposed to proattitudinal messages and low-credibility sources will be expected to develop more positive attitudes than those exposed to high-credibility sources. Note that the opposite is predicted for exposure to counterattitudinal messages: high credibility leads to greater attitude change than low credibility, the classic prediction. Again, both outcomes are expected only under conditions of low involvement or low prior knowledge.

The central route to attitude change is not limited to cognitive responses but might also involve affective or motivational factors. For instance, according to Jack Brehm's reactance theory, a restriction (or merely a threat of restriction) of a person's freedom to act, think, or feel in a way to which he or she is accustomed leads to a drive to reestablish the lost (or threatened) freedom. This might be done by counterarguing against the reasons for the restriction; evaluating more positively the focal behavior, thought, or feeling lost (or threatened); or even initiating the focal action in spite of the restriction (or threat).

Other motivational routes to attitude change can be explained by dissonance theory and impression management theory. In the former, perceived incongruities between elements comprised of thoughts, feelings, or actions lead to psychological discomfort and a drive to reduce the incongruity. This might be done by changing one's beliefs, affect, or behavior. Under impression-management theory, people present whatever attitude is needed to obtain social rewards. That is, one's own attitudes are seen as means to achieving approval from others, and attitudes are managed accordingly. *See also* COGNITIVE CONSISTENCY THEORIES.

Structural Theories

Process theories treat attitudes as undifferentiated, summary reactions toward persons, acts, or objects. A common practice is to measure attitude simply as the sum of responses to multiple SEMANTIC DIFFER-ENTIAL items (e.g., good-bad, pleasant-unpleasant, like-dislike). The *nature* of attitudes is not an issue. Instead, focus is on the antecedents of overall attitude change. Structural theories, in contrast, take the content and form of attitudes as their subject matter. Depending on the level of abstraction one assumes, attitudes can be considered as either molar or molecular representations. A *molar* attitude is one *defined* as a function of certain mental states (e.g., beliefs and evaluations) that are hypothesized to combine and aggregate according to specific rules. The mapping process between the unaggregated elements and the aggregated molar construct is nonspecific in that it does not posit a one-to-one correspondence between the elements and the molar construct. Thus, for example, the same molar attitude may be represented through different combinations of levels of the same beliefs and evaluations for any one person, and different people may achieve identical molar attitudes but react with different levels of the same beliefs and evaluations.

A *molecular* attitude is a hypothetical construct that achieves meaning through *relationships* to mental states such as beliefs and evaluations. The relationships between the molecular construct and its implied mental states are expressed through *correspondence* rules. The most common way to operationalize correspondence rules is through formative or reflective indicators (e.g., measures of beliefs and evaluations) of a latent variable (i.e., the molecular attitude) through the use of structural equation models. As with the molar attitude, the mental elements of the molecular attitude are hypothesized to combine in specific ways (e.g., additively or multiplicatively), but, unlike the molar attitude, the mapping process for the molecular attitude is specified in a one-to-one sense. For instance, any particular attitude of a person will be represented through only one combination of beliefs and evaluations at the molecular level of analysis.

Molar attitudes. Perhaps the most well-known attitude model is that of Martin Fishbein (see Figure 1), which implies that one's attitude is determined by a multiplicative integration of beliefs and evalu-

$$A_{\text{act}} = \sum_{i=1}^{n} b_i \, e_i$$

A_{act} = one's attitude toward performing a particular behavior ("attitudes toward the act")

b_i = one's belief that performance of the behavior will lead to consequence i

e_i = the evaluation of consequence i

n = the number of consequences

Figure 1. (*Attitudes*) The Fishbein model of a molar attitude.

ations of act consequences and that these information products add up to produce a singular, overall attitude.

Many researchers have attempted to discover the conditions under which attitudes and behavior are related. It has been found that attitudes and behavior relate most strongly when measures of both correspond closely as to *action*, *target* (at which the action is directed), *context* (in which the action is performed), and *time* (at which it is performed). Perhaps more important, a number of variables have been identified as moderators of the attitude-behavior relation. The relationship is enhanced when one has had direct prior experience with the attitude object or behavior, when the cognitive and affective elements of attitude are in agreement, when one holds strong confidence in one's attitude, when one is less inclined to engage in self-monitoring, and when the occurrences of extraneous, unplanned events are anticipated. Even personality variables such as need for approval have been found to moderate the relation.

Although it is possible to improve the association between attitude and behavior by considering the conditions under which both occur, one is faced with a bewildering number of minitheories explaining each contingency. Parsimony and generality are sacrificed for the proliferation of variables and theories and the pursuit of specificity.

An alternative to reliance on many contingency theories is to search for a general theory or a small number of general theories. For example, Fishbein and Icek Ajzen have proposed a general framework for explaining behavior in a wide range of contexts (see Figure 2). The Fishbein-Ajzen model has been found to explain behavior in a wide range of situations, has had significant influence on theory building in social psychology and other areas of the social sciences, and continues to receive extensive application in various applied areas such as marketing, health care, and public policy.

Nevertheless, two broad shortcomings of the Fishbein-Ajzen model limit its power as a general explanatory framework. One limitation lies in the model's internal consistency. A number of studies have challenged the hypothesized functional relations among endogenous (internal) variables in the model. For instance, intentions do not always moderate the influence of attitude on behavior, and on occasion attitude has been found directly to influence behavior. Similarly, the $\Sigma b_i e_i$ component has been found to influence intentions both directly and indirectly through A_{act}, contrary to theory. Still another anomaly concerns the possible confusion between attitudinal and normative variables. Not only has the construct validity of the normative variables been questioned, but a number of researchers have found crossover effects (often reciprocal) between A_{act} and SN, between $\Sigma b_i e_i$ and SN, and between $\Sigma (NB)_i (MC)_i$ and A_{act}.

Even the central component of the Fishbein-Ajzen model (i.e., $A_{act} = \Sigma b_i e_i$) has come under attack on the basis of theoretical and methodological arguments. For example, the purposeful-behavior conception of attitude (see Figure 3) has been shown to overcome a fundamental ambiguity in the way evaluations are represented and integrated with beliefs in the Fishbein-Ajzen model and to outperform the model empirically. Finally, potential measurement problems can be identified in the Fishbein-Ajzen model, and these will be discussed under "Measurement Issues," below.

$$B = f(I)$$
$$I = f(A_{act}, SN)$$
$$A_{act} = \sum_{i=1}^{n} b_i e_i$$
$$SN = \sum_{i=1}^{m} (NB)_i (MC)_i$$

B = focal behavior or act

I = intentions to perform the act

SN = felt subjective norm to perform act

NB = normative beliefs (i.e., expectations that specific significant others feel one should perform act)

MC = one's motivation to comply with the expectations of these significant others

m = number of significant others

f = "a function of"

Figure 2. *(Attitudes)* The Fishbein and Ajzen model for the explanation of human behavior: A person's behavior (a particular act) is a function of the person's intention to perform the act, which in turn is a function of the person's attitudes toward himself or herself performing the act and the felt subjective norm to perform the act.

$$A_{act} = \sum_{i=1}^{n} b_i P_{act/b_i}$$

A_{act} = the person's attitude toward the act

P_{act/b_i} = the subjective conditional probability that a person would perform a focal act, given that he or she believes that such a performance will lead to consequence i

Figure 3. *(Attitudes)* The purposeful-behavior conception of attitude, which overcomes certain problems with the Fishbein and Ajzen model and other formulations.

A second broad shortcoming of the Fishbein-Ajzen model is that it omits important social-psychological antecedents of behavior and is perhaps too parsimonious. At the same time, by focusing on the explanation of volitional behavior only, it fails to account for behaviors only partially under volitional control and for goal achievement. One theory that attempts to address these latter phenomena as well as behavior is the *theory of goal-directed behaviors and outcomes,* which builds on the Fishbein-Ajzen model but reformulates attitude structure and introduces new antecedents and intervening variables between attitude and goal attainment/behavior performance.

The central feature of the theory of goal-directed behaviors and outcomes is the conceptualization of attitude into three antecedents: attitudes toward succeeding, attitudes toward failing, and attitudes toward the process of trying to reach a goal or perform a behavior. Each attitudinal antecedent in turn is hypothesized to be a function of its own unique set of beliefs and evaluations of the consequences of goal attainment/behavior performance. Further, expectations of success and failure function as self-efficacy judgments (*see* SOCIAL COGNITIVE THEORY) and interact with the attitudes toward succeeding and failing, respectively, in the theory. Attitudes then influence the intention to try to reach a goal or perform a behavior. Intention is also hypothesized to be a function of social norms to strive for the goal or perform the behavior and of the frequency of having achieved the goal or performed the behavior in the past (for repeatable goals and behaviors). Next, intentions are hypothesized to initiate mental (e.g., plans) and/or physical steps toward goal attainment/behavior performance. These steps are termed *trying* in the theory and are also expected to be influenced by the frequency and recency of goal attainment/behavior performance (for repeatable goals and behaviors). Trying is then predicted to interact with actual control of the means to achieve the goal or perform the behavior to influence goal attainment/behavior performance. In addition to having greater explanatory power, the theory of goal-directed behaviors and outcomes has been tested against the Fishbein-Ajzen model and others and has outperformed them in terms of explained variance.

Molecular attitudes. The notion of molecular attitudes was first introduced in the 1980s and therefore has not received as much attention as molar and process theories of attitudes. However, molecular attitudes provide a means to perform detailed analyses of how attitudes form, what influences attitudes, and what effects attitudes have on other psychological processes and behaviors.

A molecular attitude consists of multidimensional attitudinal reactions. In the case of expectancy-value attitudes, a molecular attitude might be represented as interrelated networks of individual belief-times-evaluation products; alternatively, attitude might be conceptualized as substructures of beliefs and evaluations organized as indicators of higher-order expectancy-value latent variables. In the case of attitudes toward an act or object, attitudes most often exist as unidimensional variables. On occasion attitudes toward an act or an object might entail a molecular structure comprised of multidimensional reactions (e.g., separate but possibly associated dimensions of pleasantness, arousal, and dominance).

As an example, consider the molecular attitude one researcher discovered underlying reactions toward the act of giving blood. It was found that people's responses consisted of four distinct but interrelated expectancy-value substructures: attitudes toward immediate external physical pain (e.g., a sore arm), immediate internal sickness (e.g., nausea, dizziness), delayed costs of a means-end variety (e.g., time lost from work, reduced resistance to colds), and altruistic concerns (e.g., helping others). The first three substructures were replicated across four samples in two different cultures; the fourth was also found in two samples within one culture.

Aside from demonstrating construct validity and thus the possibility of multidimensional attitudes, what is to be gained by investigating molecular attitudes? At least four benefits can be identified. First and most generally, the basis is provided for a deeper explanation and understanding of attitude formation and the impact of attitudes on intentions, decision making, and goal attainment/behavior performance. Second, from both a pragmatic and a theoretical standpoint, the representation of molecular attitudes permits the researcher the opportunity to discover the relative effects of different attitudinal substructures on intentions, behavior, and other dependent variables. For example, given the four expectancy-value reactions noted above, the Red Cross might learn which substructure affects the decision to donate blood most strongly and thereby allocate limited promotional resources to influence the attitudinal subdimension that would be most successful in stimulating blood donations. The basic researcher might obtain a more detailed picture of the influence of attitudes and develop new hypotheses not considered before.

A third benefit, related to the second, is the framework provided for examining the antecedents of attitude in greater depth. Instead of construing the effects of communication cues and other stimuli in a global way (i.e., their effects on molar attitudes), there is a means to examine specific communication effects on deeper attitudinal responses. This could lead to research into particular mechanisms of persuasion within the context of attitude research, something lacking in the field to date. Finally, molecular attitudes allow investigation of causal or inferential relations among beliefs and evaluations. Molar attitudes, of course, obscure or confound such intricacies. But with a molecular attitudinal model one can explore the effects of a change in one belief on changes in other beliefs or the effect of a change in evaluations on beliefs, among other possibilities.

Measurement Issues

Researchers using expectancy-value attitudes have generally ignored scaling issues and have implicitly assumed ratio scale properties. The typical study either treats behavior, intentions, or A_{act} as dependent variables in a multiple regression solution, with the $\Sigma b_i e_i$ as predictor, or else bases analysis simply on the correlation between the $\Sigma b_i e_i$ and a criterion. Such an approach can be shown to be flawed in that allowable transformations of the scaling of either b_i or e_i could result in meaningless inferred relations.

One solution to the scaling problem is the use of hierarchical regression. This procedure detects valid interactions even if the variables are at best ordinal. However, hierarchical regression is sensitive to measurement error in the independent variables, and thus the possibility of Type II errors (i.e., accepting the null hypothesis when it is in fact false) exists. Contemporary advances in structural equation models overcome the measurement error limitation but still technically assume ratio scaling. More work is needed to develop a method that does not require ratio scaling yet takes into account measurement error. Until then we are in the unenviable position of relying on the findings of a vast number of previous studies that have not performed proper tests of hypotheses. For this reason it is likely that many of the time-honored assumptions, predictions, and proscriptions associated with the expectancy-value model lack empirical support.

Future Research

William J. McGuire predicted that the 1980s and 1990s would bring renewed interest in attitudes and attitude systems in general and in the structure of attitudes in particular. Indeed, a comprehensive review of the field by Shelley Chaiken and Charles Stangor supports the view that as of the mid-1980s attitude research has made a comeback from two decades of decline and shows every reason to continue unabated into the twenty-first century.

We are likely to see a greater convergence between the process and structural approaches in the years ahead. Whether this will mean that processural frameworks will incorporate structural ideas or that structural frameworks will become more processural is difficult to say. But one thing is certain: attitude theories and research have reached a new level of maturity, and they promise to enhance our understanding and practice of many forms of social communication.

Bibliography. Icek Ajzen and Martin Fishbein, *Understanding Attitudes and Predicting Social Behavior*, Englewood Cliffs, N.J., 1980; Richard P. Bagozzi, "Attitude Formation under the Theory of Reasoned Action and a Purposeful Behavior Reformulation," *British Journal of Social Psychology* 25 (1986): 95–107; idem, "Expectancy-value Attitude Models: An Analysis of Critical Theoretical Issues," *International Journal of Research in Marketing* 2 (1985): 43–60; Shelly Chaiken and Charles Stangor, "Attitudes and Attitude Change," *Annual Review of Psychology* 38 (1987): 575–630; Robert B. Cialdini, *Influence: How and Why People Agree to Things*, New York, 1984; Alice H. Eagly and Shelly Chaiken, "Cognitive Theories of Persuasion," in *Advances in Experimental Social Psychology*, Vol. 17, ed. by Leonard Berkowitz, New York, 1984; Martin Fishbein and Icek Ajzen, *Belief, Attitude, Intention, and Behavior*, Reading, Mass., 1975; William J. McGuire, "Attitudes and Attitude Change," in *Handbook of Social Psychology*, 3d ed., Vol. 2, ed. by Gardner Lindzey and Elliot Aronson, New York, 1985; Richard E. Petty and John T. Cacioppo, *Attitudes and Persuasion: Classic and Contemporary Approaches*, Dubuque, Iowa, 1981; Harry C. Triandis, *Interpersonal Behavior*, Monterey, Calif., 1977.

RICHARD P. BAGOZZI

AUDIENCE. For information on this subject viewed from varying perspectives, see the following articles.

The concept of audience is approached from a theoretical perspective in CROWD BEHAVIOR; DIFFUSION; INTERACTIVE MEDIA; MASS COMMUNICATIONS RESEARCH; MASS MEDIA EFFECTS; MODELS OF COMMUNICATION; PERSUASION; SOCIAL COGNITIVE THEORY; TASTE CULTURES.

Measurement issues are discussed in CONSUMER RESEARCH; EVALUATION RESEARCH; OPINION MEASUREMENT; POLL; PRINT-AUDIENCE MEASUREMENT; RATING SYSTEMS: RADIO AND TELEVISION.

The contributions of specific theorists are mentioned in the entries ADORNO, THEODOR; HOVLAND, CARL; LAZARSFELD, PAUL F.; LEWIN, KURT; LIPPMANN, WALTER; MCLUHAN, MARSHALL; TARDE, JEAN-GABRIEL DE.

For media influences on society, and on the media's audiences in particular, see AGENDA-SETTING; BANDWAGON EFFECTS; CULTIVATION ANALYSIS; CULTURAL INDICATORS; ENTERTAINMENT; LEISURE; OPINION LEADER; POLITICAL COMMUNICATION; POLITICIZATION; PUBLIC OPINION; SLEEPER EFFECT; VIOLENCE.

The entries CHILDREN and MINORITIES IN THE MEDIA deal with two specific audiences that have been the subject of considerable research attention.

AUDIOVISUAL EDUCATION

The provision of special learning experiences to implement and supplement the instruction that teachers can provide. The term became common early in the twentieth century when mass media—filmstrips, slides, films, sound recordings, RADIO, and television (*see* TELEVISION HISTORY)—began to be used widely for EDUCATION.

History

Though associated with modern times, audiovisual education appears to have had early precursors. There are reasons to believe that cave paintings, CLAY TOKENS, sculptures, and even some architectural forms may have served educational purposes. A more decisive advance in audiovisual instruction came after PRINTING, which encouraged the rise of LITERACY, the creation of textbooks, and the spread of schools (*see* SCHOOL). Pictures began to appear in the printed text. In 1658 Johann Amos Comenius (1592–1670), a Czech clergyman, wrote and published *Orbis Sensualium Pictus* (The Visible World in Pictures), the first illustrated textbook. It was based on the theory that the pictures would both help students establish direct links between words and things, and lead them through the process of induction to generalized knowledge.

Under the leadership of scholars like Johann Heinrich Pestalozzi (1746–1827) in Switzerland, Jean-Jacques Rousseau (1712–1778) in France, and JOHN LOCKE (1632–1704) in England, new thinking about education bloomed in the eighteenth and nineteenth centuries. More instruction was given in the mother tongue than in the classical languages, sciences began to play an active part in the curriculum, and there was a new emphasis on examining the question of how to teach (*see* TEACHING). Throughout the Western world in the second half of the nineteenth century there was an emphasis on the student's own learning activity: on learning rather than being taught.

By 1900 the new communication technology of the Industrial Revolution was reflected in study materials. The invention of cameras (*see* PHOTOGRAPHY) and of methods for printing illustrations from photographs resulted in effective pictures and maps in texts and on the walls of the CLASSROOM. Printed pictures were soon succeeded by pictures that could be viewed in a stereopticon (which produced the illusion of three dimensions), and then by filmstrips and slides that could be seen at the same time by a whole class or study group. When actual moving pictures became familiar, few educators imagined how many thousands of "teaching films" would soon be made and circulated (*see* MOTION PHOTOGRAPHY; MOTION PICTURES).

Perhaps the initial means of bringing audiovisual materials widely into schools was the establishment of cooperative arrangements between the MUSEUM and the school system. The first of these in the United States is believed to have been in St. Louis, Missouri, in 1905. Other arrangements for borrowing made it possible in many countries for teachers to show their students drawings, photographs, lantern slides, and models. As more countries took over the support of their elementary and secondary schools, the schools built up some of their own supplies of what was coming to be called "audiovisual aids." Government departments and school and college systems began to make teaching films and radio programs. In the 1920s and early 1930s a number of research projects on the effects of films and radio were organized where educational research personnel and facilities were available (*see* CHILDREN—MEDIA EFFECTS).

World War II had a positive, though unforeseen, effect on audiovisual education. The military services turned to the audiovisual resources of educators for help in training soldiers and civilians to take part in the war effort. This was notable in Germany, England, and Japan as well as in the United States, where it is estimated that more than ten thousand training films and an untold number of filmstrips, slides, and recordings were used to teach skills and shape soldiers' attitudes (*see* PROPAGANDA). Furthermore, many of the countries engaged in the war co-opted some of their best researchers to study the effectiveness of audiovisual materials, thereby setting a fashion for future educational and communications research (*see* COMMUNICATIONS RESEARCH: ORIGINS AND DEVELOPMENT).

Once the war was over, educators and researchers turned to the development of "programmed instruction"—self-teaching books and machines. This was soon adapted to the computer, and satellites were used to share television and radio lessons over wide areas (*see* SATELLITE). By the 1970s all the new communication technologies had been called on to address the problems of learning and teaching. It was estimated that by that time more than fifty thousand schools throughout the world had acquired motion picture projectors, and more than one hundred thousand schools were receiving radio and television broadcasts. Perhaps more important than numbers, however, was the fact that educational media and other materials of audiovisual instruction had been accepted and were being widely used from preschool to UNIVERSITY levels.

Effectiveness of Audiovisual Learning

Between two thousand and three thousand experiments on audiovisual learning indicate that audiovisual experience can contribute to learning in a variety of situations and for a variety of learners, and that a certain number of general propositions are supportable on the basis of present knowledge:

1. *People learn from any medium.* This does not imply that the student learns a particular skill or subject matter as well as another, from one medium or combination of media, regardless of how the desired content or skill is taught. However, the student does learn from any medium, appropriately used. This seems to hold regardless of grade level, mental ability, or age.

2. *People learn also from experience in which media play no part.* The teacher's skills usually include an ability to make good use of experiences that are not a part of formal instruction as well as those that are.

3. *People learn from media and direct experience whether we want them to or not.* Children learn behaviors their parents want them to learn and other behaviors parents do not want the children to pick up. An example of this is the way many children learn to imitate the behavior they see modeled on television (*see* SOCIAL COGNITIVE THEORY).

4. *There is no "best medium" for all learning tasks and all learning.* Many new media have been hailed as "the great one." Print was the first, television the most recent—the former because it could serve every literate person and the latter because it offered sound, speech, pictures, and movement all in one package. But learning to speak a LANGUAGE, which is perhaps humanity's greatest learning achievement, is accomplished mostly without the aid of any media. For any given task, one medium is likely to be more effective than another, but that superiority does not extend to *all* tasks.

5. *For any given learning task, some combination of media and direct experience is likely to be more efficient than others.* Print is especially useful for summarizing knowledge, pictures for visual recognition, speech or recorded audio for language learning, graphs for comparing quantities, moving pictures or television for studying motion, and so on. A teacher uses what is available and what there is time for.

6. *The events of instruction are sufficiently varied to call for a variety of media.* Every learning task requires several "events of instruction"—that is, the experiences that, in a given situation, will most efficiently contribute to a student's learning. Not only every task but even every *part* of the task is likely to call for the use of more than one medium.

7. *Consequently, a combination of media is likely to produce more learning than any one medium alone.* An ideal fit of media to learning task, therefore, is likely to require a very complex shifting back and forth among media, and the choice of audiovisual media must necessarily be a compromise with the ideal. Logistical and financial considerations must enter in, along with educational theory.

8. *Research is beginning to guide media and content choices.* Only examples can be given here. Robert M. Gagné and Leslie J. Briggs have been building instructional theory on such bases as the events of instruction. Gavriel Salomon suggested a rule for the selection of media: "The better a symbol system conveys the *critical features* of an idea or event, the more appropriate it is." The code of the audiovisual media will be most effective "if it is isomorphic to the learner's symbolic way of thinking." In other words, the symbolic "language" of the medium should make it as easy as possible for the student to interpret, store, retrieve, and ultimately use and transfer the particular lesson that is to be learned.

What Is Audiovisual Instruction Used For?

Audiovisual instruction has proved helpful in large as well as small activities—from national educational reform projects to individual study—and for short-term as well as long-term work. The following examples of larger projects in which users have reported successful results demonstrate the scope and power of the audiovisual revolution.

National educational reform. Niger has used television to upgrade the curriculum, train teachers, and expand availability of schools. American Samoa used television and expert teachers imported from the U.S. mainland to upgrade teaching while Samoan teachers and administrators were preparing to take over the system. El Salvador used television teaching to triple enrollment in the seventh, eighth, and ninth grades (*see* DEVELOPMENT COMMUNICATION).

Supplementing the school. In the United States a CABLE TELEVISION experiment in Washington County, Maryland, was launched to supply the needs of schools in which teachers of special subjects were not available. Later, cable was replaced by VIDEO recordings in each school. Colombia's national school system, mountain schools in Japan, and schools in the neighborhood of Delhi, India, all used television to upgrade the curriculum. Radio has been used to supplement teaching in upland villages of Thailand. The Central African Republic and other school systems in Africa have made use of radiovision (radio broadcast, tapes, and teacher) to improve teaching of certain subjects. In Rhodesia (now the Republic of Zimbabwe) programmed instruction was used with considerable success to augment classroom teaching.

Extending the school. The British Open University, which opened in 1969, has used correspondence study, radio, television, science kits, and short periods of residence teaching in the summer. Other countries using mostly television to make extended schools possible are the German Democratic Republic (Television Academy), the Federal Republic of Germany (Telekollegg), the Netherlands (Telemac), Poland (Television College), France (RTS), and Thailand, which now has three open universities. Australia has offered both elementary and secondary education to remote students by correspondence study and radio since 1933; many students have gone directly from this extended system into the city universities. France, the Federal Republic of Germany, Kenya, Austria, and Mexico all offer extended education by radio and/or television.

Nonformal education outside the school. Nonformal education is instruction offered outside the boundaries of the formal school system and ordinarily without academic credit. Such education puts high emphasis on local group and individual activity. Group nonformal study is stimulated by radio broadcasts in most of the radio rural forums (e.g., in Canada, India, Ghana, Malawi, Togo, and Benin). Acción Cultural Popular (Popular Cultural Action) in Colombia and several large programs in Brazil offer literacy and other elementary training to study groups totaling several hundred thousand people. A related pattern, popular in Africa, consists of groups, served by radio broadcasts and led by an *animateur,* who meet to discuss local problems, leading toward community action and learning.

The Cost of Instructional Media

Detailed figures on the cost of instructional media are scarce. There is a considerable leap in cost between "little" media (e.g., filmstrips and slides) and "big" media (e.g., television, sound films, and computer-assisted instruction). Another consideration is economy of scale. Original costs of television and radio are comparatively high, but the unit cost decreases as the amount of use increases. Some unit costs, however, do not decrease notably with extent of use; examples are motion pictures, filmstrips, and slides. A third consideration is quality. The cost of all instructional media increases with quality, but the difference is most notably apparent in the cases of television, motion pictures, computer-assisted instruction, and radio. Cost decisions, therefore, are difficult but important to a school system that is considering audiovisual instruction, and costs must be balanced against what the new technology can be expected to accomplish.

See also COMPUTER: IMPACT—IMPACT ON EDUCATION; EDUCATIONAL TELEVISION.

Bibliography. Robert M. Gagné, *The Conditions of Learning,* 2d ed., New York, 1970; Robert M. Gagné and Leslie J. Briggs, *Principles of Instructional Design,* New York, 1974; David Hawkridge and John Robinson, *Organizing Educational Broadcasting,* London and Paris, 1982; Gavriel Salomon, *Interaction of Media, Cognition, and Learning,* San Francisco, 1979; Wilbur L. Schramm, *Big Media, Little Media,* Beverly Hills, Calif., 1977; UNESCO, *The Economics of New Educational Media,* 2 vols., Paris, 1977.

WILBUR SCHRAMM

AUSTRALASIA, TWENTIETH CENTURY

The area known as Australasia has witnessed rapid change in its communication patterns since World War II, brought on by the conjunction of new media and worldwide political shifts. Although the term has never been defined precisely, *Australasia* is generally used to encompass Australia, New Zealand, Papua New Guinea, Fiji, and other island nations in the South Pacific. As with other attempts at grouping based on geographical proximity, the nations included are quite diverse in terms of population, national geography, political organization, and history.

Background. Long before European EXPLORATION in the late eighteenth century ventured farther south and east to reach what is now known as Papua New Guinea and the northern and eastern Australia coast, Polynesian, Melanesian, and other peoples had inhabited some of the islands for thousands of years. Their diverse ethnic origins, differences in LANGUAGE, and physical barriers (seas, forests, mountains, deserts) made communication among them difficult or impossible, although they were able to survive and develop indigenous cultures of varying levels of sophistication. But beginning in the late 1700s and early 1800s European COLONIZATION produced dramatic changes. Portuguese, Dutch, and English explorers were among the first Europeans to come to this part of the world, but the English established colonies of growing importance in the late eighteenth and all through the nineteenth century in Australia, New Zealand, and Papua New Guinea, constantly reinforcing them with new arrivals and a sizable military presence.

The indigenous populations suffered greatly. Their claims on ancestral lands went unrecognized, treaties were often ignored, and wars fought against them left them severely disadvantaged and much reduced in numbers. By the nineteenth century, English subjects represented a majority of the population, turning the aboriginal populations into "minorities" with limited rights and opportunities in the new societies.

The twentieth century has witnessed rapid and important changes in many areas of society within the different nations of the region. In terms of communications the tendency has been to decrease the importance of the old ties to the colonial powers—particularly England—in favor of closer and more extensive links with other countries in the area. A silent motion picture industry thrived in Australia from the late nineteenth century until the introduction of sound (*see* MOTION PICTURES). It withered because the patents covering the new sound motion picture technology were controlled by U.S. and British film-production organizations. But by and large, until midcentury it was common to look to Europe rather than to neighboring Asian and Pacific nations for everything from commodities to CULTURE. Film and broadcasting units, for example, were created and evolved following the British model. They included DOCUMENTARY film services organized by JOHN GRIERSON in Australia and New Zealand; BBC-style RADIO operations reinforced by an Empire Broadcasting Service shortwaved from England, as organized by JOHN REITH; and television experiments begun along similar lines (*see* TELEVISION HISTORY). Provided with such services, and with populations of small or moderate size, the Australasian nations were slow to develop substantial communications industries of their own. For example, Fiji and Papua New Guinea did not develop television services until the 1980s. Australia was to some extent an exception, developing a powerful press and, in the 1970s, a film industry that began to gain an international reputation. Other nations in the area increasingly looked to Australia and Australian organizations for expertise and capital.

During the postwar decades new waves of MIGRATION began to effect a rapid transformation of Australia's population. Under a postwar population program large numbers of people came from Greece, Italy, Germany, the Netherlands, Yugoslavia, Poland, Malta, Turkey, and Lebanon; others arrived from Vietnam and Malaysia. In three decades some 3.5 million immigrants arrived in Australia, and the country began to think of itself as a multiethnic, multilanguage nation, with the full range of problems this could involve. One of the major challenges was to its communications system. Australian responses to these challenges have had wide implications for Australasia as a whole.

The press in Australia is privately funded and exists with minimal GOVERNMENT REGULATION. There has been a strong trend toward concentration of ownership (*see* MONOPOLY). The major daily and weekly press is in English, and its interest is in the dominant English-speaking readership. Yet new needs and demands have arisen; in response, one or more privately funded newspapers came into being for almost every language group. Broadcasting and telecommunications, however, have faced special problems.

Almost two-thirds of Australia's 15 million people live in the southeastern coastal region. The rest are clustered in smaller regional centers or are scattered throughout the remote and often inhospitable outback. Most Aborigines live outside the major urban areas. Because of the uneven spread of the population and the vast distances involved, access to Australia's broadcasting and telecommunications services has varied markedly. Where one lives has long determined the range and quality of services.

The regulation of broadcasting and telecommunications in Australia is the responsibility of the Commonwealth government. As in Great Britain, broadcasting began noncommercially but has shifted to a dual system, with one service receiving public funds and the other supported wholly by ADVERTISING. Neither service was prepared for the complex impact of the latest population wave.

During the 1970s Australia's communication system was radically transformed by two government initiatives stemming directly from Australia's population changes and geographic dispersal. One was designed to meet the needs of the country's multiplying ethnic communities. The other was designed to overcome geographic barriers by means of a SATELLITE system—which soon acquired Australasia-wide significance.

Ethnic and multilingual broadcasting. This initiative resulted from the POLITICIZATION of members of ethnic groups and from increased sensitivity to the political and cultural consequences of media coverage. In particular the mass media were seen to be carriers of negative stereotypes of immigrants and Aborigines that both reflected and perpetuated prejudice and injustice. As an alternative to reform of the mainstream media, some ethnic and Aboriginal groups began LOBBYING for the provision of ethnic broadcasting outlets so that they would be able to broadcast their own views directly.

By the mid-1970s a number of immigrant organizations had established themselves as effective political pressure groups (*see* PRESSURE GROUP). These years saw the political mobilization of immigrant communities and the adoption by government officials of an ideology of diversity or "multiculturalism." The need for ethnic broadcasting was acknowledged on many fronts, and the stage was set for specific action to meet minority needs. *See* MINORITIES IN THE MEDIA.

An experimental access station (*see* CITIZEN ACCESS) had been set up in 1976. Though it was not specifically designed as a broadcast outlet for immigrants, many immigrant groups applied for use of the station, and within months there were regular weekly broadcasts in twenty-six languages other than English. An additional seventeen languages were broadcast from time to time. There was also a weekly program produced by Aborigines.

Soon after this access venture the government established experimental ethnic radio stations with a specific charter to broadcast to immigrants. They were to transmit community and government information to more than two million immigrants in Melbourne and Sydney—people not reached by other facilities—and were also to give recognition to the cultures and traditions of the immigrant groups and encourage tolerance and understanding among all sections of the Australian community.

The experimental seasons of ethnic radio precipitated debates about who should control the service. As a result the government created the Special Broadcasting Service (SBS). In 1980 the government initiated a multicultural television service that was designed to meet the needs of the various ethnic communities and to appeal to the wider Australian community. It aimed to increase the awareness within the whole community of the diverse multicultural nature of Australian society and increase mutual understanding among ethnic communities. It would assist in the maintenance and development of community languages and cultures and contribute to greater self-esteem and identity; at the same time it would help new arrivals to adjust to life in Australia and to learn about Australian history and culture.

Because Aborigines have resisted being described as an ethnic group, the relationship of the SBS to Aboriginal broadcasting has been ambiguous. (Aborigines have argued that they should be considered a "people" made up of a number of ethnic groups.) Although the SBS did support the production and broadcast of Aboriginal radio programs on SBS and other public radio stations, Aborigines concentrated their attention on the public broadcasting system. The Central Australian Aboriginal Media Association (CAAMA) took the initiative with a half-hour radio series. CAAMA obtained a license for an Aboriginal public radio station in Alice Springs, South Australia, and developed a network. It distributed audiocassettes containing news, interviews, and music to Aboriginal communities. It also developed VIDEO production facilities as a means of serving Aboriginal communities in the outback.

The creation of Aussat. The outlook for Aboriginal broadcasting in rural and remote areas was further enhanced by the second of the government initiatives—the Aussat satellite system. In 1977—when public discussion of a domestic communication satellite system was initiated—residents of Sydney and Melbourne had high-quality TELEPHONE, postal, and telecommunications services and access to up to twenty radio and five television stations. But for many residents of the remote outback telephone services and broadcast television were nonexistent, shortwave radio provided the only timely news and ENTERTAINMENT service, and unreliable high-frequency radio provided the only communication link for business, health, and educational services.

With the launching of Aussat's first satellites in 1985, remote homesteads and communities that could not receive television, radio, and data services by conventional means could acquire them through low-cost satellite ground stations. Outback telephone services were also improved. In addition, Aussat made possible a series of specialized video and audio services transmitted to hotels, motels, and other public places.

Aussat brought television programming into areas with the greatest concentrations of Aborigines. Research by the Australian Institute of Aboriginal Studies showed how European-style programs could be offensive to Aboriginal cultural traditions. But it also illustrated the differences between the responses of various Aboriginal groups to the same program. To ensure that Aboriginal culture was enhanced and not threatened by direct-broadcast satellite television, CAAMA created an Aboriginal consortium, Imparja, which obtained a license to engage in direct satellite-based television and was thus able to provide Aboriginal programming to South Australia and the Northern Territory, the parts of Australia with the highest concentration of Aborigines.

Although the debut of communications satellites in Australia fulfilled many expectations, the implications for Australasian communications were clearly even more far-reaching. The existence of Aussat stimulated a new evolution of the area's communication systems. For a region as fragmented as Australasia, satellite interconnection was a revolutionary technology.

Australasian vistas. The satellite's meaning for the area had already been glimpsed and discussed in the 1960s. During the following decade, the loan of a communications satellite by the U.S. National Aeronautics and Space Administration (NASA) allowed communities and schools of the region to experiment with satellite-based audio-teleconferencing, with assistance from the University of Hawaii in Honolulu and the University of the South Pacific in Suva, Fiji. These offered not only a vision of possibilities but also hands-on experience. Indonesia's launching of its PALAPA satellite system, which began operation in 1976 and likewise sought to serve a vast array of islands, offered a further model and inspiration—as did India's SITE experiments of 1975–1976, using another satellite on loan from NASA.

Regional linkages of various kinds followed the launching of Aussat. Aussat agreed to provide domestic communications links for the New Zealand

Post Office, which has jurisdiction over the nation's telecommunications services. One of Aussat's satellites can switch beam coverage to serve Papua New Guinea; there and in Fiji, the television systems are operated by Australian organizations. Further regional communications challenges and issues are being considered by the South Pacific Telecommunications Development Programme, which is part of the South Pacific Economic Commission based in Fiji. This organization has played a role in telecommunications planning and in negotiating for proposed communications services from Intelsat.

Other new technologies are also having their impact. As in Australia, various Aboriginal and other groups find in the video medium and in low-power community radio welcome instruments for self-expression. Concern about the content of imported videos and their implications for indigenous culture has encouraged interest in both local origination and local control of broadcast television. Amid this new media environment, the nations of Australasia seem to be moving toward new patterns of self-expression and interdependence.

Bibliography. Bill Bonney and Helen Wilson, *Australia's Commercial Media*, Melbourne, 1985; Allan Brown, *Commercial Media in Australia: Economics, Ownership, Technology and Regulation*, St. Lucia, Queensland, 1986; Miriam Gilson and Jerzy Zubrzycki, *The Foreign Language Press in Australia 1848–1964*, Canberra, 1967; Ian K. Mackay, *Broadcasting in Papua New Guinea*, Melbourne, 1976; Henry Mayer, *The Press in Australia*, Melbourne, 1964; Eric Michaels, *Aboriginal Invention of Television*, Canberra, 1986; Charles Moses, *Diverse Unity: The Asia Pacific Broadcasting Union 1957–1977*, Sydney, 1978; Ann Moyal, *Clear across Australia: A History of Telecommunications*, Melbourne, 1984; Ian Reinecke and Julianne Schultz, *The Phone Book*, Melbourne, 1983; Naomi Rosh White and Peter B. White, *Immigrants and the Media*, Melbourne, 1983; Keith Windshuttle, *Media*, Melbourne, 1984.

PETER B. WHITE

AUTHORSHIP

The notion of authorship centers on the act of inauguration and the complementary concept of an original inventor, composer, or author who undertakes it. The communicative impulse itself conventionally presupposes an author, a purposive initiator of the communicative process.

As far as written communication is concerned, the author traditionally appears as the individual source of a text designed to communicate specific messages to a reader or readers. From a literary standpoint the text may appear capable of transmitting more or less

directly the author's individual point of view with regard to the subject in question. And in its most intimate MODE the text may even assume the status of a virtually direct expression of the author's self, a closely personal utterance brought forth, like SPEECH, from an inner source (the word *utter* has a shared root with the word *outer*; to utter is in one sense to bring out).

This sense that the text springs from deeply personal origins has long seemed to confer rights of ownership on its author. Burgeoning "inside," the text retains a complex connection with its roots, the author's real presence, even when it moves "outside." The author can thus appear to inhabit the text as part of an intimate relationship involving dimensions far deeper than those normally at stake in the possession of property. The author may even claim, or have proclaimed on his or her behalf, a fundamental *authority* (again, the words share a common root) over the text that extends to the text's MEANING. The text means what the author intended it to mean, no less and no more.

These ideas of authorship make two literary crimes possible. The first can be termed *misinterpretation*, in which meanings other than those intended by the author are wished onto the text, which is twisted or perverted to sustain them. The second is *plagiarism*, in which the author's text is appropriated by another, and his or her proprietary rights over the words are violated.

However, these apparently straightforward and commonsensical notions rest on a number of presuppositions that have come under attack in the twentieth century as a result of developments in two particular fields, one historical and the other philosophical. In both cases a fundamentally damaging charge is laid at the door of our present notion of authorship. Far from enjoying universal validity, the notion turns out to be the result of specific pressures—social, economic, political—of our own time.

Historical Development of Concept

The briefest glance at the procedures and presuppositions governing the production of texts in the medieval period yields a notion of authorship very different from the one we take for granted (*see* MIDDLE AGES). This was a manuscript CULTURE without benefit of the PRINTING press, in which texts were produced literally by hand. Medieval books were largely collective efforts, depending on the work of armies of scribes. Having determined to produce a BOOK, the medieval "author" would be unlikely to retire to look inward and write. On the contrary, one would be far more likely to look outward, beyond the self, toward a LIBRARY. Authorship in that culture was less a question of personal creation than a matter of assembling a body of appropriate material from other books, rather like putting together the pieces of a jigsaw puzzle. In addition, both librarians and those who used the books could be expected to take part in the assembly, since, for reasons of economy, works of relatively short length would be bound together with other works to which they were not necessarily related.

If we also take into account the practice whereby a volume containing, say, twenty different pieces would end up listed under the single name of the author of the first piece, we can see that our more recent notion of authorship represents a major departure from long-established practices. The assigning of the name of an author to a text was almost an arbitrary matter in the Middle Ages. Not only were many texts unsigned or unattributed, but, as E. P. Goldschmidt makes clear, people did not attach the same importance to ascertaining the precise identity of the author of a work as they do now. To the medieval scholar the question "Who wrote this text?" was far more likely to be an inquiry concerning the identity of the scribe than of the author.

Our notion of authorship can be said to be a product of the RENAISSANCE. It reflects that age's expanding interests in individualism, self-expression, and other modes of encountering the material world in which the extension and development—even the invention—of private experience found a fruitful location. By the eighteenth century, when its first use is recorded, the term *authorship* refers primarily to an occupation or career as a writer of literary texts. So James Boswell proves anxious to preserve SAMUEL JOHNSON from any hint of a connection with one of the major literary crimes, saying that "the strength of his memory which at once detected the real owner of any thought made him less liable to the imputation of plagiarism than, perhaps, any of our writers." By the nineteenth century Samuel Taylor Coleridge could refer definitively to "the profession of literature or, to speak more plainly, the trade of authorship" and was notoriously concerned with defending himself against the charge that he had plagiarized the German writer August Wilhelm von Schlegel.

It is not surprising that the growth of this concept of authorship appears also to be concomitant with the rise of capitalism, Protestantism, LITERACY, and the printing press (*see* PUBLISHING), or that it is involved in the complex value system implicit in those developments. In the last analysis our modern, post-Renaissance notion of authorship reflects a no less modern notion of individual authority over personal property. In the process it invests that relationship with ideas of truthfulness and validity whose essential features surface in the sense of firsthand, self-sufficient, and primary authority to which we give the name *authenticity*.

Philosophical Considerations

It is precisely this notion of an authentic relationship between author and text that is brought into question by a set of philosophical considerations generally known as deconstruction (*see* STRUCTURALISM). The essence of deconstruction lies in its questioning of precisely the relationship presupposed by the notion of the text as the authentic representation of the thoughts and feelings of its author. Indeed, a deconstructionist would argue that the suggestion of an originating and authenticating "presence" beyond any SIGN, apparently serving to "authorize" its validity, instances one of the major limitations pressing upon the Western mind.

In terms of READING and WRITING, this limitation appears in the form of the persistent delusions that writing is the expression of a preexisting and deeply personalized speech, that it gives immediate access to the inwardness of its speaker, and that reading is capable of piercing the veil of writing, of traveling back through it to the inner and "real" recesses of the author, and of making contact, without mediation, with the author's originating thoughts and the "presence" that embodies them. The most devastating attack on the "metaphysics of presence" that supports these concepts has been offered by French philosopher Jacques Derrida in his *De la grammatologie* (1967) and other volumes.

The work of Swiss linguist FERDINAND DE SAUSSURE made the case that LANGUAGE creates meaning through the differences and distinctions among its terms. Any sense of a direct one-to-one correspondence between words and the "real" world to which they refer can be only an illusion, albeit a powerful one, in which certain societies have found it ideologically profitable to invest. Derrida attacks the extension of that illusion into the body of our conceptual presuppositions. At its center lies the notion that there exists somewhere, in the purest form, beyond all mediation, a pristine voice, an antecedent speaking "presence," a graspable origin, an ultimate author, one whose palpable existence guarantees the authenticity of the signs that confront us. The grip of that illusion is powerfully anesthetic; it functions effectively as a formative force, determining and limiting our apprehension of the world we inhabit. But in truth, says Derrida, that world offers no comforting, unmediated, original, and authenticating presence with which we can at last come face to face. Instead, a multiplicity of different sign systems confronts us, all referring endlessly one to another in the free play of their differences (*see* SIGN SYSTEM).

The consequences of this for our inherited notions of authorship are clearly considerable. Whereas examination of the historical point of view revealed our sense of the author's ownership of the text as a fairly recent response to specific social developments and not the universal given we tend to suppose, a deconstructive analysis similarly depletes our sense of the text's ultimate dependence on its author as the final arbiter of meaning. Released in this way, the text's innate productivity may be encouraged to flower, its suppressed meanings to blossom. And at the furthest reaches of the implications of deconstruction, the way in which the fabric of meaning has been constructed in the text may finally be revealed. To reveal the method of its construction is of course to point to its seams and to unpick them, to deconstruct the fabric along the lines of its construction and thus to show that the text leads, not back to its originating author, but only and finally to itself, or to the functioning of signs that has generated it.

The aim of deconstructive analysis therefore can hardly be the reinforcement, reconstitution, or recuperation of the author's original meaning. On the contrary, such analysis aims to demonstrate that no such meaning governs the text and that no simple process of reading can uncover it. As critic J. Hillis Miller has argued, all texts are equally unreadable "if by 'readable' one means a single definitive interpretation." By turning the presuppositions of reading on their heads, by systematically unraveling the carefully woven strands that make up the text's sense-making surface, by focusing attention on those contradictory features that the author is unable to control and that his or her writing strives always to conceal, by showing that these offer, not the guarantee of a restricted presence beyond themselves, but entry into the realm of language at large, the deconstructionist puts forward the case that all texts ultimately give priority to the free play of language over meaning. As Geoffrey Hartman expresses it, deconstruction "refuses to identify the force of literature with any concept of embodied meaning"; rather, it recognizes that words offer, not the restrictions of authorial presence, but the freedom of "a certain absence or indeterminacy of meaning."

With this, the concepts of author and authorship, and of an author's authority over the text and the authenticity of his or her relationship with it, finally expire, to be replaced by the rise of the deconstructing reader as the active and creative element in the reading-writing nexus. If the fundamental opposition of speech to writing can be dissolved (or deconstructed), as Derrida argues, to show that speech is finally merely an aspect of writing, then the cognate opposition of writing to reading can be deconstructed to show that writing is finally an aspect of reading. *See* READING THEORY.

This fundamental realignment, in which the author functions ultimately as a particular category of reader, or is even perceived as a specific and distinctive set of strategies deployed by the text itself, entirely un-dermines the property rights supposedly involved in the production of the text. And without them the two crimes mentioned above disappear from the intellectual statute book. In deconstructionist terms, plagiarism ceases to be an offense, since writing (seen by Derrida in its largest sense as the impingement of culture on nature) is a universal human activity, and a principle of radical intertextual relationships ensures that no individual text can be available for single ownership (*see* INTERTEXTUALITY). And misinterpretation ceases to be an offense, since no pure, unmediated INTERPRETATION of any text is possible. In the absence of access to the author's originating presence or to the original meaning of a text, all reading, as Harold Bloom puts it, can only be misreading. The author, conceived as the controlling factor governing the text's possibilities, thus dies, as does authorial authority, to be followed to the grave by the concept of authenticity as the ultimate guarantor of communicative good faith. Clearly the situation demands a new model of the process of communication itself.

See also ARTIST AND SOCIETY; COPYRIGHT; LITERARY CRITICISM; STYLE, LITERARY.

Bibliography. Harold Bloom, *The Anxiety of Influence,* New York, 1973; Harold Bloom, Paul de Man, Jacques Derrida, Geoffrey Hartman, and J. Hillis Miller, *Deconstruction and Criticism,* New York, 1979; Jacques Derrida, *De la grammatologie,* trans. by Gayatri Chakravorty Spivak, Baltimore, Md., 1977; Ernst P. Goldschmidt, *Medieval Texts and Their First Appearance in Print,* Oxford, 1943; Marshall McLuhan, *The Gutenberg Galaxy: The Making of Typographic Man,* London, 1962; Walter J. Ong, *Orality and Literacy: The Technologizing of the Word,* London and New York, 1982; idem, *Ramus: Method and the Decay of Dialogue,* Cambridge, Mass., 1958.

TERENCE HAWKES

AUTOBIOGRAPHY

The form of literature in which authors narrate or otherwise describe their own lives. It is a peculiarly direct, personal communication between author and reader, commonly founded on the mutual belief that whatever is recounted in an autobiography is truthful. As readers of autobiography we trust that its authors are not knowingly deceiving or misinforming us about themselves, but are confiding to us certain truths about what has happened to them in the course of their lives or about the kind of person they believe themselves to be. It is a GENRE characterized by considerable freedom so far as technique goes; the autobiographer ranks among the least constrained of writers in deciding how to represent his or her life.

Autobiography has customarily been looked on as a branch of the wider literary genre of BIOGRAPHY, even though an author writing an account of his or her own life clearly stands in a relation of greater intimacy with the subject matter than a biographer commissioned to write the life of someone previously little known or unknown to him or her. The autobiographer has the capacity—and in the modern age almost an obligation—to bring before us facts about himself or herself that no biographer could expect to discover. The evolution of autobiography has been toward an ever-greater confidentiality, with the consequence that modern readers demand revelations of the author's inner life and an ever-increasing candor, these now being seen as the specific inducements of the genre.

Unlike a DIARY or journal, an autobiography is reflective, written some time after the events it is recalling. It may well be based on written records made at the time of those events, but turning this topical record into an autobiography is a work of literary composition in which the contemporary record will be quite recast. Similarly, autobiography may be broadly distinguished from memoirs as being more concerned with the private, emotional, and intellectual life of the author rather than with his or her public activities. The great many so-called autobiographies written—or, in the past fifty or sixty years, more often ghostwritten—by famous public figures, athletes, actors, and politicians are conspicuously free from any revealing engagement with the subject's developing inner self.

If autobiography is bordered on one side by these less "literary" forms of commemorative writing, it is bordered on the other by the fully literary form of FICTION. Autobiography approximates fiction not in its content but in its NARRATIVE form. The most common form for an autobiography to take is that of a story, beginning with the author's birth or earliest memories and leading on to some appropriate end point, which may be the present moment or alternatively some conclusive landmark in the autobiographer's earlier life. But stories are not always felt by readers to be true; by adopting the narrative form the autobiographer risks the wholesale distortion of his or her life as it has actually been, since few of us experience our lives as the purposeful, causal sequence that any narrative is bound to impose on the past. This powerful element of literary artifice will seem to some to endanger the genre's reputation for complete authenticity, and in the latter part of the twentieth century a certain experimentalism has come into the writing of autobiography, whereby the narrative model is played down and the sequence of the work is determined more by the sequence in which the author remembers the past in the act of writing.

Historical development. The German scholar Georg Misch traces the origins of autobiography back even beyond the literature of Greece and Rome to commemorative practices in ancient Egypt, where the tombs of dead rulers were furnished with brief accounts of the achievements of their reigns. These accounts might be written in the first person, as if they were autobiographical, even though in fact their form was purely conventional and they were composed after the ruler's death. Such inscriptions introduce, at the outset, a principal motive in the writing of autobiography, which is to achieve a certain immortality by leaving a permanent—and flattering—trace of a particular life.

The emergence of autobiography as a literary form goes hand in hand with the slow emergence in the philosophy and literature of Greece and Rome of a sense of individuality. The first "conscious and deliberate literary autobiography," according to Misch, was the so-called *Antidosis* of the Athenian publicist Isocrates, published in 353 B.C.E., which takes the form of an imaginary speech made in his own defense in a court of law (a reminder of the rhetorical function active in all autobiography; *see* RHETORIC). Later, Roman literature produced such proto-autobiographical works as the letters of CICERO (*see* LETTER) or the *Meditations* of the emperor Marcus Aurelius.

The first recognizably modern autobiography is the *Confessions* of St. Augustine, written at the end of the fourth century C.E. when its author was the Christian bishop of Hippo in North Africa. The *Confessions* have a new unity of both form and purpose. They are narrative, insofar as they recount the story of Augustine's conversion from paganism to Christianity; they are confessional, revealing certain private facts about his life that we could not otherwise have learned and that do not necessarily do him credit (a famous episode concerns his stealing pears from an orchard as a boy); and they are exemplary, because this is a spiritual leader's account offered for the edification and encouragement of others.

It was in Italy during the RENAISSANCE that autobiography came at last into its own. Two great poets had shown the way: Dante Alighieri in the *Vita Nuova* (1295) and Petrarch in *The Secret* (1358), in which he analyzes his own nature in the form of an imaginary dialogue with St. Augustine. Later came the *Life* of the sixteenth-century sculptor, goldsmith, and bravo Benvenuto Cellini, a most competitive and vainglorious figure whose autobiography is prized for its reckless but revealing incredibility. Contemporary with Cellini was Girolamo Cardano, physician, mathematician, and gambler, whose *Life* is more sympathetic for containing, in a very capricious sequence, accounts of its author's failings, afflictions, and neuroses as well as his successes in life.

If, in autobiographies such as Cellini's, simple vanity appears to be the author's principal inspiration, in the seventeenth century a more complex, spiritual motive was introduced into the genre, reminiscent of Augustine. This was the desire, among Protestant writers, to produce accounts of their religious experience and publicly to examine their conscience. John Bunyan's *Grace Abounding to the Chief of Sinners* (1666) is an example of this peculiarly intense kind of autobiography, telling in a biblical and hortatory language of how he came to find salvation in the Christian doctrine.

In the following century it was another Protestant author who wrote what remains perhaps the most remarkable single work of autobiography: Jean-Jacques Rousseau, whose *Confessions* were published only after his death in 1778, instituting the great age of romantic autobiography in Europe (*see* ROMANTICISM). After Rousseau it no longer seemed as indecorous or egocentric as it once had to write at length about oneself, or to reveal episodes of one's past or aspects of one's nature that urbane autobiographers earlier in the eighteenth century would not have thought of including. Romantic views of the singularity and importance of the "poetic" intelligence produced much fervent autobiographical writing throughout the nineteenth century (*see* AUTHORSHIP). Notable works were produced by the German poet Johann Wolfgang von Goethe, by the French writer Stendhal, and by the English philosopher John Stuart Mill, among others. Such works may be read as monuments to an age of confident and ambitious individualism, the tone of which began to change in the twentieth century.

Changing face of autobiography. The great influence on the writing of autobiography in the twentieth century has been the development of PSYCHOANALYSIS and the theories of SIGMUND FREUD concerning the influence of early experience on human lives. Authors and readers alike have come to expect in autobiography a greater concentration on childhood and the exploration of past events. The modern autobiographer is often likely to start writing in a more consciously exploratory frame of mind than would have been the case a hundred years ago, in the hope of being surprised and enlightened by recollection. The writing of autobiography has assumed a more or less therapeutic role in the life of the autobiographer, closer to the role it has always had in the lives of those who like to read the autobiographies of others.

Autobiography exists less to bring back certain moments of the past as they were experienced at the time than to communicate to us the autobiographer's present, and thus constantly shifting, perspective on his or her past. The approximation to the forms and devices of fiction, which autobiography can never avoid, does not mean that those who read autobiographies must become skeptical about their claims to being always true; everything that they contain is autobiographical, whether or not it corresponds with the historical facts. Autobiography is a form of literature and a form of words; life is neither. Autobiography transforms life, endowing it with a pattern and consistency that as readers we find reassuring. Autobiography makes life meaningful by offering us the example of a life narrated or otherwise made sense of. It uses certain literary conventions for persuasive ends in demonstrating that our own life too is susceptible of such retrospective reordering.

Bibliography. Jerome Hamilton Buckley, *The Turning Key: Autobiography and the Subjective Impulse since 1800*, Cambridge, Mass., and London, 1984; Philippe Lejeune, *Le pacte autobiographique*, Paris, 1975; Georg Misch, *A History of Autobiography in Antiquity* (Geschichte der Autobiographie), 2 vols., trans. by E. W. Dickes, with the author, London, 1950; James Olney, *Metaphors of Self: The Meaning of Autobiography*, Princeton, N.J., 1972; William C. Spengemann, *The Forms of Autobiography: Episodes in the History of the Literary Genre*, New Haven, Conn., and London, 1980; Karl J. Weintraub, *The Value of the Individual: Self and Circumstance in Autobiography*, Chicago, 1978.

JOHN STURROCK

AVANT-GARDE

The term *avant-garde* (French for "advance guard") is military in origin but was popularized in the aftermath of the French Revolution as a figurative expression for political vanguards. In contrast to its later reference to iconoclastic and subversive cultural activities, the term was originally used in the Enlightenment context of reformist philosophies of history to refer to the cultural elites, the advance guard of progress endeavoring to organize a better society. Only since the last quarter of the nineteenth century has the term come to signify artists' iconoclastic defiance of linguistic or formal conventions, a development reflecting major changes in the function of ART in modern societies.

The current iconoclastic meaning of *avant-garde* emerged during the 1880s and 1890s when the CULTURE industry exploded in the West and when derogatory labels for art with a mass appeal (especially the term *kitsch*) were coined and gained ground in aesthetic theory and elitist cultural politics (*see* AESTHETICS). In (social) modernity and (cultural) modernism, concepts signifying "high" and "low" art are interdependent; the very meaning of each term depends on its opposite (*see* TASTE CULTURES). The increasing currency of dichotomous labels such as "avant-garde" and "kitsch" reflects a breakdown in the social function of art as envisioned by the Enlightenment and its ideological heirs, a breakdown conditioned by consumer culture. Artists began reacting against an emergent consumer culture as early as the late eighteenth century, especially in early German ROMANTICISM, which can be called the first modernist movement in art history. This reaction was strongest, however, between 1890 and 1930, a period of particularly radical experimentation with iconoclastic and hermetic forms. These four decades, which theorist Peter Bürger has termed the historical avant-garde, brought forth a wealth of avant-gardist movements, including futurism, cubism, EXPRESSIONISM, dadaism, Russian constructivism, and surrealism, the latter representing a culmination in the history of avant-garde movements.

Critics have argued that the historical avant-garde was an exclusively European event, whereas the postmodernist movement of the 1960s and 1970s was an exclusively North American phenomenon. The historical avant-garde was indeed concentrated in Europe, especially in France, Germany, Russia, and, for a short time, Switzerland. Postmodernism developed in the United States, where the term was first introduced around 1960. Yet the two movements are similar in their reaction to qualitative changes in the circulation of signs within consumer capitalism and to the defusing effect that the institutionalization of art had on the arts' critical content. The differences between the two movements are due to a sixty-year interval in the development of consumer capitalism. Nevertheless, historically and aesthetically the two phenomena clearly belong together. Even the intellectual roots of so-called poststructuralism, the major philosophical influence on Western intellectual activity of the late twentieth century, can be traced back to the avant-garde movements of the 1920s, particularly to the influence of French novelist and philosopher Georges Bataille and French dramatist and poet Antonin Artaud (see STRUCTURALISM).

Theoretical Approaches

Academic studies of the avant-garde employ two distinct conceptual approaches. The first tends to emphasize the linguistic or formal radicalism of the avant-garde's artistic practice and investigates the epistemological and sociohistorical reasons underlying its iconoclasm. The second approach focuses on the avant-garde's attack on the institution of art as a whole—its attempt to alter the function of art in modern societies—and, similarly, seeks to uncover the epistemological and sociohistorical reasons underlying this interest. It stresses the avant-garde's attempts to overcome or at least rupture the institutionalization of art as a separate, autonomous social sphere. These approaches are exemplified by two

studies: Renato Poggioli's *The Theory of the Avant-Garde* (1962) and Bürger's *Theory of the Avant-Garde* (1974).

Art and cultural renewal. According to Poggioli, linguistic hermeticism, "one of the avant-garde's most important characteristics of form and style," was designed to serve "as a corrective to the linguistic corruption characteristic of any mass culture." Linguistic hermeticism and poetic obscurity aim "at creating a treasure trove of new meanings within the poverty of common language, a game of multiple, diverse, and opposing meanings." There is indeed sufficient evidence in the history of the arts from romanticism through postmodernism to support the statement that modern artists share a preoccupation with the commodification of LANGUAGE and the resultant erosion of its expressive potential. Many modern artists see cognitive as well as linguistic atrophy induced by consumer capitalism. Thus the avant-garde's use of innovative techniques is founded on epistemological premises and cannot be ascribed simply to what U.S. art critic Harold Rosenberg called "a tradition of the new." The avant-garde does not consider language (or any other artistic material) a neutral tool that can be utilized for mimetic purposes without affecting the content of human PERCEPTION; rather, it sees language as a medium whose constitutive effect on human COGNITION cannot be erased. The avant-garde attempts to employ linguistic techniques in ways that help to reestablish critical, reflexive (imaginative, nonlogocentric) reasoning in society.

Increasingly, however, the emphasis has shifted from questions of linguistic or formal renewal, of the replacement of worn-out stereotypes with fresh expressions, to an awareness of the epistemological inadequacy of simply renewing language and to strategies whose intent is to deconstruct rather than replace established linguistic patterns of perception. Theories such as Poggioli's that overlook this shift encounter difficulties in accounting for qualitative differences between, for instance, late-nineteenth-century aestheticism and the historical avant-garde. In addition, theories emphasizing iconoclasm as the germinal feature of the avant-garde often fail to consider another fundamental obstacle to the ability of art to renew languages and forms outside its own sphere—namely, the modern institutional separation of the aesthetic from the political and economic. This institutional and, ultimately, functional separation may well preclude the ability of avant-garde works substantially to affect other activities. If, as has been convincingly argued by theorists such as MAX WEBER, social interaction and individual consciousness are indeed differentiated in terms of practices or activities (economic, moral, political, aesthetic), then a MODE of thinking or speaking in one realm may have no effect whatever on other realms. Furthermore, it is possible that contradictions between modes of expression and action are not experienced as such so long as an institutional framework keeps those modes apart. A radical mode of expression, thought, or activity in the aesthetic realm might simply compensate for its lack in other spheres of life. A formally radical artistic practice, in other words, can easily fit within the compensatory function of the aesthetic in society.

In addition to linguistic atrophy, the avant-garde fears psychological atrophy. It sees any postulation of a moral or normative effect of art as leading inevitably to psychic atrophy because any mimetic representation of life has to accept the established rules in order to achieve its desired effects. Therefore the avant-garde artist is not interested in restoring or revising identities but in producing difference. French poet André Breton, for example, worked toward "a future resolution of . . . dream and reality, which are seemingly so contradictory, into a kind of absolute reality, a *surreality*," while never suppressing the idiosyncrasy of each individual's dream state. The utopian ideal of a "surreality" remains opposed to the reformist tradition of the European Enlightenment and in accordance with an anarchistic concept of change insofar as it envisions a resolution that cannot grow out of the existing state of affairs: it presupposes a breakdown of modernity's organizational demarcations.

Although their expression is perhaps most extreme in avant-garde movements, none of these features is unique to the avant-garde. From romanticism on, with a few exceptions in nineteenth-century REALISM, the thrust of high art has been its adversarial relation to society in terms of both content and form. Underlying this tension is a pessimistic analysis of modernity culminating in the assertion that nonutilitarian, reflective thinking is increasingly sacrificed to an instrumental rationality that focuses on the human capacity to exploit nature and to make life more comfortable. A theory of the avant-garde that overemphasizes art's adversarial relation to society and its consequences for artistic forms runs the risk of blurring the distinctions between artistic movements from romanticism through postmodernism. This is where the second approach to the phenomenon of the avant-garde can offer a corrective understanding.

Art as autonomous institution. Bürger sets forth a Hegelian conception of art history in bourgeois society whose starting point is the peculiar tension within emergent bourgeois art between social concerns on the level of content (heteronomy) and separateness from society on the level of form (autonomy). Form includes the ways in which people's interactions with art are institutionalized in society. Art is invested with the specialized function of serving humanity's expressive needs in areas alien to and increasingly removed from rationalized realms of life. Thus its autonomy is the necessary result of the division of labor in capitalist societies.

The functional specialization of the arts gradually penetrated the very contents of the arts as the arts began to reflect their altered status in society. Although artists adhered to and participated in the development of the political ideals of wholeness, harmony, and community—both on the level of content, which often anticipated the golden age of true harmony, and on the level of form in the individual work of art—the institution of art was marginalized in bourgeois society as a recreational and compensatory sphere. As artists experienced the futility of their moral interventions, they began to see art's autonomous status as problematic. Art's social content began to be supplanted by the preferred content of reflecting on its form. According to Bürger, the history of art from romanticism through aestheticism can best be described as a gradual transformation of form into content. The historical avant-garde reacted to the futility of aestheticism's self-reflexive formal concerns by attacking the very institutionalization of art in bourgeois society. The avant-garde is seen in this approach as the first movement that tried to escape the developmental logic of the bourgeois institution of art by destroying or transforming it.

It is clear from an examination of both approaches to the avant-garde that an adequate theory must take into account the avant-garde's concern with both the institutional separation of art in bourgeois society and the commodification of language. Both issues address the fact that human cognition is not simply influenced but is actually constituted by established differential systems, for the system of separate institutions created by the differentiation of modern societies into functionally separate realms is as much a semiotic phenomenon as is the differential system of language (*see* SEMIOTICS). The avant-garde's epistemological concern with language is therefore not independent of its equally epistemological concern with institutions.

Modernism. Any theory of the avant-garde and postmodernism must come to terms with the basic difference between these movements and modernism. The modernist gesture of *épater les bourgeois* ("shock the middle classes") claims to criticize society from a detached, intellectual point of view. Modernists reject the revisionist optimism of the Enlightenment, yet the lack of a teleological philosophy of history does not affect the rigor and epistemological self-confidence with which they critique society. Modernism claims that the artist can inhabit a place outside society and its established discourses; modernism thus perceives itself as its own agent of linguistic and perceptual renewal. Modernism attacks modernity without reflecting on how this critique is defused by the autonomous institutionalization of its own artistic practice. Modernism, then, is the cultural complement of social modernity that cannot, however, understand its own position within modernity.

Unlike modernism, the avant-garde and its postmodern successors radically challenge the legitimacy of the organizational demarcations constituting modernity. Furthermore, the avant-garde doubts the existence of an epistemologically stable and independent vantage point from which to launch an affirmative, productive critique of society leading to meaningful reforms. A revisionist critique of established linguistic and institutional boundaries in bourgeois society always presupposes that language, logical categories, figures of thought, and disciplines exist outside and independent of history and society; that is, they are neutral tools that can be utilized for various critical purposes without affecting the nature of those purposes. Because modernism shares such epistemological premises, they offer an appropriate category by which to distinguish between modernism and the avant-garde/postmodernism. The avant-garde and postmodernism attempt to be critically effective from within established boundaries by deconstructing these boundaries. They seek to create a space from which, however fleetingly, a reflection of modernity undetermined by its established demarcations becomes possible. From the perspective of an affirmative (neo-Enlightenment) philosophy of modernity, attempts by the avant-garde and postmodernism to break down the institutional boundaries of modernity by celebrating and freeing untamed human energies (imagination, desire, madness, intensity) are bound to result in an unreflected anarchism that will destroy historical achievements without offering a substitute. Poststructuralism and postmodernism are in this view variants of the same cultural movement.

Postmodernism. Discussion of the historical avant-garde is inseparable from that of so-called postmodernism. French theorist Jean-François Lyotard sees postmodernism as a trans-avant-gardism. The justification for such a label is the premises shared by the historical avant-garde and contemporary postmodernism, the most important being that both movements see the status of art in modern societies as radically problematic. The concept of the sublime that figures most prominently in Lyotard's theory of postmodernity has in this context gained renewed importance. Lyotard notes that Immanuel Kant's aesthetic theory revolves, as do most Enlightenment theories, around the notion of community. Kant circumscribes the aesthetic as the presentation of a utopian projection of an ideal society, the only possible contemporary representation of that ideal (*see* UTOPIAS). Emphasizing that "an Idea in general has no presentation," Lyotard foregrounds a tension be-

tween a "real" and a "promise" in all representations of an ideal. This gap or tension, which Lyotard sees as constitutive of postmodernism, is for him the site of the sublime. By highlighting the gap, postmodernism questions the very possibility of representing the utopian in art. Lyotard's theory of the sublime is therefore the philosophical precipitate of postmodernism's intent to call into question the aesthetic and social project of modernity. The insistence on the sublime nature of all artistic representation is designed to remove art, at least perceptually, from its self-inflicted linguistic and institutional closure.

From the perspective of cultural politics—a perspective that lies at the very core of the avant-garde and postmodernism—the question remains whether a cultural project intending to lead art back into life is not subject to misuses that threaten its very legitimacy. Bürger maintains that the avant-garde failed in its attempt to sublate art and life in a new mode of praxis. But how is this failure to be assessed, and what are its consequences for contemporary cultural politics? The historical existence of false sublations—such as those noted by Andreas Huyssen "in fascism with its aestheticization of politics, in Western mass culture with its fictionalization of reality, and in socialist realism with its claim of reality status for its fictions"—forces later cultural movements to rethink and refine the avant-garde project.

The avant-garde's failure leads Bürger to the conclusion that critics and artists should revive the notion and practice of autonomous art and, as agents of a cultural politics, should defend art's autonomy. Such a suggestion is both nostalgic and historically impossible because it pleads for a return to traditional spatial and temporal differentiations that have been irretrievably altered or lost in postmodern societies. Moreover, it contradicts the very functionalist arguments that were its point of departure. The cultural revolution of the late 1960s and 1970s consisted, in part, of a reorganization of spatial and temporal boundaries in which demarcations between the aesthetic, public, and private spheres became blurred. One result has been that aesthetic pleasure as a publicly institutionalized activity, particularly when such activity is mediated and supported by electronic media, has become a functionally differentiated social subsystem of experiences that is no longer restricted to a functionally differentiated space. The all-pervasive presence of music in public places and the penetration of the landscape by advertising images serve as examples.

This collapse of the spatial differentiation of public spheres seems to be connected with the simultaneous replacement of actual with imaginary spaces, a process contributing, in turn, to an aestheticization of public spheres. The aestheticization of politics discussed by WALTER BENJAMIN in reference to Nazi mass rallies was by no means peculiar to Fascist societies; rather, a general aestheticization of politics seems to be one of the major effects of electronic media on social interaction. The aestheticization of the public sphere through the electronic media has led both to an erosion of moral-political discourse and to the proliferation of unconnected images. One effect of this proliferation has been the undermining of the relationship between the symbolic and the event, the image and the real. According to French theorist Jean Baudrillard, the contemporary condition is such that phenomena have lost or are in the process of losing their referential dimension. They are becoming effects of signification, that is, the reality of phenomena is increasingly grasped as a product of the structural codes organizing its perception (see CODE; SIGN). As he asserts, "All media and the official news service only exist to maintain the illusion of actuality—of the reality of the stakes, of the objectivity of the facts."

The modernist claim of resisting modernity, most pronounced in THEODOR ADORNO's theory of modernism, presupposes a mode of socialization that allows intellectuals to turn themselves into resilient, fortified entities. But if one's perspective is already informed by the circulation of images, then one cannot criticize society from a secured epistemological position outside those signs. The circulation of signs can be undercut only from a position within it. This may be why postmodern art at times seems more concerned with the parodic undercutting of signifying practices than with critical reflections on the institutional status of art in society. Both the historical avant-garde and postmodernism broke with the referential mimetic aesthetic of modernism. Yet the breakdown of institutional boundaries, which finds its most obvious example in the aestheticization of politics, has gradually rendered obsolete the avant-garde's attack on the institution of art; reality has surpassed the historical precondition for that attack.

The avant-garde's break with a referential mimetic aesthetic was motivated by the possibility of an innovative, unfettered reconnection of sign and object; postmodernism's break, by an ostensibly subversive replacing of sign with sign. Whereas the avant-garde resulted in a false sublation of the art/life dichotomy, the postmodern project has led to an ornamentalism in the style of pop art that accepts the inevitability of art's status and its compensatory function. Thus the most pressing question of a contemporary cultural politics may be whether the legacy of an avant-garde whose aim was to short-circuit signs and events that enable a working through of social experience has indeed been rendered obsolete.

See also AVANT-GARDE FILM; IDEOLOGY; VISUAL IMAGE.

Bibliography. Peter Bürger, *Theory of the Avant-Garde* (Theorie der Avantgarde), trans. by Michael Shaw, Minneapolis, Minn., 1984; Linda Hutcheon, *A Theory of Parody: The Teachings of Twentieth-Century Art Forms*, New York, 1985; Andreas Huyssen, *After the Great Divide: Modernism, Mass Culture, Postmodernism*, Bloomington, Ind., 1986; Jean-François Lyotard, *The Post-Modern Condition: A Report on Knowledge* (La condition postmoderne), trans. by Geoff Bennington and Brian Massumi, Minneapolis, Minn., 1984; Renato Poggioli, *The Theory of the Avant-Garde* (Teoria dell'arte d'avanguardia), trans. by Gerald Fitzgerald, Cambridge, Mass., 1968; Charles Russell, *Poets, Prophets, and Revolutionaries: The Literary Avant-Garde from Rimbaud through Postmodernism*, New York, 1985; Jochen Schulte-Sasse, ed., "Modernity and Modernism, Postmodernity and Postmodernism" (special issue), *Cultural Critique 5*, 1987; John Weightman, *The Concept of the Avant-Garde: Explorations in Modernism*, LaSalle, Ill., and London, 1973.

JOCHEN SCHULTE-SASSE

AVANT-GARDE FILM

An international movement of aesthetic iconoclasts whose works proclaim new modes of representation and NARRATIVE. Their existence reflects the conflict between dominant and emerging form-content codes by which the arts evolve. In film, alongside the dominant HOLLYWOOD code (conventional narrative and pseudorealism reflecting nineteenth-century storytelling norms), there exist alternative trends that parallel developments in other twentieth-century arts.

If the arts represent systems of messages, particular message systems are relevant to particular audiences—in film, a mass audience for Hollywood, a specialized audience for the AVANT-GARDE. In both cases, the messages (delivered by illusory images in illusory motion) are the fantasies, nightmares, and myths of the particular group. The transmission of meaning occurs in both content and form.

Characteristics. The parameters of opposition between the dominant Hollywood CODE and the avant-garde are clearly drawn. Most or all of the following attributes are characteristic of avant-garde films:

- The emphasis is on film as a visual rather than a storytelling medium. The VISUAL IMAGE is viewed as an active process, not as a dead record.
- The avant-garde film is made not by a committee or a team hired for the occasion by a third party but by one individual who almost always also photographs and edits it. The film is not tailored to a market for profit purposes but results from a desire for self-expression.

Figure 1. *(Avant-Garde Film)* Luis Buñuel *L'âge d'or,* 1930. The Museum of Modern Art/Film Stills Archive.

Figure 2. *(Avant-Garde Film)* Sergei Eisenstein, *Stachka* (Strike), 1925. National Film Archive, London/Sovexport.

- The "REALISM" of the commercial cinema is unmasked as neither a self-evident, ordained mode of expression nor a true rendition of reality; its seeming transparency appears fraudulent to the legatees of SIGMUND FREUD, KARL MARX, and others who have shown hidden texts underlying the "commonsense" readings of self and society. Realism is viewed merely as one possible system of representation, as much a construct as any other.

- The conventional, straightforward narrative of Hollywood is attenuated or destroyed, its horizontal progression from inception to closure superseded by vertical exploration of states of mind, atmosphere, interior universe, and the nature of film itself. Discontinuity, ellipsis, ambiguity, and aleatory elements abound—in short, a development paralleling modernism in the other arts.

- Space and time are no longer seen as separate but as a continuum; absolute space and time have disappeared. Time and space are manipulated or shattered, telescoped or expanded.

- The illusory nature of film, so carefully masked by Hollywood, is explicitly undermined by a strongly anti-illusionist stance: "This is a film, a made object." By the subverting of this hitherto unquestioned, invisible code, its underlying system of meaning-making is revealed. Thus, editing and camerawork are overt and intrusive instead of invisible; conventional punctuation and composition, insistence on "cutting on movement" or establishing direction are eliminated.

- There is a stress on improvisation and lack of polish, seen as expressions of a new artistic freedom and casualness.

- Themes are often subversive, reaching beyond the commonly accepted for the taboo. Shock is viewed

Figure 3. *(Avant-Garde Film)* Maya Deren, *Meshes of the Afternoon,* 1943. Courtesy of the Amos Vogel Collection.

as a basic tool for heightening awareness. The onscreen splitting of an eyeball in the first scene of LUIS BUÑUEL's *Un chien Andalou* (1929)—suggesting that the old vision must be destroyed before the new one can come in—is the prototypical image of the avant-garde. The shock of the unfamiliar and the violation of conventional narratives are seen as breakthroughs to new codes.

The confluence of these attributes makes it apparent that the film avant-garde is an inextricable part

Figure 4. *(Avant-Garde Film)* James Broughton, *The Bed*, 1967. Courtesy of the Amos Vogel Collection.

of the modernist impulse in the arts. Each of the modernist schools—from surrealism to abstraction, EXPRESSIONISM to cubism, dada to pop—finds its counterpart here.

Evolution and classification. The beginnings of the avant-garde movement date back to the enormously fertile period of its first wave (1919–1930), which sprang up in various parts of Europe: in France, with Louis Delluc, Jean Epstein, Germaine Dulac, Man Ray, Fernand Léger, Marcel Duchamp, Buñuel, and Salvador Dalí; in Germany, with Viking Eggeling, Hans Richter, Walther Ruttman, and Oskar Fischinger; and in the USSR, an early center of FILM THEORY and experimentation, with SERGEI EISENSTEIN, V. I. Pudovkin, DZIGA VERTOV, Aleksandr Dovzhenko, and Lev Kuleshov. During the 1930s, German fascism, Joseph Stalin's counterrevolution, and growing international tension inhibited the avant-garde. From the 1940s on, its center shifted decisively to the United States, where a second wave of the avant-garde reached its peak during the 1950s and 1960s, contributing in turn to a new European avant-garde surge and to a parallel movement in Japan.

Two main lines of development are discernible in the movement from its inception: a psychoanalytically influenced subjective-film tendency, an outgrowth of surrealism, expressionism, and dada; and a film-as-film tendency, grounded in abstract art, cubism, constructivism, futurism, and minimalism.

Subjective film includes emotive-expressive works of dream or trance states, myths (personal or collective), self-revelation, and the unconscious; they are

Figure 5. *(Avant-Garde Film)* Dusan Makavejev, *WR—Misterije Organizma* (WR—Mysteries of the Organism), 1971. The Museum of Modern Art/Film Stills Archive.

commonly symbolic, expressionist, surrealist, psychedelic, or metaphysical. Pioneers in the subjective film field were Maya Deren, Sidney Peterson, James Broughton, and Stan Brakhage in the United States; Dulac, Abel Gance, and Philippe Garrel in Europe.

Film-as-film extends from abstract to structural works. Abstract films feature rhythmically structured configurations of geometric or nonfigurative shapes and colors, offering an emotion, if not a narrative. Structural films dismantle the medium itself, exploring its very materiality (light, rhythm, projection, and image sequence). Here films no longer exist in the service of something else (the narrative), but for themselves.

While subjective film continues to use narratives, albeit modernist ones, the film-as-film tendency rejects narrative entirely. Both trends are synchronous in time, though the period from the 1920s to the late 1960s was mainly stamped by the subjective trend, with film-as-film in steady ascendancy since then. Early catalysts in this field were James and John Whitney, Robert Breer, Andy Warhol, Michael Snow, and Hollis Frampton in the United States; Eggeling, Man Ray, and Malcolm Le Grice in Europe.

Still another group bridges the two major avant-garde tendencies. Its members include collage artists, such as Bruce Conner and Stan Vanderbeek in the United States, and the directors of mixed-media presentations, filmic happenings, multiple projections, and light shows.

At various times there has also existed a semi-avant-garde in the commercial cinema, whose pioneering in form and content has been of great significance. Contributors to this movement have been Carl Theodor Dreyer in Denmark; Jean Cocteau, Robert Bresson, Jean-Luc Godard, and Alain Resnais in France; ORSON WELLES in the United States; Michelangelo Antonioni in Italy; Nagisa Oshima in Japan; Roman Polanski in Poland; Dusan Makavejev in Yugoslavia; Ranier Werner Fassbinder and Werner Herzog in the Federal Republic of Germany; and Sergei Paradzhanov and Andrei Tarkovsky in the Soviet Union.

Social position and role. Though the avant-garde attempts to set itself against the culture industry and, in fact, propounds a countermessage—in the 1960s, one reflecting oppositional lifestyles and world-views—it has always remained tied to society. The first wave of the avant-garde was ideologically linked to the rise of the socialist and anarchist movements, sharing the common goal of total social transformation, with art to serve as a means of changing consciousness. In the second wave, these radical impulses were attenuated with the decline of radical politics. They flared briefly during the youth move-

Figure 6. *(Avant-Garde Film)* René Clair, *Entr'acte*, 1924. Courtesy of the Amos Vogel Collection.

ment of the 1960s, but in the following decades they rarely made large claims regarding sociopolitical intentions or effects.

Significantly, the avant-garde appears to be concentrated largely in technologically advanced, affluent societies. Here its creations are in constant danger of becoming commodities (if found sufficiently marketable) or of being shunted to the sidelines by mass culture. The avant-garde has had its own showcases, critics, magazines, distribution collectives, archives, and festivals—but this autonomy may cloak its social ineffectuality.

It can be argued that the ever-growing power of the culture industry has signified some neutralization of the avant-garde's radical impulse. Shock need not be merely an avant-garde technique but can be domesticated by being expected, as in popular adventure or horror films. Staccato editing, fluid camera movements, and attenuated narratives can also be found in music videos, station breaks, and COMMERCIALS.

The emergence of cheaper, more mobile VIDEO cameras, the growth of the videocassette recorder market, and even the success of music videos as a format will undoubtedly contribute to the rise of new avant-garde talents. It is safe to surmise, however, that they will remain outsiders, given the growing domination of new cable and satellite markets by large corporate structures. Yet the avant-garde's delight in the unpredictable, its insistence on the deconstruction of ossified codes, its probing of the unacceptable, signify gestures of freedom in an increasingly commercialized cinema.

See also CINEMATOGRAPHY; FILM EDITING; SPECIAL EFFECTS.

Bibliography. Peter Bürger, *Theory of the Avant-Garde* (Theorie der Avantgarde), trans. by Michael Shaw, Minneapolis, Minn., 1984; David Curtis, *Experimental Cinema*, London, 1971; Renato Poggioli, *The Theory of the Avant-Garde* (Teoria dell'arte d'avanguardia), trans. by Gerald Fitzgerald, Cambridge, Mass., 1968; Hans Scheugl and Ernst Schmidt, *Eine Subgeschichte des Filmes*, Frankfurt am Main, 1974; P. Adams Sitney, ed., *The Avant-Garde Film*, New York, 1978; Parker Tyler, *Underground Film*, New York, 1969; Amos Vogel, *Film as a Subversive Art*, New York, 1974.

AMOS VOGEL

B (bī), the second letter of the Roman alphabet, ancient and modern, corresponding in position and power to the Greek *beta* and Phœnician and Hebrew *beth*, whence also its form is derived; representing the sonant labial mute, or lip-voice stop consonant. The plural has been written Bees, B's, *B*s. . . . Used, like the other letters of the alphabet, . . . to indicate serial order, with the value of *second*. . . .

BABBAGE, CHARLES (1792–1871)

English mathematician, scientist, and early experimenter with calculating machines. The son of a wealthy banker, Charles Babbage was educated at home and at Enfield before entering Cambridge University. A mathematical prodigy, he found that his knowledge of mathematics exceeded that of his Cambridge tutors. After graduation he pursued investigations into such diverse topics as actuarial tables, life insurance, lighthouse occultation, machine tools, lock picking, organ-grinding, and operations research.

Babbage is best known, however, for his work on computation by machine; his "difference engine" and "analytical engine" prefigured twentieth-century computers (*see* COMPUTER: HISTORY). While a student at Cambridge, he was frustrated by inaccuracies he discovered in mathematical tables and wondered whether calculations of trigonometric functions could be generated by a machine driven by steam. By 1820 he had roughed out a design for his difference engine and had constructed a small working model, consisting of eighteen gear wheels and three axes, with which he could calculate squares of successive numbers. His design was enthusiastically approved, and he received a promise of assistance from the Exchequer. He established a workshop in London and

hired technicians to build his machine, but almost at once ideas for improving the machine's capacity filled his mind and outstripped both his funds and the capacities of the machine shops of his day. He hoped to build a difference engine that would produce differences of the sixth order to twenty decimal places. Work on it had begun when Babbage became interested in an even grander scheme, an analytical engine that would perform arithmetic operations on any of 1,000 fifty-digit decimal numbers. This machine was to be actuated by two sets of punched cards (modeled on those developed by the French inventor Joseph-Marie Jacquard for looms)—one set containing the program, the other containing data—and would incorporate a device to record its results on copper printing plates.

An important supporter of Babbage was Augusta Ada Lovelace (the daughter of the English poet Lord Byron), who translated and added explanatory notes to an Italian article on Babbage's analytical machine. When it was published in 1843, this translation was the only English-language description of Babbage's machine. Her contributions to the computer model were deemed significant enough that a computer language, Ada, was named for her.

Because of wavering support from the Exchequer and squabbles with workers, Babbage's engines were never completed. However, the soundness of his concepts was demonstrated when a Swedish engineer, working from a description in the *Edinburgh Review* of Babbage's difference engine, built a difference calculator that was in operation for many years.

Babbage's work foreshadowed the development of computers more than a century later, incorporating many of the principles—punched cards, separate entry of data and program, retention by the machine of previous calculations for use in future calculations—that were to be used in computers.

See also COMPUTER: IMPACT.

Bibliography. Philip Morrison and Emily Morrison, eds., *Charles Babbage and His Calculating Engines: Selected Writings by Charles Babbage and Others*, New York, 1961; Maboth Moseley, *Irascible Genius: The Life of Charles Babbage, Inventor*, Chicago and London, 1964.

ROBERT BALAY

Figure 1. *(Babbage, Charles)* A portion of Charles Babbage's Difference Engine Number 1. Trustees of the Science Museum, London.

BAEDEKER, KARL (1801–1859)

German publisher, originator of the famous Baedeker guidebooks for travelers. Member of a bookselling and PUBLISHING family, Karl Baedeker started a bookshop of his own in 1827 in Essen, the city of his birth. He moved his business to Koblenz and in 1828 bought a small publishing house that was failing but had at least one popular book, a guide to the

Rhine. Baedeker revised it, preserving its scholarly content but making it more practical for the traveler, and issued his edition in 1835. Its success encouraged him to go further into guidebook publishing, especially as he observed growing numbers of British travelers coming to Europe with the new user-oriented guides published in English by John Murray III in London. The *Baedeker Guides,* in German, began with a completely new Rhineland book in 1839 and continued with volumes on Holland and Belgium (1840), one on Germany and the Austrian Empire (1842), and Baedeker's first spectacular success, on Switzerland (1844). Also in 1844 the guides began the practice of using one or more asterisks as a way of rating places to see, stay, and eat. The first Baedeker guides translated into other languages were issued in French in 1846; versions in English began to appear in 1861.

In prefaces to some early editions Baedeker acknowledged his borrowing of some features of the Murray guides: their size, to fit a large pocket; arrangement according to routes; and strong attention to facts bearing on the traveler's comfort. He tried to improve on these qualities, to make his books even more comprehensive, and to offer more frequently updated revisions. The Murray firm finally sold rights to its guides to another house, and in 1854 Baedeker adopted Murray's binding colors: raspberry red cloth with gold stamping.

Baedeker wrote in a crisp, unadorned style, objective yet reflecting his love for his subjects; he often added enlivening comments and included short essays by experts in special areas. Baedeker himself insisted that he would not write about things he had not actually seen. He checked and rechecked, traveled under assumed names, walked wherever possible. His life was exuberant but hard-driving, and he died at fifty-eight. Already, however, his name was becoming a term commonly used to denote reliability in guidebooks. Under one of his seven children, Fritz (1844–1925), the number and scope of the guides were greatly expanded.

By setting standards of comprehensiveness, Baedeker and his successors influenced all travel-guide publishing. This contributed to the growth of TOURISM, with its evolving role in enhancing both cultural relations and the lives of travelers.

See also LEISURE.

Bibliography. "Baedeker," *Supplement to the Oxford English Dictionary,* Vol. 1, A–G, Oxford and New York, 1972 ed.; "Federal Republic of Germany: Publishers," *International Literary Marketplace 86–87,* New York, 1986; "Karl Baedeker" (biographical note on Rhineland personalities), *Baedeker's Rhine* (Baedekers Autoführer-Verlag), Englewood Cliffs, N.J., 1985; Herbert Warren Wind, "The House of Baedeker" (Profiles section), *The New Yorker* (Sept. 22, 1975): 42–44, 49–85, 88–93.

CHANDLER B. GRANNIS

BAKHTIN, MIKHAIL (1895–1975)

Russian literary theorist and philosopher of dialogue. Mikhail Mikhailovich Bakhtin's place in the history of communications is secured by his lifelong insistence on the central place of dialogue in human affairs.

Bakhtin completed his education as a classical scholar at Saint Petersburg University in the revolutionary year of 1918. Then, moving to the Vitebsk area, he became deeply involved in the first of several circles that were to grow up around him. The focus of this early group was recent German philosophy, especially Marburg neo-Kantianism. In 1924 Bakhtin moved back to Leningrad, living precariously for the next five years, during which he was involved with several philosophical and religious discussion groups. He managed to publish revised versions of some earlier texts, as well as a number of new works under the names of his friends and disciples P. N. Medvedev and V. N. Vološinov, including *Freudianism* (1927), *The Formal Method in Literary Scholarship* (1928), and the magisterial *Marxism and the Philosophy of Language* (1929). Later a lively debate arose concerning the authorship of these texts, but no one disputes that Bakhtin was primus inter pares. In 1929 he succeeded in publishing *Problems of Dostoevsky's Poetics* under his own name; in the same year he was arrested as part of a roundup of religious discussion groups. He was exiled to Kazakhstan, where he continued to research and write, particularly on the theory of the novel. During this period he produced a book on François Rabelais and the essays published in English as *The Dialogic Imagination.* After his release Bakhtin spent the years of World War II in various parts of European Russia. From 1946 until 1969 he lived and taught at the Mordovian State University in Saransk. A second edition of his Dostoyevsky book in 1963 created an enormous enthusiasm for his work that led to publication of other texts and eventual translation into several languages. He died in Moscow on March 7, 1975.

In Bakhtin's earliest, "philosophical" phase (1919–1924) he worked on a number of projects, all concerned with different aspects of what he called the "architectonics of responsibility." The general project consisted in a phenomenological description of self/other relations. Bakhtin begins by assuming that no person or thing has an existence in itself: everyone and everything is interconnected by a web of relations so vast and complex that its extent and nature can never be fully comprehended. Any appearance of closure or stoppage is therefore a fiction; not only is everything and everyone connected, but the relations holding them together are dynamic, in constant flux. For human beings this interconnectedness makes itself present as our total immersion in LANGUAGE. The word *language* as used by Bakhtin has relatively little to do with the formal constructs of GRAMMAR, syntax, or PHONOLOGY. Rather, he takes pragmatics to a radical extreme, which is why much of his work is a polemic with FERDINAND DE SAUSSURE, particularly Saussure's master distinction between *langue* and *parole*. See also LINGUISTICS; MEANING; SEMANTICS.

Saussure had ascribed a great deal of freedom to the speaker; any given SPEECH act was subject not only to the vagaries of personal differences between individuals but also to the sheer contingency of the constantly changing environment in which real-life utterances are made. He concluded that speech performance was so random that it would not lend itself to scientific study: "We cannot put [individual speech performance] into any category of human facts, for we cannot discover its unity." Bakhtin, by contrast, argues that utterance is neither random nor free; the restraints present at the abstract level of language system cannot be abrogated at the particularized level of speech performance. According to Bakhtin, "Saussure ignores the fact that besides the forms of language there exist as well forms of combination of these forms." In order further to distinguish his dialogism from the practice of linguists, Bakhtin rejects the dualistic opposition between system and performance and posits *communication*—and not language as such—as the subject of his investigations. The two basic units in the study of communication as conceived by Bakhtin are the utterance and speech genres.

Utterance is Bakhtin's overall term for a simultaneity of roles that is usually obscured by the assumption that speaking and listening are unitary, mutually opposed activities, that one does either the one or the other. Bakhtin's argument is that we do both at the same time. For example, when two persons talk, speaker listens to self and to the person speaker is addressing, and listener speaks to self and to listener's internal image of the speaker even as the speaker speaks. Utterances, in Bakhtin's terminology, enact "addressivity" (*obrashchënnost'*) or the awareness of the otherness of language in general and the otherness of given dialogic partners in particular. The work of addressivity is constantly to turn a general system of language to the needs of specific experiences.

Bakhtin saw communication not only as a human activity but as a basic feature of existence. He was intensely interested in science, and throughout his work there are suggestions that the natural world seems to be organized as a series of exchanges, responses to responses in a great dialogue of being, from the interaction between subatomic particles, between the most primitive cellular organisms and their environment, to the relation that whole solar systems bear to one another. But Bakhtin's central concern was to understand better the dialogue within the world of signs (*see* SIGN) rather than the world of things (although he refuses to posit a cutoff between the two)—different interacting levels between dialogue within the individual psyche at one end of the spectrum and dialogue between social classes and whole CULTURE systems at the other. Bakhtin's dialogism may be understood, then, as a particularly capacious theory of communication with procedural implications for a broad range of the human and social sciences.

See also COMMUNICATION, PHILOSOPHIES OF.

Bibliography. Mikhail Bakhtin, *The Dialogic Imagination* (Voprosy literatury i estetiki), ed. by Michael Holquist, trans. by Caryl Emerson and Michael Holquist, Austin, Tex., 1981; idem, *Problems of Dostoevsky's Poetics* (Problemy poetiki Dostoevskogo), ed. and trans. by Caryl Emerson, Minneapolis, Minn., 1984; Katerina Clark and Michael Holquist, *Mikhail Bakhtin*, Cambridge, Mass., 1984.

MICHAEL HOLQUIST

BANDWAGON EFFECTS

In ELECTION campaigns, the tendency of some voters to join the supporters of an apparently winning candidate. In PUBLIC OPINION research the term *bandwagon effects* has come to mean such a tendency brought about specifically by exposure to public opinion polls indicating that one candidate is in the lead. In this limited version, the effect has never been demonstrated. However, PAUL F. LAZARSFELD and his associates showed in 1944 that *expectations* of who will win an election do influence voter preferences. Public opinion polls may therefore affect voter preferences by influencing expectations. But it is also considered possible that the votes of those who are motivated to jump on the leading candidate's bandwagon will be counteracted by the lost votes of supporters who no longer feel an incentive to vote (because they believe their vote is not needed) and by those moved to vote for an underdog.

Some evidence for *postelection* bandwagon effects comes from studies showing that after an election the preferences of those who claim to have voted go disproportionately to the winning candidate. The following explanation has been proposed: when a particular social group is found to have voted overwhelmingly for the winning candidate, members of the group assume, after the fact, that they too voted for this candidate, even if they did not. Such bandwagon effects may thus be explained, it has been argued, in terms of *reference groups*. That is, some voters, on the basis of later information, may unconsciously adjust their recollections to conform to the voting pattern of the group with which they identify.

In recent years the term has been extended to cover the effects of election-day projections based on early returns or exit polls (polls taken as people leave the voting place). The evidence for such bandwagon effects on voter preferences has been mixed, but the hypothesis of some effect on turnout is at least tenable.

Although no evidence exists for the classic version of the bandwagon hypothesis, wide dissemination of POLL findings can have other significant effects. In the United States they have been shown to affect the flow of financial contributions as well as the attention paid to candidates by the media. Early studies of bandwagon effects were done in a very different media environment; in the 1940s, poll results were reported neither on television nor on the radio and were seen by no more than one-fifth of the public in newspapers or magazines. Whether the now widespread broadcast dissemination of poll results likewise fails to produce effects remains an open question. Polls may also affect voter preferences in more complex ways—for example, by defining which candidates are to be considered seriously. All of these potential effects are a matter of increasing public concern.

See also OPINION MEASUREMENT; PERSUASION; POLITICAL COMMUNICATION.

Bibliography. Kurt Lang and Gladys Lang, *Voting and Nonvoting*, Waltham, Mass., 1968; Paul F. Lazarsfeld, Bernard Berelson, and Hazel Gaudet, *The People's Choice* (1944), 3d ed., New York, 1968; Elizabeth Noelle-Neumann, *The Spiral of Silence*, Chicago, 1984; Percy H. Tannenbaum and Leslie J. Kostrich, *Turned-On TV/ Turned-Off Voters*, Beverly Hills, Calif., 1983.

ELEANOR SINGER

BARGAINING

A process whereby two or more interdependent parties attempt to settle their differences through an exchange of proposals and counterproposals. A number of theorists treat *negotiation* and *bargaining* as synonyms, while others define bargaining as the exchange process taking place within the act of nego-

tiation. Here negotiation and bargaining are treated as synonyms.

Characteristics of Bargaining

Five characteristics distinguish bargaining as a form of problem solving. First, bargaining is generally treated as a subset of conflict in that the parties hold or perceive that they hold *incompatible goals* or interests. Second, the two parties engaged in bargaining are *interdependent* in that one party's gain or loss depends on the other party's choices. Within a framework of competition, then, the two parties must cooperate to reach their individual goals. Each party has the power to constrain or prevent the other from attaining a goal.

The third characteristic, *social interaction*, refers to the means through which the bargaining is carried out. Interaction can be both tacit and explicit. Explicit communication consists of the messages conveyed openly between the bargainers, such as demands, concessions, and information; tacit communication refers to hints, signs, nonverbal gestures, and other indirect messages that shape interpretations of the interaction. Tacit bargaining typically accompanies explicit messages, but in conditions of low trust, bargainers might substitute tacit maneuvers for explicit communication. Fourth, bargaining occurs through an *exchange of offers and counteroffers* that represents each party's effort to find a mutually satisfactory solution. Thus proposals, concessions, and policy arguments form the substance of the interaction. Finally, bargaining is a *strategic activity* in that both parties plot moves and countermoves based on estimates of their opponents' behavior and intentions and on their system of shared rules.

Bargaining is an activity that is found in most interpersonal, intergroup, and international contexts. At the interpersonal level, bargaining undergirds buyer-seller relations, employment negotiations, reprimand situations, legal transactions, and consumer relations. Husbands and wives negotiate household chores, subordinates bargain for salary raises, and public relations personnel negotiate with media employees. At the intergroup level, negotiations take place between racial groups, organizations involved in environmental or regulatory disputes, and departments vying for scarce resources. International negotiations provide the basis for treaty formation, hostage release, and trade contracts (*see also* TERRORISM).

The preceding types of bargaining situations differ in terms of their overall purpose; their tasks; the number, importance, and sequencing of issues; the role of constituents; the presence of deadlines and legal constraints; and the cultural norms that govern the behavior of negotiators. Thus, communicative patterns in bargaining are different in situations with different constraints. For example, a one-shot, one-issue negotiation without constituent representation differs in the type, amount, and sequencing of messages from a serial negotiation with constituent pressures exerted on multiple issues.

The Study of Bargaining

Historically, game theory and social exchange models have dominated research on bargaining. Game theory is derived from classical economics and assumes that bargainers are rational, want to maximize their gains and minimize their losses, have perfect knowledge of the possible outcomes and the values attached to each, and are able to calculate their relative advantage from the moves of their opponent.

Social exchange theory, a derivative of the pure game theory model, centers on the rewards and costs incurred from the bargaining exchange. Early studies on communication and bargaining employed game and social exchange models to test the impact of amount and medium of communication on bargaining outcomes. At first, researchers concluded that increased communication led to cooperative outcomes; but in highly competitive bargaining, more communication increased distortion and manipulation, which, in turn, heightened error and misunderstanding. Research also demonstrated that face-to-face interaction facilitated cooperative outcomes more frequently than did audio, video, or written modes of communication (see INTERACTION, FACE-TO-FACE). Thus the frequency of communication enhanced cooperative settlements only if bargainers were predisposed to be cooperative and were bargaining face-to-face.

Research on information exchange and message strategies has also adopted game theory models of bargaining. Bargainers use strategies and tactics as ways of increasing their own strength, reducing their opponents' strength, or gaining control over the negotiation context. A strategy represents the overall plan—for example, to be cooperative on problems of working conditions and to be tough on resource issues. Tactics consist of the communicative behaviors that make up a strategy, such as threats, commitments, and agreements. Bargainers reach agreements by making reciprocating concessions and by avoiding firm commitments that signal freezing into a set position. Threats and promises, while generally successful in inducing compliance, tend to intensify a conflict and make it more difficult to reach a satisfactory settlement.

Message strategies are also examined through the use of process models of communication and bargaining. Process models center on the evolution of bargaining over time. Researchers focus on behavioral patterns and regularities that indicate how bargaining goals, issues, and values change through the interaction process. Unlike game theory, this perspective assumes that bargainers have minimal knowledge of alternative outcomes and rely on types and sequences of tactics to anticipate their opponents' moves.

Process theories of bargaining frame the research on conflict cycles, information management, issue development, and phase analysis. Here discourse and conversational analysis models are used to study bargaining arguments and interaction sequences (see CONVERSATION). Studies of conflict cycles reveal that bargainers typically balance offensive and defensive maneuvers to buffer the escalation of conflict. A pattern of matching either offensive or defensive tactics, however, frequently produces uncontrollable escalation of the conflict. One type of buffer used to reduce conflict spirals is information exchange. Questions obligate an opponent to respond, a pattern that produces an information-expansion sequence of questions and short, abrupt answers. Bargaining interaction is also controlled by shifting the claims of an argument and redefining an issue. This shift in argument occurs as negotiators begin to package agenda items, drop or simplify subissues, accent or sharpen issues, and reveal their interpretations of a problem.

The study of conflict cycles has led researchers to examine phases or stages of bargaining development. Ann Douglas in *Industrial Peacemaking* (1962) uncovered three major stages of bargaining: establishing the bargaining range, jockeying for position, and precipitating the decision-reaching crisis. Not all bargaining sessions pass through the same stages, however. Procedural restrictions and deadlines may preclude a set pattern of phasic development. A spin-off of the work on phases focuses on bargaining history and the annual recurrence of bargaining events. Some organizational researchers treat bargaining as an annual rite of conflict characterized by ritualistic behavior and stories of past negotiations that are enacted in tacit and explicit communication. These studies reveal that procedural norms, nonverbal behaviors of participants, and the historical precedent of tactics and strategies become ritualized over time and affect the bargaining settlement.

Fact Finding, Mediation, and Arbitration

When the outcome of bargaining is an impasse, the conflicting parties typically turn to third-party intervention, such as fact finders, mediators, or arbitrators. Fact finders are outsiders who are called in to examine the information presented by both parties and to uncover additional data that might help move the sides toward a settlement. Mediators are primarily facilitators who control the communication process between the two sides. Mediators control topics of interaction, provide advice to both parties, offer proposals, and help the two parties to save face. Thus mediators function as communication counselors by clarifying and interpreting complex issues, providing background information, setting up the agenda, and focusing the interaction. Arbitrators, unlike fact finders and mediators, act as judges and have the power to make decisions. The two disputing parties typically bring final offers or argument briefs to the arbitrator, who rules in favor of one side or the other.

Communication is the essence of mediation activities, and it serves a dominant information-processing role in fact finding and arbitration. In bargaining, communication is also crucial: for information processing, PERSUASION, identification of patterns and regularities, and coordination of outcomes.

See also GROUP COMMUNICATION; INTERPERSONAL COMMUNICATION; NONVERBAL COMMUNICATION.

Bibliography. Samuel B. Bacharach and Edward J. Lawler, *Bargaining: Power, Tactics, and Outcomes,* San Francisco, 1981; Max H. Bazerman and Roy J. Lewicki, eds., *Negotiating in Organizations,* Beverly Hills, Calif., 1983; Ann Douglas, *Industrial Peacemaking,* New York, 1962; Jay Folberg and Alison Taylor, *Mediation,* San Francisco, 1984; Philip H. Gulliver, *Disputes and Negotiations: A Cross-Cultural Perspective,* New York, 1979; Ian E. Morley and Geoffrey M. Stephenson, *The Social Psychology of Bargaining,* London, 1977; Jeffrey Z. Rubin and Bert R. Brown, *The Social Psychology of Bargaining and Negotiation,* New York, 1975; Richard E. Walton and Robert B. McKersie, *A Behavioral Theory of Labor Negotiations,* New York, 1965.

LINDA L. PUTNAM

BARNUM, PHINEAS T. (1810–1891)

"The great American showman." Entrepreneur, circus proprietor, trickster, lecturer, politician, author, and considered by many a progenitor of modern ADVERTISING, Phineas Taylor Barnum built a career on the public's eagerness to believe and its fascination with the outrageous. He began his vocation in 1835 by exhibiting Joice Heth, a black woman who claimed that she was more than 160 years old and had been George Washington's nurse. Barnum even managed to get considerable publicity from Heth's eventual exposure as a fraud, claiming that he too had been duped. In 1841 he acquired Scudder's American Museum in New York, renaming it Barnum's American Museum. There he presented wild animals, natural history specimens, lectures, plays of a "moral" nature, novelties, oddities, and hoaxes. Exhibits included the "Feejee Mermaid," a female monkey torso

Figure 1. *(Barnum, Phineas T.)* Caricature of Phineas T. Barnum. From *Vanity Fair,* New York, September 13, 1862. National Portrait Gallery, Smithsonian Institution, Washington, D.C.

coupled with a large stuffed fish tail, and Siamese twins Chang and Eng. Finding that patrons paused too long to gawk at the presentations, Barnum erected a sign proclaiming "To the Egress," and customers in pursuit of another strange exhibit soon found themselves on the street.

In 1842 Barnum became the manager of Charles Stratton, a five-year-old midget whom he renamed General Tom Thumb. After exhibiting his discovery in the United States, Barnum toured Europe, where he and Stratton were received at the courts of London and Paris. It was this venture that truly made Barnum's name and fortune. In 1850 he engaged Jenny Lind, "the Swedish Nightingale," for a widely acclaimed and highly lucrative concert tour of the United States.

In spite of the considerable financial reward these ventures brought him, Barnum went bankrupt in 1855 as the result of an unwise investment in a clock company. He recouped much of his wealth in 1857, however, by persuading Stratton and Cordelia Howard, a nine-year-old child prodigy, to star in a production of *Uncle Tom's Cabin* that toured Britain and the Continent. By the following year Barnum had attained such celebrity status that he began to give lectures to packed houses on such topics as the art of "moneygetting" and the virtues of temperance.

Having achieved notoriety as a producer and public speaker, the self-professed Prince of Humbugs next decided to enter politics. He was elected to the Connecticut legislature in 1865 and 1866, and in 1875 he served a term as mayor of Bridgeport, Connecticut.

In 1871 Barnum entered into partnership with W. C. Coup and Dan Costello to present a huge traveling circus featuring a menagerie, a museum, and a hippodrome, as well as acrobats, clowns, and a variety of dwarfs, giants, and other special attractions. In a short time the operation had expanded into the world's first three-ring circus. Costello left the partnership after quarreling with Barnum, and in 1881 Barnum joined forces with his foremost rival, James A. Bailey, to create "The Barnum and Bailey Greatest Show on Earth." Among the circus's many famous attractions was the giant elephant Jumbo, purchased in 1882 from the Royal Zoological Society in London and exhibited by Barnum as "the only mastodon left on earth."

During the course of his career Barnum wrote a number of books, including *The Humbugs of the World*, *How I Made Millions*, and his autobiography, *The Life of P. T. Barnum*. He died on April 7, 1891. His last words were reported to be a request to know the day's circus receipts at Madison Square Garden.

See also DECEPTION; ENTERTAINMENT; SPECTACLE.

Bibliography. Neil Harris, *Humbug: The Art of P. T. Barnum*, Boston, 1973.

RICHARD PILCHER

BARTHES, ROLAND (1915–1980)

French literary critic, essayist, and semiotician. Born in provincial France, Roland Barthes studied literature at the University of Paris. After a long illness he taught at universities in Romania and Egypt, then returned to France as a member of the Centre National de la Recherche Scientifique. Barthes became director of studies at the École Pratique des Hautes Études, and in the late 1960s, as STRUCTURALISM came into fashion in France, he passed from being something of a marginal enfant terrible on the Parisian intellectual scene to the status of Parisian eminence, attracting some of the media attention and cult following previously devoted to Jean-Paul Sartre. He published numerous books, essays, and reviews and was finally honored by a professorship at the prestigious Collège de France. He died in 1980 as the result of a road accident.

From beginning to end Barthes's work displays an intense, well-nigh erotic passion for LANGUAGE, for the sheer creative act of writing, that situates it in some twilight world between full-blown semiotic theory (*see* SEMIOTICS) and imaginative FICTION. An inveterate transgressor of frontiers, Barthes cavalierly mixes the academic and autobiographical, journalism and "high" literature, scientific LINGUISTICS and baroque meditations. His early interest in semiology (*Elements of Semiology*, 1964) reflects his fascination for a discourse that indifferently traverses the jealously demarcated disciplines of the academic establishment, boldly reducing everything from Balzac to restaurant menus, Michelet to wrestling matches, to the common terrain of the rule-governed SIGN. Aware that *system* is denounced by bourgeois humanism as the enemy of *art* and *personality*, Barthes in his early years impudently schematized and manhandled the most revered cultural objects, importing Freudian PSYCHOANALYSIS into the study of the work of Jean Racine (*On Racine*, 1963), deploying intricate semiotic techniques for the analysis of popular cultural objects (*Mythologies*, 1957), and treating the Marquis de Sade's endless sexual permutations as a kind of structuralist *"combinatoire"* (*Sade/Fourier/Loyola*, 1971).

Barthes is an unrepentant formalist, convinced that it is in form rather than in semantic content that the subtlest operations of IDEOLOGY and the unconscious can be most valuably mapped. His early tour de force *Writing Degree Zero* (1953) accordingly sets out to provide a social and political history of French writing from the mid-nineteenth century on that is constructed wholly in terms of what one might call the "ideology of form," the intricate ways in which a writer's stance toward language itself speaks eloquently of his or her mode of engagement with the world. Everything for Barthes begins and ends in technique, but technique grasped in some deeply historical and political sense. Scornful in high structuralist fashion of "depth," "expression," "interiority," and "human nature," he dreams of a world of pure signs, textures, and surfaces (*Empire of Signs*, 1970) and of a writing that doubles constantly back upon itself, liberated from the deadweight of a referent. His work is in this sense a theoretical equivalent of literary modernism—not simply a theory of modernism but a modernist theory, which will overleap the boundaries between "critical" and "creative," intellectual and sensual, and put itself continuously into ironic question.

Barthes's early espousal of structuralism and semiology sprang from a fierce hatred of the "natural," which he consistently regarded as simply an alternative term for repressive ideology. His project from the outset was accordingly to unmask the received, spontaneous, and taken-for-granted as constructed artifice, no less rigorously rule-governed (and hence no less transformable) than such blatantly cultural matters as fashion in clothes (which he submitted to semiotic analysis in *Système de la mode,* 1967). From about the time of the publication of his celebrated *S/Z* (1970), a phrase-by-phrase semiotic analysis of a relatively obscure novella of Honoré de Balzac, a certain shift in his writing can be observed, parallel to the more general intellectual transition in France from structuralism to poststructuralism. Previously it had seemed to Barthes that system, artifice, and schematization were the weapons most likely to scandalize bourgeois humanism and expose its ideological prejudice; but ironically such semiotic systematization tends itself to display all the closure, inexorability, and uniformity of ideology. His work will accordingly turn increasingly to the disruptive and transgressive—to those unformalizable gestures, signifiers, and sensations that elude the mastery of closed systems and suggest some irreducible materiality that evades the grasp of MEANING. In such works as *The Pleasure of the Text* (1973) the body itself becomes symbolic for Barthes of these preoccupations; READING is now less the tracing of some stabilized SIGN SYSTEM, less a question of codes and conventions, than a ceaseless dance of signifiers, without origin, essence, or end, a fading or explosion of meaning equivalent to sexual orgasm or *jouissance.* Barthes will later explore such issues further in two apparently "confessional" texts: *Roland Barthes by Roland Barthes* (1975) and *A Lover's Discourse* (1977).

Barthes began his career as a Marxist fellow traveler, championing the work of Bertolt Brecht and writing about the political significance of cultural forms. He ends in a kind of pluralistic hedonism, expressing a libertarian distaste for all settled system and meaning, turning inward from political society to writing, pleasure, and the body. Horrified by the thought of orthodoxy, he keeps his writing restlessly on the move, endemically skeptical and provisional in its formulations, so that each of his books has about it a certain tantalizing unpredictability, a momentary resting on a topic that, like all the others, will pass quickly into the archives. Beneath this well-cultivated inconsistency, however, runs a range of repetitive themes: writing as an "intransitive" passion, unsettling all "natural" assumptions in its outrageous arbitrariness and artifice; the "death of the author," whose own intended meanings are constantly outrun and overturned by the sportive ambiguities of his or her texts; the tedium and tyranny of all realist or representational art, which fixes reality in some frozen posture and represses the artifice of its own construction (*see* REALISM). Above all, perhaps, Barthes's work is distinguished by its rare combination of delicacy and astringency, as a sensibility nervously alert to nuance is yoked to a kind of

dry, fastidious Gallic irony. His own literary style, at once somehow sumptuous and restrained, is the mark of this extraordinary blending of qualities.

See also AUTHORSHIP; FOUCAULT, MICHEL; LITERARY CRITICISM; STYLE, LITERARY.

Bibliography. Roland Barthes, *The Pleasure of the Text* (Le plaisir du texte), trans. by Richard Miller, London, 1976; idem, *Writing Degree Zero* (Le degré zéro de l'écriture), trans. by Annette Lavers and Colin Smith, New York, 1968; Jonathan Culler, *Barthes,* London, 1983.

TERRY EAGLETON

BATESON, GREGORY (1904–1980)

U.S. scholar who made contributions in anthropology, biology, psychology, AESTHETICS, learning theory, CYBERNETICS, and—drawing on all of them—communications. Gregory Bateson was born in Cambridge, England, into a family with a strong intellectual tradition. His father, William, was an important figure in the early days of genetics even before that science had its name, and other Batesons, before and after, have been members of England's Royal Society, home to the intellectual elite. Bateson received his B.A. and M.A. degrees at Cambridge and later moved to the United States and became a U.S. citizen.

Unlike many other Batesons, however, whose fame resided in one particular field, Gregory's fame and influence have a more universal character. He almost seems a dilettante, so varied were his interests, yet the thread that connects them gives evidence of a systematic development of complex ideas. Central to these have been issues related to communication, by which he meant not merely the exchange of messages between individuals but also the metaphoric transfer of information in the process of evolution. Bateson's great talent as a theorist and teacher lay in his uninhibited willingness to use the tools of other specialists that were spurned by his more narrowly focused colleagues.

He began a synthesis of his ideas, he wrote, when "in late 1969 I became fully conscious . . . that in my work with primitive peoples, schizophrenia, biological symmetry, and in my discontent with the conventional theories of evolution and learning, I had identified a widely scattered set of bench marks or points of reference from which a new scientific territory could be defined. These bench marks I have called 'steps.' " (He used the term in *Steps to an Ecology of Mind,* a book that made him something of a guru of the environmental movement.)

Bateson's first major work was conducted in Bali, much of it in collaboration with MARGARET MEAD, his first wife. An important publication during the period of their marriage was the artistically brilliant

Figure 1. *(Bateson, Gregory)* Gregory Bateson with Margaret Mead in New Guinea. The Institute for Intercultural Studies/Library of Congress.

Balinese Character: A Photographic Analysis, which foreshadowed his interest in signs (*see* SEMIOTICS; SIGN; SIGN SYSTEM) and also demonstrated the importance of still PHOTOGRAPHY and film in ethnographic research (*see* DOCUMENTARY; ETHNOGRAPHIC FILM). Bateson and Mead also collaborated in developing the science of cybernetics and in pointing out its applications in social science research. Bateson in particular applied concepts from cybernetics to problems in family therapy and ecology.

Bateson's paper "Pidgin English and Cross-Cultural Communications" (1944) provided a more explicit if aesthetically less revealing indication of his interest in signs and was followed in 1951 by *Communication: The Social Matrix of Psychiatry* (with Jurgen Ruesch). During this period and the following decade he appeared to shift from studies of South Sea cultures to work on mental illness, though the emphasis on communication ensured continuity in his writings.

Many feel that Bateson's most important contribution was the double-bind hypothesis. He applied British philosopher Bertrand Russell's theory of logical types to an analysis of communication in schizophrenics. He argued that a double bind results when the victim, usually a dependent child, is repeatedly given conflicting signals by another family member, usually a parent figure, so that no matter what the victim does it will be wrong. For example, mother asks daughter, "Have you given the gentleman a cookie?" and if daughter answers affirmatively, mother says, "What do you mean by giving away my cookies?" Or, if daughter answers negatively, mother says, "Why must you wait for me to tell you to offer our guest a cookie?" Bateson argued that it is repeated exposure to such unresolvable communicative conflicts, not unique traumatic incidents, that underlies much mental disorientation.

Parallels to the double bind are found in the animal world, but here it is a conflict such as that between fighting and fleeing that must be resolved. Young animals play-fight, but only rarely do the movements that among adults would cause blood to flow lead to violence among playing pups. Bateson addresses this issue in a 1956 article, "The Message, 'This Is Play,'" which heralds his move from a psychiatric to a zoological institute and a fully focused effort to grasp the complexities of communication in nonhuman organisms, especially whales and porpoises.

Probably Bateson's most lasting influence in studies of communication will be seen in his emphasis on the importance of METAPHOR. Ironically, this view of his is best represented by a statement from his daughter, Mary Catherine, who has concluded, " . . . we have incomplete access to the complexity that we are . . . we're just not organized to be aware of it. One reason why poetry is important for finding out about the world is because in poetry a set of relationships gets mapped onto a level of diversity in us that we don't ordinarily have access to. . . . So we read poetry as knowledge about the world and about ourselves, because of this mapping from complexity to complexity."

Bibliography. Gregory Bateson, *Naven,* 2d ed., Stanford, Calif., 1958; idem, *Steps to an Ecology of Mind,* New York, 1972; Mary Catherine Bateson, *Our Own Metaphor,* New York, 1972; idem, *With a Daughter's Eye,* New York, 1984; David Lipset, *Gregory Bateson: The Legacy of a Scientist,* Englewood Cliffs, N.J., 1980.

PETER H. KLOPFER

BEAVERBROOK, 1st BARON (1879–1964)

Canadian-born British politician and newspaper publisher. Although Beaverbrook became one of the foremost British press lords and made a fortune from his three newspapers, journalism was only a subsidiary of his highly active political and business life. He made other fortunes in the commercial world, and his newspapers were primarily adjuncts to his career in government, tools in the propagation of his essentially conservative and imperialistic views.

Born William Maxwell Aitken in Maple, Ontario, the son of a Scottish Presbyterian minister, Beaverbrook was brought up in Newcastle, New Brunswick, and demonstrated an early aptitude for business. Momentarily sidetracked into the study of law, he began his career in commerce as a stockbroker in Montreal. Three years later he had made his first fortune by using his immense energy and shrewdness to merge all the Canadian cement companies into a single industry.

Moving to England in 1910 but retaining Canadian business ties, Beaverbrook plunged at once into politics. In 1911 he won a seat in Parliament as a Conservative member from Ashton-under-Lyne in Lancaster. As private secretary to Andrew Bonar Law, the new member immediately found himself in a position of power after Law became party leader a year later. From that point on, Beaverbrook's career offers a curious paradox of success and failure. Knighted in 1911 and in 1916 made a baronet, then baron, he became an influential figure in David Lloyd George's cabinet, but from the beginning he was unsuccessful in bringing about the political reforms he dedicated most of his life to pursuing and to which his newspapers were devoted.

After serving as minister of information in Lloyd George's wartime cabinet, Beaverbrook turned his attention to journalism as soon as World War I ended. He had gained financial control of the *Daily Express* in 1916 and placed himself in full charge at the end of 1918. At the same time, he founded the *Sunday Express* to expand its mass readership, and in 1923 he completed his small empire with the acquisition of the *Evening Standard*. In a short time the *Daily Express* became the most widely read newspaper in the world.

Beaverbrook's papers were the British equivalent of JOSEPH PULITZER's nineteenth-century newspaper in the United States, the New York *World*. They were sensational in their news and feature columns (although mild by late-twentieth-century standards) and politically outspoken on their editorial pages. But whereas Pulitzer's views were liberal, Beaverbrook tirelessly promoted what he called Empire Free Trade, by which he meant separating Britain from its foreign trade arrangements to concentrate on

Figure 1. *(Beaverbrook, 1st Baron)* Lord Beaverbrook. The Bettmann Archive/BBC Hulton.

Commonwealth interests. In spite of an editorial stridency not since surpassed by the London press, his campaign was not a success. Beaverbrook won only small victories despite the power generated by his newspapers.

Beaverbrook was also overshadowed journalistically by rival press lord ALFRED NORTHCLIFFE, who founded the *Daily Mail* and the *Daily Mirror* and introduced sensationalism to the British press. Beaverbrook's papers were, however, unusually well written and edited for his time. After his death they lost some of their idiosyncratic character, which had reflected Beaverbrook's personality, but continued to flourish in varying degrees as mass-circulation papers. In addition to his newspapers Beaverbrook left such books as *Politicians and the Press* (1925), *Don't Trust to Luck* (1954), and *Men and Power* (1956).

See also NEWSPAPER: HISTORY; NEWSPAPER: TRENDS—TRENDS IN EUROPE.

Bibliography. Thomas E. N. Driberg, *Beaverbrook: A Study in Power and Frustration*, London, 1956; Logan Gourlay, ed., *The Beaverbrook I Knew*, London and New York, 1984; A. J. P. Taylor, *Beaverbrook*, London, 1972; Evelyn Waugh, *Scoop*, London, 1938.

JOHN TEBBEL

BELL, ALEXANDER GRAHAM (1847–1922)

Scottish-born inventor of the TELEPHONE. In 1875 Alexander Graham Bell achieved the first electrical transmission of SPEECH, and during the following year he gave demonstrations widely, including performances at the Centennial Exposition in Philadelphia. His Bell Telephone Company expanded quickly into a powerful system that included the American Telephone and Telegraph Company (AT&T), organized in 1884 to wire the nation and link it, in the words of its charter, "with the rest of the known world." The possibility of instant communication with any part of the globe revolutionized the way people thought of their world and their place in it. But Bell's achievement had still further implications. In his patent application he described the invention as a system for "transmitting vocal and other sounds telegraphically." His demonstrations included diverse elements. An audience in Boston was invited to hear "telegraphically" a singer in Providence performing arias from *The Marriage of Figaro*. Demonstrations in other cities relayed an exhortation by evangelist Dwight Moody, a gospel hymn sung and played by Ira David Sanky, a dramatic reading of Hamlet's "To be or not to be," and a woman singing "Kathleen Mavourneen." Such cultural services, seen by some as the real destiny of the telephone, soon yielded to the more profitable servicing of two-way talk. But Bell foreshadowed the age of broadcasting as well as that of universal telephony, and AT&T would return in due time to the rest of the agenda (*see* RADIO).

Bell was the son and grandson of noted elocutionists. His father invented the first accurate ALPHABET for the recording of speech sounds; he called it "visible speech." The family moved to Ontario when Bell was twenty-three, in a successful effort to restore his health. Soon after, Bell moved to Boston and opened a school to teach methods of training the deaf to speak. By 1872 his interest in recording and communicating speech had broadened to include mechanical apparatuses. He began by using modulations in an electrical circuit to stimulate sounding rods, to reproduce a melody over telegraph wires; this work led to a system of multiple TELEGRAPHY, partially patented in early 1875. Bell then synthesized the principle of induced current used in his multiple telegraph with the use of a flexible diaphragm to transform sonic vibrations into electromagnetic impulses, utilizing a magnetic driver for the diaphragm based on the principle of variable resistance (what Bell called "undulatory current").

Bell's invention of the telephone precipitated legal struggles. Western Union, which had for decades enjoyed lucrative MONOPOLY control over telegraphy in the United States—and therefore over rapid long-distance communication—did not at once see Bell's invention as a threat. When Bell offered his 1876 patent to Western Union for $100,000, the offer was scornfully refused. Soon afterward Western Union saw its peril and launched a determined patent war but in 1879 gave up the struggle and settled with Bell's company. Ironically, Bell's victory made it far more powerful than Western Union had been, setting a pattern for the trusts that would develop during the first decades of the twentieth century. *See* TELECOMMUNICATIONS NETWORKS.

After his active involvement in the telephone company ended in 1880, Bell turned his energies to a dozen fields of invention, ranging from medical instruments to underwater detection, from hydrofoil ships to geodesic homes. Of these later researches, two are most relevant to communications. Bell and his colleagues developed the floating-stylus phonograph, the first commercially successful version of THOMAS ALVA EDISON's invention. About the same time, Bell also patented a "photophone," which used light beams as a communications carrier. This invention eventually became practical with the development of the laser and optical fiber (*see* FIBER OPTICS).

Bibliography. American Telephone and Telegraph, *The Bell Telephone*, New York, 1908; Robert Bruce, *Alexander Graham Bell and the Conquest of Solitude*, Boston, 1973.

HARTLEY S. SPATT

BENJAMIN, WALTER (1892–1940)

German Marxist and theological thinker. Born in Berlin of prosperous middle-class parents, Walter Benjamin came under the influence of the romantic and neo-Kantian thought prevalent in Germany in the years before World War I and took a deep interest in Jewish mystical and apocalyptic writing, becoming for a while a member of the Jewish youth movement. His early essays reveal a preoccupation with messianic conceptions of social REVOLUTION, laced with an element of anarchic violence influenced to some degree by the French radical theorist Georges Sorel. But he was also fascinated from the very outset of his intellectual career with the idea of LANGUAGE, and in such writings as the early *On Language as Such and the Language of Man* (1916) he explored esoteric notions of a primordial, prelapsarian language in which SIGN and object, word and deed, were harmoniously united. A conception of language as essentially mimetic rather than semiotic (*see* SEMIOTICS) was to thread its way through Benjamin's writing career, with complex relations to cabalistic notions of scriptural INTERPRETATION on the one hand and Marxist doctrines of the unity of theory and practice on the other.

After an early, brilliant essay on Johann Wolfgang von Goethe's *Elective Affinities* (1922), Benjamin produced his first major work, a profound, esoteric, and markedly idiosyncratic study of German baroque TRAGEDY, which was published in 1928 as *The Origin of German Tragic Drama*. Neo-Kantian and cabalistic in critical method, the work develops a startlingly original theory of allegory, viewing the German baroque DRAMA as the sluggish, melancholic record of a world that has sacrificed metaphysical truth to corrupt political intrigue. Aspects of Benjamin's theory of allegory were to pass later into his Marxist notions of the commodity, and his fascination for the multileveled, fragmentary, self-conscious dramatic forms of baroque THEATER prefigures his later championship of the Marxist poet and dramatist Bertolt Brecht. The work was written as Benjamin's postdoctoral thesis, but he withdrew it from examination, having been privately advised that his examiners had not understood a single word of it. At the time of its appearance as a published book, it was greeted with silence, irritation, or incomprehension throughout Germany. Deprived of an academic career because of the failure of his thesis, Benjamin eked out a modest existence for the rest of his life through literary journalism, devoting a large part of what little money he made to his consuming passion for collecting.

In the mid-1920s, partly under the influence of the Russian revolutionary theater director Asja Lacis, Benjamin began to turn slowly toward Marxism, without abandoning his Judaic beliefs. He was greatly stirred by the Hungarian philosopher and literary critic György Lukács's *History and Class Consciousness* and became a friend of the Marxist theologian Ernst Bloch, whose "philosophy of hope" paralleled many of the motifs of his own messianic thought. Another close friend was the Jewish theologian Gershom Scholem, who disapproved of Benjamin's shift toward revolutionary politics. That shift was first reflected in his collection of fragments *One-Way Street* (1925–1926), which broke boldly with conventional book format and proclaimed the literary critic as "strategist of the literary struggle." Benjamin struck up an intimate collaboration with Brecht and was the first critic to grasp and appreciate his revolutionary dramaturgy. *See also* LITERARY CRITICISM.

Caught precariously between Brecht's deliberately "crude" political commitment and the arcane theological interests represented for him by Scholem, Benjamin fled to Paris in 1933, when Adolf Hitler came to power in Germany, and began work on the major project of his life: a detailed study of nineteenth-century Paris, focused on the poet Charles Baudelaire and known today as the Arcades project. The work brings together "allegorical" and cabalistic interpretation, Freudian PSYCHOANALYSIS, and historical materialism, moving with dialectical dexterity from Parisian ARCHITECTURE to the structure of the commodity, from poetic imagery to the peculiarities of the modern psychical and perceptual apparatus. In Paris Benjamin also fell under the thrall of surrealism, and in his classic essays "The Author as Producer" (1934) and "The Work of Art in the Age of Mechanical Reproduction" (1936) he boldly defended AVANT-GARDE artistic experiment against traditional ART forms. During this period Benjamin was kept financially afloat by the Institute for Social Research, center of the so-called Frankfurt school of Marxism, which was then in exile from Germany in New York.

Benjamin's last major piece of writing, the 1940 "Theses on the Philosophy of History," wove together messianic notions of redemptive apocalypse and politically revolutionary views of history to combat what he saw as a ruling-class IDEOLOGY of history as homogeneous continuum. In 1940 he fled before the advance of the Nazi troops into Paris to the Franco-Spanish frontier, where he was arrested. On being told that he was to be handed over to the Gestapo the following morning, Benjamin took his own life.

Benjamin's astonishingly varied, fertile writings, largely ignored in his own lifetime, are recognized today as among the most vital documents of Western Marxism. That Marxism was always deeply idiosyncratic, shot through with esoteric reflections on history and language; but from this unstable compound of intellectual motifs, Benjamin was able to produce searching insights into such diverse topics as the revolutionary uses of nostalgia, the materiality of the sign, the cultural potential of modern technology, and the "redemption" of precious objects by quotation, collection, miniaturization, and hallucinogenic PERCEPTION. His writing, distinguished by its cryptic, indirect, tenaciously detailed attention to stray minutiae, is a strange blending of the High German traditional intellectual and the revolutionary avant-gardist devoted to "shock effect," discontinuity, and estrangement. Like his close friend THEODOR ADORNO, he believed in "breaking open" the dreary continuum of ruling-class cultural and political history by a technique of violent "constellation," in which (as with avant-garde methods of montage) strikingly disparate or scattered images are forced suddenly into fresh, revelatory interrelations. Each of Benjamin's works represents such an unorthodox "constellation," raiding a history collapsing into barbarism for the odd bits and pieces that, properly wrenched out of context and put to use, could be deployed as weapons against the Fascist enemy from whom, as he once remarked, "not even the dead are safe."

See also MARXIST THEORIES OF COMMUNICATION.

Bibliography. Walter Benjamin, *Charles Baudelaire: A Lyric Poet in the Era of High Capitalism* (in German), trans. by Harry Zohn, London, 1973; idem, *Illuminations* (Illumi- nationen, Frankfurt, 1955), ed. with an intro. by Hannah Arendt, New York, 1969; Richard Wolin, *Walter Benja- min: An Aesthetic of Redemption*, New York, 1982.

TERRY EAGLETON

BENNETT, JAMES GORDON (1795–1872)

U.S. editor and publisher. Considered by his contem- poraries and by journalism historians as the founder of modern journalism, James Gordon Bennett was a leader in developing the "penny press," a new style of newspaper for "the great masses of the commu- nity." Born in Newmill, Scotland, he emigrated to Canada in 1819 and then to the United States. Ben- nett began his newspaper career in 1823 at the age of twenty-eight as a reporter and correspondent for such papers as the *Charleston Courier*, the New York *National Advocate*, and the *Morning Courier and New York Enquirer*. He later served briefly as editor and publisher of the New York *Globe* and the Phil- adelphia *Pennsylvanian*.

Bennett began publishing the *New York Herald* in 1835 at a time when U.S. society was rapidly moving toward including the average working-class citizen in the political, social, and economic system of the country. Through extensive reporting of political ac- tivities and campaigning for the rights of the general public, the *Herald* became a newspaper that catered to the interests and concerns of the working class. Sensational in style, the *Herald* reflected the mood of a country whose language, thought, and demo- cratic politics were rapidly changing.

Bennett's newspaper soon gained the reputation of being the most aggressive in news gathering and could be expected to contain the latest "intelligence" from New York and other places throughout the United States and the world. Bennett was one of the first U.S. newspaper publishers to report financial, sports, social, and religious news on a regular basis. An innovator in news gathering at a time when editors sat in their offices and waited for news to come to them, Bennett sent his enterprising staff into the field to gather the news and rush it back for publication by any means available—carrier pigeons, pony express, steamboat, special trains, and eventu- ally the new telegraphic system (*see* TELEGRAPHY). He forced his competitors to compete or lose out in the circulation wars in New York and the nation as a whole. The *Herald*'s reporting of the U.S. Civil War reflected Bennett's style of journalism at its peak. At various times during the war the *Herald* would have over sixty correspondents in the field, more than all other New York newspapers com-

Figure 1. *(Bennett, James Gordon)* Cartoon showing James Gordon Bennett of the *New York Herald* and his chief rivals in New York's "penny press"—Horace Gree- ley of the *New York Tribune* and Henry Raymond of the *New York Times*—whose witches' brew of aggressive journalism was a frequent "botheration" to government. *Vanity Fair*, October 5, 1861. From Don C. Seitz, *The James Gordon Bennetts: Father and Son*, Indianapolis: The Bobbs-Merrill Company, 1928, opposite p. 216.

bined. Through his efforts he helped to establish the pattern for modern wartime reporting.

Bennett also developed ADVERTISING as a major source of income, thereby keeping the cost to the reader at a reasonable rate. At first he sold his newspaper on the street for one cent per copy, later raised it to two, and eventually to three cents.

Even among his contemporaries Bennett was the undisputed leader in news gathering. Bennett's com- petition drove Henry Raymond, founder of the *New York Times*, to say it would be worth a million dollars "if the Devil would come and tell me every evening what the people of New York would like to read about next morning." HORACE GREELEY's biog- rapher, James Parton, wrote in 1866 that "it is impossible any longer to deny that the chief news- paper in New York is the *Herald*." At Bennett's death Greeley himself, Bennett's bitterest competitor for newspaper supremacy, admitted that it was as a "collector of news that Bennett shone conspicuously."

Bennett himself saw the newspaper's role as something far more than news collecting. He was given to grandiose statements about the social role he thought newspapers were destined to play:

Books have had their day—the theatres have had their day—the temple of religion has had its day. A newspaper can be made to take the lead of all these in the great movements of human thought and human civilization. A newspaper can send more souls to Heaven, and save more from Hell, than all the churches or chapels in New York—besides making money at the same time.

As *Herald* publisher and editor Bennett was succeeded by his son, James Gordon Bennett, Jr., who in 1887 started the famous Paris edition of the *Herald*.

See also NEWSPAPER: HISTORY; NEWSPAPER: TRENDS—TRENDS IN NORTH AMERICA; PRINTING—HISTORY OF PRINTING.

Bibliography. Oliver Carlson, *The Man Who Made News: James Gordon Bennett*, New York, 1942; Don C. Seitz, *The James Gordon Bennetts*, Indianapolis, Ind., 1928.

PERRY J. ASHLEY

BENSHI

Japanese motion picture "explainer," a man who, through the entire era of silent film and even after, sat at one side of the screen and explained, commented upon, and often acted out the accompanying film. So great was the popularity of these men that the film can be truly said to have merely accompanied them. During the first three decades of the twentieth century the benshi were often a greater audience attraction than the film. The audience would come to see Musei Tokugawa or Raiyu Ikoma (two of the most famous) "in," for example, *Way Down East* (United States, 1920).

Not only foreign films needed benshi, though here their role was plainly to help explain novel foreign ways. Japanese motion pictures also used their talents, so much so that a certain incoherence in a film did not seem to matter much; inconsistencies could always be explained away by the benshi. Inconsistencies were also created by this system. Since benshi were STARS, each wanted to be unique. Individual interpretations of a given film varied widely. Seeing a film with one benshi was quite different from seeing it with another.

Historically, Japan has always favored a storytelling mode of NARRATIVE (the Bunraku doll-drama, some Kabuki, and such popular entertainments as

naniwabushi and the *kodan*, and the vaudevillelike *yose*), and so it was natural that the benshi should have made their appearance and proved so durable. Their demise was not caused by lack of popularity but was the result of technological change. Though the sound film was bitterly fought by the benshi, in the end the soundtrack drove them from their place beside the screen. Not right away, however: the benshi took to turning down the sound and talking over it, or actually used the new apparatus to record themselves onto a dubbed version. One such print, a benshi version of *Der blaue Engel* (The Blue Angel, 1930), still exists.

In the end, the new order triumphed and the benshi were rendered obsolete. They remained only as rather self-conscious adjuncts to occasional evenings of nostalgia, comparable to "an old-fashioned night at the flickers."

See also MOTION PICTURES—SILENT ERA; MOTION PICTURES—SOUND FILM.

Bibliography. Joseph L. Anderson and Donald Richie, *The Japanese Film: Art and Industry*, Rutland, Vt., and Tokyo, 1959.

DONALD RICHIE

BERGMAN, INGMAR (1918–)

Swedish filmmaker and stage director. Son of a stern Lutheran minister, Ernst Ingmar Bergman drew heavily on theological and metaphysical preoccupations in his work. To filmgoers throughout the world he communicated a vision of Sweden as a starkly beautiful panorama marked by loneliness, as in *Smultronstället* (Wild Strawberries, 1957); by explosions of sexuality, as in *Jungfrukällan* (The Virgin Spring, 1960); by occasional rollicking humor, as in *Sommarnattens leende* (Smiles of a Summer Night, 1955); and always by the presence of an inscrutable deity who never answers humankind's most searching questions, a theme reflected in *Tystnaden* (The Silence, 1963).

Born in Uppsala, Bergman studied ART and literature at the University of Stockholm. After directing plays he began a scriptwriting apprenticeship at Svensk Filmindustri in 1943. The success of his first screenplay, *Hets* (Torment, 1944), won him a directing assignment in *Kris* (Crisis, 1946). Bergman went on to direct more than forty major films. During the years after World War II he gained international standing, especially through the impact of *Det sjunde inseglet* (The Seventh Seal, 1957), a medieval allegory set in the time of the Black Death; it won the Grand Prize at the Cannes Film Festival. Its gaunt leading performer, Max von Sydow, became a fixture in

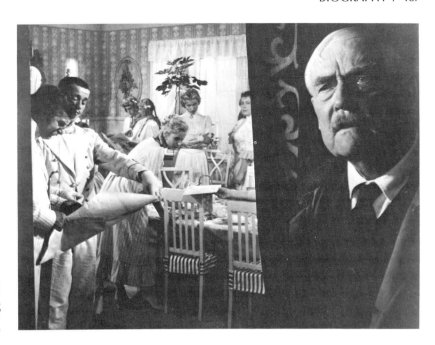

Figure 1. *(Bergman, Ingmar)*
Smultronstället (Wild Strawberries),
1957. The Museum of Modern Art/
Film Stills Archive.

many Bergman films, including *Såsom i en spegel* (Through a Glass Darkly, 1961) and *Nattvards-gästerna* (Winter Light, 1963).

During most of his career Bergman kept together a virtual stock company, which performed in films during summer months (sometimes on desolate Fårö Island) and in stage productions during the winter at Stockholm's Royal Dramatic Theater. Bergman was especially brilliant in his direction of women, and many of his films focused on dilemmas and emotional crises of women, including *Persona* (1966), *Viskningar och rop* (Cries and Whispers, 1973), and the six-hour television series *Scener ur ett äktenskap* (Scenes from a Marriage, 1973). Such actresses as Harriet Andersson, Eva Dahlbeck, Bibi Andersson, Ingrid Thulin, and Liv Ullmann gave memorable performances in Bergman films. Cinematographers Gunnar Fischer and Sven Nykvist helped give Bergman's films a keen visual sense and imagery, often presented in bleak natural surroundings with almost a DOCUMENTARY style. *See also* ACTING; THEATER.

Many of the conflicts running through Bergman's work seemed to find a final summation in *Fanny och Alexander* (Fanny and Alexander, 1982), a saga of two interlocking families—one theatrical and loving, the other clerical and self-righteous—as seen through the eyes of two children. In an introduction to his published screenplays Bergman offers further insight into the drives behind these themes:

A child who is born and brought up in a vicarage acquires an early familiarity with life and death behind the scenes. Father performed funerals, marriages, baptisms, gave ad-vice and prepared sermons. The devil was an early ac-quaintance, and in the child's mind there was a need to personify him. This is where my magic lantern came in. It consisted of a small metal box with a carbide lamp—I can still remember the smell of the hot metal—and colored glass slides: Red Riding Hood and the Wolf, and all the others. And the Wolf was the Devil, without horns but with a tail and a gaping red mouth, strangely real yet incomprehensible, a picture of wickedness and temptation on the flowered wall of the nursery.

He received his first film projector at the age of ten. It became his "first conjuring set."

See also CINEMATOGRAPHY; MOTION PICTURES.

Bibliography. Peter Cowie, *Ingmar Bergman: A Critical Biography*, New York, 1983; Frank Gado, *The Passion of Ingmar Bergman*, Durham, N.C., 1986; Vernon Young, *Cinema Borealis: The Art of Ingmar Bergman*, New York, 1975.

RICHARD PILCHER

BIOGRAPHY

It could be argued that literature began with biog-raphy. One of the oldest human impulses is to record for posterity something of the lives of one's fellows, and its expression is found on prehistoric slabs of stone and scraps of papyrus. No more splendid bi-ography has been written than the four words carved on the tablet commemorating the English architect Christopher Wren in his masterpiece, St. Paul's Ca-thedral in London: *Si monumentum requiris, circum-*

spice (If you seek his memorial, look round you). The significance of the lives of others for one's own life has been a theme of the finest biography.

Similarly, the elegiac poem (JOHN MILTON's *Lycidas*, 1637; Percy Bysshe Shelley's *Adonais*, 1821) and the funeral oration are forms of biography. Even the humble journalistic obituary can be admirable ART when composed by an old friend of the deceased. Brief lives of those deemed worth remembering continue to be recorded in successive volumes of *Who Was Who* and the necrologies in the annual reports of learned societies throughout the world.

The dividing line between biography and FICTION has always been hazy. The great Greek and Roman epics are, in an important sense, biographies. They begin, as later biographies often do, with a brief profile of their subjects: Odysseus (Ulysses), "that ingenious man, who saw the cities of many peoples, and knew their minds"; Aeneas, the founder of Rome, "who, exiled by Fate, first came from the shore of Troy to Italy, much buffeted on sea and land by divine power and the unsleeping wrath of Juno." Even the Iliad, dealing with a far shorter period of time than the other two, proposes a psychological biography of its central character: the work, we are told at the start, is to be about the source and progress of the anger of Achilles, which had such direful consequences for the Greeks and Trojans.

For centuries during the MIDDLE AGES the careers of these and other great, sometimes more historical, figures—Alexander, Charlemagne, King Arthur, and their illustrious companions—were the subjects of innumerable popular romances (*see* ROMANCE, THE). In both epics and romances, as in modern popular biographies, the family lives and encounters of the central characters are not neglected: Aeneas's meeting with his mother, Venus, and his affair with Dido; Odysseus's involvements with the temptress Circe and the nymph Calypso, with his faithful wife, Penelope, his father, Laertes, and his son Telemachus; Arthur's with his unfaithful Guinevere and her lover, Lancelot. The epics and romances are the ancestors of the modern novel, and their quasi-biographical origin should be kept in mind.

We now think of a biography as a prose NARRATIVE, based on serious historical investigation—though INTERPRETATION and judgment by the author are expected—of the life, achievements, and milieu of some individual prominent enough to arouse a general wish for more detailed knowledge than appears in the official accounts. Among the best early ones are Xenophon's biography of Socrates; Suetonius's scandal-filled lives of the twelve Caesars; Tacitus's fine life of his father-in-law, Agricola; and, above all, Plutarch's *Parallel Lives* of eminent Greeks and Romans, regarded for centuries as the classic of biog-

raphy. The Middle Ages contributed that curious branch of biography called *hagiography*—the lives of the saints. Since canonization requires the performance of miracles, miracles abound in them. Nevertheless, the Middle Ages did furnish some serious attempts at biographies of historical figures, such as Eginhard's of Charlemagne and Asser's of King Alfred, even though they and their like could not always resist including such delightful, if apocryphal, stories as those of Roland's far-heard horn and Alfred's burning the cakes he had been set to watch.

Biography blossomed in the RENAISSANCE and after. Giorgio Vasari's monumental *Lives* (1550–1568) of the great Italian painters was a landmark. From England came William Roper's charming life of his father-in-law, Sir Thomas More; Izaak Walton's lives of five famous contemporaries, including John Donne (1640) and Richard Hooker (1665); and John Aubrey's *Brief Lives,* published first in 1813 and filled with hilarious anecdotes of eminent figures of his time. It was in the seventeenth century that the word *biography* (from the Greek *biographia,* "life-writing") was introduced into English by John Dryden, in the preface to his translation of Plutarch. Around this time, too, the subbiographical GENRE of ana began to flourish—records of casual conversation or "table talk" of eminent people. First, and most famous, was that of MARTIN LUTHER; then, in France, of Gilles Ménage, the collection of whose witticisms, *Ménagiana,* gave birth to the name of the genre. In England the *Table Talk* (1689) of jurist John Selden and, later, of poet Samuel Taylor Coleridge were popular; in Germany there was Johann Eckermann's *Conversations with Goethe.* James Boswell ends his *Journal of a Tour to the Hebrides with Samuel Johnson* (1785) with a defense of it as a specimen of this worthy genre. Nevertheless, the temptation for the compiler of ana to include quips (sometimes found in old jest books) dubiously attributable to the subject is often hard to resist. One eminent biographer of Luther warns that the serious scholar will not use a remark found in *Table Talk* unless the opinion expressed in it is confirmed from Luther's own writings.

At this time, too, multivolume dictionaries of biography began to be published, later culminating in such tremendous works as the French *Biographie universelle* and such ongoing enterprises as the British *Dictionary of National Biography* and the *Dictionary of American Biography,* with similar national biographical dictionaries in many other countries. Nor should the very competent biographical content of many encyclopedias be overlooked.

The eighteenth century in England experienced what has been regarded, perhaps with some exaggeration, as a revolution in the theory of biography.

Previously the justification had been that biography's purpose was to teach morality by giving its readers, on the one hand, examples of virtuous lives to be imitated and, on the other, examples of vice and folly to be avoided. Plutarch goes so far as to recommend that the biographer conceal from the reader occasional lapses from strict virtue by a subject presented as a model. SAMUEL JOHNSON, in perhaps the greatest statement on the subject of biography ever composed, his *Rambler* essay No. 60, rejected both the doctrine that the only proper subjects for biography are individuals who have become publicly famous and the doctrine that the biographer, in the cause of promoting morality, should suppress factual information about the subject:

I have often thought that there has rarely passed a life of which a judicious and faithful narrative would not be useful. We are all prompted by the same motives, all deceived by the same fallacies, all animated by hope, obstructed by dangers, entangled by desire, and seduced by pleasure.

The scholar, the merchant, the priest are at least as worthy of attention as some military conqueror or enterprising politician. This is because the reader is better able to identify with and empathize with such a subject. And, for the same reason, it is not the public triumphs of the military or political hero that the biographer should be chiefly concerned with, but the seemingly minor, even if undignified, details of the subject's private life. Johnson's essay was a manifesto for what later became known as *psychological biography*.

Johnson practiced his own preaching in his early biography of his friend, the obscure writer Richard Savage (1744), who was a good deal of a psychopath, talented but continually self-defeating. The analysis of motivation is also important in the biographical parts of Johnson's fifty-two *Prefaces, Biographical and Critical, to the Works of the English Poets* (1779–1781; usually, but inaccurately, called *The Lives of the Poets*). To be sure, Johnson may only have been formulating what had long been felt unconsciously by dedicated biographers. For all Plutarch's insistence on the didactic purpose of biography, Dryden notes that he enjoys and lets his readers enjoy minor and seemingly (though Johnson would argue, not really) irrelevant details in the lives of his subjects. So did Johnson's contemporary Voltaire, in his life of Charles XII of Sweden (1731), which Johnson greatly admired.

The nineteenth century became the age of the "official biography"—what Lytton Strachey deplored as "those two fat volumes . . . with their ill-digested masses of material, their slipshod style, their tone of tedious panegyric." Readers in the early twentieth century were shocked when Strachey pro-

mulgated what is essentially Johnson's view—"Human beings are too important to be treated as mere symptoms of the past. They have a value which . . . is eternal, and must be felt for its own sake"—and then in 1921 went on to write a life of the sacrosanct Queen Victoria that treated her as a human being.

The popularity of Strachey's *Queen Victoria* inspired, in the 1920s and 1930s, a flood of semifictional biographical works, sometimes containing invented conversation, factual inaccuracy, and amateur psychologizing. Gamaliel Bradford's *George Washington* he described as a *psychography*. (The later term *psychobiography* refers to a specialized technique that employed a narrowly Freudian approach, finding nearly everything in the later life of the subject accounted for by psychic trauma in youth; the best-known example is Erik Erikson's *Young Man Luther*.) There were justified objections to some of this output, but those who dismissed it as "debunking," as when attention was called to Washington's problems with his ill-fitting false teeth, missed Johnson's and Strachey's point.

In the late twentieth century the popularity of ephemeral biography was never higher. A new semifictional work by Irving Stone about Michelangelo or Freud or Pissarro became an instant best-seller. Biographies of film or rock STARS were similarly profitable. Many candidates for high public office felt the need for a "campaign biography." How much of this mass production would ever be read more than a year or two after publication remained a question. At the same time, a higher standard prevailed for serious biography, at once scholarly, perceptive, and readable. A long list of titles could be given to support this claim; one example is Richard Ellmann's masterly *James Joyce* (1959).

The problem of the dividing line between biography and fiction became acute when, in the 1920s and later, Boswell's enormous cache of private diaries was discovered and began to be made available to the public. Boswell's *Life* of Samuel Johnson, published in 1791, seven years after Johnson's death, was proclaimed by the historian Thomas Babington Macaulay in a striking journalistic review to be the greatest of biographies and Boswell the greatest of biographers. Macaulay's ranking of the work was accepted almost without question for more than a century. But with the publication of the original DIARY jottings from which Boswell constructed his recension of 1791, doubts began to be expressed—as well as the complaint that what Johnson was doing during long periods in his later life was not recorded. Contrary to what many have thought, Boswell, whose home was in Edinburgh, not London, spent only a limited time in Johnson's company; sometimes whole years passed without any contact between them, and the gaps are often filled with undated and unauthenticated anecdotes passed on to Boswell by acquaintances. And even what Boswell, in the *Life*, asserts to have been said by Johnson in his presence sometimes turned out, on inspection, to vary widely from what his diary recorded as having been said at the time.

Such complaints were answered by defenders of Boswell on the grounds that his final version is very amusing and appealing—is, in fact, a great work of art—and that, in any case, no biographer can possibly reproduce the past exactly as it was; that any modern "Samuel Johnson" must be some writer's construct, and "none has pleased so many or so long as Boswell's." To which their opponents have replied that biography is, in the end, a branch of history rather than fiction and that the biographer's primary responsibility must always be to try to arrive as closely as possible to the truth, not to provide entertainment, however delightful; that indeed the intelligent reader of biography will get greater enjoyment from the account of an incident in the subject's life that one knows probably happened than from one it is suspected did not. The debate continues.

See also AUTOBIOGRAPHY; LETTER.

Bibliography. James L. Clifford, ed., *Biography as an Art: Selected Criticism 1560–1960*, New York, 1962; Samuel Johnson, "The dignity and usefulness of biography" (*Rambler*, No. 60), "Biography, how best performed" (*Idler*, No. 84), in *Essays from the "Rambler," "Adventurer," and "Idler,"* ed. by W. J. Bate, New Haven, Conn., and London, 1968; Jeffrey Meyers, ed., *The Craft of Literary Biography*, New York and London, 1985; Harold Nicolson, *The Development of English Biography*, New York, 1928; John A. Vance, ed., *Boswell's Life of Johnson: New Questions, New Answers*, Athens, Ga., 1985.

DONALD GREENE

BOAS, FRANZ (1858–1942)

U.S. anthropologist. Because of the breadth of his research, and his editorial positions, teaching, and contributions to the professionalization of the discipline, Franz Boas did more than anyone else to shape the course of American anthropology. His research in all the subdisciplines of anthropology and his ground-breaking work in American Indian ART, FOLKLORE, and LINGUISTICS have been invaluable to scholars in communications.

Born in Minden, Germany, Boas studied geography and physics at Heidelberg and Bonn and received a Ph.D. in 1881 from the University of Kiel. His first fieldwork was among the Central Eskimo on Baffin Island in 1883, and later studies involved

Figure 1. *(Boas, Franz)* Franz Boas. The Bettmann Archive, Inc.

the Indians of British Columbia (particularly the Kwakiutl). Boas's long association with the American Museum of Natural History began in 1889, and ten years later he became Columbia University's first professor of anthropology, a position he held for thirty-seven years. He was a founder of the American Anthropological Association and participated in the creation of the American Association of Physical Anthropologists and the Linguistic Society of America. He and his students, including Ruth Benedict, MARGARET MEAD, EDWARD SAPIR, and Alfred L. Kroeber, developed American anthropology into a professional discipline.

Boas redefined anthropology as the study of all aspects of human life and experience. He emphasized the importance of fieldwork among living cultures, particularly nonliterate cultures. He did not accept the prevailing notion of geographical determinism and showed that the same environment does not always produce the same type of CULTURE; the evolution of human society involves more than adjustments to natural habitat. To study human society, one must gather three types of data—biological, linguistic, and cultural—and analyze them individually as well as comparatively. Boas was trained in MATH-EMATICS as well as in physics and geography and was skilled at applying statistical methods to anthropological and archaeological data.

Through his own linguistic work and the work of his students, Boas effected major changes that defined the field of linguistic anthropology. His early fieldwork convinced him of the importance of studying each LANGUAGE on its own terms instead of in terms of some "preconceived abstract scheme." He objected to the categorizations of languages according to some "arbitrary classification" based on an evolutionary hierarchy of language types. Boas felt that linguistic description and analysis should be grounded in empirical data in the form of texts collected and transcribed by the field-worker. He took advantage of the technological advances in SOUND RECORDING to collect many of his texts. He stressed the importance of studying American Indian languages, many of which were nearly extinct. Boas was a founder of the *International Journal of American Linguistics* and the editor of the *Handbook of American Indian Languages*. In his own research Boas brought a new depth and diversity to the study of phonetics and morphology, discovering new evidence of borrowing among languages and emphasizing the need to study the differences as well as the similarities among languages.

In addition to his ethnographic and linguistic fieldwork, Boas studied American Indian folklore and art. He was also one of the first anthropologists to use PHOTOGRAPHY in ethnographic fieldwork and in fact took both still photographs and films. Through his example he showed students the importance of including cameras in their fieldwork equipment and also encouraged at least one of his native informants to become a photographer. Although stressing the primacy of text collection in fieldwork, Boas felt that some kinds of data, such as documentation of physical types, artifacts (*see* ARTIFACT), and BODY MOVE-MENT, were best "described" visually.

Boas's career was multifaceted, and his contributions have had an impact on several academic disciplines and research traditions, including the field of communications. In spite of all his accomplishments his name has never been associated with a particular school or method; there is no "Boas school" of anthropology. Nevertheless, his work continues to influence American anthropology and the way in which anthropologists and others study language and culture.

Bibliography. Franz Boas, *Race, Language and Culture*, New York, 1940; Walter R. Goldschmidt, ed., *The Anthropology of Franz Boas: Essays on the Centennial of His Birth*, Washington, D.C., 1959; Melville Herskovits, *Franz Boas: The Science of Man in the Making*, New York, 1953; Ira Jacknis, "Franz Boas and Photography," *Studies in Visual Communication* 10 (1984): 2–60; George W. Stocking, Jr., "The Boas Plan for the Study of American Indian Languages," in *Studies in the History of Linguistics: Traditions and Paradigms*, ed. by Dell Hymes, Bloomington, Ind., 1974; idem, *Race, Culture, and Evolution*, New York, 1968.

BODY DECORATION

The decoration of the body provides a means of expression for our innermost thoughts and also conveys information about the society in which we live. Body painting, tattooing, scarification, and altering the shape of the body are all forms of behavior that communicate information by means of a culturally defined CODE. As a form of NONVERBAL COMMU-NICATION this behavior is governed by rules similar to those found in language. Among many peoples this is acknowledged explicitly. The Indians of Paraguay say that the undecorated body is "dumb"—it has no message to convey.

Contexts of Body Decoration

The act of body decoration distinguishes a person as a social being and as a member of a particular group.

Figure 1. *(Body Decoration)* Nuer from eastern Africa between Waat and Akobo. Dr. J. F. E. Bloss/Anthro-Photo.

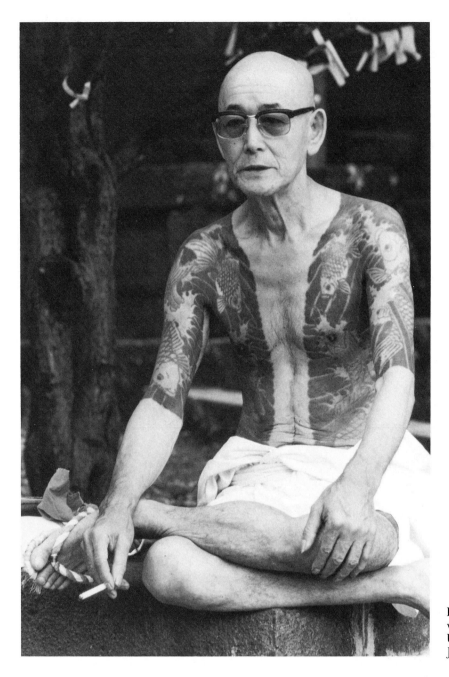

Figure 2. *(Body Decoration)* Man with an elaborate tattoo, Tokyo. United Nations photo 148563/Bruno J. Zehnder.

People who do not observe the same practices are seen as outsiders and sometimes as not fully human.

Christopher Columbus's account of his discovery of America makes only brief mention of the local peoples he encountered, and these brief descriptions are scattered throughout lengthy accounts of the peculiarities of the landscape. As Tzvetan Todorov points out in his study of the discovery of America, Columbus saw the inhabitants of these lands as features of the countryside. Doubtful that creatures so different from his notion of what was distinctively human could be men, Columbus described them in the same terms used for the elements of the landscape, such as dogs, houses, and trees.

The distinction between the human and the animal world is frequently based on the human capacity to care for, decorate, or alter the shape of the body. The Nuba of Sudan say that humans differ from animals because they can shave their heads and bodies. It is said that in the past, monkeys had their own language and could speak like humans. People differed from animals only because they cared for their bodies. The Roro of Papua New Guinea also make a distinction between those who do and those who do not decorate. They say that a person who does not have tattoos is "raw," like uncooked meat. This notion provides a striking illustration of CLAUDE LÉVI-STRAUSS's comparison of raw and cooked meat on the one hand and fresh and rotten fruit on the other. The former is transformed by a cultural process, the latter by a natural one. The Roro see the tattooed man as "cooked," transformed by a human process and given a social identity. *See also* FOOD.

The aim of different forms of decoration, paint, tattoo, and accessories and modifications of the body's morphology is the creation of a social identity. The identity of an individual as a social being requires a physical appearance that conforms to a culturally defined model. The process begins at infancy and continues throughout a lifetime. Among some American Indians of the Northwest Coast, a high, domed forehead was considered beautiful and also something that distinguished tribe members from neighboring groups. The Kwakiutl, the Salish, and the Nootka peoples bound a board against a child's head to produce the sloping forehead that they considered a mark of beauty. Minor variations in the technique distinguished members of one group from others.

Such practices transform a biological entity into a

Figure 4. *(Body Decoration)* Young man dressed in punk style, London, 1985. Reuters/Bettmann Newsphotos.

Figure 3. *(Body Decoration)* Kayapo with penis sheaths, Brazil. Joan Bamberger/Anthro-Photo.

member of society. For example, the asymmetrical facial tattoos of a Cudeveo woman of Brazil obscure her features but also proclaim her membership in a particular social group. As Lévi-Strauss has noted, the design creates the individual and confers upon him or her a social identity. The body, transformed from its natural state, makes a statement about CULTURE.

Anthropologists have focused on the nature/culture dichotomy and the role of society in transforming certain "natural" processes, such as childbearing, into socially defined and regulated patterns. Social control is also manifested in the treatment of the body. In parts of Africa female excision is practiced as a way to control women's sexuality and to regulate childbearing. Moreover, a child whose mother has not been excised is considered not fully human and may be killed at birth. Such operations impose limitations on a woman's sexual activity, which itself is often seen as a potential threat to the social order.

Such practices, expressed and enacted upon the physical body, reinforce other nonverbal as well as verbal messages about social control over behavior. As anthropologist Terence Turner has shown, Kayapo men of Brazil wear a penis sheath that restricts sexual activity to socially approved contexts; in this

Figure 5. *(Body Decoration)* "La Parisienne," from the Palace of Knossos, Crete. Reconstruction after a fresco. Minoan, ca. 1500 B.C.E. Marburg/Art Resource, New York.

way potentially disruptive behavior is brought into a framework and controlled by a cultural process.

Body decoration is a form of RITUAL behavior that, like all ritual behavior, expresses a desire to gain mystical power. As Edmund Leach, the British anthropologist, has noted, such behavior is "potent in itself in terms of the cultural conventions of the actors but not potent in a rational technical sense. [It] is directed towards evoking the potency of occult powers even though it is not presumed potent in itself." In some cases body decoration equips the individual with the mystical protection necessary to withstand the threats of everyday life. The spirit medium of Ghana who claims that the white lines painted on her forehead deflect the evil invoked by her enemies relies on the magical substances from which the paint is made and also on the design itself.

The objects used in adornment are a means to invoke the magical powers believed inherent in the natural world. They enable a person to generate the powers he or she wishes to possess. A man adorns himself with feathers in the hope that he will be as successful in his quest for wealth as the eagle is in its predatory forages. By painting his body with the

spots of a leopard or by donning bird-of-paradise feathers, he endows himself with the powers of those creatures, extending his own powers beyond the world in which he lives and stepping beyond the limits of his own identity.

Objects with symbolic value are seen as highly desirable accessories. As anthropologists Andrew Strathern and Marilyn Strathern have pointed out, the Mount Hageners of Papua New Guinea wear aprons made of pigs' tails painted with red ocher; they paint their bodies and accessories with wavy white lines and put red and white feathers in their hair. These objects and colors are associated with money and wealth, and their "brightness," like the red flowers of a tree known to attract birds, is said to attract more of the same things. Mount Hageners use these objects because they represent success and are thought to be instrumental in attracting good fortune.

In Western societies body decoration allows people to "borrow" the qualities they wish to possess for themselves. Fashions in CLOTHING and cosmetics change from season to season. The use of cosmetics is necessary to create the fashionable "look," which is, in the 1980s, explicitly associated with wealth, youth, and glamour. Sometimes one person becomes the personification of all these qualities and acquires a flock of look-alike admirers. Aesthetic reasons may be primary, but one important reason behind this form of imitation is the desire for the less tangible qualities associated with the prototype's success.

The use of cosmetics dates back far into the past. In Egypt cosmetics have been found in very early burial sites. The traces of substances found on cosmetic palettes and the portraits of men, women, and children show that the use of eye paint, FACE paint, cleansing cream, and perfumed oils was widespread.

Clay palettes, often with animal motifs and a hole pierced at the top for suspension, were used to grind the pigments. The most frequently found substances were malachite and galena, which were mixed together to make eye paint, or kohl, which in addition to highlighting the EYES was also said to provide protection from the sun and sand.

Lip paint, made from red ocher and oil, was also in common use. The so-called erotic Turin papyrus shows a woman painting her lips with a brush. On a relief from the Middle Kingdom a woman is applying rouge, probably made from hematite, with a pad. In Greece and at Knossos in Crete these same substances were used to make lip and face paint.

Another popular form of cosmetic in Egypt, and later in Rome, was henna. This plant substance was made into a paste and applied in a decorative pattern on the soles of the feet, the nails, and the hair; when washed away it left a lasting stain. The practice continues in present-day Arab countries, where women paint their hands and feet with elaborate, fanciful patterns.

In ancient times body decoration was used to render the individual more beautiful, but it also conveyed a specific message about the place of the individual in society. Archaeological evidence demonstrates that women associated with temples who were dancers and musicians tattooed their bodies. The earliest example comes from a well-preserved mummy of a dancer who had tattoo marks on her thighs, upper arms, and chest. Such marks seem to have been considered erotic and are found on the small statuettes known as the "Brides of the Dead" that were buried in the tomb of a man and were believed to arouse his procreative powers. Later examples of women musicians with tattoos have also been found on Islamic paintings in Egypt dating from the eleventh and twelfth centuries. In one painting a female figure holding a lute in one hand and a cup filled with red liquid in the other has tattoos on her face, breasts, hands, and feet. The tattoos almost certainly had erotic associations, but they were also perhaps associated with particular professions.

Body decoration plays an important part in the presentation of status and role. Officeholders are identified by the possession of objects that represent and, at the same time, validate their positions. The body is also a field upon which people may demonstrate personal wealth. It is a display counter for objects that are in themselves worthy of display. Their value is superimposed on the physical body, and in their social presentation the two are inextricably linked. Marriage ceremonies, particularly in societies with dowry requirements, provide an example of the way in which the human body, usually the bride's, becomes an index of the transfer of wealth from her family to that of her husband.

Body decorating also identifies the individual's status within society, portraying in visible terms the individual's progression from infancy through puberty to adulthood. The outward signs of physiological development are not enough; they are also accompanied by ritual acts. Once the rites are accomplished, the individual is permitted to adorn himself or herself with objects considered appropriate to the new grade or status.

Among the Kayapo a man's age is marked by the size and shape of his lip plug. In their society PUBLIC SPEAKING is the prerogative of men, and only males have their lips pierced. Shortly after birth a male child's lip is pierced, and the hole is kept open with beads and a piece of shell. As he grows toward manhood, the size of the lip plug increases. Adult men, who have many dependents and who have the authority to speak publicly, wear the largest lip plugs. Elderly men, who have a less active role in community affairs, wear a lip plug of rock crystal. Its clear or milky color is associated with age and with ghosts; it refers to the place of the elder, whose age puts him beyond the arena of social conflict and competition.

In many societies the physical maturing of the individual is accompanied by rites of passage. Male initiation rites performed at the onset of puberty vary in their complexity but usually begin with a period of seclusion when the youth is removed from his former way of life and taught the knowledge he will need as an adult. The ordeals he undergoes demonstrate his courage and worthiness to enter the adult world and sometimes include circumcision or scarification. The rites are carried out during a period of seclusion, when the youth is removed from everyday community life. His return from this seclusion is regarded as a form of rebirth. Among the Ndembu of Zambia, the boys' return to town is a joyous occasion; the women brew quantities of beer to greet them, and they pretend not to recognize their sons in the "men" who have returned.

As the transition is marked on the physical body,

Figure 6. *(Body Decoration)* Kayapo male wearing large wooden disc in lower lip, Brazil. Joan Bamberger/Anthro-Photo.

the inner person is changed too. The possession of new and esoteric knowledge, the long period of seclusion, and the often painful and terrifying rites distance the new "adult" from his former way of life. The change is partially achieved through physical pain that is visible on the skin. The experiences of the physical body and the inner man are marked permanently on the flesh.

The relationship between the inner self and the individual's social identity is expressed by the use of accessories as well as by permanent marks on the body. In Mount Hagen, on certain occasions, people decorate themselves in order to hide their personal identities. A dancer at a formal ceremony takes pride in disguising himself beyond recognition. The decorations hide the individual, and the spectators "read" the message that the dancers wish to portray: wealth, health, and fertility.

The presence of the ancestors is also invoked by the appearance of the dancers. People adorn themselves with valuable shells and anoint their skin with oil to give it a healthy shine. This display of wealth

Figure 7. *(Body Decoration)* Paloic Dinka from Melut. Africa. Dr. J. F. E. Bloss/Anthro-Photo.

and well-being is credited to the intervention of the ancestors, and their presence is indeed visible to the observers in the material success of their descendants. Objects of value adorn their bodies and represent the powerful spiritual support of the ancestors. In this manner abstract qualities associated with inner well-being are projected into a social occasion.

The individual projects an inner reality onto the external environment. The self is bound to the outside world by imposing personal desires and thoughts onto the environment. Among the Shipibo of Peru this outward manifestation of an inner reality has a particularly compelling and pervasive character. Houses, boats, kitchen utensils, textiles, pottery, and people are all decorated with elegant geometric designs. These designs are seen as visible representations of the shamans' songs that float through the air, bringing health and well-being to the village. These patterns impose upon the Shipibo universe a harmonious unity based on the inner reality and profound knowledge of the shamans.

Outward Appearances and Inner Values

If body decoration implied anything less profound than an expression of an inner reality, we would not react so strongly to physical differences between ourselves and others. It is not simply that we are confused by individuals whose physical appearance differs from ours; our reactions are often stronger than that. Outward and physical variations from the familiar often seem to indicate a depth of difference that cannot be bridged by shared perceptions or values. Conversely, we are reassured by someone who resembles us; since this person also observes the same outward conventions, we assume that he or she shares the same value system. Making judgments about people based on their physical appearance has consequences for the individual and for societies—everything from misplaced trust in a well-dressed con artist to the violence directed toward minority groups.

Colonial history offers numerous examples of such behavior (*see* COLONIZATION). Officers and missionaries frequently gave detailed descriptions of the physical appearance of the people among whom they lived. Often at the same time that they recorded these practices they were trying to repress them as a necessary step in dismantling a people's belief system. By citing the Bible to claim that man is created in God's image, and therefore this divinely inspired endowment should not be altered, or by creating laws to ban ritual behavior, missionaries and colonial government officials succeeded in imposing their own vision of the human body. They were able to "remake" the people according to their own stereotypes.

Artists too portrayed unfamiliar peoples to conform with their own stereotypes. A nineteenth-cen-

a   *b*

Figure 8. *(Body Decoration)* Tom Torlino, a young Navajo *(a)* in 1882 and *(b)* in 1884. From the Carlisle Indian School Collection of the Cumberland County Historical Society, Carlisle, Pennsylvania, 17013.

tury portrait of a South Pacific Marquesas Islander by a British painter depicts an individual who appears to be Mediterranean. His tattoos, for which the Marquesas Islanders are well known, make a brightly colored design resembling a French military uniform. The artist has succeeded in suggesting the specific qualities of the inner man—that of an aristocratic and noble "other"—by relying on signs from his own society (*see* SIGN; SIGN SYSTEM). The tattoos become a high-collared shirt, and the subject's profile is markedly European. The distinctive appearance of the Marquesan was effaced by the artist's imagination; he acquired the features and dress of societies that were more familiar to the artist yet still slightly exotic.

Our perception of others is based at least partly on assumptions about physical appearance derived from our own cultural background and personal experience. These assumptions serve as a point of reference when we encounter others. They may vary over time in response to changing values and people's sense of invention and innovation, but the forms remain basically the same for long periods. Using the forms in radically different ways—for example, a man dressed as a woman at carnival time—makes a strong statement about the liminal nature of that particular occasion, and the message comes across so clearly because the rule it violates about male and

female dress is so fundamental. In other situations, if a person's appearance does not conform to the expectations of his or her society, the incomprehensible nature of the message is in itself significant as an expression of antisocial sentiment.

The central point here is that an understanding of body decorations allows one to communicate information at several different levels. It demonstrates participation in a society and also refers to status, material and spiritual well-being, and the expression of aesthetic values (*see* AESTHETICS). The specific message, however, can be understood only when placed in the context of an assemblage of verbal and nonverbal means of communication.

Bibliography. Robert Bianchi, "The Tattoo in Ancient Egypt," in *Marks of Civilization: Artistic Transformations of the Human Body*, ed. by Arnold Rubin, Los Angeles, 1987; Victoria Ebin, *The Body Decorated*, London, 1979; James Faris, *Nuba Personal Art*, Toronto, 1972; Angelika Gebhart-Sayer, *The Cosmos Encoiled: Indian Art of the Peruvian Amazon* (exhibition catalog, Center for Inter-American Relations), New York, 1984; Dalu Jones, "Notes on a Tattooed Musician: A Drawing of the Fatimid Period," *Art and Archeology Research Papers* (AARP) 7 (1975): 1–14; Edmund Leach, *Culture and Communication: The Logic by Which Symbols Are Connected*, Cambridge and New York, 1976; idem, "Ritualization in Man,"

Philosophical Transactions of the Royal Society, Series B, Vol. 251, London, 1966; Claude Lévi-Strauss, *Structural Anthropology*, 2 vols., New York, 1963–1976; A. Lucas, *Ancient Egyptian Materials and Industries*, 4th ed., rev. and enl. by J. R. Harris, London, 1962; Andrew Strathern and Marilyn Strathern, *Self-Decoration in Mount Hagen*, Toronto and Buffalo, N.Y., 1971; Marilyn Strathern, "The Self in Self-Decoration," *Oceania* 49 (1979): 241–257; Tzvetan Todorov, *La conquête de l'Amérique: La question de l'autre* (The Conquest of America, trans. by Richard Howard, New York, 1984), Paris, 1982; Terence Turner, "The Social Skin," in *Not Work Alone*, ed. by Jeremy Cherfas and Roger Lewin, Beverly Hills, Calif., 1980; idem, "Tchikrin: A Central Brazilian Tribe and Its Symbolic Language of Body Adornment," *Natural History* 78 (1969): 50–59, 70; Victor Turner, *Ndembu Divination: Its Symbolism and Techniques* (The Rhodes-Livingstone Papers, no. 31), Manchester, Eng., 1961.

VICTORIA EBIN

BODY LANGUAGE. *See* BODY MOVEMENT; KINESICS.

BODY MOVEMENT

Studies of body movement and posture range from anatomical and physiological to a focus on their communicative functions. Posture and body movement are part of a continuum from FACIAL EXPRESSION to GESTURE. They can be analyzed at the level of individual behaviors, uses of postures and gestures in group activity, or as patterned by cultural traditions. They can also be studied from the standpoint of human biological evolution, as possible reflections of our primate ancestry. Posture and body movement serve not only practical locomotor and other somatic functions, but also an immense variety of social or cultural ends. The ability of human beings to imitate or learn from the movements of others is extremely well developed.

The Greek historian Xenophon (ca. 431–ca. 352 B.C.E.) attributed to Socrates the notion that emotions and personality traits were reflected in postures and facial expressions. In England, philosopher Francis Bacon (1561–1626) noted the importance of gestures. By the seventeenth century gesture and posture were the subject of systematic investigation, especially in connection with rhetoric. RENAISSANCE and post-Renaissance realism in painting and SCULPTURE also focused attention on bodily "attitudes," but it was PHOTOGRAPHY that enabled investigators to collect more accurate data. CHARLES DARWIN used photographs in his pioneer work on the expression of the emotions in animals and humans (1872). French physiologist Étienne-Jules Marey began to record body movement with the camera in 1882, and in

1887 Eadweard Muybridge, working in the United States, instituted a major photographic project on animal and human body movement (*see* MOTION PHOTOGRAPHY). While such studies provided accumulating data on body movement, serious research into its communicative aspects was slow to develop. In the 1920s and 1930s, psychologists such as Gordon W. Allport and P. E. Vernon in the United States were studying "expressive movement" (1933). Marcel Mauss wrote an important programmatic paper, "Les techniques du corps," in 1935.

These and other studies led to a long controversy. Are the differences among groups in posture, movement, and gesture the outcome of innate human predispositions, or are they culturally determined? That some could be innately programmed or predisposed and others clearly acquired was a middle position rarely taken. U.S. anthropologist Weston La Barre argued for almost total cultural causation. In Germany, I. Eibl-Eibesfeldt, with considerably more empirical evidence, argued the reverse. Some postures, body movements, and gestures seem to have, as Darwin believed, deep phylogenetic roots, and others are recent, even deliberate, inventions and also geographically limited, as in the case of the Nilotic one-legged standing position. The interplay of biological determinants and predispositions and cultural factors is one of the reasons scholars find this field so challenging.

Approaches to the Study of Body Movement and Posture

Muybridge photographed both humans and nonhumans in motion, testifying to a widespread and probably very ancient human interest in animal and human locomotion. Nonhuman animals, including many invertebrates, utilize postures and distinctive movements for communication. In many species, GENDER often affects or determines postures and movements. A commonplace example is the difference between urination postures in male and female dogs. Sex differences in human sitting postures are widespread cross-culturally. Both pelvic dimensions and fat distribution have well-known effects on differences in gait (especially in running) between most men and women. Cultural elaborations, derived from the division of labor, patterns of male dominance, CLOTHING, and the like, have intensified such differences.

Much of the distinctiveness of human body movement and posture arises from the bipedal stance and gait of our species. Walking and running have been studied mainly by physical educators, physiologists, and orthopedists, although walking and running styles may present individual, cultural, or other elements. Human beings also crawl, go on all fours, leap,

Figure 1. *(Body Movement)*   Martha Graham in *Letter to the World*, 1944. Photograph by Barbara Morgan. International Museum of Photography at George Eastman House.

climb, swim, or dive, all in ways subject to anatomical, physiological, psychological, and cultural factors. The achievement of full bipedalism is a step in the development of human children probably recognized as significant in all cultures and is seen as a criterion of humanness, despite the existence of bipedalism in birds and a few other vertebrates. Occasional bipedalism in bears seems to have been a factor in the phenomenon of bear ceremonialism, a widespread and ancient cultic practice in which they are regarded as mysteriously humanlike. Human beings, judging from mythology and folklore, as well as from frequent dream experiences, have long been envious of the flying ability of birds—a locomotor deficiency that probably does not trouble any other nonflying species.

Even as neonates, human infants are sensitive to body movements of others and to some gestures as well. There has been much study of motor activity and development in PLAY. Young children are often trained to conform to cultural postural and motoric norms, notably with respect to eating habits, including such matters as careful avoidance of the use of the left hand. School is often another agency of postural training of the young.

Standing and walking impose energetic burdens on the human body. Much of the time we sit, squat,

kneel, recline, or lie down, and it is especially with these postures that cultural factors lead to remarkable variations. These have been plotted geographically, and they exhibit significant regional differences. Here gender differences are very evident, along with the effects of clothing (including footgear), work habits, housing, furniture, ground cover, and climate, although what is cause and what is effect may not always be apparent. While no environmental barriers would seem to preclude the worldwide occurrence of cross-legged ground-sitting postures, these are not in fact universal. Special meditation postures (as in yoga) are resting positions of a sort, but they are not found in all human cultures. Some cultures also have breathing exercises involving special postures and movements, likewise of limited geographic distribution.

Different cultures or subcultures may have different standards for what constitutes "good" or "bad" posture or movement. Postures acceptable in children or adolescents may be considered undignified in older individuals. A style of walking that may be admired in a cabaret hostess may seem improper in a female schoolteacher.

Postures and movements may be important indexes of health or symptoms, sometimes highly diagnostic, of illness, including mental illness. Catatonic

Figure 2. *(Body Movement)* Fourteen-year-old Nadia Comaneci from Romania performing during the XXI Olympic Games, July 21, 1976. UPI/Bettmann Newsphotos.

schizophrenia produces bizarre postural effects. Drugs may affect posture and locomotion, and even slight deviations from normal body movement are used in law enforcement to detect drunkenness. Obesity, illness, old age, strong emotion, and deformities produce obvious postural or body movement effects. Actors are expected to be able to simulate these effects or to exaggerate them for dramatic purposes, as in the traditional roles of Falstaff, Lear, Richard III, or Camille. *See also* ACTING; DRAMA—PERFORMANCE.

Sleeping postures and movements have been studied but mainly from the standpoint of physiology and dream behavior. Cultural differences in sleeping postures may result from the use of headrests, pillows, bedclothing, and hammocks, or the need to protect coiffures. Burial or mortuary postures are often intentional simulations of sleeping positions. The deliberate burials of Neanderthal times, eighty thousand to forty thousand years ago, in which the corpse was flexed on its side, have been described as being in a fetal position. This is in fact the earliest evidence of culturally patterned placement of the human body, but there is no real evidence to connect it with the position of the fetus in utero and whatever that might symbolize.

Copulatory and other sexual postures and movements have been described and depicted in many different cultures, in some cases in famous treatises such as the Kama Sutra and in sculpture and painting from many periods and cultures as well: ancient Greek and Roman, medieval Indian, Chinese and Japanese, among others. Scientific studies have tended to focus on physiological and psychological aspects of such postures and movements rather than on their positional and motoric features. In this area of behavior, our species seems to exhibit greater complexity and creativity than other animals. Postural and motor effects of pregnancy and lactation have received little attention. Birth postures, sometimes dictated for the convenience of obstetricians in the Western world, have recently begun to be studied from a cross-cultural standpoint. Delivery with the mother in a squatting or sitting position is more common worldwide than the supine position characteristic of Western hospital births.

Postures used for excretion have received some ethnographic notice, as has the associated furniture, if any. There are gender differences, although it is by no means universal that males stand to urinate. Clothing affects excretory postures, and clothing design may be affected in turn. Remains of Roman public lavatories show that chair-sitting postures, rather than squatting, were customary, at least in cities.

Body orientation with respect to others in small-group situations has been exhaustively investigated. This topic has constituted the focus of research in PROXEMICS and INTERPERSONAL DISTANCE.

Despite some sharp departures from widespread nonhuman primate patterns, human postures and movements of dominance and submission show many similarities to what may be observed in other animals, suggesting that they have very old evolutionary origins. Etiquette in many cultures requires the subordinate to occupy a physically lower level, especially by lowering the head to the superior. A more general principle would seem to be that of least effort on the part of the superior, who may either remain standing while others bow or prostrate themselves or remain seated or reclining while inferiors stand. Bowing, curtsying, and kowtowing are only a part of this branch of deference behavior. Ways of tying up or torturing victims or criminals may also involve their assuming demeaning postures, with parallels in sadomasochistic practices.

Figure 3. *(Body Movement)* His Highness the Thakore Sahib, ruler of Palitana, with Her Highness and five children, all sitting in the cross-legged position. The Bettmann Archive, Inc.

Clothing and ornament, as noted, may affect posture and gait, for example, because of stiffness or weight (as with corsets or suits of armor) or because of precarious balance (as when very high-heeled shoes are worn). Chinese foot-binding represented an extreme effect of this sort on women's gait. There has not been much serious study of such phenomena, although actors in historical costume dramas are presumably familiar with some of these bodily constraints. *See also* BODY DECORATION.

Occupation or work habits may affect posture and movement in two main ways. First, certain tasks may require special postures or movements for maximum efficiency. This is the field of ergonomics research. Second, habitual work postures or movements associated with particular jobs may produce characteristic health problems. Carrying heavy burdens and prolonged bending over work tables are common examples. Less damaging to health but occupationally characteristic are the rolling gait of sailors and the bowlegged outcome of a lifetime of horseback riding, though both may be cultural stereotypes rather than significantly frequent occupational stigmata.

Religious and related RITUAL activities commonly include prescribed postures or movements. These range from prayer positions, genuflection, and prostration to flagellation or meditation poses. Many ritual postures or movements seem to be extensions of submissive or deferential social behaviors.

DANCE is an activity involving social communication, postures, movements, and gestures, often of great complexity. Its cross-cultural analysis by Alan Lomax and others has revealed some unexpected correlations of dance style with other aspects of culture, including the overall complexity of sociopolitical structures. There has also been some work on postures and movements associated with the playing of different musical instruments, Western and non-Western. *See also* CANTOMETRICS; CHOREOMETRICS.

Formal elaboration of movements and postures reaches a high point in many SPORTS activities, among them martial arts, gymnastics, tennis, and golf. In many forms of athletic competition, style in the performance of movements is a major criterion of excellence.

In many cultures, as mentioned in relation to eating behavior, there are specified "proper" ways of handling objects, presenting them to others, and the like. The predominance of right-handedness means that left-handed persons are at a persistent physical disadvantage with many common artifacts designed for the right-handed majority, from bolt-action rifles to schoolroom desk chairs. The proper way to mount a horse also favors the right-handed.

Sources of Data for the Study of Body Movement

Complexities and variety of phenomena related to human body movements and postures are reflected in the diversity of methods used to investigate them.

Figure 4. *(Body Movement)* Worker shoveling coal into a furnace at the Bethlehem Steel Company. F. W. Taylor was hired to reorganize this company in 1907. From his time and motion studies, he learned ways to maximize worker efficiency. Brown Brothers, Sterling, Pennsylvania.

However, many aspects of body motion and postures have been studied without reference to their possible social communicative functions. Habitual squatting produces distinctive facets on knee and ankle joints, so that the characteristic resting postures of some ancient populations can be determined from skeletal remains. Does this provide evidence for postural behavior in prolonged small-group interactions? The striding gait of three australopithecine hominids at Laetoli in northern Tanzania nearly four million years ago has been recorded in footprints, indicating two persons of different size walking side by side in a way still characteristic of modern human pairs. Evidence from later prehistoric sites often reveals the layout of working floors in relation to hearths and hut entryways. This may shed some light on ancient proxemic habits and the spatial patterning of domestic activities, from food processing and eating to toolmaking and sleeping. Sitting or sleeping platforms, benches, and occasionally stools, chairs, thrones, and other furniture found in archaeological sites provide data on ancient postural habits. Stairs and ladders in ancient sites show us that people in many different parts of the world solved the problems of ascending or descending from different levels in the same ways.

Much richer data on past postures, gestures, and movement come from figural art, providing a data base going back to the Upper Paleolithic in some regions. Art historians have been assiduous students of posture and gesture and their symbolic communicative aspects. Certain art traditions are especially rich sources of information on postures ranging from ordinary productive tasks to court or priestly ritual, as in that of pharaonic Egypt. Literary sources are generally less helpful, but they have been used for some kinesic research. Photography, cinema, and their offshoots have produced the most complete record, but one that only began around 1840. Videotape is one of the most valuable recent recording tools. Several systems of movement, gestural, and postural notation have been devised, such as those of Rudolf Laban, Ray Birdwhistell, and Rudolph Benesh. Finally, data relating to posture and movement can be collected from interviews and questionnaires, especially to elicit responses to illustrations of posture or body movement.

See also BODY MOVEMENT NOTATION; KINESICS; NONVERBAL COMMUNICATION; TOUCH.

Bibliography. Michael Argyle, *Bodily Communication*, London, 1975; Jack Blacking, ed., *The Anthropology of the Body*, New York and London, 1977; Adam Kendon, ed., *Nonverbal Communication, Interaction, Gesture*, The Hague, 1981; Mary Ritchie Key, ed., *The Relationship of Verbal and Non-verbal Communication*, The Hague, 1980; Marianne LaFrance and Clara Mayo, *Moving Bodies: Nonverbal Communication in Social Relationships*, Monterey, Calif., 1978; Desmond Morris, *Manwatching: A Field Guide to Human Behaviour*, London, 1977; Gerard I. Nierenberg and Henry H. Calero, *How to Read a Person Like a Book*, New York, 1971; Ted Polhemus, ed., *The Body Reader: Social Aspects of the Human Body*, New York, 1978; Albert E. Scheflen, with Alice Scheflen,

Body Language and the Social Order, Englewood Cliffs, N.J., 1972; Klaus Scherer and Paul Ekman, eds., *Handbook of Methods in Nonverbal Behavior Research*, Cambridge, 1982; Karl Sittl, *Die Gebaerden der Griechen und Römer*, Leipzig, 1890; Aaron Wolfgang, ed., *Nonverbal Behavior: Applications and Cultural Implications*, New York, 1979.

GORDON W. HEWES

BODY MOVEMENT NOTATION

A system of notation is very important for the systematic study of the role of BODY MOVEMENT in communication. Once movements are transcribed into graphic form it becomes possible for an investigator to read and analyze those movements without being confined to the rapid flow of real space and time. In addition to being a recording device, a notation system provides for the development of important conceptual skills—ways of thinking with and about human movement.

Different disciplines in Western academic contexts define human movement in very different ways. For example, fundamental differences such as those between biological/physiological modes of explanation and the discourse of the social sciences or humanities have led to two major differences in ways of measuring and recording movement. Investigations of the biological/physiological kind are usually concerned with metric measurement and involve such notions as angles of displacement, muscle force, velocity, and principles of mechanics. They are generally found in kinesiological and biomechanical contexts and, in contrast to social-scientific/humanistic investigations of human movement, are ways of measuring movement that do not attempt to deal with units of MEANING.

Extant records suggest that simple notation systems began to appear in the fifteenth century (in Europe at least) as mnemonic devices for social dances. As these DANCE forms changed and more detail of steps and floor patterns was required, other systems came into being, such as the Beauchamp-Feuillet system in France around 1700. There followed a period when the ability to read dances was an expected skill of any educated person in the courts of Europe. This brief excursion into dance literacy seems to have passed with the decline of the aristocracy during the French Revolution as more elaborate theatrical dance forms developed separately from social dance forms and as nonliterate persons became theatrical dancers. Many European and later U.S. choreographers attempted to develop new notation systems. Some utilized stick-figure representations;

others relied on musical notation with various combinations and abstractions.

Dance is not the only context in which the notation of movement has been attempted. For example, a system was developed in 1806 by Gilbert Austin for the notation of gestures and body positions during PUBLIC SPEAKING. Many of these notation systems have been little used because they were developed to meet the needs of one particular movement form, dance style, or research project. The problem has been to develop a script capable of writing all anatomically possible bodily action that will preserve the identity of the movement, make possible accurate reproduction of it, and maintain its semantic content.

It is only in the twentieth century that such generalized systems have emerged. Some of the fundamental issues involved in this process are discussed here with reference to three of these extant systems: Labanotation (1928), Benesh notation (1955), and Eshkol-Wachmann notation (1958). These have continued the earlier attempts to record dances, but they also have more ambitious goals. By the 1970s, in addition to the recording of choreography, these systems began to be applied to such diverse contexts as social/cultural anthropology, physical therapy, SIGN LANGUAGE studies, kinesiological analysis, and the historical study of dance and dance composition, as well as animal behavior studies and computer GRAPHICS.

Notation Systems

It is important to note that the inventors of the Laban, Benesh, and Eshkol-Wachmann systems had different aims for their notation systems, came from different cultural backgrounds, and were familiar with different movement systems. These factors affected the choices they made in solving the problems that will be mentioned below.

Labanotation. Labanotation was invented by Rudolf Laban (1879–1958), a choreographer and dancer. Working in Austria and Germany around 1926, he set out to devise a notation system that could record any human movement, although initially it was a system for use in choreographic contexts. Laban was intrigued by Greek concerns with MATHEMATICS, the movements of planetary spheres and crystal forms, and the Bauhaus movement in visual art and ARCHITECTURE in Germany. He had wide interests in movement in diverse situations, from the physical working environment to MIME. His later work in England focused particularly on the analysis of dynamic components of manual work in industrial environments. Labanotation, or Kinetography Laban as it is known in Europe, came to be used primarily for the recording and preservation of professional THEATER dance works in the United

States and in Europe and the traditional dances of eastern Europe. More recent applications are in social/cultural anthropology, sign language studies, and kinesiology. The dynamic analysis known in the United States as Effort-Shape, mentioned below, has been used in child development studies, creative dance in education, dance therapy, and personality analysis.

Benesh notation. In contrast, Rudolph Benesh, an artist and accountant, and Joan Benesh, a ballet dancer, were both involved in the professional world of ballet in England. Benesh notation was designed specifically at its outset to record one movement language and its "dialects": the ballet. Not unexpectedly, therefore, the writing system itself underlines many of the principles of ballet, such as a concern with line and the visual results of movement. Applications apart from the recording of ballet and modern dance choreography are in social anthropology and physical therapy with handicapped children.

Eshkol-Wachmann notation. Noa Eshkol, an Israeli choreographer and dancer, and Abraham Wachmann, an architect, were the inventors of the Eshkol-Wachmann system. Eshkol's interests lay in choreography that was free of a priori connotations. Both were interested in the cognitive and creative potential of a notation system that could refer to the complex articulation of any kind of object in space. The notation has therefore been used in nonhuman contexts such as computer graphics, architectural design, and animal behavior studies as well as the recording of traditional and modern dance compositions and Israeli sign language.

The Notation Problem

Any movement notation system has to resolve several difficult technical issues. The problem is not only how to represent all the parts and surfaces of the body with two-dimensional graphic signs but also how to organize the writing of those signs when some or all of those body parts are moving simultaneously and/or sequentially in three dimensions of space. All of this necessarily takes place through time and may occur in relationship to other persons who are also moving.

The body. Solutions to the problem of representing parts and surfaces of the body on paper have included the use of words or abbreviations of words, pictographic representations, stick-figure diagrams, system-specific symbols, numbers or letters representing joints and/or limbs, and specified columns on a page for each body part. The overall number of signs required is greatly reduced in those notation systems that utilize abstract symbols rather than pictographic representations.

Space. The medium in which the parts of the body move also must be made finite in some way. Problems arise with conventional numerical measurement because a baseline or point is needed from which to measure. In a number of studies of GESTURE and other aspects of communicative body movement attempts have been made to measure movement by plotting successive positions of a moving body part on a grid superimposed on a projected film image of the movement. Such an approach leaves out the third dimension and in effect removes the movement itself by treating it as a succession of static positions.

A different approach was developed by Laban. Utilizing a Euclidean view of space, he conceived of the body as being surrounded by a sphere of space, as if inside a balloon. This space divides into three dimensions via three axes perpendicular to each other (up/down, front/back, left/right), the body being in the center of the sphere. Each major direction and various intermediate divisions are assigned a symbol. This same scheme provides a framework for determining the direction of individual limbs and smaller body parts by locating smaller imaginary spheres at each joint. An important feature of this approach is that it allows spatial direction to be written according to the mover's perspective rather than from the standpoint of an observer.

The Eshkol-Wachmann system is based on a similar approach. The same imaginary sphere of space is divided into two planes, horizontal and vertical (each plane being a two-dimensional surface). These planes are in turn segmented into sections, and directions are assigned numbers. As with Labanotation, the basic division of space for the whole body in the Eshkol-Wachmann system applies in miniature for movement of each limb and parts of a limb, the planes being located at each joint. In both these notation systems spatial directions are represented with a small and finite set of characters that apply to all situations and to all body parts.

Other systems use part symbol, part placement on a visual representation of the mover's space. In the Benesh system, for example, the up/down and left/right dimensions are represented iconically. Representation of the third dimension relies partly on visual perspective and partly on symbols for "in front," "level with," and "behind." Characters for details such as FACIAL EXPRESSION and hand and finger movements were a later addition to the system, and the set of symbols devised for these operates on principles different from those used for the rest of the body.

Time. Scripts of all kinds deal with time by assigning a direction for reading—an axis for the sequential flow of sound or movement (e.g., left to right, bottom to top of page). In contrast to spoken language scripts, however, and because of the simultaneous actions of the body's multiple articulators, a movement script must be able to distinguish between

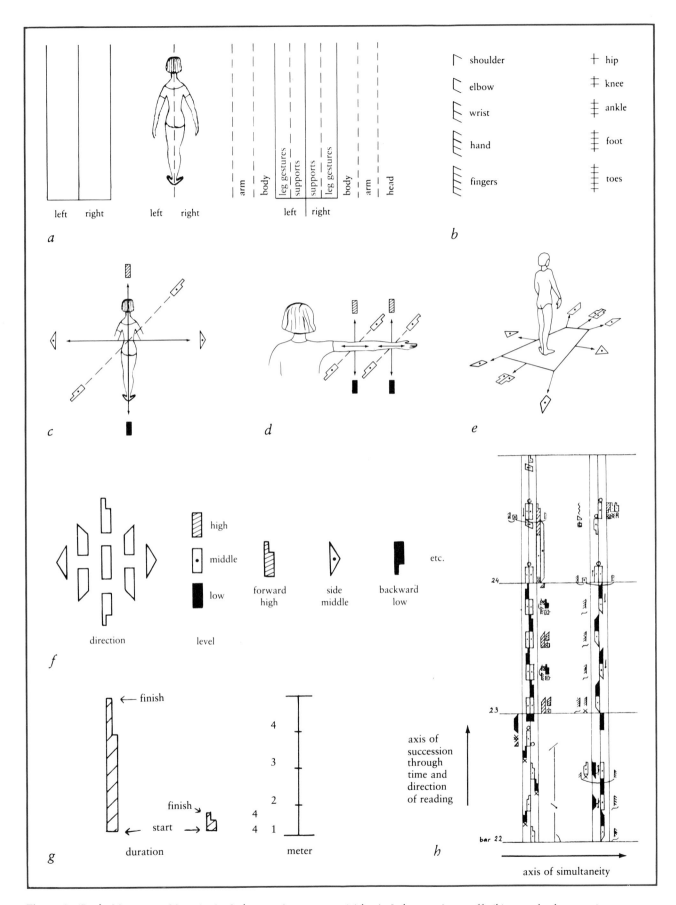

Figure 1. *(Body Movement Notation)*   Labanotation system: *(a)* basic Labanotation staff, *(b)* some body part signs. Redrawn after Ann Hutchinson Guest, *Dance Notation*, New York: Dance Horizons, 1984, pp. 82, 83. *(c)* Main cross of directions centered in the body, *(d)* local cross of axes located in joints of body part, *(e)* direction of steps into the displacement space. Redrawn after Brenda Farnell. *(f)* Spatial organization, *(g)* timing, *(h)* example of writing. Redrawn after Ann Hutchinson Guest, *Dance Notation*, New York: Dance Horizons, 1984, pp. 83, 84.

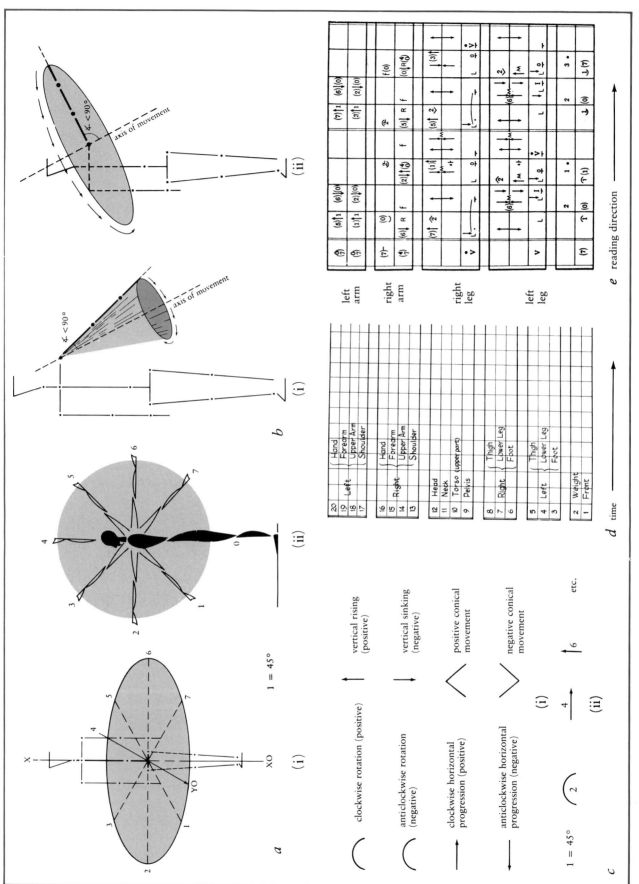

Figure 2. (*Body Movement Notation*) Eshkol-Wachmann notation system: (*a*) organization of space: (i) coordinates of the vertical plane; (ii) coordinates of the horizontal plane; (*b*): (i) Conical movement; (ii) planal movement. Redrawn after Noa Eshkol and Abraham Wachmann, *Movement Notation*, London: Weidenfeld and Nicolson, 1958, pp. 11, 10. (*c*): (i) Signs for motion; (ii) numbers are added to each of the signs for motion to state the degree of displacement. Redrawn after Ann Hutchinson Guest, *Dance Notation*, New York: Dance Horizons, 1984, p. 111. (*d*) The full staff; body parts. Redrawn after Noa Eshkol and Abraham Wachmann, *Movement Notation*, London: Weidenfeld and Nicolson, 1958, p. 3. (*e*) Example of writing. Redrawn after Ann Hutchinson Guest, *Dance Notation*, New York: Dance Horizons, 1984, p. 109.

206

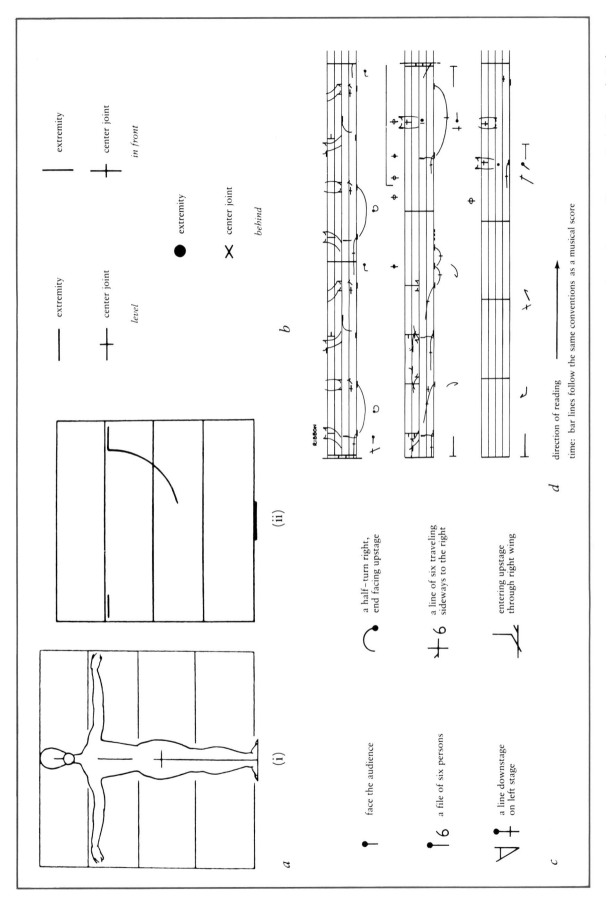

Figure 3. (*Body Movement Notation*) Benesh notation system: (*a*) body parts and staff: (i) matrix representing the performer; (ii) arm raised sideward. Redrawn after Joan Benesh and Rudolph Benesh, *An Introduction to Benesh Dance Notation*, New York: Pitman, 1956, p. 11. (*b*) Direction symbols for the third dimension. (*c*) Signs under the staff indicate stage direction faced, turning, stage location, and direction traveled. Redrawn after Ann Hutchinson Guest, *Dance Notation*, New York: Dance Horizons, 1984, pp. 99, 100. (*d*) Example of writing. From Julia McGuinness-Scott, *Movement Study and Benesh Movement Notation*, London: Oxford University Press, 1983, p. 117.

simultaneous and sequential action. If movement is externally motivated by music or rhythmic divisions, the time axis can be divided up in a similar manner to musical notation.

Dynamics. A movement always involves some degree of muscular tension or strength; thus acceleration and deceleration may be an important feature; the impetus or initiation point for the action might be of significance; accents, vibration, and so on can be relevant. Symbols that can capture these dynamic aspects are often useful additions to the notations for body, space, and time aspects mentioned above. Although Labanotation includes symbols for these dynamic aspects, Laban also created a detailed classification of movement dynamics that has become known as Effort-Shape. An additional Effort-Shape notation system has been developed that attempts to capture the intention or attitude of the mover toward action. Effort elements identify attitudes toward weight (strong/light), time (quick/slow), space (direct/indirect), and flow (bound/free). Shape involves relationships between the body and space in categories such as shape-flow (opening/closing), arc- and spokelike directional movement, and three-dimensional shaping in space. The emphasis on inner attitude has made this system of interest in areas such as dance therapy, child development studies, creative dance in education, and personality analysis. Assumptions of universality, however, are highly problematic, as these movement dynamics are named and classified according to values that Western cultures attach to spatial directions and bodily use.

Choosing a Notation System

Semantic concerns relating to concepts of the body and the spatial orientation of the mover can be an important consideration, especially in anthropological contexts in which notation according to the cultural concepts of the persons moving is an important goal. The "frame of reference" keys and choice of symbols in the Labanotation system provide a means for subtle alternative descriptions of movements that look alike but semantically are quite different. The iconic commitment of the Benesh system would appear to limit movement description to an observer's point of view.

In the history of writing it is widely agreed that iconic or picturelike devices that represented ideas or objects were the forerunners of systems in which the graphic marks represent units of the spoken languages themselves. In relation to writing systems for movement this suggests that greater referential value, an economy of symbols, and less ambiguity over interpretation can be achieved when graphic marks relate to elements of the medium of movement itself.

Arguments have been advanced, however (e.g., by Benesh), that because movement is perceived visually, its representation should be visual; that is, an iconic relationship between SIGN and denotatum is desirable. Indeed many dance notation systems have used some form of stick-figure representation of the body (e.g., Arthur Saint-Léon, *La sténochorégraphie*, Paris, 1852; Friedrich Albert Zorn, *Grammatik der Tanzkunst*, Leipzig, 1887; Valerie Sutton, *Sutton Movement Shorthand*, U.S., 1973; Joan Benesh and Rudolph Benesh, *An Introduction to Benesh Dance Notation*, U.S., 1955). These rely on perspective and/or use extra symbols to suggest the third dimension. However, just as in alphabetic writing systems the relationship between sound and the graphic sign that represents it is a conventional one, so there can be a conventional relationship between a movement and its written representation that need not have anything to do with visual perception. Movement notation systems that follow this principle gain greatly in symbol economy and ease of representation. *See also* PERCEPTION—STILL AND MOVING PICTURES; VISUAL IMAGE.

These systems and others that have appeared during the twentieth century continue to vie with one another for supremacy. Unfortunately, arguments for the superiority of one system over another have tended to revolve around practical considerations such as the speed of production, ease of reading, correlation between notators, and accurate reproduction. For example, the first International Congress on Movement Notation, held in Israel in 1984, focused largely on pragmatic aspects and diversity of application rather than on the many theoretical issues that require consideration. It would seem that wider academic recognition of movement notation systems will depend on attention to the creative and intellectual potential of literacy in relation to movement in addition to concerns over the historical preservation of choreographic invention.

See also CHOREOMETRICS; KINESICS.

Bibliography. Gilbert Austin, *Chironomia: A Treatise on Rhetorical Delivery*, ed. by Mary M. Robb and Lester Thonssen, Carbondale, Ill., 1966; Joan Benesh and Rudolph Benesh, *An Introduction to Benesh Dance Notation*, New York, 1955; David Best, *Philosophy and Human Movement*, London, 1978; Noa Eshkol and Abraham Wachmann, *Movement Notation*, London, 1958; Nelson Goodman, *Languages of Art*, 2d ed., Indianapolis, Ind., 1976; Ann Hutchinson Guest, *Dance Notation: The Process of Recording Movement on Paper*, New York, 1984; idem, *Labanotation*, 2d ed., London, 1970; Klaus Scherer and Paul Ekman, eds., *Handbook of Methods in Nonverbal Behavior Research*, Cambridge, 1982; Drid Williams, *The-*

ories of the Dance, Metuchen, N.J., 1987; Drid Williams, Dixie Durr, and Brenda Farnell, *Labanotation for Non-Dancers,* forthcoming.

BRENDA FARNELL

BOOK

With the exception of SPEECH itself, no human invention has played so important a role in communication for so long a time as the book. Nothing else has been so prevalent and effective a means of storing and transmitting to others the records, knowledge, literature, speculations, and entertainments characteristic of human society.

In the twentieth century the idea of "the book" is embodied in the printed codex. Each of its paper leaves contains two pages (recto and verso). Each two-page leaf may or may not be joined to another leaf. The leaves themselves are brought together into gatherings, normally of thirty-two leaves. Then groups of gatherings are sewn or glued together at their back or spine and cased in paper or board covers. On the majority of its pages the modern book normally contains photolithographic images of ideographic or alphabetical word- or letterforms. Illustrations, variously created and reproduced, may also be printed with these letterforms, either on the same or on separate leaves.

However, the book has taken this form only very recently. For the preceding several hundred years it had, in the West, contained images of letterforms reproduced not photolithographically but by relief. Its leaves might be paper, but, particularly in the fifteenth century, they might instead be prepared animal skin (vellum or parchment). They were not cased but bound, joined physically both to one another and to the boards and animal skins covering and protecting them by sewn cords and glue. *See also* WRITING MATERIALS.

For more than a thousand years before that the book's letterforms had been created not by mechanical processes but by hand. But books had, in the West, already taken on the codex form that they still use, and their texts were written generally on vellum. Earlier still, however, books had usually looked nothing at all like what we recognize as books. Their texts were written or painted on leather or papyrus, which was then rolled for storage. Other forms of the book were chiseled or written on tablets of clay or wood, or on bark, leaf, linen, or metal, and they were stored variously as the nature of their materials demanded.

The printed book in codex form is only an episode in the long history of the book. As these words are written the future of this form is open to speculation.

Electronic and digitalized storage and retrieval mechanisms, still at a very early stage in their own history, may well affect how people continue to seek and to preserve the information, literature, history, records, and entertainment for which they have long used books. *See also* ARCHIVES; DATA BASE; ELECTRONIC PUBLISHING; LIBRARY.

Early History

Basic to the creation of books, whatever their physical shape or means of production, are the various WRITING systems in which their contents are embodied. These can be traced back to a period beginning roughly in 3500 B.C.E. Pictographic, ideographic, syllabic, and alphabetic writing systems were devel-

Figure 1. *(Book) The Bookseller.* From Annibale Carracci, *Le arti di Bologna,* 1646, plate 44. Facsimile, Rome: Edizioni dell'Elefante, 1966.

Figure 2. *(Book)* Greek tax roll from Theadelphia (Fayyum), 166 C.E. Papyrus. The reproduction depicts column 14; the others are rolled up. Staatliche Museen zu Berlin (DDR), Papyrussammlung, P11651.

oped over several millennia by the peoples of western Asia *(see* ALPHABET*)*. Not only Near Eastern, North African, and European writing systems derive from these early developments, but also Indic and even Chinese systems have been hypothesized to derive from them.

From the very earliest periods of which we have knowledge, writing appears to have functioned in the ways it has continued to function ever since. Commercial and government records dominate, along with those created in the service of the local RELIGION. But we also find literature, high and low, and mathematical, astronomical, and medical texts. It pleases users of alphabetical systems to regard them as almost the evolutionary end product of the various writing systems thus far devised. It also appears to be historically true that alphabets were the latest of the writing systems to develop. But all systems seem equally capable of adaptation to all forms of record-keeping and literary pursuits. Various modern oriental writing systems still employ some tens of thousands of ideographs instead of the twenty-six characters and assorted punctuation marks of the Roman alphabet. They sufficiently indicate the adaptability of such systems.

In North Africa, the eastern Mediterranean, and Europe the papyrus roll eventually emerged as the dominant form of the book. The codex succeeded the roll early in the Christian era, though only with some difficulty. The papyrus industry, well established, involved much capital investment and many laborers. At the same time, the production of vellum, fraught with technical problems, took centuries to become established on a large scale. These impediments might have proved less obstructive to the triumph of the codex form had the papyrus codex been adopted for secular literature prior to the vellum codex. But for reasons not entirely understood, the vellum codex was adopted first. Moreover, the vellum codex appears to have been invented in Rome at a time when Rome was dominated by a culture—Greek—for which only the roll meant a book. These factors reinforced a conservatism long characteristic of books and writing. Yet between the first and the fifth centuries C.E. the change from roll to codex occurred. Of the surviving exemplars of Greek secular literary and scientific writings 100 percent of those now dated to the first century are found in roll form, while almost 90 percent of those now dated to the fifth century are found in codex form. The third century saw the adaptation of books to the codex form in significant numbers. By the beginning of the fourth century the codex had achieved something like parity with the roll.

Early Christian communities evidently possessed a different idea of the book. By the second century the Christian Bible seems always to have appeared in papyrus codices. Noncanonical Christian writings also appeared more frequently in codex than in roll form. The adoption of the papyrus codex by Christian communities may have served to differentiate their writings, both scriptural (*see* SCRIPTURE) and noncanonical, from Jewish and pagan writings—an unusual validation of the critical cliché that relates form and content. Christians had shifted to the codex by about the end of the first century. It may thus seem that the eventual triumph of the codex is directly related to the triumph of Christianity in the West. But certain practical concerns had already initiated the shift from roll to codex. These include the compact portability of the codex, its ability to bring together within one set of protective covers perhaps six times as much text as a roll could contain, and its ease of use for reference. Christianity merely gave final impetus to a change already under way.

The production of papyrus in Egypt did not cease until about the twelfth century, but papyrus had long before largely given place to vellum in bookmaking. In China a new writing material, paper, made from mulberry and bamboo bark and probably with additional vegetable fibers, had been announced as early as 105 C.E. by Ts'ai Lun. It is uncertain whether he was the inventor of paper or the official who conveyed word of its discovery. By the eighth century the technique had reached the eastern Islamic world. The Moors brought paper to Europe late in the eleventh century, when its manufacture began in Spain. Paper mills were established in Italy in the thirteenth century; in France and Germany in the fourteenth century; and in Switzerland, England, and Austria in the fifteenth century. By the sixteenth century paper was also made in Holland and Russia.

Some form of ink may have been used in China as early as the third century B.C.E. But development of the classic Chinese ink used in writing and printing is most commonly ascribed to Wei Tan (d. 251 C.E.). *See also* EAST ASIA, ANCIENT.

Printing

Also of oriental invention was the mechanical reproduction of word- or letterforms, that is, PRINTING. Early in the eighth century C.E. Chinese artisans appear to have begun printing from woodblocks. Later in that century the technique reached Japan, where in 770 Empress Shotoku ordered a million copies of a Buddhist text printed for public distribution. Some copies still survive. The earliest surviving printed book, the *Diamond Sutra* (868), also made from blocks, is Chinese. It is, incidentally, preserved in roll rather than codex form. By the eleventh century the Chinese had developed individual, movable, ideographic types. The first experiments, undertaken by Pi Sheng between 1040 and 1048, used clay rather than metal. Tin and wood types followed. Some wooden types in the Uigur script of central Asia, dated about 1300, survive. Type molds were developed in Korea early in the fifteenth century.

Evidence can be found for the routes from East to West taken by papermaking techniques. It leaves no doubt that paper was an invention of China, even though later papermakers certainly modified Chinese techniques. In part their customers needed other kinds of papers. But in part, too, they had to take account of the different materials available to them from which to make their products. The routes taken by

Figure 3. (*Book*) *Maestricht Book of Hours*, Flemish, thirteenth century. By permission of the British Library.

ink or printing from movable types are far less certain. These techniques appear to have been independently reinvented in the West.

JOHANNES GUTENBERG is popularly known as the inventor of the printing press, but his real contribution seems to have been the development of the type mold. This hand-held device permits the manufacture, from a molten alloy of lead, tin, and antimony, of bits of metal type, uniform in height but varied in width to accommodate letterforms of varying width. On the top of each bit (or sort) stands a letterform in reverse relief. Western printing also relied, in contrast to oriental methods, on the screw press, a technology known in Europe since the first century C.E. Such presses could transfer mechanically, under pressure, inked impressions from type to vellum or paper. Gutenberg seems also to have created an oil-based ink that would adhere to the metal surfaces of his types. His technique required a heavier paper than that needed for printing by rubbing paper over woodblocks covered with water-based inks. This form of printing, perhaps borrowed from Asia, had been used in Europe from at least the 1420s.

The new art spread rapidly, although not all early printers managed to establish stable commercial enterprises. By 1471 presses had been at work in Bamberg, Cologne, Nuremberg, Augsburg, Basel, Subiaco, Rome, Foligno, Venice, Seville, and other cities. By 1480 printing had reached many cities throughout the Germanies, the Italian peninsula, France, and the Low Countries, as well as Budapest, Prague, Wrocław, and Kracow; numerous locations throughout Spain; and, in England, London, Westminster, Saint Albans, and Oxford. By the end of the fifteenth century books had been printed in Portugal, Sweden, and Denmark, and presses continued to be established at new locations within western and central Europe. By 1539 a press was established in North America, in Mexico City. One hundred years later the English brought a press to Massachusetts.

Impact of Books

The impact of the printed book is easy to theorize about but difficult to demonstrate. A great deal of the history of the West since the end of the fifteenth century seems intimately connected to the spread of printed books. But definition of that connection is far from simple. It has, for instance, been proposed that the reproducible illustrations that printed books contain and disseminate are a far more significant factor in the retention and spread of scientific and technical knowledge than their texts. Such a suggestion is not farfetched. The difficulties that might face a botanist, an engineer, or an architect using books with no illustrations at all, or books whose hand-made illustrations were drawn by a copyist or gen-

erations of copyists with no special expertise or firsthand knowledge of the objects to be illustrated, are obvious. Outside of scientific or technological fields, printed images, whether within books or issued separately, functioned to disseminate popular piety and conventional morality. Intriguing though this line of investigation may be, not enough is currently known to do more than raise questions about the effects of reproducible illustrations. Obviously, however, books also have an impact even when, like MARTIN LUTHER's Theses, Thomas Paine's *Common Sense*, Adam Smith's *The Wealth of Nations*, KARL MARX's *Das Kapital*, or Adolf Hitler's *Mein Kampf*, they are unillustrated.

Manuscript texts existed only in unique or few copies. By comparison printed texts, clearly more numerous, were more widely disseminated and more readily accessible. Amenable to standardization and correction, they offered inducements to rationalized organization of data, not only through such devices as exactly repeated page numbers and tables of contents but also through alphabetized indexes, dictionaries, atlases, and so forth. An index found in a manuscript, by contrast, could refer only to the particular exemplar within which it was found; it had no necessary relationship to other manuscript exemplars of the same text. Printing also improved data presentation. Textual corruptions could be corrected, "standardized" texts augmented, and new knowledge rapidly incorporated in old texts as they were reissued again and again. On the one hand, the existence of multiple, dispersed copies of texts and, on the other, the freeing of their contents from the sort of substantive degeneration through repeated copying to which manuscript texts were forever and inevitably subject made possible the preservation of knowledge, new and old, in a manner impossible with the manuscript book. The low rate of survival of literature in all fields from antiquity and the textual corruptions with which many surviving texts are afflicted illustrate these basic advantages of printing.

Conversely, the dissemination of outdated knowledge and old texts dressed in the authority of print could act as a brake on the development of new approaches to knowledge. The domination of scientific knowledge by ARISTOTLE characteristic of the late MIDDLE AGES, for example, was by no means ended with the introduction into Europe's intellectual economy of printed books. Moreover, the increased accessibility of books made possible by printing is also easy to overestimate. A Cambridge don who died in 1569, more than a century after Gutenberg's invention, thought it worthwhile to provide an inventory of his personal library of only 159 books in his will. Had he sought additional books in his university's library, he would have found, even as late as the end of the sixteenth century, that it contained fewer than a thousand of them. Books remained expensive for a very long time. Libraries were uncommon, rarely well stocked, and open but briefly to few people. Even if the ability to read was more widespread within early modern societies than has long been supposed, relatively few could have read the libraries' contents, whether in learned or vulgar languages. LITERACY was not to become widespread till very near our own times.

Such caveats suggest the necessity of a cautious approach to gauging the impact of printed books. Yet some aspects of this impact are discernible. Even the RENAISSANCE itself, the period when Gutenberg's invention was developed and spread, felt its effects. Without the preservative capabilities of print, the pre-Gutenberg Italian Renaissance might have proved as limited in effect and duration as the Carolingian or twelfth-century renaissances that preceded it. An institutionalized or perpetual renaissance, so to speak, was inaugurated only by the post-1450 spread of printing. Multiplied and dispersed in printed form, texts might now act as continuing prods to further scholarship instead of dropping from sight to await rediscovery in a monastic library. One scholar suggests that even that sense of self, of the significance of the individual that Swiss cultural historian Jakob Burckhardt regarded as a hallmark of the Renaissance, may be a consequence of the new fixity permitted by printing.

Religion, too, was profoundly affected by printing. Reformation historians have long realized that the reformers' ideas gained widespread circulation because of the press. But printing, in use for almost seventy years before Luther posted his Ninety-five Theses, affected Roman Catholicism just as deeply. It permitted the "standardization" of theological positions by freezing them in printed form, hardening the distinctions between viewpoints whose coexistence an earlier church had tolerated without serious strain. The dissemination of vernacular versions of

Figure 4. *(Book)* Muhammad bin al-Wahid, frontispiece, Qur'an of Sultan Baybars II, Egypt, 1304. By permission of the British Library.

Capitulum III

uidebateí dimna:contraeíus dignitatem . Hunc autem quicumcp veſtrum penes ſe
aliquod haberet teſtimonium. aut nouerit aliquid ſuper hoc.referat nobis illud.vt z
nos omnia regi referamus.quoniam non eſt ſuipropoſiti interficere quemcp: niſi p̃
acquiſitionem diligentem et ſufficientem examinationem. Hon enim vult ipſe iudi/
care ſecundum propriam voluntatem.nec faciem cognoſcere in ſuo iudicio. Et ait iu
der. Reſpicite et attendite bene omnia:que legalis leopardus locutus eſt . nec aliquis
veſtrum occultare debet quod nouit de iſta materia.ſiue cauſa. z hoc propter multas
cauſas. Prima quidem eſt:quia nullus veſtrum dedignari debet ſententiam que la /
ta fuerit.ſiue bona.ſiue mala. Hec velitis aliquid mutilare de eo quod ſcitis Ha mo/
dicum veritatis maximum eſt.et precipue apud deum.vt rex non interficiat innocen/
tem et abſcz culpa verbis ſeductoriis et mendacie . Secunda cauſa eſt . quia quando
punitur peccator iuxta peccatum ſuum:reliqui audientes:timebunt et cauebunt ſibi .
ne in ſimili incidant peccato. z hoc redundat in bonum regis exercitus et populi. Ter
tia cauſa eſt.quia quando perditur malus et ſeductor exercens mendacia et dolum:eſt
maxima tranquillitas regi:et exercitui ſuo. Ham ſua conuerſatio cum eis in maximũ
et grauem turbationem redundat. Hunc igitur dicat vnuſquiſcz veſtrum quod no 9
uit. necx celet veritatem.et confirmet falſitatem. Cumcp audiſſent viri exercitus ver /
ba hec:reſpiciebant vnuſquiſcz ad inuicem et tacebant. Dixit dimna . Quare tacetis?
dicat vnuſquiſcz veſtrum quod nouit.quoniam non credatis mihi diſplicere.ſi omnia
que ſcitis dixeritis. Ham ſi ego deliquiſſem gauderem vticz pro veſtro ſilencio: Uex
tamen ſcio me eſſe innocentem. Et ideo in eo quod ſcitis loquamini. Scitote tamẽ cũ
veritate.quia ad omnia eſt reſponſum. Et ideo cauete:ne aliquod quod neſcitis:profe
ratis. Ham ei qui putat vidiſſe quod non vidit:et audiuiſſe quod non audiuit; dignũ

Figure 5. *(Book) Directorium
humanae vitae.* Printed by Johann
Prüss, Strassburg, 1488. PML 56, The
Pierpont Morgan Library, New York.

the Bible as well as the encouragement of new editions of scriptural texts, and hence of editorial examination of them, helped call into question the very
lexical bases of faith. Ultimately printing contributed
to a hardening of many differences between Roman
Catholic and Protestant cultural and political worlds,
quite apart from the religious distinctions that separated post-Reformation Europe.

The scientific revolution also bears witness to the
impact of printing. Many recent historians have
pointed out medieval advances in such fields as computation, astronomy, and mechanics. But too often
such advances remained isolated and sterile. Far from
provoking a progeny of further advances, they were
likely to remain limited in circulation. When circulated, they were likely to travel in inaccurate, inexact
copies because of the difficulties that technical manuscripts posed for scribes. Only works disseminated
by print, permitting widespread cumulative augmentation of knowledge instead of its haphazard creation
and preservation, could promote rapid scientific advance. Even the publication of older, unreliable scientific books, retrograde from some points of view,
proved an essential propaedeutic to scientific progress. Such books gave postprint scientists a stable,
commonly held basis of knowledge—and error—on
which to build. Merely publishing tables of numbers—standard distances, for instance, or logarithmic
tables—freed investigators from some of the drudg-
ery that quantitative studies can entail.

The increase in the dissemination of knowledge to which printed books gave rise was almost immediately understood, but it was not regarded as an unmixed blessing. Truth and knowledge could now easily circulate, but so could error. Evidence of efforts by ecclesiastical and government authorities to control the printing of and the trade in books is found very early. Precedents existed in the efforts of ecclesiastical authorities to guarantee the integrity of texts in the manuscript era. Trade in Lollard books was a punishable offense in Henry VIII's England; attempts to curb the traffic in both Protestant and Roman Catholic treatises and vernacular Bibles persisted throughout sixteenth-century English history. Copies of Copernicus's *De Revolutionibus* (1543) with passages blacked out to accommodate the censor may easily be found. The *Index Librorum Prohibitorum* is only the most notorious of many efforts to regulate what were frequently perceived as the pernicious effects of the printed book's easy circulation. Political as well as religious objections might be raised to the publication of a book; so might moral objections. A complicated industry grew up around the borders of Enlightenment France to see to the publication and smuggled import into that country of books denied license. Books published within France needed to carry some sort of announcement that they had appeared with approbation ("avec privilège et permission du Roi"). *See* CENSORSHIP; COPYRIGHT.

Yet the effect of the printed book has been constantly to beat back such restrictive impulses. As books have circulated in increasing numbers the most unconventional ideas have circulated with them. Even a barely educated miller in the Friuli might, in the sixteenth century, attract the attention of the Inquisition because of his too public espousal of heterodox religious ideas garnered, in part, from printed books. As more books have circulated, the pressures to become literate so as to be able to read them have also grown. Such developments certainly did not occur in lockstep with one another. Mass literacy, at least in the West, is a phenomenon only of the late nineteenth century. But its coming was assisted by several book-inspired pressures, among them the Protestant Reformation, with its insistence on the ability to read Scripture; the growth of broad-based liberal political systems, which required a literate electorate; and the demands of an increasingly technological culture, in which the illiterate could not function and to whose progress they could contribute very little.

Figure 6. *(Book)* "The Preparation of Pasta for Nightingales," from Giovanni Pietro Olina's *Uccelliera*, Rome, 1684. The Houghton Library, Harvard University.

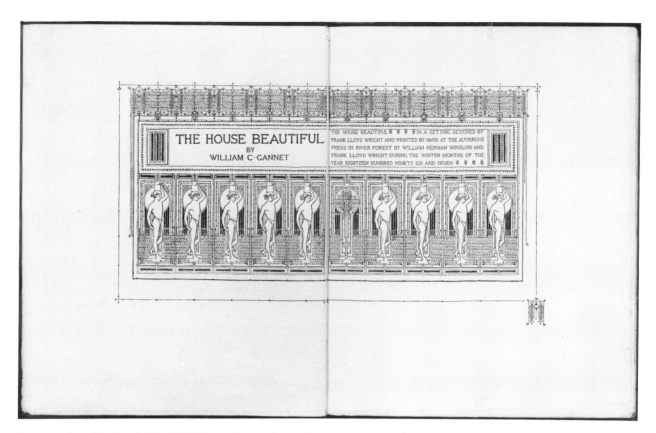

Figure 7. *(Book)* Frank Lloyd Wright, title page for William Ganne[t]t's *The House Beautiful*, Illinois, 1897. Courtesy of the Rare Book and Special Collections Division, Library of Congress.

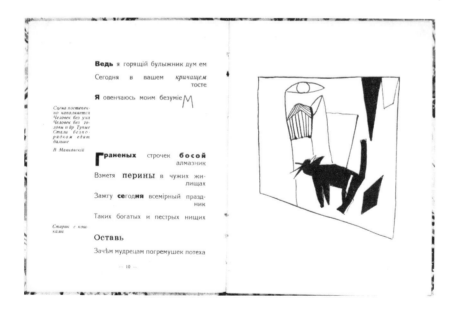

Figure 8. *(Book)* Page 10 and facing illustration from David Burliuk and Vladimir Burliuk, *Vladimir Mayakovsky—A Tragedy*, 1914. By permission of the British Library.

New Technologies

Growth in literacy has meant a growth in the market for print. Consequently, book production has experienced significant technological alteration since Gutenberg's day. The product of a conservative trade, books did not undergo much more than cosmetic and stylistic alterations from the fifteenth through the eighteenth centuries, nor did their mode of production change significantly. But in the nineteenth century many changes occurred. The most significant altered printing from a handpress to a machine-press industry. Powered by human beings since the time of Gutenberg, the press was provided new sources of power: water, steam, electricity. Machine presses produced print in quantities impossible for the older wooden or even metal press driven by human beings. The adoption of stereotypes—steel plates that reproduced entire forms of type with much-improved durability—in association with rotary presses gave an additional boost to productivity. The cutting and setting of type was removed from human hands and relegated to machines. Efforts to increase the availability and cheapen the price of paper, long an expense even greater than the labor for which printers also paid, were successful. Experiments enabled papermakers to shift from rag to vegetable fibers for their product, and new machinery transformed papermaking from an artisanal craft to an industry.

In the twentieth century additional changes have occurred making it possible to eliminate typesetting, whether by machine or hand, altogether. Word- or letterforms are set by computer-driven photographic processes and then printed lithographically. Hot type, deriving a letter's image from metal, has given way to cold type, from which a letter that is an image only may be reproduced. This and other related processes now dominate an industry that in the United States alone produces more than fifty thousand new books each year.

Its typography, its illustration, its binding, and its design are all aspects of the book's history that this brief survey has neglected. Studies of the book as an object of artistic interest fill many volumes. But most books are merely serviceable, not beautiful. They are meant at best to be unobtrusive while they are read. The book's function is preeminently that of container and communicator, not of object. In fulfilling this function the book has had and continues to have an inestimable effect on human history.

See also AUTHORSHIP; PUBLISHING; TYPOGRAPHY.

Bibliography. David Cressy, *Literacy and the Social Order: Reading and Writing in Tudor and Stuart England*, Cambridge, 1980; Robert Darnton, *The Literary Underground of the Old Regime*, Cambridge, Mass., 1982; Elizabeth L. Eisenstein, *The Printing Press as an Agent of Change: Communications and Cultural Transformations in Early Modern Europe*, 2 vols., Cambridge and New York, 1979; Lucien Febvre and Henri-Jean Martin, *The Coming of the Book: The Impact of Printing, 1450–1800* (L'apparition du livre), trans. by D. Gerard, London, 1976; Philip Gaskell, *A New Introduction to Bibliography*, Oxford and New York, 1972, reprint (with corrections) 1974; idem, *Trinity College Library: The First 150 Years*, Cambridge, 1980; Carlo Ginzburg, *The Cheese and the Worms: The Cosmos of a Sixteenth-Century Miller* (in Italian), trans. by John Tedeschi and Anne Tedeschi, Baltimore, Md., 1980; Geoffrey Ashall Glaister, *Glaister's Glossary of the Book*, 2d ed., Berkeley, Calif., and London, 1980; Harvey J. Graff, ed., *Literacy and Social Development in the West: A Reader* (Cambridge Studies in Oral and Literate Culture, No. 3), Cambridge, Mass., 1981; Rudolf Hirsch, *Printing, Selling and Reading, 1450–1550*, 2d ed., Wiesbaden, 1974; William M. Ivins, *Prints and Visual Communication*, London, 1953, reprint Cambridge, Mass., 1969; F. G. Kenyon, *Books and Readers in Ancient Greece and Rome*, 2d ed., Oxford, 1951; J. C. T. Oates, *Cambridge University Library: A History from the Beginnings to the Copyright Act of Queen Anne*, Cambridge, 1986; Colin H. Roberts and T. C. Skeat, *The Birth of the Codex*, London, 1983.

DANIEL H. TRAISTER

BROADCASTING. *See* RADIO; RADIO, INTERNATIONAL; RELIGIOUS BROADCASTING; TELEVISION HISTORY.

BUÑUEL, LUIS (1900–1983)

Spanish-born film director. Creator of more than thirty films in a career that spanned five decades, Luis Buñuel is one of the most celebrated and iconoclastic directors in the history of the cinema. He is among only a handful of directors who have managed successfully to impose their personal artistic vision onto the process of commercial filmmaking, thereby extending the limits of what we define film to be.

The eldest son of a prosperous bourgeois family, Buñuel was raised in the Aragon region of Spain. Although his early years were spent within the confines of a traditional Catholic upbringing, he left that world behind when he began studies at the University of Madrid. He lived at the Residencia de Estudiantes, where he befriended the poet Federico García Lorca. After graduating from the university in 1924, Buñuel moved to Paris to pursue his new interest in THEATER. There he discovered the potential of filmmaking and apprenticed himself to director Jean Epstein.

When his first film, *Un chien andalou*, written with the painter Salvador Dalí, was released to shocked Parisian audiences in 1928, Buñuel became identified with the aesthetic and political radicalism of surrealism. *Un chien andalou* and his next film, *L'âge d'or* (1930), in their juxtaposition of images to create a dreamlike logic, were to have a profound influence on AVANT-GARDE FILM. From the beginning Buñuel's work combined a pointed satire of the bourgeoisie and the Catholic church with the director's continuing fascination with the eroticism that lies beneath the surface of everyday life.

Following the triumph and scandal of his first two films, Buñuel went on to direct a remarkable and diverse series of productions in Spain, Mexico, and France, beginning with *Las Hurdes* (Land without Bread, 1932), a harsh, ironic DOCUMENTARY of the landscape and poverty in one area of his native Spain. He returned to documentaries during the Spanish civil war, after which he lived in the United States and worked at various film-related jobs. In 1946 he moved to Mexico and began directing again. There he completed his internationally acclaimed *Los olvidados* (The Young and the Damned, 1950), in which a surrealistic view of the world is mediated by a seemingly natural narrative. Still in Mexico during the 1950s, Buñuel directed commercial narrative melodramas invested with a critical vision that exposed hypocrisies and neuroses that destroy individual lives; films from this period include *Él* (1952), *Nazarín* (1958), and *The Young One* (1960). In 1960 Buñuel returned temporarily to Spain to produce *Viridiana* (1961), a brilliant narrative whose characters reveal a vulnerability hidden by a naive religious belief. The film demonstrates Buñuel's characteristic surrealist twist, especially in the remarkable scene in which a group of beggars assume the pose of Leonardo da Vinci's *Last Supper*.

Buñuel returned to the more explicit surrealism of his earlier films in *El ángel exterminador* (The Exterminating Angel, 1962). This was followed by a series of outstanding works including *Belle de jour* (1966), *Tristana* (1970), and *Le charme discret de la bourgeoisie* (The Discreet Charm of the Bourgeoisie, 1972), which are marked by a polished mise-en-scène in which the language and trappings of bourgeois life are subverted by the unconscious fantasies of the characters. In his final film, *That Obscure Object of Desire* (1977), finely crafted dialogue and ACTING delineate an imaginary journey through the urban geography of an irrational modern world.

Buñuel's artistic economy, surreal representation of individual desires, and satire of social institutions created a compelling narrative style that exerted a powerful and lasting influence on directors of the new narrative cinema of the 1970s and 1980s in Europe, the United States, and South America.

See also CINEMATOGRAPHY; MOTION PICTURES.

Bibliography. J. Francisco Aranda, *Luis Buñuel: A Critical Biography*, New York, 1976; Luis Buñuel, *My Last Sigh* (Mon dernier soupir), trans. by Abigail Israel, New York, 1983; Raymond Durgnat, *Luis Buñuel*, London, 1967; Gwynne Edwards, *The Discreet Art of Luis Buñuel*, London, 1983; Joan Mellen, ed., *The World of Luis Buñuel: Essays in Criticism*, New York, 1978.

JOHN G. HANHARDT

BURKE, KENNETH (1897–)

U.S. literary critic, rhetorician, and philosopher. Born in Pittsburgh, Pennsylvania, Kenneth Burke briefly attended Ohio State University and Columbia University but was largely self-educated. He began his career as a poet and FICTION writer in the 1920s but soon turned to LITERARY CRITICISM (in *Counterstatement*, 1931) and later, from the mid-1930s on, to social and cultural criticism rooted in ideas about LANGUAGE. His more than a dozen published books range over large areas of history, philosophy, and literature, but his interest in the nature of human communication and the role of language in the drama of human affairs is present in all of them.

Such themes run through *Permanence and Change* (1935) and *Attitudes toward History* (1937), in which he developed his theory of tropes (*see* METAPHOR). In *The Philosophy of Literary Form* (1941) he presented his theory of language as symbolic action and took DRAMA as his model for the study of human relations. His early speculations were systematized in *A Grammar of Motives* (1945), *A Rhetoric of Motives* (1950), and other essays in which he developed his dramatistic theory of language and human behavior and worked out a comprehensive dialectics, RHETORIC, and POETICS. In *The Rhetoric of Religion* (1961) Burke moved away from the system building of the *Motives* books and developed logology, a universal methodology for the study of language and of humans as symbol-using animals. *Language as Symbolic Action: Essays on Life, Literature, and Method* (1966) is an omnibus collection of Burke's ideas about language up to that point.

Burke's major contribution to the study of communication is the concept of symbolic action and the consequent development of dramatism and dramatistic analysis. Dramatism was designed (and used by such scholars as ERVING GOFFMAN and Hugh Dalziel Duncan) to study the function of symbols in society, social relations, literature, and human motivations. Arguing that action, as distinct from mere physical motion, is behavior interpreted in a symbolic context, Burke concluded that symbolic action always has material existence but is not reducible to it. In order to have a symbolic act, which can be almost any human act that means something other than its physical motion component, there must be an agent, a scene, an agency (i.e., means or medium employed by the agent), and a purpose (otherwise it is an accident, not a symbolic act). These five terms form the dramatistic pentad on which dramatism as a nomenclature and method of analysis is based.

Burke's definition of humankind—from an article in *The Hudson Review*—provides a key to much of his thinking:

Man is
the symbol-using (symbol-making, symbol-misusing) animal
inventor of the negative (or moralized by the negative)
separated from his natural condition by instruments of his own making
goaded by the spirit of hierarchy (or moved by the sense of order)
and rotten with perfection.

Among his most resonant speculations are those that center on the negative—the *no*, the *don't*—that "marvel of language." The negative, Burke points out, cannot exist in nature: the absence of a stone or bison or river is an idea that can exist only in the SYMBOLISM of language. In this extraordinary human invention Burke finds the wellspring of many aspects of language and of the development of the human species.

Burke argues that the beginnings of language cannot have stemmed from an impulse to name *things*. For our primal ancestors calling attention to danger—"Stop!" "Beware!"—would have been far more significant. The primal ancestor, thinks Burke, would be closer to a verb than to any other part of speech—and the verb would be used with hortatory, admonitory connotations. It might begin with a mere tonal gesture for calling attention. Burke sees language as essentially hortatory—a means by which people control other people—and this function naturally leads to hierarchies. It looks to the future, to action, and—as in drama—to resolution, fulfillment. Thus Burke sees the evolution of language as essentially dramatistic.

Modern societies honor the resolutely positive over the negative and celebrate such terms as *freedom*. Burke, examining dictionaries for the meaning of freedom, finds it explained in terms of an array of negatives: "Exempt from subjection . . . not under restraint, control, or compulsion . . . not dependent . . . not under arbitrary or despotic government . . . not confined or imprisoned . . . not subjected to the laws of physical necessity . . . guiltless . . . innocent . . . unconstrained. . . ." Can it be that the idea of freedom can exist only on a foundation of negatives and that they provide the generating force behind the concept? Burke gives various other linguistic dualities a similar analysis (*see* LINGUISTICS).

Burke sees humankind as not only symbol using, symbol misusing, and symbol making but also as "symbol-made." He sees many aspects of human affairs emerging from the positive-negative dualities: religion, social hierarchy, conflict, the quest for order, the quest for perfection. He sees humans goaded by their symbols to perfect what they have begun, to take the next step, to go to the end of the line, even if it may have disastrous results.

Bibliography. Hugh Dalziel Duncan, *Communication and Social Order*, New York, 1962; Armin Paul Frank, *Kenneth Burke*, New York, 1969; Frank Lentricchia, *Criticism and Social Change*, Chicago, 1983; Trevor Melia and Herbert Simons, eds., *The Legacy of Kenneth Burke*, Madison, Wis., 1987; William H. Rueckert, *Kenneth Burke and the Drama of Human Relations*, 2d ed., Berkeley, Calif., 1982; idem, ed., *Critical Responses to Kenneth Burke, 1924–1966*, Minneapolis, Minn., 1969; Hayden White and Margaret Brose, eds., *Representing Kenneth Burke*, Baltimore, Md., 1982.

WILLIAM H. RUECKERT

BYBLOS

The ancient Levantine coastal city that gave the Greeks their word for "papyrus," "papyrus roll," and "book." Derivatives of this Greek word, *byblos* (later *biblos*), abound in the vocabulary of modern European languages, such as the English, French, and German words *bibliography, bibliothèque*, and *Bibliothek*. A plural of the Greek diminutive *ta biblia* (literally "the books") was early applied to sacred scriptures, especially those of the Christians, and thus yielded the word *bible* in its various forms and compounds in later languages.

Byblos, situated about twenty-six miles north of Beirut on the Mediterranean coast, was a center for the shipping trade from as early as 3000 B.C.E. The site had been occupied much earlier, at the end of the Stone Age; excavations provide evidence for trade with Egypt from the very earliest period of Egyptian history. This trade with Egypt, which was the source of the papyrus rolls from as early as 1500 B.C.E., continued throughout the early history of the city, until the decline of the Egyptian Empire and the subsequent assertion of Phoenician independence (ca. 1000 B.C.E.). Along with Sidon, Byblos played a leading part in the great period of Phoenician expansion, before the submission of the city to the series of conquests by the Assyrians, Babylonians, Persians, Greeks, and Romans.

Some of the very earliest Phoenician inscriptions, which is to say, some of the earliest intelligible writing in a linear alphabetic script, are from tombs at Byblos (eleventh or tenth century B.C.E.). A small body of earlier writings from Byblos have survived; carved on bronze plates, they contain a nonalphabetic script—the Byblian hieroglyphic texts (not related to EGYPTIAN HIEROGLYPHS). These early second-millennium texts have so far resisted decipherment.

Bibliography. Maurice Dunan l, *Byblia Grammata,* Beirut, 1945; idem, *Fouilles de Byblos,* Vols. 1–3, Paris, 1937–1950; Siegfried H. Horn, "Byblos in Ancient Records," *Andrews University Seminary Studies* 1 (1963): 52–61; Pierre Montet, *Byblos et l'Égypte,* 2 vols., Paris, 1928–1929; James Bennett Pritchard, ed., *Ancient Near Eastern Texts Relating to the Old Testament,* 2d ed., Princeton, N.J., 1955.

DELBERT R. HILLERS

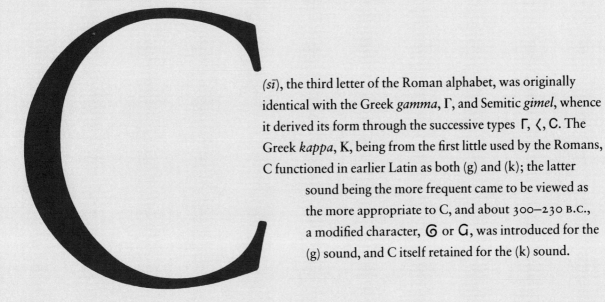

(sī), the third letter of the Roman alphabet, was originally identical with the Greek *gamma*, Γ, and Semitic *gimel*, whence it derived its form through the successive types Γ, ⟨, C. The Greek *kappa*, K, being from the first little used by the Romans, C functioned in earlier Latin as both (g) and (k); the latter sound being the more frequent came to be viewed as the more appropriate to C, and about 300–230 B.C., a modified character, Ɠ or Ǥ, was introduced for the (g) sound, and C itself retained for the (k) sound.

CABLE TELEVISION

Begun after World War II to provide a television service that supplemented broadcast television, retransmitting programs of over-the-air stations by cable to homes in fringe reception areas, cable television gradually came to be seen as a potentially independent service, challenging broadcast television's hegemony over media (*see* TELEVISION HISTORY). As cable technology developed, some forecasters even saw it as the core of a revolution in telecommunications. Together with everything represented by conventional television, they saw it becoming the "one wire" that would bring into the home TELEPHONE service, computer access, facsimile capability, interactive merchandising, burglary protection, and other as yet barely imagined services. By the 1980s it was clear that such ideas were technically feasible. But even while the visions began to take shape, cable television found its position threatened by other rising technologies in an increasingly complex communications arena.

Technology. The basics of cable technology are suggested in its original name, community antenna television (CATV). Signals are received from a SATELLITE antenna, a microwave ground link, or, in the case of a local broadcast station, over the air. These signals are then retransmitted from an originating point, known as the system's headend, usually over coaxial cable, to numerous receiving points. Receivers are slightly modified conventional television sets. Although coaxial cable uses a broad band of frequencies, lying between five (5) and six hundred megahertz on the radio SPECTRUM, most cable systems are capable of sending signals in one direction only, emanating outward from one source, the headend, to subscribers' receivers. Early coaxial cable could carry only three channels; later capacity grew to twelve, long the industry standard. The majority of systems carried twenty or fewer channels for many years, though more technologically sophisticated systems carried one hundred or more. Some hybrid systems mixed coaxial cable and telephone lines as a cost-saving measure. Most local telephone lines, however, are narrow-band and cannot efficiently carry video or high-speed data signals. Some cable systems have been INTERACTIVE MEDIA, allowing users to respond by means of a keypad or terminal to signals from the headend. A pioneer in this technology was the QUBE system designed by Warner-Amex Cable Communications.

National policies. National approaches to cable development have differed widely. In the early 1980s France, the Federal Republic of Germany, Great Britain, and the United States all enacted national cable policies. At that time the first three countries had few, if any, cable systems in operation, but their

political authorities made an attempt to envision cable in industrial as well as cultural policy terms. The design, manufacture, and installation of advanced cable technology were seen to benefit the domestic economy, both as productive industrial activities in a key high-technology sector and as ways to establish a modern telecommunications infrastructure, which was strategically vital to further participation in international telecommunications markets. Culturally, cable policy in France, the Federal Republic of Germany, and Great Britain was part of a policy of liberalization that broke the traditional state-owned MONOPOLY broadcast systems. This in turn portended a greater demand for programming that might promote increased opportunities for a nation's own producers. France was especially aggressive in developing cable and committed large sums of public money to experimental projects. *See* TELECOMMUNICATIONS POLICY.

The policy situation in the United States was quite different. Few new media captured the attention of U.S. policy researchers more fully than cable. A succession of studies and reports was supported by such groups as the Rand Corporation and the Sloan Foundation and came also from congressional committees, the executive Office of Telecommunications Policy, and the Federal Communications Commission (FCC). They appeared in popular periodicals and books, recommended a host of policies for cable regulation, and gave cable almost unprecedented visibility.

In 1959 the FCC ruled that because cable was neither broadcast nor common-carrier communication the commission lacked jurisdiction over it. From about 1962 until 1978, a period when cable's penetration of television households in the United States grew steadily from 2 to 20 percent, the FCC imposed a variety of restrictive regulations on it. By 1984, with the Cable Communications Policy Act, Congress had formally circumscribed government authority over cable to a minimum. Arguably, the turn from broadcast protectionism to market power in U.S. cable regulatory policy reflected a perception that the rapid growth of the cable industry was an indicator of future prosperity, while over-the-air networking appeared to be growing slowly obsolete, especially for advertisers seeking smaller, more homogeneous audiences. U.S. regulatory policy, lacking a widely accepted or historically consistent view of cable—unlike western European approaches—has largely been reactive, conforming to pressures of political and economic power.

Programming, services, and ownership. Cable offers subscribers far greater potential for choice than did the earliest community-antenna systems. The turning point is generally acknowledged to have occurred in the 1970s when Time, Inc.'s Home Box

Office (HBO) began using satellites to distribute movies to cable systems scattered throughout the United States. This brought about the practice of offering "tiers" of programming and services and established the practicality of networking cable program services, thereby permitting cable to grow rapidly into a major national and transnational industry.

The economics of cable programming became perhaps more like that of the film industry than of broadcasting. Cable system operators generally buy programming for an amount based on the total number of their subscribers; subscribers, in turn, pay the cable system operator for services received. In countries where regulations permit, programming services may be partly or wholly subsidized by ADVERTISING. To reduce costs, trends toward multiple-system ownership and cross-media enterprise have been widespread. Multiple ownership of cable systems has developed rapidly in the United States, along with linkages of cable system and program service, network and program service, motion picture studio and program service—in each case with notable successes and failures. In Great Britain the country's largest wholesaler of newspapers and magazines became a major presence in cable programming. Rupert Murdoch's Sky Channel was a program service on the Continent even before he purchased the U.S. Twentieth Century-Fox studios and Metromedia television in the United States. And a German cable channel, owned in part by the Bertelsmann communications conglomerate, derived its news from local newspapers. *See also* HOLLYWOOD; MAGAZINE; NEWSPAPER: HISTORY.

Competition with cable programming emerged in several forms. Videocassette recorders (VCRs) could be used to screen tapes of movies and other programming available for purchase or rental through stores and clubs (*see* VIDEO). Direct broadcast satellites (DBSs) transmitted signals directly to the home, avoiding the need for a cable hookup. Low-power television (LPTV), intended for small, local audiences, and multichannel multipoint distribution services (MMDSs), using microwave links to offer a limited number of channels off the air, were less capital-intensive than cable television. Satellite master-antenna television (SMATV), also known as private cable, offered a cable system in miniature to large multiple-dwelling buildings. Relatively inexpensive home dish antennas could receive at no cost the signals programmers intended for cable systems—until programmers began scrambling or encoding the signals.

The global pattern of cable ownership has been varied. The French cable system was designed, installed, and maintained by the nation's ministry of post, telegraph, and telephone (PTT). Local communities, however, in cooperation with national authorities, were responsible for financing construction. Within general guidelines communities also had authority for programming. In the Federal Republic of Germany, while the Bundespost (its PTT) encouraged national cable development, formal authority for cable decisions resided with the länder (states). Great Britain established national policy and set up a cable authority, but no public money was committed to build systems or to provide programming, which was considered a corporate task. A single company, Robert Maxwell's British Cable Services, quickly acquired nearly three-quarters of the cable systems in the United Kingdom.

In the United States ownership of cable systems became concentrated fairly early. By the early 1980s the top ten multiple-system operators (MSOs) served nearly half of all cable subscribers. Vertical integration and cross-media ownership were common, and MSOs tended to swap systems so as to consolidate their holdings within geographic regions. The ability to adapt cable programming from other media, such as magazines, reduced programmers' costs and at the same time made programming more recognizable and thus more attractive to many viewers. Some programmers had exclusive agreements with Hollywood studios to carry their films, or they coproduced films with studios or actually became their own production houses. By the late 1980s several of the largest U.S. MSOs were considered worth more than a billion dollars each.

Extent of cable television. The plenitude and novelty of cable programming made steady inroads into broadcast television viewing. In the United States, for example, the network share of the television audience declined from about 93 percent in 1975 to 80 percent in 1985; some evidence suggested that in homes with pay television the network share may have dropped to 50 percent. By the middle 1980s nearly half of all U.S. television households had cable television. Large areas of the country, however, especially rural and inner-city locations, were neglected. In Great Britain there was uncertainty at the outset about whether cable would ever be able to attain the 30 percent penetration necessary for financial viability. Other countries, in contrast, had historically high cable penetration. By the mid-1980s Belgian cable reached eight out of ten households, and in the Netherlands the figure was six out of ten. These countries plus Switzerland then represented only about 8 percent of western European homes in general but approximately two-thirds of all homes with cable television. About 60 percent of Canadian homes with television subscribed to cable. Around the same time there was no cable television development in Italy. In the less developed countries cable made few inroads; VCRs, satellite dishes, and conventional broadcasting systems expanded instead.

One factor in the up-and-down fortunes of cable television has been its continuously derivative nature. It has brought its subscribers more and clearer programming, but the offerings have largely echoed those of other media. The disconnect rate has been high. Yet vistas of a more extraordinary future, with one-wire systems encompassing an unprecedented array of two-way services, persist. These visions are based on the capabilities of FIBER OPTICS, far exceeding those of coaxial cable to deliver multiple streams of communication. The technology seems ready to revolutionize not only cable television but also telephone service and TELECOMMUNICATIONS NETWORKS. Whether these will merge or one will absorb the others, and what the social implications of any such developments might be, are questions for the next century.

See also GOVERNMENT REGULATION; VIDEOTEX.

Bibliography. Mary Louise Hollowell, ed., *Cable/Broadband Communications Book*, Vols. 1–4, Washington, D.C., 1977–1985; idem, *Cable Handbook, 1975–1976*, Washington, D.C., 1975; Don R. Le Duc, *Cable Television and the FCC*, Philadelphia, 1973; Mary Alice Mayer Phillips, *CATV: A History of Community Antenna Television*, Evanston, Ill., 1972; Ralph Lee Smith, *The Wired Nation*, New York, 1972; Christopher H. Sterling, "Cable and Pay Television," in *Who Owns the Media?* ed. by Benjamin M. Compaine, Christopher H. Sterling, Thomas Guback, and J. Kendrick Noble, Jr., White Plains, N.Y., 1982; U.S. Congress, House of Representatives, Committee on Interstate and Foreign Commerce, Subcommittee on Communications, *Cable Television: Promise v. Regulatory Performance*, Washington, D.C., 1976.

JAMES MILLER

CALENDAR

Calendars have been devised in various ways by societies throughout the world to serve in the reckoning of time; the scheduling of recurrent agricultural, religious, and other activities; and the transmitting of seasonal observations and conclusions to later generations. Early calendars were a tool of communication guiding the management of crops and the breeding of livestock. As cultures progressed, most used celestial events as the basis for their calendars.

Three celestially determined periods have traditionally marked time: the day, the month, and the year. The day—measured, for example, from one sunrise to the next—is determined by the rotation of the earth and is thus slightly variable. The month—the period between one full moon and the next—averages a little more than 29.53 days. The year is the period between, for example, one summer solstice—when the midday sun is highest in the sky—and the next. This tropical year is about 365.2422 days, although in remote times it was slightly longer.

The day, the month, and the year are not commensurable; that is, the month and the year are not simple multiples of the day, and the year is not a simple multiple of the month. Calendar makers using these celestial periods often have taken the month to the nearest whole day and used an arbitrary value for the year, have taken the year to the nearest whole day but used some arbitrary value for the month, or have taken somewhat arbitrary values for both the month and the year.

Babylonian calendar. The Babylonians, who formulated a calendar used from the third to the first millennium B.C.E., regarded the day as extending from one sunset to the next and the month as the period from one first crescent moon visible after sunset to the next. Their month, governed by the phases of the moon, was twenty-nine or thirty days long. The Babylonians recognized quite early that twelve such months made up almost a year of the seasons. However, after three calendar years of 354 or 355 days the calendar was seen to be running about a month ahead of the seasonal year, so every now and then the Babylonian kings decreed a thirteenth, intercalated month in the calendar year. By about 500 B.C.E. the Babylonians discovered that nineteen years of the seasons contained almost exactly two hundred thirty-five lunar months, so they included an intercalated month in a regular pattern seven times in a nineteen-year cycle, later named the Metonic cycle in honor of the fifth-century B.C.E. Greek astronomer Meton.

After the Babylonian exile period of Jewish history, dating from the sixth century B.C.E., Jews adopted the Babylonian calendar with some modifications (*see* JUDAISM). For example, the Babylonian year began in spring, corresponding to the Jewish Passover, but the Jewish new year begins in autumn. The ancient Greeks also may have borrowed several calendars from the Babylonians.

From at least the second century B.C.E. the Chinese had a calendar basically similar to that of the Babylonians. The Chinese calendar featured months of twenty-nine and thirty days in rough alternation and had seven intercalated months in a nineteen-year period. However, the Chinese new year began some weeks earlier than the Babylonian new year, and the Chinese years were structured in a twelve-year cycle based on the orbit of Jupiter, with each year given the name of a sign of the Chinese zodiac—the rat, the tiger, the ox, and so on.

Egyptian calendars. Before about 3000 B.C.E. the Egyptians had their own calendar based on the cycles of the moon, but about 2800 B.C.E. they introduced a calendar for civil purposes as well. This new calendar had a 365-day year and twelve thirty-day

a

b

Figure 1. *(Calendar)* Two scenes from a Roman pictorial agricultural calendar in mosaic: *(a)* a sacrifice to Ceres, and *(b)* a man placing loaves in the oven. Giraudon/Art Resource, New York.

months, plus five epagomenal days outside the months. Each month was divided into three ten-day weeks, the first example of a standardized weekly cycle operating independently of lunar activity. The civil months, although derived in an approximate way from the phases of the moon, did not keep in step with them. Because the year according to the civil calendar was about one quarter-day shorter than the year of the seasons (determined by the regular flooding of the Nile, which made possible the planting of crops), over centuries the first day of the year moved steadily forward through the seasons, from the flooding of the Nile to the growth of crops to harvest. Thus, although the civil calendar may have been useful for administrative purposes such as the duration of office holding or the collection of taxes, it was poor at guiding agrarian activities.

Roman calendars. The Roman calendar, from which the modern calendar descends, underwent a series of alterations. Before about 700 B.C.E. the Roman calendar year consisted of ten named and two unnamed months, totaling perhaps three hundred fifty-five days. The named months were Martius, Aprilis, Maius, Iunius, Quintilis, Sextilis, September, October, November, and December. The first was named after Mars, the god of war; the second relates to the greening of the earth on the eve of spring; the third is named for Maia, Mother Earth; and the fourth for Juno. The last six names mean fifth month, sixth month, and so on to tenth. The two unnamed winter months were later called Ianuarius, after Ianus, the god of gateways; and Februarius, for the purification festival Februa.

After 450 B.C.E. the republican or pre-Julian calendar was in force, consisting of four months with thirty-one days, seven with twenty-nine days, and one, Februarius, with twenty-eight days. Occasionally Februarius was shortened to twenty-three or twenty-four days, and a twenty-seven-day month, Intercalaris, was let in. The decision on this matter was in the hands of the Pontifex Maximus, who for political reasons often failed to take action when it was necessary. As a result the calendar got badly out of step with the seasons.

In 46 B.C.E. Julius Caesar, then Pontifex Maximus, instituted a radical reform by adding ninety days to that year, thus restoring the seasons to their traditional places. He allotted thirty-one days to seven months, thirty days to four others, and twenty-eight to Februarius except in every fourth year, when it was given an extra day after the twenty-fourth. This brought the ordinary year to 365 days and the leap year to 366. A grateful senate decreed that the month Quintilis should thereafter be known as Iulius. Iulius's successor, Augustus, later arranged for the month Sextilis to be given his name.

The Julian year is slightly longer than the year of the seasons, so that by the late sixteenth century the spring equinox, important in determining the date of Easter, was occurring around March 11 instead of on March 21 as had been decreed by the Council of Nicaea in 325 C.E. In 1582 Pope Gregory canceled ten days by declaring that the day after October 4 that year would be October 15. He further ordered that in centurial years not divisible by 400 February should not have an extra day. Over a 400-year period

Figure 2. *(Calendar)* Pietro Crescenzi, detail of a medieval manuscript showing the labors of the months from January through August. Condé Museum, Chantilly, ms. 603. Giraudon/Art Resource, New York.

Figure 3. *(Calendar)* Aztec calendar, Mexico City. The Bettmann Archive, Inc.

the average Gregorian year thus works out to 365.2425 days, which is about .0003 day too long.

Other systems. There is much cultural and historical variation among methods of time reckoning. For example, an Indian calendar in the first millennium C.E. adopted the Julian year and, more recently, the Gregorian year. This calendar has had three sets of twelve months: one based on the phases of the moon, which has months of twenty-nine or thirty days with an intercalated month let in seven times in nineteen years; another with solar months marked by the sun's passage through a sign of the zodiac and with lengths of from twenty-nine to thirty-two days; and a third with a system of civil months, five of which have thirty-one days with the other seven having thirty days (one has thirty-one days every fourth year).

Early in the first millennium C.E. the Arabs had a calendar of twelve lunar months with an intercalated month let in on an arbitrary basis. Muhammad proscribed intercalation and fixed the months in a strict twenty-nine- and thirty-day alternation, with the twelfth month having twenty-nine days on nineteen occasions and thirty days on eleven. This yielded a month of 29.53 days (very close to lunar months) and a year of 354.36 days. The Islamic year advances through the year of seasons in about 33.56 years.

Modern Iran has had three calendars. The national calendar, based on the Egyptian civil calendar and with a sixth day outside the months every four years, was brought back after the Persian conquest of Egypt in 526 B.C.E. The Parsis took with them a modified version of this calendar when they migrated to India. Iranians use the Islamic calendar for religious purposes and the Gregorian calendar for business.

In Central America the Mayan calendar had eighteen months of twenty days and five days outside the months, an arrangement unrelated to any celestial phenomena. Complex cycles were generated first by pairing the number of each of thirteen divinities with the names of the twenty days, yielding a count of 260 days, and then by matching the names of the eighteen months and of the five-day period with the day number, resulting in a total of 365 days. Putting the two cycles together, a calendar round was completed in 18,980 days in which each day had four indicators. *See also* AMERICAS, PRE-COLUMBIAN— WRITING SYSTEMS.

Calendar features often are the result of historical or cultural conventions. For example, years have been variously dated from the beginning of the reigns of Babylonian kings, from the foundation of Rome, from the birth of Christ, and from the flight of the Prophet Muhammad.

The seven days of the week and the twenty-four-

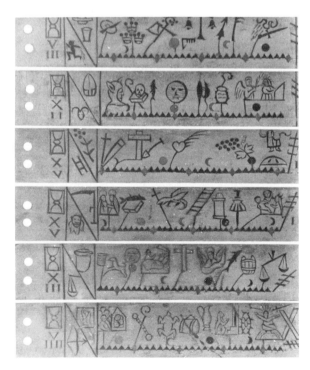

Figure 4. *(Calendar)* Perpetual pocket calendar. Front and back views of the six leaves of a wooden "fan" calendar that belonged to the English archbishop William Laud (1573–1645). The twelve sides of the six leaves correspond to the twelve months of the year. Along the bottom of each leaf, a row of triangles (black for weekdays, red for Sundays) represents the days of the month. The symbols probably indicate church festivals. Museum of the History of Science, Oxford.

Figure 5. *(Calendar)* French decimal calendar issued during the French Revolution. The Bettmann Archive, Inc.

hour day are also arbitrary creations. The seven-day week has origins both in the Jewish cycle based on observance of the Sabbath and in the planetary or astrological week introduced to the West by Rome. With the rise of Christianity these traditions were blended. The twenty-four-hour day was derived from the Egyptians, who divided the sunlight period into twelve parts and the sunset-to-sunrise period into twelve parts. These temporal "hours" varied in length with the seasons. They were in use in Europe until the development of the mechanical CLOCK, which could operate only with near-constant hours. In other cultures the day has conventionally started at different times such as sunrise, midday, sunset, or midnight, resulting in different ways of calculating the length of the day. The Babylonians, for instance, divided the day into twelve *berus;* the Indians, into sixtieths.

Revolutionary calendars. The basic role played by time measurement in the formation of group identity and the maintenance of social structure can be seen clearly in instances in which calendars have been radically altered as a result of REVOLUTION. In 1793 the French republican government established a revolutionary calendar based on the decimal system. It consisted of twelve thirty-day months, each divided into three ten-day weeks called *décades,* and five days outside the months. The days of the week were given Latin numerical names: Primidi, Duodi, Tridi, and so on up to Decadi. Each day was divided into ten hours, each hour into 100 minutes, and each minute into 100 seconds. This rational and scientific system was intended to counter the influence of Christianity on the weekly cycle governing religious and economic life in France. Accordingly, the new calendar replaced religious holidays with civil holidays and discouraged traditional Sunday observances. The attempt to alter the fundamental underpinnings of French society was ultimately unsuccessful, and in 1805 Napoléon Bonaparte formally restored the Gregorian calendar as part of a broader reconciliation with the Catholic church.

Another notable postrevolutionary calendar change—again to subvert the powerful role of religion—took place in the Soviet Union in 1929. The Soviet revolutionary calendar kept the twelve Gregorian months, but each month consisted of six five-day weeks. The days of the week were not named but numbered. The rationale for the new five-day week was to maximize industrial growth by instituting a continuous cycle of production, which was accomplished by staggering the weekly cycle so that no more than one-fifth of the population had the same day of rest. In effect the Soviet government replaced the seven-day week with five different five-day weeks—a move with devastating results for Soviet family and social life. The introduction of the *nepreryvka* ("uninterrupted"), which required that workers rest every fifth day rather than every seventh, also made traditional religious worship impossible for members of the three main Soviet faiths: Christianity, Judaism, and Islam. After a series of piecemeal calendrical reforms, by 1940 the Gregorian calendar was reinstated in the Soviet Union.

See also RELIGION.

Bibliography. William M. O'Neil, *Time and the Calendars,* Sydney, Australia (2d printing, with corrections), 1978; Alan E. Samuel, *Greek and Roman Chronology,* Munich, 1972; Eviatar Zerubavel, *The Seven Day Circle,* New York and London, 1985.

WILLIAM M. O'NEIL

CANTOMETRICS

Term coined by Alan Lomax, meaning the measure of SONG, or song as a measure of CULTURE. Cantometrics views singing styles as NONVERBAL COMMUNICATION about culture and social relations and defines their salient characteristics so that they can be compared and interpreted cross-culturally. This standardized, multiscalar rating system, which has a consensus level of more than 80 percent, has been applied to the analysis of over four thousand songs from more than four hundred cultures. It is one of several such methods (*see* CHOREOMETRICS) developed in the Columbia University Cross-Cultural Study of Expressive Style, initiated in 1961.

Computer operations using the numerical PERFORMANCE profiles of cantometrics have produced two principal fields of information: (1) a classification of song performance into stylistic regions and areas that match the main geographic distributions of human culture as seen by archaeology and ethnography, and (2) a body of cross-cultural correlations of cantometric scales with standard measures of social structure that account for these variations.

The cantometric method was invented in the 1960s by Alan Lomax and Victor Grauer when, for the first time, a corpus of authentic field recordings made the music of the whole world available for comparative analysis (*see* SOUND RECORDING). These data afforded a unique opportunity to examine one type of human communication on a global scale. Field recordings provide direct behavioral data that can be studied repeatedly. The holistic, systems approach of cantometrics was designed to identify audible patterns such as those that differentiate OPERA from country or black African from Amerindian performances. These stylistic patterns are composed of sets of highly redundant, systems-maintaining qualities that persist all the way through sets of performances.

Earlier, anthropologist Ray L. Birdwhistell had suggested that such qualities could be roughly quantified, and linguist Norman Markel had demonstrated that their relative prominence could be reliably scaled and rated by teams of judges.

The quantitative scales needed to define these salient characteristics were tested on a global sample of song. The most dependable and efficient measures were incorporated into a set of teaching tapes in which the steps along each scale were illustrated with examples from a variety of musical traditions.

Classroom testing of these style-defining tapes produces a high level of consensus among listeners. Moreover, the tapes quickly acquaint students with the full range of human song and with a reliable method for the cross-cultural analysis of the cultural meanings of song performance. One teacher reports that after a month of classroom work students were able to identify the world source of any new recording and to comment on its cultural content.

Figure 1 presents the cantometric rating system and exhibits the contrasting modal profiles of two regional styles—African gatherers (the main modes in ovals) and urban East Asia (the main modes in rectangles). The ensemble-oriented, multipart, unified, repetitious, unornamented, and clear-voiced gatherer style reinforces the egalitarian, complementary, sharing tradition of the communal band. The exclusive, solo, virtuosic, elaborate, orchestrated, vocally idiosyncratic, oriental style mirrors the highly stratified, male-dominated, urbanized societies of the irrigation empires. Visual inspection showed that every main cultural region has such distinctive profiles, consisting of a core of stable features on some scales and typical ambiguities on others.

These discoveries were confirmed and enriched when the cantometric data were computerized and subjected to factor analysis. A large and well-distributed set of cantometric profiles was clustered into ten regional groupings. The resulting regional style map (see Figure 2) presents a layered historical geography of song style and culture.

Regional styles 1 and 2 link the multipart singing of the African gatherers to isolated pockets of similar style in Austronesia and South America. Region 3 defines the Siberian homeland of the glottalized solo style of the prehistoric big-game hunters, which turns up again in Patagonia at the terminus of their American migration. Style region 4 comprises the Circum-Pacific, peopled in the last glacial age, when North America, Melanesia, and Australia were linked to Asia by land bridges. Regional style 5, Nuclear America, outlines the zone in which agricultural civilizations arose in Middle America and the Andes. In region 6, the tropical gardener style, characterized by cohesive, polyphonic choralizing, runs all the way from Oceania to black Africa. The text-heavy choral styles of region 7, the Malayo-Polynesian cluster, appear to trace the spread of Malay culture from Southeast Asia into the Pacific and its merger there with style 6. Regional style 8 was *Old High Culture* because its solo, ornamented, heavily orchestrated style links together all the zones shaped by ancient urban civilization, from East Asia to the Mediterranean. Region 9, Central Asia, is the heartland of a simpler but related solo style. Region 10, Europe, though closely allied to regions 8 and 9, still shows its ancient affiliation with Siberia in the north and with the polyphonic gardener zone of the south.

A framework of explanatory hypotheses for these and other song-style variations has emerged from the study of the powerful correlations among cantometric scales and standard measures for social structure, derived from ethnographic compendiums. The many relationships can only be summarized here.

Style. Song style tends to grow more articulated, ornamented, heavily orchestrated, and exclusive as societies grow bigger, more productive, more urbanized, and more stratified. Specifically, (1) the level of text repetition decreases directly as productivity increases, (2) the level of precision of enunciation increases as states grow in size, (3) the prominence of small intervals and embellishments indicates the level of stratification, (4) orchestral complexity symbolizes state power, and (5) melodic size and complexity reflect the size and subsistence base of a community.

Organization. The organization of the performing group varies with community organization: (1) the cohesiveness of singing groups reflects and reinforces the level of social solidarity in other aspects of social organizations, (2) solo or individualized choruses are characteristic of network-oriented and individualized social webs, and (3) polyphonic choral performance, in which two or more independent melodic parts coincide, is characteristic of sexually complementary cultures in which women have a productive role equal to or greater than that of men.

Vocal quality. Vocal noise and tension vary with GENDER roles: (1) harsh-voiced singing is typical of cultures in which boys are trained for aggression, and (2) vocal tension, as measured by nasality and vocal narrowness, tends to be high where sexual sanctions are severe, whereas relaxed, open voices are common where relatively permissive sexual standards prevail.

Rhythm. It appears likely, though a smaller sample was tested, that rhythmic and phrasal preferences may be shaped in childhood: (1) regular rhythms and phrases of moderate length are characteristic of cultures in which discipline imposes regular habits early in life; (2) on the other hand, irregular meters and long phrases are more frequent in cultures in which weaning is long deferred and children are reared indulgently.

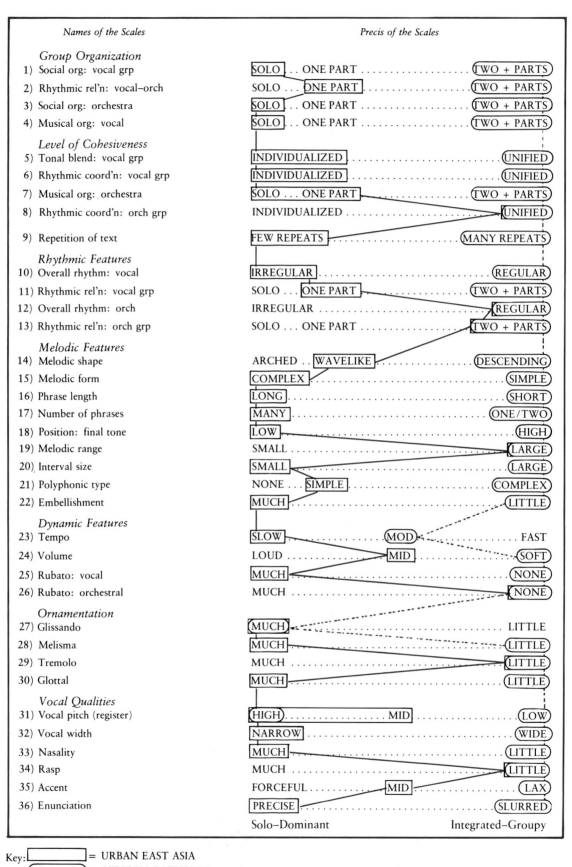

Names of the Scales   Precis of the Scales

Group Organization
1) Social org: vocal grp   SOLO ... ONE PART .... TWO + PARTS
2) Rhythmic rel'n: vocal–orch   SOLO ... ONE PART .... TWO + PARTS
3) Social org: orchestra   SOLO ... ONE PART .... TWO + PARTS
4) Musical org: vocal   SOLO ... ONE PART .... TWO + PARTS

Level of Cohesiveness
5) Tonal blend: vocal grp   INDIVIDUALIZED .... UNIFIED
6) Rhythmic coord'n: vocal grp   INDIVIDUALIZED .... UNIFIED
7) Musical org: orchestra   SOLO ... ONE PART .... TWO + PARTS
8) Rhythmic coord'n: orch grp   INDIVIDUALIZED .... UNIFIED

9) Repetition of text   FEW REPEATS .... MANY REPEATS

Rhythmic Features
10) Overall rhythm: vocal   IRREGULAR .... REGULAR
11) Rhythmic rel'n: vocal grp   SOLO ... ONE PART .... TWO + PARTS
12) Overall rhythm: orch   IRREGULAR .... REGULAR
13) Rhythmic rel'n: orch grp   SOLO ... ONE PART .... TWO + PARTS

Melodic Features
14) Melodic shape   ARCHED .. WAVELIKE .... DESCENDING
15) Melodic form   COMPLEX .... SIMPLE
16) Phrase length   LONG .... SHORT
17) Number of phrases   MANY .... ONE/TWO
18) Position: final tone   LOW .... HIGH
19) Melodic range   SMALL .... LARGE
20) Interval size   SMALL .... LARGE
21) Polyphonic type   NONE ... SIMPLE .... COMPLEX
22) Embellishment   MUCH .... LITTLE

Dynamic Features
23) Tempo   SLOW .... MOD .... FAST
24) Volume   LOUD .... MID .... SOFT
25) Rubato: vocal   MUCH .... NONE
26) Rubato: orchestral   MUCH .... NONE

Ornamentation
27) Glissando   MUCH .... LITTLE
28) Melisma   MUCH .... LITTLE
29) Tremolo   MUCH .... LITTLE
30) Glottal   MUCH .... LITTLE

Vocal Qualities
31) Vocal pitch (register)   HIGH .... MID .... LOW
32) Vocal width   NARROW .... WIDE
33) Nasality   MUCH .... LITTLE
34) Rasp   MUCH .... LITTLE
35) Accent   FORCEFUL .... MID .... LAX
36) Enunciation   PRECISE .... SLURRED

                                  Solo-Dominant   Integrated-Groupy

Key: ☐ = URBAN EAST ASIA
     ⬭ = AFRICAN GATHERER

Figure 1. (*Cantometrics*) Outline of the cantometric scales and their use in contrasting two regional styles: African gatherers and urban East Asia. Courtesy of Alan Lomax.

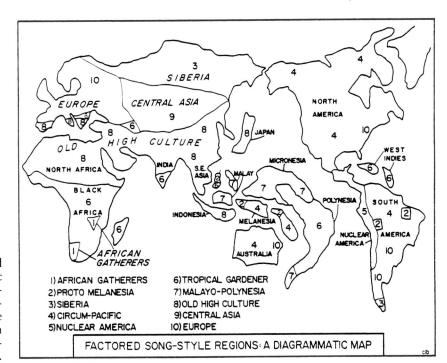

1) AFRICAN GATHERERS   6) TROPICAL GARDENER
2) PROTO MELANESIA   7) MALAYO-POLYNESIA
3) SIBERIA   8) OLD HIGH CULTURE
4) CIRCUM-PACIFIC   9) CENTRAL ASIA
5) NUCLEAR AMERICA   10) EUROPE

FACTORED SONG-STYLE REGIONS: A DIAGRAMMATIC MAP

Figure 2. *(Cantometrics)* Factored song-style regions: a diagrammatic map. From Alan Lomax, *Cantometrics: An Approach to the Anthropology of Music*, Berkeley, Calif.: The University of California Extension Media Center, 1976, p. 32. Copyright © 1976 Alan Lomax.

Dynamic level. Finally, the dynamic levels of song, DANCE, and orchestra are highly intercorrelated. Emphasis on loudness is characteristic of the music of large polities that put a high value on military glory.

These propositions, based in correlations of a high order of probability, have been extensively tested since they were first reported in the 1960s. Parallel concepts have been found in the analysis of other expressive systems. Altogether they portray some ways in which expressive systems reflect and change with culture patterns, as wholes. Thus the rhythmic arts seem to have important roles to play in the reinforcement of the basic structures of society. The comparative success of the cantometric experiment suggests that prime universals of communication, usually sought at the linguistic level, are to be found at the nonverbal level through cross-cultural analysis.

See also ETHNOMUSICOLOGY; MUSIC, FOLK AND TRADITIONAL; MUSIC PERFORMANCE; MUSIC THEORIES.

Bibliography. Herbert Barry, Irvin L. Child, and Margaret Bacon, "A Cross-Cultural Survey of Some Sex Differences in Socialization," *Journal of Abnormal and Social Psychology* 55 (1957): 327–332; Ray L. Birdwhistell, *Kinesics and Context: Essays on Body Motion Communication,* Philadelphia, 1970; Alan Lomax, *Cantometrics: A Method in Musical Anthropology*, Berkeley, Calif., 1977; idem, "The Evolutionary Taxonomy of Culture," *Science* 177 (1972): 228–239; Alan Lomax et al., *Folk Song Style and Culture*, Princeton, N.J., 1968; Norman Markel, "The Reliability of Coding Paralanguage: Pitch, Loudness, and Tempo," *Journal of Verbal Learning and Verbal Behavior* 4 (1965): 360–368; George Peter Murdock, *Ethnographic Atlas*, Pittsburgh, Pa., 1967; George Peter Murdock and Douglas R. White, "Standard Cross-Cultural Sample," *Ethnology* 8 (1969): 329–368.

ALAN LOMAX

CANTRIL, HADLEY (1906–1969)

U.S. social psychologist. The research of Albert Hadley Cantril ranged over many aspects of human nature and society, but most of it was directly or indirectly related to communication and PUBLIC OPINION.

After graduating from Dartmouth College in 1928 and receiving a Ph.D. from Harvard University in 1931, Cantril taught briefly at Dartmouth, Harvard, and Columbia University. In 1936 he started a twenty-year career at Princeton University, where he organized the Office of Public Opinion Research and served as chairman of the psychology department. He was enormously popular as a lecturer, earning the enthusiastic loyalty of his students. In 1955 he became the full-time chairman of the board of the Institute for International Social Research, which was established with an endowment from the Rockefeller Brothers Fund.

During World War II Cantril was a consultant to the secretary of war and the Office of War Information. From 1940 to 1945 he conducted polls on the war effort for Franklin D. Roosevelt. He subsequently served as director of the UNESCO Tensions Project in Paris and, in 1955–1956, as a consultant to the White House. His work in applying the social sciences to political problems is engagingly set forth in *The Human Dimension: Experiences in Policy Research* (1967).

Cantril made noteworthy contributions to several areas, including PERCEPTION, PERSUASION, and audience research. He was a founder of a transactional psychology that emphasized the interplay between an individual's assumptions and intentions and the external environment in shaping each person's unique "reality world."

The Psychology of Radio (1935), written with Gordon Allport, anticipated the flood of audience studies that were to follow during the next decades. Program preferences of different population groups, ratings given male and female voices, and uses of RADIO in the classroom were among the topics it examined. Further contributions to audience research, incidental to investigations of other subjects, were made in *The Invasion from Mars* (1940) and *The Psychology of Social Movements* (1941).

The study of audiences, as well as of PROPAGANDA and public opinion, was likewise advanced by Cantril's basic work on ATTITUDES and perception, which began with his monograph *General and Specific Attitudes* (1932). This work was carried forward by *The Psychology of Ego-Involvements, Social Attitudes and Identifications* (1947), written with Muzafer Sherif, and by extensive research on perception. In one experiment (with Albert Hastorf) he exposed Princeton and Dartmouth students to a film of a foul-plagued football game between the two institutions. As expected, the students tended to see mainly the violations committed by the other side's team.

During World War II and after, Cantril focused some of his work directly on propaganda and public morale. One of his papers on the U.S. information program, "What Should Our Message Be?" (1951), was reprinted in the *Congressional Record*. In *Soviet Leaders and Mastery over Man* (1960) he analyzed Soviet assumptions about human nature and techniques of persuasion resulting from them.

Public opinion research interested Cantril throughout his career. His *Gauging Public Opinion* (1944), which may have been the first book-length treatment of survey methods, remains one of the best. With F. P. Kilpatrick he developed an ingenious technique for measuring attitudes, which he called the "self-anchoring striving scale." This technique was used by his Institute for International Social Research in surveys throughout the world.

Two major volumes reporting on Cantril's polling activities (*see* POLL) are *The Pattern of Human Concerns* (1965) and *The Political Beliefs of Americans* (1967), the latter written with his research partner at the institute, Lloyd A. Free. The former volume summarized people's aspirations, and progress in achieving them, in thirteen countries on five continents.

Underlying Cantril's thinking was a basically optimistic view of prospects for the human condition. "Whatever the circumstances," he wrote, "the human design will in the long run force any institutional framework to accommodate it."

See also COMMUNICATIONS RESEARCH: ORIGINS AND DEVELOPMENT.

Bibliography. F. P. Kilpatrick, "Hadley Cantril (1906–1969): The Transactional Point of View," *Journal of Individual Psychology* 25 (1969): 219–225.

W. PHILLIPS DAVISON

CARICATURE

The creation of satirical images in visual form, often with a political theme. By emphasizing certain outstanding features of the subject, whether a person or an event, caricature communicates in a way that is at once humorous and critical. The caricaturist does not perform, but instead locates the performance for an audience.

Beginnings

The development of caricature was facilitated by the existence of a language of relatively fixed iconographic types in ART (*see* ICONOGRAPHY). The growth of a language of types in art took place during the RENAISSANCE and Reformation periods and involved artists in Italy, Germany, France, the Netherlands, and other parts of Europe. Social and political conflicts along with geographic factors all offered fertile conditions for the emergence of caricature.

During this widespread revolution the political print as the bearer of caricature came into its greatest use. There are earlier examples of caricature, many dating from the invention of the woodblock and printing (*see* PRINTING). But it was MARTIN LUTHER, the great German theologian, who first used the political print in pictorial PROPAGANDA on a large scale, for the purposes of his revolutionary movement. Luther employed wood engravers and was an excellent pamphleteer; his fly sheets circulated in Germany throughout the sixteenth century, inspiring satires of Luther himself (see Figure 1).

Caricature, in the sense of a critical and exaggerated portrait of an individual, is frequently associated with the work of the Carracci family in Bologna in the late 1500s. To the Carraccis, caricature meant to penetrate reality or get to the truth about a person by using as little detail as possible to construct a recognizable picture. They linked certain distortions to qualities of character and personality so that a

Figure 1. *(Caricature)* Erhard Schoen, *The Devil's Bagpipe*, 1525. Courtesy of Lawrence H. Streicher.

smirk might mean a deceitful person, or a crouch of the body a cunning outlook. The *ritratto carico*, or portrait caricature, had emerged.

The focus of activity next moved to the Netherlands, which claimed many of the skilled engravers and artists in Europe at that time, including Anthony Van Dyck and Peter Paul Rubens. The considerable degree of freedom from persecution in the Netherlands of the seventeenth century made it a general place of refuge for political malcontents and religious dissenters. This was especially true for French citizens who fled from the tyranny of Louis XIV. The Netherlands became the launching station for satirical prints directed largely against Louis and his policies. The inscriptions on some of these Dutch prints appear in both French and English, suggesting that they were to serve and to ally at least two groups of readers.

Emergence as an Art

Professional caricaturists had not yet made an appearance in eighteenth-century Europe. Although oc-

casional practitioners produced identifiable personal satire in Italy and the Netherlands, there was not yet a systematic statement or a professional stance that helped to distinguish the caricaturist from the comic artist. In part, this stance was supplied by William Hogarth, the great British dramatic artist. Hogarth did not wish his works to be confused with the crude excesses of caricature, yet he is often called the father of caricature for his role in setting and defending standards of engraving, thus raising the prestige of prints. He considered *caricatura* per se to be crude, exaggerated, and contradictory to his expressive realism.

Hogarth saw himself as a moralist rather than a political partisan. Even his well-known print *Gin Lane* (1751) is a moral stricture, although it was intended to support a ministerial act against the unlimited sale of gin (see Figure 2). Hogarth satirized, but in a comic manner that provoked good-humored laughter. His work brought together the burlesque and exaggerated depictions of Italian caricature and the allegorical satire practiced by Dutch artists such as Romeyn de Hooghe, thereby helping to define the art of caricature itself.

The upheavals of the French Revolution and the Napoleonic Wars gave political caricature in Britain the opportunity to come into its own. The classic

Figure 2. *(Caricature)* William Hogarth, *Gin Lane*, 1751. Courtesy of Lawrence H. Streicher.

age of British caricature began with the work of Thomas Rowlandson, a watercolor artist who became known primarily for his social satire. Rowlandson's contemporaries included Isaac Cruikshank, who designed and etched some of the earliest caricatures of Napoléon Bonaparte, and Isaac's son, George Cruikshank, who became more famous as a caricaturist, especially after the death of James Gillray.

Gillray was the outstanding British political caricaturist of the early nineteenth century, and his work exemplifies the development of caricature into a powerful political weapon. In the old emblematic prints, people had been depicted by the use of signs, inscriptions, and analogies. The Carraccis had made people recognizable as personalities. Gillray's satires of George III and Napoléon also were easily recognizable as personal or portrait caricatures without the use of excessive symbolism (see Figure 3). Gillray sometimes identified the personalities of his subjects with particular animal attributes, resulting in unmistakable definitions of character. The label "Little Boney," referring to Napoléon, was Gillray's invention.

For the most part, caricatures were printed on separate sheets and exhibited to the public in shops that served as outlets for an artist's work. Print shops achieved the status of institutions during the late eighteenth and early nineteenth centuries, and publishers and exhibitors of caricature played an influential role in the formation of PUBLIC OPINION. The development of lithography in 1798 made possible the mass production of images and set the stage for the widespread use of caricatures as illustrations in the press (*see* GRAPHIC REPRODUCTION; NEWSPAPER: HISTORY).

Caricature and the Mass Press

The union of caricature and journalism, which increasingly helped to organize public response to political acts, occurred in the context of repression and social unrest in Europe. In Spain, corrupt leadership had reduced the country to a state of economic and political collapse. In 1799 the painter Francisco Goya y Lucientes published a collection of eighty etchings, *Los caprichos*, depicting the great changes taking place in the structure of Spanish society. In each plate actors perform, as on a stage, some scene graphically illustrating the manners and moral abuses of the time. Goya often used such grotesque imageries as owls, bats, giant cats, and nightmarish monsters in his dramatic caricatures (see Figure 4).

Political caricature was all but suppressed in France during the early part of the nineteenth century. In 1830, however, Charles Philipon, a journalist and lithographer, founded *La caricature*, a journal dedicated to satire. Philipon created one of the best-known caricatures of the nineteenth century, a sequence in which King Louis-Philippe's heavy face is transformed into a pear. *La caricature* was banned in 1835 after a series of legal battles but was replaced in the same year by another famous Philipon publication, *Le charivari*. In 1838 Philipon founded *La caricature provisoire*, another addition to his group of innovative illustrated publications. Their success inspired similar ventures in Europe and the United States, including, in 1841, the establishment of the British periodical *Punch*.

One of the most famous contributors to Philipon's publications was Honoré Daumier, a painter, lithographer, and caricaturist. Daumier's caricature of Louis-

Figure 3. (*Caricature*) James Gillray. Original caption: "The Plumb-pudding in danger;—or—State Epicures taking un Petit Souper. 'The great Globe itself, and all which it inherit' is too small to satisfy such insatiable appetites.—*Vide* Mr. Windham's eccentricities in the *Political Register*." Published by H. Humphrey, February 26, 1805. Courtesy of Lawrence H. Streicher.

Philippe as "Gargantua" (see Figure 5) was violently disliked by the monarchy and landed the artist in prison for six months in 1832. The drawing shows the king's ministers collecting taxes from the people in panniers and feeding them into Gargantua's open maw, while from under the chair of the figure come privileges and monopolies for the bourgeois business class in whose interests the government was conducted.

Like Hogarth, Daumier did not wish to be known as a caricaturist. He preferred painting in simplified form and using subjects who were easily recognizable types. Unfortunately for his ideals, this genre became easily adapted to caricature. Daumier's *portraits-chargés* (portrait caricatures) of identifiable individuals helped systematize the use of political caricature in the mass press.

Modern political caricature in Germany dates from the revolution of 1848–1849 and the founding of a number of publications devoted to satire, including *Kladderatsch* in Berlin and the Munich-based *Fliegende Blätter* and *Punsch*. Wilhelm Busch, a prominent draftsman who got his start on the *Fliegende Blätter*, was known for his satirical drawings accompanied by short rhymes criticizing human weaknesses. Adolph Oberlander, who became the chief artist for the *Fliegende Blätter*, relied on pure caricature without the use of captions. Thomas Theodor Heine was associated with the famous periodical *Simplicissimus*, established in 1896. Heine and his colleague Eduard Thöny were noted for their satires of Prussian Junkers, the kaiser, and "political loudmouths."

The U.S. Civil War and its turbulent aftermath provided unique opportunities for the growth of

Figure 4. *(Caricature)* Francisco Goya, *El sueño de la razón produce monstruos* (The Dream of Reason Produces Monsters). "Imagination deserted by reason creates impossible, useless thoughts. United with reason, imagination is the mother of all art and the source of all its beauty." *Los caprichos*, 1799. Courtesy of Lawrence H. Streicher.

Figure 5. *(Caricature)* Honoré Daumier, *Gargantua. La caricature,* 1831. Courtesy of Lawrence H. Streicher.

caricature in the United States. Thomas Nast emerged as the outstanding graphic satirist of this period (see Figure 6). Drawing for *Harper's Weekly*, Nast left an enduring legacy of political symbols, including the Republican elephant and the Democratic donkey. His successful fight against the corrupt Tweed Ring in New York made him a national figure.

Caricatural expression in Japan was influenced by the artist Besaku Taguchi, who drew for the great humor magazine *Marumaru chinbun*. As its editor, Taguchi also had the opportunity to meet important political figures of the 1890s and was thus in a unique position to further the development of Japanese caricature.

World War I afforded many examples of the power of caricature to propagandize. One of the most notable was the work of the Dutch artist Louis Raemaekers, whose depictions of the kaiser and the German forces had a profound effect on wartime sentiment in Britain and later in the United States.

Figure 6. *(Caricature)* Thomas Nast. Original caption: "A Group of Vultures Waiting for the Storm to 'Blow Over.'—'Let Us Prey.' " *Harper's Weekly*, September 23, 1871. Courtesy of Lawrence H. Streicher.

In the first half of the twentieth century, caricature expanded to encompass new genres and forms, including COMICS and film ANIMATION. At the same time, political caricature thrived, in part because of the growing tension in international relations. One outstanding political caricaturist of this period was Sir David Low, who achieved international prominence on Lord Beaverbrook's London *Evening Standard* from 1927 to 1949 (*see* BEAVERBROOK, 1ST BARON). Low injected the news of the day into his work and combined a global outlook with impish humor. One of his most famous inventions was Colonel Blimp, a stereotypical figure summing in a synecdochic form some characteristics of the fool as a social type. Despite his title, Colonel Blimp was a political rather than a military figure, representing muddled thinking on the part of all parties and concerns. Low's clever drawings were especially effective in rallying public opinion against Adolf Hitler and Benito Mussolini before and during World War II (see Figure 7).

Japan produced a number of noteworthy political satirists, including Keiichi Suyama and Masamu Yanase. Suyama drew leftist caricatures for the *Musansha shimbun* (Proletarian News) and regularly contributed to the magazines *Tokyo Puck* and *Nap*. His later work appeared almost entirely in book form and elaborated the history of Japanese cartooning. Yanase drew for the *Yomiuri* newspaper in Tokyo; his sympathies were with working people, and much of his satire was directed at corrupt bosses as well as Prime Minister Tanaka and Japanese militarists. Yanase became a member of the Japanese Communist party in 1931 and was blacklisted in 1932 along with other members of the proletarian movement. He was prohibited from drawing cartoons and turned to oil paintings.

Political caricature in the Soviet Union is associated with several important names. Mikhail Cheremnykh, one of the founders of *Krokodil*, the famous Soviet satirical weekly, created anti-Nazi propaganda posters during World War II, as did many caricaturists of that period. Viktor Denisov ("Deni") was the permanent editorial cartoonist of *Pravda*. Boris Yefimov, one of the Soviet Union's most popular artists, became internationally known for his wartime cartoons of Hitler and Mussolini in comic situations adapted from Russian folktales. Kukryniksy, probably one of the most famous signatures in Soviet caricatures, is the pen name of three artists—Mikhail Kupriyanov, Porfiry Krylov, and Nikolai Sokolov—whose collaborative career began with anti-Franco cartoons during the Spanish civil war. Although they are best known for their vicious drawings of Hitler and JOSEPH GOEBBELS, the Kukryniksy team continued to satirize international events well into the cold war period (see Figure 8).

Figure 7. *(Caricature)* Sir David Low, *The Girls He Left Behind Him.* London *Evening Standard,* May 10, 1935. Courtesy of Lawrence H. Streicher.

Social Caricature

Caricature is not limited to political themes; it also focuses on social and cultural issues. Its wide range of subject matter is matched by the different countries and local backgrounds from which artists take their ideas. Twentieth-century caricaturists known for their portrayals of representative social types and situations include Juan Carlos Alonso of Argentina, Norman Alfred Lindsay of Australia, James Ensor of Belgium, Alvaro Cotrim of Brazil, and Fritz Jürgensen of Denmark. England's extensive history of social caricature yields such figures as Max Beerbohm, famous for his insightful drawings of personalities, and Sidney Strube, whose "Little Man" represented Britain against all odds.

Mexican artist Miguel Covarrubias produced geometric and sculptured caricatures of notables such as the Prince of Wales, CHARLES CHAPLIN, and Franklin D. Roosevelt. Covarrubias's unique style influenced, among others, Albert Hirschfeld, whose caricatures of film and stage celebrities appeared regularly in the *New York Times* during the 1930s and 1940s.

Since the early 1960s, some of the best-known social caricature in the United States has been produced by David Levine. Levine's contributions to the *New York Review of Books* are characterized by their accuracy and incisiveness and by a virtuoso pen-and-ink technique that has been likened to that of Thomas Nast. Many of his drawings illustrate topical book reviews, although he caricatures political personalities with equal and deadly joy (see Figure 9). Levine's work shows that, while the art of caricature may be used to expose and subvert, it can also be sympathetic and supportive.

See also HUMOR; MAGAZINE; POLITICAL COMMUNICATION—HISTORY; POLITICAL SYMBOLS.

Figure 8. *(Caricature)* Kukryniksy, *They Croaked.* "The foreign press does not conceal that Kennedy's conversations with Eisenhower, Nixon, and Truman discussed plans for preparation of a new aggression against Cuba. A flock of former presidents and vice-presidents flew to Washington and croaked like ravens." *Pravda,* April 30, 1961. From Michael Milenkovitch, *The View from Red Square,* New York: Hobbes-Dorman, 1966, p. 88. Courtesy of Lawrence H. Streicher.

Figure 9. *(Caricature)   Eisenhower, Kennedy, Johnson, Nixon, Thieu.* Drawing by David Levine. Reprinted with permission from *The New York Review of Books.* Copyright © 1969 Nyrev, Inc.

Bibliography. Hans Dollinger, *Lachen streng verboten! Die Geschichte der Deutschen im Spiegel der Karikatur,* Munich, 1972; William Feaver, *Masters of Caricature,* New York, 1981; Richard Fitzgerald, *Art and Politics: Cartoonists of the "Masses" and "Liberator,"* Westport, Conn., 1973; Jules Fleury [Champfleury], *Histoire de la caricature antique,* 5 vols., Paris, 1865–1880; Eduard Fuchs, *Die Karikatur der europäischen Volker,* 2 vols., Munich, 1902, 1921; Mary Dorothy Gordon George, *English Political Caricature: A Study of Opinion and Propaganda, —to 1792* (Vol. 1), and *1793–1832* (Vol. 2), Oxford, 1959; Edward Lucie-Smith, *The Art of Caricature,* Ithaca, N.Y., 1981.

LAWRENCE H. STREICHER

CARTOGRAPHY

Efficient communication about the relative geographical location of things, the nature of places and regions, and the variations of phenomena from place to place requires maps. All these reduced surrogates of geographical space portray reality to some extent, some diagrammatically, others by artful use of line, shading, and color to evoke the essence of a distribution or the subjective character of a landscape. Each map is a mix of scale, projection, data selection, generalization, symbolization, graphic elements, and names. Four overlapping classes of maps have evolved with distinct communication objectives: topographical, travel, figurative, and thematic. There are great differences between the large-scale and small-scale varieties in each class.

Topographical maps. These maps show an assortment of features in an area. The earliest Western map dates from about 3800 B.C.E.; a more sophisticated Eastern relic is from the second century B.C.E. Principles for their preparation were proposed by Claudius Ptolemy (ca. 90–160 C.E.) in Alexandria and Pei Hsiu (224–271 C.E.) in China. Mapmaking advanced in China while it lagged in the Western world until the fifteenth century, when the Ptolemaic writings were introduced to Europe. The development of PRINTING and the expansion of geographical EXPLORATION led to greatly increased production of maps as separates, in cosmographies, and in atlases. Map publishing became big business in the sixteenth and seventeenth centuries.

The era of national topographical mapping, which involved careful measurement and portrayal of detail on large-scale maps, began in the eighteenth century. The symbolism has remained relatively standard since then. One vexing problem has been the portrayal of the three-dimensional land-surface form on two dimensions. It was highly diagrammatic until the nineteenth century when hill-shading, hachuring, and contouring were developed.

Travel maps. Charts for mariners to determine location, course, and safety have ancient origins, but the earliest extant are of the early 1400s in both Europe and China.

The portolan charts of the Mediterranean region, with no known prototypes, were characteristically crisscrossed with numerous lines of wind or compass directions. They included amazingly accurate coastlines with many coastal names. They soon became decorative and colorful. Early Chinese charts were much simpler and did not develop further.

Independent chartmakers in the West practiced until the nineteenth century, but in the sixteenth century competition in exploration and trade caused governments and quasi-private companies to organize bureaus to collate information and maintain quality. Marine charts showed not only coastlines, depths, and hazards as clearly as possible, but also numerous identifying sketches of the shore features. Since the nineteenth century almost all marine charts have been officially produced. Aeronautical charts

Figure 1. *(Cartography)* The "Psalter" *mappa mundi,* twelfth century, an example of figurative maps. (East is at the top.) By permission of the British Library.

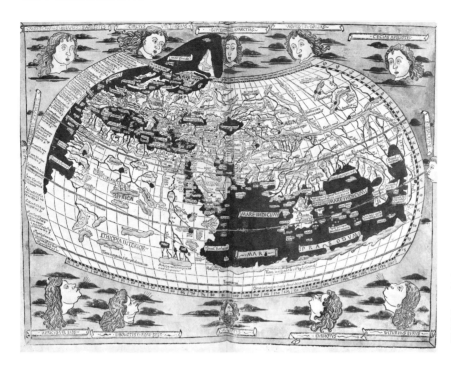

Figure 2. *(Cartography)* Ptolemaic map of the world. From the Ulm (Germany) edition of Ptolemy's *Geography*, 1482. Courtesy of the Library of Congress, Geography and Map Division.

for visual flying were produced in the late nineteenth century, but as aircraft and electronics advanced, so did the variety of charts.

Road maps date back at least to Roman times. One dating from about 500 C.E. shows roads throughout the empire schematically with distances written on the map (*see* ROMAN EMPIRE). Medieval road maps for pilgrims and merchants based on itineraries were often diagrammatic *strip maps* with the routes shown relatively straight. By the seventeenth century road maps drawn to scale became common.

In the nineteenth century the advent of rail travel added railroad maps to the class. The development of automobile travel demanded maps of all usable roads, categorized by quality and identified first by name and symbol and later by numbers and letters. Millions of such maps are produced annually.

Figurative maps. In this genre geographical space is used as the vehicle to communicate matters of faith, to promote economic or nationalistic ends, or to provide a striking display of selected information. In many cases, geographical reality is intentionally distorted or selectively portrayed.

The earliest examples are the medieval *mappae mundi*, didactic metaphorical representations of ecclesiastic cosmology. Examples in illuminated manuscripts include small and large displays, but all give substance to abstract concepts.

In the age of exploration and COLONIZATION, optimistic maps supported such ideas as the theory of a navigable northern passage from Europe to the Far East or encouraged settlement and the development

of plantations. The rise of nationalism brought propaganda maps to support claims of wrongs that needed righting; on some, potentially aggressive areas were made to resemble ominous animal shapes. After railways evolved, many diagrammatic maps were produced to portray favorably a line or the proposal for one.

Schematic maps or cartograms systematically distort the geographical base by substituting some other quantity, such as population, for geographical area.

Thematic maps. In the late seventeenth century, maps appeared that concentrated on the distribution of particular elements such as ocean currents, winds, or magnetic variation. They required new symbolism to communicate geographical variations in quantities and qualities.

Before 1800 most thematic maps dealt with natural phenomena. As censuses were taken and attention focused on such diverse topics as political economy, industrialization, trade, and epidemic disease, the need for effective methods of portrayal became critical. The first half of the nineteenth century, a period of unusual ingenuity in graphic symbolism, saw the innovation of such devices as the choropleth, isotherm, isopleth, and other isolines, as well as proportional shading, circles, and lines. Problems of comparability of data were severe. For example, the

Figure 3. *(Cartography)* Mateo Prunes, a portolan chart ▷ of the Mediterranean Sea, 1559. (West is at the top.) Courtesy of the Library of Congress, Geography and Map Division.

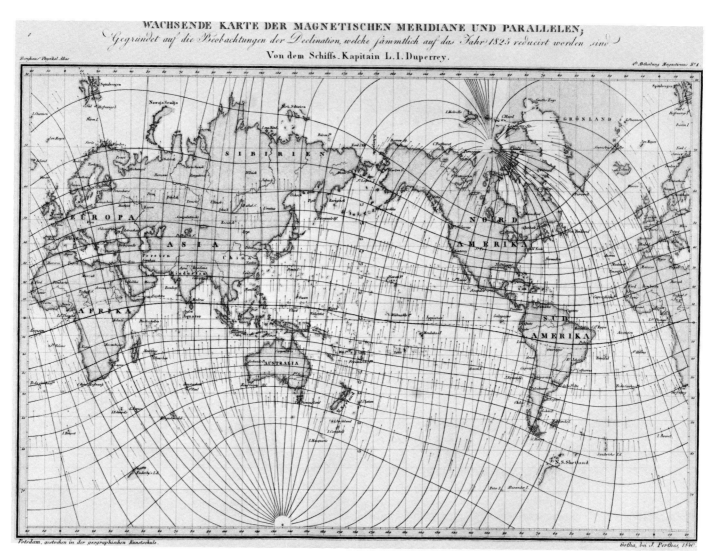

Figure 4. *(Cartography)* Map of the magnetic meridians and parallels. From Heinrich Berghaus, *Physialischer Atlas*, 1845. Courtesy of the Library of Congress, Geography and Map Division.

synoptic weather map required simultaneous information from places far apart. This was solved by the advent of TELEGRAPHY; a century later SATELLITE technology made possible real-time displays of sensed data such as cloud coverage, precipitation patterns, vegetation character, and floods.

Technology. The attractiveness and efficiency of communication by maps were greatly constrained by technology until the mid-1900s. Before duplication by woodcut and copper engraving was introduced in the late 1400s, all maps were handmade originals. Woodcut for relief printing tended to be coarse, while the finer copper intaglio engraving allowed more detail. When color was used, it was applied by hand. In the nineteenth century lithography added versatility at lower cost, and color printing became common after about 1860. A variety of other techniques, some incorporating PHOTOGRAPHY, were developed. Cerography, engraving in wax to produce a relief printing plate, was widely used well into the twentieth

century. The production of line, shade, and color by lithography and video displays is no longer subject to significant technical restriction.

See also GRAPHICS; MAP PROJECTION.

Bibliography. Leo Bagrow, *History of Cartography*, rev. and enl. by R. A. Skelton, London, 1964; Arthur H. Robinson and Barbara Bartz Petchenik, *The Nature of Maps*, Chicago, 1976; Arthur H. Robinson, Randall D. Sale, Joel L. Morrison, and Phillip C. Muehrcke, *Elements of Cartography*, 5th ed., New York, 1984; David Woodward, ed., *Five Centuries of Map Printing*, Chicago, 1975.

ARTHUR H. ROBINSON

CARTOON. *See* ANIMATION; CARICATURE; COMICS.

CAXTON, WILLIAM (ca. 1422–1491)

English merchant, diplomat, courtier, translator, publisher, and the first printer in England. A member of the Mercers' Company (cloth merchants), William Caxton spent some thirty years on the Continent, mainly at Bruges, where he was governor of the English residents and thus a member of the court of Margaret of Burgundy, the sister of Edward IV. With her encouragement Caxton began to translate *The Recuyell of the Historyes of Troye,* a popular romance. During a brief political exile in Cologne, in 1471–1472, he first saw printers in action and decided to learn the new art. On his return to Bruges he established a press; his first BOOK was his own translation of the *Recuyell,* published in 1475. In 1476, having printed six books, Caxton returned to England, where he set up his press in Westminster.

Caxton printed some one hundred books and other works. They included editions of Chaucer, Malory, Lydgate, and Gower; books of hours, missals, and indulgences; Aesop, CICERO, and Boethius; schoolbooks such as Aelius Donatus's popular Latin grammar; reference works such as Ranulf Higden's *Polychronicon* (a history of the world from the Creation to 1360) and the *Chronicles of England;* and popular literature such as *Reynard the Fox, The Golden Legend,* and *Godfrey of Boloyne.* Many were translations from Latin or French, generally his own; during a period of twenty-three years he translated twenty-three books, totaling some fifty-six hundred pages. He also wrote lengthy prologues and epilogues to some of his books, often containing valuable biographical, bibliographical, and historical information. Many of the translations and their printed editions were supported by wealthy patrons, to whom Caxton dedicated them (*see* TRANSLATION, LITERARY).

During the late 1480s, when he fell from court favor and had to publish at his own risk, he turned mainly to standard school and liturgical books and to long devotional works, which had a secure market. When he gained the support of Henry VII he was commissioned to translate and print the *Faytes of Arms,* a fifteenth-century rendering of Vegetius's fourth-century *De re militari* and various later works on military tactics. He also printed the statutes of Henry's first three parliaments, in 1485, 1487, and 1489–1490. His last book for a named patron was an edition of a prayer book, *The Fifteen O's, and Other Prayers,* commissioned by the queen and issued in 1491.

Caxton remained vigorous and active until the end of his life. At the time of his death he was working on a translation of the *Vitas patrum,* a collection of the lives of the Desert Fathers, an enormous work of about 350,000 words.

Few printers have been as prolific or as influential as William Caxton. His importance lies less in his having been the first English printer than in what he chose to print and the language he employed for it. Many fifteenth-century printers—JOHANNES GUTEN-

Figure 1. (Caxton, William) Detail of a page from *The Fables of Aesop,* printed by William Caxton. Woodcut. From David Bland, *The Illustrations of Books,* London: Faber and Faber, 1951, p. 45.

BERG and Nicolas Jenson, for instance—were better at their craft than Caxton. But as a publisher and scholar he is almost unequaled. He ranks with Geoffrey Chaucer as one of the great influences in establishing written English as a legitimate—even literary—language, through his choice of vernacular texts to print and through his translations.

See also PRINTING; PUBLISHING—HISTORY OF PUBLISHING.

Bibliography. George D. Painter, *William Caxton,* London and New York, 1976.

JAMES M. WELLS

CB RADIO. *See* CITIZENS BAND RADIO.

CENSORSHIP

This entry is composed of three sections:
1. **Survey of Entries**
2. **Government Censorship**
3. **Nongovernment Censorship**

1. SURVEY OF ENTRIES

In addition to the major articles below, there are many entries in this encyclopedia touching on forms and effects of censorship—often under rubrics other than *censorship.* The article on GOVERNMENT REGU-

LATION, for example, examines a large range of regulatory devices, variously named, affecting the flow and content of ideas but having purposes or proclaimed purposes other than censorship: protecting national security (by measures shielding government secrets); protecting children (by film distribution controls); protecting individuals and groups from defamation (by laws against libelous expression); preventing private monopolies (by antitrust legislation). These forms of regulation, or censorship, are discussed in the articles on SECRECY, HOLLYWOOD, LIBEL, and MONOPOLY, respectively.

The subject of monopoly has further ramifications. Many modern media have inherently monopolistic features in that they involve allocation of limited resources (orbital slots, broadcast frequencies) or limited privileges (the right to dig up city streets for cable laying, or a place at major government press conferences). The censorship implications of these monopolistic features are discussed in such articles as CABLE TELEVISION, CITIZEN ACCESS, GOVERNMENT-MEDIA RELATIONS, NEW INTERNATIONAL INFORMATION ORDER, NEWS AGENCIES, RADIO, SATELLITE, and SPECTRUM.

Aspects of the historical evolution of censorship practices are discussed in COLONIZATION; COPYRIGHT—THE EVOLUTION OF AUTHORSHIP RIGHTS; ISLAM, CLASSICAL AND MEDIEVAL ERAS; MARXIST THEORIES OF COMMUNICATION; MIDDLE AGES; PRINTING; RELIGION; REVOLUTION; ROMAN EMPIRE; and TOKUGAWA ERA: SECLUSION POLICY.

Themes around which censorship disputes often revolve are discussed in CHILDREN—MEDIA EFFECTS, PORNOGRAPHY, SEXISM, and VIOLENCE. Modern censorship patterns in various parts of the world are touched on in the multipart entries COMPUTER: IMPACT and NEWSPAPER: TRENDS as well as in such regional surveys as AFRICA, TWENTIETH CENTURY; ASIA, TWENTIETH CENTURY; AUSTRALASIA, TWENTIETH CENTURY; ISLAMIC WORLD, TWENTIETH CENTURY; and LATIN AMERICA, TWENTIETH CENTURY.

As the technology and organization of the media become more complex, more individuals find their freedom of expression curtailed or negated. Sometimes the roles of the censor and the censored become confused. The television SPONSOR, though often thought of as a censor, may be seen by the business community as a victim of PRESSURE GROUP censorship. Censors exist at all media levels, but all avoid the word, adding semantic confusion to an inherently intricate and controversial topic.

2. GOVERNMENT CENSORSHIP

A tool in the hands of authorities to shape and perpetuate an official version of "the truth." It can extend to any medium and any expression—artistic, scientific, or political—that is perceived as potentially subversive.

Official suppression of expression has a long history; it was practiced in many ancient civilizations. But censorship in the modern sense developed with the rise of the modern state and the invention of the PRINTING press. This narrower definition of censorship focuses on decisions made prior to publication about which works will be licensed to appear in public and under what conditions.

History

The potential of printing to challenge authority became apparent during the Reformation. The Catholic church identified the tracts that poured forth from the Wittenberg presses as one of the critical means by which MARTIN LUTHER's revolt developed into a REVOLUTION. Consequently the governments of Europe and the church each established elaborate systems designed to control and regulate the impact of the printing press on society.

Threatened, the church gradually accelerated its condemnation of heresies and heretics until, in 1571, Pope Pius V established the Congregation of the Index, a body specifically assigned to make decisions about censorship. The Index itself, which had been published in 1559, was the first in a series of more than fifty lists of censored manuscripts issued by the church from the sixteenth through the twentieth centuries, when the practice was discontinued.

Secular authorities employed similar means. England published its first list of prohibited books in 1529. In 1557 the Stationers' Company was established, composed of printers and sellers of manuscripts. Thus British censorship took a quasi-voluntary or semiprivate form. The crown granted the stationers MONOPOLY over the production and distribution of printed matter, and they, in turn, "were readily persuaded" to take upon themselves not only the protection of their own advantages but also the suppression of all printing that was in that day considered "dangerous to authority." This particular form of censorship, calling for cooperation among the crown, the church, and private printers, resulted in a highly effective mechanism of suppression. In the second half of the seventeenth century suppression through censorship became more and more difficult, and in 1694 Parliament decided to let the Censorship Act expire. However, it was not repealed out of commitment to free speech. The act merely expired because of "difficulties of administration" and because of the restraints it had placed on the trade of books. During the eighteenth and nineteenth centuries the press in England was not controlled through licensing procedures, but suppression of expression was continued by other means. The same goals were pursued through taxation of the press and prosecution for seditious LIBEL.

French censorship similarly started in cooperation with the church. An early sixteenth-century royal decree assigned the prerogatives of censorship to the Faculty of Theology of the University of Paris. This prerogative was partially withdrawn in the seventeenth century as the king asserted more secular power over publications. Later, as the general level of suppression rose, the police were assigned the task of censorship. Toward the end of the ancien régime, as the king felt more vulnerable, he sought still higher levels of repression. Nevertheless, compliance was low, and the clandestine market for books flourished. Censorship lacked a uniform policy and was weakened by internal politics and corruption. With the French Revolution and the Declaration of the Rights of Man, censorship was prohibited. Thus, in contrast to the British, who abandoned censorship for pragmatic reasons, the French terminated censorship as a matter of principle, in keeping with the libertarian values of the Revolution. After the demise of the First Republic, however, censorship through licensing was restored. It was abandoned by the Third Republic with the enactment of the 1881 press law.

The history of censorship in western Europe parallels the shift from the absolute to the liberal, or constitutional, state. It reflects the passage from the authoritarianism of the MIDDLE AGES, dominated by king and church, to the Age of Enlightenment, inspired by science, reason, and the belief in progress.

The philosophers of the Enlightenment viewed censorship as a hindrance to freedom and progress. They developed justifications for free expression: the importance of free speech in the search for truth, the function of free expression in developing the potential of individuals (self-fulfillment), and the role of free speech in democratizing the state (self-rule). The negative impact of censorship on the development of human creativity and its role in helping to hide the abuse of power by government officials were used to illustrate the evil of suppression and the link between censorship and reactionary worldviews.

In the nineteenth century John Stuart Mill eloquently summarized the importance of free speech for the good of society and the damage censorship inflicts upon it. Censorship, Mill argued, assumes the infallibility of the censor's view, an infallibility that is highly improbable. Censorship stifles intellectual processes and prevents the expansion of knowledge. It also prevents the exposure of the abuse of power. Further, Mill argued, even if the censor's view does reflect the good and the true, this truth may stagnate; unchallenged, it will ripen into prejudice. Formalized official truth, even if inherently good, will inevitably lose its vitality and keep humanity in the fetters of mental slavery.

The principle of free expression has long been and continues to be an important justification against censorship, particularly political censorship. But there is another cause for the decline of censorship in the West: the idea of rule of law. In the absolute state public law was conceived as a set of tools to be used at the discretion of the rulers to satisfy their interests. In the liberal-constitutional state the legitimacy of the government action depended on consistent, legal principles. These principles opposed the practice of censorship, which was discretionary, often arbitrary, and administrative, rather than adjudicatory. The idea of the rule of law was applied to the censorship issue in the doctrine against prior restraint articulated by the noted jurist Sir William Blackstone in the eighteenth century. Blackstone's doctrine delegitimized such censorship systems and called for the regulation of expression through the criminal law, thereby providing for the uniformity of laws in the liberal legal system.

Censorship in the Twentieth Century

In the twentieth century the functional equivalents of censorship existed everywhere—often using other terminology. Three models of censorship, characteristic of three styles of government, can be identified: liberal-constitutional, authoritarian, and bureaucratic-ideological.

Liberal-constitutional regimes. The liberal-constitutional model is typified by the presence of a constitutional principle against censorship. It prevails in modern liberal democracies such as the United States, Sweden, and Australia. Official censorship is proscribed. However, some functional equivalents of censorship do exist. For example, in the United States information is withheld through an extensive system of classification and by administrative restrictions on the right of public employees to talk to journalists. In addition, there is a measure of cooperation between the government and the press. The press will self-censor newsworthy items if the editors are persuaded that publication might damage national security. On the eve of the 1961 U.S. invasion of Cuba, the *New York Times* voluntarily censored a story that an invasion organized and led by the CIA was imminent. Still, at least in the United States, when such voluntary measures fail the legal system generally will not assist the government in its quest to suppress information. In the only episode in which the government asked the Supreme Court to enjoin a newspaper from publishing top secret materials (the Pentagon Papers case), the Court declined, invoking the doctrine against prior restraint.

Variations on the theme of voluntary censorship appear in other countries where the legal system is more sympathetic to limitations on free speech. In the United Kingdom a D-Notice system is in operation. The D-Notices are letters sent by the Services,

Press, and Broadcasting Committee to editors requesting that material related to certain defense matters not be published. Failure to comply with a D-Notice may result in prosecution for breach of Britain's tough Official Secrets Act.

In Israel the draconian censorship regulations introduced by Britain during the colonial period are replaced in practice by a voluntary agreement between the censor and the editors. The agreement limits censorship to matters of security and includes a supervisory mechanism and disciplinary proceedings for violations. However, Arab newspapers published in Israel and other newspapers whose editors are not part of this agreement are still subject to the stricter censorship regulations.

While the liberal state allows a large measure of freedom in the area of political speech, it is sensitive to conventional morality. Film censorship is legal in many liberal democracies, although it is generally applied only to very violent or pornographic content. PORNOGRAPHY and obscenity, in both the print and electronic media, are areas still widely regulated, either through censorship or through criminal measures designed to deter publication, particularly when the sexual depiction of children is involved.

All liberal-constitutional regimes have employed censorship during periods of war, partly to prevent information from reaching the enemy and partly to pursue intelligence activities. Censored information includes ship, plane, and troop movements; information related to pending military operations; the location and description of fortifications and defenses; certain war production elements; the weather; and movements of the chief executive. Usually a code detailing these items is distributed to the press, which refrains from publishing such information or, in case of doubt, submits information for the censor's approval. Although violation of the censorship code usually constitutes a criminal offense, it is safe to expect a high level of cooperation during such periods of crisis, particularly if there is consensus about the necessity to fight the war. During World War II the Allied countries enjoyed a high level of compliance with their (by and large voluntary) system of censorship. The dates of the Allies' invasions of North Africa and Normandy, as well as the invention of radar and the atom bomb, were effectively kept secrets. Wartime censorship for intelligence purposes applies to telegrams, the TELEPHONE, and the mail in order to discover enemy agents and intercept economic or military information.

It is important to note that, while the core purpose of wartime censorship is to shelter military information, it does not always stay within such limits. Thus a military censorship board may become politicized and be used to stifle criticism of the government or to suppress information about the blunders and delinquencies of the government. For example, during the Algerian war the French government consistently attempted to smother the critical leftist press. During World War II news of the U.S. naval defeat off Savo Island was not released until nine weeks after the battle.

Authoritarian regimes. The authoritarian model is exemplified by Third World regimes that exercise considerable control over their communications media. For example, most African governments own their newspapers and thereby control the information disseminated to the public. Usually this system is not fortified by the addition of a censorship board. *See* AFRICA, TWENTIETH CENTURY.

The authoritarian regimes of Latin America do not generally use a formal system of censorship. But they have regularly sought to control public discourse by terrorizing and intimidating journalists and editors into suppressing news unfavorable to the regime (such as information about conflicts within the military, the activities of the security apparatus, and resistance to the regime). *See* LATIN AMERICA, TWENTIETH CENTURY.

South Africa provides an excellent example of how censorship intensifies as anxiety deepens. For years South Africa has maintained a formal censorship board for books, periodicals, films, plays, and records. Interference with the press was kept to a minimum in an effort to maintain the image of a democracy that respects the rule of law. In 1986, as domestic unrest increased and international PUBLIC OPINION turned more hostile, the government launched a war against the press, desperately hoping that "killing the messenger will also kill the message." Powers of censorship were invested in the commissioner of police, prohibiting "the announcement, dissemination, distribution, taking or sending within or from the Republic of any comment on or news in connection with any conduct of a force or any member of a force regarding the maintenance of the safety of the public or the public order or the termination of the state of emergency." Further, the regulations prohibited "the presence of journalists for the purpose of reporting in any black residential area or any other area in which unrest is occurring except with the prior consent of the . . . commissioner." As a result, journalists could not publish a wide range of statements from any government opponent, were prohibited from photographing protests or reporting government efforts to suppress them, and were not even allowed to enter the black townships.

Bureaucratic-ideological regimes. One example of the bureaucratic-ideological model is the Soviet Union immediately after the 1917 Revolution. V. I. Lenin advised the Communist press to "learn, organize, propagandize." He viewed the press as "a powerful instrument . . . no less dangerous than bombs and machine guns." The Soviet press, accordingly, was to be controlled by the Communist party, and the theoretical groundwork was laid for the operation of the press in the Soviet Union and Soviet-inspired regimes. This type of control over the press goes beyond authoritarianism, in the sense that it both suppresses information inimical to the power elite and indoctrinates the population to internalize a specific worldview. In the Soviet Union the Central Committee Propaganda Department and the censorship board (Glavlit) work in tandem. Glavlit alone employs an estimated seventy thousand censors. The actual operation of Glavlit is highly bureaucratized, subjecting the content of every article to a successive number of reviews before it finally receives the stamp of approval. This aspect of censorship is crucial in guaranteeing effective control over information and encouraging conformity. It not only exhausts writers, who have to obtain the approval of numerous functionaries, but also circumscribes their creativity. It remains to be seen whether the policy of openness introduced by Soviet leader Mikhail Gorbachev will have long-term effects on the Soviet press.

Insight into the operation of censorship as a tool to promote IDEOLOGY is provided by the Black Book of Polish Censorship, the 1976 censorship code of Poland. The book instructs the censor: "Information on the licenses that Poland has bought from capitalist countries [e.g., Leyland engines, Fiat automobiles] should be eliminated from the mass media." Another censorial device eliminates specific types of information from the popular press (such as information about epidemic cattle diseases) but permits popular articles that discuss the existence of the diseases though not their occurrence in Poland. The code's section on CULTURE reveals the subtle indoctrination achieved through censorship. A person of literary or scientific reputation who becomes persona non grata is never to be mentioned in a positive manner. However, the existence of such persons, the subject of their work, and criticism of that work are permitted. Censorship codes are kept secret, and newspapers may not indicate that the contents were subjected to censorship. The purpose of the system—to shape public opinion rather than merely to prevent criticism—is evident from the fact that a special unit in the censorship apparatus is in charge of transmitting to the government those items that were censored. Thus the authorities have access to information unavailable to the public—a sophisticated device to maintain control over the society. The system creates a privileged class of persons who are better informed and who frequently enjoy higher social status.

It is the close link between PROPAGANDA and repression that clearly distinguishes the authoritarian model from the bureaucratic-ideological model. In the former censorship is used mainly to prevent expression of dissent. In the latter it is a sophisticated mechanism to shape ideology. However, such attempts cannot be entirely successful. Censorship itself becomes a haven for those in society who wish to know. In addition, the existence of the samizdats (underground publications) and a black market in forbidden literature attest to the fact that even under optimal conditions censorship cannot be entirely effective.

Government censorship implies political, military, or moral insecurity. When feeling vulnerable, those in power will censor the information they consider subversive. But, to succeed, such censorship depends on an efficient bureaucratic structure. Once such a structure is erected it becomes resistant to peaceful change. According to the noted press scholar Fred S. Siebert, it took eighty years to build up the system of censorship in England but more than two hundred years to tear it down.

Both the purposes and the achievements of government censorship have for centuries been attacked by writers and politicians, often in memorable terms (see MILTON, JOHN). But the desire to control and suppress has been equally persistent, and systems of government censorship of one sort or another continue to exist worldwide.

Bibliography. Albert Bachman, *Censorship in France from 1715 to 1750: Voltaire's Opposition*, New York, 1934, reprint 1971; Jane Leftwich Curry and Joan R. Dassin, eds., *Press Control around the World*, New York, 1982; Edward De Grazia, *Banned Films: Movies, Censors, and the First Amendment*, New York, 1982; Thomas I. Emerson, *The System of Freedom of Expression*, New York, 1970; Dina Goren, *Secrecy and the Right to Know*, Ramat Gan, Israel, 1979; Pnina Lahav, ed., *Press Law in Modern Democracies: A Comparative Study*, New York, 1985; John Stuart Mill, *On Liberty*, London, 1849, reprint (annot. and ed. by David Spitz) New York, 1975; Saul K. Padover, trans. and ed., *Karl Marx on Freedom of the Press and Censorship*, New York, 1974; George Haven Putnam, *The Censorship of the Church of Rome and Its Influence upon the Production and Distribution of Literature*, New York, 1906–1907, reprint 1967; George Schöpflin, ed., *Censorship and Political Communication in Eastern Europe*, New York, 1983; Fredrick S. Siebert, *Freedom of the Press in England, 1476–1776: The Rise and Fall of Government Controls*, Urbana, Ill., 1952.

PNINA LAHAV

3. NONGOVERNMENT CENSORSHIP

Official or government censorship makes up only a small part of the actual censoring activity in any society. All established systems of knowledge and social order are secured by social controls that provide methods for identifying and censoring deviance. In some societies these methods are sanctioned by legal codes and enforced by formal administrative bodies, police, censorship boards, judiciaries, and so on. However, all social structures back up and supplement their formal systems of control with social pressures, rites, conventions, and institutional practices that deter deviance. Censorship is therefore always pervasive, intractable, and sociologically significant.

Liberal and sociological approaches to censorship. Since the Enlightenment Western liberals have conceived of censorship as a regressive or unenlightened practice that inhibits the development of democracy and hampers the advancement of knowledge. Liberals acknowledge that censorship has existed in all previous societies and that censorship continues to operate in nonliberal and liberal societies alike, but they maintain that reforms can bring an end to the cycle of repression. Western liberal conceptions of censorship and free speech continue to exercise significant influence over the ways issues of freedom and control are conceived and debated throughout the world.

Sociological models of science, knowledge, and social order, on the other hand, support the view that knowledge, order, and deviance are social constructions—processes and products of human communications and communities. Proponents of social constructivist models such as ERVING GOFFMAN and David Rothman in sociology, Mary Douglas in anthropology, Michael Polanyi and Thomas S. Kuhn in the philosophy of science, and MICHEL FOUCAULT in epistemology have reasoned that if communication and community are integral, then examination of the ways a particular social structure defines and polices deviance can explain how its members create and sustain both social and cognitive order. Social constructivist perspectives therefore treat censorship as a crucial category for analysis.

Social constructivist conceptions of censorship are supported by studies in cognitive psychology (*see* COGNITION) and LINGUISTICS that suggest that the mind's capacity to process information is limited by its vulnerability to overload as well as by the range of the linguistic categories, GRAMMAR, and semantic resources available to it (*see* SEMANTICS). These studies indicate that in order to process information at all humans must simplify it. Moreover, they suggest that these simplifications are culturally patterned or programmed and that, as a result, PERCEPTION itself is "languaged" (*see* LANGUAGE). In sum, these linguistically informed studies in cognitive psychology provide empirical support for LUDWIG WITTGENSTEIN's dictum, "The limits of my language are the limits of my world."

The social constructivist rethinking of censorship

conceives of censoring and sense making as two loops in the dialectical knot that binds power and knowledge. This conception appears to be consistent with both the etymology of the term and the social history of the practice. The word *censor* derives from the Latin root *cense,* from the Latin *censure,* "to estimate, rate, assess, judge, reckon." Historically censorship has played an important part in all attempts to assemble and codify learning. Censorship has drawn the lines that establish and mark the boundaries between good and evil, truth and falsity, the rational and the irrational. It has defined the limits of knowledge and provided mechanisms for policing epistemological outlaws.

Encyclicals have been issued and encyclopedias have been written to secure correct views and discredit ignorance or misinformation. Heretics have been persecuted to encourage virtue and discourage departures from dogma. Sense is made by censoring nonsense. The Enlightenment did not eliminate this paradox. Negation continues to secure affirmation even in a scientific age. Thus, for example, textbooks on scientific methods are written to identify the principles and procedures of good science and to censure the breaches of bad science. The constructivist perspective revises and inverts the liberal equation by acknowledging that while censorship is frequently an obstacle to knowledge, it is also a constituent of knowledge.

Censorship and criticism. Censorship is an exercise of the critical faculty and carries the sanction of some form of authority. Censorial authority may be secured by social customs; by the practices of political, economic, religious, educational, or cultural institutions; by established semantic conventions; or by prevailing rules of reason. The temptation to proscribe fallacious or dangerous views is the underside of the desire to proclaim and propagate factual or felicitous views. Consequently those who care most fervently about ideas are frequently tempted to suppress opposing ideas. In ancient Greece, for example, the primary advocates of censorship were philosophers, not kings. PLATO advocated banishing poets from the ideal republic because he believed that fictive symbols misrepresent reality and inhibit the development of civic virtues. He also believed that rhetoricians and natural scientists should be outlawed because their views are deceptive and erroneous.

No modern society outlaws POETRY, RHETORIC, or science, although some treat these disciplines as especially worthy of surveillance. However, in modern republics poets, rhetoricians, and scientists play an active role in the surveillance process. They help draw the boundaries, articulate the canons, set the agendas, and craft the paradigms that codify correct views and censor incorrect views (*see* AGENDA-

SETTING). They define and enforce the prescriptions and proscriptions that regulate their disciplines. Because communication, community, and CULTURE cohere, disciplinary self-censorship is not free of contamination by external powers, nor is its influence contained within the disciplines.

When churches, colleges, corporations, and cultural institutions can effectively propagate right thinking and police the erroneous, governments do not need to maintain censorship offices. Editors will do the censors' work. Furthermore, poets, rhetoricians, and scientists who want to publish will try not to transgress the boundaries established by the canons, conventions, paradigms, and professional standards of their disciplines. Until the collective voice of the discipline or communication community is ready to redraw the boundaries, the inner voices of most members of that community will not permit them to realize the motto of the Enlightenment: "Dare to know." Some questions will not be asked for fear of censure; others will not be asked because the cognitive categories and semantic resources available to the community render them inconceivable.

Organizational self-censorship. These pragmatic economic, psychological, sociological, and linguistic pressures create what Elisabeth Noelle-Neumann has termed a "spiral of silence." They conserve established opinion and discourage dissent. However, in heterogeneous societies informal controls are usually too ambiguous fully or effectively to contain potentially dangerous ideas. Moreover, modern scientific, cultural, and industrial organizations need to provide means for encouraging the development of new ideas, technologies, and commodities without undermining their own power bases. They also need to develop mechanisms for protecting themselves from as well as responding to government and pressure groups that find their messages objectionable (*see* PRESSURE GROUP). As a result of these conflicting demands, media organizations frequently find it necessary to identify and formally articulate the rules of proscription and prescription under which their members operate. Editorial policies, broadcast standards and practices manuals, and film industry production codes are responses to these demands (*see* HOLLYWOOD).

Such articulations of organizational rules sometimes consist of general statements of principles that can be enforced or ignored at the discretion of management. In other cases they may entail detailed "do" and "don't" checklists that guide the production process. In liberal societies newspaper editorial policies typically embrace tenets of press freedom, but they also articulate those tenets in ways that usually attract like-minded editors and reporters (e.g., a reporter with socialist sympathies is not likely to seek or find a career opportunity on a newspaper that caters to a business market). In all societies film and broadcast media have been much more subject to rigid external controls and self-censorship than print media because of the heterogeneity of their audiences and because of the amount of capital involved in production. Thus, for example, the production code of the Motion Picture Producers and Distributors Association of America, which operated as an effective agent of self-censorship in the U.S. film industry for three decades, proscribed material dealing with first-night scenes, miscegenation, branding, surgical operations, white slavery, sexual hygiene, and much more. In addition, it offered detailed instructions for presentation of the flag, the marital bed, national feelings, sin, and other sensitive topics.

Media self-censorships are enforced by organizational reward systems, hiring, firing, promotions, professional prizes and awards, and so on; by work routines that socialize practitioners to pursue some subjects and ignore others; and by marketing decisions that emphasize some material and some markets and ignore others. In addition, the discipline that operates within individual media organizations may be supplemented by industrywide sanctions enforced by trade associations. In the Soviet Union membership in a writers' union is required in order to publish; expulsion is equivalent to excommunication. In liberal societies maverick media organizations might be fined or denied access to media distribution systems, and offending individuals might be subject to industrywide blacklisting. In the United States during the 1950s thousands of writers, journalists, printers, linotype operators, actors, producers, and other communications workers were denied further employment in media industries by media organizations because of government and internal questioning of their political loyalties.

Overt interventions in media operations depart from the normal routines of media self-censorship in liberal societies. Such interventions are usually responses to political, economic, or social crises in the larger society. When self-regulatory mechanisms are operating normally, control systems are almost invisible. Liberals would say this is because the controls are secured in consensus. Marxists would say it is because the controls are secured by a hegemonic system that operates automatically.

The concept of self-regulation is an ideological extension of the democratic ideal of self-government. The difference is that governance is transferred from public to private control. By definition, self-regulation is intended to operate in the interests of the regulators. Media industries are capital-intensive industries. When self-regulation is undertaken by a capital-intensive industry, profit considerations usually act as effective muzzles. As Joseph Breen, chief officer of the Production Code Administration of the Motion Picture Association of America, pointed out to a representative of Universal Studios in 1946, "20,000,000 people have to see every picture Universal makes before you get five cents of your salary. We can't afford to offend anybody!" In media supported by ADVERTISING rather than by box-office or newsstand receipts, audiences become commodities to be sold to advertisers. Media marketing is rationalized, but media organizations become more directly responsive to advertisers than to audiences. Members of audiences, offended by media messages, may discover that the power of the box office must now be exercised in the supermarket or department store. Organized consumer resistance may express itself through boycotts of advertisers' products rather than theaters, newsstands, or programs. Some advertisers view consumer boycotts as abridgments of their freedom of expression.

The conservative bias of capital seeks safe investments. Audience segmentation of some media permits some diversity in cultural production. Minority voices are not strongly represented in mass media, but they may comprise a targeted market served by individual RADIO stations, ethnic magazines, or specialized newspapers. Local television stations may allocate some time to community groups representing minority interests (see CITIZEN ACCESS; MINORITIES IN THE MEDIA). However, media addressed to national audiences frequently avoid risks by avoiding the concerns of minorities. Formulaic plots and stereotypical characters usually provide low-risk investments. In the United States and other heterogeneous societies they also tend to reproduce the racial, ethnic, gender, religious, and ageist biases that circulate in the larger society. Those who are offended by these messages may seek to propagate more positive images of minorities in the media. They may propose media guidelines for portrayal of minorities, launch campaigns to purge language of racist or sexist usages (see SEXISM), or seek revisions of textbooks (see TEXTBOOK). These efforts may, in turn, be experienced as threats to free expression by those who support mainstream values, conventions, and prejudices. The logic of capital seeks the largest market possible. It supports the majority view and exerts strong pressures toward homogeneity. Some suggest that this logic supports a kind of market censorship.

The paradoxes of self-censorship underscore the hazards of ignoring either loop in the knot that binds power and knowledge. Power relations provide the auspices for dissent as well as consent. For this reason security measures are written into the birthrights of all compelling ideas.

See also GOVERNMENT REGULATION; MINORITY MEDIA; POLITICAL SOCIALIZATION.

Bibliography. Mary Douglas, *Purity and Danger: An Analysis of Concepts of Pollution and Taboo*, New York and London, 1966, reprint 1978; Michel Foucault, *Discipline and Punish: The Birth of the Prison* (Surveiller et punir), trans. by Alan Sheridan, New York, 1977; Erving Goffman, *Asylums: Essays on the Social Situation of Mental Patients and Other Inmates*, Garden City, N.Y., 1961; Thomas S. Kuhn, *The Structure of Scientific Revolutions*, 2d ed., enl. (International Encyclopedia of Unified Science, Foundations of the Unity of Science, Vol. 2, no. 2), Chicago, 1970; Jonathan Miller, *Censorship: The Limits of Permission*, London, 1962; Elisabeth Noelle-Neumann, *The Spiral of Silence*, Chicago, 1984; David J. Rothman, *The Discovery of the Asylum: Social Order and Disorder in the New Republic*, Boston, 1971; Dallas Smythe, *Dependency Road: Communications, Capitalism, Consciousness and Canada*, Norwood, N.J., 1981; Ludwig Wittgenstein, *Tractatus Logico-Philosophicus* (1921), trans. by D. F. Pears and B. F. McGuinness, with an intro. by Bertrand Russell, London and New York, 1961, reprint 1971.

SUE CURRY JANSEN

CETI

Communication with extraterrestrial intelligence. Human interest in communicating with other forms of life has been recorded throughout history. Legends abound with tales of talking creatures, angels, and demons. Speculations about other intelligent forms of life that might reside in planetary systems around the distant stars are a popular topic of SCIENCE FICTION.

Recent discoveries in astronomy and biology indicate that the processes that produced life on Earth may have occurred in hundreds of millions of other solar systems throughout our galaxy. Advances in RADIO astronomy and communications technology have stimulated scientists and engineers to conduct experiments designed to search for evidence of extraterrestrial intelligent life. The search for extraterrestrial intelligence (SETI) has become a serious endeavor.

If we assume that extraterrestrial intelligent (ETI) civilizations are "out there," we might then wonder how they would choose to contact others across the vast distances that separate stars. EXPLORATION and ultimate contact via space travel is one option, but that choice is extremely costly. The energy and time required to transport mass across interstellar distances are enormous. In contrast, the transmission of information using massless photons (e.g., light or radio waves) requires much less energy, and the signals travel at the speed of light. The kinetic energy of an electron traveling at half light speed is 10 billion times the energy of a microwave photon. To some SETI proponents, interstellar communication is far more likely to occur than interstellar travel.

A comprehensive SETI must examine a number of basic dimensions of search space that include the

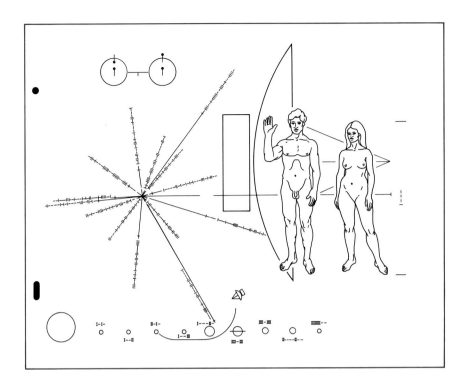

Figure 1. *(CETI)* *Pioneer 10* plaque, 1971. The plaque includes *(top left)* a drawing of the hydrogen atom showing the length of the radio wave emitted by its transition from one state to another (used as a base length in depicting the height of the *Pioneer* and the man and woman); *(middle left)* a pulsar map indicating the location of the solar system; *(middle right)* human figures incorporating characteristics of all races, shown in front of a drawing of the spacecraft to provide scale (the man's hand is raised in greeting); and *(bottom)* a diagram of the solar system showing the *Pioneer* trajectory and the relative distances of the planets from the sun. Courtesy of the National Aeronautics and Space Administration.

direction and distance to the source as well as the power, frequency, modulation, and polarization of the signal. The observational limits within which ETI signals might exist remain largely unexplored. It is virtually impossible to search for all plausible signals at all frequencies from all directions with maximum sensitivity. Tradeoffs must be made between the sensitivity and signal character on the one hand and the spatial and frequency ranges covered by the search on the other. The challenge is to select the most effective strategy within the constraints imposed by time and resources: SETI must be manageable and affordable.

Microwave frequencies in the range 1 to 100 gigahertz (1 GHz = 1 billion cycles per second) are thought to be most advantageous for interstellar communication. Stars do not shine brightly at these wavelengths. Interstellar gas and dust do not absorb microwaves as they do visible and infrared photons. Microwaves are easy to transmit because the energy of each photon is low. Finally, the galaxy is quiet at microwave frequencies, the only noise being the cosmic background, the relict radiation from the big bang. The most detectable signals are those in which the energy is packed into a narrow bandwidth and transmitted as pulses or as a continuously present tone; either method produces an attention-getting signal that contrasts with the natural emissions from the cosmos.

Other civilizations need not intentionally direct their transmissions at Earth to be detectable. Earth has been advertising itself to the universe for decades.

A cacophony of radio, television, and radar signals has escaped the planet since the 1930s. Those signals now fill an enormous bubble that expands at the speed of light and extends more than fifty light-years from Earth. (A light-year is the distance light travels in one year, about 6 trillion miles.) One may question the wisdom of these "shouts in the jungle." We may very well discover that we are among the technological infants in our galaxy. It is perhaps fortunate that such signals as AM, FM, and television broadcasts are extremely difficult to detect at stellar distances. In contrast, extant radio astronomical technology is quite capable of detecting intentional microwave beacons. An instrument such as the radar facility at Arecibo, Puerto Rico, is capable of transmitting to a twin of itself over distances of thousands of light-years if we only knew where and when to point it.

Search space can be explored with existing radio telescopes outfitted with receivers and microelectronic signal-processing systems (*see* MICROELECTRONICS). Two complementary search strategies have been proposed by the National Aeronautics and Space Administration (NASA). One is a targeted search that by concentrating on approximately eight hundred nearby stars is able to cover a wide frequency range with high sensitivity at the sacrifice of complete sky coverage. The second is a survey that achieves still wider frequency coverage and complete sky coverage by sacrificing sensitivity.

The search volume of these two strategies is approximately two hundred thousand times as great as the sum of all prior searches. It is so great that

Figure 2. *(CETI)* Aerial view of the Arecibo Observatory, Puerto Rico, showing the 305-meter-diameter radio/radar telescope. The observatory is part of the National Astronomy and Ionosphere Center, which is operated by Cornell University under contract with the National Science Foundation. Courtesy of the National Astronomy and Ionosphere Center.

searching with a single-channel receiver would take millions of years to complete. NASA plans to solve this difficulty by constructing specialized digital processing systems that will divide large segments of the spectrum into tens of millions of channels of data. Each of the channels will be simultaneously analyzed and searched for signals as the observations are under way. The data flowing through the system are so numerous that only a tiny fraction can be saved. Data that pass a stringent series of candidate-signal verification tests will be saved for further analysis; most will be discarded.

When and if the first detection of an interstellar signal is made, it will rank among the most profound discoveries in human history. It will inform us that we are not alone in the universe. It will mark the transition from SETI to CETI, and we will be faced with the task of deciphering its content. Some scientists speculate that the message might consist of simple repetition of a prime number, for example, which would catch the recipient's attention. Others reason that more information could be communicated by sending groups of binary digits, which form patterns or mosaic pictures when the groups of digits

are arranged in rows and columns. And still others speculate that artificial languages might be encoded and taught to the recipient via progressive lessons embedded in the text.

Time will also play an important role. Traveling at light speed, signals could take tens, hundreds, or thousands of years to propagate from one site to another. Our concept of a dialogue may expand to include communication from generation to generation. The communication might be one-way if the distance is great enough; the senders might not even exist when we finally receive their transmitted legacy.

Recent debates have gone beyond questions of search strategies and message decoding to the fundamental question of whether there can be anyone out there to talk to at all. Do enough long-lived stars have planets on which life might have begun? What are the odds of life—let alone technological civilizations—developing elsewhere? Would other species feel the same desire to make contact as we do? The discussions have grown more intense in recent years as theorists have proposed ways by which humans might someday travel to the distant stars. If star travel is possible, these scientists ask, then why has

Earth apparently never been visited? On serious inspection the evidence for so-called close encounters, past or present, is poor indeed.

Some prominent scientists have suggested that we will someday build robot space probes that will be able to build copies of themselves when they arrive at distant star systems and then send those duplicates onward to other star systems. The release of one such probe could, in principle, eventually lead to copies in every star system in the galaxy within 10 million years, just .1 percent of the age of the galaxy. Why then have we not discovered such probes sent by older civilizations in our solar system? This quandary has been called "the great silence" of the Fermi paradox, after the twentieth-century U.S. physicist Enrico Fermi, who asked, "Where *is* everybody?"

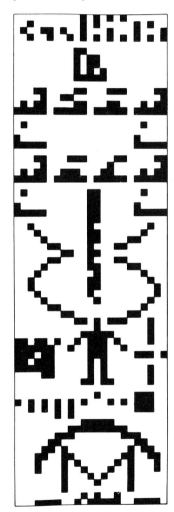

Figure 3. *(CETI)* The decryption of the Arecibo message of November 1974. The message is written as seventy-three groups of twenty-three characters. From Carl Sagan et al., *Murmurs of Earth: The Voyager Interstellar Record*, New York: Random House, 1978, p. 61. Copyright © 1978 by Carl Sagan. All rights reserved. Reprinted by permission of the author.

Bibliography. John Billingham, ed., *Life in the Universe*, Cambridge, Mass., 1982; Glen David Brin, "The 'Great Silence': The Controversy concerning Extraterrestrial Intelligent Life," *Quarterly Journal of the Royal Astronomical Society* 24 (1983): 283–309; International Astronomical Union 112th Symposium, *The Search for Extraterrestrial Life: Recent Developments*, ed. by Michael D. Papagiannis, Boston, 1985; Thomas R. McDonough, *The Search for Extraterrestrial Intelligence: Listening for Life in the Cosmos*, New York, 1987; Margaret Poynter and Michael J. Klein, *Cosmic Quest: Searching for Intelligent Life among the Stars*, New York, 1984; Carl Sagan et al., *Murmurs of Earth: The Voyager Interstellar Record*, New York, 1978.

MICHAEL J. KLEIN AND GLEN DAVID BRIN

CHANNEL. *See* MODELS OF COMMUNICATION.

CHAPLIN, CHARLES (1889–1977)

British actor and filmmaker. Sir Charles Spencer ("Charlie") Chaplin gained extraordinary popular and critical acclaim during the silent-film era (*see* MOTION PICTURES—SILENT ERA). As an actor and a director he created moments of comic genius that have rarely been equaled. He became one of the most universally known artists in the world.

Born to struggling music-hall entertainers, Chaplin first performed onstage at the age of five. Following his father's death and his mother's breakdown he and his half brother, Sydney, lived in orphanages, boarding schools, and sometimes the streets. At seventeen Chaplin joined the Fred Karno troupe, a music-hall company, and began to hone his comic talents. While on tour in the United States with Karno, Chaplin was spotted by Mack Sennett, who hired him in 1913 to act in the Keystone Company's slapstick comedies. By his second film, *Kid Auto Races at Venice* (1914), Chaplin was already beginning to develop the character of the tramp, the little fellow whose baggy trousers, battered shoes, and cane belied his debonair and gallant demeanor, and who, at the end of a film, was likely to be seen walking down the road away from the camera, with an air of optimism. It was a character he retained and refined for the next quarter-century.

The success of his early films enabled Chaplin to direct, and often write, his own pictures. He signed with a series of film companies, each time at a large increase in salary, until in 1919 he joined Douglas Fairbanks, Mary Pickford, and D. W. GRIFFITH in forming United Artists, a company organized to distribute the work of independent producers. From 1923 to 1952 Chaplin released eight feature films through this organization.

Chaplin's first generally acknowledged masterpiece, *The Tramp* (1915), mixed broad physical com-

Figure 1. *(Chaplin, Charles)* Charlie Chaplin in *The Rink*, 1916. National Film Archive, London/Black Ink Films.

Figure 2. *(Chaplin, Charles)* Charlie Chaplin in *Limelight*, 1952. National Film Archive, London/United Artists.

edy with a note of pathos. He continued that style in his first feature-length film, *The Kid* (1921), which had a sentimentality unusual in a comedy of the period. *The Kid* was hugely popular, bringing in greater profits at the box office than any other film up to that time except Griffith's *Birth of a Nation.* In 1925 he produced *The Gold Rush,* the brilliant tale of the tramp in the Far North. The film, which contains some unforgettable moments—including Chaplin consuming a boiled shoe as if it were a gourmet dinner—frequently appears on critics' lists of all-time great motion pictures. His next film earned him a special Oscar from the first Academy Awards (1927–1928), presented for "versatility and genius in writing, acting, directing and producing *The Circus.*"

In spite of the advent of sound in film (*see* MOTION PICTURES—SOUND FILM), Chaplin used only SOUND EFFECTS and a musical score, which he composed and conducted, in making *City Lights* (1931). It was a great success commercially and artistically, as was his next (primarily) silent film, *Modern Times* (1936), a lampoon of the machine age.

The little tramp last appeared in *The Great Dictator* (1940), a satire on fascism in which Chaplin appeared as both a Jewish barber and a caricature of Adolf Hitler. *Monsieur Verdoux* (1947), a pacifistic black comedy that drew parallels between a mass murderer and international warfare, and *Limelight* (1952), the portrait of a pathetic clown, did not win popular success.

Chaplin's personal life and political views frequently came under attack from conservative voices. Some were offended by his stormy marriages to much younger women, and his identification with liberal ideology and supposed subversive causes led to his being denied reentry to the United States in 1952. Chaplin settled in Switzerland with his wife, Oona (the daughter of playwright Eugene O'Neill), and their children. His bitterness toward the United States is evident in *A King in New York* (1957). He made only one other film, *A Countess from Hong Kong* (1967), a disappointing romantic comedy.

Chaplin returned to the United States in 1972 to receive a special Oscar for his contribution to the cinema. In 1975 he was knighted by Queen Elizabeth II. He died in Corsier-sur-Vevey, Switzerland, in 1977.

See also HOLLYWOOD.

Bibliography. Maurice Bessy, *Charlie Chaplin,* New York, 1985; Charles Chaplin, *My Life in Pictures,* New York, 1975; Wes D. Gehring, *Charlie Chaplin: A Bio-Bibliography,* Westport, Conn., 1983; Gloria Kamen, *Charlie Chaplin,* New York, 1982; David Robinson, *Chaplin: His Life and Art,* London, 1985.

RICHARD PILCHER

CHERRY, COLIN (1914–1979)

British telecommunications engineer and a leader in the development of the English school of INFORMATION THEORY. The work of Edward Colin Cherry, notably his book *On Human Communication* (1957), was instrumental in introducing scholars in a variety of fields to the emerging discipline of communication.

During the depression, while serving as a laboratory assistant with the General Electric Company of England, Cherry began studies in electrical engineering at Northampton Polytechnic Institute in London, receiving his B.Sc. in 1936. During World War II he was engaged in flight testing of microwave radar systems. He joined Imperial College, University of London, in 1947 as a reader and was appointed Henry Mark Pease Professor of Telecommunication in 1957.

Following his early research in electronics and circuit theory, Cherry directed his attention to mathematical theories of information based on a general statistical principle stating that the information conveyed by a SIGN, message, or symbol in a set of events decreases as its frequency of occurrence increases in the set. In an influential history of the subject published in 1952, Cherry traced the origins of LANGUAGE statistics to fourteenth-century Europe, where military strategists used letter-frequency tables in deciphering secret codes (*see* CRYPTOLOGY). However, not until the 1920s and the development of telegraphic channel analysis could information "quantities" be formulated precisely, giving rise to the modern mathematical theory of communication. From the early 1950s on, Cherry, along with his colleagues Donald McKay and Dennis Gabor, contributed extensively to this emerging field; he was also an organizer of four of the first International Symposia on Information Theory.

Cherry also made significant contributions in the psychology of aural PERCEPTION and the acoustics of SPEECH. Prompted by the realization that communications engineers knew vastly more about communication equipment than about the abilities of its human users, Cherry began studies of the human being as a component in the aural communication channel. He identified characteristics of binaural hearing, with special attention to the human ability to detect an information-carrying signal whose intensity is below that of the background noise ("the cocktail party effect").

On Human Communication, first published in 1957 and revised in 1966 and 1977, was one of the first attempts to introduce elementary concepts in the field of communication and to show the convergences in a range of problems from fields as diverse as LINGUISTICS, MATHEMATICS, SEMIOTICS, and psychology. Although Cherry devoted much of the book to the explication of the mathematical theory of communication, he emphasized the difficulties that beset attempts at quantitative description or study of human communication. He maintained that theories of information based on the statistical rarity of signals, as conceptualized in the Shannon-Weaver measure of information and in NORBERT WIENER's model of information processing in biological systems, were inappropriate in dealing with questions of semantic information or MEANING (*see* SHANNON, CLAUDE; WEAVER, WARREN). Examinations of meaning in human communication situations must take account of signs and their uses, in context.

Cherry's definitions of communication, information, message, and context, as well as his emphasis on pragmatic aspects of meaning, have been of considerable value to ethologists (*see* ETHOLOGY) studying the functions of ANIMAL SIGNALS. They have found particularly useful his suggestion that meaning can be operationally defined as the response selected by the recipient of a message from all the responses open to it.

The later phase of Cherry's work was devoted to the sociology of telecommunication and to the relevance of new communications technologies to international development and education. In *World Communication: Threat or Promise?* (1971) Cherry expressed concerns about the consequences of complex TELECOMMUNICATIONS NETWORKS for the stability of existing social orders. He cautioned that increased human communication per se does not guarantee increased agreement and that the centralization of power resulting from telecommunications networks may contribute to the decreased importance of the individual (*see also* TELECOMMUNICATIONS POLICY). In 1978, a year before his death, Cherry was awarded the fourth Marconi International Fellowship for his achievements in the field of telecommunications.

Bibliography. Claude E. Shannon and Warren Weaver, *The Mathematical Theory of Communication*, Urbana, Ill., 1949, reprint 1964.

JANE JORGENSON

CHILD ART

Before the twentieth century the traditional concept of ART was based so much on refined technique and circumscribed subject matter that it would have been inconceivable to apply the honorific term *art* to the rough sketches and clumsy daubs of children. However, the middle of the nineteenth century saw the rise in Europe of an attitude challenging the prevailing view of art as an exercise in craft and execution. The academies of art, which up to then had been highly influential in the training of artists and in the administration and regulation of the art world, came under attack by painters such as Edouard Manet, Claude Monet, Paul Cézanne, and Vincent van Gogh.

The first impressionist shows were attacked by conservative critics who made derogatory comparisons between the crude work of the AVANT-GARDE and the equally crude work of children. However, at about the same time, the French poet Charles-Pierre Baudelaire and the painter Eugène Delacroix praised the aesthetic attitude of the child as a sort of prototype for the artist. Thus, with the demise of the values and criteria associated with European academic art, and as the concept of art became broader, the way was left open for considering all sorts of people as artists, including non-Western tribal peoples ("primitive art") and children.

A second important factor facilitated the conception of the child as artist: the romantic notion of the child as a creature of nature uncorrupted by adult society. This view, which had its origins in the work of philosopher Jean-Jacques Rousseau, remains a powerful force in shaping attitudes toward children's visual work. *See* ROMANTICISM.

Characteristics of Child Art

The constraints that help to create the look of child art—its crudeness, boldness, and unconventionality—are imposed by development and lack of experience with a medium. The constraints that help to shape the formal and thematic aspects of adult art, on the other hand, have been consciously chosen by the artist. The element of self-conscious choice is the most telling difference between the work of adults and that of children. Many important twentieth-century artists such as Joan Miró, Paul Klee, and Jean Dubuffet have complicated matters considerably by imitating the forms, organization, and subject matter of children's art (Figure 1).

Two important components contribute to the look of child art: developmental factors, which are universal and arise through the interaction of the child's mental capacities and the unalterable constraints inherent in working on a two-dimensional surface; and cultural factors, which have an increasingly profound influence on the child's choice of images and subject matter. Children's drawings change systematically and predictably over time, making it easier to identify the culture of the child making the drawings.

Drawing development starts with the child's discovery of mark making. Out of the growing capacity to repeat, vary, and organize simple marks on a surface emerges the next stage in graphic development: the use of closed forms, generally irregularly shaped circles or ovals. By about age four, children can produce combinations of simple and complex

Figure 1. *(Child Art)* Paul Klee, *La belle jardinière*, 1939. Giraudon/Art Resource, New York.

closed forms. In some cultures pure forms (circles, squares) are used interchangeably with symbols derived directly from the ICONOGRAPHY of the culture. Brent Wilson and Marjorie Wilson found, for example, that four- and five-year-old Egyptian children draw the human figure using a crescent moon shape taken from the coat of arms on the Egyptian flag.

At the point where the child can produce and organize closed forms, cultural influences begin to make themselves strongly felt. The most powerful influence in Western culture is adult concern about what the child is trying to represent. That is, it is taken for granted among adults that the child is trying to make a picture. Children quickly oblige by turning most of their energies to visual representation. They begin to use culturally given formulas for various subjects: rainbows, smiling faces, cartoon and television characters. Children also start to copy formulas from one another. In the 1920s and 1930s there was a vogue among youngsters in the United States for drawing a person in a profile view with two full-face EYES. This stereotype of a human figure was found to have virtually disappeared from the drawing repertoires of U.S. children by the 1980s, which suggests that the two-eyed profile was a cul-

tural rather than a developmental phenomenon. *See* REPRESENTATION, PICTORIAL AND PHOTOGRAPHIC.

Theorist Viktor Lowenfeld has identified four stages in drawing development. In the "pre-schematic period," from about four to seven years of age, the child begins to develop the visual formulas that will be used for representation and struggles with establishing schemata for people, animals, and objects. During the "schematic period" (ages seven to nine) the child has a vocabulary of fixed visual forms and has established certain basic patterns of representation that can be produced as required. The "gang age" (nine to twelve years) marks the predomination of concerns with REALISM and spatially accurate rendering. This is the point at which many Western children become increasingly dissatisfied with their drawing ability. They expect to be able to draw realistically—that is, in proportion and according to the canons of classical perspective. Drawings from this period and from the "pseudo-naturalistic" stage (twelve to fourteen) are characterized by their generally stunted appearance. Figures and objects are labored over, space is used with great concern for realistic canons—but not as dramatically or as freely as with the younger child.

The constraints that affect the development of graphic skills can be characterized as a series of changing rules governing all aspects of constructing representational pictures. As children meet and master problems in representation, their initial solutions tend to be simple, additive, and local, while their later approaches to the same problems tend to be differentiated, integrated, and coordinated.

The shift from addition to integration. Figure 2 illustrates this developmental shift in the construction of individual objects. The child artist started out drawing the head, ears, and neck of the horse as separate entities and then later began to subsume all elements within the same outline. Similarly, a child may start out drawing a person as an agglomeration of simple shapes and then, with practice, shift from this composite image to a drawing enclosed by a single continuous outline.

The shift from separate objects to interaction. A rule that children observe when they first start to draw or paint is that each object should have its own place, uninterrupted by other objects. In Figure 3 the child starts out isolating horse and rider; an older child integrates the two but loses the sense of them as two distinct entities.

The construction of pictorial space. Much like shopping lists, children's early drawings itemize important objects but do not contain information about how the objects relate to each other in space. The first spatial ordering principle is the concept of objects inside and outside a space or container. Thus children will often indicate pregnancy by showing

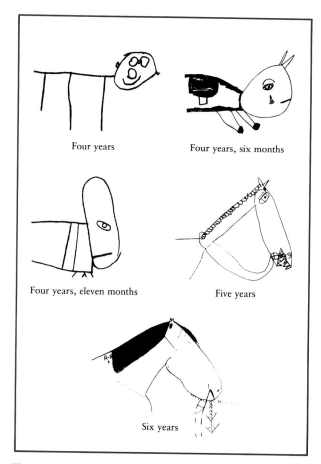

Figure 2. *(Child Art)* Drawings of horses' heads. From Sylvia Fein, *Heidi's Horse,* 2d ed., Pleasant Hill, Calif.: Exelrod Press, 1984, p. 138.

Figure 3. *(Child Art)* Equestrians and elephant rider. From Rudolf Arnheim, *Visual Thinking,* Berkeley and Los Angeles: The University of California Press, 1969, p. 264. © 1969 The Regents of the University of California.

Figure 4. *(Child Art)* Pregnant woman. Drawing by a five-year-old boy.

the baby inside the mother (Figure 4). These drawings are not intended as cutaway or X-ray views; they result from the child's use of line as a boundary separating things outside an area from things within. A later, more articulated organizational principle is the deployment of individual images along horizontal, vertical, or even diagonal axes.

The construction of a coordinated system of representation. The shift from local relationships between objects to more comprehensive and coordinated pictorial relationships can be seen in the way young children typically draw a house so that the axis of the chimney is at a right angle to the slope of the roof (Figure 5). It is only after children have learned to coordinate all the elements of the picture that they can see that the perpendicularity of the chimney is determined not just by its immediate relationship to the roof but also by its relation to the entire picture.

In the West expectations of representational competence are very high; photographic realism is the commonplace criterion for being a good artist. The ubiquity with which this standard is upheld and the relatively low priority given to drawing instruction

result in most children giving up on artistic expression in despair and disgust. Yet not all cultures require adult artists to pass the test of realistic or photographic accuracy. An Australian anthropologist reported the case of a native Australian boy raised by a farming couple in the outback, who by puberty was drawing farmhouses and country scenes in modified perspective just like his schoolmates. However, as soon as the Aboriginal youth was initiated into his own tribe as an adult, he ceased drawing in the European style and used the more abstract forms of his clan for representing mythic events.

Child Art and the Symbolic Process

The point at which the child assigns meaning to a mark signals the realization that marks, like sounds,

Figure 5. *(Child Art)* Typical houses with chimneys.

Figure 6. *(Child Art)* Toy airplane, which is transformed into a rabbit. Drawing by a ten-year-old girl.

can serve to refer to things. Young children who have just begun to assign meaning to their marks are capable of quite sophisticated visual symbolization. A child may make a "picture" of a person by indicating the facial features, limbs, and stomach using only lines placed appropriately on the page. Children may also show a striking disregard for the cultural convention that a picture exists on only one side of the picture surface. A belt may be indicated by a line that goes across the front of the page and across the back, because this piece of clothing goes *around* the person. At this stage of graphic development, the salient aspects of an object, for purposes of representation, are the location and relative position of features rather than any more visual information, such as the distinctive shapes of eyes, nose, or hands.

Georges H. Luquet, who studied child art in the 1920s, identified two systems by which children assign meaning to their drawings. Young children may identify a likeness between their drawings and other graphic images, which Luquet referred to as a *homologie graphique*. A scribble that happened to resemble a comic-strip character would be a good example of this. Meaning can also be assigned on the basis of likeness between the drawing and some real-world object—what Luquet called *analogie morphologique*. These two systems of assigning meaning appear to be operative in even very young children. A good illustration of this shift in interpreting forms can be seen in Figure 6. The first drawing is a careful outline of a toy airplane, a "realistic" likeness; the second is a transformation of the first. By rotating the picture ninety degrees to the right and adding

details such as ears, whiskers, eyes, and a carrot, the ten-year-old artist turned the three-quarters view of an airplane into a full-face view of a comic-book rabbit. This child has demonstrated intuitive understanding that symbols do not exist independently of the systems that give them meaning. By applying different rules of interpretation to the sketch, she succeeds in radically altering its meaning.

In the course of a century of interest in child art there have been significant shifts in what is considered authentic child art. In the 1930s and 1940s some art educators argued that true child art looked naive and was always a spontaneous expression of the child's personal concerns. In the 1960s and 1970s others maintained that much of what a child painted or drew was derivative of adult work. The fact that the concept of child art has changed radically within a few decades is further evidence that it is a social construct reflecting conventional assumptions about art itself.

See also AESTHETICS; ARTIST AND SOCIETY; CHILDREN—DEVELOPMENT OF COMMUNICATION; CHILDREN—DEVELOPMENT OF SYMBOLIZATION; VISUAL IMAGE.

Bibliography. Alexander Alland, *Playing with Form: Children Draw in Six Cultures*, New York, 1983; Rudolf Arnheim, *Visual Thinking*, Berkeley, Calif., 1969; Howard Gardner, *Artful Scribbles: The Significance of Children's Drawings*, New York, 1980; Jacqueline Goodnow, *Children Drawing*, Cambridge, Mass., 1977; Rhoda Kellogg, *Analyzing Children's Art*, Palo Alto, Calif., 1969; Viktor Lowenfeld and W. Lambert Brittain, *Creative Mental*

Growth, 5th ed., New York, 1970; Georges H. Luquet, *Le dessin enfantin*, Paris, 1927; C. P. Mountford, "Contrast in Drawings Made by an Australian Aborigine Before and After Initiation," *Records of the South Australian Museum* 6 (1938): 111–114; Nancy R. Smith, *Experience and Art: Teaching Children to Paint*, New York and London, 1983; Ellen Winner, *Invented Worlds: The Psychology of the Arts*, Cambridge, Mass., 1982.

DAVID A. PARISER

CHILDREN

This entry consists of four articles:
1. Development of Communication
2. Development of Symbolization
3. Use of Media
4. Media Effects

1. DEVELOPMENT OF COMMUNICATION

Communication may be the most important domain of development during childhood, the prerequisite to much of children's other learning. The ability to communicate, using both the linguistic and the nonlinguistic communicative systems of society, is the accomplishment that enables children to take their places as members of society and as full participants in their CULTURE.

Normal Development

The newborn infant's survival depends on his or her capacity to solicit appropriate caretaking from adults. The newborn is equipped with powerful, though rather minimally differentiated, communicative tools: some that signal hunger, pain, and other forms of distress, and "positive" signals such as smiles, quiet vocalizations, and neutral facial expressions that signal positive affective states (*see* FACE; FACIAL EXPRESSION).

Within a few weeks after birth the infant's social repertoire expands enormously, although considerable controversy exists about whether these newly developed behaviors are communicative or simply social. Three-month-olds show considerable attention to human faces. They respond to faces and voices with smiles, laughs, vocalizations, and characteristic gestures (*see* GESTURE), as well as with change of state (altering) and of affect (often from fussy negative to positive, though the infant can shift from positive to negative if the adult stimulation becomes intense and/or intrusive).

The infant's vocal communicative capacities may show the most extreme development during this first year of life—from minor vegetative noises just after birth, to coo- or goo-like sounds at about three months of age, then to a wide variety of nonsyllabic or monosyllabic vocalizations, often alternated with exploitation of a variety of prosodic patterns (e.g., highly variable screaming sorts of noise). Finally, at some time around six to eight months of age seemingly intentional babbling emerges, its onset marked by the production of duplicated syllables (*ba-ba, ma-ma,* and *ya-ya* are among the frequent early ones). The duplication of syllables is evidence for the infant's intentional production of the sound sequence, and his or her exploitation of increasing motor control in the service of vocal articulation. At the same time, it provides good evidence to the attentive parent that the child is converging on the adult LANGUAGE system by starting to make wordlike noises. In fact, almost every culture described so far supports parents in this belief by providing "baby talk" words that match the patterns produced in early babbling (e.g., *mama, dada, boo-boo,* and *yum-yum* in English). *See also* LANGUAGE ACQUISITION.

Use of gestures. Sometime between eight and twelve months of age most infants start down a new path in their development of communication: the use of gesture. Babbling may start to become highly elaborated (e.g., "jargon babblers," who produce long babbled strings with the prosody of complete sentences) and may eventually be incorporated into conversationlike interactions with adults. But at the same time, infants start to engage in a new set of related behaviors that very strikingly change the babies' interactive status by making them much more interpretable. These behaviors are typically gestural, some object-mediated (showing objects, reaching for objects, pointing to objects) and some clearly the product of social modeling and training (waving bye-bye, indicating body parts on request). *See* SOCIAL COGNITIVE THEORY.

Parental training of and reaction to these gestures raises an interesting question. Most people would agree that language is primarily a vocal phenomenon, and indeed, until the complex and clearly linguistic rule systems that characterize American Sign Language (ASL) were explicated, use of the vocal channel was identified as a language universal (*see* SIGN LANGUAGE). Nonetheless, the earliest efforts of parents to promote language and their earliest effective communicative interchanges with their children are gestural, not vocal. This fact would seem to reflect an unconscious accommodation to infants' greater skills and ease in using gesture for communication. Children raised in bilingual homes in which one of the two languages is gestural (e.g., ASL) are generally reported to be quite precocious in ASL as compared to the spoken language. First signs have been noted as early as six months, whereas first words in the same children do not appear until some months later. These reports suggest that infants are predisposed to use gesture as a way of communicating. Discovering the possibility of exploiting the vocal channel for communicative purposes, despite its long availability for playful babbling, seems to be more difficult (*see* SPEECH).

First words. At some point, though, typically around twelve months of age, infants produce their first word, an event that has considerable impact on the infant's status as a communicator. There are interesting cultural influences on the nature of the first word, since this word is not a product of the child's cognition alone but of a consensual process by which caretaker and child negotiate both form and meaning of the early words. In North America *mama* is often expected as a first word, though research tells us that *daddy* is much more frequent. Among the Kaluli of Papua New Guinea, the first words are described by U.S. anthropologist Bambi Schieffelin as culturally prescribed; *bo* (breast) and *nɔ* (mother) must be produced before anything else the child might say is credited with being a word. Among the Samoans the first word is identified as *fae,* a curse word expressing the infant's inherently antisocial nature.

Although the naive assumption about children's early words is that they name things (mommy, daddy, baby, juice, cookie, nose, hair, etc.) and although in fact many of the earliest words acquired are typically names for salient objects or people in the child's experience, it is not at all clear that those words function for the child as *referential,* that is, the way nouns function for adults. When a child says "cookie," his or her primary intent may not be to *name* the cookie but to request it. Similarly when a child says "nose," this may constitute a purely social act—taking a turn in a well-practiced game of naming body parts—rather than a referential act.

With their earliest words, and even earlier when they have acquired the behaviors of reaching and pointing, children are engaging in expressing a variety of communicative intentions or speech acts: requesting objects, requesting help, requesting social interaction, greeting social interactants, marking completion, marking change, marking appearance or disappearance, and requesting repetition are a few commonly noted ones. All these communicative acts can be expressed with gestures or single words, though between the ages of twelve and forty-eight months almost all children will learn more conventional forms for expressing and for differentiating among these speech acts, utilizing their growing control of syntax, the lexicon, and the pragmatic rules governing the use of markers of politeness, respect, and indirection.

A major task of researchers studying the development of communication and of language is to explain why children, who at a relatively early age and with a relatively primitive control of the language system can accomplish a wide variety of communicative acts, bother to acquire the complexities of the linguistic

system at all. The great bulk of research on language development has looked at the period after eighteen months, at which point children's communicative skills are already quite elaborate even though their language system might be limited to the use of a fifty-word lexicon in single-word utterances. Furthermore, this research has focused more on children's growing control of the linguistic system—production and comprehension of word order, morphological markers for plurality, tense, possession, pronominal reference, conjunctions, and similar issues—than on children's elaboration and growing control of communicative skills. However, new communicative skills emerge during this period and continue to develop (some differentially across individuals) into adolescence and adulthood: persuading, teasing, complimenting, conveying sympathy, arguing, preaching, teaching, joking, insulting, and many more. Differences in the accomplishment of these skills can have a major impact on adults' lives—their perceived talents, their capacity for success in a variety of social situations, even their personalities. Unfortunately, we know very little about how such skills develop, what factors facilitate their development, or how they relate to each other or to other capabilities individuals possess.

Disruption of the Normal Process

The picture sketched above—of development from protocommunicative skills such as babbling, smiling, laughing, or preintentional gesturing, through primitive but intentional communicative gestures, to words, exploitation of the linguistic system for communicative needs, and finally a differentiated control of a wide variety of communicative skills—fits the majority of children despite enormous differences among them and the environments in which they grow up. Communicative development, of which language development is a major subcategory, is a highly buffered system that rarely fails. Nevertheless, some children have a harder time discovering and developing the skills of communication, and it can be instructive to consider what factors or situations impede this process.

First, some organic problems interfere with full or normal communicative development. For example, serious mental retardation and autism may block the development of any normal communicative functions; in fact, one theory of autism identifies it as a complex of emotional and intellectual consequences of a basic, severe language disorder. Less severe language disorders in children may result in delayed language acquisition or in persistent difficulties with certain kinds of language tasks. It remains unclear, however, whether these developmental language disorders involve communicative deficiencies or deficits specific to the linguistic system, not to the system of communicative *intents* that normally serves as a substrate for language development.

Other organic problems can impede the development of language—and of communication somewhat less directly—by interrupting the normal channels through which communicative skills are acquired and elaborated. Children born with hearing impairments need suffer no communicative deficits at all, unless their parents are unable to adopt and help the child to learn a gestural communicative system. Blind children often have problems in understanding that language is a means of communicating MEANING, since the terms and events they hear adults talking about are mysterious to them because they are invisible. Furthermore, the interpersonal component of communicative development—the games, protoconversations, and sharing of affect that are typical of interaction with infants—relies on eye contact as a major channel (*see* EYES). Blind infants (or others, such as those with Down's syndrome, who tend to avoid eye contact) not only miss this experience with their caretakers but often are reported to "turn off" caretakers, who expect and are rewarded by the experience of recognitory eye contact that such children cannot provide.

Mechanisms of Development

The major unanswered question about communicative development is, of course, how does it occur? Is communication primarily a social accomplishment, a cognitive achievement, or a biological inevitability? To what extent is it possible to dissociate communicative skills from strictly linguistic skills? What features of the child's environment are prerequisite to the development of communication?

Answering any of these questions requires taking a stand on a highly vexed issue: the definition of *communication* itself. The six-week-old infant's biologically programmed production of certain gestures in combination with certain facial expressions, or differentiation of behavior to people and to objects, is interpreted as communication by researchers such as Colwyn Trevarthen who identify communication with social interaction and emphasize the biological contribution to communicative development. The role of the caretaker in interpreting and presenting to the child conventionalized expressions of the child's own intentions and emotions is stressed by researchers such as John Dore and Daniel Stern, who see communication as a basically interpersonal achievement. The role of the caretaker in setting up contexts for interaction within which the infant's preintentional acts can be treated as intentional is identified as crucial by Jerome Bruner, John Newson, and Catherine Snow. The co-occurrence of certain milestones of communicative and cognitive development is taken as evidence by researchers such as Elizabeth Bates and Susan Sugarman that communication derives from cognitive accomplishments such as understanding causality, being able to combine two schemata for action, and decentering.

In later stages of development slightly more evidence is available concerning the factors that facilitate communicative development (*see* FAMILY), though here as well too little is known about the mechanisms of development through which environmental factors have their effect.

Cultures differ from one another in their selection of which of the more advanced communicative skills everyone is expected to develop or which garner their possessors respect or other rewards. Certain sorts of communicative skills, specifically skills in presenting information so that it is comprehensible by a generalized audience with no access to interaction with the communicator (this mode had been commonly called "decontextualized," "literate," and "disembedded"), are clearly valued by Western schools (*see* READING). Children are expected to read, to write, and even to speak in this way at school—for example, during sharing time, when writing research reports, or when writing short answers "using complete sentences." The skills that go into producing decontextualized prose may be very different from the skills that make one an effective face-to-face conversationalist, and the two sets of skills may be learned in very different ways.

See also LITERACY; WRITING.

Bibliography. Margaret Bullowa, ed., *Before Speech: The Beginning of Interpersonal Communication*, New York, 1979; Roberta M. Golinkoff, ed., *The Transition from Prelinguistic to Linguistic Communication*, Hillsdale, N.J., 1983; M. A. K. Halliday, *Learning How to Mean*, New York and London, 1975; H. R. Schaffer, ed., *Studies in Mother Infant Interaction*, London and New York, 1977; Ronald Scollon and Suzanne B. K. Scollon, *Narrative, Literacy, and Face in Interethnic Communication*, Norwood, N.J., 1981; Rachel E. Stark, *Language Behavior in Infancy and Early Childhood*, New York, 1981; Daniel Stern, *The First Relationship: Mother and Infant*, Cambridge, Mass., 1977.

CATHERINE E. SNOW

2. DEVELOPMENT OF SYMBOLIZATION

The study of symbolic development entails an effort to trace the steps whereby normal individuals gain fluency in handling the various symbol systems of their CULTURE. An additional goal is the specification of factors that cause this developmental sequence to unfold in the ways in which it does.

Symbol Systems

Once philosophers became aware of the ubiquity of symbols, they devised various typologies of symbol systems. Among the best known is the distinction drawn by CHARLES S. PEIRCE between *indices* (which signal the occurrence of an event), *icons* (which bear a physical resemblance to a referent), and *symbols* (which have only an arbitrary, or conventional, connection to a referent). Susanne K. Langer contrasted discursive symbols like LANGUAGE—in which individual elements are combined to produce more complex MEANING—with presentational symbols like pictures, which must be apprehended as a single indivisible unit. Workers in fields such as LINGUISTICS and psychology have debated whether these varieties of symbols operate in essentially the same fashion or whether each type of symbol exhibits its own characteristic features. From the perspective of linguistics, ROMAN JAKOBSON considered language the most prototypical and central of all symbol systems, whereas Noam Chomsky stressed the differences between language (with its rule-governed syntax) and other symbol systems.

In an effort to clarify such discussions, philosopher Nelson Goodman has proposed a novel and powerful description of symbol systems. First, Goodman suggests that symbol systems either approach or deviate from a set of criteria, which he terms *notationality*. Systems presenting discrete characters that can be unambiguously mapped onto a frame of reference—for example, musical notation—are fully notational (*see* MUSIC THEORIES—NOTATIONS AND LITERACY). In contrast, systems like paintings, which have neither separate characters nor unambiguous reference to discrete entities, violate both the syntactic and semantic properties of notationality (*see* REPRESENTATION, PICTORIAL AND PHOTOGRAPHIC). While pictorial and verbal symbols do exhibit certain differences, Goodman stresses other symbolic functions that they share, such as their capacity to *denote* or refer to entities (e.g., the word *dog* and a certain line configuration both denote the concept *dog*) and to *express* certain properties (e.g., a painting, a poem, or a musical passage can be described as sad or triumphant, depending on the mood it is said to evoke or exemplify metaphorically).

Theories of Symbolic Development

The major theorists of developmental psychology have offered contrasting formulations about the course of symbolic development. A *unitary* point of view was advanced by JEAN PIAGET, who claimed that all children pass through a symbolic, or semiotic, stage between the ages of two and five (*see* SEMIOTICS). According to Piaget's account, the ability to imitate a display or an action internally (without having to carry it out explicitly) lies at the heart of all symbolic representation. Piaget considers language, PLAY, dreams, and mental imagery all manifestations of the same underlying "semiotic function."

Psychologists Heinz Werner and Bernard Kaplan consider symbolic development a process of increasing differentiation and hierarchical integration among four separate components: the *addressor* (or communicator), the *addressee* (or recipient of the message), the *vehicle* (the symbolic form that carries information), and the *referent* (the object or topic about which communication is occurring). In Werner and Kaplan's framework, only in mature symbolization are these entities fully uncoupled from one another. Jerome Bruner outlined a three-stage sequence of acquisition, beginning with enactive (motoric) representation during infancy, passing through an iconic mode in the third and fourth years, and culminating in an arbitrary, purely symbolic form of representation at about six or seven years of age.

Finally, LEV VYGOTSKY, ALEKSANDR LURIA, and other members of the Soviet school of psychology speak about a *second* signal system that builds upon but eventually supersedes the initial stimulus-response links: secondary signaling systems like language come to exert a controlling influence on a child's behavior. In one respect the Soviet point of view is reminiscent of behaviorist or learning theory accounts, in which symbols are seen merely as stimulus-response links with an intervening or "mediating" response. In contrast to this conservative view, however, the Soviet school considers behavior to be ultimately dominated by various symbol systems, and all thought to be an internalized reflection of the symbol systems of the surrounding culture.

Harvard Project Zero

One of the most comprehensive studies of symbolic development was carried out in the late 1970s and early 1980s at Harvard Project Zero, a research group initially convened by Nelson Goodman. The Project Zero group, under the direction of Howard Gardner and Dennie Wolf, distinguishes among the following stages in symbolic development.

Presymbolic stage (ages 0–1). During the first year of life the child is already an effective "knower" of the world. However, this knowledge is completely "practical" (i.e., tied to specific sensory and motor schemas), and it has no independent symbolic status. The child is able to appreciate that certain events cause or signal other events but can manifest this appreciation only when the eliciting circumstances are present.

Mundane symbolization (ages 1–2). By the end of the first year of life the child can appreciate relationships between a single symbol and a single referent.

Children at this age appreciate that a word can stand for an object or concept and that a set of lines can depict an object or entity in the world.

Early symbolization (ages 2–5). During this crucial period the child proceeds from a phase in which he or she has only the most rudimentary understanding of individual symbols to one in which he or she can produce organized works or integrated symbolic products. Thus, while the two-year-old is restricted to two-word phrases and simple scribbles, the five-year-old can relate a coherent story or draw an organized scene.

During this period of early symbolization children exhibit two fundamentally different classes of processes, some of which are specifically restricted to particular symbolic domains and have been termed *streams of symbolizations.* Examples of streams include the working out of elementary pitch relations in the domain of music, the mastery of two-dimensional spatial relations in the area of drawing, and the construction of the "plus one" operation in the realm of numbers. Characteristic of a streamlike process is its tendency to remain within a particular symbolic domain.

Other processes, called *waves of symbolization,* may originate in one particular symbol system but characteristically invade other domains of development. At least three specific waves of development have been isolated during this period. At about the age of two, children exhibit the wave of *event-* or *role-structuring:* the knowledge that agents carry out actions upon objects and that these actions have certain consequences. Having originally exhibited this knowledge in the area of language and symbol play, children may transfer the same processes even to areas in which they are not conventionally appropriate. For example, a child asked to draw a truck will instead convert the marker into a motor vehicle and drag it along imitating the truck's roar. Here the marker has been transformed into the object *truck,* with the child acting as its controlling agent.

A second wave of symbolization occurs around the age of three. Called *topological mapping,* this wave entails the capacity to encode various topological relations such as relative size, dominance, proximity, and numerosity. The original arena for topological mapping is two- and three-dimensional representation in which, for the first time, the child becomes able to draw or mold representational forms. Once again, however, children manifest these basic operations in other domains, even when they would be deemed inappropriate (e.g., a number of characters in a story are collapsed into two—a good guy and a bad buy—or a complex tune is converted into a set of relatively high or low notes).

A third wave of symbolization, occurring around the age of four, is called *digital mapping.* At this time the child can count small quantities accurately and can effect precise one-to-one correspondence between objects and number words. This readily noted ability to assess quantity can be observed in other symbolic domains, ranging from rendering the correct number of fingers in a drawing to producing appropriate symbolic rhythms in a newly learned song. While digital mapping basically represents a cognitive advance, an excessively rigid adherence to quantity may result in the child's neglecting or minimizing the expressive aspects of a symbol (e.g., in an effort to include the correct number of toes the young artist may forget to depict the happy mood or playful stance of a birthday child).

Notational symbolization (ages 5–10). At about the age of five the child has attained a rudimentary knowledge of the various symbol systems in the environment. At this point two new sets of processes begin to manifest themselves within most cultures. The first is the proclivity to acquire or to create new "second-order" symbol systems, which Project Zero termed *notational systems* (a symbol system that itself refers to other symbol systems that may not be fully notational in Goodman's sense). The most familiar examples in Western culture are the systems for written language and for written numerals, but musical scores, tally systems (*see* NUMBER), and many other formal codes also qualify as second-order symbol systems. In devising such systems the child uses "first-order" symbolic knowledge and then proceeds to reduce it, systematize it, and make it accessible to other individuals.

The second process, which begins to take effect around the age of five, involves the demarcation of different functions within a particular symbol system. Exploring the "channels of symbolization," the child now discovers or learns various telltale divisions within a particular symbol system. Thus, rather than telling all narratives in the same manner, the child learns to distinguish between a fictional account, a fantasy, a straightforward account, a newspaper report, and other genres of narration (*see* NARRATIVE). Within the area of graphic symbolization, the child comes to distinguish among such channels as a realistic drawing, an impressionistic painting, a diagram, a chart, a map, and other variants. More generally, children at this stage employ techniques that are appropriate to a particular symbolic system or code and honor the boundaries between various symbol systems.

The details of notational symbolization, and the extent to which all adults within a culture actually achieve mastery of these systems, have not yet been ascertained. Definitions of LITERACY are ever changing both within and across cultures. Even in an advanced culture or subculture, most individuals may fail to achieve a high degree of literacy with any but the most familiar symbol systems. Finally, two main hypotheses have been proposed to deal with the extent to which spontaneous efforts at creating notations appear in cultures that themselves are preliterate or prenotational: (1) insofar as individuals in such cultures produce incipient notational systems, we can infer that these systems reflect *mental models* already constructed by the subject; and (2) the absence of notational efforts in cultures without literacy indicates that *internal representation* may depend on the internalization of culturally provided notational systems (*see* READING).

Acquisition of Symbol Systems

Given this overview of symbolic development, the question arises about why humans acquire the variety of symbol systems in the manner that they do. It is now widely accepted by behavioral scientists that human beings as a species have a strong proclivity to use various kinds of symbols for communicative, expressive, and conceptual purposes. At least one symbol system—that of natural language—is universal, and others, such as graphic depiction or music making, seem nearly universal. It is probably necessary for the survival of human cultures that individuals attain skill in apprehending various symbolic products (e.g., the stories, songs, and rituals of their culture) and eventually become able to transmit these forms of knowledge to their progeny. Moreover, the processes whereby language and other symbol systems are acquired in early childhood seem sufficiently similar across cultures (despite some clear variations) to be considered part of the human genetic program. At the same time it must be stressed that many other symbol systems (e.g., higher mathematical codes) are far from universal and must be explicitly taught. The very symbol systems relied on in one culture prove quite different from those featured in another. While symbol making, symbol use, and the processes of acquiring certain symbol systems appear pervasive among humans, there are clearly individuating patterns of use and training.

It is important to indicate certain limitations in the present treatment of symbolic development. To some investigators—for example, those in the psychodynamic tradition, such as SIGMUND FREUD, CARL JUNG, René Spitz, and Donald W. Winnicott—symbolic development is a phenomenon that is highly affect-laden and linked to motivation. On this account all symbol use reflects basic desires, and symbolic development reflects the operation of unconscious factors. Other investigators favor a view of symbolic development different from the one detailed here; for example, Dan Sperber questions the wisdom of grouping together a system like natural language, whose processing is rule governed and strictly limited

in scope, with symbol systems that allow or encourage endless mental association, such as dreams or rituals. Indeed, a possible weakness in the Project Zero formulation is that after infancy cognitive development becomes virtually synonymous with symbolic development. In response to this criticism it can be pointed out that human beings are so prone to invest objects with expressive and/or referential significance, and to systematize their knowledge into some kind of symbolic or notational form, that it is difficult to conceive of mature cognition apart from a symbolic activity. Moreover, investigators have little choice but to investigate the child's knowledge through the window of his or her symbol use.

While some critics embrace different definitions of symbolization, others question the naturalistic or developmental approach in which one stage is inevitably followed by another stage, with the latter exhibiting a higher degree of organization. Those of an empiricist (behaviorist) persuasion highlight the role of the environment in shaping all forms of knowledge; they question whether *any* development can occur apart from specific shaping of responses. By contrast, those of a nativist persuasion claim either that all knowledge is essentially present at birth or that milestones result from purely endogenous factors (e.g., the maturation of a new brain region). In both cases the interactive or epigenetic model of biological development is questioned.

Although these lines of analysis may be tenable for certain forms of behavior, they seem inadequate to account for the full range and complexity of human symbolic activities like music, drawing, or DANCE. The area of symbolic development is so complex that its full dimensions are unlikely to be understood until our knowledge of both culture and the nervous system has been greatly enhanced. Separate analysis of specific symbol systems, as well as studies of the ways in which symbolic competence develops, will continue to be needed.

Bibliography. Jerome S. Bruner, Rose R. Olver, and Patricia M. Greenfield, eds., *Studies in Cognitive Growth*, New York, 1966; Noam Chomsky, *Reflections on Language*, New York, 1975; Jerry A. Fodor, *Representations*, Cambridge, Mass., 1981; Norman Freeman, *Strategies of Representation in Young Children*, New York, 1982; Roman Jakobson, *Essais de linguistique générale*, Paris, 1963; Philip N. Johnson-Laird, *Mental Models: Towards a Cognitive Science of Language, Inference, and Consciousness*, Cambridge, Mass., 1983; Aleksandr R. Luria, *The Making of Mind*, ed. by Michael Cole and Sheila Cole, Cambridge, Mass., 1979; Jean Piaget, *Play, Dreams, and Imitation in Childhood*, trans. by C. Gattegno and F. M. Hodgson, New York and London, 1962; Don Rogers and John A. Sloboda, eds., *The Acquisition of Symbolic Skills*, New York and London, 1983; Gavriel Salomon, *Interaction of Media, Cognition, and Learning*, San Francisco, 1979; Dan

Sperber, *Rethinking Symbolism,* trans. by Alice Morton, Cambridge, 1974; René Spitz, *No and Yes: On the Genesis of Human Communication,* New York, 1957; Lev Semenovich Vygotsky, *Mind in Society,* ed. by Michael Cole, Cambridge, Mass., 1978; Heinz Werner and Bernard Kaplan, *Symbol Formation,* New York, 1963; Donald W. Winnicott, *Playing and Reality,* London, 1971.

HOWARD E. GARDNER

3. USE OF MEDIA

In MASS COMMUNICATIONS RESEARCH, the "powerful effects" notion of MASS MEDIA EFFECTS—according to which children and adults alike are passively affected by the media—has given way to alternative conceptions of audiences as active processors and interpreters of media messages (see section 4, below). The view that media users, and children especially, cannot and do not influence the way the media affect them has been replaced by one that argues that children are active "consumers" of media in at least five distinctive ways: (1) in their choice of what to expose themselves to, (2) in the amount of their exposure, (3) in the selection of information they attend to, (4) in the ways in which they cognitively process that selection, and (5) in the way they ultimately comprehend it. Thus the study of how children become active media consumers assumes a reciprocal, interactive process involving the child and the media. Factors such as age, social context, and cognitive development on the one hand and the diverse qualities of media on the other operate to affect children's media consumption.

Media Selection

Children are able, from a relatively young age, to select the media they become exposed to on the basis of a number of factors. Two of the first studies investigating the impact of television on children— by Hilde Himmelweit and her associates in Great Britain (1958) and WILBUR SCHRAMM and his colleagues in the United States (1961)—found that medium choice greatly depends on the balance between expected rewards and effort required, that is, on the utility function of accessible alternatives. When a medium is easily available and is perceived to offer satisfaction of certain needs (e.g., escape, information, reality testing, material for imagination) with little effort expenditure relative to the alternatives, it is likely to be preferred. Television is often selected over other media because it easily meets such criteria, given its accessibility, the attractiveness of its pictorial symbolic forms, and its relatively stereotypic (and therefore easier-to-process) structure and story grammar. However, with age, children's needs, interests, and inclinations become more differentiated and specialized, and their choice of media moves from those that serve equivalent functions (i.e., serve similar social or psychological functions) to those that fulfill alternative functions. The criterion of effortless accessibility, although still present, is gradually replaced by that of differential need and interest satisfaction.

Other factors are more socially anchored. A child's choice of a medium is closely related to the home environment (*see* FAMILY) and the kinds of media use explicitly or implicitly encouraged there. In general children watch less television in homes in which books and other print materials dominate and watch more in homes in which television is a constant background presence in family life (*see* LEISURE).

Amount of Exposure

As children get older they become more selective in their exposure to media like television and cinema, as well as in their use of print materials, computer games, and so on. In general, amount of exposure is a reflection of factors such as educational level, need for achievement, and educational aspirations. In pre-television days children who were low on these characteristics were among the highest in cinema attendance, and in the television era poorly educated children tend to be the heaviest viewers and less selective in their choice of content. For many of them READING is a demanding and unsatisfying activity, especially when compared to television viewing. Very heavy exposure to television, as well as excessive reading or total immersion in computer activities, may be the result of tensions, loneliness, difficulties in coping with the daily demands of home and peers, and possibly also failure in SCHOOL.

When television viewing patterns are observed over a span of several years, it becomes clear that the kinds of content one chooses for exposure at an early age remain relatively stable at an older age. Consistency tends to be related to three major types of choices: (1) strong stimulation (e.g., action-adventure, VIOLENCE), (2) intellectual, "highbrow" material (e.g., documentaries, news, biographies), and (3) SPORTS. One also chooses more exposure to media material within one's preferred area of interest. A number of studies in a variety of countries have shown that children of higher ability and with a wider range of interests and needs tend to select more exposure to a variety of media: they watch more television, read more, and listen more to the radio.

Attention

Most media materials are sufficiently rich in quality and detail that no person—child or adult—can attend to everything available to the senses. Attention is thus necessarily selective (see SELECTIVE RECEPTION), and numerous factors determine what materials are attended to or ignored.

One such factor is called attentional inertia: the longer one attends to a medium (e.g., television), the longer one is likely to continue to do so. Children's comprehension of the material is another factor, because sustained attention is a function of comprehension rather than the other way around. Material that signals to the child through particular sounds (e.g., children's voices) and sights (e.g., ANIMATION) that it might be comprehended is attended to. Auditory stimuli in television, including spoken language, has been shown to be quite important in capturing children's attention, even that of the very young. Younger children, who are generally more stimulus-bound than older children, appear to be more attracted to salient features like colors, movement, certain sounds, and SPECIAL EFFECTS. Younger children can be said to "explore" the material from the bottom up, guided by its salient features, whereas older children can be described as being actively engaged in a top-down, self-controlled "search" for MEANING thanks to their richer cognitive schemata (see COGNITION). Thus older children are able to distinguish well between the central and peripheral elements in a story.

Ways of Processing

The child's cognitive processing of media material is determined jointly by the nature of the material and by his or her cognitive structure. A question of special interest is how deep, mindful, or effortful is the processing, that is, the degree to which mental activities such as elaborations, inference generation, and active, organized (rather than episodic) commitment of the material to memory are involved.

Media clearly differ in terms of cognitive demands. Although television relies on what appear to be relatively familiar and nonabstract codes and formal features, it typically provides "crowded," fast-moving material that may not allow enough time for reflection, inference generation, and deeper processing. By contrast, print and even orally presented stories (see SPEECH) may allow for or even demand more mindful processing because of their linear, abstract nature, which requires serial integration, the generation of integrated images, and logical sequential thinking. Younger children's processing of television material, and of stories in general, tends to be fragmented and relatively unorganized until about eight or nine years of age, when more complex and abstract mental operations become involved in the processing of media messages.

The child's active choice of how much mental effort should be spent in actual processing is another factor. When older children are expecting easy entertainment or have learned to recognize that television stories share similar structures, they often choose to rely on "automatic" processing requiring little mental effort. In this processing mode comprehension tends to be shallow and stereotypic, influencing what the child will take away from that program or material.

Comprehension

Comprehension is based on children's general knowledge schemata ("world knowledge"); knowledge of a medium's codes, formal features, and conventions; and knowledge of the structure of stories and other classes of materials. As one result of the parallel development of knowledge structures and attention and processing capabilities, comprehension becomes less dependent on the specific features of a medium or a particular program or story, and the child's knowledge, capabilities, and inclinations come to play a larger role.

Up to middle childhood there is low comprehension of media materials. The difficulties are evident in children's deficient temporal and logical integration of stories (e.g., those read to them or viewed on television), lack of inferences concerning motives, absence of connections between events in a story and their consequences, and so on. These shortcomings reflect a general difficulty in shifting attention from one dimension to another and connecting between them (a problem called centration) and in being able to go beyond the specific information given. A similar difficulty has been identified in the comprehension of the commercial intent underlying advertisements (see COMMERCIALS), although the use of salient production features, repetition, and familiar (i.e., easy-to-process) contents increases comprehension and recall. Making children aware of the internal structure of stories has a similar facilitating effect. It is interesting to note that children, even young ones, tend to spontaneously generate more inferences and make more connections to their world knowledge when read a story than when viewing it on television. Whether this results from greater effort expenditure in a medium perceived to be more serious, the imagery-demanding nature of language, or other factors is an open question.

The potential for becoming sophisticated media consumers increases as children mature but still depends considerably on their choice of mindful over mindless exposure. Children who choose to invest more mental effort in processing media messages become increasingly aware of hidden meanings, implied connections between events, the differences between FACT AND FICTION, and the various intentions underlying different types of messages.

Educating for media consumption. A variety of activities designed to be implemented in the home, the community, and the school have been developed with the explicit intention of educating children to become mindful and critical media consumers, especially of television. Instruction on the nature of the media, their typical materials, and alternatives for their intelligent consumption are included in the curriculum. Although these programs are relatively successful in their intended goals, questions remain about the degree to which children actually apply these skills and information when exposed to the media in unsupervised situations.

Bibliography. Jennings Bryant and Daniel R. Anderson, eds., *Children's Understanding of Television: Research on Attention and Comprehension*, New York, 1983; Takeo Furu, *The Function of Television for Children and Adolescents*, Tokyo, 1971; Patricia Marks Greenfield, *Mind and Media: The Effects of Television, Video Games, and Computers*, Cambridge, Mass., 1984; Hilde T. Himmelweit, A. N. Oppenheim, and Pamela Vince, *Television and the Child*, London, 1958; Daniel Lerner and Lyle M. Nelson, eds., *Communication Research: A Half Century Appraisal*, Honolulu, Hawaii, 1977; Gavriel Salomon, *Communication and Education*, Beverly Hills, Calif., 1981; Wilbur L. Schramm, Jack Lyle, and Edwin B. Parker, *Television in the Lives of Our Children*, Stanford, Calif., 1961; Dorothy G. Singer, Jerome Singer, and Diana M. Zuckerman, *Getting the Most Out of Television*, New York, 1981.

GAVRIEL SALOMON

4. MEDIA EFFECTS

Historically it has been assumed that lack of adultlike cognitive skills and life experiences renders children particularly vulnerable to symbolic messages. Such assumptions earned children status as a "special" audience at least as early as PLATO's *Republic*, which urged careful control over the stories and ideas presented to children. Their special status has been renewed periodically, often when new communications media emerge to make "new" stories and ideas available.

As the historical trend toward widespread EDUCATION created a growing audience of young readers, concern with the possible impact of print emerged (*see* PRINTING; READING). Many twentieth-century publishers of the Grimm fairy tales took care to eliminate themes they feared might harm children—for example, themes of abandonment and VIOLENCE. In the mid-1950s, the U.S. Senate voiced objections to crime and horror comic books (*see* COMICS), and reports of public disputes about which books and magazines should be available to children in SCHOOL, public libraries, and even bookstores remain common.

Similar concerns appear in calls for controls over popular music heard on the RADIO by adolescents, whether the problem is with rock and roll as a sociopolitical threat, as in the Soviet Union in the 1950s and 1960s, or with sexually explicit and violent song lyrics, as in the United States in the 1980s (*see* CENSORSHIP; MUSIC, POPULAR). The new communications media—with their blend of the storage and programming capabilities of the computer and the print and audiovisual display capacities of more traditional mass media—have aroused almost identical fears (*see* COMPUTER: IMPACT).

Audiovisual Media

The most intense and enduring scrutiny, however, has been reserved for the audiovisual media. Because the combination of sound and moving pictures provides children with symbolic messages they can "understand" at a much earlier age than is the case with other media (see sections 1 and 2, above), and because the nature of the production and distribution systems of both film and television tends to ensure that a significant proportion of their messages portray a world that children might not normally encounter (at least until they reach adulthood), these media seem particularly threatening.

The first systematic research on MASS MEDIA EFFECTS on children was undertaken in response to the rapid growth in popularity of MOTION PICTURES in the United States in the 1920s. The Payne Fund Studies, published in 1933, addressed questions about the impact of motion picture content on children's moral beliefs and ATTITUDES. The studies are remarkable both for their methodological sophistication and for their articulation of research questions that remain at the core of scientific studies of children and the mass media. The Payne Fund Studies used seventeen different motion pictures to test (in both naturalistic and experimental settings) various emotional, cognitive, and attitudinal responses of several thousand children ranging in age from eight years through the mid-teens. The studies reported some of the earliest empirical evidence that changes in physiological measures of emotional response (e.g., heart and breathing rate, galvanic skin response) varied with the action portrayed on-screen. They documented enormous amounts of children's learning from motion pictures and demonstrated that specific films (e.g., *Birth of a Nation; All Quiet on the Western Front*) could change children's beliefs about war, crime and punishment, and various racial, ethnic, and national groups. Moreover, these changes in attitudes were shown to persist over several months, and the effect was found to be cumulative, with exposure to several films dealing with the same issue increasing the amount of belief and attitude change obtained. Thus the Payne Fund Studies foreshadowed subsequent research in their consistent findings that the influence of films—whether measured as emotional response, amount of learning, or attitude change—varied dramatically with characteristics of the audience: boys reacted differently from girls, urban children differently from rural children, younger children differently from older children, and so on. *See* COMMUNICATIONS RESEARCH: ORIGINS AND DEVELOPMENT.

Television. Television research dominates the literature on children and the mass media. More than any other medium, television threatens parents' control over their children's received view of the world. In addition to the cognitive accessibility of the message inherent in its audiovisual symbol system, the rapid DIFFUSION of television sets into most U.S. households created widespread physical accessibility to the medium (*see* TELEVISION HISTORY). This combination of an accessible message system in a ubiquitous medium almost guarantees children's exposure to ideas, information, and attitudes different from those manifested within the immediate environment, if only because multiple information sources increase the probability of divergent messages (*see* CULTURAL INDICATORS). This, in turn, undermines the gatekeeping role that parents (then neighbors, then local institutions) have traditionally exercised over the information reaching young children. Public questioning of the role television plays in the lives of children has continued uninterrupted from the medium's inception.

Three large field studies greeted television's emergence as the dominant mass medium in the industrialized nations at the end of the 1950s. Hilde Himmelweit and her colleagues in Great Britain, WILBUR SCHRAMM and his associates in North America, and Takeo Furu in Japan all compared the behavior of children with and without and/or before and after acquiring access to television. Studies of this type, in which the "treatment" is access to television, are well suited to addressing questions about the impact of the medium as opposed to the impact of particular kinds of television content. Thus, for example, all three studies found that television dramatically altered how children spent their time, particularly time previously devoted to functionally similar activities. Television use greatly reduced both comic book reading and cinema attendance, had a lesser effect on the use of print FICTION, and had very little impact on nonfiction reading. The smaller effect on dissimilar media, as well as evidence that once the novelty of television wears off adolescents tend to return to the movie theater (whose function for them is probably quite different from the function of television viewing), supports a displacement hypothesis based on functional equivalence. So, too, does Himmelweit's finding that television most affected children's unstructured, marginal activities. The medium delayed bedtimes in all three countries (from ten to twenty-five minutes) but reduced homework time only in Japan. It is interesting to note that subsequent examinations of the introduction of television into various communities in Canada, Australia, and South Africa report substantially the same kinds of findings as this early work. *See* LEISURE.

These first studies also found little negative impact of the medium on school performance in either the United States or Great Britain. Rather, in the two Western countries television seemed to promote significant, albeit short-lived, increases in general knowledge and vocabulary among young, less bright children. A positive academic impact was also reported in Japan, but only on the girls' science achievement scores. Among Japanese boys, particularly those in grades five through seven, television brought significant declines in reading ability (*see* EDUCATIONAL TELEVISION).

Subsequent work on the relationship between television viewing and academic achievement has altered these early findings only slightly. Typically there is a negative relationship between amount of television viewing and various measures of academic achievement. But when such third variables as parental socioeconomic status, personal and social problems, and intelligence are taken into account, most of the overall relationship disappears. There is a small but persistent negative correlation between television viewing and reading achievement, but this is highly dependent on characteristics of the children. For example, a review of twenty-three studies by Patricia A. Williams and colleagues (published in 1982) found that the negative effect begins only after children reach ten hours of viewing per week and reaches a ceiling around forty hours per week. The effect appears to be greater on more intelligent children and on females and tends to depend on age. There is also evidence that when socioeconomic status is controlled, conditions within the home that foster educational achievement (e.g., when there is a great deal of print material available and when reading is encouraged) tend to eliminate any relationship between viewing and reading achievement. Finally, a few findings point to the possibility that some children from highly impoverished environments may gain from television viewing—the medium providing something educationally valuable that otherwise would be missing from their experience.

Contrary to popular expectations, none of the early field studies produced compelling evidence that television generated major changes in children's emotions, attitudes, or social behavior (e.g., the medium did not appear to make children more passive). The British study reported that adolescent girls who watched a great deal expressed slightly more anxiety about the future and that some children raised their career aspirations and reduced their willingness to make value judgments about foreigners as a function of having television. But none of the studies was able to demonstrate an increase in children's aggressive behavior as a result of television, nor were any other major forms of social behavior shown to be directly affected by the medium. *See* SOCIAL COGNITIVE THEORY.

It is important to note, however, that these early studies were ill suited to examining such "content-related" outcomes. As indicated earlier, most concern about the effects on children of any symbolic medium usually derives from assumptions about exposure to content transmitted via the medium. It was not storytellers but particular kinds of stories that Plato feared. So it is with television. Most questions about how television influences children assume that influence derives from specific kinds of content: news and public affairs (*see* TELEVISION NEWS); violence; prosocial actions; portrayals of racial, ethnic, or sex-role stereotypes; and so forth. In other words, most research on television's impact on children tends to be problem-centered, and types of content tend to define the problems.

Testing of hypotheses based on such assumptions requires an assessment of exposure to specific content that can be related to subsequent behavior or beliefs that might logically follow from such exposure. This was not the case with most field studies, whose overriding criterion of presence or absence of a television set in the home was, at best, only a gross indicator of exposure to a given kind of content. Thus, for example, their failure to find a relationship between viewing television and aggressive behavior does not address the question of whether there might be a relationship between viewing television *violence* and aggressive behavior. A more content-specific approach is required, and it is well exemplified in subsequent studies of television's effect on antisocial and prosocial behavior.

The issue of television's influence on children's aggressive behavior dominated research in the 1960s and early 1970s. The violence research aptly illustrates the importance of a carefully delineated linkage between content, exposure, and outcome. For example, laboratory experiments, which ensure that all children in a treatment group pay relatively close attention to a violent stimulus and which remove normally operating sanctions against aggressive behavior, are therefore almost unanimous in finding a causal link between viewing violence and subsequent aggressive behavior. Field experiments, in which exposure is more problematic to measure and in which various sanctions against aggressive behavior usually operate, report less clear-cut results, their numbers almost equally divided between those finding no relationship between viewing violence and aggressive behavior and those finding that viewing does lead to aggression.

Finally, results of various correlational studies seem even more equivocal. They report relationships between viewing and aggressive attitudes or behavior that range from zero to moderately positive. However, when arranged in order of sensitivity to their respective measures of viewing violence (e.g., from owning a TV set, to hours of TV viewing, to preference for violent shows, to amount of actual violence viewing), a pattern of reliable, positive relationships emerges. Even though discussions of the policy implications of the violence studies are marked by controversy, primarily because of disputes over the generalizability of their results, there is ample evidence that when viewing of violence per se is guaranteed and sanctions against aggressive behavior are removed, viewing violence does lead to aggression. Moreover, the same kind of generalization can be drawn from studies of the effects of many other types of television content. Viewing portrayals of prosocial behavior, commercial appeals, displays of ethnic and racial stereotypes, and so on, has been shown to influence similar classes of attitudes and actions.

Prosocial behavior. Both laboratory and naturalistic experiments demonstrate that television programs can encourage a variety of positive behaviors. Children ranging from preschool through high school age understand and learn from prosocial television content. They learn more when the messages are explicitly designed to promote positive behavior and values, particularly when the portrayals are interesting enough to attract attention and concrete enough to be comprehensible. The introduction into preschool curricula of programs designed to teach prosocial behavior (e.g., "Mister Rogers' Neighborhood," "Sesame Street") increased at least some viewers' displays of cooperation, friendly interaction, helpfulness, willingness to share, and self-control. The CLASSROOM setting tends to facilitate such positive outcomes, especially when viewing is combined with supplementary activities endemic to the classroom, such as role playing and verbal labeling. Evidence that children respond to prosocial themes in programming produced primarily to entertain also mounts. Commercial programs selected for prosocial content and not supplemented by other activities have also led to increases in cooperation and helping behavior among children as old as ten or eleven.

Commercials. Numerous empirical studies show that children attend to, learn from, and change their behavior as a result of television COMMERCIALS. Commercials are particularly apt to influence children because they are brief, entertaining, and concrete; they focus on a single act; they promise big rewards; and they establish clear connections between the television image and real situations. Exposure to commercials has been shown to lead preschoolers to prefer an advertised toy to playing with friends in a subsequent choice situation, and the annual barrage of Christmas commercials that occurs in many countries has been found to overcome the defenses of even the most initially resistant children. In short, commercials aimed at children do what they are designed to do: they create an awareness of and a desire for the advertised products.

Television content has been shown to affect children's beliefs, attitudes, and knowledge on a variety of other issues and topics, including occupational knowledge and expectations; sex-role stereotypes; knowledge of and attitudes toward science; information about health, safety, and nutrition; political information and beliefs; and so on. For example, a growing body of literature indicates that viewing news and public affairs programs increases adolescents' levels of political information—although, consistent with findings for adults, the relationship between exposure and political information is even higher when the stimulus is newspapers or newsmagazines (*see* POLITICAL SOCIALIZATION). Correlational studies have found that children who watch more television tend to be more accepting of traditional sex-role stereotypes. Such results are consistent with the majority of television portrayals of females and also with evidence that frequent television viewers are likely to hold more traditional sex-role attitudes. However, results from experimental procedures also indicate that counterstereotypical portrayals of women excerpted from commercials and ENTERTAINMENT programming (e.g., women engaged in male-dominated occupations) can influence sex-role attitudes and expectations in less traditional directions; viewers become more accepting of women in male-dominated occupations and in leadership roles. For example, a long-term evaluation of "Freestyle," a U.S. television series specifically designed to reduce sex-role stereotyping, found viewers more accepting of such things as girls performing mechanical tasks, men helping with housework, and girls in leadership roles. Some of the findings held only for girls, others only for boys, and some of the targeted attitudes and expectations remained unchanged. Nevertheless, it is clear from this study, as well as from work concerned with programs as diverse as "Sesame Street," "3-2-1 Contact," or the "National Citizenship Quiz," that when programming is designed to teach, it may be quite successful regardless of whether concern is with preschoolers learning the alphabet, grade-schoolers learning science, or high schoolers learning to discount traditional sex-role stereotypes. *See* AUDIOVISUAL EDUCATION; GENDER; SEXISM.

Qualifications. This is not to say that all television teaches all children the same things all the time. On the contrary, several important qualifications are necessary for most of the preceding generalizations. Indeed, perhaps the most important changes in research on media and children since the early 1980s have

been a reduction in the number of studies examining the effects of specific kinds of content and a dramatic increase in work concerned with *how* children process mass-mediated messages. Contemporary research focuses on such general processing outcomes as exposure, attention, comprehension or sensemaking, and memory, and the factors that mediate differences in such outcomes. These studies make clear that what is learned, by which children, and whether such learning is translated into action vary with characteristics of the television content, the child, and the environment (see section 3, above).

A second set of conditions mediating effects pertains to the viewers. There is tremendous variation among children, and to the extent that they have different needs, interests, and past experiences, they learn different things from the medium. Boys and girls focus on different program elements; children from urban and rural environments or from differing social or ethnic backgrounds interpret a given portrayal in very different ways; children with personal problems use television quite differently from their less troubled peers.

Differences in cognitive abilities, generally indexed by age, locate particularly significant variations in responses to television content (*see* COGNITION). Although some studies illustrate that young children understand a good deal more than was previously thought, differences in how preschool, grade school, and high school children process symbolic information remain dramatic. Before seven or eight years of age, children's attention spans and memory capacities are limited. They tend to focus on the perceptual attributes of programs (e.g., action sequences, scene changes, SOUND EFFECTS), respond to concrete portrayals, interpret discrete scenes, and often fail to notice implicit content or to interpret noncontiguous events. Younger children often confuse realism and reality, and they "make sense" of television content in their own terms, not those of their older counterparts. By contrast, older children are able to respond to more conceptual program elements such as motives underlying actions, abstract issues such as responsibility and justice, and implicit relationships. They tend to integrate scenes into larger wholes and begin to understand that even the most realistic drama is fiction. Hence, portrayal of the police subduing and jailing a criminal at the end of a program may teach an adolescent that crime does not pay, but a ten-year-old may learn that good guys have the right to punish bad guys, and a five-year-old may simply fail to relate the punishment in Act 3 to the crime in Act 1.

It is also important to distinguish between learning and performance. Although almost all social behavior is learned, not everything learned is translated into overt behavior. Children's behavior depends on the situation in which they find themselves and on their learned expectations about what is right or wrong, good or bad, wise or foolish, possible or impossible. In other words, television cannot create situations, but it can influence the expectations and norms children bring to situations. Thus a fact, attitude, or behavior that a child learns from television may not be displayed until he or she encounters an appropriate set of conditions in a different context—perhaps weeks, months, or even years after viewing. Similarly, then, the likelihood of a child performing behaviors learned from television increases as the portrayed setting or conditions become more similar to the actual world of the child. And finally, the likelihood that a given child will be affected by television content increases as opportunity for direct experience or availability of competing messages dealing with the same topic decreases. That is, the more "distant" the material television presents—regardless of whether that distance is spatial, temporal, social, or psychological—the more likely a child is to be influenced by the portrayal.

The mass media in general and television in particular have become an integral part of contemporary culture, shaping our children in much the same way that schools, churches, and families do. Insofar as socialization refers to children's learning about the world in which they must operate, all of those institutions, including the media, are socialization agents. It is important to keep in mind that mass media effects on children do not occur in a vacuum. Media are only one of many contributors to children's beliefs about and behavior in the world. However, the evidence is clear that they are extremely important contributors.

Bibliography. Jennings Bryant and Daniel R. Anderson, eds., *Children's Understanding of Television*, New York, 1983; George Comstock, Steven Chaffee, Nathan Katzman, Maxwell McCombs, and Donald F. Roberts, *Television and Human Behavior*, New York, 1978; Hilde T. Himmelweit, A. N. Oppenheim, and Pamela Vince, *Television and the Child*, London, 1958; Michael J. A. Howe, ed., *Learning from Television: Psychological and Educational Research*, London and New York, 1983; Robert M. Liebert, Joyce N. Sprafkin, and Emily S. Davidson, *The Early Window: Effects on Children and Youth*, 2d ed., New York, 1982; Edward L. Palmer and Aimee Dorr, *Children and the Faces of Television: Teaching, Violence, Selling*, New York, 1980; David Pearl, Lorraine Bouthilet, and Joyce B. Lazar, eds., *Television and Behavior: Ten Years of Scientific Progress and Implications for the Eighties*, 2 vols., Washington, D.C., 1982; Ruth C. Peterson and L. L. Thurstone, *Motion Pictures and the Social Attitudes of Children*, New York, 1933; Donald F. Roberts and Nathan Maccoby, "Effects of Mass Communication," in *The Handbook of Social Psychology*, Vol. 2, 3d ed., ed. by Gardner Lindzey and Elliott Aronson, New York, 1985; Wilbur L. Schramm, Jack Lyle, and Edwin B. Parker, *Television in the Lives of Our Children*, Stanford, Calif., 1961; Tannis M. Williams, ed., *The Impact of Television: A Natural Experiment in Three Communities*, New York, 1986.

DONALD F. ROBERTS

CHOREOMETRICS

A method for describing what is most typical in the varied DANCE traditions of the world. Unlike dance notation systems, choreometrics does not record sequences of dance steps or gestures so that they may be reproduced from scores. Instead it describes distinctive patterns of BODY MOVEMENT and interaction so that dance styles may be compared and classified cross-culturally. Choreometrics was the coinvention of Irmgard Bartenieff, Forrestine Paulay, and Alan Lomax, working with concepts from the Laban Effort Shape System, the kinesic studies of Ray Birdwhistell, and the cultural methodologies of anthropologists George Peter Murdock, MARGARET MEAD, Conrad Arensberg, and others. *See also* KINESICS.

The choreometrics system consists of more than one hundred standardized scales for recording body part use, body attitude, trace forms, dynamics, the composition and organization of the dance group and orchestra, the audience, the degree and kind of synchrony employed, step and GESTURE style, GENDER differentials, and patterns of dance form and rhythm. These scales of measurement and the traits they comprise were chosen and tested for their reliability and effectiveness in the study of a set of films representing the main cultural areas. Careful verbal definitions of these measures were set down in a coding book. The measures were also defined visually in teaching films that illustrate each scale point with examples from a variety of cultures. These films incorporate a world perspective on important qualities of movement style and have produced a high level of agreement among raters (over 80 percent).

Operating from this platform of agreement, movement analysts then applied the choreometric system to a global sample of several hundred DOCUMENTARY and ethnographic films, creating numerical profiles that were entered into computer files for comparison (*see* ETHNOGRAPHIC FILM). These dance profiles came from four hundred cultures representing 80 percent of the cultural provinces in the standard ethnographic world sample for which codified information is also available on work, climate, social organization, and musical style. The computer programs devised to handle this socioaesthetic data bank produced a geographic taxonomy of movement style regions and a set of correlations to social structure like those found in the song style study (*see* CANTOMETRICS). The many discovered structural relations between dancing and music making suggest that an underlying set of factors fundamental to cultural structure is at work in both of these rhythmic expressive systems.

The correspondence between the regions of expressive style and those found by historians of culture indicate that these patterns of movement, dynamics, timing, phrasing, posture, and interaction are learned early in life and passed on generationally. This may explain why the known historical movements of culture—Europe to America, Africa to America, North Africa to Andalusia, South Asia to Southeast Asia—are reflected on the choreometric grid.

Of interest here are the many parallels between choreometric distributions and those established by archaeology. For example, choreometrics analysis finds that clear differential patterns run through all the dance styles of aboriginal America and link this pan-American tradition to Siberia (as per the film *The Longest Trail*). Both choreometric and cantometric data confirm the evidence of modern archaeology concerning the spread of Paleo-Indian culture across the land bridge that once linked the Siberian Arctic to Alaska and the subsequent isolation and specialization of traditions in the New World. In the same way, the stylistic evidence matches the findings of culture historians about the peopling of the Pacific from Asia and the southward spread of black culture from the Sudan into sub-Saharan Africa. It begins to appear that the spread and differentiation of culture traditions may be traced not only by potsherds but by PERFORMANCE profiles as well.

See also BODY MOVEMENT NOTATION.

Bibliography. William Laughlin and Albert B. Harper, eds., *The First Americans: Origins, Affinities, and Adaptations*, New York, 1979; Alan Lomax et al., *Dancing*, Lincoln, Neb., forthcoming; idem, *Folk Song Style and Culture*, Princeton, N.J., 1968. **Filmography.** Alan Lomax and Forrestine Paulay, *Dance and Human History*, Berkeley, Calif., 1976; idem, *The Longest Trail*, Berkeley, Calif., 1986; idem, *Palm Play*, Berkeley, Calif., 1979; idem, *Step Style*, Berkeley, Calif., 1979.

ALAN LOMAX

CICERO (106–43 B.C.E.)

Roman lawyer, politician, and philosopher. Living in the last decades of the Roman Republic, including its breakup in civil war (49–45 B.C.E.), Marcus Tullius Cicero developed ORATORY into a high art. With his imposing presence, his appeals to emotion, his dramatic delivery, and his long periodic sentences that featured parallelism, balance, and complex interweaving clauses, Cicero manipulated his audience's attention and devastated his opponents in the courtroom and the political arena. According to Cicero a free society is one in which political power is exercised through the persuasive techniques of RHETORIC, not through violence (*see* PERSUASION). Throughout subsequent history Cicero has served as a model for public speakers.

Cicero left several instructional works on oratory that, together with his example, have influenced not only PUBLIC SPEAKING but also PROSE style—especially during the RENAISSANCE—and even the art of ACTING during its more declamatory periods. As a philosopher Cicero was influential not so much for the originality of his thought—which, like his oratory, owed much to Greek influence—but because he was a vital link in transmitting Greek philosophy to the Latin MIDDLE AGES and the Renaissance.

Born at Arpinum into the equestrian class—not the highest nobility but, in his family's case, wealthy—Cicero received one of the best possible educations. He studied law, oratory, literature, and philosophy in Rome, Athens, and Rhodes with some of the leading teachers of his time. Politically ambitious, Cicero rose through several lesser offices to the rank of consul. But he identified with the conservative aristocracy, which proved incapable of stemming the anarchy that overwhelmed the republic.

During periods when Cicero was out of office he retired to one of his spacious villas and sought the consolation of philosophy. He studied the Greek philosophers, favoring the Academics and Stoics, and wrote numerous eclectic volumes reflecting their thought. Many of his philosophical works are dialogues in which the speakers are leaders of Rome and the listeners students. Conflicting views are presented, and the exchanges are sometimes heated and emotional but never rise to violence. Cicero's works on oratory include *De oratore* (55 B.C.E.), *Brutus* (46 B.C.E.), and *Orator* (46 B.C.E.). More than eight hundred extant letters written by Cicero—approximately half to his close friend Titus Pomponius Atticus (109–32 B.C.E.)—reveal more about Roman life and politics than any other source now available. *See also* LETTER.

During the civil war Cicero opposed Julius Caesar, but the victorious Caesar granted him amnesty. Although Cicero did not participate in the plot to assassinate Caesar, he certainly approved of the event. Afterward, in fourteen speeches known as the *Philippics* (44–43 B.C.E.), Cicero attacked Caesar's friend Mark Antony in the senate. When Antony joined forces with young Octavian, the future emperor, they put Cicero on their proscribed list. Antony's men seized Cicero as he fled his Tusculum villa. The great orator's severed head and hands were later displayed on the speaker's stand in the Roman Forum.

Bibliography. D. R. Shackleton Bailey, *Cicero*, New York, 1971; Gaston Boissier, *Cicero and His Friends: A Study of Roman Society in the Time of Caesar*, trans. by Adnah D. Jones, New York, 1897, reprint 1970.

CINÉMA VÉRITÉ

Film technique in which lightweight hand-held cameras and portable synchronized sound recorders are used. It was made possible by the technological breakthroughs in camera design in France in the late 1950s and in the United States in the early 1960s. The term also embraces innovative approaches to DOCUMENTARY filming in the same period, best represented by the work of Jean Rouch in France and Drew Associates in the United States.

Cinéma vérité represents an attempt to get closer than other film genres to the untempered reality of life. It avoids using professional actors to play roles and depicts instead the lives of real people in real situations. It disavows the artifice and reconstructions of the documentaries of the 1940s and 1950s and tends to reject both commentary and music. The *cinéma vérité* film has no preplanned script, but rather relies on spontaneity. *Cinéma vérité* is, in a sense, "found" on the editing table, where the material must be organized in sequence.

History. The ideological roots of *cinéma vérité* can be traced to the writings of the Soviet filmmaker DZIGA VERTOV—whose newsreel *Kinopravda* (Film Truth; see Figure 1) inspired the French term—and to the influence of the U.S. documentary pioneer ROBERT FLAHERTY. In his essays Vertov denounced the fiction film and asserted that the proper material for film was to be found in the ongoing events of life. Flaherty's contribution lay in his emphasis on nonpreconception and on the necessity for filmmakers to be open to all the nuances of a situation. He emphasized detailed observation—the key to *cinéma vérité*—and the role of the editing process for "finding" the film.

The practice and theory of what is termed *cinéma vérité* actually varies enormously from filmmaker to

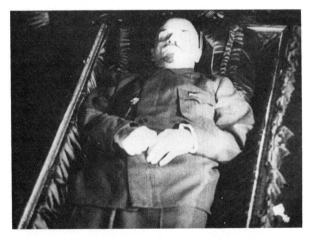

Figure 1. *(Cinéma Vérité)* Dziga Vertov, *Kinopravda* (Film Truth), 1922. Lenin in his casket. National Film Archive, London/Sovexport.

filmmaker and from country to country. The term was first used in reference to *Chronique d'un été* (Chronicle of a Summer, 1961), made by anthropologist filmmaker Jean Rouch together with sociologist Edgar Morin. The film follows the lives and concerns of a group of Parisians in the summer of 1960 (*see* ETHNOGRAPHIC FILM).

Rouch's work in *cinéma vérité* reflected a belief in the camera as a catalyst that could encourage people to reveal their true selves. It involved considerable intervention and probing by the director. Although *Chronique* was edited to its final version from twenty-one hours of filming, Rouch also declared that editing was wrong and that material should not be lost in the cutting room, since that falsified reality.

The pioneers of *cinéma vérité* in the United States—reporter Robert Drew and photographer Richard Leacock—used it in a somewhat different way, which is often termed *direct cinema*. Unlike the Rouch method, direct cinema avoids all directorial influence on the filmed events. Theoretically the filmmakers are like flies on the wall, totally uninvolved in the scene being filmed.

Leacock, who had been cameraman for *Louisiana Story* (1948) and had been deeply influenced by its director, Flaherty, began his collaboration with Drew in 1957. With the support of the Time-Life broadcasting organization, they modified their equipment to allow a freer style of shooting. Later they were joined by Albert and David Maysles, Donn A. Pennebaker, and Gregory Shuker, and under the banner of Drew Associates made a group of films using *cinéma vérité* methods that defined the dominant path for *cinéma vérité* in the United States for the next decade.

The most important of their films was *Primary* (1960), which covers the struggle between Hubert H. Humphrey and John F. Kennedy during the Wisconsin primary election in the 1960 U.S. presidential campaign. What was new was the intimacy of the filming, the sense of place and character, and the humanization of the electoral process. Drew Associates then made four one-hour documentaries for ABC Television's "Close Up" series and another ten films between 1961 and 1963 for Time, Inc., under the title "The Living Camera." These films include *Jane* (1962), which follows Jane Fonda rehearsing in a Broadway play, and *The Chair* (1962), about the possible reprieve of a man sentenced to death. Most of the films show what critic Stephen Mamber calls a synthesis of *cinéma vérité* techniques and fictional concepts of character, action, and structure. This can be observed in the films' dependency on a crisis structure in which people are seen living through pressure situations that are resolved in the last minutes of the action.

A third pioneering example of *cinéma vérité* is represented by the work of a National Film Board of Canada unit under Roman Kroitor and Wolf Koenig, who proposed a series of experiments for television under the title "The Candid Eye." Intimacy and spontaneity were to be emphasized, and no formal scripts were to be submitted—merely a list of titles and sequences. The films were to be shot as freely as possible and structured in the editing room. The first film released in the series was *The Days before Christmas* (1958), about people's activities just prior to the holiday. At least six filmmakers directed sequences for it. While Kroitor, Koenig, and producer Tom Daly set the tone, undoubtedly one of the most interesting filmmakers to emerge was Terence Macartney-Filgate. His two films—*Blood and Fire* (1958), about the Salvation Army, and *The Back Breaking Leaf* (1959)—are often regarded as the highlights of the series.

A number of the unit's filmmakers had an influence on foreign *cinéma vérité* work. Macartney-Filgate, for example, was also on the Drew team that shot *Primary*. Another occasional member of the group, French Canadian Michel Brault, was the principal camera operator on Rouch's *Chronique d'un été*.

While the Drew films used the crisis element to provide a certain structure, form was generally the one problem that the "Candid Eye" films failed to solve, even with the help of occasional narration. A film that did work well in this regard was one of the last films in the series, *Lonely Boy* (1962; see Figure 2). Directed by Koenig and Kroitor, this portrait of pop singer Paul Anka foreshadowed later pop portraits such as Pennebaker's *Don't Look Back* (1964), about Bob Dylan, and *Gimme Shelter* (1970), by the Maysles brothers and Charlotte Zwerin, about the Rolling Stones.

Apart from various show business portraits such as *Meet Marlon Brando* (1966), the Maysles brothers also produced an extraordinary portrait of four Bible salesmen in *Salesman* (1969; see Figure 3) and a humorous, complex description of a mother-daughter relationship in *Grey Gardens* (1975). The Maysles's work was characterized by an attempt to break away from the Robert Drew crisis formula and use *cinéma vérité* in a more open and nondramatic fashion.

One criticism of the Drew-Leacock-Maysles films was that they failed to use *cinéma vérité* to address social issues in any depth. This was remedied in the United States by the work of Frederick Wiseman, a lawyer turned filmmaker. Wiseman's first film, *Titicut Follies* (1967), gives a searing picture of an institution for the criminally insane. This was followed by fourteen films over the next decade and a half, including *High School* (1968) and *Law and Order* (1969; see Figure 4). Wiseman's films deal with the main tax-supported institutions of U.S. society and tend to examine the ways in which bureaucratic power is manipulated within these institutions. As

Figure 2. *(Cinéma Vérité)* Wolf Koenig and Roman Kroitor, *Lonely Boy*, 1962. National Film Board of Canada.

Figure 3. *(Cinéma Vérité)* Albert and David Maysles, *Salesman*, 1969. Maysles Films.

277

Figure 4. *(Cinéma Vérité)* Frederick Wiseman, *Law and Order,* 1969. National Film Archive, London. © Zipporah Films, Inc.

one critic put it, Wiseman's films offer an unparalleled social history and critique of daily life in the United States in the 1960s and 1970s.

In Great Britain a similar sociological thrust could be seen in the films of Roger Graef, an expatriate American known especially for two television series. "The Space between Words" (1972) dealt with communication problems in both family and work situations. "Decisions" (1976), made for Granada Television, focused on decision-making processes in huge corporations and served to demystify the way in which big businesses were run and governed.

An early influence on Graef was the Canadian filmmaker Allan King, who in 1966 made *Warrendale,* a landmark *cinéma vérité* film about a Toronto center for emotionally disturbed children. Two years later King made *A Married Couple,* which was shot in Toronto over the course of ten weeks. The film, which explores the marital difficulties of Billy and Antoinette Edwards, was edited out of chronological order and creates what King has called "an emotional fiction" rather than a true portrait of a marriage. King's exploration of the intimacies of marriage was copied in many other *cinéma vérité* films.

Criticism. During the 1970s the theoretical basis for *cinéma vérité* received increasingly sharp criticism. The four most serious objections concerned its structure, meaning, truth, and ethics. Regarding structure, although many of the original *cinéma vé-*

rité pioneers claimed that the form had broken the shackles of the standard fiction film, *cinéma vérité* seemed to succeed best when it simply copied fictional structures (e.g., "The Living Camera" series). Concerning meaning, it has been claimed that while these films offer interesting social and political observations, as in the films of Wiseman, they lack the context or meaningful perspective that would normally be supplied by commentary. On the issue of truth, many critics claim that *cinéma vérité*'s vaunted search after truth and transparency is futile inasmuch

Figure 5. *(Cinéma Vérité)* Claude Lanzmann, *Shoah* (Holocaust), 1975. Henrik Gawkowski, Polish locomotive engineer. The Museum of Modern Art/Film Stills Archive.

as all documentaries are fictions. They argue that there is no clear window onto reality and that all filmmakers fabricate meanings and present subjective selections of images. The last objection to *cinéma vérité* is that the intimacy of its technique and its tendency to invade the private family world inevitably have an impact on, and in some cases have disrupted and even destroyed, the lives of the films' subjects. In the mid-1970s this moral and ethical critique became a subject of fierce debate among writers and filmmakers.

Later developments. The essence of pure *cinéma vérité* is indirect address, with an audience coming to a conclusion about a subject unaided by implicit or explicit commentary. This style was largely superseded in the 1970s—particularly in a number of political and feminist documentaries—by the use of direct address. This mainly took the form of witness-participants telling their stories directly to the camera, prompted by an interviewer who might be seen or unseen, heard or unheard. Among the most notable of these films were *Le chagrin et la pitié* (The Sorrow and the Pity, 1970) by Marcel Ophuls, about French collaboration with Nazi Germany, and *Shoah* (Holocaust, 1975; see Figure 5), by Claude Lanzmann, about the operation of Nazi death camps. In both cases the directors elicited testimony from numerous individuals who had long had reason to keep their roles secret. The films represented a further stylistic development of the 1970s and 1980s, in the increase of self-reflexivity in the documentary, with the filmmakers' presence becoming much more visible and explicit.

In the 1970s and 1980s the rapid rise of VIDEO, with its increasingly compact and portable equipment, gave *cinéma vérité* unprecedented new opportunities and led to increased use of the form. Videotaped *cinéma vérité* sequences or "minidocumentaries" became a normal ingredient in television newscasts. The genre had become just one among many techniques available to filmmakers.

Bibliography. M. Alí Issari and Doris A. Paul, *What Is Cinéma Vérité?* Metuchen, N.J., 1979; Stephen Mamber, *Cinéma Vérité in America*, Cambridge, Mass., 1974; Louis Marcorelles, *Living Cinema*, New York and London, 1973; Alan Rosenthal, *The Documentary Conscience*, Berkeley, Calif., 1980.

ALAN ROSENTHAL

CINEMATOGRAPHY

The process of recording and creating images on motion picture film. Cinematography plays an essential role in a film's overall meaning and effect. In manipulating the image the cinematographer employs three broad types of techniques involving three kinds of choices: photographic, framing, and shot duration.

Photographic Techniques

Cinematography shares with PHOTOGRAPHY the photochemical process of recording light rays reflecting from an object. Consequently, cinematography manipulates a number of photographic resources.

Tonalities. Different black-and-white and color motion picture film stocks vary in their degree of sensitivity to light, amount of grain, and so on. By selecting a specific film stock, the cinematographer controls the range of contrast, color rendition, textural detail, and other aspects of the image. The image can be manipulated during laboratory processing as well. Filters, latensification, solarization, and other photographic techniques can also affect tonal qualities and create expressive effects. During the 1920s, for example, HOLLYWOOD cinematographer John F. Seitz pioneered the use of gauze filters and low-contrast developing to create a soft, sensuous image.

Spatial relations. Every motion picture lens has a particular focal length, which affects the depth of field of the resultant image. By using a lens of a specific depth of field and adjusting the focusing component of the lens, the cinematographer can control the degree of focus in the image. An image can utilize shallow focus, in which one plane is sharp and the others fall into a blur, or the image can present a series of planes all in sharp focus. U.S. cinematography of the studio period favored shallow focus for close shots of STARS, but Gregg Toland, cinematographer for ORSON WELLES's *Citizen Kane* (1941), popularized the use of deep focus, even on closer views (Figure 1).

The focal length of the lens also affects the image's perspective qualities. A short-focal-length lens takes in a wide angle of view and exaggerates distances between planes. Such lenses were pioneered by German and Soviet cinematographers of the late 1920s and became common in Hollywood after Toland's extensive use of them. A long-focal-length lens takes in a narrow angle of view and minimizes distances between planes, producing a flatter image; the telescopic magnification of such lenses can be seen throughout the history of NEWSREEL photography.

Finally, SPECIAL EFFECTS can also affect the image's spatial relations. Some effects are quite simple and can be done in the camera, such as the superimposition (a double exposure) or the glass shot (a painted pane of glass depicting portions of a set, placed between the camera and the filmed object). More complex is projection-process work, whereby the actor is filmed against a screen upon which

Figure 1. *(Cinematography)* Orson Welles, *Citizen Kane,* 1941. The Museum of Modern Art/Film Stills Archive.

another film is projected. In the studio era this procedure was usually featured in shots showing characters in moving vehicles. Most sophisticated of all are the various matte processes. Here several strips of film, each holding a portion of the final image, are jigsawed together in the printing process. Matte work is common in SCIENCE FICTION films. Through special effects the cinematographer can create a wholly artificial image, one that records no single existing spatial whole.

Speed of motion. Unlike the photographer, the cinematographer records continuous movement. This parameter can be manipulated through adjustment of the camera's drive mechanism. Normally, 16-mm and 35-mm sound films are projected at 24 frames per second (fps), so if the cinematographer wants a natural impression of movement, that is the rate at which the film should be exposed in the camera. Exposing fewer than 24 fps will yield fast motion, an effect used by some silent cinematographers when they "under-cranked" for comic or kinetic effect. Exposing more than 24 fps will yield slow motion, an effect pioneered by SPORTS and nature cinematographers of the silent era and used to artistic ends in DZIGA VERTOV's *Chelovek s kinoapparatom* (The Man with the Movie Camera, 1928; cinematographer Mikhail Kaufman), Leni Riefenstahl's *Olympia* (1938), and Kon Ichikawa's *Tokyo Olympiad* (1965).

Lighting. Although not strictly part of camera technique, in studio filmmaking the cinematographer usually has charge of the lighting. U.S. studio practice standardized a three-point lighting pattern in which actors were lit by a key light (the light of greatest intensity, coming from an oblique frontal angle), a fill light (a less intense light filling in the shadows created by the key), and a backlight (a light coming from behind and above that outlined the player's body). Throughout the studio period this scheme was supplemented by atmospheric "low-key" lighting, which reduced the ratio of fill lighting to create sharper shadows and greater chiaroscuro. Examples can be seen in the work of George Barnes on *Bulldog Drummond* (1929), Stanley Cortez on *The Magnificent Ambersons* (1942; Figure 2), and John Alton on several low-budget crime thrillers of the 1940s. Other outstanding experimenters in lighting include Charles Rosher, for his diffusing gauzes and scrims in *Sparrows* (1926); Toland, for his use of arc lights to increase depth of field in *Citizen Kane;* and Raoul Coutard, who employed ordinary daylight without diffusion to obtain brilliant saturated color in several films for Jean-Luc Godard.

Framing

As in still photography, cinematography demands decisions about how the image will be composed within its frame. Again, several variables can be manipulated.

Frame shape and proportions. Very early in the history of the cinema, the image was standardized as a rectangle of 1:1.33 proportions. The development of wide-screen cinema in the 1950s created new, narrower formats, the most common being CinemaScope, 1:2.55 in its magnetic-sound version. Since the 1970s the generally accepted standard has been 1:1.85, although other formats are still used. Independent of these official standards, cinematog-

Figure 2. *(Cinematography)* Orson Welles, *The Magnificent Ambersons,* 1942. The Museum of Modern Art/ Film Stills Archive.

raphers have long experimented with the shape of the image. Silent filmmakers used masks—circles, triangles, keyhole shapes, and others—to alter the frame's shape. For D. W. GRIFFITH's *Intolerance* (1916), G. W. "Billy" Bitzer emphasized a soldier's fall from a parapet by masking the image to create a narrow shaft of space in the center. More ambitiously, Abel Gance's *Napoléon* (1927) introduced Polyvision, a wide-screen format that joined three images horizontally (Figure 3), anticipating the multiple-frame imagery of later films like *Twilight's Last Gleaming* (1977).

Camera position. The framing of the image necessitates decisions about where the camera will be placed in relation to the filmed object. The camera may be placed on a level axis or a tilted one; if the

Figure 3. *(Cinematography)* Abel Gance, *Napoléon,* 1927. National Film Archive, London.

Figure 4. *(Cinematography)* Louis Lumière, *Arrivée d'un train à La Ciotat* (Arrival of a Train at La Ciotat Station), 1895. National Film Archive, London.

latter, a canted framing will result. The camera may be set at a low, high, or straight-on angle. It may also be placed at any distance from the filmed object, ranging from an extreme long shot to an extreme close-up. From the very beginning of cinema, film-makers have recognized that camera position is a powerful means of guiding the spectator's attention, clarifying or emphasizing certain aspects of the object, and evoking attitudes to the filmed material. In Louis Lumière's *Arrivée d'un train à La Ciotat* (Arrival of a Train at La Ciotat Station, 1895), the oblique angle and medium-long-shot framing bring out the depth of the tracks and the bustle of passengers (Figure 4) (*see* LUMIÈRE, LOUIS AND AUGUSTE). By contrast, the early films of Georges Méliès are quite theatrical in placing the camera perpendicular to the playing space, and the long-shot distance simulates the view of an audience member. Some film-makers have made particular choices about camera position an integral part of their style. Welles habitually used canted low angles, while Howard Hawks relied on straight-on, normal framings. Carl Theodor Dreyer's *La passion de Jeanne d'Arc* (1928) was composed almost completely of detailed close-ups (Figure 5), but Chantal Akerman's *Les rendezvous d'Anna* (1978) was filmed almost entirely in long shot.

Camera movement. The motion picture camera can change its framing during filming, providing a continuously unfolding space and time. A pan consists of swiveling the camera horizontally; a tilt is swiveling it vertically. A tracking shot (also called a trucking, dollying, or traveling shot) consists of moving the camera forward, backward, laterally, or diagonally. A crane shot, usually made from a mobile crane arm, consists of raising or lowering the camera on the vertical axis. In the silent era some camera movements, such as those in Giovanni Pastrone's

Cabiria (1913) and Griffith's *Intolerance,* conveyed the volume of a vast set. German cinematographer Karl Freund executed many virtuosic following shots in F. W. Murnau's *Der letzte Mann* (The Last Laugh, 1925), and his efforts were arguably surpassed by Rosher and Karl Struss in Murnau's *Sunrise* (1927). Complex camera movements, especially crane shots, became important in German and Hollywood musicals of the 1930s (*see* MUSICAL, FILM), with the crane coming into use in dramatic productions in the United States and Japan at the end of the decade. By the late 1950s, most cinematographers around the world were mounting the camera on a mobile dolly, usually a "crab dolly" that could execute tight turns and move in virtually any direction. The development of portable cameras like the Arriflex in the postwar era made hand-held camera movements feasible, and these found their way not only into DOCUMENTARY work but also into fiction filmmaking (e.g., the opening of *Seven Days in May,* 1964).

Shot Duration

As the record of an unfolding event, cinematography can control the duration of the shot. Many filmmakers, including Soviet and U.S. directors of the 1920s, filmed brief shots that would be assembled in the editing phase. Other directors have insisted on prolonging the shot beyond its normal length, using the resultant "long take" to develop an action or scene. When the shot constitutes a complete scene in itself, it is usually called a *plan séquence* (shot sequence). The long take may allow the actors to build up a continuous performance, or it may be used to generate tension and suspense. Both Welles and ALFRED HITCHCOCK used the long-take technique on occasion; Hitchcock's *Rope* (1948) was shot entirely in long takes. Other filmmakers identified with the tech-

Figure 5. *(Cinematography)* Carl Theodor Dreyer, *La passion de Jeanne d'Arc* (The Passion of Joan of Arc), 1928. National Film Archive, London.

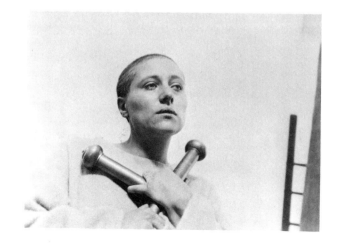

nique include Dreyer, Kenji Mizoguchi in Japan, and Miklós Jancsó in Hungary. Long-take directors usually make extensive use of camera movement, which may function as an equivalent for editing in directing the viewer's attention to various parts of the action.

See also AVANT-GARDE FILM; FILM EDITING; MOTION PICTURES; PERCEPTION—STILL AND MOVING PICTURES.

Bibliography. Brian Coe, *The History of Movie Photography*, London, 1981; Linwood G. Dunn and George E. Turner, *The ASC Treasury of Visual Effects,* Hollywood, Calif., 1983; Leonard Maltin, ed., *The Art of the Cinematographer,* enl. ed., New York, 1978; H. Mario Raimondo Suoto, *The Technique of the Motion Picture Camera,* 3d ed., New York, 1977; Leslie J. Wheeler, *Principles of Cinematography,* 4th ed., New York, 1969.

DAVID BORDWELL

CITIZEN ACCESS

The word *access* has many communications uses but in general implies a privileged position in relation to a restricted resource. In reference to *citizen access* (or *public access*) it has become a banner word for groups and individuals demanding a meaningful, active role in the broadcast media, not as a privilege but as a democratic right. They focus on these media because of the monopolistic nature inherent in any medium based on licensing authority.

The citizen access movement points to the early history of the PRINTING press, when European rulers sought to control its output and block heretical and other unwelcome ideas by instituting licensing systems. Anyone wishing to communicate with the public through the new medium needed a royal license (and often ecclesiastical approval) or the cooperation of a printer already possessing such a license. These licensees became gatekeepers of the established order.

This form of CENSORSHIP was difficult to enforce and was philosophically protested, as by JOHN MILTON in his *Areopagitica* (1644), printed defiantly without the seal of approval. Over several centuries press licensing was abandoned in most leading nations, while the philosophical objections to it became enshrined in such documents as the First Amendment to the U.S. Constitution, with its guarantee of freedom of the press. To its authors this meant freedom from licensing. They were determined that in the new nation no one would need government permission to communicate ideas to a wide public.

It is ironic that the RADIO broadcasting boom of the 1920s, raising the same issues, led to different results. The new medium needed licensing arrangements to prevent SPECTRUM chaos. Governments everywhere took charge and assigned channels. But the implications were the same: licensees became a new kind of gatekeeper. To protect their status they were inclined to be cautious.

The necessity of the arrangement was soon taken for granted, but as radio and television (*see* TELEVISION HISTORY) became for many people the main sources of ideas about the world and its problems—and about proposed solutions—the gatekeeper control fueled increasing dissatisfaction and stimulated citizen access movements. A number of governments and licensing commissions sought ways to accommodate the pressures and protests.

Access devices. Various access mechanisms have been proposed and tried. An especially unusual plan was developed in the Netherlands and has governed its radio and television policies. The government decided to operate the transmission facilities itself but divided the programming role among major citizen groups representing diverse interests such as politics, religion, and organized labor. New groups can win a share of the time by achieving a required scale of membership. Each group has produced programs designed to reach the widest possible audience while keeping them in harmony with its own ideals and beliefs, which are only occasionally articulated. The system provides access on a group basis; the individual, to gain access, must look to his or her group.

A number of countries—Great Britain and the Federal Republic of Germany, among others—have provided arrangements for individual access by setting aside time periods under such titles as "Open Door" and "Free Time" to accommodate statements from individuals on a large range of topics. Some commercial stations in the United States have likewise established arrangements for "speak out" or "free speech" messages, sometimes between programs. The selection of such messages has generally been determined by a panel chosen for this purpose.

Another approach, which has gained momentum in a number of countries in the decades since World War II, has been the authorization of noncommercial stations with very limited power and range, so that many can be accommodated. The most extreme example has been the Japanese "mini FM stations," which do not even require a license if radiation is confined to a half-mile radius. They tend to become neighborhood projects and are felt to develop a community ethos. The United States has developed analogous "community stations," mostly volunteer operated. An important transition is felt to be made when citizens become shapers (not merely consumers) of messages. A critical media awareness is generated. The stations tend toward programming that challenges commercial norms in content and form.

A limitation in all such devices is that while giving scope to dissent they also segregate it. They have been compared to Britain's traditional Hyde Park corner, where dissenters were permitted to let off steam with little peril to established institutions. At the same time, such access devices have provided media experience and created a determination to widen it. Far from diffusing the access movement, they have intensified it.

Right to reply. An important phase of access movements has revolved around the right to reply to one-sided uses of media by licensed broadcasters. A number of countries have enacted laws establishing such a right, especially when defamation is involved, but sometimes permitting wider application, as illustrated by the Fairness Doctrine in the United States. Initiated as a policy statement by the Federal Communications Commission (FCC), it was enacted as law in 1959. It required licensees to deal with "issues of public importance" and to air "conflicting views." Commercial broadcasters protested that this formula would actually inhibit vigorous journalism or pad it with "fairness filler." The doctrine may have done so, but it was also credited with unusual achievements. In 1967 Washington lawyer John Banzhaf III argued before the FCC that broadcasters accepting cigarette advertising, which persistently linked cigarettes with romance and vigor, should be obliged to give comparable time—free, as a matter of the public interest—to data about the relation of cigarettes to lung cancer and other diseases. In the context of the fairness law the FCC upheld this view, and a wave of messages from health agencies began to assault the cigarette so effectively that Congress decided to ban cigarette advertising from the air after 1970.

Another Fairness Doctrine achievement involved a major television station in the South, the NBC outlet WLBT-TV in Jackson, Mississippi. The population of its area was 45 percent black. But a fairness complaint pointed out, on the basis of a months-long monitoring study under the Reverend Everett C. Parker of the New York headquarters of the United Church of Christ, that the station totally ignored the black segment of its audience. It carried no news of events, local or national, about blacks. Network bulletins on the Martin Luther King campaigns for racial justice were interrupted with the notice "Sorry, Cable Trouble." No blacks, on or off the air, were involved in station programming. A number of white ministers, but no black ministers, received airtime. The station was accused of presenting "a distorted picture of vital issues," a disservice to whites and blacks alike. The FCC, reprimanding the station, still decided to renew its license, but the United Church pursued the matter through litigation, and the station license was voided through court action—a rare occurrence that brought sweeping changes in hiring and program policies at many stations.

Broadcasters continued to denounce the law as an unwarranted government intrusion and a violation of freedom of the press. The FCC itself, taken aback by what it had set in motion, pressed for repeal of the law. In the 1980s, a time of deregulation, the law was seldom implemented.

Cable access. Meanwhile access groups focused on an arena of rising importance: CABLE TELEVISION. Early cable systems had carried only about a dozen channels. In the 1970s cable operators in the United States, seeking licenses in major cities, were proposing systems of a hundred channels or more, made feasible by evolving technologies. Access proponents argued that in any such system at least one channel should be devoted to public access—on a first-come, first-served basis. A number of cities adopted the idea as a license requirement, and public access channels became a feature of more than a thousand cable systems. In many the system was required to maintain a studio for the purpose.

Results were mixed. In some cases there were hours of talking heads. Yet by the middle of the 1970s vigorous groups in every state were making their own television and gaining momentum. In 1976 they formed the National Federation of Local Cable Programmers, which served as a valuable coordinating organization, furthering the access philosophy and establishing liaisons with access groups elsewhere, especially in Europe and Latin America. Program exchanges were arranged. The impact achieved by some of the groups enabled them to raise funds, engage paid staff, organize rigorous training sessions, acquire more sophisticated equipment, and keep it in good order. Because of the importance of the equipment factor, some groups tended to become dominated by technologically skilled individuals inclined to favor technical quality over content. A quest for large audiences also became noticeable in some groups. It became the role of the federation to counter such tendencies and, in national conferences and local workshops, to reemphasize the original purpose of the access movement: an alternative to dominant communication trends and systems. In fulfilling this mission, another new medium became an invaluable adjunct.

Access by video. The VIDEO medium, like cable, started as something different from what it would become. Beginning as a technology used by networks to make copies of live telecasts for rerun or archive storage (*see* ARCHIVES), it gradually blossomed into an independent means of communication. Its use for public service purposes was especially pioneered by the National Film Board of Canada (NFB). In 1967 the NFB formed a unit called Challenge for Change, instructed to "create a dialogue between the ordinary citizens of Canada and those public servants shaping social programs that influenced so many of their lives." Film, the medium first chosen for these "mediated dialogues," proved too expensive, slow, and cumbersome. Also, film meant that community members had to rely on professional operators to record and edit their messages. By switching to video portapaks, which arrived from Japan in the late 1960s, the Challenge for Change staff found that people could quickly become their own mediators. Submerged and isolated population groups began to communicate meaningfully with government and in the process acquired a new sense of their own identity. Cable systems, at this time proliferating in Canada, began to welcome some of their productions. As video technology improved and achieved broadcast quality, the programs also found niches on Canadian stations and networks.

In the United States independent filmmakers likewise turned to video. For a time they were content to show their works in closed sessions in their own lofts, campus and community centers, and small theaters. But they too began to find outlets in cable television and occasionally on-the-air television. They saw themselves as a new AVANT-GARDE movement. They were determined to "demystify the media." A self-styled guerrilla television movement developed, with its own publication, *Radical Software*.

But video meant more than access to cable systems, stations, and networks. It could also bypass these licensed media. With video players winning a place in millions of homes, schools, union halls, churches, and other centers, it meant that videocassettes and series could reach far-flung audiences without benefit of gatekeepers. Distribution systems would be needed, by subscription or otherwise, but official licensees were no longer an obstacle. The genie was out of the bottle. The linking of religious, labor, and other groups via video gained momentum in various parts of the world, as in the Islamic countries (*see* ISLAMIC WORLD, TWENTIETH CENTURY) and Latin America. In Brazil video groups of various kinds became linked in an organization called Video Popular.

That media under a licensing system inevitably reflect the values of dominant groups has long been taken for granted but never quite accepted. Access movements are fueled by the politics of dissent. In many areas of political turbulence, including the Middle East, Central America, and parts of Africa and South Asia, they produce the phenomenon of clandestine stations, beyond official control. Even in more settled regions unlicensed, illegal stations spring up from time to time and are sometimes ignored by authorities unless they are felt to go too far. In the 1980s Spain had a rash of such low-power ventures, largely tolerated, occasionally raided. Elsewhere dissident groups probe for openings in standard broadcasting but may also make use of such specialties as amateur radio and CITIZENS BAND RADIO to promote their ideas. The extraordinary worldwide dominance of the broadcast media seems a guarantee that concerns over access will continue to produce criticism and experimentation.

See also AGENDA-SETTING; ETHICS, MEDIA; GOVERNMENT REGULATION; MINORITIES IN THE MEDIA; MINORITY MEDIA.

Bibliography. Kirsten Beck, *Cultivating the Wasteland*, New York, 1983; Mary Louise Hollowell, ed., *The Cable/Broadband Communications Book*, Vols. 1–4, Washington, D.C., 1977–1985; Lorenzo W. Milam, *Sex and Broadcasting: A Handbook on Starting a Radio Station for the Community*, 3d ed., Los Gatos, Calif., 1975; Jennifer Stearns, *A Short Course in Cable*, New York, 1981.

GEORGE C. STONEY

CITIZENS BAND RADIO (CB RADIO)

A two-way RADIO service used by private citizens in the United States for personal or business-related voice communication. Transmissions take place in the VHF band at 27 megahertz (MHz). The Citizens Radio Service was authorized by the Federal Communications Commission (FCC) in 1949 as a democratic experiment in short-range point-to-point radio. Although the public has always owned the airwaves in the United States, transmission privileges have been limited mostly to a small number of licensed broadcasters charged to transmit in the public interest as defined by the FCC and the courts as well as to some other groups concerned with protecting property and public safety. Over three decades Citizens Radio grew from a tiny service used mostly by small-business owners, truckers, farmers, and a few other individuals into the largest radio service administered by the FCC. As CB lore and practice became an arena of mass CULTURE in which millions of Americans participated, the FCC was forced to abandon its efforts to restrict Citizens Radio to a narrow range of uses and to implement a populist rather than paternalistic ethos of personal radio use. *See* TELECOMMUNICATIONS POLICY.

Radar research during World War II dramatically expanded the portion of the electromagnetic SPECTRUM available for radio transmission, inspiring the FCC to imagine many new peacetime radio services. Among them was a cheap, widely available service requiring minimal technical proficiency and intended to assist citizens in their pursuit of work and LEISURE activities. Authorized originally in the 460–470 MHz band (UHF), the Citizens Radio Service had two classes. Class A was used by industrial and public service operators able to afford the expensive equipment required for reliable operation at this frequency. Class B users were small businesses and individual operators. A third class, C, was assigned to 27.255 MHz for remote-control operation of garage-door openers and model boats and airplanes. In Class B the FCC expected small entrepreneurial establishments like bakeries and dry cleaners to communicate with local delivery truck fleets, and individuals to conduct radio communication to facilitate work and recreation. The FCC considered idle chit-chat an improper use of the service from the beginning. Nevertheless, some operators used it for this purpose, and over the years this became its most popular use.

Although Class A prospered in the 1950s, citizen adoption in Class B was minimal. Few manufacturers found a profitable market for Class B gear since affordable equipment was technically unreliable. The FCC began to phase out Class B in 1958 and reallocated most of the 460–470 MHz band to the industrial radio services. Twenty-three channels between 26.96 MHz and 27.23 MHz, a bandwidth roughly the size of a single television station, were reallocated from the Amateur Radio Service (ham radio) to a new Class D for individual personal use. Users were limited to a maximum output of four watts of power (giving them an operating range of fifteen to thirty miles) and a time limit of five minutes on each transmission followed by two minutes of silence.

Almost as soon as reliable, easily operated, inexpensive gear came on the market the FCC found itself in conflict with a large group of Class D users who ignored rules for both message content and calling procedures. According to long-standing FCC policy, hobby use was restricted to the Amateur Radio Service, where technically sophisticated and disciplined operators were licensed by examination. Class D users were often neither disciplined nor obedient to FCC rules. There is some evidence that despite its democratic rhetoric the FCC assumed Class D would attract mainly affluent users, such as physicians, for whom radio would be convenient in their work or in elite leisure pursuits such as flying, yachting, and mountain climbing. Many Class D hobbyists, in fact, were rural or blue-collar operators with little interest in an official radio etiquette that enforced upper-middle-class standards of propriety.

Radio etiquette was not the only source of conflict between the FCC and Class D users. Possession of a license was not a precondition for the purchase of radio equipment, and licenses were often delayed in the administrative backlog created by the band's growing popularity. Increasing numbers of users operated without licenses and without any knowledge of FCC rules and policies. The use of rural dialect forms, ham radio lingo, identifying nicknames called "handles" in lieu of call letters, and the police-10 CODE also created groups that operated by their own conventions, many of which violated FCC rules. Some groups engaged in informal self-policing to minimize disruption. By 1961 the Citizens band was the fastest growing of all radio services.

For a time the FCC attempted to control wayward users. It issued stricter regulations and adopted a license application fee (see GOVERNMENT REGULATION). It imposed disciplinary actions for violations such as using obscene language and broadcasting above prescribed power limits. It dismissed repeated petitions for more permissive rules that it said were not in the public interest. The emergence of a few dominant manufacturers by the late 1960s created an atmosphere of greater accommodation on both sides. To protect its $300 million market (estimated at $2 billion at the peak of CB popularity in the late 1970s), the industry attempted to promote more responsible user operation. In turn, the FCC began to relax its more restrictive rules.

This development was interrupted by the Middle East oil embargo in 1973, which struck a decisive blow to FCC control of Citizens Radio. During the embargo CB radios were used by truckers to communicate about availability of scarce gasoline supplies and to coordinate widely publicized traffic blockades that protested the lower speed limits imposed during the oil crisis. Thousands of motorists began to buy and use CB radios to avoid speeding tickets. In the first year after the oil embargo nearly a million Class D licensees and several million more unlicensed operators were estimated to be active on the Citizens band. The FCC was overwhelmed by new license applications. It had scant enforcement staff to attend to widespread rule violations by licensees and no power to move against unlicensed operators. These last came within the jurisdiction of the Federal Bureau of Investigation, for whom CB abuse was a relatively unimportant priority. Serious channel congestion, reduced operating range, and television interference resulted.

Ironically, the mass invasion of CB airwaves caused by the oil crisis crowded off the air many small CB communities that had previously angered the FCC by engaging in idle chitchat. These were small groups of mutually acquainted operators who communicated mostly among themselves. New operators put the band to imaginative and often illicit uses. Antibusing demonstrators in Boston organized activities by CB radio. Coffee thieves in San Francisco used it to advertise their wares at discount prices. Evangelists used CB radio to coordinate Bible distribution, and prostitution rings used it to solicit clients. Private volunteer groups also monitored CB transmissions to assist in relaying aid to motorists in distress.

In 1975 the FCC dropped its rule against casual communication. Major revisions were enacted in 1976 when the Citizens Radio Service became the Personal Radio Service. Class A was renamed General Mobile Radio Service, and Class D became Citizens Band (CB). In 1979 the Safety and Special Services Bureau, which administered the original Citizens Radio Service, was reorganized as the Private Radio Bureau. Seventeen new frequencies were assigned to the congested CB service, raising the total number of channels to forty.

From a base of 4 million authorized transmitters before 1973, a peak of 45 million authorized transmitters was operating by 1979. Until 1978 the FCC kept records of both authorized stations and transmitters. Licenses were issued to stations, which might operate multiple transmitters. From 1973 to 1977 the ratio of stations to transmitters was between one to three and one to four. After 1978 the FCC no longer kept figures for transmitters. Following a peak of almost 15 million stations in 1979, however, the number of authorized stations dropped sharply, leveling off to about 10 million by 1981. The extent of unlicensed operation has never been determined, but estimates during the period of peak CB popularity consistently added tens of millions of illegal transmitters to authorized-use figures. In 1983 the FCC delicensed CB radio altogether. Arguing that the paperwork burden required to administer licensing outweighed any public benefit to be derived from it, the FCC authorized individual Citizens band operation without individual licenses and shifted enforcement efforts to STANDARDS for technical equipment.

Although most widespread in the United States, CB radio also exists in the Federal Republic of Germany, Sweden, France, Italy, Holland, Canada, and Mexico. Except for certain restricted business practices, CB radio is generally illegal in these countries; it is entirely illegal in Mexico.

See also CITIZEN ACCESS; INTERACTIVE MEDIA; TELECOMMUNICATIONS NETWORKS.

Bibliography. Erwin G. Krasnow, Lawrence D. Longley, and Herbert A. Terry, *The Politics of Broadcast Regulation*, 3d ed., New York, 1982; Carolyn Marvin and Quentin J. Schultze, "The First Thirty Years: CB in Perspective," *Journal of Communication* 27 (1977): 104–117.

CAROLYN MARVIN

CLASSICISM

The terms *classic* and *classicism* are applied to works in virtually any medium of expression, ancient or modern. They can come into play in discussing or analyzing public buildings, fashion designs, films, ORATORY, music, furniture, or works of literature. Behind the terms is the view that artistic excellence can best be approximated by the imitation of approved models from a particular period. These are to be studied in terms of their forms, moods, attitudes, and the kinds of ideas or feelings they communicate. The architects who built the first Greek temples must have had a working theory (although no written record survives) governing the proportions of length, breadth, and height, and the most

satisfactory combination of the building's parts (*see* ARCHITECTURE). Architects who have imitated such buildings have kept within a limited set of mathematical relationships and have used the same structural ingredients, individual expression being confined to certain details of ornament.

Origins

The first clear formulation of classicism is found in Greek stylistic RHETORIC, the main treatises being *On Style*, attributed to one Demetrius (second century B.C.E.); *On the Ancient Orators* and *On Literary Composition*, by Dionysius of Halicarnassus (early first century B.C.E.); *On Sublimity*, by one Longinus (first century C.E.); and *On Types of Style*, by Hermogenes (second century C.E.). The procedure in all these treatises is the same; certain qualities of style are defined, such as the grand, the elegant, the plain, and the forceful (with their opposites, the frigid, the affected, the arid, the unpleasant). The writer then breaks up style into its linguistic components—vocabulary, arrangement of words, syntax, rhetorical figures—and shows how each of these is treated in each of the main styles. The treatises are illustrated

Figure 1. *(Classicism)* Donato Bramante, the Tempietto, 1508. San Pietro in Montorio, Rome. Alinari/Art Resource, New York.

Figure 2. *(Classicism)* Annibale Carracci, *Polyphemos*, 1596–1600. Detail of ceiling frescoes in the Farnese Gallery, Farnese Palace, Rome. Alinari/Art Resource, New York.

Figure 3. *(Classicism)* Robert Adam, furniture designs for the villa of Kenwood, mid-eighteenth century. Giraudon/Art Resource, New York.

with quotations from a wide range of literature, from Homer to the Greek version of the New Testament, and the budding writer is encouraged to imitate the best authors. In Dionysius the concentration on approved models results in the formulation of the canon of the "ten Attic orators," who are analyzed in terms of the traditional rhetorical concept of the hierarchy of styles (high, middle, and low) and whose work as a whole constitutes a corpus of classical expression and defines the range of correct writing. *See* STYLE, LITERARY.

The Greek stylistic rhetoric books all date from the Hellenistic period (*see* HELLENIC WORLD). Rhetoric was then establishing itself in Rome, and an educational system based on it was evolving that was to spread throughout the ROMAN EMPIRE and, after the RENAISSANCE, throughout the West. Two crucial formative elements in this system were the analysis of the components of style, especially in the CLASSIFICATION of expressive devices known as the rhetorical tropes and figures (*see* METAPHOR), and the TEACHING of composition by the graded imitation of models. In the *progymnasmata* (preliminary exercises taught in the grammar schools) pupils started with simple forms such as the fable, the maxim, and mythological NARRATIVE and learned how to collect material, organize it according to the rules of each GENRE, and illustrate it with appropriate devices. This technique of *imitatio* took in more complex forms, such as encomium, denunciation, speeches in character or impersonation, and even works in the style of a given author.

When Renaissance educationalists revived the

Greco-Roman teaching methods, these composition exercises became a fundamental part of school curricula, and an "Allusion to Horace" or an "Imitation of Juvenal" was a recognized form of POETRY up to the time of the British writers Alexander Pope and SAMUEL JOHNSON in the early eighteenth century, and indeed later. The school exercises of the German dramatist Georg Büchner at the gymnasium in Darmstadt in the 1820s included speeches imagined to be spoken by Menenius Agrippa to the Roman people and by Cato in his own defense. The French novelist Gustave Flaubert, in the lycée in Rouen a few years later, wrote six "narrations" (stories set in some past period) that count among his earliest compositions. The imitation of classical models was a basic educational method up to the end of the nineteenth century, and its influence was often beneficial. As the French scholar Gérard Genette has noted, the writer setting out on a career could regard the early years of that career not as a rupture with years spent at school but as their fulfillment.

Expression in the Arts

The value of imitation has often been disputed, especially since ROMANTICISM gave rise to an alternative procedure, but it can be said in its defense that fostering artistic inspiration around extant models does not necessarily inhibit individual expression. The history of painting since the Renaissance shows that drawing from life or obeying the conventions of fixed-point perspective has not erased differences among artists. The rediscovery of antiquity in the Renaissance generated a massive phase of imitating classical models that produced distinctly individual ART works. The plays of Seneca were imitated throughout Europe, but the results range from the truly academic Latin DRAMA of the Jesuits to the static closet drama of the French and the bloodthirsty revenge tragedies of the English popular THEATER. In music the Florentine Camerata, at the end of the sixteenth century, were inspired by an attempt to imitate Greek music (see MUSIC HISTORY). Renaissance humanism, essentially a language-based movement, had already emphasized the importance of the meaning of the words being set to music, and the Camerata applied this principle polemically, attacking medieval polyphony on the ground that several voice parts singing at once and at different rates could only obscure the sense. Guided by what they thought Greek texts to mean, the Camerata introduced monody, the principle of one voice singing or declaiming over an accompaniment, the resulting new relation between words and music leading to the invention of OPERA.

The examples of Senecan drama and Florentine monody show that classicism can produce quite un-expected artistic consequences, great variations within a form, and even the invention of new forms. They also illuminate two further aspects of this movement: first, that the "classic" is a relative concept with widely different meanings in different geographical or historical contexts; and second, that resort to classicism is an artistic choice that can imply a rejection of other choices. Renaissance humanists consciously rejected the AESTHETICS of the MIDDLE AGES (if not always to the extent they claimed), returning to classical models to find styles and genres that would better fulfill the requirements of unity, coherence, and expressiveness. The discovery of fixed-point perspective in early quattrocento Florence is one sign of a new demand that works of art should cohere, and it is no accident that the first theorist of this movement, Leon Battista Alberti, was deeply influenced by classical rhetoric and that his two treatises, De Pictura (1436) and De re Aedificatoria (1450–1472), passed on to the language and the thought of artists many of the formative principles of rhetoric.

Throughout these three centuries the ideas formulated by such classic writers as Longinus and Hermogenes, CICERO and Quintilian, Horace and Pliny, continued to form the way painters, sculptors, and architects thought about their art. The rhetorical theories were supplemented by specific ancient texts that provided practical models. The rediscovery of the Roman architect Vitruvius's De architectura, written in the first century B.C.E., and its diligent study by Renaissance architects and theater designers led to a second wave of classicism as the work of the Italian architect Andrea Palladio, for instance, influenced English architects from Inigo Jones in the seventeenth century to William Wilkins in the Greek Revival of the early nineteenth century.

Just as the notion of the classic shifts, so do the chosen models within the pantheon. If Roman architecture was the inspiring phase for the Renaissance, baroque classicism looked more toward Hellenism, with the treatises of Hermogenes and Longinus influencing poetry, painting, and music. In the movement known as neoclassicism, which dates from the mid-eighteenth century, a new impetus came from the excavations just begun at Pompeii and Herculaneum; ornamental motifs from the wall paintings discovered at these sites soon found their way into interior decorators' pattern books (see MURAL). The Italian artist Giambattista Piranesi's engravings of ancient Rome, both real and imaginary, were another element, as were the aesthetic treatises of the German painter Anton Raphael Mengs and the German art historian Johann Winckelmann, both steeped in Roman antiquities. Classicism now had more explicitly formulated ideals of simplicity, grace, and harmony, as can be seen in the paintings of

Figure 4. *(Classicism)* Giambattista Piranesi, *The Arch of Constantine and the Colosseum*, 1770s. From the *Views of Rome.* Alinari/Art Resource, New York.

Figure 5. *(Classicism)* Thomas Jefferson, Monticello, Charlottesville, Virginia, 1770–1806. The Bettmann Archive, Inc.

Figure 6. *(Classicism)* Antonio Canova, *The Three Graces*, ca. 1790. Alinari/Art Resource, New York.

Figure 7. *(Classicism)* Pablo Picasso, *The Three Bathers*, 1922. Art Resource, New York.

Jacques-Louis David and the SCULPTURE of Antonio Canova. Yet during this period the attempt to evaluate the literature of the past according to neoclassical literary theory (*see* LITERARY CRITICISM), as evolved in France by Nicolas Boileau-Despréaux and André Dacier and in England by John Dryden and John Dennis, produced a critical dilemma. William Shakespeare was venerated as the greatest of dramatists, but once the theoretical expectations of neoclassicism (such as the separation of TRAGEDY and COMEDY, the maintaining of decorum, the avoidance of puns) were applied to Shakespeare, his work could only be found wanting. In romanticism, with its rebellion against rules and systems, Shakespeare came to be seen as a writer "without art," a distortion of the true estimate of his work albeit in the opposite direction.

Legacies

If classicism emerged in the Renaissance as a reaction against medievalism, it has been reacted against in its turn by romanticism, REALISM, and modernism (*see* AVANT-GARDE). Concepts that had been of value in helping the writer to establish a style and to unify material now came to be seen as restrictive, a system

from which the artist had to be liberated in order to be authentic or to express his or her own experiences directly. Yet when romanticism came to be seen as having overextended itself, as having exhausted the expressive possibilities of personal subjectivity, some artists in the 1920s returned to classical motifs, forms, and styles. The graphic work of Pablo Picasso and the music of Igor Stravinsky and Paul Hindemith are examples of this third wave of classicism. In the early literary theory of T. S. Eliot more personal motives, such as the wish to preserve a sense of his own privacy, led to an aesthetic of impersonality, of the absorbing of individual talent into the tradition. In this phase classicism shows more strongly than ever its inherent conservatism, its rejection of the contemporary for some previous and better existence. Classicism is not necessarily, but can become, reactionary.

Yet as an ideal expressed above all in architecture, classicism will always be with us. The public buildings of many great Western cities are modeled on the Greek temple, yet they were built at any time between 1800 and 1940. And "classic" is a concept that can be used to subsume other period labels, in the sense that classical music, as a category distinguished from jazz or popular music, includes works by both romantic and modern composers, just as the epithet "classic" can be applied to filmmakers or fashion designers who are nothing if not contemporary.

See also POETICS.

Bibliography. K. Borinski, *Die Antike in Poetik und Kunsttheorie vom Ausgang des klassischen Altertums bis auf Goethe und Wilhelm von Humboldt*, Leipzig, 1914–1924; T. S. Eliot, "Tradition and the Individual Talent," in *Selected Essays, 1917–1932*, 3d enl. ed., London, 1972; idem, *What Is a Classic?* London, 1945; Michael Greenhalgh, *The Classical Tradition in Art*, London, 1978; Hugh Honour, *Neoclassicism*, Harmondsworth, Eng., 1968; Erwin Panofsky, *Renaissance and Renascences in Western Art*, Stockholm, 2d ed., 1965, reprint London, 1970; Dominique Secrétan, *Classicism*, London, 1973; C. C. Vermeule, *European Art and the Classical Past*, Cambridge, Mass., 1964; Brian Vickers, *In Defence of Rhetoric*, Oxford, 1987; Roberto Weiss, *The Renaissance Discovery of Classical Antiquity*, Oxford, 1969; René Wellek, "The Term and Concept of Classicism in Literary History," in *Aspects of the 18th Century*, ed. by Earl R. Wasserman, Baltimore, Md., and London, 1965.

BRIAN VICKERS

CLASSIFICATION

Classification is intrinsic to the use of LANGUAGE, hence to most if not all communication. Whenever we use nominative phrases we are classifying the designated subject as being importantly similar to other entities bearing the same designation; that is, we classify them together. Similarly the use of predicative phrases classifies actions or properties as being of a particular kind. We call this *conceptual* classification, since it refers to the classification involved in conceptualizing our experiences and surroundings. A second, narrower sense of classification is the *systematic* classification involved in the design and utilization of taxonomic schemes such as the biological classification of animals and plants by genus and species. Both senses of classification are important to the conceptualization and communication of knowledge, in ordinary social and cultural intercourse as well as in science. Closely related are the notion of conceptual frameworks and ideas about their role in cultural and linguistic relativity. Theories about conceptual and systematic classification have conditioned our understanding of the communication of fact and interpretation within science, as well as their dissemination to the public.

Theories about Classification

Beginning with the seminal works of PLATO (ca. 428–348/347 B.C.E.) and ARISTOTLE (384–322 B.C.E.), philosophers have developed theories about the nature of classification.

Conceptual classification. To say that two or more things are of the same kind—that they are chairs, for example—is to say that they share some common essence or *universal*. Theories about the nature of conceptual classification have centered traditionally on analyses of such universals. *Realism* maintains that such universals exist in their own right no matter how people conceptualize their experiences: if the essence of being a chicken is being a feathered biped, then two chickens belong in the same classification by virtue of possessing the properties of being feathered and bipedal regardless of whether anyone has so conceived chickens. By contrast, *conceptualism* maintains that such universals or essences are mind-dependent, and thus two things are correctly classified as chickens only if they conform to a general mental concept—for example, they both conform to the concept of a feathered biped. Such general concepts, according to this view, are inherent in our sensory experience of chickens. *Nominalism* denies that there is *any* common essence or universal the possession of which is the basis for classifying things as being of the same sort: all that is shared by chickens is that we use the same word, *chicken*, with reference to each of them. *Resemblance theories* also deny that there is any common essence, mental or physical, by virtue of which things are classified as the same kind; rather, things are classified together by virtue of a family or other shared resemblance. Thus some chickens may be plucked and others legless, and so they are not classified together by virtue of the shared feathered biped essence; resemblance theories argue that, plucked or not, legged or not, they resemble each other and so are classified together.

There is considerable unresolved controversy about which is the correct theory of universals. That controversy is reflected in conflicting views of what are the correct definitional forms to use in establishing systematic classifications in science.

Systematic classification. Biological classification is the paradigm. Individual classes known as taxa are organized into a scheme—typically a hierarchical classification scheme with such levels as species, genus, family, order, class, phylum, and kingdom; each individual organism belongs to exactly one taxon on each level of the hierarchy. Not all systematic classifications or *taxonomies* are hierarchical. For example, Mendeleyev's periodic table of the chemical elements has eight groups, but these are just the taxa, and each element occurs in exactly one of them. Taxonomies typically provide fairly specific membership criteria or definitions for taxon membership.

Aristotle, who wrote the first treatise on systematic classification, *De partibus animalum*, and introduced the notions of genus and species, required that the definitions of species taxa specify the essences of the species. After the RENAISSANCE this was expanded to the idea that definitions should give necessary and sufficient conditions for taxon membership. Depending on the conditions chosen, the taxonomies were viewed as natural or artificial—the latter typically not involving specifying essences. Different theories of universals favor different interpretations of what these essences consist in, hence of natural and artificial taxonomies. For example, Aristotle had a realist view of essences, whereas the Comte de Buffon (1707–1788), a French naturalist, held a nominalist position and denied any natural taxonomies. Michel Adanson (1727–1806) held a resemblance theory and distinguished natural from artificial taxonomies on the basis of the sorts of affinities shared by members of the same taxon.

The joining of evolutionary biology and genetics in the twentieth century raised serious challenges to the idea that taxa always can be defined in terms of necessary and sufficient conditions. As evolution works on a species, the diagnostic phenotypic characteristics used to characterize the species may undergo changes so radical that what once were definitive markers of the species fail to be possessed by members of later generations. Thus there may be no necessary features for species membership, just an open-ended variety of clusters of sufficient conditions. Other philosophers, such as LUDWIG WITTGENSTEIN (1889–1951), argued that there are many classes (e.g., games) whose members do not share one common or essential characteristic. Peter Achinstein (1935–) argued that concepts defining many natural taxa lack jointly sufficient conditions and suggested that at best such cluster concepts can be defined by listing a set of relevant concepts of which a good number must be possessed to qualify for taxon membership. Out of these observations emerges the idea that the choice of appropriate definitional form for taxon membership is not a matter of logic or a priori considerations but, rather, of the sorts of empirical regularities that obtain between diagnostic characteristics and species- or other taxon-making characteristics. Numerical taxonomists maintain that these relationships are no more than statistical correlations.

These diverse views about suitable definitional forms for taxa have been put to interesting empirical tests. Attempts by numerical taxonomists to use statistical "cluster analysis" to generate biological taxonomies have had rather uneven results. Although trial attempts to classify artificial organisms have been quite successful, when the techniques are used with real specimens, the taxonomies generated often cannot be replicated easily; similarly, attempts to use cluster analysis in medical diagnosis and disease classification have proved fairly unsatisfactory. On the other hand, in certain social science studies, such as the Kinsey Institute study of types of homosexuals, tax-

onomies generated by cluster analysis have proved highly replicable. ARTIFICIAL INTELLIGENCE attempts to develop computer programs for medical diagnosis and other forms of classification have experimented with a number of definitional forms. Attempts based on definitions of taxa in terms of essences have not proved very successful. The most promising approaches generate taxa on the basis of causal and other discovered empirical relationships. Collectively, these results strongly suggest that developing criteria for taxon membership is more a matter of developing scientific theories than of forming definitions.

Conceptual Frameworks, Classification, and Relativity

A language carries with it conceptual classification schemes often called *conceptual frameworks*. Different languages have different conceptual frameworks, and so it is easier to express certain ideas or view things in a particular way in one language than in another (*see* LANGUAGE IDEOLOGY; LANGUAGE VARIETIES). For example, one of the fascinations with pre-Socratic Greek philosophers comes from reading their struggle to express ideas for which the language provided no ready means of straightforward expression. Heracleitus (ca. 535–ca. 475 B.C.E.), for example, resorted to puns to get at ideas for which there was no abstract vocabulary. German is far better suited for expressing G. W. F. Hegel's ideas than is English. Some ideas may be virtually impossible to express in the conceptual framework of one language, whereas those of other languages may be quite congenial. For example, modern quark theory or quantum theory in physics is quite expressible in contemporary scientific English but would be impossible to render in the conceptual framework of classical Greek.

Thus there is a considerable degree of conceptual and classificatory relativity among languages. Some scholars have gone much further in the degree of cultural relativity they claim for different languages. U.S. linguist BENJAMIN LEE WHORF (1897–1941) claimed that a language's conceptual framework determined one's ontology—that users of different languages could live in different worlds. While users of standard European languages live in a world populated with things that undergo *activities*, the conceptual frameworks of languages such as Eskimo and Hopi create a world in which *processes* are the basic ontological furniture. Whereas Europeans and users of related language families live in a world with walruses that *do* various things, the Eskimo, for example, live in a world populated with various characteristic walrus activities or walrus*ings*, such as walrus-sunnings, walrus-fishings, and walrus-eatings.

Whorf further claimed that it would be virtually impossible for "process languages" to develop science as we know it. The evidence for such extreme forms of cultural relativity is not compelling, but the more modest forms of linguistic relativity do obtain and have important implications for communication and the sorts of intellectual achievements a particular culture can easily accomplish. *See also* LINGUISTICS.

Classification in Scientific Method

One of the most characteristic features of science is that it concentrates its attention on only a few selected variables, ignoring most aspects of the studied phenomena. Thus Newton's laws ignore all aspects of bodily motions other than forces, positions, and momenta of the involved objects, treating them as frictionless point-masses acting in a vacuum. Similarly, in the nontheoretical, more descriptive parts of experimental science, a few variables are selected for study, and all other aspects of the phenomena are rendered irrelevant by means of experimental or statistical controls.

The choice of a set of variables for scientific study of a phenomenon tacitly involves the imposition of a classification scheme. The class of phenomena chosen for study constitutes a taxon in some implicit classificatory scheme—as, for example, Newton's decision to study the motions of systems with a finite number of interacting massive bodies. And the choice of a select set of variables to use in studying these phenomena typically involves the implicit claim that these variables, if not constituting the essence of the phenomena, at least are characteristic of any and all phenomena within the studied class or scope of the investigation.

In the twentieth century it has been commonplace to require that such implicit classificatory schemes be developed as systematic classifications or taxonomies as a precondition to scientific investigation or theorizing—in other words, that science must define its terms prior to commencing study. Operationalism and logical positivism in the philosophy of science, and behaviorism in the social sciences, are related intellectual movements that have made such definition essential to their conceptions of what it is to be scientific. All three share the following central ideas. Science must be grounded in observation, and any theoretical variables or terms that refer to phenomena that are not directly observable must be *operationally defined* in terms of what is observable. Initially operational definition was construed as the specification of necessary and sufficient conditions for the variables. This is tantamount to defining the theoretical variable as a taxon in which the definition specifies the essence of taxon membership. Later the notion of operational definition was loosened to in-

clude partial definitions that merely specify jointly sufficient conditions or even just clusters of potentially relevant observable diagnostic markers. (The latter correspond to the sorts of definitions of taxa discussed above that have emerged in modern biological taxonomy.) Thus, in these related views scientific theorizing has at its heart the establishment of a systematic taxonomy with theoretical taxa. In nontheoretical contexts, such as statistical descriptive studies, it similarly was required that theoretical constructs be operationally defined in ways that amount to the specification of a systematic taxonomy. Intelligence (IQ) tests operationally define intelligence in ways that establish a taxonomy of intelligences, and studies of mental health using the Minnesota Multiphasic Personality Inventory (MMPI) operationally define mental disorders in ways that establish a systematic classification scheme.

The demand that science proceed by establishing a systematic taxonomy through operational definition of terms as a precursor of empirical or theoretical study can be seriously challenged on a number of fronts. First, the most successful portions of physical science often do not proceed in this way. Operational definition of theoretical variables in physical science often does not occur until the later stages of a scientific investigation, well after the theory is in a stage of mature development. At the same time it must be noted that the development of a systematic taxonomy may be the essence of scientific theorizing, as in the periodic table of elements, which is itself a scientific theory. Second, scholars such as Thomas Kuhn (1922–) have argued that it generally is impossible to define operationally the basic variables of global scientific theories such as Newtonian physics or quantum mechanics. To the extent that these arguments are persuasive, it is impossible to require explicit development of taxonomies as a precursor to scientific theorizing. Third, if indeed the criteria for taxon membership are disguised patterns of empirical regularity best uncovered by empirical investigation, the proposal reduces to vicious circularity: it amounts to demanding definition of the variables as a precursor to doing the empirical investigations needed to uncover the patterns of regularity constituting the definitions in question.

The fact that the development of systematic taxonomies is not a necessary preliminary to doing good science does not imply that classification is not at the heart of doing science. For science to operate and for scientists to communicate with one another, it is essential that practitioners share a common way of looking at phenomena and a vocabulary for talking about them. Systematic taxonomies provide only one way of meeting this necessity. A number of contemporary philosophers of science, such as Kuhn, have argued that science proceeds from within a conceptual framework that performs this function and that, unlike systematic taxonomies, these frameworks, or weltanschauungs, cannot be explicitly formulated or articulated. Rather, they are more like what Wittgenstein calls a "form of life" that must be learned. Kuhn describes the process of training a scientist as a method of indoctrinating a fledgling scientist into coming to see the world and using vocabulary to describe it in the same way as do full-fledged members of the scientific community. Kuhn sees this process as being not unlike TEACHING a child to learn to use, think in terms of, and experience the world through the framework provided by a particular natural language (*see* CHILDREN—DEVELOPMENT OF COMMUNICATION; LANGUAGE ACQUISITION). That is, it is a process of coming to possess a conceptual classification scheme and associated language without the definitional development of a systematic classification scheme. While many of the specifics of Kuhn's view of science are controversial, he does make a convincing case that conceptual classification schemes are necessary for, and part and parcel of doing, science but need not always be obtained through the development of systematic taxonomies.

Classification and the Dissemination of Scientific Knowledge

Although the conceptual frameworks and classification schemes found in science are descended from those found in natural languages, they are different in content. Even when science borrows terminology from ordinary language, its expropriation involves its undergoing what Stephen Toulmin (1922–) calls a "language shift." Thus the Newtonian sense of "force" descends from the common pugilistic sense but has a different meaning, and quark "color" is quite unlike the colors of a sunset. Language shifts are involved in both the conceptual and the systematic classifications science employs. This poses a problem for the dissemination of scientific knowledge to nonscientists who have not undergone the acculturation through the training that Kuhn describes. To avoid communicative entropy in presenting science to the public, the public must be educated about the classifications science uses. Sometimes this is done by METAPHOR, analogy, or other heuristic means. Sometimes informal definitions "give the idea" of how science uses key vocabulary; these are rarely operational definitions but instead are glosses. Most important, things themselves—the objects of scientific study—are not that dissimilar for students, so teachers build on the students' experiences and experiments. Rather than burying students under masses of definitions, teachers give them exercises and problems to solve and thereby teach them to think and to experience the world through the classification

scheme of science. The questions asked and the background information utilized as presuppositions of science also invoke classifications and ways of viewing and approaching phenomena. In teaching students what questions to ask, scientists teach them how to classify and organize their experiences as fellow scientists do.

Classification and the Emergence of Modern Science

Conceptual classification has been seen to permeate the development of modern science just as it permeates all cognitive and communicative activity. Science characteristically refines and sophisticates its conceptual classifications as it matures. Thus there is an important sense in which *conceptual* classification is an essential component of the emergence of science, just as it is in the emergence of all knowledge. On the other hand, the role of *systematic* classification in the emergence of modern science is more variable. In some instances it has been the vehicle for major scientific advances: the periodic table, Carolus Linnaeus's (1707–1778) binomial system of taxonomy, soil classification schemes, and qualitative analysis in chemistry are examples. Other major scientific developments seem to eschew the explicit development of taxonomic schemes; this is characteristic of much of physics. In still other areas premature preoccupation with taxon definition and the development of taxonomic schemes seems to have hindered the development of modern science; phrenology and medical nosologies not based on common etiology are good examples. On the other hand, the selection of key variables to investigate and research questions to pursue is crucial to the success of a scientific investigation. To the extent that these choices implicitly invoke conceptual or systematic classificatory schemes, classification is at the very heart of the emergence of modern science.

See also CONTENT ANALYSIS; MODE.

Bibliography. Peter Achinstein, *Concepts of Science*, Baltimore, Md., 1968; D. M. Armstrong, *Universals and Scientific Realism*, 2 vols., Cambridge and New York, 1978; Carl G. Hempel, *Fundamentals of Concept Formation in Empirical Science*, Chicago, 1952; Paul Henle, ed., *Language, Thought, and Culture*, Ann Arbor, Mich., 1958; David L. Hull, *The Philosophy of Biological Science*, Englewood Cliffs, N.J., 1974; Linnean Society of London, *Lectures on the Development of Taxonomy 1948–1949*, London, 1950; Kenneth Schaffner, ed., *Logic of Discovery and Diagnosis in Medicine*, Berkeley, Calif., 1985; R. R. Sokal and P. H. A. Sneath, *Principles of Numerical Taxonomy*, San Francisco, 1963; Frederick Suppe, ed., *The Structure of Scientific Theories*, 2d ed., Urbana, Ill., 1977; Jerzy A. Wojciechowski, *Conceptual Basis of the Classifi-*

cation of Knowledge (Ottawa Conference on the Conceptual Basis of the Classification of Knowledge, 1971), Munich, 1974.

FREDERICK SUPPE

CLASSIFIED ADVERTISING

A special form of ADVERTISING, most common in print media, consisting of small notices classified according to theme (e.g., sale items), target audience (e.g., people looking for employment), or other criteria. Classified advertising, or something quite like it, has been traced back to "want ads" inscribed on papyrus in Egypt more than three thousand years ago (*see* EGYPTIAN HIEROGLYPHS), as well as to inscriptions on the walls of the Roman city of Pompeii (*see* ROMAN EMPIRE). In postmedieval Europe, handwritten notices known as *siquis* (from the Latin, "if anybody") appeared in England during the fifteenth century; they were used primarily by professionals of various trades. In the seventeenth century the term *advices* became increasingly common. The King James Bible, published in 1611, used *advertisement* to mean notification or warning. Book publishers and printers started to use the same term as a heading for commercial messages.

In the British North American colonies, classified advertising first appeared in the *Boston News-Letter* in 1704, when an ad offering a reward for the return of two anvils was printed (*see* NEWSPAPER: HISTORY). The New York *Sun* has been credited with the first grouping of small advertisements into a "want ad" section in 1830, starting what is known as the classified advertising section of modern newspapers. The emergence of the penny press (*see* DAY, BENJAMIN H.) helped develop the use of classified advertising by the reading public and also gave rise to the policy of charging for the messages (usually by the word, by the line, or by the column-inch).

Classified advertising can be characterized as "person-to-person" communication, in contrast to retail and national advertising, which are considered "business-to-person." Its advantages include low cost (because each ad uses only a few lines of copy), flexibility (because it can be used in many ways), and selectivity (because the reader may go directly to items of interest or need). It is subject to the same restrictions and regulations that pertain to other types of advertising in a print medium. Most of the restrictions are based on the principle that the publisher has the right to accept or reject ads that do not conform to house policies. Newspapers and magazines have been criticized for ads in their "personals" section because of the explicit or implicit content (e.g., ads for "escort services" or "massage parlors" as fronts for prostitution).

Classified advertising can be divided into two broad categories: professional and personal. The former is usually sold on a volume or contract basis and accounts for approximately 75 percent of the income from classifieds. The latter is generally sold on a single-message basis to individual customers. A further division arises from the manner in which the business is obtained. In some cases people call or bring in their own ads, while other ads are gathered by solicitors, who make their contacts by personal visits or telephone calls.

Most newspapers have a classification system that helps the reader find specifically what is needed. Typically the format includes some broad categories such as "Help Wanted," "Housework," and "Office Work," as well as other more specific labels (e.g., under "Help Wanted" a section for "Carpenters," under "Office Work" a section for "Secretaries"). In major cities it is extremely important to have a workable system of classification, whereas in smaller cities the system can be less complex. In general, the easier it is for readers to find what they need, the more readers the columns will attract.

On average more than 80 percent of classified revenue comes from automotive, real estate, and employment ads. It is estimated that more than 50 percent of people who are shopping for a car, nearly three-fourths of those looking for a house, and four out of five people seeking a job use the classified columns.

In most of the larger newspapers around the world the computer is already being used for composition, billing, credit checks, page makeup, updating and correction of ads, and improvement of the classification system. Some newspapers have started accepting ads directly from personal computers to the newspaper's mainframe computer (*see* COMPUTER: IMPACT).

On the international scene, a survey of sixteen newspapers in eight countries revealed no basic differences in the patterns of classified advertising from those of U.S. newspapers in terms of pricing, display of ads, typefaces, or marketing methods. One pronounced difference was that some papers mixed editorial and classified ad pages, instead of confining the classifieds to just one section.

Some newspapers have established ties with CABLE TELEVISION companies to reach larger audiences for classified advertising, as a way of facing increased competition from other print media such as telephone directories, "shoppers," and other specialized publications. In a number of countries experiments have been made with "electronic classified" advertising through teletext and VIDEOTEX. Although these systems have not yet had substantial success, they may hold long-range importance.

Bibliography. Association of Newspaper Classified Advertising Managers, *Principles and Practices of Classified Advertising*, Danville, Ill., 1985; Morton J. A. McDonald,

How to Use Classified Advertising to Sell More Real Estate, Englewood Cliffs, N.J., 1957; Morton J. A. McDonald and Bert Reh, eds., *Principles and Practices of Classified Advertising,* 2d ed., Culver City, Calif., 1952.

BILLY I. ROSS

CLASSROOM

For many children in the world the classroom is a critical site of transition and transformation between the intimate world of the FAMILY and the more impersonal, bureaucratized world of the larger society. Social scientists analyzing schools around the world (*see* SCHOOL) have identified certain characteristics that distinguish contemporary forms of interaction in the classroom from other forms of EDUCATION. In contemporary mass education—as opposed to education mainly for social, economic, political, or religious elites in older societies and civilizations—the human potential to be realized by individual students is the acquisition of knowledge and skills that will be related to later work and life status. Students compete for opportunities to perform as individuals, and there is no expectation that all will succeed. Teachers evaluate performance at immediate and long-term intervals by means of grades, promotion, and selection for higher levels of education (e.g., from high school to the UNIVERSITY level).

Patterns

The most common pattern of classroom communication is the recitation, in which the teacher interacts with a group of students, controlling the selection of topics and the allocation of turns (*see* INTERACTION, FACE-TO-FACE; INTERPERSONAL COMMUNICATION). Topics covered may have been predetermined by a school, district, state, or nationwide decision, and groups are typically homogeneous in terms of age and one or more measures of achievement as well.

Recitations usually consist of three parts: teacher initiation (often with a question), student response, and the teacher's evaluation. Teachers typically talk two-thirds of the time, and the remaining one-third is unevenly distributed among the students. In general, questions request factual answers retrievable from memory, student answers are short, and student comments or questions are ruled out of order unless they are perceived by the teacher as relevant and not an interruption.

Another common pattern of classroom social organization is more individualized. Children work alone on tasks assigned by the teacher, who monitors their progress either by circulating among them or by allowing them to approach the teacher's desk for help and evaluation. U.S. linguist Marilyn Merritt has called student-teacher conversations in these settings "service-like encounters," to suggest similarities to exchanges between customers and clerks in large service or commercial institutions such as banks, supermarkets, and government offices. Communication between the students—at least that approved by the teacher—is much less frequent.

Limitations. Schooling grounded on these most common types of classroom interaction has been a constant in the Western world since the nineteenth century, spreading to former colonies and newly formed nations (*see* COLONIZATION). Its pervasive presence suggests a functional fit with processes of industrialization (e.g., by allowing potential factory workers to gain skills needed for employment, such as LITERACY). However, critics have pointed out certain limitations. First, the recitation format biases the curriculum toward a conception of knowledge as emanating from authority, rather than constructed and critically analyzed anew by each learner. When teachers are poorly trained and classrooms lack adequate resources (e.g., blackboards, pictures, maps), the rote learning of words at the expense of deeper comprehension is a likely result (*see* AUDIOVISUAL EDUCATION).

Second, both the typical school content and the typical patterns of communication seem to be more useful for children of educated parents, who come to school already equipped with the cultural capital that schools assume and require. In these terms, mass education has both a hidden curriculum and an invisible culture. Third, education via words—removed from practical action—may have cognitive effects separable from the effects of literacy, but the very separation from the contexts of everyday life may impede the transfer of what is learned in the classroom to the out-of-school world (*see* COGNITION).

Special Issues

Two other issues deserve special mention: language of instruction and computers. With regard to the former, in many countries more than one language may be heard in each classroom, and teachers, researchers, and policymakers are still trying to discover why certain combinations seem to work so well in some contexts but not in others. As for computers, they are becoming a regular addition to an increasing number of classrooms (*see* COMPUTER: IMPACT—IMPACT ON EDUCATION). Their most common use is as providers of additional drill and practice—in effect, an electronic workbook. Their more complex applications make possible a return to the master-apprentice model of learning at its best, with opportunities for student questions and expert computer responses owing to imaginatively designed software. In addition, access to data bases (*see* DATA BASE) provides a rich source of information for posing and solving problems, and the capacity to communicate electronically from one classroom to another—whether next door or anywhere in the world—makes for a substantially richer learning environment.

See also TEACHING; TEXTBOOK.

Bibliography. Douglas Barnes, *From Communication to Curriculum*, London, 1976; Courtney B. Cazden, *Classroom Discourse*, London and Portsmouth, N.H., in press; Courtney B. Cazden, Vera P. John, and Dell Hymes, eds., *Functions of Language in the Classroom*, New York, 1972, reprint Prospect Heights, Ill., 1984; Elizabeth G. Cohen, *Designing Groupwork: Strategies for the Heterogeneous Classroom*, New York, 1986; A. D. Edwards and V. J. Furlong, *The Language of Teaching: Meaning in Classroom Interaction*, London, 1978; Shirley Brice Heath, *Ways with Words: Language, Life, and Work in Communities and Classrooms*, Cambridge and New York, 1983; Hugh Mehan, *Learning Lessons*, Cambridge, Mass., 1979; Michael Stubbs, *Language, Schools, and Classrooms*, 2d ed. (Contemporary Sociology of the School), London and New York, 1983.

COURTNEY BORDEN CAZDEN

CLAY TOKENS

The Neolithic cultures of western Asia created a system of clay tokens to count and keep track of goods. These three-dimensional symbols, which stood for units of merchandise, were a means of supplementing language and represent an early step toward WRITING. They foreshadow Sumerian CUNEIFORM writing in their use of clay, in which markings were incised or impressed.

Description. Tokens were of fifteen types, which are classified by shape: spheres, disks, cones, tetrahedrons, biconoids, ovoids, cylinders, bent coils, triangles, paraboloids, rectangles, rhomboids, vessels, animals, and miscellaneous. The smallest tokens are about one or two centimeters across, the largest three to four centimeters.

The manufacture of the artifacts was simple. It consisted in pinching a small lump of clay between the fingers. Markings were added by incising one or several strokes or lines with a pointed tool such as a stylus while punctations were apparently made by impressing the blunt end of the stylus. Because they were handmade, each token reflects the style of its maker. Differences are mainly in craftsmanship, quality of clay, firing, and size. Some tokens were made with great care and show a crisp contour, while others are sloppy, exhibiting uneven edges. During the Neolithic and Chalcolithic periods, 8000–3500 B.C.E., the clay sometimes included gravel or even small pebbles. In the Bronze Age, about 3500–3100 B.C.E., the clay was usually fine, suggesting that it was subjected to a treatment process. Analysis of tokens

of various periods shows that they were fired at relatively low temperatures, never exceeding 600° C. Differences in firing apparently account for the various shades of color in the tokens, from buff to pink, red, gray, and black.

Symbols for communication. The meaning of some tokens can be deduced from early Sumerian pictographs, which followed the tokens in their use of symbols. It appears that the cone and the sphere represented two different measures of grain, that an ovoid stood for one jar of oil, and that a disk with a cross stood for one sheep. The token system marked an innovation in the use of symbols. It contrasts, for instance, with the symbolism exhibited by Paleolithic and Neolithic art. The paintings in the caves of Lascaux or in the Catal Hüyük shrines seem to express a complex and fabulous cosmology. The tokens, on the other hand, functioned as a precise code for the storage and communication of economic data.

The tokens can be considered word signs. Although they did not seek to duplicate speech and never acquired phonetic value, they shared some fundamental features of linguistic units. The tokens, like words, could refer to transactions in the present, the past, or the future. Tokens could be arranged in all possible combinations to accommodate any transaction. New tokens could be created at will to express additional economic concepts. Also, like words, the tokens were abstract, and their meaning had to be learned by cultural transmission.

The unique advantage of the token system over language was that it was durable. The three-dimensional tokens gave a solid and tangible expression to oral concepts. The system was, therefore, a revolution in communication technology. By functioning as a CODE that could be translated into speech at all times, the token system made it possible to collect large amounts of data without burdening the mind. Tokens made it possible to store information indefinitely since the data they yielded could be retrieved at any time by anyone who understood the system. The tokens were light and small and could be easily transported, facilitating transactions that occurred over great distances. Perhaps most important of all, the token system provided a method for sorting and organizing information. Because tokens were easy to manipulate, they could be ordered and reordered according to all possible criteria. This made it possible to scrutinize and analyze information for rational decision making.

Like writing, the system lent permanence to speech and served as an extension of the mind. Its major drawback was three-dimensionality. Since each concept needed its own form, there was a risk of overburdening the system. Although the tokens were small, the use of large numbers made the system unwieldy. It was thus limited to concise recordkeeping, without possibility of even the simplest syntax.

Precursor of writing. It is not yet possible to identify the original homeland of the token system. The earliest assemblages of tokens, dated about 8000–7500 B.C.E., come from such sites as Tell Aswad and Tell Mureybet, in Syria, and Tepe Asiab and Ganj-Dareh Tepe, in Iran (see Figure 1). In other words, by the first half of the eighth millennium B.C.E., the token system was already in use at both ends of the Fertile Crescent. At the time it consisted of nine types, including spheres, disks, cones, tetrahedrons, ovoids, and cylinders, with an occasional triangle, rectangle, or animal head. Markings were rare. It is probably not a coincidence that the earliest tokens of Mureybet were excavated at a level associated with the first evidence of the domestication of plants. This suggests that the need for recordkeeping was related to the rise of agriculture.

Tokens from the seventh millennium B.C.E. are found in practically every excavated site from Turkey to Israel and from Syria to Iran. Throughout this area the token system is remarkably uniform (see Figure 2). A few regional variations can be observed, such as a type of carinated cones typical of the Jeitun culture in Russian central Asia. During the seventh to fifth millennia the system shows no major transformation, suggesting little modification in its use.

In the middle of the fourth millennium B.C.E., which is characterized by the rise of cities, the token assemblages of urban centers such as Susa and Chogha Mish in Iran, Habuba Kabira and Tell Kannas in Syria, and Tello and Uruk in Iraq exhibit major changes. New shapes occur—biconoids, bent coils, paraboloids, rhomboids, vessels, and miscellaneous naturalistic renderings of tools. Triangles, rectangles, and animal heads are common. Perhaps the most characteristic feature of this period is the proliferation of markings on all types of tokens (see Figure 3). These form various patterns of incised lines (single or grouped), punctations, pitted surfaces, nicks, and, less frequently, pinched edges or appliqué pellets and coils. These fourth-millennium tokens, characterized by a greater diversity of shapes and markings, are referred to as *complex tokens*, as opposed to the *plain tokens* of the former periods.

The site of Uruk in Iraq provides a chronology for the evolution of the token system in the fourth millennium B.C.E. and the steps that led to Sumerian writing. At Uruk complex tokens were found at a level that also marks the beginning of monumental architecture. It seems, therefore, that the appearance of complex tokens corresponded to the rise of a new political system and an increase in bureaucracy. A number of tokens became perforated, seemingly in order to string together tokens belonging to the same account.

Still later, about 3250 B.C.E., tokens relating to the same transaction were grouped together in clay envelopes in the shape of hollow balls (see Figure 4). These envelopes provided a convenient clay surface upon which to impress the seals used by the Sumerian bureaucracy or private individuals. The seals were small stones carved with a motif that left a recognizable design when impressed on clay. Some envelopes bear as many as four different seals, probably identifying levels of the Sumerian bureaucracy or the parties involved in the transaction.

The envelopes had the disadvantage of being opaque, which concealed their contents. As a result, accountants started impressing each token on the surface of the envelopes in the same way that seals were impressed. The impressions on the surface of the envelopes gave information about the tokens inside. It soon became clear that the tokens inside were really superfluous and that markings on a surface might suffice. The shift in emphasis from the three-dimensional tokens to two-dimensional surface markings may be thought of as the beginning of writing.

Precursor of numerals. A counting device inevitably reflects the mode of counting of the culture using it. The token system may illustrate, in particular, a stage in the evolution of counting known as *concrete counting*.

A comparison of the token system with the abacus may give some insight into counting in protoliterate western Asia. Both the token system and the abacus are simple computing devices using movable counters. In the case of the abacus, the beads are uniform and can be used to compute any possible item because the system is based on abstract numbers, which are universally applicable. In contrast the token system, as seen in Figure 2, is characterized by counters of different shapes to count different items. Cones were used to count small measures of grain and spheres to count large measures of grain; ovoids represented jars of oil. In other words, each token fused together the concept of "one" and the concept of a unit of a good. Because these concepts could not be separated, two jars of oil had to be expressed by two jar-of-oil tokens—two ovoids—three jars of oil with three ovoids, and so on. The token system thus illustrates concrete counting, which relied not on abstract numbers but on different symbols to count different classes of merchandise.

Numerals—symbols for abstract numbers—first occur on the Sumerian pictographic tablets of 3100–3000 B.C.E., when plurality is no longer expressed by repeating units of goods in a one-to-one correspondence (see Figures 5 and 6). One jar of oil, for instance, is expressed by two different signs: "1" and "jar of oil." Similarly, six jars of oil is expressed by two different signs—"6" and "jar of oil"—thus

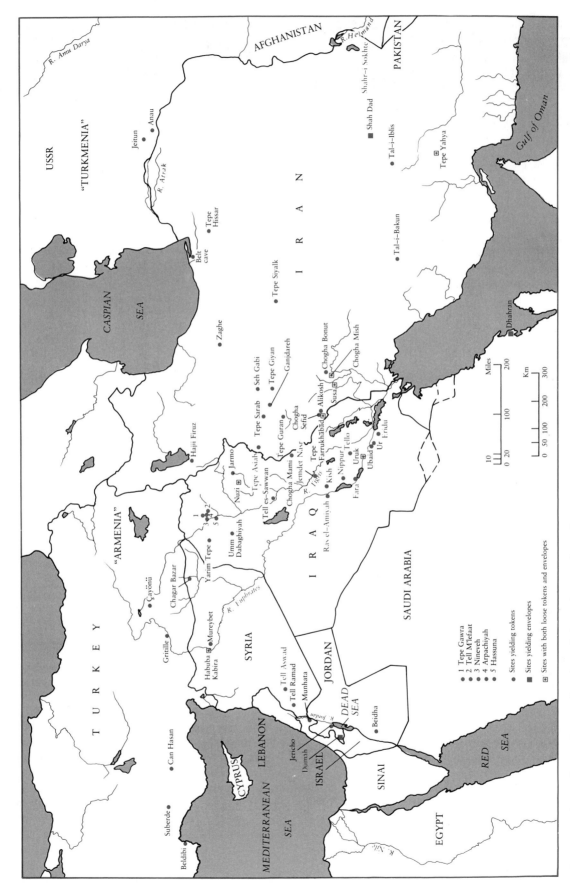

Figure 1. (*Clay Tokens*) Excavation sites of clay tokens and envelopes.

300

Figure 2. *(Clay Tokens)* Tokens from Seh Gabi, Iran, fifth millennium B.C.E. Courtesy of the Royal Ontario Museum, Toronto, Canada.

Figure 3. *(Clay Tokens)* Complex tokens from Susa, Iran, ca. 3300 B.C.E. Courtesy of Musée du Louvre, Département des Antiquités Orientales.

Figure 4. *(Clay Tokens)* Envelope with its content of tokens from Susa, Iran, ca. 3200 B.C.E. Courtesy of Musée du Louvre, Département des Antiquités Orientales.

Figure 5. *(Clay Tokens)* Impressed tablet from Susa, Iran, ca. 3100 B.C.E. Courtesy of Musée du Louvre, Département des Antiquités Orientales.

Figure 6. *(Clay Tokens)* Pictographic tablet from Godin Tepe, Iran, ca. 3000 B.C.E. Courtesy Godin Project, Royal Ontario Museum, Toronto, Canada.

creating an economy of notations. It is remarkable that the Sumerian numerals for one and six are shown by a wedge and a circular marking that derived from the tokens in the form of cones and spheres used for counting measures of grain. This suggests that instead of creating new symbols for numerals, the signs expressing measures of grain were assigned a secondary abstract numerical value. The cone and the sphere formerly used to count concrete measures of grain ultimately led to the expression of abstract numbers. Therefore, the to-kens may be considered symbols that preceded and led to the invention of numerals.

The simple invention of clay counters to compute and keep track of goods in Neolithic villages of western Asia opened new avenues of tremendous importance to the human mind. The tokens were the first step in the process that ultimately led to the first writing system in Sumer; the Sumerians, in originating the symbols that expressed abstract numerals, brought about the beginnings of MATHEMATICS.

See also NUMBER.

Bibliography. Denise Schmandt-Besserat, "The Envelopes That Bear the First Writing," *Technology and Culture* 21, no. 3 (1980): 357–385; idem, "From Tokens to Tablets: A Re-Evaluation of the So-Called 'Numerical Tablets,'" *Visible Language* 15, no. 4 (1981): 321–344; idem, "The Emergence of Recording," *American Anthropologist* 84, no. 4 (1982): 871–878; idem, "Before Numerals," *Visible Language* 18, no. 1 (1984): 48–60.

DENISE SCHMANDT-BESSERAT

CLOCK

Clocks and watches measure what we loosely call time by dividing it into discrete portions such as hours, seconds, and nanoseconds. Timekeepers have as their primary function the communication of these discrete divisions of time for different purposes. Since its invention the clock has reflected the status of its owner and maker, reinforced notions of the divine order of society, measured periods of short duration (such as a footrace), and communicated specific points in time when collective action should be taken (such as the departure of a train). Indeed communication beyond simple conversation and handwritten notes is nearly impossible outside the context of measured time. Thus the technical history of clocks and watches—increasingly accurate timekeepers—reflects their contributions to communication in general.

Early history. The mechanical clock (and its portable form, the watch) was undoubtedly the greatest mechanical invention of the MIDDLE AGES and perhaps the single most important invention since the wheel. Before the clock, time had been measured in various parts of the globe by water, sand (or eggshells), fire, and the sun. But clepsydras (water clocks),

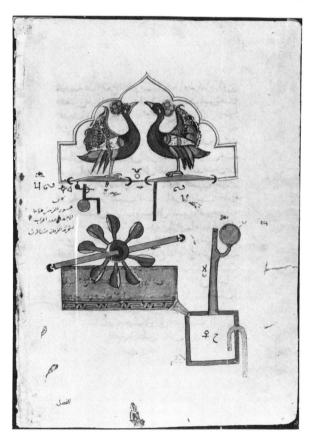

Figure 1. (*Clock*) Peacock waterclock. Miniature from the *Automata* of al-Gazari. Probably Syrian, 1314 C.E. The Metropolitan Museum of Art, New York, Rogers Fund, 1955. (55.121.15)

Figure 2. (*Clock*) Domestic alarm clock, sixteenth century. Weight driven and iron framed, this clock had a revolving dial with holes for fitting the alarm peg. Reproduced by courtesy of the Trustees of The British Museum.

sandglasses, incense and candle clocks, and sundials all had serious technical drawbacks that severely limited their accuracy.

When the mechanical clock appeared in the monasteries of northern Europe about 1275–1300, it was first used to communicate the appropriate time to pray. The clock quickly spread to towns and almost immediately became both a personal and a civic status symbol. It was soon a standard feature in cathedrals and public buildings.

These first public clocks were not designed primarily to tell time—they were too inaccurate to do so reliably—but rather to drive very complicated astronomical mechanisms. Richard of Wallingford spent thirty years building such a clock about 1330. These mechanical models of the universe were great technological and scientific marvels. Cities and churches that could afford them took pride in the status these mechanical wonders brought.

By the mid-sixteenth century the art of clockmaking, especially in Germany, had developed on a broad scale along with the other arts of the RENAISSANCE. These clocks reflected the wealth and status of their owners, but, more important, they also communicated a sense of political, social, and religious order that had been challenged during the preceding centuries. The clock became a mechanical metaphor for the universe, the state, and the individual.

In addition to their intellectual impact, Renaissance clocks, inaccurate though they were, formed the basis for the most important science of the Renaissance: astronomy. Contemporary astronomers sought a more accurate timekeeper than the verge and folio escapement, which often beat only every two seconds. In 1657 the application of the pendulum as the regulator of the mechanical clock suddenly made it accurate enough for science, particularly astronomy. Christiaan Huygens's invention made the clock accurate within fifteen seconds per day and transformed it from a work of art to a machine of science.

As the political and military leadership shifted from central to western Europe, so too did economic and technological leadership. The English quickly took up the pendulum clock and by the early eighteenth century had dramatically improved its accuracy with the development of the anchor escapement and temperature-compensated pendulums. Within a century of its invention the pendulum-regulated mechanical clock was accurate to within a few seconds per day.

Much of the effort to improve timekeeping was made in the seafaring nations of western Europe in order to solve the problem of longitude (*see* CARTOGRAPHY). Finding latitude (one's position above or below the equator) at any place on the globe is relatively easy, but finding longitude required knowing the precise time at a place of known longitude and comparing that time with local time. The technical problem was to build a clock accurate enough to take to sea. It was not until about 1780 that the necessary technological innovations were perfected. By 1800 these chronometers, being produced on a large scale in Britain, provided the accuracy necessary to determine longitude at sea. Transoceanic communication became not only cheaper and easier but also routine.

Modern innovations. The development of increasingly accurate clocks continued throughout the nineteenth and twentieth centuries. Electric impulses replaced mechanical impulses, carefully controlled vacuum chambers eliminated atmospheric interference, and new pendulum materials removed temperature errors. The accuracy of this generation of precision clocks approached the thousandth part of a second per day.

The quartz crystal, which vibrates a hundred thou-

Figure 3. *(Clock)* Carillon clock by Isaac Harbrecht, 1589. Reproduced by courtesy of the Trustees of The British Museum.

Figure 4. *(Clock)* Christiaan Huygens presents his pendulum clock, 1657. The Bettmann Archive, Inc.

sand times per second, and the cesium-beam atomic clock have redefined the very basis of time measurement. The second is no longer the basic fraction of the solar day or year.

The quartz-crystal clock was a development from early RADIO broadcasting and was based on the oscillatory effect of alternating current on certain crystals. Quartz clocks were eventually used to regulate computers, through which all electronic communication takes place (*see* COMPUTER: HISTORY). Quartz watches, whose accuracy far surpasses that of the best mechanical timekeepers, became mass-produced items that were sold cheaply worldwide.

Whereas the technical history of watches and clocks is a history of increasing accuracy, the impact of these developments changed the nature of society and its methods of communication. For example, until late in the nineteenth century every city and town had its own local time. Noon was defined locally as the time when the sun reached its zenith. As long as communication and transportation were slow, local time was satisfactory. British and continental railroads used the telegraph (*see* TELEGRAPHY) to transmit time signals along their routes, thus establishing a standard time to which each particular firm adhered.

With the transcontinental expansion of American railroads local time no longer sufficed. Train travel was scheduled, and scheduling was notoriously difficult between towns using different times. The con-

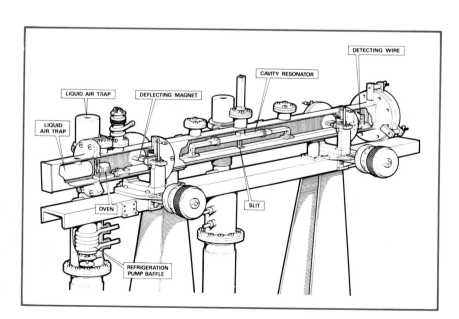

Figure 5. *(Clock)* Caesium clock. The atomic beam chamber for the caesium frequency standard. Trustees of the Science Museum, London.

fusion over various local times led to the development of standard time in 1883. This system divided the world into twenty-four distinct time zones beginning with Greenwich, England. Localities within each time zone used a common time based on the time in Greenwich.

In the seven centuries since the invention of the mechanical clock timekeepers have always communicated the status of their owners. The adoption of equal hours brought a new time consciousness to western Europe during the late Middle Ages and the Renaissance, and clocks became prized articles of trade throughout the world. In the seventeenth century Jesuit missionaries used them to gain a foothold in China. In the nineteenth century Americans pioneered the mass production of clocks and watches. Eventually everyone could own a clock or watch, and the Western world became obsessed with time and being on time. Modern communications would be impossible without our current notions and accurate methods of measuring time.

See also CALENDAR.

Bibliography. *Antiquarian Horology* (Journal of the Antiquarian Horological Society), Sussex, Eng., 1953–; *Bulletin of the National Association of Watch and Clock Collectors*, Columbia, Pa., 1943–; David S. Landes, *Revolution in Time: Clocks and the Making of the Modern World*, Cambridge, Mass., 1983; Klaus Maurice and Otto Mayr, *The Clockwork Universe: German Clocks and Automata, 1550–1650* (Die Welt als Uhr), trans. by H. Bartlett Wells, New York, 1980.

DONALD HOKE

CLOTHING

The set of all items worn on the human body. Such issues as how clothing items (and their combinations) function as signs, how the assemblage of clothing items of a given CULTURE forms a signaling system, and what kinds of MEANING can and cannot be conveyed through clothing are relevant for theories of communication. *See also* SIGN; SIGN SYSTEM.

Functions of clothing. Clothes are worn, first of all, for temperature regulation and protection from the environment. The distribution of types of clothing in relation to different climatic zones and the variation in clothes worn with changes in weather conditions show their practical, protective function. Sun helmets, sou'westers, down-filled anoraks, neoprene suits, and space suits are examples of clothing items that are primarily protective in function. However, even in identical environmental conditions, people wear different kinds of clothes. Furthermore, types of clothing vary with types of social occasions, which indicates that the wearing of clothes is also subject

to sociocultural norms. The gentleman's tuxedo and the lady's long gown, worn at a banquet, are not chosen in response to weather conditions but in response to social expectations. An even more extreme example is a king's majestic coronation robe with its long train. Such a garment is quite impractical; it is heavy and hot, and it impedes movement. In such cases the practical functions of clothes are subordinated to their signaling functions. In general the clothing of persons who must produce practical results—the furnace cleaner, the production worker—is designed and organized primarily to facilitate (or at least not hinder) the production of such results. The clothing of persons who are confirming or transforming their social relationships—as in processions, parades, marriage rituals, and graduations—is organized primarily in relation to impression management, and its sign function is thus predominant.

Both of the above types of clothing use and design have the quality of signs, because they are systematically associated with something else for which they stand (*aliquid stat pro aliquo*). The wearing of a bearskin, a poncho, or a down anorak in certain weather conditions can be interpreted as a symptom of the wearer's biological response to the environment, that is, the wearer feels cold. This interpretation does not presuppose any culture-specific knowledge, because the symptom is here causally related to circumstances. To the extent to which the responses to the biological needs of protection and temperature regulation are subject to additional culture-specific values, norms, or expectations, the responses attract further meanings. These can be decoded only by using culture-specific knowledge. Such responses assume the status of arbitrary, conventional symbols. The practical thing becomes a culturally meaningful thing. For example, to the outsider the blue or charcoal *Mutze* of the Amish male is just a jacket. To someone who knows the clothing norms of Amish culture, however, the *Mutze* signals that the wearer is Amish, that he is baptized (which usually takes place at the age of sixteen), and that he defines the situation as not an everyday event. If the *Mutze* is blue the wearer is between sixteen and thirty-five years of age; if it is charcoal the wearer is over thirty-five. To the outsider the Russian *kalbak* is just a brimless red hat; to the insider it signals that the wearer is a doctor. Examples of this sort make possible the following conclusion: if clothing can be seen as a signaling system, it must be seen as the signaling system of a social unit, not of an individual person or of humans in general.

Like LANGUAGE, the signal system *clothing* is part of the acquired knowledge shared by members of social units. In further analogy to verbal signaling systems (natural languages), the signaling system *clothing* can be said to be made up of varieties:

Figure 1. *(Clothing)* Teenagers in punk clothing, Dallas, Texas, 1984. UPI/Bettmann Newsphotos.

cultural varieties (Bedouin versus western European clothing), regional varieties (Scottish versus Bavarian folk costume), social varieties (bohemian versus bourgeois), sexual varieties (male versus female), functional varieties (ceremonial versus work clothing), and personal varieties (an individual's particular selection among socially sanctioned—and unsanctioned—options) used to project personal identity versus social identities of various kinds.

Clothing as a signaling system. First, consider the properties of the channel in which clothing signals are transmitted. This determines the kinds of meanings the system can and cannot convey. Clothing signals are transmitted by vision. For this reason they function only when people can see each other. In addition clothing signals remain present throughout an interaction. Unlike the sounds of speech, they do not fade rapidly and so make way for new signals. Clothing is thus unsuitable for the rapid coding of new messages but well suited to the coding of messages that remain constant through an interaction. Further, with speech a person's full linguistic repertoire is available in any interaction, but with clothing what is available is only that part of the clothing repertoire that is actually brought to an interaction. Thus new messages with clothing can be encoded in an interaction within these limits—for example, doffing a hat, putting on a coat, performing a striptease, or throwing down a glove when challenging someone to a duel.

Second, consider the properties that allow clothing to be defined as a signaling system. The basic units of clothing are clothing items such as top hat, waistcoat, Bermuda shorts, or swallowtails. Such items can be analyzed as particular combinations of features, including type of material, color, shape, and size. Such combinations are not random, however, but are governed by certain situational restrictions. For example, only a hat of cylindrical form covered with black or gray silk is a top hat appropriate for wearing at weddings, funerals, or the royal enclosure at Ascot. A hat of cylindrical form but made of uncovered cardboard or covered in red silk would be a different garment and would have a different significance. This suggests that a repertoire of clothing items could be analyzed as a set of features organized in certain combinations according to combination rules. On this level the relationships among features are simultaneous ones, much like the relationships among the distinctive features of a phoneme in a language.

Clothing items, in turn, can be classified into sets whose members can substitute for one another in

Figure 2. *(Clothing)* Isaac Oliver, *Richard Sackville, Earl of Dorset*, 1616. Miniature. Courtesy of the Board of Trustees of the Victoria and Albert, London. ▷

Figure 3. *(Clothing)* Bloomer girls, ca. 1845. The Bettmann Archive, Inc.

filling one of the several clothing slots that divide the body: head, neck, chest, abdomen, legs, and feet. These slots are contiguous on one level and also may be layered; undershirt, shirt, vest, jacket, and coat occupy layered slots in the clothing ensemble of a man, for example. Cultures vary in how clothing slots divide the body; the toga and caftan fill a single slot in some cultures that is divided into several slots in other cultures. Clothing items that can be substituted for one another in one slot (as sandals, shoes, boots, or slippers can substitute for one another in the slot "foot covering") can be said to have a paradigmatic relationship to one another, much like members of a word class (e.g., nouns) in spoken language. Cultures differ in the range of items that are members of a given paradigm. The bowler, boater, helmet, bearskin hat, and cap are acceptable English fillers for the slot "head covering" but not the fez, cowboy hat, or turban. These items belong to the head-covering paradigms of other cultures.

Just as clothing features cannot combine randomly, so clothing items are restricted in the ways in which they may combine. For example, an admiral's cocked hat is not normally worn with a tuxedo, Bermuda shorts, or cowboy boots. The unacceptability of such combinations in ordinary everyday life,

Figure 4. *(Clothing)* Child in Ghana, Africa. The Bettmann Archive, Inc.

Figure 5. *(Clothing)* William Hogarth, *The Graham Children*, 1742. Reproduced by courtesy of the Trustees, The National Gallery, London.

in contrast to the inverted worlds of carnival (*see* FESTIVAL; SPECTACLE), shows that social constraints affect the combinations that are theoretically possible. Thus clothing items stand in paradigmatic and also in syntagmatic relationships.

The above considerations show that clothing is not just a repertoire of elements (features and items) but that three types of relationship obtain among the elements. Like all phenomena that have a repertoire of elements plus a set of relationships, clothing has the status of a system. In order to show that a system is a signaling system, another type of constraint must be considered. Within the community the norms must be uncovered that determine which items and item combinations may, shall, or must be worn by whom on which occasion. If such norms are discovered, it means that the items and item combinations stand for something that they themselves are not (who, what occasion). Clothing is not only a system; it is also a signaling system, that is, a CODE.

Meaning conveyed through clothing. The specific properties of clothing codes make them suitable for signaling some types of meaning but unsuitable for other types. The limited number of slots limits the "length" of the "utterance" and makes clothing codes unsuitable for the coding of complex messages. In this respect they contrast with language, in which an indefinitely large number of sentences can be pro-

Figure 6. *(Clothing)* At the Chester races, 1926. Ullstein Bilderdienst, West Berlin.

Figure 7. *(Clothing)* A group of women in Kabul, Afghanistan, 1962. The older women are wearing the *chadari*. United Nations photo 79046/JL/MOJ.

duced and arranged in an indefinitely long text. Also in contrast to language, clothing codes are intrinsically unsuitable for making statements about, or for referring to, the outside world, be it part of the situation ("that man," "that chair over there") or outside the situation ("in nineteenth-century Britain"). Clothing codes thus cannot convey what in language has been called descriptive, referential, or cognitive meaning. Furthermore, and again unlike language, clothing codes cannot be used reflexively; that is, clothing cannot be used to refer to itself.

Basically clothing codes are limited to communicative functions connected to the regulation of interaction and the relationships among interactants. Combinations of clothing items produced in accordance with the norms for given types of occasions help to set the stage for an event. By wearing particular types of clothing combinations, people can indicate what sort of social occasion they are participating in. Clothing can also be used to convey information about the wearer. On the one hand, such signals can give cues about the sender's social identity—sex, age, status, tribe, clan, gang, organization, PROFESSION, and the like—by illustrating adherence to the clothing norms that apply to such categories. On the other hand, by exploiting the full range of options, by modifying or even transgressing the established norms, the sender may seek to express particular individual characteristics. Clothing signals can also indicate to the receiver what behavior in respect to the wearer should be. The sheriff's uniform and the prostitute's garb may be meant as a call to order and an invitation, respectively, and may be decoded accordingly.

Clothing codes can be used for creating false impressions. One may feign an identity by wearing the uniform of a profession not one's own. Creating a false impression may be regarded positively in some circumstances, negatively in others. The professional disidentification of a floorwalker or a plainclothes detective as someone else is generally accepted or at least tolerated. In still other contexts deliberate mis- and disidentification are negatively seen and negatively sanctioned, such as the thief dressed as a meter reader or the private outfitted in a captain's uniform. Creating false impressions with clothing is actually quite common, as illustrated by such acts as removing a wedding ring, wearing a borrowed fur coat, or trying to pass off imitation diamonds as the real thing. *See also* DECEPTION.

The number of terms commonly used to refer to different types of clothing indicates that clothing is not regarded as a homogeneous signaling system. Terms such as folk costume, uniform, robe, livery, and fashion label varieties and imply that they are used differently by different groups or not at all by some. Tribal societies and tradition-oriented subcultures of contemporary industrial society have been

Figure 9. *(Clothing)* Design for a summer suit. From *Esquire*, June 1941. From O. E. Schoeffler and William Gale, *Esquire's Encyclopedia of 20th Century Men's Fashions*, New York: McGraw-Hill Book Company, 1973, p. 23. Copyright © 1941 by Esquire Associates.

slow to change their traditional garb. The members of primary groups such as gangs and clubs tend to project their sense of we-ness through collective acts of symbolic identification, such as wearing certain clothing items and insignia. Many organizations impose clothing regulations on their employees in order to distinguish visibly both agents of the organization from clients and also members of its hierarchy from nonmembers. They may even assign uniforms that stigmatize their wearers, such as those worn by inmates of prisons and concentration camps.

Figure 8. *(Clothing)* Kaigetsudo Doshin, *Beauty Arranging Her Hair*. Japan, early eighteenth century. The Los Angeles County Museum of Art, The Shin'enkan Collection. L.83.50.33.

Bibliography. Roland Barthes, *Système de la mode* (The Fashion System, trans. by Matthew Ward and Richard Howard, New York, 1983), Paris, 1967; Petr Bogatyrev, *The Functions of Folk Costume in Moravian Slovakia*, The Hague, 1971; Justine M. Cordwell and Ronald A. Schwartz, eds., *The Fabrics of Culture*, The Hague and Paris, 1979; Erving Goffman, *The Presentation of Self in Everyday Life*, New York, 1959, reprint Woodstock, N.Y., 1973; idem,

Figure 10. *(Clothing)*   Men on a park bench, Algiers, Algeria. The Bettmann Archive, Inc.

Stigma, Englewood Cliffs, N.J., 1963, reprint Harmondsworth, Eng., 1970; Mary Lou Rosencranz, *Clothing Concepts: A Social-Psychological Approach*, New York and London, 1972.

WERNER ENNINGER

CODE

A system for the generation and communication of meanings within a society. This means that every aspect of our social life is encoded—everything we say, see, hear, or do. Codes underlie all aspects of life in society: everything made or manufactured, from cars to cosmetics; all activity, from playing football to going to school; even the way nature is understood. In fact, social life consists of an intricate, omnipresent network of codes. It may be impossible to provide an exhaustive typology of codes, but we can detail the elements that constitute a code and offer a broad taxonomic structure with which to categorize and thus understand them. *See also* MODE.

The first distinction is between codes of behavior and signifying codes. The primary purpose of codes of behavior, such as the legal code or the codes that many professional bodies such as advertisers or doctors draw up to regulate the conduct of their members, is social control. These codes do, of course,

generate and communicate MEANING—for instance, what justice means in a particular society or what it means to be a doctor—but their primary function is regulatory rather than communicative.

Communicative codes exhibit the following features:

1. They consist of a paradigmatic dimension, that is, a set of units (or signs) from which a choice is made (*see* SIGN).
2. They are ordered by syntagmatic conventions, which determine how a chosen unit or sign can be combined with others in a meaningful way.
3. They construct and convey meaning: their units are signs that refer to something other than themselves.
4. They are socially produced and depend on a shared social background or agreement among their users.
5. They are transmittable by appropriate and available media of communication.

Analog and digital codes. An analogic code is structured along a continuum; a digital code consists of discrete units or signs. Nature, or reality, consists of continua; a culture's way of making sense of nature is to digitalize or categorize it. Thus a watch with hands is analogic: the movement of the hands around the dial is continuous and is analogous to the continual movement of natural time. A digital watch, on the other hand, divides this continuum up and codifies it into hours, minutes, and seconds. The marks or numbers around the rim of an analog watch digitalize the movement of the hands, and so do the words or figures by which we communicate the time (e.g., 3:30 P.M.). Making sense of nature and making that sense communicable involves digitalizing, categorizing, and codifying it. Thus INTERPERSONAL DISTANCE is a natural continuum. We make sense of it by codifying it into the intimate (within about three feet), the personal (about three to eight feet), and the public. Growing old is a continuous process, but we codify age into categories and often construct elaborate boundary rituals to make the passage from one digital category to another. Turning nature into CULTURE and thus making it understandable and communicable involves codifying it digitally.

Presentational and representational codes. Representational codes are used to produce texts, which are messages with a physical existence that is independent of the social context within which they were produced. Presentational codes convey meaning only within the context of their transmission and reception. Thus a BOOK is composed of the representational codes of written LANGUAGE, punctuation, typeface, and design. These codes work in any appropriate social context. The presentational codes of, for instance, oral language, tone of voice, FACIAL EXPRESSION, and dress (*see* CLOTHING) can work only in the immediate social context of their use. Presentational codes are typical of INTERPERSONAL COMMUNICATION, representational codes of mediated or mass communication.

The human body is the main transmitter of presentational codes, of which there are three main types:

1. Behavioral, learned codes (e.g., facial expression). These are acquired through social experience and often work below the threshold of awareness or of deliberate intention. Nonetheless, they can be brought within the control of the encoder, if only with difficulty.
2. Commodity codes (e.g., dress). Culturally produced commodities can elaborate the bodily presentational codes. These are entirely within the control of the encoder.
3. Genetically produced bodily codes (e.g., physical size). These depend on physical features and lie largely beyond the control of the user.

Each type of presentational code can be called upon to convey one or more of the following four types of meaning:

1. Meanings about relationships: the attitude of one person toward another and the relations of liking or of domination-dependence between them.
2. Meanings about social affiliation: the class or social group membership that we signal in any particular situation.
3. Meanings about identity: the presentation of individual differences within group or class affiliation.
4. Expressive meanings: meanings about the emotional or internal states of the people involved.

British social psychologist Michael Argyle listed ten of the behavioral presentational codes that the human body transmits:

1. *Touch.* Whom, where, and when we TOUCH can codify meanings of affection or social closeness.
2. *Proxemics.* The distance between people encodes meanings about the intimacy of the relationship (*see* PROXEMICS).
3. *Orientation.* The angles at which people orient themselves to each other convey social meanings. For example, facing each other closely signifies intimacy or aggression; being at 90 degrees to another signifies cooperation.
4. *Appearance.* This is basically a genetic code but is listed here because we can control our appearance to a degree by diet, hairstyle, BODY DECORATION, and so on. Appearance conveys meanings about personality, social status, and social conformity.
5. *Head nods.* These work mainly to manage interaction, particularly turn taking in CONVERSATION.
6. *Facial expression.* This can be further divided into the codes of eyebrow position, eye shape, mouth shape, and facial size (*see* FACE), which can be combined in various ways to convey a wide range of personal, emotional, and social meanings.
7. *Gestures* (KINESICS). Hands, arms, head, and feet can all be used to convey a wide range of meanings (*see* GESTURE).
8. *Posture.* Ways of sitting, standing, or lying can convey expressive meanings, interpersonal attitudes, or social status.
9. *Eye movement and eye contact.* The eyes convey particularly powerful meanings about relationships but also work to manage interaction or turn taking and to express inner feelings.
10. *Nonverbal aspects of speech.* Pitch, tone, volume, accent, and stress can all affect not only the meanings of the words but also the social meanings of the relationship within which they are spoken.

These codes use the physical abilities of the human body to generate and communicate meanings, and they can be culturally extended and elaborated. Hair, for instance, is the most easily changeable of our natural features, and thus hairstyles become highly charged with meaning. Cosmetics too are used to extend the signifying potential of the body. But these are close to commodity codes. *See also* NONVERBAL COMMUNICATION.

The communicative function of a huge range of consumer goods is to act as metaphoric extensions of the human body. Clothes, houses, furniture, and cars all have a functional purpose—to keep us warm, dry, comfortable, and mobile—but this is a baseline function that is taken for granted. The significant consumer choices are those among a variety of goods that serve their functional purpose equally well but differ widely in their communicative purpose. The real choices are among encoded meanings of social relationships, social membership, and individual identity.

Then there are the other aspects of the human body that are genetically rather than culturally determined. These include such characteristics as race, skin color, physical size, and GENDER. In general these characteristics are not within the control of the individual, and therefore the paradigmatic choice is not made by the encoder but rather occurs on the social level only. Thus no individual can choose to be encoded as white, black, or yellow, or as male or female, but society can and does choose what meanings and values to give to these physical differences.

Sometimes, of course, people do try to exercise choice over genetic presentational codes. These attempts range from relatively superficial alterations, such as changing hair color or changing eye color by wearing contact lenses, to more fundamental ones, such as changing signs of race (eye shape or hair texture) or of gender.

Representational codes are technologically based transformations of the presentational codes that free them from the context of the here and now. The kind of meanings the codes can convey is extended to include the absent, the abstract, and the general. Verbal language is our most complex and highly developed representational code. In its spoken form it may perform some of the functions of a presentational code, but its distinctive feature is its ability to conceptualize, to theorize, and to produce general principles. It can achieve this in both its oral and written forms.

The formal characteristics of representational codes are determined both by the properties of the medium by which they are to be transmitted and by the conventional uses that society makes of them. The form of WRITING came to be determined by its need to be produced manually by a sharp instrument on a thin, light material for easy transportation and storage. Then the technical needs of movable print produced new letterforms, and the needs of computers have produced yet others. Originally this medium was expensive in time and was used only for messages deemed to be of social importance. Thus the conventions of written language differed from those

of oral language and became more formal, more constrained by rules. Written language also required the code of punctuation as a means of reproducing the presentational codes of inflection and pauses. So representational codes are influenced by both technical and social forces. *See also* COMPUTER: IMPACT; PRINTING; WRITING MATERIALS.

The contemporary medium of television can serve as an example of how the medium-specific representational codes (both technical and conventional) work and how they relate to the presentational. An event, such as a scene in a drama, is televised. This event consists of a complex web of presentational codes. The technological processes and conventional practices are then brought to bear upon the event in such a way as to make it electronically transmittable and recordable, electronically decodable by the television receiver, and then culturally decodable by the viewer (see Figure 1).

All the media of communication have their own medium-specific technical and conventional codes, and insofar as the media are similar, so too will their codes resemble one another. Thus the codes of film and television have many similarities, some of which they share with RADIO and others with PHOTOGRAPHY. The codes of radio are similar in some ways to those of audio recording and in other ways to those of newspapers. Thus the various media differ in their technical codes but resemble one another in their conventional codes, so that the cultural competencies required to decode them are relatively easily acquired by social experience. *See also* MOTION PICTURES; NEWSPAPER: HISTORY; SOUND RECORDING; TELEVISION HISTORY.

Denotational and connotational codes. Codes do not just transmit messages over time or distance; they also generate and circulate meanings in a society. Meanings are complex phenomena, and different sorts of meaning require different sorts of codes. At one end of the scale are denotational meanings, that is, meanings that are grounded in a sense of universal reality that is the same for everyone in every society. The code of MATHEMATICS (e.g., $2 + 3 = 5$) is perhaps the purest example. These codes are objective and impersonal, and their meanings work solely within the rational, logical area of our minds. But humans are social, moral, and emotional as well as rational beings, and there is a huge range of meanings (and the codes to convey them) of this type. These codes are called connotational. Connotation occurs when denoted meanings meet the value system of a culture or the emotional system of a person. Scientific codes try to give priority to denotational over connotational meanings. Aesthetic codes, on the other hand, prefer the connotational over the denotational. Connotative meanings are specific to a culture or subculture. Thus a painting may connote harmony and beauty in one culture but not in another. A word

An event to be televised consists of
presentational codes, e.g.:

Appearance, Dress, Makeup, Environment, Behavior, Speech,
Gesture, Expression, Sound, etc.

which are encoded electronically by
technical representational codes, e.g.:

Camera, Lighting, Editing, Music, Sound Effects, Casting

which transmit the
conventional representational codes, e.g.:

Narrative, Conflict, Character, Action, Dialogue, Setting, etc.

which are organized into coherence and social acceptance by the
ideological codes, e.g.:

Individualism, Patriarchy, Race, Class, Materialism,
Capitalism, etc.

Figure 1. *(Code)* The process of codification in television.

like *colonial* will have negative connotations in a country like Britain, which is trying to escape its colonizing past, but will have positive values, particularly in ARCHITECTURE, in the United States or Australia with their quite different social histories. Most social codes convey denotational and connotational meanings in varying proportions. Therefore, although the British and U.S. connotations of *colonial* may differ, its denotational meaning will be shared much more closely between them.

A photograph is composed partly of the denotational codes (largely technological) by which the appearance of the object is transferred to the photograph and recognized (decoded) by the viewer. But it also employs connotative (conventional) codes, such as those of framing, focus, lighting, or graininess of the film, by which the denoted object is given social meanings, values, and expressiveness. Any choices made by the photographer are grounded in photographic conventions and result in the use of connotational codes. Denotational codes convey identical meanings for all their users and require understanding. The meanings of connotational codes vary according to the social conditions of their use and require interpretation.

Ideological codes. Connotational codes are not random. They are organized according to a deeply structured set of ideological codes that constitute the most taken-for-granted, natural-seeming meanings of a society. All societies have deep, invisible sets of ideological codes that shape the social values that, in turn, determine their connotational and aesthetic codes. In Western industrial democracies some of these codes or shared systems of meanings and values given to central areas of social life can be given names, such as individualism, freedom, progressivism, materialism, patriarchy, and scientism. *See also* IDEOLOGY.

Broadcast and narrowcast codes. Despite these widely shared ideological codes, there are social differences in any society and between societies. Broadcast codes are ones that emphasize common social experience, and thus shared conventions, in order to circulate meanings around as many social groups as possible. Narrowcast codes are those with a narrower social use and a more restricted set of conventions. Within written language, journalese is a broadcast code, legalese a restricted code; pop music (*see* MUSIC, POPULAR) is a broadcast code, OPERA a narrowcast one. Broadcast codes tend to be simpler, in that they tend to have a smaller "paradigm" of signs and simpler syntagmatic rules for combining them. Broadcast codes are acquired through social experience; narrowcast codes frequently require formal instruction or training. Popular ART, of whatever form, tends to use broadcast codes; highbrow art uses narrowcast ones.

Codes and society. By their ability to generate and circulate shared meanings and values codes produce and maintain the sense of community and shared interests on which any society depends for its coherence and stability. They perform this function at every level of social organization, from the smallest—dyadic communication—up to the largest—national or international communication. They even operate within the individual to make a coherent and socially communicable sense of self. They form the interface among the personal, the social, and the technological and are thus the core of any social system.

See also SEMIOTICS; SIGN SYSTEM.

Bibliography. Michael Argyle, *The Psychology of Interpersonal Behaviour*, 4th ed., Harmondsworth, Eng., 1983; Basil Bernstein, *Class, Codes, and Control*, Vol. 1, 2d rev. ed., London, 1974; Colin Cherry, *On Human Communication* (1957), 3d ed., Cambridge, Mass., 1978; John Fiske, *Introduction to Communication Studies*, London and New York, 1982; Pierre Guiraud, *Semiology* (in French), trans. by George Gross, London, 1975; Edward T. Hall, *The Silent Language*, New York, 1959, reprint 1973; Robert A. Hinde, ed., *Non-Verbal Communication*, Cambridge, 1972.

JOHN FISKE

COGNITION

The activity of knowing; the acquisition, organization, and use of knowledge. Under this general heading many different topics are studied. For example, some scholars focus on how CHILDREN develop the abilities to perceive, remember, and think; others focus on the organization of knowledge systems that make it possible to store and recall information; and still others focus on the way in which knowledge is used to solve problems such as making a strategic move in a game of chess. The many different approaches to the study of cognition are united in the assumption that it is possible to study the complex processes that occur in a cognitive system as it obtains, stores, transforms, and uses information about the environment in which it functions. Terms such as *thinking, sensation, problem solving,* PERCEPTION, *recognition, imagery,* and *recall* are commonly used to refer to stages or aspects of this functioning.

History

The roots of the study of cognition are often traced to German philosopher Immanuel Kant's analyses of the schema and concept in the late eighteenth century, and many scholars would trace these origins back to ARISTOTLE. However, it was not until the twentieth century that the study of cognition emerged as a specific area of inquiry. From World War I until the 1960s various behavioristic and psychoanalytic theories so dominated psychology that cognitive processes were largely ignored. To the extent that they were studied during this period, they were usually studied by Gestalt psychologists. However, like behaviorists, Gestalt psychologists devoted relatively little attention to specifying the complex activities and processes that are now seen to characterize cognitive systems. *See also* PSYCHOANALYSIS.

The appearance of computers changed this. Their importance in inspiring an interest in cognition did not stem primarily from their role in gathering and analyzing empirical data. Rather, it stemmed from the fact that computer operation came to be viewed as having important parallels to human cognitive processes. This suggested that complex cognitive processes were real and could be studied in terms of programs, routines, subroutines, storage, input, output, retrieval, and so forth. *See also* COMPUTER: HISTORY; COMPUTER: IMPACT.

It is largely because of this influence of computers, as well as associated developments in INFORMATION THEORY and CYBERNETICS, that cognitive and information-processing approaches came to be important subdisciplines of psychology in the 1960s and 1970s. The interest in computers was also instrumental in the emergence of new, related disciplines such as ARTIFICIAL INTELLIGENCE and cognitive science. Researchers in these disciplines are typically even more concerned with issues of computers and computer programming than are researchers from cognitive and information-processing psychology. In particular, they have been concerned with delineating general principles of intelligence and cognition that apply to computers as well as to humans.

Two general sets of claims have emerged about the relationship between human and machine (i.e., computer) intelligence. Some scholars have focused on the use of computers and computer programs to simulate human cognitive processes. Their claim is that by carrying out such simulations it is possible to gain insight into human psychological processes. Even though the philosophical validity of this claim has been questioned, it continues to underlie much of the research carried out in cognitive psychology, information-processing psychology, and cognitive science. In contrast, other scholars have focused their attention on programming machines that can perform tasks efficiently and intelligently, without considering the ways in which humans might carry out the same tasks. This latter approach tends to be more characteristic of studies in artificial intelligence. The various efforts devoted to the study of cognition in humans and machines are often referred to under the general heading of *cognitivism.*

Major Approaches to Cognitivist Analysis

During the short history of cognitivism, many different schools of thought have emerged. One of the major criteria distinguishing one school from another is the choice of a unit of analysis. Virtually all cognitivist models are alike in assuming that a unit of analysis must reflect the fact that human and other cognitive systems deal with a potentially infinite range of contextually specific situations by using generalized categories. They differ, however, in what they consider to be the appropriate analytic unit for understanding these categories. Some of the major analytic units underlying accounts of cognitive processes are concepts, features, prototypes, propositions, schemata, and simple processing elements.

Concepts. The notion of a concept is probably the most widely used unit of analysis in studies of cognition. Various notions of a concept have been invoked in order to deal with a fundamental, defining property of human and computer cognitive systems, namely, the tendency to treat phenomena that differ in some way as similar or equivalent. For example, even though no two roses are identical, they are often treated as interchangeable members of the category of roses; even though a rose and a dandelion are still more dissimilar, they are treated as interchangeable members of the category of flowers; and even though a rose, a dandelion, and an oak tree are quite unlike one another, they are all treated as members of the category of plants. In some way or another this fundamental property of cognitive systems must be a part of any complete account of their functioning, and the notion of a concept is frequently and widely invoked in an attempt to meet this requirement.

Various accounts of concepts differ in the particular way they approach this tendency of cognitive systems to classify experience. Some approaches argue that LANGUAGE of some sort is essential for CLASSIFICATION. In these approaches the key to understanding the use and development of concepts can be found in the structure or function of language. Other approaches argue that concepts need not be linguistically based. For these the key to concepts may be in motor or perceptual activity. Still other approaches try to consider both nonlinguistic and linguistic factors in accounting for concepts. In such views different kinds of concepts may be tied to these two factors, or nonlinguistic concepts may lay the groundwork for complex cognitive functioning during development, and this groundwork may be transformed with the emergence of language.

Features. In most cognitivist accounts of concepts is an assumption that concepts are interrelated in a complex system. In trying to describe this system it became apparent to many researchers that some analysis of the internal structure of individual concepts was necessary. This in part led to the proposal that features could serve as basic units of analysis. Instead of viewing concepts as unstructured wholes, feature analysis decomposes them into a set of iso-

lable, abstract properties. Such an approach allows researchers to describe and predict ways in which cognitive processes are affected by features. For example, the fact that robins, canaries, and ostriches all share certain common features (e.g., being animate, having feathers, having wings, having a head) suggests a way to account for the tendency of subjects to group or cluster them together in memory tasks involving lists of words from a variety of general categories (e.g., birds, mammals, furniture, clothing, plants). Findings such as these on clustering suggest that memory is organized in terms of features.

Some approaches that take features as the basic unit of analysis assume that a concept is a logical, clearly defined entity whose membership is defined by an item's possession of a single set of criterial features. Such straightforward approaches have been called into question, however, on the grounds that they lack the power and flexibility to deal with many of the contextually situated items typically encountered by cognitive systems. Cognitivists have responded to this observation in several ways. Some have tried to retain the basic tenets of feature theory but have argued that more sophisticated and variegated lists of features are needed. For example, it has been argued that some features may be defining (i.e., essential for an item's being included under a conceptual heading), whereas others may be only characteristic (i.e., nonessential). Thus the features of being animate, having feathers, having wings, and having a head are defining for the concept of bird, but the features of being able to fly and being able to sing are only characteristic, because they are present in certain birds (e.g., canaries) but not in others (e.g., ostriches).

Prototypes. Another way researchers have tried to overcome the weaknesses in feature theory is tied to the third unit of analysis: the prototype. Instead of viewing a concept as a particular set of features, prototype analysis is organized around prototypical exemplars or "best representatives." In this view members of a conceptual category may vary in their distance from the prototypical exemplar, and category membership is a matter of degree rather than an absolute.

Even though prototype theory emerged for the same reason as certain refinements in feature theory, it is fundamentally different in its assumptions. The basic representational mechanism in feature theory is a set of abstract, isolable features, and the issue is whether concrete items have the criterial features specified by these representational types. In the case of prototype theory, the basic representational mechanism is an image of a concrete object or event, and the issue is the degree to which other concrete items are similar to it.

Propositions. The fourth basic type of analytic unit is the proposition, an abstract MEANING representation that relates two or more concepts. It is abstract in the sense that it is not tied to any particular linguistic form. Thus the same propositional representation (hit John Bill), which involves the relation of hitting and the arguments (concepts) of John and Bill, may be encoded in English, French, Russian, or any other language. Furthermore, within a language this propositional representation is not tied to any particular linguistic form; thus it may properly be encoded in English either as "John hit Bill" or "Bill was hit by John." One of the major motivations for accepting an abstract propositional representation as a unit of analysis is that empirical research has demonstrated that humans often store and recall the propositional content of a spoken or written passage but not its actual linguistic form. Because propositions are treated as abstract representational types by cognitivists, they are similar to features and unlike prototypes. However, propositions differ from features (and concepts) in that they involve relations among arguments, or concepts, as well as the arguments themselves.

Schemata. A fifth basic unit of analysis is the schema. A schema is a generalized pattern of action that guides humans or other cognitive systems as they obtain and process information about the environment and act on that environment. In more computer-oriented terms, a schema is a large-scale data structure that guides the INTERPRETATION of input data, the storage and transformation of information in memory, and the execution of action on the environment. Schemata are variously thought of as generalized plans, recipes, or formats that guide perception, thinking, memory, and motor action. For example, it has been claimed that there are generalized schemata for actions such as going to a restaurant, listening to a folktale, and remembering the spatial layout of an apartment (*see* SPATIAL ORGANIZATION). In addition to schema, the terms *frame* and *script* are often used in cognitivist literature to refer to such patterns of action.

Cognitivists introduced the notion of schema in an attempt to formalize the observation that humans often recognize and deal with situations in terms of a general, routinized pattern of action. In this view such a pattern of action cannot be broken down into smaller units such as simple concepts or stimulus-response links without losing sight of the crucial facts about its overall, holistic nature. Evidence for the role of schemata in cognitive processes comes from a variety of sources. For example, many studies have demonstrated that scripts or schemata influence the memory for written or spoken texts. This influence is manifested in subjects' tendency to "remember" information that in fact was not in a passage but could be expected to be there on the basis of a familiar script. Conversely, subjects often systemati-

cally forget or distort information that is not consistent with the scripts that usually guide their processing.

Each of the five units of analysis mentioned so far (concepts, features, prototypes, propositions, schemata) has been proposed in one or another model as the appropriate construct on which to build a general theory of cognition. However, as cognitivist research has expanded, the notion that any one of these analytic units can provide the underpinnings for a comprehensive theory has been called into question. In some cases, the idea that a single unit can underlie functioning in the variety of task settings encountered by a cognitive system has been criticized. Such criticisms often are associated with the claim that cognitive systems require the flexibility of having access to different units for different situational demands. In this connection, various combinations of the five units of analysis outlined above, as well as others (e.g., temporal strings, spatial images), have been proposed.

Simple processing elements. Other cognitivists have argued that a fundamentally different level of analytic unit is required to create an integrated theory of cognitive processes. Some researchers have proposed the notion of a simple processing element. Theoretical approaches that take the simple processing element as their basic unit of analysis differ from most others in certain crucial ways. The importance of these differences is indicated by the basic META-PHOR that they take to be guiding their work. Whereas cognitivist approaches concerned with the first five analytic units are generally motivated by some sort of computer metaphor, approaches grounded in the simple processing element are based on a brain metaphor. In many respects the simple processing element is modeled after the neuron. For this reason, such approaches are sometimes called "neurally inspired."

A basic operating principle of such approaches is that representations associated with analytic units such as concepts or schemata reflect an emergent property of large aggregates of simple processing elements (or simply "units") acting together. Instead of a one-unit, one-concept or one-unit, one-schema approach, the assumption is that the unit's job is simply to receive input from other neighboring units and, as a function of the inputs it receives, to compute an output value that it sends on to its neighbors. The system in which these units operate is viewed as functioning in an inherently parallel (as opposed to sequential) fashion in that many units can carry out their computations at the same time. Furthermore, processing is distributed throughout the system. For these reasons such approaches are sometimes grouped under the heading of parallel distributed processing (PDP) models.

PDP models were proposed because of various

dissatisfactions with existing cognitivist models based on other analytic units. For example, the observation that human cognitive functioning typically involves multiple, simultaneously activated concepts, schemata, and so forth implies that approaches that cannot provide a principled account of parallel processing are likely to be unable to provide an adequate simulation of human cognition. Also, it has been widely observed that although activity at the level of individual neurological events proceeds at a much slower speed in humans than in modern computers, humans solve many complex problems faster than computers do. With an eye toward simulation of human cognition, approaches that assume parallel and distributed processes may be able to resolve this seeming contradiction.

Much of the cognitivist research concerned with the six units of analysis outlined here has been grounded in computer simulations and in laboratory experiments with human adults. (In spite of the fact that research concerned with elementary processing units is grounded in a brain metaphor rather than a computer metaphor, the use of computer simulation applies to it as much as to research concerned with other analytic units.) In all cases, the methodology typically involves the computer simulation of a cognitive process as well as the experimental study of adult subjects' execution of that process. Each of the two sets of findings generates hypotheses and provides validation checks for the other.

Other Approaches to the Study of Cognition

In addition to these procedures, other major methodologies exist for the study of cognition. The most important are concerned with developmental (i.e., ontogenetic), cross-cultural, and clinical issues. For a variety of reasons having to do with the practicalities of dealing with certain kinds of subjects, these approaches tend to focus on more naturalistic settings for gathering data rather than on laboratory experiments and the computer simulations that go with them. Even though the same general set of analytic units mentioned above is studied in one or more of these more naturalistic approaches, the methodologies are often so different from laboratory experimentation and computer simulation that the subdisciplines of developmental psychology (especially cognitive development), cross-cultural psychology (also psychological anthropology), and clinical psychology (including studies of neuropsychology and developmental disabilities) have made unique contributions to the study of cognition.

Developmental. A fundamental tenet of most approaches to developmental psychology is that cognitive processes are best understood by analyzing their origins and development. The most influential version of this claim can be found in JEAN PIAGET's account of "genetic epistemology." In this approach the roots of human cognition may be traced to the elementary sensorimotor schemata of the infant. These schemata guide the individual's assimilation of new information and experience while simultaneously developing and accommodating to the demands of the reality that surrounds the child. The functional invariants of assimilation and accommodation of schemata (together called adaptation) characterize all stages of cognitive development, according to Piaget.

Theories such as Piaget's take an "interactionist" approach to cognitive development. Such approaches assume that cognition is shaped by the forms of interaction that occur between an active subject and its environment. In this view human cognitive processes are neither innately specified nor determined simply by a passive subject's accumulation of information about the environment. Such interactionist approaches avoid the classic pitfalls of both Cartesian rationalism and simple empiricism.

Major differences exist among interactionist approaches in what are considered relevant aspects of the environment and hence in what can be predicted about how human cognition will be shaped by subjects' interaction with it. Some focus primarily on the physical environment and arrive at an account of cognition that looks much like the logico-mathematical foundations of modern science. Since the aspects of the physical environment at issue in such approaches are the same everywhere, these approaches tend to focus on universal cognitive structures and processes. Others are more concerned with social and cultural aspects of the environment. Their account sees major differences among cultures and social groups in the cognitive processes that result. For example, some of these latter approaches concentrate on the way in which the structure and function of language may influence cognition. Since such linguistic factors differ widely among speech communities, these approaches tend to be more sensitive to social and cultural differences that may emerge in cognitive processes.

Cross-cultural. In cross-cultural methodologies for studying cognition, cultural and social groups are studied in an attempt to identify commonalities (and hence universal human tendencies) as well as differences in cognition. Because cross-cultural approaches typically deal with settings that differ from those studied in the West, they often begin with an account of the setting (called an ethnography) and then attempt to identify the cognitive correlates of it. Relevant aspects of this setting include factors such as the language used and the forms of institutional activity in which people engage. These two aspects of the environment are often examined in tandem. For example, several important studies have been done on the cognitive consequences of using language in the ways associated with formal instructional activity. One of the advantages of studying this issue cross-culturally is that it allows the investigator to separate the influence of schooling from the effects of maturation. This separation can be made because, unlike in Western industrial societies, in which there is a high, positive correlation between child's age and exposure to formal instruction, children in many other sociocultural settings do not regularly have increasing experience with formal schooling as they grow up. *See also* SCHOOL.

Clinical. Like cross-cultural studies, many clinical approaches to the study of cognition assume that it is possible to learn a great deal about cognitive processes by making comparisons among groups of subjects. There are two additional issues. First, since the primary consideration in clinical practice is the diagnosis and remediation of patients' performance, research in this area generates different kinds of data from those generated in other approaches. Second, many clinical studies are motivated by the desire to learn more about the relationship between the brain and cognitive processes—for example, the studies of specifiable neurological impairments and related disturbances in cognitive performance. Indeed, during much of the twentieth century most information about what areas of the human brain are involved in various cognitive tasks came from studies of what cognitive impairments emerged with specific kinds of brain damage.

Social groups and cognitive processes. In general, cognitivist approaches have made some impressive contributions to knowledge. However, several issues have traditionally received little or no attention. One of these is how cognitive processes can be carried out by social groups. Most studies in cognitivism are grounded in the assumption that cognition is a property of individuals, not groups. This assumption is reinforced by the nature of the analytic units employed in these studies; concepts, features, prototypes, and so forth are almost always assumed to be notions that apply to individual, not social, activity. Several investigators have proposed alternative analytic units that would allow the study of group as well as individual cognition. Such challenges are often particularly important in developmental studies in which some approaches emphasize the social origins of individual cognitive activity.

Artifacts. Another sometimes neglected issue in cognitivism is the role of artifacts, or cultural devices used to mediate human activity (*see* ARTIFACT). The importance of artifacts for cognitivism derives from the claim that much of human cognitive activity can be accounted for only if we understand the cultural devices used to mediate it. In this connection the use of tools and sign systems (e.g., natural language), rather than internal, individual cognitive processes,

is viewed by an increasing number of scholars as holding the key to understanding human cognitive functioning (*see* SIGN SYSTEM). The role of social groups in cognitive processes and the role of artifacts are examples of issues whose investigation would require increased collaboration between cognitivists and scholars from disciplines such as anthropology, history, and SEMIOTICS. While cognitivists have often called for increased interdisciplinary collaboration, such collaboration remains largely a promise of the future rather than a present reality.

Bibliography. Frederic C. Bartlett, *Remembering: A Study in Experimental and Social Psychology*, New York and Cambridge, 1932; John D. Bransford, *Human Cognition: Learning, Understanding, and Remembering*, Belmont, Calif., 1979; Michael Cole and Sylvia Scribner, *Culture and Thought: A Psychological Introduction*, New York, 1974; John H. Flavell and Ellen M. Markman, eds., *Cognitive Development*, Vol. 3, *Handbook of Child Psychology*, 4th ed., Paul H. Mussen, general ed., New York, 1985; Aleksandr R. Luria, *The Working Brain: An Introduction to Neuropsychology* (in Russian), trans. by Basil Haigh, New York, 1973; Ulric Neisser, *Cognition and Reality: Principles and Implications of Cognitive Psychology*, San Francisco, 1976; Jean Piaget, *The Psychology of Intelligence* (in French), trans. by Malcolm Piercy and D. E. Berlyne, London, 1950, reprint Totowa, N.J., 1969; Lev Semenovich Vygotsky, *Myshlenie i Rech': Psikhologicheskie Issledovaniya* (Thinking and Speech: Psychological Research), Moscow and Leningrad, 1934, reprint (ed. and trans. by Eugenia Hanfmann and Gertrude Vakar, Thought and Language) Cambridge, Mass., 1962.

JAMES V. WERTSCH

COGNITION, ANIMAL

The debate over the nature of COGNITION in animals and humans has a long and acrimonious history, and one of the more controversial topics in this debate has been the question of whether animals could learn to use and understand human LANGUAGE. The results of many of the early studies that sought to answer this question were difficult to interpret because, among other reasons, the experiments were not well designed and did not test what they purported to test. More recent research has tried to define and control more carefully what is being tested, what counts as language learning, and what effect the context and the experimenter's behavior might have on the behavior of the animal during the experiment.

Thus far, after fifteen years of experimentation, no nonhuman has acquired a language comparable to human language. This cannot be a surprise; even humans who are deficient in language cannot be taught normal human language. When children who fail to acquire language in the first place and adults who acquire but then lose language through neurological damage are trained with the same procedures

Figure 1. *(Cognition, Animal)* Dr. H. S. Terrace and Nim. Dr. Terrace: "Mine," Nim: "Me/hat" (simultaneous signs). Animals Animals © Dr. H. S. Terrace.

used with species of apes, both apes and humans learn a similar system, one in which there is no evidence of grammatical classes or recursion, properties that set human language apart. *See also* LANGUAGE ACQUISITION.

Although earlier failures to teach language to chimpanzees—for example, that of K. J. Hayes and C. Hayes—can be discounted on the grounds that chimpanzees cannot produce human SPEECH sounds, more recent failures cannot be so discounted. The languages Allen Gardner and Beatrix Gardner and David Premack attempted to teach chimpanzees were not based on speech. The Gardners used a simplified form of American Sign Language (ASL), and Premack used an artificial language in which metal-backed pieces of plastic serving as "words" were placed on a magnetized slate in sentencelike strings. The work of the Gardners and Premack was soon duplicated by others but with no essential change in either procedure or outcome. *See also* SIGN LANGUAGE.

The chimpanzee can learn to observe word order both in producing sequences of "words" and in comprehending the sequences given it. For instance, it can be taught to "describe" simple conditions. A red card placed on a green one will be "described" as "red on green" (not "green on red"). Similarly, the animal can be trained to request food by "writing," "Mary give Sarah apple"; it will react quite differently to "Sarah give Mary apple." In the latter case it may carry out one or two requests but will soon reject others, either knocking the words from the board or stamping its own name, "Sarah," vigorously on each piece of apple (as a child might lay claim to its property by shouting, "Mine! Mine!"). Because the chimpanzee can be trained to use word

order in this manner, why deny that it has language?

The basic reason concerns the use of grammatical categories such as subject and predicate. Does the chimpanzee use such categories in forming or understanding its "sentences" (as the human clearly does, for human sentences cannot be formulated without recourse to such categories)? We have no evidence that it does. The sentencelike sequences of the chimpanzee can be formed with the use of categories far less abstract than that of subject or predicate—categories of perhaps a semantic (e.g., agent, recipient) or, more likely, merely a perceptual nature (e.g., object, action, property). Of course, it is not inconceivable that evidence for grammatical categories in nonhumans will yet be demonstrated, but none has been so far.

At the level of the sentence, evidence for animal language is unrelievedly negative; the evidence is more positive and interesting at the level of the word. Animals (and not only humans) store mental representations of their perceptual experience. Moreover, when chimpanzees are taught names for the items whose mental representations they store, they can retrieve the representations with the "words." For instance, when given the word *apple* (a small blue triangular piece of plastic), the chimpanzee can think of or picture an apple and will identify properly all its properties—taste, seed, stem, shape, color, and so forth. This ability enables the chimpanzee to engage in what is sometimes considered the hallmark of language: "displacement," or talking about things that are not there. In addition, the chimpanzee shows what has been called the Markman effect, an interesting characteristic of word use in children. When a child is shown a picture of, for example, a dog and is asked to match it with either a picture of a different dog or a picture of a bone, the child typically chooses the bone, a thematic rather than a categorical (taxonomic) associate. However, if the word *dog* or even a nonsense word is spoken when the child is shown the pictures of the dog and the bone, the child tends to choose the dog, the categorical associate. Chimpanzees show the same shift from thematic to categorical associate both when the sample is accompanied by its name and when it is accompanied by a nonsense word (a piece of plastic, wordlike in its features but never actually used as a word). Moreover, the chimpanzee that has not been taught words does not show the effect.

The major benefits of animal language research actually have less to do with language per se than with other facets of intelligence. For instance, tests indicate that chimpanzees "read" simple actions in a humanlike way. When shown videotapes of simple actions, such as Bill cutting an orange, they can learn to place distinctive markers on Bill (agent of the action), orange (object of the action), and knife (instrument of the action), thus identifying precursors of basic semantic concepts. In addition, the animal can complete incomplete representations of action. For example, when given the sequence apple-blank-cut-apple, it chooses knife (not pencil or water); when given sponge-blank-wet-sponge, it chooses water (not pencil or knife). Finally, the animal appears to be able to attribute states of mind—such as want and belief—to someone other than itself. When shown an actor confronting a problem, it consistently chooses photographs that constitute a solution to the problem. In order to choose a solution one must first see a problem. And a problem can be perceived as an individual who is seen as wanting something and believing that he or she can get it by acting in a certain way.

See also ANIMAL COMMUNICATION; HUMAN-ANIMAL COMMUNICATION.

Bibliography. Noam Chomsky, *Reflections on Language*, New York, 1975; Ellen M. Markman and Jean E. Hutchinson, "Children's Sensitivity to Constraints on Word Meaning: Taxonomic versus Thematic Relations," *Cognitive Psychology* 16 (1984): 1–27; Steven Pinker, "Formal Models of Language Learning," *Cognition* 7 (1979): 217–283; David Premack, *Gavagai! or the Future History of the Animal Language Controversy*, Cambridge, Mass., 1986.

DAVID PREMACK

COGNITIVE CONSISTENCY THEORIES

A variety of social psychological theories sharing the assumption that people have an inherent tendency to reduce inconsistency among the items of information they hold about the world and themselves. The items of information, called cognitions, include beliefs, AT-TITUDES, opinions, affective responses (liking and disliking), and behavior. These theories argue that when relationships among cognitions are perceived as inconsistent, people will initiate mental processes or behavioral changes designed to reduce or eliminate such inconsistencies. Specifically, cognitive consistency theories predict when people will be particularly receptive or resistant to persuasive communications and when they will try to persuade other people (*see* PERSUASION). What defines inconsistency of cognitions, what other dimensions of cognitions must be considered, and what are the psychological consequences of inconsistency distinguish the major theories of cognitive consistency.

Balance Theory

Fritz Heider's balance theory, derived from principles of Gestalt psychology, holds that our perception of people and things tends to be organized in terms of two dimensions, *unit* and *sentiment* relations. Unit relations may be either positive or negative. A positive unit relation occurs when a person is tied to another person or thing through any of a number of psychological, sociological, or physical variables, such as causation, ownership, membership, and proximity. Specific examples would include a house and its owner, a book and its author, and two people in a relationship. A negative unit relation exists when people and objects are not tied to one another, as when an adult and a child are unrelated or the person does not own the house. Similarly, sentiment relations are positive (e.g., liking) or negative (e.g., disliking) in character.

Cognitive balance is defined from a perceiver's point of view. If the perceiver's unit and sentiment relations toward an object are both positive or both negative, balance exists (e.g., if Joe likes the car he owns or if he dislikes the car he does not own). Imbalance exists if the unit and sentiment relations have opposite signs (e.g., if Joe hates his car or likes the car he does not own). When considering the relations between two people, the analysis becomes slightly more complicated because in addition to those unit and sentiment relations described above, the perceiver will also note whether the observed person likes or dislikes the perceiver. Considering sentiment relations alone, cognitive balance exists when two persons like each other or dislike each other, and imbalance exists when one likes the other and is disliked in return.

The definition of balance when there are three persons, or two persons and an object, is generally clear, especially when only sentiment relations are considered (see Figure 1). Among three relationships balance exists when all are positive or when two are negative. If Joe likes Jane and Sue, then Jane and Sue

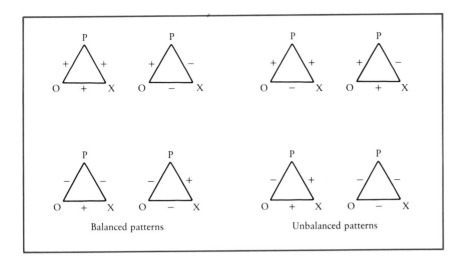

Figure 1. *(Cognitive Consistency Theories)* Balanced and unbalanced patterns in Fritz Heider's balance theory. P and O represent persons, X an attitude object. The lines between elements represent either *unit* or *sentiment* relations. Balanced or unbalanced states are defined here from P's point of view. From Stuart Oskamp, *Attitudes and Opinions*, p. 194. © 1977. Adapted by permission of Prentice-Hall, Englewood Cliffs, N.J.

must like each other for balance to exist. Similarly, if Joe likes Jane and dislikes Sue, then balance is produced by Jane disliking Sue. But note that if Jane and Sue are roommates balance will be difficult to achieve by one disliking the other because of the positive unit relationship. Note also that in these examples reciprocal sentiment relations have not been considered (although Theodore Newcomb's theory of symmetry in interpersonal relationships provides such an analysis). The analysis of cognitive balance even among three people can be quite complicated when all possible sentiment and unit relations are taken into account. The analysis of cognitive balance among more than three persons requires mathematical solutions such as that offered by Dorwin Cartwright and Frank Harary.

Heider assumes that a perceived state of balance is preferred to a perceived state of imbalance. Thus when imbalance occurs, there will be a tendency on the part of the perceiver to see or produce change toward cognitive balance. The individual who is disliked by someone he or she likes may come to dislike that person, and the individual who dislikes the house he or she owns may sell it or come to like it.

Perhaps the major implication of balance theory for the understanding of communication processes concerns agreements or disagreements that people have about any kind of attitude issue. Agreement with a disliked person or disagreement with a liked person produces imbalance and a consequent tendency to attain balance. Thus people may come to change their attitudes about issues in order to achieve balance, or they may change their liking for others.

Congruity Theory

Explicitly about communication processes and their effects on attitudes, congruity theory was generated by CHARLES OSGOOD and Percy Tannenbaum in the mid-1950s. It predicts changes in attitudes toward a communicator and toward the idea or object about which the communicator made an evaluative statement. For example, if a respected clergyman asserted that prostitution was good, the incongruity would tend to produce changes in one's attitude toward both the clergyman and prostitution. As this example implies, congruity theory is quite similar to Heider's balance theory. Although it is more limited than balance theory in that it applies only to those situations in which a source makes an evaluative assertion about a concept (person, object, idea), it is more refined than balance theory in that it predicts amounts of attitude change as a function of the degree of incongruity.

The theory assumes that it is possible to measure the extent to which a person approves or disapproves of a communicator and of the concept about which the communicator makes an assertion. The assertion is conceived as being either for or against the concept without regard to its strength. As will be apparent a strongly positively regarded communicator making a supportive statement about a strongly approved concept constitutes a state of congruity. As long as the assertion favors the concept, incongruity occurs to the extent that (1) regard for the communicator is less than strongly positive or (2) the concept is less than strongly approved. If either the attitude toward the communicator or the attitude toward the concept was negative, strong incongruity would exist. Alternatively, if the assertion is against the concept, a strongly positively viewed communicator and concept would produce maximal incongruity. Incongruity would then be decreased to the extent that (1) regard for the communicator is less than strongly positive or (2) the concept is less than strongly approved.

The theory assumes that when incongruity exists there will be a psychological drive to reduce it. In general, incongruity can be reduced by changes in attitudes toward the communicator and/or the concept in the direction of greater congruity. These changes will not necessarily be equal between the attitudes toward the communicator and the attitudes toward the concept. When a source makes an assertion about a concept, there will be a general tendency for the attitude toward the concept to be more affected than that toward the source. Finally, when the assertion made by a source is very surprising (e.g., a clergyman advocating prostitution), there will be a tendency to disbelieve the assertion or its apparent significance, thereby reducing incongruity.

Congruity theory has obvious utility in considering those situations in which the persuasive effect is due more to the (positive or negative) prestige, reputation, or attractiveness of the communicator than to the persuasiveness of the message. It therefore complements theories that bear on the persuasive effects of a communicator's trustworthiness and expertness as well as theories that concern the persuasive content and structure of a communication.

The Theory of Cognitive Dissonance

This theory was formulated by Leon Festinger in the mid-1950s and subsequently inspired hundreds of research projects and considerable debate and commentary. It was provocative because it turned the commonly accepted positive relationship between incentives and behavior on its head, asserting that under certain conditions behavioral tendencies would be strengthened in *inverse* proportion to the magnitude of rewards or punishments. The theory noted that not only do attitudes guide behavior—as was always assumed—but that behavior also guides attitudes. Thus cognitive dissonance theory essentially stipulates a set of conditions under which attitudes will become more consistent with behavior.

The theory is stated in terms of cognitions, defined as items of information that a person has about the self and the world. Examples of cognitions are one's awareness of a liking for ice cream, attitudes toward nuclear disarmament, perception that a friend is authoritarian, knowledge that the world is round, and recollection of how one voted in the last election. When one cognition (e.g., I am eating ice cream) "follows from" another (e.g., I like ice cream) the two cognitions are said to be *consonant*. When one cognition (I like ice cream) is inconsistent with another (I have just refused to eat some ice cream) the two cognitions are said to be *dissonant* with each other. This definition of a dissonant relationship approximates what has been used to test empirical derivations, whereas the original, more general and formal definition—that one cognition follows from the obverse of another—has been criticized for imprecision. Given any pair of cognitions, it is not always possible to say whether they are consonant, dissonant, or simply irrelevant to each other. There

are nevertheless many instances in which consonant and dissonant relationships can be specified, thus allowing tests of the theory and its application to the understanding of psychological processes.

Dissonance theory takes an important step beyond other theories of cognitive balance by specifying that cognitions are resistant to change. First, the theory assumes that perceptions are responsive to reality (e.g., it would be very difficult to "see" a circle as a square). At the same time, some realities are more ambiguous than others, and to the extent that a reality is ambiguous its corresponding cognition will be less resistant to change. An object perceived through a heavy mist might be seen as a tree, a building, or an elephant, and changing what it is that one "sees" would be quite easy. In addition to perceiving realities in different ways, one can change a cognition by changing its corresponding reality. In this case resistance to changing the cognition results partly from the difficulty of changing the reality. If one sees oneself as fat, that cognition may be changed by becoming thinner through exercise, intake control, and so on.

One more variable that must be specified in order to understand the implications of dissonance theory is the relative importance of cognitions. No formal definition is given, but the variable is accessible intuitively. For example, the cognition that I have just broken my pencil is less important than the cognition that my car has been stolen, and the cognition that the day is cloudy is less important than the cognition that a friend has just died. Cognitions must therefore be weighted according to their importance.

When a person holds two or more cognitions that are in a dissonant relationship to each other, the person is said to experience dissonance, a motivational state that, like hunger, urges behavior designed to reduce or eliminate it. The centerpiece of the theory, then, is the statement that relates the determinants of the magnitude of dissonance to the ways in which a person will try to reduce dissonance. The magnitude of dissonance associated with a given cognition is a direct function of the number of cognitions dissonant with it, each weighted for importance, and an inverse function of the number of cognitions consonant with it, each weighted for importance. In other words, the magnitude of dissonance associated with a given cognition is a direct function of the ratio of dissonant to consonant cognitions (see Figure 2). A person who experiences dissonance can reduce it by reducing the number of dissonant cognitions or their importance and by increasing the number of consonant cognitions or their importance. In general, what cognitions will be changed in order to reduce dissonance will be determined by their resistance to change, as described above.

In order for this formulation to be sensible the

$$\text{The magnitude of dissonance associated with any one counterattitudinal statement} = \frac{\text{Related dissonant cognitions} \times \text{the importance of the cognitions}}{\text{Related consonant cognitions} \times \text{the importance of the cognitions}}$$

Figure 2. (Cognitive Consistency Theories) From Leon Festinger's theory of cognitive dissonance, a framework for calculating the magnitude of dissonance generated by counterattitudinal statements. From Mary John Smith, *Persuasion and Human Action, A Review and Critique of Social Influence Theories*, Belmont, Calif., p. 122. © 1982 by Wadsworth. Reprinted by permission.

cognition in regard to which the magnitude of dissonance is calculated must have very high resistance to change. Hence it is in regard to irrevocable behaviors that the implications of the theory have been most clear. The selection of one of several alternatives when one cannot reverse the selection, or the decision to comply or not with pressure to behave in a certain way, provides a clear cognition with high resistance to change and thereby allows specification of the magnitude of dissonance and how dissonance will be reduced. For example, the choice to vote for political candidate A rather than B will create dissonance to the extent that candidate A has negative characteristics (e.g., he or she knows little about foreign policy) that candidate B does not have, and to the extent that candidate B has positive characteristics (e.g., he or she is an expert on crime and delinquency) that candidate A does not have. Note that irrationality is not assumed in the decision; on balance candidate A is perceived as better than candidate B. The reduction of dissonance resulting from the voting decision can proceed in any or all of the following ways. Positive characteristics of A can be seen as more important, and new positive characteristics can be found. Negative characteristics of A can be seen as less important. Conversely, positive characteristics of B can be made less important, negative characteristics can be made more important, and new negative characteristics can be found.

Implications regarding the communication process are many. After a dissonance-arousing vote, for example, the voter will welcome almost any kind of supportive information about the chosen candidate. The voter will be pleased if the candidate won, not only because the candidate was preferred but also because winning shows that other people agree with one's decision. At the same time, the voter will avoid or discount any negative information about the chosen candidate and welcome negative information about the rejected candidate.

The induction of behavior that a person would normally avoid, called "forced compliance" by Festinger, also has implications for the understanding of communication processes. However, the implication that has received major attention focuses on self-persuasion as opposed to persuasion of others. When by the promise of a reward or the threat of punishment for noncompliance a person is induced to uphold an attitudinal position that is discrepant with what he or she privately believes, the magnitude of resulting dissonance will decrease as the magnitude of the reward or threat increases. That is, because the initial attitude and the behavior are dissonant with each other and are constant, as the number of reasons for engaging in the behavior increases, the ratio of dissonant to consonant (weighted) cognitions will decrease. Because it is difficult to deny that one has engaged in counterattitudinal behavior, dissonance will tend to be reduced by changing one's attitude so that it more nearly corresponds with one's behavior. Thus when people are induced to engage in counterattitudinal behavior, the *less* the magnitude of the inducement (e.g., money or threat), the greater will be the attitude change in the direction of the induced behavior. This is an interesting insight into self-persuasion processes and relates to phenomena such as brainwashing and religious conversion.

A more relevant implication of dissonance theory for the understanding of communication processes comes from an audience's "forced compliance." Whenever an individual exposes himself or herself to persuasions or points of view that would normally be avoided, some dissonance should be experienced that should result in a tendency to become more positively disposed toward the avoided communications. ADVERTISING is a good example. Watching television (especially in commercial mass media systems) involves an almost inevitable exposure to COMMERCIALS and occasional public service persuasive messages. Interestingly enough, the dissonance formulation holds that the magnitude of dissonance and consequent tendency for positive attitude change toward the advertised product will increase as the entertainment value of the program *decreases*—up to the point, of course, at which one does not watch at all. From the perspective of dissonance theory, having a very good reason for enduring ads (or any persuasive messages) makes them less persuasive as long as the reason is irrelevant to the content of the ad or message. More generally, whenever a person exposes himself or herself to a discrepant point of view, the less good the reasons for doing so, the greater the dissonance and consequent positive change toward the discrepant position. This is perhaps the most important and general of the implications from dissonance theory for the understanding of communication processes.

One final derivation of dissonance theory deserves mention. No matter how dissonance has been created in a person, a method for reducing dissonance that is likely to be available is the procurement of social support. In some instances this will be most easily attained by selective association with people expected to have a point of view consonant with one's behavior. In other cases persuasion will be necessary. Those in whom dissonance has been aroused will attempt to persuade others of the validity of what they have done. Hence dissonance can produce persuasive communications as well as make people more or less prone to accept them.

Assessment

Although cognitive consistency theories have been criticized as mechanistic, simplistic, not applicable outside the laboratory, and as viewing people as passive rather than active processors of information, the theories must be judged as having made a major contribution to our understanding of human behavior. Dissonance theory, in particular, opened new frontiers for research and changed our fundamental understanding of how promises of reward and threats of punishment affect values and behavioral tendencies. While the major thrust of research that followed the theories of cognitive consistency centered primarily on *how* information is processed, the current trend is to return to the question of *why* information is processed. Theories of cognitive consistency integrated these two questions to a remarkable degree.

Bibliography. Robert Abelson, Elliot Aronson, William McGuire, Theodore Newcomb, Milton Rosenberg, and Percy Tannenbaum, eds., *Theories of Cognitive Consistency*, Chicago, 1968; Leonard Berkowitz, ed., *Advances in Experimental Social Psychology*, Vol. 9, New York, 1976; Leon Festinger, *A Theory of Cognitive Dissonance*, Stanford, Calif., 1957; Fritz Heider, *The Psychology of Interpersonal Relations*, New York, 1958; Gardner Lindzey and Elliot Aronson, eds., *Handbook of Social Psychology*, 2d ed., Reading, Pa., 1968, and 3d ed., New York, 1985; Charles E. Osgood, George J. Suci, and Percy H. Tannenbaum, *The Measurement of Meaning*, Urbana, Ill., 1957; Robert A. Wicklund and Jack Brehm, *Perspectives on Cognitive Dissonance*, Hillsdale, N.J., 1976.

JACK W. BREHM

COINS

Coins have existed since the seventh century B.C.E. in the eastern Mediterranean and were minted somewhat later elsewhere in the Middle East, India, and China. As an alternative to coins, paper money was printed in China from about 1000 C.E. for four hundred to five hundred years but only appeared in the rest of the world much later. While coins and paper currency served important functions in trade and finance, they also furnished a means of communication by carrying pictorial and verbal messages. In most cases, the design of coins and notes included not only the monetary value, the name of the issuing authority, and the date, but also decorative elements with some sort of political or religious message.

Origins

Early coins featured a wide range of symbols and figures, including animals, humans, and gods and goddesses, but the first clear examples of the political use of coins appeared in Persia in the sixth century B.C.E. The figure of the monarch, arrayed for war as the defender of his people, adorned the obverse of gold darics and silver sigloi from the beginning of Persian coinage until the demise of the Persian Empire in the fourth century B.C.E. The Parthians, who eventually succeeded the Persians, presented their monarchs with the attributes of gods on the reverse of their drachmas and larger coins. The kings bore weapons, just as they did on Persian coins, and were intended to be viewed as defenders of the nation. Such concepts dominated Parthian coinage from approximately 250 B.C.E. to 250 C.E.

In Greece coins issued by individual cities celebrated civic identity and pride. For instance, the staters of Metapontum, which were decorated with an ear of wheat, probably referred to the agricultural wealth of the town. The frequent inclusion of protective deities sacred to a particular polis also served to identify and celebrate the town. *See* HELLENIC WORLD.

Ancient Rome

Ancient Rome furnishes many examples of the symbolic use of coin illustrations. At its zenith, the Roman Empire encompassed an area of nearly 1 million square miles, with a population approaching 100 million. The empire was composed of dozens of different peoples, each with its distinctive language, religion, and way of life. As part of a strategy to retain dominance, it was important for the Roman state to make its rulers and their power widely known. Some form of mass communication had to be found, and coinage was one of the few available possibilities. *See* ROMAN EMPIRE.

Another reason for the use of coins was the political insecurity of the emperor. By placing his portrait on coins, by referring to his personal virtues and political accomplishments, the emperor hoped to enhance his prestige and political legitimacy.

Some of the Roman coins glorified both emperor and state. For example, a brass sestertius during the reign of Nero (54–68 C.E.) depicted a seated figure of the goddess Roma. The other side of the coin featured a portrait of the emperor. Other coins that celebrated the state were struck during the reign of Philip (244–249), which included a celebration of the one-thousandth anniversary of Rome's supposed founding. Since contests between wild animals were a prominent feature of the celebration, their depiction on coins was used to commemorate the festivities.

Nonetheless, the primary purpose of messages on Roman coins was to support and draw attention to the emperor. The head of the reigning monarch graced the obverse of most Roman imperial coins; the reverse frequently displayed a personal characteristic of which the ruler was particularly proud. The mild-mannered Antoninus Pius (r. 138–161) celebrated his piety, clemency, and sense of justice by using allegorical figures, labeled with the name of the virtue being celebrated. Since Nero fancied himself a great builder and beautifier of the empire, he commemorated his modernization of the port of Ostia on an issue of sestertii, which unsuccessfully attempted to combine an aerial view of the harbor with a perspective view of the ships within it. This ruler also paid homage to his supposed skills as a musician: on a copper struck late in the reign, he poses as Apollo, complete with lyre.

Trajan, whose reign (98–117) coincided with the greatest geographical extent achieved by the empire, commemorated his conquest of the nation of Dacia with an issue of silver denarii that featured a seated captive on the reverse along with the inscription *DACCAP* (for "Dacia Capta"). The seated figure resembles others modeled in stone, seen on Trajan's Column in Rome.

Because the question of succession constantly plagued the Roman state and its emperors, the intended line of succession was sometimes indicated on the coins. A gold aureus of Septimius Severus (r. 193–211) depicted the emperor on its obverse and his wife and sons on the reverse, perhaps to accustom the populace to his plan.

Other Roman coins rendered tribute to various organs of the Roman state, such as the senate or the army. Coins featuring two soldiers and a military standard, carrying the legend *Gloria Exercitus* ("To the glory of the army"), became very common in the troubled fourth century. The message may have been intended to shore up the morale of a Roman army that was increasingly falling prey to external invasions. The design became so popular that the invaders eventually adopted it on their own coins.

Still other coins extended recognition to various Roman provinces. They usually had a seated or reclining female figure with the name of the province around or beneath it. This type of coin was quite prominent during the reign of Hadrian (117–138).

Later, a different sort of message appeared on Roman coins, one that reflected the religious currents sweeping the late-classical world. By the 390s, Christianity had become the sole legal religion of the empire, and this was reflected on the messages carried by Roman coins. Crosses began to appear, and traditional figures representing Victory metamorphosed into Christian angels. On later coins, a hand from heaven appeared in the act of crowning the ruler with God's favor (see Figure 1). This closely paralleled an aureus of Trajan, on which a figure of Jupiter conferred his blessings on the emperor, represented by a much smaller figure (see Figure 2). The close identification of the ruler and the Christian faith on coins soon ended in the Christian West, but it endured for many centuries on the coins of the Byzantine East.

Middle East and Islam

Rome was not the only empire that employed coins for the communication of political and cultural change. Early in the third century C.E., the Parthian Empire was succeeded by a new, more authentically Persian state, the Sassanian Empire. The rulers of the new regime wished to emphasize that they were a native dynasty, with a legitimacy superior to that of the "alien" Parthians. The coins of the region, previously founded on Greek models with Greek inscriptions, were now inscribed in Pehlevi, the language spoken by the people. In addition, the ruler was depicted on the coins in native headdress. The reverse of the coins emphasized the king's piety and his attachment to Persian traditions by depicting him, usually with his son, at an altar taking part in a rite of the Zoroastrian faith, which was the prevailing religion of Persia.

Early in the seventh century a new force, Islam, arose in the East and in time led to the demise of both the Byzantine and Sassanian states (*see* ISLAM, CLASSICAL AND MEDIEVAL ERAS). Although the Arab peoples were acquainted with the concept of coinage at the time the conquests began, they had little experience in producing their own coins. As they spread out of the Arabian Peninsula in the 630s and 640s, they tended to use whatever coins came their way, usually Byzantine and Sassanian issues. By the 650s, having conquered vast regions, they found it necessary to produce their own coins on a large scale.

Two types of coins resulted, both strongly imitative of earlier types. Arab-Byzantine coins resembled the Byzantine coins before the conquest, but with

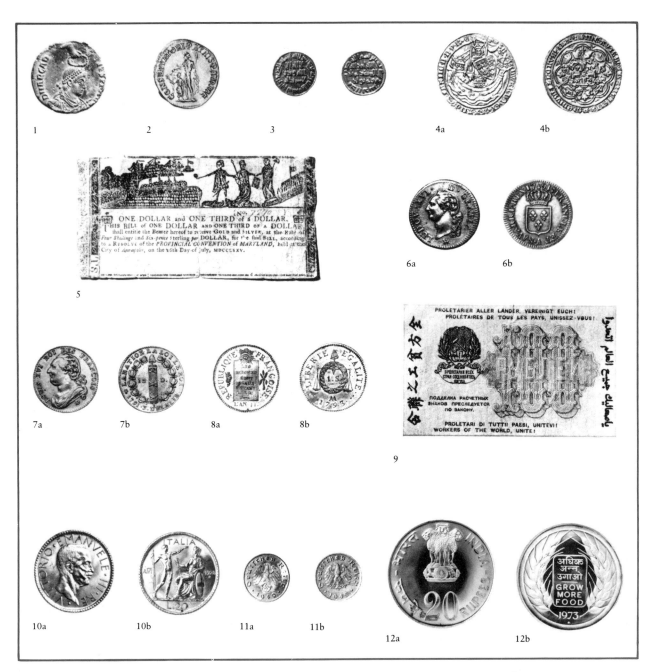

Figures 1–12. *(Coins)* (**1**) arcadius, Rome, 378–383 c.e.; (**2**) aureus, Rome, 112–117 c.e.; (**3**) dinar, Syria, a.h. 80 (699–700 c.e.); (**4**) noble, England, 1356–1361, *a:* obverse, *b:* reverse; (**5**) one and one-third dollar, Maryland, America, 1775; (**6**) sol, France, until 1791, *a:* obverse, *b:* reverse; (**7**) sol, France, 1791, *a:* obverse, *b:* reverse; (**8**) sol, France, 1793, *a:* obverse, *b:* reverse; (**9**) 100 rubles, Russia (RSFSR, or Soviet Russia), 1920; (**10**) 20 lire, Italy, 1928, *a:* obverse, *b:* reverse; (**11**) 10 pfennig, Germany, *a:* 1940, *b:* 1945; (**12**) 20 rupees, India (United Nations Food and Agricultural Organization), 1973, *a:* obverse, *b:* reverse. Courtesy of the American Numismatic Society, New York.

important alterations. Christian crosses were replaced by globes on poles. Brief Arabic legends supplemented those in Greek. PORTRAITURE remained a feature of the coins, even though it violated Islamic laws prohibiting the use of images. In the Arab-Sassanian coins, legends continued to be in Pehlevi, with the addition of brief inscriptions in Arabic.

While active conquest continued, violations of Islamic law in the form of portraits on coins were overlooked. By the 690s, however, the Islamic Califate was an established power, and the faithful demanded that it reform the coinage. In A.H. 77 (696–697 C.E.) the Umaiyad caliph ʿAbd al-Malik introduced a completely new gold coin, the dinar (see Figure 3). It was soon joined by the silver dirhem and the copper fals. None of them bore images of any kind; they were decorated solely with religious inscriptions. These new coins had the greatest purely religious content of any coins in human history.

Coins of this type, struck in mints from Spain to the gates of China, dominated the Islamic world for the next several centuries. They accurately reflected the new faith and left a lasting imprint on later coins in Islamic areas.

Medieval and Early Modern Europe

In the early MIDDLE AGES, coins became less important because trade, especially between distant regions, declined. The collapse of the Roman Empire was as much economic as it was political. As a result, virtually no coins were being made in the Christian West by the middle of the sixth century. Byzantine gold solidi from Constantinople were used for exceptionally large purchases, but daily business was carried on by simple barter. By the seventh and eighth centuries, a few coins were once more being produced; their numbers increased after approximately 790, particularly in France and Britain. A new denomination, the denier or penny, had appeared in both countries by that time, and its use spread eastward in the following centuries.

Even though more coins were made as the Middle Ages continued, the coins were very small and thin and contained only modest amounts of precious metals. Silver and gold were in short supply at that time and continued to be scarce until the thirteenth century; almost no gold coins appeared in the West until about 1250. Understandably, the modest size of the early medieval coin limited its design possibilities, as did the penchant—which increased after 1000—for creating dies with a small number of tiny, simple punches.

The coin appears to have been considered only an economic tool, not an artistic communicative medium as it had been in the days of ancient Greece and Rome. The decoration on early medieval coins was abbreviated or absent. There were crosses, of course, but they formed a simple design rather than an aggressive religious or political statement. The occasional Carolingian attempt at realistic portraiture of the king probably had a political purpose, but the quality of portraiture on most early medieval coins remained poor for many centuries to come.

By about 1200, trade between and within the states of the West accelerated, and new and larger coins were needed. The first of these was the grosso, a silver coin from Venice. By the middle of the thirteenth century, gold coins were being struck in western Europe, essentially for the first time since the fall of Rome. These new, more valuable coins did not characteristically have elaborate decorations, although there were exceptions. One was the English noble (see Figure 4), introduced in the 1340s by Edward III (r. 1327–1377). On the obverse of this coin, Edward was depicted on a ship, defending himself with sword and shield, upon which were blazoned the quartered arms of France and England. It is thought that the ship may have symbolized the English naval victory at Sluys in 1340, one of the earliest battles in the Hundred Years' War between England and France, and that the use of the French and English arms together reflected Edward's political aspirations on the Continent. The coin might be considered a numismatic declaration of war.

By the 1300s, the basic design elements on coins had settled into patterns that continued to modern times. The obverse generally contained a picture of the ruler, with a legend listing the ruler's titles. The reverse of larger coins was usually a heraldic reference to the state; smaller coins were decorated with crosses or other simple devices.

In the Germanies coins had assumed a commemorative function by the latter half of the sixteenth century; the large, silver thalers, first struck around 1500, adapted themselves well to this purpose. A Danish version of the thaler, called a krone, dating from 1659, depicted an arm from heaven cutting off a (Swedish) hand which is reaching for the Danish crown. And in England a series of coins with English rather than the traditional Latin legends commemorated the beheading of Charles I and the foundation of Cromwell's Commonwealth in 1649. During the English Civil War the Parliamentary forces put the pious motto "God with Us" on their issues. When Charles II returned to the throne in 1660, his reemployment of Latin on coins was one symbol of the restoration of the old regime.

American and French Revolutions

The communicative function of coins found another numismatic medium in paper money. Paper notes were used in the English colonies of North America, where the inclusion of both subtle and blatant messages on paper money served to propagate colonial aims. National issues (called Continental currency) used allegorical figures to make political statements. The issues released by the individual states were often even more obvious in their political statements. One issue from South Carolina had an engraving of an American Hercules strangling a British lion. A one and one-third dollar note from Maryland presented the following scene: on the left, George III sets fire to an American city while trampling on the Magna Carta; to the right, Britannia receives a petition from America, represented by a woman stepping on a scroll marked "Slavery"; to the extreme right, American troops march to the rescue of the burning city (see Figure 5). The reverse showed Britannia and America reconciled, with the hopeful motto *Pax Triumphis Potior* ("Peace is preferable to victory").

French coins also reflected that country's revolutionary struggles. Until 1791, however, the French copper coin known as the sol or sou retained the designs and legends it had carried since the beginning of Louis XVI's reign (see Figure 6). It had a portrait of the king on the obverse and the Bourbon fleur-de-lis on the reverse. Legends were given in Latin and referred solely to the king and his possessions, not to the French people. In 1791, when Louis XVI became a constitutional monarch, the sol was redesigned with an unflattering but realistic portrait of the king replacing the earlier idealized one (see Figure 7). On the reverse, a fasces topped by a liberty cap was substituted for the fleur-de-lis of the Bourbons. Changes were also made in the legends. For the first time, Louis was called king of the French, not of France, and the language was French, not Latin. The reverse legends referred to "Nation, Law, and King," in that order, and the date on the coin (1791) was termed—according to the new revolutionary calendar—the third year of liberty.

In the autumn of 1792, when France was at war with the monarchies of Europe, the sol was once again redesigned (see Figure 8). The obverse featured an Eye of Providence above a tablet with the inscription *les hommes sont egaux devant la loi* ("All men are equal before the law"); the date was expressed as the year II. The reverse had a scale of justice and the date expressed according to the traditional calendar. The date on the reverse was soon dropped, however, and for approximately the next decade all French coins bore dates expressed only in terms of the revolutionary calendar.

Other countries also marked their revolutions and anticolonial struggles with new coin designs. In Latin America, when insurgents ousted the Spanish and Portuguese in the early nineteenth century, they invented new, nationalist designs for their coins. Typically the name and arms of the new country adorned the obverse, while the reverse often contained information about the coin's value, place of mintage, and metallic purity. Occasionally, as in Bolivia and Argentina, these reverse elements were replaced by portraits of national heroes.

Twentieth-Century Coins

The designs of coins bear witness to the political and social upheavals that occurred in Europe in the first half of the twentieth century. During the civil war that followed the establishment of the Soviet regime in 1917, neither Soviet nor anti-Soviet factions struck coins to any extent; they relied on paper currency. Communist slogans and allegories became a constant feature on the notes (and on postage STAMPS, which were frequently used as money during those turbulent years). One noteworthy example of the use of currency for political purposes is a series of notes issued in 1919–1920. Referred to as Babylonians by collectors, they include the slogan "Workers of the World Unite" in Russian, German, French, Arabic, English, Chinese, and Italian, along with the revolutionary symbol of hammer and sickle (see Figure 9). The multilingual text may have expressed the belief that many other countries were about to follow the Soviet example.

By the early 1920s, sufficient order had been achieved in the Soviet state so that coins could once again be produced and remain in circulation. On a 1924 ruble, the obverse featured the arms of the regime along with the slogan noted above, while the reverse depicted one worker leading another into a "Revolutionary Dawn." Soon after V. I. Lenin's death in 1924, his portrait appeared on many of the coins and virtually all the paper money.

New coins were also issued in Italy in the 1920s when Benito Mussolini came to power (see Figure 10). Because Italy was still a monarchy whose king was very much part of the political scene, Mussolini could not hope to place his own image on the coins. This problem was addressed in two ways. First, the fasces, the symbol of Mussolini's political organization, appeared on most Italian coins and notes through the end of the regime in 1943. Second, consistent with Mussolini's references to Italy's past greatness, coins were issued that were reminiscent of ancient Roman issues. These were some of the most beautiful and artistic coins of the twentieth century. They featured classical motifs and a new dating system (expressed in Roman numerals), which gave the year of the Fascist regime along with the date according to the Christian calendar.

Similar uses of coin symbols occurred in Adolf Hitler's Third Reich. The swastika appeared on most forms of official communication from 1933 until the demise of the National Socialist regime in 1945. At first it occupied a subordinate position on coins, but by 1936, supporting the German eagle, it had become the dominant obverse symbol on silver coins and was soon extended to all other coins as well (see Figure 11).

Since 1945 new and developing countries have employed coins as part of their efforts to forge a sense of national identity. For example, when Ghana achieved independence in 1957, its name, which was representative of its precolonial history, replaced the old name, Gold Coast. The new name also appeared on its coins and currency, as did a portrait of the new leader, KWAME NKRUMAH, replacing the picture of Britain's Queen Elizabeth II. Other emerging nations displayed native flora and fauna on their coins and native scenes on their notes, to emphasize the country's uniqueness in the eyes of citizen and foreigner alike. Still other nations paid homage to heroes of the struggle against colonial regimes. Some states renamed their currency units, replacing denominations imported by a colonial power with new names that recalled indigenous traditions. Thus, in the 1960s, Ghana replaced the pound with the cedi, which derives from the Ghanaian word *sedie*, the cowrie shell used for money by the coastal tribes.

Another form of coinage that has emerged since World War II is the commemorative, usually issued in economically developed countries. Such issues are in part attempts by governments to gain extra income from collectors, but also to achieve the same communication goals mentioned above, to forge a sense of unity among disparate groups by illustrating a shared history and national identity.

Since the early 1970s there have been issues of coins and, to a lesser extent, notes by many countries, representing causes that transcend national boundaries. Thus far there have been issues on behalf of conservation of endangered wildlife species and in support of the United Nations Food and Agriculture Organization's campaign against world hunger (see Figure 12). Approximately one hundred countries issued coins on behalf of the latter campaign. In both cases, although the coins featured a marked emphasis on indigenous themes, there was at the same time an effort to circulate coins with an international message. The success of such worldwide numismatic campaigns ensures further issues of this sort.

See also ARTIFACT; HERALDRY; POLITICAL SYMBOLS.

Bibliography. R. A. G. Carson, *Coins: Ancient, Mediaeval & Modern*, 2d ed., rev., London, 1970; Richard G. Doty, *Money of the World*, New York, 1978; Anthony Dowle and André de Clermont, *Monnaies modernes, de 1789 à nos jours*, trans. by Robert Lapassade and Pierre-Yves Lathoumetie, Paris, 1972; J. Rufus Fears, *Princeps a Dis Electus: The Divine Election of the Emperor as a Political Concept at Rome*, Rome, 1977; Michael Grant, *Roman Anniversary Issues: An Exploratory Study of the Numismatic and Medallic Commemoration of Anniversary Years, 49 B.C.–A.D. 375*, Cambridge, 1950; idem, *Roman History from Coins*, Cambridge, 1968; Leslaw Morawiecki, *Political Propaganda in the Coinage of the Late Roman Republic (44–43 B.C.)*, Wrocław, Poland, 1983; Walter Trimmlich, *Familienpropaganda der Kaiser Caligula und Claudius: Agrippina Maior und Antonia Augusta auf Munzen*, Berlin, 1978.

R. G. DOTY

COLONIZATION

The establishment of political and economic control by one country over another, or over a relatively unsettled area, usually accompanied by the settlement abroad of a number of people who remain loyal to the colonizing country and represent its system of governance and its economic interests. Thus, colonization differs from ordinary MIGRATION in the official relationship of the countries involved, and the effectiveness of the colonial situation is directly dependent on the communication system that joins the colonizing country and the colony. All subsequent communication patterns are, in turn, affected by the colonization process.

Colonization followed roadways and sea paths and moved through underwater cable systems and on overland railroad networks. It has all but disappeared in the age of air travel and telecommunications, a time when the worldwide spread of technology, the universalization of the nation-state, and the substantial population of all inhabitable land have changed our concepts of space, distance, and the exercise of power. The very term *expansion*, so frequently used in the early twentieth century to describe the colonial process as movement outward from a central point, no longer has geographical meaning. Accompanying romantic terms like *frontier, open space*, and *empty land* are archaic as well.

Territorial colonization is therefore largely a historical fact, not a possible future condition of major significance. (Only space colonization assures the term continued contemporary usage.) *Imperialism*, a word frequently used in conjunction with colonization, implies any form of outside domination by foreign state or private institution, such as a corporation. It can be direct, as in the instance of military intervention, or it can be indirect, as in economic control or cultural assertion. What clearly distinguishes colonization from imperialism, however, is the former's special characteristic: the presence of individuals of different cultural or natural origin who directly assert their state's authority or whose legal and social position in the territory is guaranteed by that authority. Colonization may

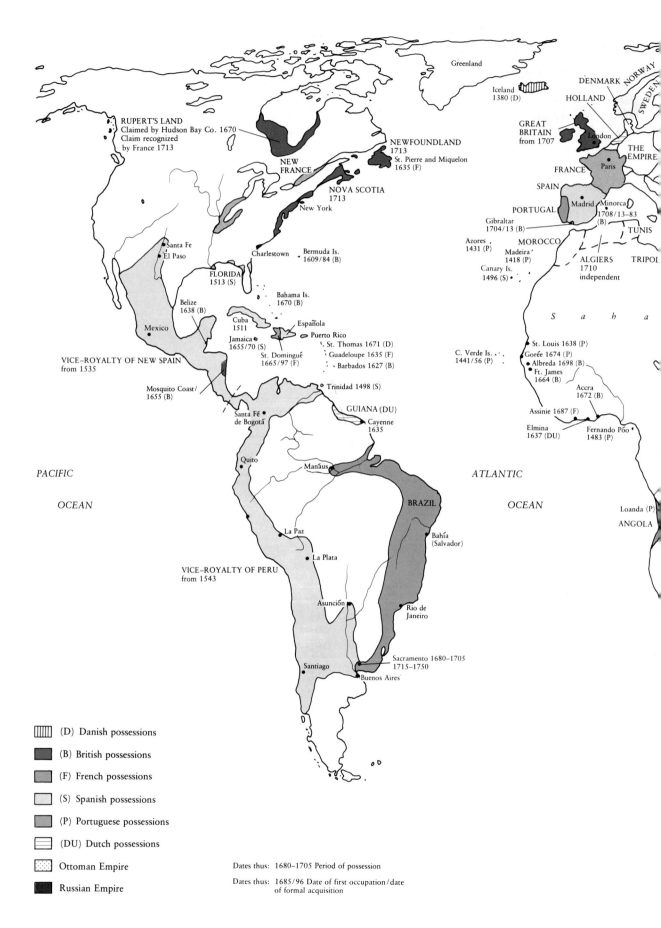

Greenland

Iceland
1380 (D)

NORWAY
SWEDEN
DENMARK
HOLLAND
London
GREAT
BRITAIN
from 1707
THE
EMPIRE
FRANCE
Paris
SPAIN
PORTUGAL
Madrid
Minorca
1708/13-83
(B)
Gibraltar
1704/13 (B)
TUNIS
Azores
1431 (P)
MOROCCO
Madeira
1418 (P)
ALGIERS
1710
independent
TRIPOL
Canary Is.
1496 (S)

RUPERT'S LAND
Claimed by Hudson Bay Co. 1670
Claim recognized
by France 1713

NEWFOUNDLAND
1713
St. Pierre and Miquelon
1635 (F)

NEW
FRANCE

NOVA SCOTIA
1713
New York

Charlestown
Bermuda Is.
1609/84 (B)

FLORIDA
1513 (S)

Santa Fe
El Paso

Bahama Is.
1670 (B)

Belize
1638 (B)

Cuba
1511
Española
Jamaica
1655/70 (S)
Puerto Rico
St. Thomas 1671 (D)
Guadeloupe 1635 (F)
Barbados 1627 (B)

Mexico

St. Domingué
1665/97 (F)

VICE-ROYALTY OF NEW SPAIN
from 1535

Mosquito Coast/
1655 (B)

Trinidad 1498 (S)

GUIANA (DU)

Santa Fé
de Bogotá

Cayenne
1635

Quito

PACIFIC

OCEAN

Manáus

BRAZIL

La Paz

VICE-ROYALTY OF PERU
from 1543

La Plata

Asunción

Santiago

Sacramento 1680-1705
1715-1750

Buenos Aires

Rio de
Janeiro

Bahía
(Salvador)

ATLANTIC

OCEAN

S   a   h   a

St. Louis 1638 (P)
Gorée 1674 (P)
Albreda 1698 (B)
Ft. James
1664 (B)

C. Verde Is.
1441/56 (P)

Accra
1672 (B)

Assinie 1687 (F)

Elmina
1637 (DU)

Fernando Póo
1483 (P)

Loanda (P)

ANGOLA

(D)	Danish possessions
(B)	British possessions
(F)	French possessions
(S)	Spanish possessions
(P)	Portuguese possessions
(DU)	Dutch possessions
	Ottoman Empire
	Russian Empire

Dates thus: 1680–1705 Period of possession

Dates thus: 1685/96 Date of first occupation/date
of formal acquisition

332

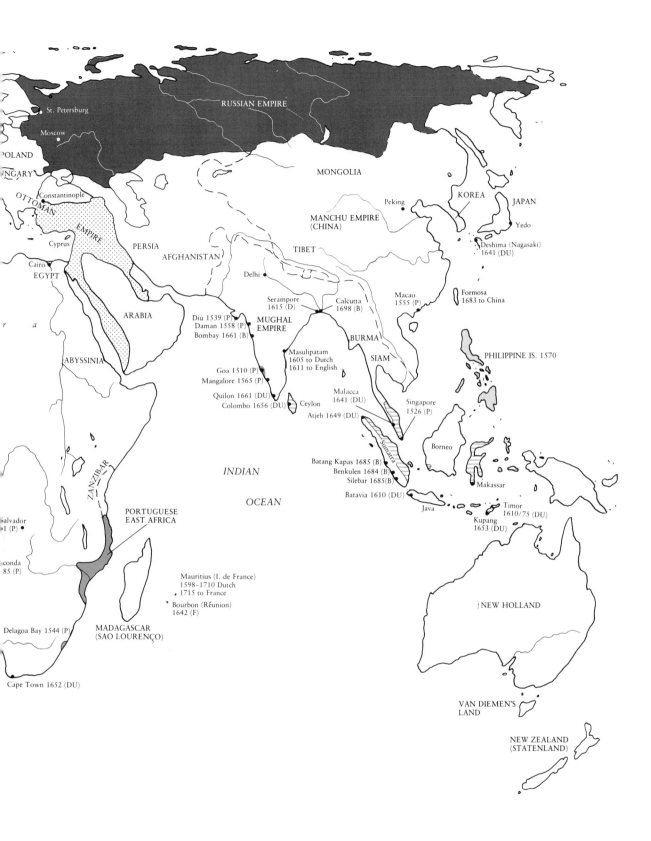

RUSSIAN EMPIRE

St. Petersburg

Moscow

POLAND

NGARY

OTTOMAN

Constantinople

EMPIRE

Cyprus

Cairo

EGYPT

PERSIA

AFGHANISTAN

ARABIA

ABYSSINIA

MONGOLIA

Peking

KOREA

JAPAN

MANCHU EMPIRE
(CHINA)

Yedo

TIBET

Deshima (Nagasaki)
1641 (DU)

Delhi

Serampore
1615 (D)

Calcutta
1698 (B)

Macao
1555 (P)

Formosa
1683 to China

Diu 1539 (P)
Daman 1558 (P)
Bombay 1661 (B)

MUGHAL
EMPIRE

BURMA

Masulipatam
1605 to Dutch
1611 to English

SIAM

Goa 1510 (P)
Mangalore 1565 (P)

Quilon 1661 (DU)
Colombo 1656 (DU) Ceylon

PHILIPPINE IS. 1570

Malacca
1641 (DU)

Singapore
1526 (P)

Atjeh 1649 (DU)

ZANZIBAR

INDIAN

OCEAN

Borneo

Batang Kapas 1685 (B)
Benkulen 1684 (B)
Silebar 1685(B)

Batavia 1610 (DU)

Makassar

alvador
1 (P)

conda
85 (P)

PORTUGUESE
EAST AFRICA

Java

Timor
1610/75 (DU)

Kupang
1653 (DU)

Mauritius (I. de France)
1598–1710 Dutch
1715 to France

Bourbon (Réunion)
1642 (F)

NEW HOLLAND

Delagoa Bay 1544 (P)

MADAGASCAR
(SAO LOURENÇO)

Cape Town 1652 (DU)

VAN DIEMEN'S
LAND

NEW ZEALAND
(STATENLAND)

Figure 1. *(Colonization)*   The world ca. 1714. Redrawn after *Third World Atlas,* prepared by Ben Crow and Alan Thomas, Milton Keynes, Eng., and Philadelphia: Open University Press, 1983, p. 37.

therefore be considered an expression of imperialism, but not the only one.

Forms of colonization. Although the general motives for colonization are economic, beginnings have tended to take three different forms. One was the settlement colony, of which the British North American possessions of the seventeenth and eighteenth centuries are good examples. There, the colonist was principally a tiller of the soil or a manager of the land. Elsewhere the settlement colony was characterized by the plantation or the estate: the latifundia of Roman days, the encomienda of Spanish-American days, and the large farms of French Algeria and British Kenya. All these represent land masses mainly devoted to agriculture overseen by European colonists.

Second was the commercial or trade colony in which settlement was incidental. Residence was for the purpose of generating trade. The Phoenician Empire, with its trading cities scattered around the Mediterranean, is an example from the ancient world. Later, in the fifteenth and sixteenth centuries, the Portuguese extended a maritime empire across the waters of the Eastern Hemisphere. Its geographical characteristic was the coastal enclave, a place like Goa on the Indian coast or Macao on the Chinese coast. These small territories, municipal in political size, were warehouses for the merchandising and storage of goods both brought and carried away by the Portuguese mercantile fleet. Dutch and British ventures in Asia likewise began as trading companies, which grew into something more of the third type.

Third was the administrative colony, the most widespread and, later, the most criticized. In such a colony a small number of Europeans administered a large territory from which the colonizing power, usually through private companies, hoped to gain economic advantages, often in the form of raw materials. Included within this grouping were the African colonies of the late nineteenth century, large land masses with generally sparse populations. Colonies of this sort conferred on the individual colonial officer great authority, such that the terms *chief* and *feudal lord* were occasionally used to describe his position. In theory the administration was responsible for maintaining the colony at peace in order for economic activity to take place.

In the development of colonies in each of these categories Western civilization has been more active than any other. It first spread around the rim of the Mediterranean Sea, then along the Atlantic coast of western Europe, and thereafter rounded the African capes in what has been called the Vasco da Gama epoch in honor of that Portuguese explorer's trip around the Cape of Good Hope in 1497.

The outstanding era of colonization occurred between the fifteenth and nineteenth centuries, when European maritime technology made seaborne communications the most extensive and effective and when the European urge to know the world—explore, map, and exploit its resources—was first intensely expressed. *Terra incognita*, a term prevalent on medieval maps (*see* CARTOGRAPHY), was used less and less frequently, until it disappeared altogether in Joseph Conrad's bitter commentary on nineteenth-century colonial Africa, *The Heart of Darkness* (1902):

It had got filled since my boyhood with rivers and lakes and names. It had ceased to be a blank spot of delightful mystery—a white patch for a boy to dream gloriously over. It had become a place of darkness.

One of the major characteristics—and problems—in the history of colonization was its tendency to be unidirectional. In simple metaphor, colonization was the grounding of power. The complaints of colonized peoples (the indigenous populations over whom colonial rule was also established) were later followed by the complaints of colonists over the colonial state's inclination to dominate, to impose willfully, and not to negotiate out of understanding or appreciation.

With its locus of political power hundreds or even thousands of miles away, with authority delegated usually in the person of a governor, and with metropolitan interests always heavily outweighing colonial ones, the settlement colony eventually became the scene of two opposing forces: in one direction the autocratic pull of the government toward the homeland, and in the other the effort of the colonists to situate authority and responsibility locally. Over time, as new generations were born in the colonies, the sense of place and purpose was even more strongly localized. A distinctive subculture emerged, the nuances of difference expressed in vocabulary and accent. This process of colonial maturation and its consequences were described aptly by the eighteenth-century French statesman Anne-Robert-Jacques Turgot: "Colonies are like fruit which remains on the tree until ripened, at which time it falls off."

Probably no one in the era of colonization ever assumed that the colonial relationship would be interminable. Most theorists and practitioners anticipated a future, however distant, in which the colony would be politically transformed, either integrated into the extended political system of the colonial power or granted autonomy, perhaps even independence. Colonization was thus accepted as a long-enduring but not permanent relationship, a condition expressed in such familiar terms as *mother country, tutelage,* and *trusteeship*. Only the ROMAN EMPIRE had a quality of permanence about it. Its four-hundred-year existence was largely a result of cultural assimilation, effective administration, excellent engineering, and a legal system that encouraged citizenship.

In addition to Rome, the exceptions to the general historical pattern of transient development include China, which, during the Han dynasty (beginning 206 B.C.E.), expanded in such a manner that it rivaled Rome administratively in the geographic reach of its authority and chronologically in the endurance of that authority. In the modern era the United States and the Soviet Union have been successful colonizing powers, emerging as both unitary states and continental monoliths whose political domains reach to the two major oceans. The geographical direction and particular motivation were different in each instance, but the general pattern was the same. Westward expansion in the United States and subsequent colonization were intensified by the quest for gold and the search for new land, places for settlement of a mobile population. The "prairie schooner," the famous covered wagon, was aptly named because many Americans saw their movement as a voyage similar to that undertaken by colonists who crossed seas. The advent of the transcontinental railroad in 1869 and the rapid spread of TELEGRAPHY, the TELEPHONE, and, later, roads assured this new continental empire of unity through ample networks of communication. For Russia the construction of the Trans-Siberian Railroad between 1891 and 1904 was not noticeably different in purpose and effect. Russian colonization had pushed eastward since the seventeenth century, with fur, not gold or land, as its objective. In the nineteenth century peasants in search of land, particularly after their emancipation from serfdom in 1861, moved as colonists into Siberia. The new railroad was a means of linking these newly colonized territories with European Russia. Telegraphy and the telephone eventually reinforced the process.

Railroads. Everywhere in the colonial world of the nineteenth century railroad building was designed to assume the function that the road system had performed in the Roman Empire: a swift and sure means of overland communication by which political authority could be asserted and products easily shipped. Cecil John Rhodes, the great English empire builder of the late nineteenth century, argued that "the rail is less costly than the cannon and it goes farther." Rhodes himself proposed a Cape-to-Cairo railroad to unite on a north-south axis the British possessions in the eastern sector of Africa. The French had a plan of similarly grand proportions: a Trans-Saharan railroad that would unite French North Africa with French West Africa. Neither scheme was realized, but extensive railroad networks were one of the major legacies of the modern colonial empire, even giving structural unity to a country as vast as India.

The technologies of communication and transportation were a constant factor in empire building. Before the advent of electronic communications, dis-

patches and letters were carried overland and overseas. At the beginning of the nineteenth century communication between England and India took many months. By the middle of the century ocean steamers were plying between Liverpool and Halifax in two weeks, while the sea route from England to India, with overland passage of the Isthmus of Suez, could be completed in a month. On the occasion of her Diamond Jubilee in 1897, Queen Victoria was able to telegraph greetings around the British Empire so that her message was received in the course of the day in every major colonial city.

The intensification of communications suggested a world of new cultural and geographical proportions. By the late nineteenth century critics were arguing that "time distance" was the proper measure—not the number of miles to be covered, but the number of hours to negotiate a journey, to transmit a message. Jules Verne's famous novel *Around the World in Eighty Days* (1872) was representative of this new attitude. Henceforth, or so many colonial theorists thought, large territories, loosely held together, might be more tightly bound by the iron of railroads and the copper of telegraph wires.

The advent of the air age in the twentieth century made colonial empires look upward for both communication and domination. The German government had dramatically sought to send relief to its embattled colony of East Africa during World War I by dispatching a huge zeppelin laden with fifteen tons of supplies. The first instance of aerial bombing occurred before that war when the Italians hand-dropped bombs from an airplane in Libya in 1911. By the 1930s all the colonial powers had air service throughout their empires; *time distance* had become a most useful term.

However, better communications (i.e., improvements in technologies) did not necessarily mean better communication. The social and psychological distance between colonizer and colonized in the modern European empires increased as the mechanical and electronic means of communication became more sophisticated.

Decolonization

The history of decolonization is in considerable measure the history of opposition organized along new lines of communication, whether through the press, the legal system, the political rally, or an underground network of militant activity generally described as TERRORISM or guerrilla warfare. Such communication networks encourage the creation of an IDEOLOGY and community of the oppressed. Famous examples include the Committees of Correspondence that were initially formed in 1772 in the British North American colonies under the leadership

Greenland
(to Denmark)

Iceland
(to Denmark)

Spitzbergen
(to Norway)

ALASKA

CANADA

NORWAY

SWEDEN

DENMARK

GERMAN
EMPIRE

UNITED
KINGDOM

FRANCE

AUSTRO-
HUNG.

St. Pierre
and Miquelon(F)

Minorca
1708/13–83 (B)

ITALY

SPAIN

UNITED STATES

PORTUGAL

Gibraltar (B)

Malta (B)

Azores (P)

SPANISH MOROCCO

TUNISI

Bermuda Is.
(US)

MOROCCO
1912

Madeira (P)

SPANISH SAHARA 1912

ALGERIA

LIBY

Canary Is. (S)

RIO DE ORO
1884

S

A

H

A

MEXICO

CUBA

DOMINICAN
REPUBLIC

Bahama Is. (B)

FRENCH WEST
AFRICA
from 1904

Puerto Rico (US) 1898

Cape
Verde Is. (P)

Jamaica (B)

St. Thomas (DU)

BR. HONDURAS

St. Croix
(DU)

GAMBIA (B)

GUATEMALA

HAITI

Guadeloupe (F)

PORTUGUESE
GUINEA (P)

NIGERIA
1914

HONDURAS

St. Lucia (B)

Barbados (B)

SIERRA LEONE (B)

CAMEROO
1884

NICARAGUA

SALVADOR

Trinidad and
Tobago (B)

LIBERIA

COSTA RICA

VENEZUELA

BRITISH

GOLD COAST
TOGO 1884/89

RIO MUNI

PANAMA
CANAL
ZONE
1903 to U.S.

DUTCH

GUIANA

Fernando Póo (S)

FRENCH

FRENCH

COLOMBIA

Cabinda

PACIFIC

ECUADOR

OCEAN

BRAZIL
from 1889 United States of Brazil

ATLANTIC

OCEAN

PERU

GERMAN
SOUTHWEST
AFRICA 1884

BOLIVIA

CHILE

PARAGUAY

ARGENTINA

URUGUAY

(US) United States possesions

(B) British possesions

(F) French possesions

(S) Spanish possesions

(P) Portuguese possesions

(DU) Dutch possesions

German possesions

Falkland Is. (B)

Italian possesions

Belgian possesion

Ottoman Empire

Russian Empire

336

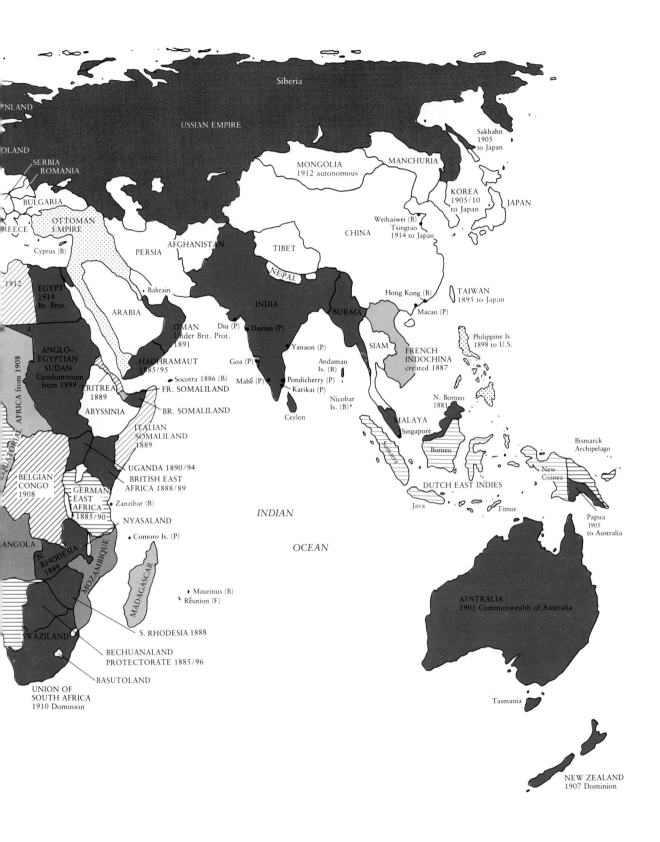

The Pacific Islands are not included in this map.

Figure 2. *(Colonization)* The world ca. 1914. Redrawn after *Third World Atlas,* prepared by Ben Crow and Alan Thomas, Milton Keynes, Eng., and Philadelphia: Open University Press, 1983, p. 41.

of John Adams. Organized in each colony, the committees were "to state the rights of the colonists . . . as men, as Christians, and as subjects." This well-designed network helped arouse anticolonial sentiment that was further fired by the publication in 1776 of Thomas Paine's PAMPHLET titled *Common Sense,* which denounced King George III as the "Royal Brute of Great Britain." The pamphlet was widely read and highly influential, among the first in a long series of literary protests against colonialism. Ho Chi Minh, later to become president of North Vietnam, followed in that tradition when his 1923 pamphlet, *The Case against French Colonialism,* was published in French in Paris.

The nineteenth-century communications revolution made printed materials cheaply and widely available and LITERACY a popular objective. The first newspaper published in Hong Kong began in 1828; the first printing press in Black Africa was introduced in 1829. By the 1930s an opposition press was established in most of the major European colonies (*see* NEWSPAPER: TRENDS). Through this press and the new political movements it so often represented, a new social element appeared: a political elite versed in European language and thought. These people were lawyers, doctors, schoolteachers, journalists—all trained in the European educational system, all part of the European colonial structure. The nationalism they soon defined was essentially anticolonial, with its arguments derived from Western liberalism, communism, and the European sense of historical consciousness.

The political rally was one of the most effective means of direct communication with large segments of the indigenous population and of creating visible discomfort in the ruling power (*see* DEMONSTRATION). No one used this device more successfully than MOHANDAS GANDHI in the 1930s, when he protested against continued British rule in India. Gandhi's was a policy of nonviolent, passive resistance—*satyagraha,* a word Gandhi often defined as "soul force." The policy was effective in confronting the British with a situation not easily resolved by military intervention. It was particularly effective as a means of gaining widespread attention because of the press coverage given in many countries to Gandhi's activities. In 1930 alone, some forty-five articles appeared in English-language journals on Gandhi's political activities. With the wide distribution of the NEWSREEL at this time, Gandhi became the first anticolonial figure to be widely recognized.

Contemporary development. In the early years of the twentieth century the international conference was used as an institution of solidarity and protest. Among the most famous was the series of Pan-African conferences, the first of which was held in Paris in 1919, organized by the American black leader W. E. B. DuBois, who was concerned to make the African colonial question an important one at the peace conference following World War I. Another meeting of international significance, this time amplified by wider media coverage, was the Bandung Conference of 1955, held in the Indonesian city of that name, attended by the representatives of twenty-nine Asian and African nations, and the first such occasion for the new nationalist leaders in the African colonies to discuss their common interests.

The effect of PUBLIC OPINION, international as well as colonial, was a powerful force on decolonization. Certainly such opinion was a contributing factor after World War II, when the European colonial powers, having suffered the imperialism of Nazi Germany, were more sensitive to the aspiration of their colonial peoples. The United States and the Soviet Union, although subscribing to different ideologies, were both opposed to the continuation of colonial empires.

Strong RHETORIC was joined by weakening resolution. The colonial powers no longer could command the political authority they once had. None remained a "great power." This change in status was marked by the fact that at the war's end the second-largest Allied navy belonged to Canada, theoretically under the rule of the British crown. As colonial opposition increased and militant action in the form of guerrilla warfare occurred more frequently, the metropolitan states conceded independence to most of their colonies. In the thirty-year period following Great Britain's withdrawal from India in 1947, about sixty new nations stood where colonies had existed before.

The world's economic situation also suggested the outdated condition of colonial empires. The appearance of multinational corporations with their own highly advanced TELECOMMUNICATIONS NETWORKS made colonial rule seem an inefficient instrument to conduct business in other nations. In addition, technology transfer proved a major factor in the rearrangement of global power. Manufacturing and trade were no longer dominated by the European nations and the United States. Japan, militarily divested of its Pacific empire during the course of World War II, became the second-largest industrial power by 1980, building its economic might on applied research and new management and production techniques. Soon a leader in electronic communication technologies, it established new links with many nations.

Colonization belonged to another era, when the battleship commanded the seas and the ocean liner was the swiftest form of intercontinental travel. As the farthest territorial extension of sea power, the colony was at once part of and removed from the metropolitan state. This unusual condition of long-distance subservience was not only political but economic. In seventeenth- and eighteenth-century theory, colonies were made by and for the colonizing power. The English Navigation Acts of 1650 and 1651 and the French *Exclusif*, a policy inaugurated around the same time, attempted to restrict colonial trade to the mother country. Defining the prescribed economic relationship, an author of the French *Encyclopédie*, published between 1751 and 1775, stated that colonies were "established for the sole benefit of the metropolitan state."

Racism. Later expressions of colonial authority were more dangerous and pernicious because of the racism that intruded into them. Supported by pseudoscientific theories of evolutionary development, aggravated by technological differences that allowed the Europeans to assume that they were "advanced" peoples, and furthered by careless observation of other cultures, racism in the late nineteenth century added to the ideology of imperialism and the justification of colonial empire. The assertion that Europeans had a "civilizing mission" or that they ought to take up "the white man's burden" gave to colonization, particularly in Africa, a false moral justification and allowed a strikingly unequal division of labor. In a frequently expressed organic metaphor, colonial theorists stated that the European would provide the brain and the "native" the muscle by which economic development would proceed.

The social encounter in the modern colonial empire was therefore characterized by no sense of respect or equality, but by mutual misunderstanding and frequent condescension and contempt on the side of the colonists. Daily communication was hindered by a language problem: few of the Europeans became conversant in local dialects, and only a small, well-educated indigenous elite spoke the European language proficiently. In colonial Africa one of the most valuable administrative services was provided by the local interpreter, the one who mediated between the two linguistically restricted parties to the colonial act.

A rich literature attempting to evaluate the psychological and cultural significance of this encounter emerged at the end of the colonial era. It has centered on the cultural deprivation that the Europeans were accused of having caused, the personality disorders that occurred among Africans, Asians, and Native Americans in the colonial situation as they sought to define themselves in the face of an alien culture. What stands out from all of this literature is the lack of authenticity in the roles colonizer and colonized were required by the peculiar circumstances to play.

The principle of equitable treatment almost never obtained in the history of colonization. An exception may be found in the Northwest Ordinance, passed on July 13, 1787, an act that set the conditions of subsequent U.S. continental colonization. The ordinance defined the conditions under which newly settled regions could become states. Of greater importance, it sought to guarantee the same civil rights and liberties that prevailed in the original states, and it prohibited slavery (*see* SLAVE TRADE, AFRICAN).

Elsewhere, particularly in the colonies acquired in Africa and Asia, paternalism and segregation prevailed. The cultural vocabulary that contained terms like "backward races" and "primitive peoples" and the domestic vocabulary that made common use of the term "boy" reveal the reason for the concept of tutelage in administrative thought. The most modern of the colonial political devices, the protectorate, of which French domination of Tunisia (from 1881 to 1956) and Morocco (from 1912 to 1956) are examples, explains in its very name the colonial ideology of political dependency.

There was no effective bridging of interests in the modern colonial empires situated in Africa and Asia. The social levels of the participants were too sharply different. The "location theory" of modern urban geography has particular relevance for this social disparity. The Europeans sought the high land, established hill stations in India, of which the summer residence of the viceroy, Simla, was the most famous. The French in Dakar, Senegal, established themselves on the "plateau" of that city, thereby establishing it as an urban place. The British in Sierra Leone moved up the mountains from the bay defining Freetown. Although most of these moves were predicated on nineteenth-century medical theories—primarily the notion of airborne disease—they were also expressive of the thought that the two peoples should not live together. Geographic and social segregation were common characteristics of the twentieth-century colonial world.

The era of colonial empire effectively ended in the decade following World War II. Yet, as an activity that has worked its way through the course of world history, colonization must be measured as a crucial episode in the history of human communication, one that has profoundly affected many aspects of the modern world.

See also AFRICA, TWENTIETH CENTURY; ASIA, TWENTIETH CENTURY; DEVELOPMENT COMMUNICATION; DIFFUSION.

Bibliography. Raymond F. Betts, *Uncertain Dimensions: Western Overseas Empires in the Twentieth Century*, Minneapolis, Minn., 1985; Daniel R. Headrick, *The Tools of Empire: Technology and European Imperialism in the Nineteenth Century*, New York, 1981; Harold A. Innis, *Empire and Communications* (1950), rev. by Mary Q. Innis, foreword by Marshall McLuhan, Toronto, 1972; James Morris, *Farewell the Trumpets: An Imperial Retreat*, New York and London, 1978; Tzvetan Todorov, *The Conquest of America*, New York, 1985.

RAYMOND F. BETTS

COMEDY

Comedy is derived from the Greek *kōmōidia,* which comes from two words: *kōmos* (a banquet, revel, or FESTIVAL) and *ōidia* (from *aeidein,* "to sing"). The origin of the word indicates the status of comedy as celebration, especially in relation to a RITUAL, festival, banquet, or procession. Comedy is always social or societal, and the *Oxford English Dictionary* lists a possible derivation from *kōme* ("village"). The origin of the word suggests that the comic SONG or play was used to mark a special occasion and was part of general rejoicing.

Some of the ritual significance of comedy survives in the comedies of Aristophanes (ca. 450–ca. 388 B.C.E.), which are generally referred to as Old Comedy. These plays are more like skits or revues with very rudimentary plots. Two large ideas or values are generally set against each other—peace versus war, youth versus age, right reason versus wrong reason, Euripides versus Aeschylus. At the center of the play there is an *agon,* or debate, in which the idea favored by the playwright is made to prevail. Old Comedy is also highly political, and Aristophanes never tired of attacking the dictator Cleon. In *Lysistrata,* Aristophanes' best-known play, the women's sex strike is directed against the war with Sparta that is crippling Athens.

Middle Comedy is associated with Menander (ca. 342–ca. 292 B.C.E.), most of whose plays are lost, but its influence is felt through New Comedy, especially in the works of Terence (ca. 185–ca. 159 B.C.E.) and Titus Maccius Plautus (ca. 254–184 B.C.E.), who wrote in Latin and imitated Greek originals. Terence was popular in the MIDDLE AGES and RENAISSANCE, but Plautus did the most to establish the conventions of New Comedy. Unlike Old Comedy, New Comedy is heavily plotted, often with a romantic interest in the young hero's trying to win a girl or at least buy her away from a curmudgeonly pimp. In this project he is aided by a clever and resourceful slave or parasite, who will do anything to win a favor and eat a copious dinner. He becomes the center of the action. Plautus's plots tend toward farce, with a good deal of disguise, mistaken identity, and mix-ups of all kinds. The characters are types, mechanized by the energy of the comic action. Adaptations of Plautus have been popular in the modern THEATER (e.g., *The Boys from Syracuse* and *A Funny Thing Happened on the Way to the Forum*), and the influence of New Comedy formulas is powerful in television situation comedies and in the intricate plotting of soap operas (*see* SOAP OPERA).

Genres of comedy. Of the various genres and kinds of comedy, the most pervasive is satire (*see* GENRE). The Roman satirists Horace (65–8 B.C.E.) and Juvenal (ca. 55 or 60–in or after 127 C.E.) wrote

Figure 1. *(Comedy)* Actors in Old Comedy: two drunken slaves or revelers. Greek terra-cotta statuettes, mid-fourth century B.C.E. Staatliche Museen zu Berlin (DDR).

poems that hold up the follies, vices, and hypocrisies of their times to scorn and ridicule. Horace was more genially ironic than the biting Juvenal, but both contrasted the deplorable conditions and manners of their times with some ideal standard. Satirists are generally defenders of right reason against the abuses of rationality, and they tend to display a reformer's zeal to set things right and bring back the golden age. Comic dramatists use satire to ridicule the absurdities of their society, as in Jean-Baptiste Molière's (1622–1673) portraits of the miser (Harpagon), the religious hypocrite (Tartuffe), the misanthrope (Alceste), and ignorant pretentious physicians. Ben Jonson (1572–1637), in his comedy of humors, used satire to bring eccentric and obsessive characters to their senses, in other words, to some awareness of social decorum and utility.

Most comedy has a satiric component, although separate genres may be distinguished from satire proper. The comedy of manners flourished in late-seventeenth-century (Restoration) England and thrived on the sharp split between the elegant court party and the middle-class Puritans. In the plays of George Etherege (ca. 1635–ca. 1692), William Wycherley (ca. 1640–1716), and William Congreve (1670–1729) there is a strong opposition between wits and fools, and the manners of the court are taken as a standard of elegance and refinement. The wits are often young libertines who speak and act with studied insouciance and artificiality. Oscar Wilde (1854–1900) nostalgically evokes the Restoration comedy of manners in *The Importance of Being Earnest* (1895).

Romantic comedy is associated with William Shakespeare, who drew on romances for many of his plots. Typically the setting is remote, the characters are highly stylized, and the plot sets up obstacles to true love, which nevertheless triumphs in the end. In Shakespeare's pastoral romances, such as *The Winter's Tale* (ca. 1610), the characters are shepherds and shepherdesses (or shepherds and shepherdesses in disguise), and the action celebrates the simple life away from the corruption of courts and cities. The myth of the golden age is strongly linked with pastoral romance. The charm of romantic comedy lies in its distance from the concerns of ordinary life and its ability to generate fantasies of pure innocence and absolute beauty. It is a perfect setting in which young love can flourish. There is a cultivated artificiality in romantic comedy that encourages both a feeling for lyric POETRY and a sense that this is a self-conscious world of play that is set apart.

In contemporary DRAMA, black comedy and the comedy of the absurd have tended to dominate all other genres. Black comedy borrows many assumptions and devices that traditionally have been associated with TRAGEDY. Irish playwright Samuel Beckett's *Waiting for Godot* (1952) and *Endgame* (1958) draw on the existentialist doctrine of absurdity, which is embodied in characters who have no specific purpose and speak as if the world were coming to an end. In English dramatist Harold Pinter's comedies of menace, such as *The Homecoming* (1965), all of reality outside one's own space or room is sinister and threatening. But both Beckett and Pinter use comic materials to define their tragic world. Swiss playwright Friedrich Dürrenmatt's *The Visit* (1956) is a farcical account of a small town's murder of a scapegoat victim, strongly reminiscent of the Nazi era. Black comedy presents a series of entertaining but disorienting fables that are close to tragedy in theme but wholly comic in treatment. Tom Stoppard uses parody, or a mocking rewriting and reechoing, of well-known works of literature to produce shocking and disturbing effects. Thus Shakespeare's *Hamlet* is seen from the point of view of Rosencrantz and Guildenstern in Stoppard's *Rosencrantz and Guildenstern Are Dead* (1966). The comic distortion defines contemporary absurdist values.

Theories of comedy. Among the many theories of comedy, a few of the more significant ones may be singled out. The older superiority theory is associated with German philosopher Immanuel Kant (1724–

Figure 2. *(Comedy)* Buster Keaton in *The General*, 1926. The Museum of Modern Art/Film Stills Archive.

1804) and English political philosopher Thomas Hobbes (1588–1679). Hobbes said that "laughter is a sudden glory," meaning that laughter marks that delicious moment when one triumphs over one's adversary. There is much in the cynical maxims of François de La Rochefoucauld (1613–1680) to support this idea. If laughter is, physiologically, an involuntary muscle spasm, then the person who makes you laugh against your conscious will does in some literal sense triumph over your resistance. The recent theater of cruelty, associated with Antonin Artaud (1896–1948), Peter Weiss (1916–1982), and Jean Genet (1910–1985), uses grotesque comedy to enforce its meanings about the absurdity and capriciousness of the modern world. The superiority theory of comedy offers a plausible explanation for comic aggression and the large role that cruelty plays in black comedy.

SIGMUND FREUD's views on comedy, especially in *Jokes and Their Relation to the Unconscious* (1905), depend heavily on dreams, fantasies, and the seemingly involuntary workings of the unconscious. Laughter releases suppressed and censored material, so that Freud would also find a sudden glory in being relieved of the burden of repression. Freud's book on comedy is an offshoot of his major work on the interpretation of dreams, and jokes function very much like dreams, with a sharp contrast between the latent and the manifest content. For Freud laughter is a therapeutic mechanism that helps us release and therefore master anxiety. We laugh for reasons that lie deep in our psyche. *See* HUMOR.

Henri Bergson's (1859–1941) treatise *Laughter* (1900) is perhaps the most influential single book on comedy. Using examples from daily life and from the comedy of manners (especially Molière), Bergson tries to locate the cause of laughter in an incongruous relationship between the mechanical and the living. We laugh when something mechanical or mechanistic seems to be stuck onto something human or, in other words, when something human behaves as if it were a machine. There is a corresponding humor in machines behaving as if they were sentient human beings. Both sides of the equation are brilliantly exploited in CHARLES CHAPLIN's movie *Modern Times* (1936). Bergson is concerned with the ways in which human beings lose their characteristically human qualities, as, for example, in professional deformation, in which one speaks and acts in the narrowly technical jargon of one's occupation. Like Freud, Bergson also sees laughter as therapeutic—it reminds us not to abandon our precious humanity.

Recent theories of festive comedy have a strongly anthropological basis. Most important is MIKHAIL BAKHTIN's work on François Rabelais (ca. 1483–1553). Everything in Rabelais is closely connected with the society of his time and all of its festivals, rituals, carnivals, and communal celebrations. Going back to root meanings of comedy, Bakhtin stresses the grossness and animality of comedy and its inseparable link with the lower material bodily stratum. In *Shakespeare's Festive Comedy: A Study of Dramatic Form in Its Relation to Social Custom* (1959), C. L. Barber locates Shakespeare in relation to the life of his time. Barber makes important use of folk rituals, which figure prominently in such plays as *The Merry Wives of Windsor* (ca. 1598).

Comedy is closely related to PERFORMANCE not only onstage but also in the telling of stories and jokes. The ending, or punch line, is crucial, and it

Figure 3. *(Comedy)* William Shakespeare, *Much Ado about Nothing.* Diana Wynyard as Beatrice and John Gielgud as Benedick in a scene from Gielgud's production at the Phoenix Theatre, London, 1952. The Bettmann Archive/BBC Hulton.

Figure 4. *(Comedy)* Samuel Beckett, *Waiting for Godot*, 1952. Scene from a performance at the Théâtre de Babylone, Paris, 1953, directed by Roger Blin. Courtesy of the French Embassy Cultural Services.

needs surprise to work its effect. In shaggy-dog stories there is a sudden deflation at the end that reverses our expectations for a snappy conclusion. Jokes very often depend on unexpected wordplay that brings together incongruous meanings. Tall stories draw on consistent hyperbole and exaggeration; we laugh at their extravagance and wildness. Sick jokes, too, and all forms of black humor encourage the listener's participation with the teller in an assault on moral norms and rational behavior. Comic invective goes even further to test the limits of permissible expression. Freud would explain all anarchic and uncensored humor as an attack on inhibitions, which releases energies otherwise engaged in suppression.

The line between comedy and tragedy has grown very thin in contemporary comedy, and there has been a general rehabilitation of the value of comedy. Although attempts have been made to reconstruct ARISTOTLE's theory of comedy as if it were a counterpart to the theory of tragedy in *The Poetics*, comedy is no longer subordinated to tragedy in the hierarchy of genres, nor do critics still think that comedy strives to perfect itself in becoming more like tragedy. We no longer tend to sentimentalize the clown in the "Pagliacci syndrome," laughing on the outside, crying on the inside. Perhaps it is more fruitful to see comedy and tragedy as separate and autonomous systems that do not need each other to complete one single meaning. By a natural evolution comedy seems to be taking over the large territory formerly staked out for tragedy.

See also MUSIC THEATER; MUSICAL, FILM.

Bibliography. Mikhail Bakhtin, *Rabelais and His World* (Tvorchestvo Fransua Rable i narodnaia kul tura srednevekoṽ ia i Renessansa), trans. by Hélène Iswolsky, Cambridge, Mass., 1968, reprint Bloomington, Ind., 1984; C. L. Barber, *Shakespeare's Festive Comedy*, Princeton, N.J., 1959; Maurice Charney, *Comedy High and Low*, New York, 1978; idem, ed., *Comedy: New Perspectives*, New York, 1978; George Duckworth, *The Nature of Roman Comedy*, Princeton, N.J., 1952; Leo Salingar, *Shakespeare and the Traditions of Comedy*, London and New York, 1974; Richard Keller Simon, *The Labyrinth of the Comic*, Tallahassee, Fla., 1985; Wylie Sypher, ed., *Comedy*, Garden City, N.Y., 1956.

MAURICE CHARNEY

COMICS

A distinct blending of VISUAL IMAGE and text that borrows elements from both ART and literature to produce a NARRATIVE told by means of a sequence of pictures, a continuing cast of characters (*see* SERIAL), and the inclusion of dialogue or text within the picture. As in MOTION PICTURES, the flow of images and narration in comics is dynamic and aims at the creation of movement. The ties between the comics and film extend beyond similar artistic origins and commercial considerations to the merging of both forms in the animated cartoon (see ANIMATION). Since the birth of the comics as a popular GENRE in the beginning of the twentieth century, they have constituted a sociological phenomenon contributing to everyday LANGUAGE, cultural ICONOGRAPHY, contemporary FOLKLORE and mythology, and every area of communication from ADVERTISING to politics.

Development

The comics were heralded by a long succession of portents, from the cave paintings of Altamira and Lascaux through the Egyptian bas-reliefs and the Pompeii frescoes to the *Biblia pauperum* of the MIDDLE AGES (see MURAL). The roots of the comics are closer to us, however, in the work of eighteenth-century English cartoonists like William Hogarth, Thomas Rowlandson, and James Gillray (see CARICATURE). These artists told stories through sequences of drawings, or "cartoons" (from the French *carton*, meaning a sketch on pasteboard), and even made extensive use of the balloon, an enclosed space containing dialogue issuing from the mouths of characters. This technique is exemplified in the work of Rowlandson, especially in *The Tour of Dr. Syntax* (1809), in which the story is told in text and pictures, speech balloons are used throughout, and the char-

acters are well developed. All that is needed to make it a genuine comic strip is continuity.

This technique soon spread to the Continent, and in the course of the nineteenth century Europe witnessed a flood of pictorial narratives. These stories did not make use of the British cartoonists' innovations—none of them employed the balloon, for example—but they contributed in various ways to the development of the comics. Swiss artist Rodolphe Töpffer's *Histoires en estampes* (1846–1847) was a collection of brilliant graphic narratives woven around a redundant text; the illustrated poem "Max und Moritz" (1871) earned the German Wilhelm Busch lasting fame and inspired "The Katzenjammer Kids"; and in 1889 Frenchman Georges Colomb ("Christophe") created "La famille Fenouillard," regarded as the direct forerunner of the modern comic strip (Figure 1).

However, it was in the United States that the comics eventually were born. U.S. cartoonists did not rely on the written word as did European artists, and therein lay their strength. Throughout the nineteenth century U.S. newspapers and magazines evinced a robust vitality (see MAGAZINE; NEWSPAPER: TRENDS—TRENDS IN NORTH AMERICA), and U.S. cartooning was correspondingly more innovative and iconoclastic than its European counterparts. The enormous influx of immigrants from eastern and southern Europe speaking many different languages gave visual communication a steadily growing public. New talent came forward to answer the increasing demand for illustrators and cartoonists. Circulation wars

a

b

Figure 1. *(Comics)* Christophe, "La famille Fenouillard," 1889. *(a)* Being in need of a change of clothes, Mr. and Mrs. Fenouillard return home. Mrs. Fenouillard would like to break out in bitter complaints, but because her mouth is full of cheese she maintains a dignified calm. *(b)* In the evening, now that she has finished swallowing her cheese, Mrs. Fenouillard tells her husband that from now on she won't listen to him when he tries to tear her away from her home on the pretext of a trip. From Pierre Couperie and Maurice Horn, *A History of the Comic Strip,* New York: Crown Publishers, 1968, p. 14.

among newspapers, epitomized by the struggle between publishers JOSEPH PULITZER and WILLIAM RANDOLPH HEARST for control of the New York market, resulted in increasingly garish Sunday supplements to daily newspapers that aimed to attract wider audiences.

These hopes proved well founded: the new picture stories drew an enormous readership. In 1896, when Richard Outcault's "Yellow Kid" (which inspired the term *yellow journalism*) proved its worth as a circulation builder for Pulitzer's New York *World*, Hearst simply brought artist and character over to his new Sunday supplement, the *American Humorist*. It was in this periodical (self-described as "eight pages of polychromatic effulgence") that Rudolph Dirks's "The Katzenjammer Kids" first appeared in December 1897. "The Katzenjammer Kids" was the first feature to integrate all the elements of the contemporary comic strip and to make full and systematic use of the speech balloon.

The Language of Comics

What distinguished the comics from other cartoons appearing in turn-of-the-century Sunday supplements was a specific set of conventions. The most widely employed and instantly recognizable of these was the balloon, which at first played only a utilitarian role in conveying the utterances of various characters and thus endowing them with the faculty of speech. The balloon's dual nature—a dramatic device by function but a graphic form by design—created possibilities that innovative cartoonists were quick to explore. By using the graphic elements of the balloon (shape, lettering, symbols) in a literal way, they were able to translate the more complex aspects of language such as tone, intensity, rhythm, pitch, and accent. The balloon can also transcend speech, addressing itself to the naked thought or conveying interior monologue in thought balloons, usually configured by scalloped contours. The balloon can even free itself from all the restraints of organized expression, as when it changes form, slowly dissolving or suddenly exploding. It can be used variously as a ploy, a tool, a mask, a shield, or a weapon; the possibilities are endless.

The comics have at their disposal an impressive array of signs and symbols, often in the form of word pictures and visual puns. Thus a lighted bulb comes to represent a bright idea, a black cloud hovering over the head of a character is a feeling of grief or despair, a succession of *z*'s means loud snoring. Onomatopoeias abound, colorfully mimicking the sounds of action and ordinary life. "Pow," "vroom," "kaboom," and "splat" are easily recognized phonetic equivalents, just as "#@*%!!!" has become universal shorthand for a variety of expletives.

In addition to an extensive vocabulary, the comics have evolved a complex syntax and GRAMMAR of their own. The most original feature of the form is its blending of component elements—text and artwork—into one organic whole. The basic element in the language of the comics is the panel, a single drawing with or without accompanying text or dialogue, usually enclosed in a square or rectangular frame. It stands both apart from and in close relation to the other panels in the strip or page, like a word in a sentence. The contents of the individual panel are usually perceived by the eye as one unit. The panels themselves are grouped into strips (usually a horizontal succession of panels) or into pages presenting a vertical and horizontal combination of frames. These strips and pages are in turn organized into sequences and episodes.

The Genre Matures

The newspaper comics grew in number and quality in the first decade of the twentieth century. This was the time of James Swinnerton's "Little Jimmy" (1905), F. B. Opper's "Happy Hooligan" (1900) and "And Her Name Was Maud!" (1905), and Outcault's wildly popular "Buster Brown" (1902), whose name and likeness were used to advertise shoes, hats, buttons, and even cigars and whiskey. This was also the time during which the comics became an art form, with the short-lived creations of the German-American painter Lyonel Feininger, "The Kin-der-Kids" and "Wee Willie Winkie's World" (both 1906), and especially with "Little Nemo in Slumberland" (1905), artist Winsor McCay's most celebrated creation (Figure 2). The year 1907 marked a further milestone in the history of the medium: H. C. "Bud" Fisher's "Mutt and Jeff" definitively established the daily newspaper strip.

In the second decade of the century the comics consolidated their position as a mass medium. The syndicate system (*see* SYNDICATION) became generalized and helped ensure the phenomenal success of such strips as George McManus's archetypal "Bringing Up Father" (1913), which achieved universal fame, was translated into many languages, and was made into a number of films and stage plays. In 1911 George Herriman created "Krazy Kat" (Figure 3), a richly symbolic and highly artistic feature that earned its author the respect and admiration of intellectuals all over the world.

From about 1910 to the end of the 1920s the comics also developed a unique narrative MODE that combined the literary continuity of the novel with the visual pacing of the movies. Weekly and, later, daily continuity was not new to the comics; the earliest strips, such as "The Katzenjammer Kids," used it in the sense that occasionally one Sunday

Figure 2. *(Comics)* Winsor McCay, "Little Nemo in Slumberland." From Pierre Couperie and Maurice Horn, *A History of the Comic Strip*, New York: Crown Publishers, 1968, p. 24. © McCay Company.

page would pick up where the preceding one had left off. The tempo picked up after 1910 with a smattering of strips using continuing stories, usually humorous adventures like those of Charles Kahles's "Hairbreadth Harry" (1906), or burlesques of silent films such as Harry Hershfield's "Desperate Desmond" (1910–1914). Continuity was used mainly as an added fillip, but Joseph Patterson, president of the Chicago Tribune Syndicate (and later publisher of the *New York Daily News*), saw in the device a novel way to gain and keep the loyalty of new readers. He started with the feature that was to become the syndicate's flagship, "The Gumps," which Sidney Smith tailored to his boss's specifications in 1917. The success of the series, which earned its author the industry's first million-dollar contract, gave rise to more story strips from the syndicate. Frank King's "Gasoline Alley" (1919), Frank Willard's "Moon Mullins" (1923), and particularly Harold Gray's "Little Orphan Annie" (1924) proved Patterson's foresight.

Patterson was responsible for another trend in the

Figure 3. *(Comics)* George Herriman, "Krazy Kat," December 15, 1935 (single frame). From J. O'Sullivan, *The Art of the Comic Strip*, New York: A. Colish, 1971, p. 26. © King Features Syndicate.

1920s: the proliferation of so-called FAMILY strips focusing on domestic life and everyday events instead of slapstick and buffoonery. The family comics were tailored to attract a largely untapped female readership, and Patterson tied the new strips to story lines not unlike those of the popular radio SOAP OPERA of a later time. Indeed, "The Gumps" was made into one of the first daytime radio serials. The most successful family strip of all time, Chic Young's "Blondie," turned up in the following decade and for the rival King Features Syndicate (Figure 4).

"Blondie" was the exception, however. The 1930s became known as the comics' decade of adventure, ushered in on the same day in 1929 by Phil Nowlan and Dick Calkins's "Buck Rogers" and Harold Foster's "Tarzan." Their immediate success firmly established the genre. The Great Depression and heightening international tensions gave the U.S. public an unprecedented appetite for escape. Favorite avenues of escape included the exotic adventure strip (Milton Caniff's "Terry and the Pirates"), western adventure (Fred Harman's "Red Ryder"), aviation adventure (Noel Sickles's "Scorchy Smith"), space adventure (Alex Raymond's "Flash Gordon"; Figure 5), detective adventure (Chester Gould's "Dick Tracy";

Figure 6), and even medieval adventure (Foster's "Prince Valiant").

With the onset of World War II most of the heroes rushed to the defense of home and country. After the war, however, the comic strip adventurers faced changing public tastes and diminishing newspaper space. HUMOR was again in the ascendancy with new and successful strips such as Mort Walker's "Beetle Bailey" (1950) and Hank Ketcham's "Dennis the Menace" (1951). Al Capp's "Li'l Abner," which debuted in 1934, also enjoyed its greatest popularity in the 1940s and 1950s.

A new, more sophisticated brand of humor sprang onto the scene in this period, heralded by Walt Kelly's delightful series of fables, "Pogo" (1948), and Charles Schulz's "Peanuts" (1950), a phenomenal artistic and popular success (Figure 7). Other strips of the same intellectual bent include Mell Lazarus's "Miss Peach" (1957) and "Momma" (1970), Johnny Hart's "B.C." (1958), and Jeff MacNelly's "Shoe" (1978). More decidedly political were such strips as Jules Feiffer's "Feiffer" (1956) and "Doonesbury" (1970), by Garry Trudeau, the first comic strip artist to be awarded a Pulitzer Prize in cartooning; they were later followed by Berke Breathed's "Bloom County" (1980). Traditional humor was also well represented in U.S. newspapers of the 1970s and 1980s with series like Dik Browne's "Hagar the Horrible" (1973) and Jim Davis's "Garfield" (1977).

The Comic Book

For many years newspapers were almost the exclusive outlet for comics. It was not until the 1930s that comic books (comic strips in booklet or magazine form, usually sold separately on newsstands) came on the scene. At first they reprinted newspaper strips, but soon they branched out into original production. The phenomenal success enjoyed by *Superman*, created in 1938 by Jerry Siegel and Joe Shuster, established the new medium for decades to come. Hordes of superheroes, including *Batman, The Human Torch,* and *Captain America,* were among the hundreds of

Figure 4. *(Comics)* Chic Young, "Blondie." From R. Reitberger and W. Fuchs, *Comics: Anatomy of a Mass Medium*, London and Harlow: Little, Brown and Company, 1971, p. 10. © 1933 King Features Syndicate.

FLASH GORDON

BY-
ALEX RAYMOND

DALE IS BRINGING FOOD WHICH HER FELLOW SLAVE, KHAN, HAS POISONED--SEEING FLASH AT THE TABLE, AND NOT WISHING TO POISON HIM, SHE TRIPS HERSELF---

INSTANTLY, THE GUARD WOMAN IS OVER DALE, CUTTING VICIOUSLY WITH HER CRUEL WHIP---

DON'T BEAT THE GIRL--SHE COULDN'T HELP TRIPPING!

HO, GUARD! BRING SLEEP GAS!

BEFORE THE GUARD CAN BRING HIS GAS-GUN INTO USE, FLASH DROPS HIM WITH THE FLAT OF HIS SWORD---

ARE WE TO BE FRIENDS OR ENEMIES, AZURA?

FRIENDS, FLASH--I'M SORRY I LOST MY TEMPER---

OH, DON'T YOU LOVE ME ANY MORE, FLASH?

WHY, I DON'T EVEN KNOW YOU, GIRL!

1935, King Features Syndicate, Inc. Great Britain right

LATE THAT NIGHT, AS FLASH TOSSES IN TROUBLED SLUMBER, THE WITCH QUEEN TEACHES DALE---OBEDIENCE!

NEXT WEEK: "WAR IN THE CAVES"

6·2

348

comic book titles that appeared in the late 1930s and early 1940s. The comic books were immensely popular during World War II, when they were read by youngsters and adults (mainly enlisted men) alike. After the war, with an initial drop in readership, publishers turned to other themes like VIOLENCE and horror to increase sales. Some followed the lead of William Gaines, later publisher of *Mad* magazine, who released such titles as *Crypt of Terror, The Vault of Horror,* and *The Haunt of Fear.* This resulted in a public outcry that grew more strident during the 1950s. To fend off impending CENSORSHIP, publishers set up the Comics Code Authority, a self-regulating body with broad policy powers. If it saved the industry from probable ruin, the comic book code also resulted in a devitalization of the medium that lasted many years.

In the 1960s the comic books started experimenting again. This was the time of Marvel Comics' "superheroes with problems," such as the Fantastic Four, the Incredible Hulk, and especially Spider-Man (Figure 8), who became a symbol for a whole generation of college students. Yet the foremost innovators of the medium proved to be the so-called underground cartoonists, including Robert Crumb, Gilbert Shelton, S. Clay Wilson, and Art Spiegelman,

Figure 6. *(Comics)* Chester Gould, "Dick Tracy." From Pierre Couperie and Maurice Horn, *A History of the Comic Strip*, New York: Crown Publishers, 1968, p. 62. Reprinted by permission: Tribune Media Services.

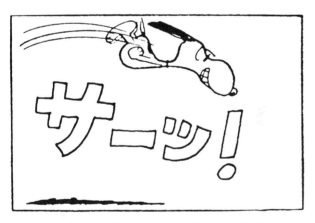

Figure 7. *(Comics)* Charles Schulz, "Peanuts." The Japanese translation of "Swoop!" under Snoopy is well presented visually. From R. Reitberger and W. Fuchs, *Comics: Anatomy of a Mass Medium*, London and Harlow: Little, Brown and Company, 1971, p. 27. Reprinted by permission of United Feature Syndicate.

Figure 5. *(Comics)* Alex Raymond, "Flash Gordon." From Judith Robinson, *The Comics: An Illustrated History of Comic Strip Art*, New York: A. Colish, 1974, p. 136. © 1935 King Features Syndicate.

Figure 8. *(Comics)* Spider-Man. From S. Lee, *Origins of Marvel Comics,* New York: Simon and Schuster, 1974, p. 139. Copyright © 1974 by Marvel Comics Group.

who all combined great freedom of subject matter with a simple cartooning style reminiscent of the early years of the comics. Eventually they attracted public notice and came up from the underground, notably Crumb, whose creations Fritz the Cat and Mr. Natural earned him lasting fame. Working outside the established comic book channels, the undergrounders were able to develop themes—sex, drugs, social protest—that remained taboo to mainstream comic book writers, hedged in as they were by the strictures of the Comics Code. The underground comic books, most often printed in black and white, created a sensation and spawned a long line of epigones up to the new wave cartoonists of the 1980s, among whom Rick Geary, Futzie Nutzle [Bruce Kleinsmith], and Gary Panter are the most representative. Bridging the gap between the two generations is Spiegelman, author of the critically and popularly acclaimed comics novel *Maus* (1986).

By the 1980s falling comic book sales had led to the increasing reliance of major U.S. publishers (DC Comics and Marvel Comics) on comic book specialty stores catering mainly to confirmed fans and collectors. This growing phenomenon also gave rise to a number of independent publishers whose frequently more adult productions competed directly with those of the established comic book companies.

The International Scene

There has been considerable production of comic features outside the United States, particularly since World War II. In Europe, Japan, and Latin America the main vehicle for the dissemination of comics has been the magazine (*see* FOTONOVELA). Often comics from these publications are collected in book or album form, allowing them to reach a wide international audience. "Tintin" (Figure 9), by Belgian artist Georges Rémi ("Hergé"), and "Astérix," by Frenchmen René Goscinny and Albert Uderzo, have been particularly popular. Another influential French cartoonist is Moebius [Jean Giraud], who settled in the United States. Among the very prolific Italian comic strip artists of the postwar era are Guido

Figure 9. *(Comics)* Hergé, "The Adventures of Tintin." "Quick, Captain, let's jump out! Our car has got loose and is going to roll back down the slope!" "Jump, quick!" From Pierre Couperie and Maurice Horn, *A History of the Comic Strip*, New York: Crown Publishers, 1968, p. 202.

Figure 10. *(Comics)* Peter O'Donnell and Jim Holdaway, "Modesty Blaise." From R. Reitberger and W. Fuchs, *Comics: Anatomy of a Mass Medium,* London and Harlow: Little, Brown and Company, 1971, p. 202. © London Evening Standard.

Crepax ("Valentina," "The Story of O") and Hugo Pratt ("Carto Maltese"). In the 1970s Spanish cartoonists like Esteban Maroto, José Gonzales, Fernando Fernández, and Jordi Bernet began to make their presence felt internationally. Even the British, whose production in the first half of the century had been devoted almost entirely to children's comics, came up with such popular creations as Reginald Smythe's "Andy Capp" and Peter O'Donnell and Jim Holdaway's "Modesty Blaise" (Figure 10).

Since the early decades of the twentieth century Latin America has had a local, if modest, comics production. Three countries have been especially active in the field: Mexico, perhaps best known for the satirical creations of Rius [Eduardo del Rio], whose tongue-in-cheek primers—*Castro for Beginners, Lenin for Beginners*—are widely published outside his native country; Brazil, noted for Mauricio de Souza's winsome creations, such as "Monica"; and Argentina, which produced the notable humor strip "Mafalda," described as a feminist "Peanuts," by cartoonist Quino [Joaquín Lavado]. Argentina can also boast of such remarkable artists as José-Luis Salinas (who for a long time drew "The Cisco Kid" for the U.S. market), Chilean-born Arturo del Castillo, and the highly original Alberto Breccia.

Comics readership is nowhere as widespread as in Japan. In 1980 the top five comics magazines had between them weekly sales of almost nine million copies. The resurgence of comics in postwar Japan was due almost entirely to one artist, Osamu Tezuka, who was acclaimed by the Japanese as "the god of comics." His many creations, especially Tetsuwan Atom (Astroboy) and Jungle Tatei (Kimba the White Lion), are well known outside his homeland. Following Tezuka, other Japanese cartoonists have gained international repute, including Reiji Matsumoto, Sampei Shirato, and Keiji Nakazawa, author of the moving "Gen of Hiroshima."

See also LITERATURE, POPULAR.

Bibliography. Stephen D. Becker, *Comic Art in America,* New York, 1959; Bill Blackbeard and Martin Williams, eds., *The Smithsonian Collection of Newspaper Comics,* Washington, D.C., 1977; Javier Coma, ed., *Historia de los comics,* 4 vols., Barcelona, 1982–; Pierre Couperie and Maurice Horn, *A History of the Comic Strip* (Bande dessinée et figuration narrative), trans. by Eileen B. Hennessy, New York, 1968; Denis Gifford, *The International Book of Comics,* New York and London, 1984; Irene Herner, *Mitos y monitos,* Mexico, D.F., 1979; Maurice Horn, ed., *The World Encyclopedia of Comics,* New York, 1976; Jeff Rovin, *Encyclopedia of Superheroes,* New York, 1985.

MAURICE HORN

COMMERCIALS

Short messages broadcast between programs or in intervals within programs, usually with the purpose of furthering the sale of a product or service or enhancing the image of a corporation or organization. The term is used mainly for messages broadcast in periods that have been purchased for the purpose. In RADIO, commercials began as simple spoken announcements, but in television they have evolved into complex productions that often cost more than the programs with which they share the schedule. In the United States it is not unusual for sums in excess of $100,000 to be spent to produce a thirty-second television commercial, and additional millions to be spent to air it on stations and networks. Such messages, in filmed or recorded form, are generally rebroadcast many times and may appear internationally in various language versions. Thus, despite initial outlay, an advertiser may consider them economical when calculated on a cost-per-thousand-viewers basis. *See* TELEVISION HISTORY.

Because commercials embody an advertiser's central purpose in broadcasting, no efforts are spared in their planning and preparation. In countries with major commercial television industries, top-ranking

"BETTER WITH CHUNKS"
:30 TV COMMERCIAL

CHARLES NELSON REILLY: We hafta
talk about this.

I think you need va-ri-ety in your men-u
. . . so I have kibbles!!!

Oh, dear Doggie, this is new
Purina Kibbles and Chunks!

Kibbles taste better
when they come with chunks!

Crunchy kibbles. . .mmmmmmmm

Chew-wee chunks

mmmmmmmm. . .yummmmmm. . .
New Purina brand
Kibbles and Chunks dog food.

Two kinds of crunchy kibbles

taste better with two chewy chunks!

CHARLES: Whadaya say. . .

Purina Kibbles and Chunks
. . .better with chunks?

(CHARLES LAUGHS)
Better with chunks!

CHECKERBOARD ADVERTISING COMPANY
A Subsidiary of the Ralston Purina Company

© Ralston Purina Company, 1985

Figure 1. *(Commercials)* A storyboard: sketch for a thirty-second television commercial. Courtesy of CAC Advertising, a division of Ralston Purina Company.

performers, directors, writers, composers, arrangers, designers, and technicians may be enlisted in these miniproductions. Some STARS for a time resisted involvement in commercials, but this reluctance gradually gave way to an eagerness to participate, not only for financial reasons but because an uncertain professional status was sometimes reinvigorated by an amusing or stylish thirty-second performance, widely disseminated. By the mid-1970s the members of HOLLYWOOD's Screen Actors Guild were earning more from commercials than from appearances in television films and theatrical films combined.

Historic Background

At the start of the radio broadcasting boom in 1920 (set off by radio bulletins of KDKA Pittsburgh, reporting on the presidential election that sent Warren G. Harding to the White House), few people imagined that ADVERTISING would play a major role in broadcasting. In fact, Herbert Hoover, who became Harding's secretary of commerce and thus acquired control over the issuing of station licenses, called it "inconceivable that we should allow so great a possibility for service to be drowned in advertising chatter." In spite of this dictum, Hoover posed no obstacle when the American Telephone and Telegraph Company (AT&T) in 1922 proposed a plan for a chain of advertising-supported stations. The first such station, which AT&T likened to a "phone booth" for public messages, became WEAF New York. Its first revenue was a fee of fifty dollars for a message promoting a suburban apartment-house complex. The AT&T plan took hold slowly and was angrily denounced by diverse interests, but it gradually became a central feature of American radio and later television. The idea raised similar resistance in other countries, but in many the high cost of broadcasting—particularly with the advent of television—and effective LOBBYING by advertising interests gradually turned the tide. The commercialization was introduced with various restrictions, such as limits on the length, frequency, and positioning of commercials. Many government-operated systems were among those that eventually adopted plans for selling time for advertising. Some decided to cluster commercials in time periods designated for that purpose, without relation to specific programs. The intention was to insulate programming decisions from direct advertising influence. Some indirect influence was felt to be inevitable. The sale of time for electioneering purposes, which became permissible in the United States, was banned in most European countries as giving finance an undue influence in politics.

Types of Commercials

Diverse genres of commercials evolved over the years, developing along parallel lines in most countries adopting commercial broadcasting. Commercial genres generally reflected dominant programming genres. The following variations appeared worldwide:

1. *Minidramas.* An individual faces a crisis in romance, business, or community status; the day is saved by Product.
2. *Musicals.* The infectiousness of SONG, sometimes supported by brisk choreography, is used to surround Product with a favorable atmosphere.
3. *Documentaries.* Quasi-DOCUMENTARY demonstration of Product in action, sometimes buttressed by charts and GRAPHICS, stresses its technical virtues.
4. *Testimonials.* The great and famous recommend Product as their personal choice among all available alternatives.
5. *Fantasy.* ANIMATION is enlisted to create imaginary creatures whose magic powers are associated with the magic of Product.
6. *Actuality.* Ordinary citizens, apparently observed unaware in restaurant, café, or other locality, discover and exclaim over the unique qualities of Product. *See* CINÉMA VÉRITÉ.
7. *Humor.* Comedians, promoting Product in unconventional ways, are permitted some of the liberties of the court jester. *See* COMEDY; HUMOR.
8. *News.* An announcer reveals that a new improvement makes Product even better than it has always been, assuring its continued supremacy over all competition.

Aspects of all the above genres are also used in diverse combinations.

Effects

Controversy over effects of commercials has been ever present. Commercials have been attacked on psychological, sociological, aesthetic, and political grounds. They are accused of exploiting and building personal anxieties, overemphasizing the material side of life, and distorting human and ethical values. It is argued that while they sell merchandise, they also sell a way of life, one that is linked to wasteful use of the world's finite resources and environmental pollution.

Such accusations are sometimes combined with charges of misleading advertising. Statements made verbally in television commercials are, however, seldom found false. In a visual medium, verbal tests of truth or falsity may have little meaning. When commercials feature SPORTS idols in cigarette or beer commercials, some viewers may consider this to be assurance that smoking and alcohol are compatible with radiant and vigorous health, though no assurance of this sort has been verbalized. The success of such strategies, amid rising cancer and accident statistics, have led a number of countries to ban broadcast advertising of cigarettes and alcoholic beverages. In the United States cigarette advertising on the air became illegal in 1970.

Commercials have been categorized as *hard sell* or *soft sell.* Both extremes persist. In the early 1980s hard-sell advertising began to feature *negative advertising*—attacks on competing products or companies, identified by name. The trend was widely deplored, but also praised as providing an "informed choice."

For the resolute opponent of commercials, various remote-control "mute" mechanisms have long been available, and their sale has caused some anxiety among advertisers. However, there is little evidence of any widespread anticommercial revolt in the general public. There is, on the contrary, evidence that commercials have won acceptance not merely as an information medium but also as skilled entertainment. Some phrases and slogans from commercials pass quickly into everyday use. Commercial jingles sometimes become popular songs and seem to turn into a species of modern folk music. In many countries commercials have apparently become an important component of popular culture.

See also CHILDREN—MEDIA EFFECTS; CONSUMER RESEARCH; FACT AND FICTION; MASS MEDIA EFFECTS; RATING SYSTEMS: RADIO AND TELEVISION; SPONSOR; VIDEO.

Bibliography. Leo Bogart, *Strategy in Advertising,* 2d ed., Chicago, 1985; Stuart Ewen, *Captains of Consciousness: Advertising and the Social Roots of the Consumer Culture,* New York, 1976; Bruce Kurtz, *Spots: The Popular Art of Television Commercials,* New York, 1977; Tony Schwartz, *The Responsive Chord,* New York, 1974.

ARTHUR ASA BERGER

COMMUNICATION, PHILOSOPHIES OF

The major ideas philosophers have developed about communication can be grouped under pragmatics, hermeneutics, existential communication, and prereflective communication. All have histories that reach back to antiquity and are, in this sense, classical.

Pragmatics

The word *pragmatics* was introduced by CHARLES MORRIS in 1938 to refer to the study of the users and contexts of signs (*see* SIGN; SIGN SYSTEM). Philosophers then were not interested in Morris's broad sense of pragmatics as involving all kinds of signs. They restricted the term to signs of LANGUAGE, but even within this restriction they could not agree on a definition. The one that is most accepted states that pragmatics is concerned with the ways in which language functions as a communicative system. The flourishing of pragmatic studies since the early 1960s makes it seem as if philosophers had begun only recently to study the pragmatic aspects of language, but this is not so. Morris had launched the term pragmatics in reference to the work of CHARLES S. PEIRCE, WILLIAM JAMES, JOHN DEWEY, and GEORGE HERBERT MEAD. These philosophers shared a communal view of reality, in which communication by way of arguments and such notions as "agreement" and "disagreement" had pivotal roles. But as for argumentation being essential to any procedure for justifying truth claims, philosophic reflections about communication are as old as philosophy, originating roughly in what German philosopher Karl Jaspers called "axial time" (ca. 800–200 B.C.E.) with Vedantism and Buddhism in India, Confucianism and Taoism in China, and classical Greek philosophy in Europe. Among these, PLATO offers the most explicit philosophy of communication.

Plato: dialectic, rhetoric, sophistic. Plato believed that philosophical understanding is dialectic; that is, it implies the ability to demonstrate itself in argumentation. Beliefs have to be justified in discussion, and discussion, in turn, has to be based on the search for truth. This sets philosophical dialectic apart from RHETORIC as the art of PERSUASION and from sophistic as the art of argumentation in the service of public goals and interests. Plato thought that truth must be demonstrated by way of inner or outer SPEECH, so rhetoric is intrinsic to the acquisition of truth only as long as it remains in the service of truth. The same is true of sophistic, which, as long as it is subordinated to the search for truth, is assimilated to virtue defined as "the right usage of knowledge," which consists essentially in being a good citizen. Under these circumstances, Plato regarded both sophistic and rhetoric as necessary conditions for communicating one's knowledge effectively, and for knowledge to be communicated effectively, it has to be accepted by the listener or reader.

Aristotle: the search for first principles. ARISTOTLE saw in Plato's dialectic the pragmatic setting for formal logic. He believed that without agreement on premises for starting points of an argument there could not be any philosophical communication. If communicators mistakenly assume that their audience agrees with their premises, they commit petitio principii—they beg the question. The argument miscarries not because of a logical error ("if *p*, then *p*" is logically valid) but because of an error in communication, that is to say, argumentation.

Cicero and Italian humanism: rhetoric and common sense. CICERO transmitted the classical Greek philosophical concern with communication to the RENAISSANCE. His legacy to the Italian humanists was a view of communication as basically grounded in common sense and in the popular language that accompanies it.

This led in the fourteenth century to a revival of natural local languages, beginning with the work of the Italian poet Dante, who communicated his vision not in Latin but in the "vulgar" popular language of his time. He emphasized the role of pragmatic parameters in communication, such as time and place of utterance, speakers and addressees, and the larger context of the particular communication situation, and he was followed in this by the Italian humanists. In the twentieth century LUDWIG WITTGENSTEIN in Austria and John Austin in England picked up this tradition by viewing philosophy as being essentially conversational in the sense that the meanings of words are determined by the way people actually communicate and by the specific contexts of communication.

Deictic or indexical words. To analyze the context of communication some philosophers have been interested in deictic or indexical words. These are words whose INTERPRETATION depends on an analysis of the context in which they are used. Words like demonstratives (*this, there*), pronouns (*I, you*), and indicators of tense (*was, will be*) belong to this category. Peirce was the first to call them "indexical signs." He characterized the relationship between these signs and their referents as "existential." The English philosopher Bertrand Russell called them "egocentric particulars" and argued that in principle all indexicals refer to some kind of subjective experience. Hans Reichenbach, a German philosopher, saw indexicals as token reflexives: they refer to themselves. For example, the word *I* would refer to "the person uttering this token of the word *I*."

The most widely accepted philosophic approach to indexicals makes a distinction between the MEANING of an utterance and the proposition it expresses. Meanings are functions from contexts to propositions; propositions are functions from possible worlds to truth values. For example, a sentence like "I am forty-nine years old" has an invariable meaning, but the proposition picked out by this sentence differs depending on who is saying it, how (e.g., with irony), when, and where. In this theory pragmatics is preliminary to SEMANTICS, but the whole approach focuses mainly on those indexicals that are amenable to truth conditions. Some are not, such as performative indexicals like "I *hereby* . . ." or emphatic indexicals like "*This* is it."

Speech acts. In speech act philosophy, advanced first by Austin and subsequently systematized by the English philosopher John Searle, a large portion of speech is seen as a kind of action. For example, if I

say to someone, "I promise," I do not describe something true or false, but rather *do* something, namely, promise. I am engaged in a PERFORMANCE that Austin called an *illocutionary act,* whose force derives from social conventions. He distinguished two other kinds of speech acts: the *locutionary act,* which is achieved by the assertion of sense and reference, and the *prelocutionary act,* which includes all the effects an utterance may cause in a specific situation. Although these three kinds of acts are not always clearly separable, most philosophers have concentrated on illocutionary speech acts, probably because these acts clearly demonstrate that it is not truth conditions but social conventions that are central to our understanding of how we communicate. However, it is notoriously difficult to survey these conventions, and it is not likely that a comprehensive theory can be found.

Speaker meaning versus sentence meaning. Another philosophy of communication, proposed by the English philosopher H. Paul Grice, starts from the premise that it is not so much the culturally given illocutionary force of an utterance that is basic to communication but the communicative intention with which an utterance is conveyed and received. Communication is achieved by the mutual recognition on the part of sender and receiver of their intention to communicate. Only when such mutual knowledge of each other's communicative intention is present can we properly speak of successful communication. Grice distinguished between *natural meaning,* as in "This storm means trouble," and *nonnatural meaning* or *meaning-nn,* which is the meaning conveyed by a communicative intention. Grice emphasized that what a speaker means by an utterance is not necessarily the meaning of the utterance, as in cases of irony or METAPHOR. This discrepancy can be taken care of by distinguishing between *speaker meaning* (Grice's meaning-nn) and *sentence meaning* or (which is the same) between *conveyed meaning* and *literal meaning.* Pragmatics is interested mostly in speaker meaning, while semantics is concerned mainly with sentence meaning.

Conversational implicature. The notion of *conversational implicature* bridges the gap between semantics and pragmatics, between what an utterance conveys as a sentence and what it conveys in terms of the mutual knowledge of the communicators. The theory of conversational implicature attempts to make explicit basic assumptions guiding successful conversations. Grice formulated general guidelines for people to follow to achieve efficient communication: they should be cooperative, rational, and efficient; that is, what they say should be true, informative, relevant, and clear. This is not to say that we always communicate this way, but we *implicitly* act under these assumptions when we communicate (hence the notion of implicature). For example, when we do not understand a remark, we often ask for clarification, which illustrates Grice's point that we expect clarity in communication. This applies even to the use of figurative forms of communication, such as irony: the temporary bafflement of receivers who do not immediately get the point attests to the fact that they expected straightforward talk. The theory of conversational implicature is thus at least partly extendable to tropes (figures of speech). Its major constraints seem to come from those forms of communication that are systematically uncooperative, such as cross-examinations in a court of law. But even here one could argue that this form of noncooperativeness is conventionally sanctioned and in those terms precisely cooperative. *See also* LAW AND COMMUNICATION; TESTIMONY.

Universal pragmatics. The widest sense of pragmatics is to be found in the work of the German philosopher Jürgen Habermas, in which it assumes the status of a comprehensive theory of communicative action. Habermas sees communication as all socially coordinated activities through which the human species maintains itself as human, that is, rational. Rationality, in turn, is the ability to seek agreement by way of argumentative reasoning. Arguments contain validity claims, and Habermas's universal pragmatics addresses four universal validity claims that he sees as being necessarily presupposed by communication. Persons acting communicatively claim to be (1) *uttering* something understandably, (2) giving the hearer *something* to understand, (3) making *themselves* thereby understandable, and (4) coming to an understanding *with another person.* Although these validity claims are universal and as such are applicable to any type of communication, communicators always stand in culture-bound and language-specific traditions that support their "lifeworlds"; they in turn renew and transmit these traditions by acting communicatively. Communication theory is thus for Habermas equivalent to *critical social theory,* in which any human action deserving that title becomes communicative action. Most critics of Habermas tend to agree with the notion of universal validity claims but are quick to point out that the apparent strength of such a view, its universality, is precisely its weakness in terms of how such claims can be validated empirically.

Hermeneutics

Hermeneutics, named after the Greek messenger god Hermes, developed in the Renaissance originally as the art of reviving classical and theological texts by means of written commentaries. But in the nineteenth century the German theologian Friedrich Schleier-

macher extended the art to CONVERSATION and speech, because he claimed that understanding texts implied communicating with their authors. In the twentieth century Schleiermacher's discourse-oriented notion of hermeneutics provided the basis for a hermeneutic philosophy of communication whose central notion is that of the hermeneutic circle.

According to German philosophers Martin Heidegger and Hans-Georg Gadamer, communicators bring their own culture-bound preconceptions, biases, and prejudices to bear on their understanding of a communicative event. Insofar as listeners or readers always understand messages in terms of their own prior understandings, communication contains a circular structure. Awareness of this structure improves the awareness communicators have of their own biases. It forces them to acknowledge their own cultural traditions and preconceptions as important influences on what they understand. Each message, besides coming from the other, is also a self-fabrication in terms of the receiver's own input of interpretation. In this way the hermeneutic circle lets speakers come face to face with themselves precisely when they communicate with others. *See also* CULTURE.

Existential Communication

While for hermeneutics the reflexive element of one's own self-projection is an integral element in communication, the confrontation with one's self in and through the act of communication can become the sole purpose of communication. This is the case in existential communication, whose best-known forms are known as maieutic communication, indirect communication, and oracular communication.

Plato's maieutic communication. In Plato's dialogue *Phaedrus,* Socrates saw in written communication a misleading implication that truth could be found outside the communicator's own soul. Plato thought to remedy this situation by writing in the form of dialogue in which Socrates practiced the art of "midwifery"—in Greek, *maieutike*—which involves asking questions in such a way that the listeners find the answers to the questions within themselves. In maieutic communication receivers are reminded that they are already in possession of the truth and that communication merely evokes that truth in them. In the *Meno* Plato demonstrated how Socrates elicited from an ignorant slave boy important mathematical information simply by asking him questions and drawing diagrams in the sand. Communication is here seen not as transferring knowledge from sender to receiver but as eliciting knowledge that the receiver already has but is not aware of and therefore is induced to recollect by the sender.

Besides evoking potential knowledge, maieutic

communication also aims at creating in communicators an attitude of passion for the truth, since the relationship to truth can only be a personal one in each case. Thus the search for truth is a search for one's true self. The Danish philosopher Søren Kierkegaard called this type of communication indirect communication.

Kierkegaard's indirect communication. For Kierkegaard, indirect (also called dialectical or existential) communication works against itself in the very act of communicating in order to facilitate the receiver's access to an ethical-religious existence. To live in the ethical order, individuals have to realize their own inwardness, in which what is objectively uncertain or even impossible is held fast by the infinite passion of faith. To lead individuals to such radical subjectivity, communicators have to lead, but at the same time they should remove themselves as leaders. In addition, since indirect communication should result in a realization of freedom and not an increase in knowledge, communicators must *be* what they teach and receivers must *become* what they are taught. Truth is not a doctrine but an existential transformation, and indirect communication is existence communication. To be existentially transformed is to stand alone in a relationship to God, but ironically one can be helped toward this inner one-to-one relationship with God by someone else. The other is therefore in a sense deceiving, since the other only seems to teach. In reality it is only God who can teach how to exist. This necessary ironic element of DECEPTION in indirect communication is very similar to the psychoanalytic view of communication, which the French psychoanalyst Jacques Lacan characterized as oracular communication.

Lacan's oracular communication. If for Kierkegaard the only teacher is ultimately God, for Lacan it is the Freudian unconscious. The unconscious is an effect of language, specifically of the way its binary semantic oppositions split the mind into states of "allowed/forbidden," "present/absent," "reality/fantasy," and the like. One side of these oppositions tends to be repressed and assumes its role as permanent other, whose heterogeneity is desired as such; that is, the self desires its own difference and absence as a constitutive part of itself. This is essentially Hegelian, and Lacan's reformulation of psychoanalytic communication turns out to be a unique blend of G. W. F. Hegel, Kierkegaard, and Heidegger, concisely expressed by Lacan's formula of communication: Human language constitutes a communication in which the sender receives its own message back from the receiver in an inverted form. The message relates to the necessity of difference in the very constitution of the speaking subject. Senders get their own difference back from receivers and thereby show the structural necessity of communication: we communicate because who we are is always forthcoming from the other. *See also* FREUD, SIGMUND; PSYCHOANALYSIS.

Other Minds: Preverbal Criteria of Communication

The philosophical problem of the existence of other minds is, strictly speaking, not a philosophy of communication, but it can be viewed as addressing the foundation of a philosophy of communication, namely, the existence of other minds capable of communicating. Moreover, the way some philosophers, such as Wittgenstein and Frenchman Maurice Merleau-Ponty, addressed the problem carries with it a description of communication that is preverbal and prereflective. Wittgenstein believed that to understand first-person sentences we should see them as being similar to natural, nonverbal expressions of sensations. "My knee hurts," for example, replaces such behavior as crying, limping, holding one's knee; it does not describe it. First-person speech acts are seen as substitutes for original, natural expressions of sensations. Merleau-Ponty said similar things about gestures. The meaning of a GESTURE is not something "behind" it; it is the gesture itself. For example, a gesture indicating a fit of anger does not make one think of anger; it is anger itself. Merleau-Ponty called this type of communication *primordial*, because the act that communicates anger is anger itself and does not refer to some psychological state apart from it.

Philosophy as Communication

A strong philosophical tradition, ranging from Plato through Hegel to Heidegger, sees philosophy itself as an act of ongoing communication between self and other, identity and difference. For these philosophers communication is always in the service of truth, although they have different conceptions of truth. More recently U.S. philosopher Richard Rorty has claimed to see in philosophy a kind of communication that consists in the ability to sustain a conversation, generating ever-new descriptions of ways of looking at things, rather than a kind that is concerned with truth. Communication, in this view, is connected and concerned with itself rather than with the world.

See also MARXIST THEORIES OF COMMUNICATION; POETICS.

Bibliography. Hans-Georg Gadamer, *Truth and Method* (Wahrheit und Methode), trans. from 2d ed. by Garrett Barden and John Cumming, New York, 1975, reprint 1986; Jürgen Habermas, *Communication and the Evolu-*

tion of Society, Boston, 1979; Søren Kierkegaard, *Journals and Papers,* Vol. 1, A–E (Papirer, 1909), Bloomington, Ind., 1967; Jacques Lacan, *Écrits,* Paris, 1966, reprint (trans. by Alan Sheridan) New York, 1977; Stephen C. Levinson, *Pragmatics,* Cambridge, 1983; Richard Rorty, *Philosophy and the Mirror of Nature,* Princeton, N.J., 1979; C. J. Rowe, *Plato,* New York, 1984.

EUGEN BAER

COMMUNICATION MODELS. *See* MODELS OF COMMUNICATION.

COMMUNICATIONS, STUDY OF

The study of communications focuses on a process fundamental to the development of humans and human society—interaction through messages. By means of communication we share ideas and information, live in infinitely varied cultures, and extend knowledge and imagination far beyond the scope of personal experience. It is not surprising, therefore, that the study of communications in one form or another has long been of deep human concern. Philosophy, RHETORIC, POETICS, HOMILETICS, LINGUISTICS, SEMANTICS, and SEMIOTICS are just a few of the branches of learning that have dealt with aspects of communication.

However, organized academic programs in communications are relatively recent. The impetus for their establishment came from the growth of the mass media and other new communication technologies, which made possible the rapid mass production and distribution of messages and images. Thus, although lectures on journalism were being given at Leipzig University in 1672 and a doctoral dissertation on the press was presented there in 1690, such developments were few and far between, and the impact of communication studies was not widely felt until the twentieth century.

Modern media-oriented studies began with practical training in journalism, film, RADIO, SPEECH, television (*see* TELEVISION HISTORY), ADVERTISING, PUBLIC RELATIONS, and similar activities. These studies are often conducted as apprentice training by the media themselves or in connection with professional and trade organizations, unions, and government agencies. Communication or communications (often in combination with related terms, for example, speech communication or journalism and communication) is an area of scholarship and research whose purpose is to contribute to the critical understanding of interpersonal and social communication and its policies as well as to the practical skills of media production.

The broadening of communication studies from skills training to research and analytical and critical inquiry was a result of changes in social, artistic, and technological conditions. Early print had been a mo-

nopoly of literate elites, but cheap newspapers became a mass medium (*see* NEWSPAPER: HISTORY). Film and radio bypassed the need for LITERACY. Television completed the transition of modern media from "class" to "mass." It also created the first media environment to pervade the home and fill the LEISURE hours of millions of people of all ages. New media also gave rise to new forms and styles of expression, socialization, and governance, challenging traditional modes of social analysis and cultural study.

The availability of relatively cheap (and cheaply printed) stories and pictures (including COMICS) in the late nineteenth and early twentieth centuries added fuel to the ancient debate about new modes of communication debasing the old and corrupting the impressionable and vulnerable. Each new MODE or medium also stimulated research, as well as controversy, about the consequences for CHILDREN, the "lower classes," and CULTURE in general. The results of research enriched the scholarly basis of the new discipline and hastened its emergence. *See also* COMMUNICATIONS RESEARCH: ORIGINS AND DEVELOPMENT.

In several European countries cinema studies began in the 1920s to address more specialized literary and artistic issues raised by the new medium. A tradition of media scholarship and criticism was initiated in independent centers only loosely connected, if at all, with academic institutions. This tradition of media studies eventually led to two distinct developments: the semiotic (or semiology) approach to analysis, especially in France and Italy, and the movements in screen EDUCATION and media studies in the United Kingdom and other countries.

In the United States the study of communications gained a relatively early entry into colleges and universities mostly as a "practical," vocationally oriented course. However, in an academic environment it was forced to broaden its scope. Students of media had to take courses in philosophy, history, politics, and other liberal arts subjects. With the acceptance of communications in the academy and the development of graduate programs of research and analysis came a growing acceptance of the concept of communication as the core of a distinct academic discipline able to contribute to knowledge about human development, society, government, and the arts.

United States

The spread of communication studies in the United States reflects the prominence of communication media in the everyday life of its citizens. In the late 1980s more than six hundred U.S. colleges and universities (about 20 percent) had formal programs (schools, departments, or other units) in communication media studies, employing more than seventeen hundred full-time faculty members. These programs included journalistic, artistic, and scientific approaches to the study of practice and policy in press, film, radio, television, advertising, public relations, speech, and telecommunications (the study of new communication technologies).

More than six out of every ten of these academic units grant bachelor's degrees, two out of every ten have graduate programs leading to the master's degree, and about 4 percent confer the Ph.D. The University of Iowa approved the first doctoral programs in 1945. Within ten years communications doctoral programs existed at the Universities of Illinois, Wisconsin, and Southern California, and Stanford University. By the late 1980s there were twenty-four doctoral programs in communications and related studies. More than five thousand students pursue graduate studies in communication fields, and about fifteen hundred graduate degrees in these fields are awarded each year by U.S. universities.

From journalism to communication scholarship. Germany was the first country to offer the study of journalism in its universities. The United States, however, pioneered in the nineteenth- and twentieth-century development of academic journalism.

In 1869 Robert E. Lee, hero of the Confederacy, who became president of Washington University (later renamed Washington and Lee in his honor), supported a university program for training journalists, which he called "journalism and printing," that was meant to aid in the rebuilding of the South. Editors disagreed about the appropriateness of the idea. Henry Watterson of the Louisville *Courier-Journal* declared firmly, "There is but one school of journalism and that is a well-conducted newspaper office." E. L. Godkin of *The Nation* and HORACE GREELEY of the New York *Tribune* lined up with Watterson. JOSEPH PULITZER of the New York *World* and Whitelaw Reid of the *Tribune* were on Lee's side. The program was not a great success and was disbanded before the end of the century.

The University of Missouri gave a course in the history and materials of journalism as early as 1878. The Wharton School of Business at the University of Pennsylvania offered a business journalism major from 1893 to 1901, under Joseph French Johnson, who had been financial editor of the *Chicago Tribune.* The first separate *school* of journalism was founded at Missouri in 1908, with longtime journalist Walter W. Williams as dean. The Pulitzer School at Columbia University, established in 1912 (later renamed the Columbia Graduate School of Journalism), was founded with an endowment from Pulitzer of about $2.5 million.

Developments came rapidly. In 1910 there had been only one school (Missouri) and four departments of journalism. In 1917, 84 institutions were offering work in journalism. In 1934 there were 455 such institutions and 812 teachers. By 1987 more than 300 institutions offered degree-granting programs in journalism or journalism and mass communications, and nearly twice as many conducted some work in these and related communication subjects.

The American Association of Teachers of Journalism (AATJ) was founded in 1912, with Willard G. Bleyer as its first president. Administrators of journalism programs founded the American Association of Schools and Departments of Journalism (AASDJ) in 1917. The development of a formal accrediting program resulted in the establishment of the American Council for Education in Journalism in 1939 and a rival group, the American Society of Journalism School Administrators, in 1944. To resolve the confusion and to place leadership in the hands of teachers, the Association for Education in Journalism (AEJ) was formed in 1950, and it added "and Mass Communication" to its name (becoming AEJMC) in 1982. Other organizational mergers and alliances gave the field a coherent professional and scholarly structure, and it grew in total membership from the founding group of eighteen to more than two thousand members and from 14 college and university departments to 173 in 1987.

By 1924 the new field had a scholarly journal, the *Journalism Bulletin,* which in 1930 was renamed the *Journalism Quarterly* and is still published. In the first five years typical articles in the *Bulletin* were "Proof Errors Analyzed" and "Comparing Notes on Courses," but beginning in 1930, when Frank Luther Mott became editor and the name changed from *Bulletin* to *Quarterly,* tougher standards were applied. In the first five years of Mott's editorship the number of articles on the teaching of journalism was halved from the preceding five years, and the number of articles on international communication and the foreign press tripled.

Other scholarly journals joined the *Journalism Quarterly* to serve the field, such as the *Film Quarterly, Journal of Broadcasting and Electronic Media, Journal of Communication,* and *Quarterly Journal of Speech,* to name only a few. An *Index to Journals in Communication Studies through 1985,* published by the Speech Communication Association, listed fifteen scholarly journals, and four more have been started since 1985. Organizations such as the Association for Education in Journalism and Mass Communication, the International Communication Association, the Speech Communication Association, the Society for Cinema Studies, and the Broadcast

Education Association promoted scholarship as well as professionalism in the field. Clearly the academic face of journalism had changed.

Other changes took place as well. A few institutions began to call themselves schools of journalism and communication (or communications). Among these were some of the pacesetters, such as Wisconsin and Minnesota. Illinois combined journalism and several other departments into a school of communication, headed by a dean. By 1986 more than eighty-six thousand students were reported in 180 schools as majoring in journalism and mass communications.

The change in names had a dual significance. First, it signaled the broadening of the new field from newspaper journalism to all media and modes of communication. For example, when Stanford established a department of communication it included radio and film. Nonjournalism departments were affected also. At the University of Iowa the Department of Speech renamed itself the Department of Communication, but the school of journalism was left with its old nameplate, Journalism and Mass Communication.

A second and deeper effect of the name change was that a social science name—communication— replaced a vocational one. This change announced to the rest of the university that the practical study of journalism—like business and education—had joined academia and was looking at its problems and conducting its research with the same rigor that other social sciences insisted on.

Supporting the academic study of communications was the development of communications research as an academic specialty. Research until the 1960s concentrated on specific media and was sporadic and noncumulative. Its rapid consolidation was based on research undertaken during and immediately after World War II. The need to consolidate research findings and to plan further research led to the establishment of institutes for communications research, which were usually attached to schools or departments of communication. These attracted social scientists and research grants and made it easier for communications to claim disciplinary status among academic disciplines and to launch graduate programs leading to the Ph.D., a major scholarly recognition of such status. Communications doctoral programs trained researchers and scholars who prepared the way for the next advance: the introduction of communications as a fresh approach to the liberal arts, with subject matter necessary for all citizens in a media-dominated society. The doctoral programs became the chief training grounds for the critical and analytical approach to the new media environment. Their graduates were sought by many colleges and universities in order to expand old and to launch new undergraduate programs.

A significant opportunity for progress in the new direction came with the establishment of graduate programs not dependent on undergraduate media training and free to chart their own courses. The first such opportunity arose when Walter H. Annenberg, prominent publisher and U.S. Ambassador to the Court of St. James, founded The Annenberg School of Communications at the University of Pennsylvania in 1959. The newly assembled faculty of media scholars and social scientists designed an innovative graduate curriculum focusing on three areas of communication study: analysis of the codes and modes of structuring images and messages, research on the behavior of parties to the communication process, and the study of communication systems, institutions, and policies. The new concept and its productivity in scholarship and publications contributed to the trend toward making communication study an integral part of the academic organization of knowledge.

Speech communication. Parallels between the university development of communication studies in speech and journalism are striking, although, of course, the study of journalism accompanied the mass media, whereas the study of speech goes back at least as far as the Greek and Roman rhetoricians and the Elder Sophists.

The classical rhetoricians provided a foundation in the first century B.C.E., and rhetorical studies in the early European universities built on that base. Rhetoric was part of the first curriculum of Harvard University in 1636. Princeton University, the University of Pennsylvania, and the College of William and Mary all taught rhetoric in the eighteenth century. In those years it was usually a part of the Department of English.

In 1910 seventeen teachers of speech walked out of the annual meeting of the National Council of Teachers of English and formed their own association. By 1914 they had created a National Association of Academic Teachers of Public Speaking, which later became the Speech Communication Association (1968).

Film. Film as the medium of MOTION PICTURES attracted the interest of artists, critics, educators, businesspeople, and students from the time THOMAS ALVA EDISON's kinetoscope peepshows first became popular in New York in 1894. Soon films were being studied as the artistic expression of leading filmmakers, as vehicles of social protest, as instruments of revolutionary PROPAGANDA, as reflections of cultural tendencies, as instruments of education and information, and as historical documents.

European schools of filmmaking and film criticism

centered on such leading personalities as SERGEI EISENSTEIN and Aleksandr Dovzhenko (Russia), JEAN RENOIR and Jean-Luc Godard (France), F. W. Murnau and Rainer Werner Fassbinder (Germany), and Lucino Visconti and Michelangelo Antonioni (Italy). Training and study were for the most part conducted outside universities.

U.S. universities were somewhat more hospitable to film studies. The first known listing of a university course on motion pictures was one at Columbia University in the 1916–1917 academic year, initiated by Victor Oscar Freeburg but taken over by Frances Taylor Patterson when Freeburg left for war duty. Two pioneering textbooks emerged from this beginning: Freeburg's *The Art of Photoplay Making* (1918) and Patterson's *Cinema Craftsmanship: A Book for Photoplaywrights* (1920). The University of Southern California (in the shadow of the HOLLYWOOD film industry) first offered a course on the photoplay in 1929. By 1932 it had programmed a sequence of courses for a B.A. in film studies and by 1935 a sequence for an M.A. After World War II the growth in the number of courses dealing with motion pictures in U.S. colleges and universities was swift.

The first adoptions of film studies programs were in departments of education (in which film was studied as an audiovisual aid to TEACHING), speech, and DRAMA. Critical and empirical research approaches were represented by adoptions in departments of English, literature, and history and later in departments and schools of communication. From the beginning, filmmaking and production courses were very popular, as were courses on the history and AESTHETICS of the cinema and on the social and psychological aspects of films.

Radio and television. The first master's degree in broadcasting (which at that time was limited to radio) was offered by the University of Wisconsin in 1931. By the end of the 1950s eighty-nine universities and colleges offered bachelor's degrees in radio-television, forty-five offered master's degrees, and sixteen awarded doctorates.

By that time, of course, television had become the dominant audiovisual medium of modern times, attracting a nightly audience greater than the weekly attendance at movies when they were most popular, and more scholarly attention than either radio or films ever received. Craft and critical approaches to the three newest media tended to merge. Because of the importance of news and information to the broadcast media, graduates of schools and departments of journalism increasingly found employment with them. Researchers in radio and television found themselves studying parallel problems. Although cinema studies retained much of their AVANT-GARDE flavor and critical tendencies and continued as a

separate line of scholarship (as indeed do all the subdisciplines of communications), the ferment in communication studies in the 1980s led to the absorption and integration into the new discipline of many of the insights derived from film scholarship. Thus although their differences are as apparent as ever, the audiovisual media are reaching the end of the century with their patterns of study more unified than ever before.

Advertising. More than half of the world's advertising expenditures are in the United States and Canada, and, not surprisingly, the majority of programs of professional training and study are in North America as well. There was, however, little activity in advertising education before 1900 despite the long history of advertising itself. The advent of printed media (see PRINTING) in the seventeenth century greatly stimulated the use of advertising, and, in turn, advertising became the business subsidy that supported commercial media in capitalist countries.

The first university course labeled "advertising" was one offered by New York University during the 1905–1906 school year. In 1908 both the University of Missouri and Northwestern University offered their first courses in advertising. The Northwestern course was taught by Walter Dill Scott, a psychologist who wrote the first well-known textbook in the field—*Psychology of Advertising*—and later became Northwestern's president. The first major in advertising was offered at the University of Missouri around 1913. By 1930 more than thirty colleges and universities listed at least one course in advertising in their catalogs.

Advertising education, like all communication study, grew from varied roots: the interest of the advertising community in training, of psychologists and other social scientists in the effects of PERSUASION, of business organizations and schools of business in marketing, of new schools of journalism and communication in the economic mainsprings of commercial media, and of historians and social scientists in exploring advertising's influence on society and on individual lives.

In the United States an estimated five hundred institutions of higher learning offer some courses in advertising. Forty or more institutions have major programs in advertising. Among the students in schools of journalism and/or journalism and communication who have declared majors, about 18 percent chose advertising compared to about 30 percent who chose editorial journalism. Among graduates, about 8 percent go into advertising, 10 percent into public relations, and 14 percent into broadcasting; 12 percent work for daily newspapers, and some 10 percent get other media-related jobs. Nearly half do not find (or seek) careers in these areas.

Canada

Canadian scholars such as HAROLD INNIS and MAR-SHALL MCLUHAN pioneered in the economic and cultural policy approaches to the study of communication, but early university education in the field followed the patterns established in the United States. Spurred by the demand for journalism education after World War II, three universities established journalism departments in Canada: Carleton University in Ottawa, the University of Western Ontario in London (Ontario), and Ryerson Institute of Technology (now Ryerson Polytechnical Institute) in Toronto. In 1965 Loyola College in Montreal started a course in mass communications, and soon many universities followed suit, including Windsor, Toronto, Saskatchewan, Simon Fraser, Concordia, McGill, Montreal, and Laval. The work and fame of McLuhan attracted students to the University of Toronto, which continues a McLuhan Centre for Culture and Technology.

By the late 1970s at least thirty universities and forty community colleges offered degree and diploma programs in communications or journalism. Graduate programs lead to a master's degree in communications at ten universities and to a diploma in journalism at three universities. Programs leading to a Ph.D. in communications were established at McGill and Simon Fraser universities and in a bilingual (French-English) program jointly conducted by the Université de Montréal, Université du Québec à Montréal, and Concordia University. The scholarly Canadian Communication Association was formed in 1980 and the Association de Recherche en Communication de Québec shortly thereafter.

Europe and the USSR

The study of communications in Europe tends to reflect the varied history and cultural context of its development. University lectures on press history were given in Germany as early as 1672. After World War I journalism training was promoted in England by the newspaper industry for former armed forces personnel. Practical and professional media studies developed rapidly in eastern Europe and the Soviet Union after World War II.

The Institute of Journalists, a trade organization, supported the establishment of the first graduate diploma course in journalism at London University in 1919. Not until 1970 was there another specialized professional program, the Centre for Journalism Studies at University College, Cardiff, a part of the University of Wales. A Chair of Film was set up at London University in 1967. By that time organized research programs in mass communication had been launched at the Universities of Leicester, Leeds, and Birmingham, and at the London School of Economics and Political Science. By the late 1980s at least twelve universities, including several important polytechnic institutions, were offering organized degree programs in various aspects of communications, and more technical courses were offered by press and broadcast industry training programs.

Although the roots of communication study in Germany are very old, continuous study of the field began around World War I. MAX WEBER's proposal for the sociological study of the role of the press in PUBLIC OPINION formation was turned down at a Congress of Sociology in 1912. Instead, the German Institute for the Study of the Press was established in Berlin by professional associations and major publishers. However, the practical journalism training offered in Berlin and a growing number of other centers was not considered an appropriate function for universities. Therefore, *Zeitungswissenschaft* ("press science") at Leipzig and other centers of learning was considered a major subject, legally recognized for the granting of university degrees, and was closely related to history, politics, economics, and law, rather than to the skills and techniques of journalism.

In the 1920s sixteen German universities were offering study programs in press science, and the example was noted and followed in a number of other European countries. Between the wars *Zeitungswissenschaft* began to seem less appropriate as a title because of the growing influence of radio, especially in Germany, where public opinion and propaganda, rather than press history and press law, were beginning to dominate thinking about the media. After World War II the term *Publizistik* (which might be translated as "public communication") had begun to replace *Zeitungswissenschaft* as a name for the academic field.

In other western European countries the structure of communication study showed similar signs of change. The Institut für Zeitungswissenschaft at the University of Vienna changed its name to the Institut für Publizistik and also changed its research emphasis from press history and law to mass communication in general and began to concentrate on empirical approaches. In France an Institute of Press Science was established before World War II. It closed during the war, and its successor was eventually superseded by the Institut Français de Presse (French Institute of the Press), which was founded in 1951 and which became attached to the Sorbonne in 1957. In 1966 it was granted the power to award diplomas and degrees. Two influential programs in practical journalism were begun after World War II by the University of Bordeaux and the University of Strasbourg. In Strasbourg the program was connected with an International Center for Advanced Training in Journalism, established in 1956 with UNESCO's help, and it offered refresher courses for teachers of journalism and practicing journalists as well as aspiring journalists from Europe, Africa, and the Middle East. The "cultural approach" (involving the development of STRUCTURALISM), also practiced at the University of Birmingham's Centre for Contemporary Cultural Studies, thrived in the 1960s and 1970s at the Centre d'Études de Communications de Masse (CECMAS) in the École Pratique des Hautes Études in Paris. Government attention to the new communication technologies stimulated new training and research programs in the 1980s.

By the 1970s every European country was offering practical training in journalism in addition to the more academically oriented courses. Prominent centers of communication studies included the Universities of Madrid, Barcelona, Bilbao, and Pamplona in Spain, Naples and Bologna in Italy, Amsterdam and Nijmegen in the Netherlands, and Oslo, Lund, Göteborg, Helsinki, and Tampere in the Scandinavian countries.

Cinema and broadcasting, as might be expected, were added to the subject matter of communication study somewhat later than the press. Further, practical training in the audiovisual media was less likely to be given by universities than by institutes or film and broadcasting studios. It is generally observed that the coming of television after World War II not only stimulated and broadened mass media studies in Europe but also boosted research on the social use and effects of mass communication in general (see MASS MEDIA EFFECTS). Similarly the new approach to film studies in the writings of Gilbert Cohen-Séat, especially his philosophy of the cinema described as "filmology" that combined the cultural-aesthetic and social-psychological approaches to the film and stimulated the establishment of the Institute for Filmology at the Sorbonne, sparked an interest in studies of social communication in general, especially in France, Italy, and Belgium. Thus by the 1970s mass media studies, practical and theoretical, were well known in western Europe.

In the USSR the study of communication started outside the universities and concentrated on journalism and other media training. Its direction was strongly influenced by V. I. Lenin's concept of the press as "collective organizer." There was thus a practical political as well as a scholarly reason for an early start to education in communication.

Journalism and film training were established in Moscow shortly after the October Revolution. The State Institute of Journalism was founded in Moscow in 1921, reorganized in 1923, and largely supplanted by the establishment of university units after World War II. The first university department of journalism was founded at the University of Leningrad in 1946 as a Section of Journalism in the Faculty of Philosophy. At the Lomonosov State University of Moscow

a Section of Journalism was organized in the Faculty of Philology in 1947. Five years later it was transformed into a faculty (in U.S. university terminology, a school), the first such faculty in the country. It has grown tremendously since the early 1950s and continues to be the leading institution of journalism education in the country.

The three types of journalism education in the USSR all lead to a diploma: a full-time five-year course, evening classes for six years that meet three or four times a week, and correspondence courses with twice yearly individual examinations for practical journalists living outside Moscow or other major university centers.

The University of Moscow's Faculty of Journalism is divided into departments that include newspaper and MAGAZINE journalism, news agency journalism (see NEWS AGENCIES), radio and television journalism, and book PUBLISHING so that students can choose their specializations. Faculty members are divided among departments (called chairs) that include theory and practice of the Soviet press, foreign press and literature, history of Russian and Soviet journalism, sociology of the mass media, LITERARY CRITICISM, and stylistics of the Russian language. The general curriculum is a combination of liberal arts, Russian socioeconomic disciplines, and applied journalistic skills. Ten weeks of practice between summer and fall semesters at local newspapers, radio stations, and television stations is required of all students. (Specialization in radio and television journalism began in the mid-1960s and has been playing an increasingly important role in the system of journalism in the USSR.)

After the school of journalism was established at the University of Moscow, other universities throughout the country quickly followed suit. There are more than twenty schools and departments of media education in the USSR, in the capital cities of almost all the republics as well as in other major cities such as Leningrad, Sverdlovsk, Voronezh, and Vladivostok.

Moscow University's Faculty of Journalism has approximately twenty-five hundred students and about five hundred graduates each year. In the USSR as a whole the number of graduates is not much greater than six thousand, which falls far short of the country's needs. For this reason many journalists are drawn from other backgrounds and professions, such as teaching, economics, engineering, and writing, and they often draw on their specialized knowledge in their work as journalists. See also NEWSPAPER: TRENDS—TRENDS IN THE SOVIET PRESS.

The All-Union State Institute for Cinematography was established in Moscow in 1919 to give training in drama and CINEMATOGRAPHY, screenwriting, directing, producing, and cinema economics. Cinema training is also offered by similar institutions in Minsk, Tbilisi, Tashkent, Kiev, and Leningrad. These institutions are not universities, but their diplomas have an equivalent status to the degrees of universities. Most of the academic units provide a full-time five-year education for future producers, camera operators, scriptwriters, actors, cinema critics, and cinema executives.

Czechoslovakia, the German Democratic Republic (DDR), Poland, and Yugoslavia began university-based journalism training after World War II. These universities combined practical training with academic teaching and research. One outstanding example is the journalism faculty of Karl Marx University in Leipzig in the DDR. The course aims at providing a basic orientation in journalism, followed by additional specialization in print media, radio, or television and a content area (foreign politics, political economy, cultural politics, etc.). Influential teaching and research institutions include the Press Research Center in Krakow and the film school in Lodz, Poland; the department of journalism and communication at the University of Ljubljana, Yugoslavia; and the Mass Communication Research Center of Hungarian Radio and Television, Budapest, Hungary.

Journalism studies in some of the socialist countries of eastern Europe were caught up in the political and ideological upheavals of the post–World War II era. An example is the history of such studies in Czechoslovakia.

University-level studies of journalism were introduced into the Higher School of Political and Social Science in Prague soon after the liberation of Czechoslovakia from Nazi occupation in 1945. The school was reorganized in 1950 and abolished in 1952. Although departments of "journalism and libraries" were organized in the philosophy faculties of both Charles University in Prague and Comenius University in Bratislava, the hybrid units did not last long. Problems with finding a satisfactory balance of practical, ideological, and scientific training at the universities led the Union of Journalists to organize its own independent Institute of Studies in Journalism in Prague in 1953 and one in Bratislava in 1955. In 1960 Charles University responded by launching its Institute of General Education and Journalism. That institute was reorganized as a faculty in 1965 and renamed in 1968 the Faculty of Social Sciences and Publicity to indicate its newly acquired social-scientific orientation. Some critics called the new unit "trendy" and lacking in critical rigor as well as practical applicability. In 1972 a new Faculty of Journalism was established at Charles University (and a similar faculty at Comenius University) and was charged with preparing "ideologically mature and politically conscious future specialists in different editorial boards." Their departments include propaganda, history of

journalism, broadcast journalism, press agency journalism, and socialist advertising and publicity. The faculties select each year about forty candidates in Prague and twenty candidates in Bratislava and give them full scholarships, including family stipends. The Prague faculty also maintains an Institute of the Theory and Practice of Journalism to coordinate research in the field.

Australasia

The development of communication studies in Australia reflects the long dependence of Australian universities on British and U.S. imports and European trends. The fifteen degree-granting programs in communications and media studies, spread over eighteen universities and fifty colleges or advanced institutes, have little in common. In the older universities the field was still struggling for recognition in the late 1980s, and there were no chairs (full professorships) in it. Work was mostly print oriented and eclectic, with media policy studies likely to be located in departments of sociology or politics with the focus on special topics such as television VIOLENCE and children.

The number of colleges of advanced education and institutes of technology has increased since the 1960s. These schools were designed to offer more skills-oriented programs. In fact, however, they became staffed with two groups. One was following the U.S. speech communication model, usually under the titles of interpersonal, organizational, and business communication, and more recently such specialties as health communication. The other group was influenced by the British screen education movement and the Birmingham school of critical "cultural studies," and it focused on political economy, semiotics, feminism, and issues of language and power.

In New Zealand there are five general communications courses in polytechnics and one chair of telecommunications. Work in communications in both Australia and New Zealand is also carried on by individual scholars working in departments ranging from the social sciences and anthropology to economics, business, and law. Most courses are underfunded, and many applicants compete for relatively few places.

See also AUSTRALASIA, TWENTIETH CENTURY.

Asia

In Asia, as in most other parts of the world, much of the training for work in the mass media is given on the job. However, Asia has more institutes and academic units providing formal education for communications than any other region of the world except North America. A 1975 tabulation by the

Asian Mass Communication and Research Center (AMIC) listed 210, and most of the unofficial tabulations since that time have placed the total at 250 or more.

The growth of Asian institutions for communication study has been rapid, particularly since midcentury. For example, in the late 1930s there were fewer than twenty journalism courses in all of Asia; by the middle 1970s there were four times that many. Furthermore, the variety of communications training and research organizations in Asia is quite remarkable, particularly among the institutions designed to support communication for social change and planned development (see DEVELOPMENT COMMUNICATION).

Slightly more than half of these schools, departments, and institutes (around 140) follow what might be called the U.S. pattern; that is to say, like schools of communications or journalism in the United States, they are organized as part of a university or college, offer degrees at the baccalaureate or graduate level or both, and combine academic study or research with practical preparation for work in the media.

The first professional school in Asia is believed to be the one founded in 1932 at the Department of Journalism in the Faculty of Letters of Jochi (Sophia) University in Tokyo. The four-year undergraduate program prepares candidates for the journalistic profession, and the two-year graduate program trains researchers. The second Asian professional school of communication was a branch of the Far Eastern University, founded in 1934 in Manila, and was built around a four-year course leading to a B.A. in speech arts, THEATER arts, or mass communication. In 1935 the third communication institution in Asia—National Chengchi University—was founded in China "to offer academic preparation for careers in communication research and mass media practice." When the Nationalist Chinese moved to Taiwan, the university moved with them and set up its new home in Taipei in 1954. Indonesia, the Republic of Korea, and other states joined in, and by 1950 approximately twenty schools, departments, and institutes of various kinds in Asian countries offered specializations in communication study. That number had doubled by 1960 and is still increasing.

India—with more than twenty thousand journals (including more than fourteen hundred daily newspapers), written in sixteen principal languages and seventy-five other languages, and also large broadcasting and film industries—has the largest number of communication programs in Asia. Newspapers prefer to train their own journalists, but the central and state governments rely increasingly on university-educated communication specialists.

The first regular journalism department was established at Punjab University in 1941 with "a one-year course in journalism and related areas such as advertising, graphic arts, and public relations." First located in Lahore, the university moved to Delhi in 1947 at the time of India's independence and then to Chandigarh, the new capital of Punjab. Other early departments were founded at Madras in 1947, Calcutta in 1950, Mysore in 1951, Nagpur in 1952, and Osmania in 1954.

The government-supported Indian Institute of Mass Communication was set up as an advanced center for training and research in 1965. Of the thirty-seven other university courses and institutes that offer mass communication study programs, nine offer graduate work leading to a master's degree. The inaugural issue of the *Indian Journal of Communication* was published in 1986. Despite this impressive growth, several commissions have called attention to a shortage of resources for research and training to meet the needs of the vast subcontinent.

A major trend in Third World communication education, development journalism (the use of communications to support national development) received much of its initial impetus at the Philippine Press Institute in 1963. With the help of UNESCO and other United Nations (UN) organizations, development journalism is now being taught and implemented in many Third World countries.

Communication study in China began at the turn of the century with the translation of foreign books on journalism. The first formal journalism course was offered at Beijing University in 1918. The following year the first Chinese book on journalism appeared. Journalism education developed rapidly after that.

Journalism departments were established in the 1920s at six universities: Beijing, Yenching, Fudan, Jinan, and People's University in Beijing. After the setbacks of the turbulent 1930s and World War II, the People's Republic revived journalism study on the Soviet model. The Cultural Revolution again disrupted study until 1978. However, by the end of the next decade more than sixteen universities had journalism departments, some offering graduate work leading to the M.A. and Ph.D. degrees and employing nearly four hundred faculty members. The Beijing Broadcasting Institute also offered courses of study. National and provincial journalism research societies were established. Communication study in China broadened to include broadcasting and film training in several universities as well as in some independent institutes and to encompass the critical and empirical approaches to research on media content and effects.

Japan, which, as noted, established the first department of journalism in Asia at Sophia University in 1932, has for the most part chosen to found communication institutes and programs outside the university. However, in addition to the department at Sophia, the University of Tokyo has a well-known and well-staffed Institute of Journalism that was founded in 1949 and has an impressive output of research. This institute offers both M.A. and Ph.D. degrees.

Keio University in Tokyo has a program in communication study, founded in 1946. Osaka University of the Arts has a faculty for training and research in broadcasting. But much of Japan's visibility in communication studies derives from production-related organizations, including the Japanese Broadcasting Corporation (NHK), which has training programs and also maintains research programs, including the Radio and Television Culture Research Institute; and the Japan Newspaper Publishers and Editors Association (NSK), which has its own research organization and cooperates with the Japanese press in training staff members.

One of the interesting developments in communication study within Asia is the appearance of strong and influential institutes, most of which are entirely outside universities and offer no academic degrees. For example, Asia has at least twelve film and/or television schools, including the large and elaborate Indian film and television institute at Poona. There are eight schools for the study of educational communication, either audiovisual or print. At least six schools specialize in the improvement of communication for economic and social development. One of the most impressive of these is India's National Institute of Community Development, at Hyderabad. This organization maintains a large research program, provides consulting services, serves as a clearinghouse of information concerning community development, and issues a large number of publications. A somewhat parallel program to the one just mentioned is the Development Support Communication Service, financed largely by UN agencies (UNDP, UNFPA, and UNICEF) and headquartered in Bangkok. The purposes of the organization are to design and produce, or help in the production of, communication materials intended to ensure the adoption of development innovations and to build up national capabilities to support total development programs. Like the Indian institute, it has a large research program and offers training and advisory services.

One distinctive pattern in Asian communication institutes and programs is joint founding by a national agency and an agency from outside the country. For example, the Thompson Foundation of Great Britain has worked with Xinhua, the international news agency of China, to operate a journalism training center in China. We have already mentioned AMIC (located in Singapore), which is jointly sponsored by the Singapore government and the Friedrich-Ebert Stiftung (foundation) of the Federal Republic of Germany. This serves as a regional information center for media and media-related programs in Asia, sponsors research, and organizes conferences and training activities.

Still another not entirely common use of communication institutes and programs in Asia has been to meet needs that governments or media organizations find hard to handle. For example, in Indonesia a communication group trained Department of Information personnel in information science skills. In Taiwan a department of journalism was asked to prepare students to become public relations officers in the armed services. A Philippine research institute provided research on the progress of the government's program for community development.

See also ASIA, TWENTIETH CENTURY.

Latin America

Latin America's remarkably early start in professional training for journalism is almost without precedent in the Third World. Brazil and Argentina had schools of journalism in the mid-1930s; Colombia, Ecuador, Mexico, Peru, and Venezuela established them in the 1940s. Twenty-five more schools were organized in the 1950s. By the end of the 1960s eighty-one schools of journalism were active in Latin America. One reason for this early start is that most South and Central American countries received their independence earlier than many other Third World countries. Another reason is the example provided by the U.S. model of school-based training rather than apprenticeship. And third, the schools have been popular because professional education represents a road to upward mobility.

The large number of schools and their relatively early beginnings represent disadvantages as well as advantages. Most schools are not well financed. Many of the teachers teach only part-time and are not well trained in the academic requirements of professional instruction. Many of the schools are poorly equipped, even regarding typewriters and books. Not much research is carried out in the typical journalism school, and the curriculum is usually so brief that little opportunity remains for a broad educational background.

Signs of change have appeared. For one thing, a federal decree passed in Brazil in 1969 required all new entrants into a number of journalistic occupations to have a baccalaureate degree from "an approved school of journalism." Second, there has been a lively wave of writing and discussion in Latin America about the New World Information Order (*see* NEW INTERNATIONAL INFORMATION ORDER) and its import for the mass media, a development that represents a broadening of interest in both the mass media and the education people will require. Third, the efforts of the Centro Internacional de Estudios

Superiores de Periodismo para América Latina (CIESPAL, International Center for Advanced Studies in Journalism in Latin America) have borne fruit.

CIESPAL is a regional center established with help from UNESCO to improve education in journalism and other media. Its primary target, therefore, has been teachers, rather than students, of communication. It has conducted high-level regional and national seminars and courses, many of them drawing foreign teachers and scholars. Through CIESPAL's influence new communication-oriented subjects previously unknown in Latin America, including the sociology of communication, the psychology of collective information, public opinion, and, especially, the scientific investigation of mass communication, have been introduced. CIESPAL also has helped to organize and accumulate in Latin America a collection of books and journals about communications and has distributed bibliographies and abstracts.

Also of great help in raising the quality of communication teaching and research have been agricultural organizations such as the Instituto Interamericano de Ciencias Agrícolas (IICA, Interamerican Institute of Agricultural Sciences), which, with assistance from U.S. universities with agriculture programs, have helped support the extension of Latin American rural development.

In Latin America, as in many other regions, the support of leading newspapers and other media organizations has been instrumental in initiating and maintaining the quality of communication study. The editors of two highly respected newspapers in Buenos Aires, *La prensa* and *La nación,* proposed as early as 1901 that a school of journalism be established in Argentina. Thirty-two years later journalists from *La prensa* helped organize such a program at the National University of La Plata. Courses were first offered in 1934, and the school began to function in 1935.

The first professorship of journalism in Brazil was established in the Faculty of Philosophy and Letters at the new Federal University of Rio de Janeiro. When this university was replaced by a new University of Brazil in 1943, the course in journalism was moved there. The first school for professional training in journalism was established at the Catholic University of São Paulo in 1947.

One of the most elaborate programs of media studies in Latin America is at the School of Communications and Arts at the University of São Paulo. All students in this school take an introductory semester of seven courses. Then there are two main teaching streams: "communications" (journalism, editing and publishing, publicity and propaganda, radio and television, library science and documentation) and "arts" (cinema, theater, music, and plastic arts).

Argentina, Brazil, and Mexico were the three Latin American countries to begin university training in journalism before World War II. The first school in Mexico was established at the Universidad Femenina (Women's University) de México in Mexico City. One of the most interesting programs is the one at the Universidad Nacional Autónoma de México (National Autonomous University of Mexico), which takes five years to complete and is described as "a career in information sciences." It covers both theoretical and technical aspects of journalism, public relations, publicity, radio, television, cinema and press agencies, the psychology of information, sociological aspects of mass communication, journalism history and ethics (*see* ETHICS, MEDIA), law in relation to journalism research techniques (including historical and social research, CONTENT ANALYSIS, and the use of documentary material), and some technical and administrative subjects.

See also LATIN AMERICA, TWENTIETH CENTURY.

Africa and the Middle East

Since the MIDDLE AGES traditional communication geared to the needs of religious leaders has been taught at the center of Islamic studies in Cairo's al-Azhar University. A modern course in journalism started at the American University in Cairo in 1937. A few years later Cairo University established an Institute of Journalism, which in 1975 became the Faculty of Mass Communication. Three provincial university communication departments followed. In Israel sophisticated mass communication research and training of a modern kind are in progress at the Communications Institute at Hebrew University in Jerusalem.

The first degree program for media professionals in South Africa was launched in 1960 in the University of Potchefstroom. Since then some dozen universities have started programs in various aspects of communication study, and the Human Sciences Research Council established an institute to support media studies.

The first institute of journalism in North Africa was established in Tunis in 1964 and was followed in 1967 by the Institut de Presse et des Sciences de l'Information (Institute of the Press and Information Sciences) of the University of Tunis. In 1964 Algeria started its Institut National Supérieur de Journalisme (National Institute of Journalism), which became the Institute of Political and Communication Sciences within the framework of the University of Algiers in 1976. The University of Baghdad established a Department of Journalism in the Faculty of Arts in 1964. It suspended its courses in 1971 but resumed them in 1974 as a Department of Communications.

The Omdurman Islamic University in Sudan started the Journalism and Information Department in 1965.

The Lebanese University in Beirut set up its Institute of Journalism in 1967, renamed it Faculty of Communications in 1971, and then transformed it into a Faculty of Mass Communications and Documentation in 1975. The American University at Beirut opened its Department of Communication in 1970. In Saudi Arabia the University of Riyadh started its Department of Communication in 1972. In Libya the Unis Campus of the University of Benghazi established its Department of Communication Studies in 1975. In 1976 a Department of Communication was opened at the King Abdul Azziz University in Jidda, Saudi Arabia. The Higher Institute of Islamic Communication was established by the Imam Mohamed Ibn Saud Islamic University in Riyadh, Saudi Arabia, in 1976 with branches in Mecca and Medina. Damascus University in Syria established a communication department in 1986.

That is one side of the diverse picture of communication study in Africa and the Middle East. What must be remembered is that the entire African continent had only four independent countries in 1950 but thirty-six by 1970. Consequently, many of these newly independent countries have experienced extraordinary pressures for modernization, as well as political, social, economic, and even linguistic changes, that have forced them to turn to new measures in order to bring about these changes more quickly.

Radio, of course, is the mass medium that seems ideal when literacy is low and the bulk of the population is rural. The number of radio transmitters in Africa increased from 151 to 330 between 1955 and 1964, and the number of radio receivers from 350,000 to 12 million. The colonial or former colonial powers stepped in to help train communication staffs to operate the broadcast equipment and prepare the programs. The United Kingdom set up a small British Broadcasting Corporation (BBC) in each of its former colonies. France designated three places—Dakar, Brazzaville, and Paris—to broadcast regionally. The United Kingdom, France, and other countries provided "attachments," fellowships, and study grants to help talented prospects from the new countries travel abroad for study and practice. U.S. and Soviet universities provide many scholarships for African and other Third World students of communications. The Prague-based International Organization of Journalists (IOJ) maintains the International Institute for the Training of Journalists in Budapest.

The new countries set up study and practice centers of their own as soon as it was possible. Such a training center for East African countries was at Nairobi; another, for Francophone countries, was at Yaoundé, in Cameroon. The African countries found that they needed to study the uses of radio for development and to teach journalism and broadcasting skills as well. Zambia, for example, created an innovative program for a literacy campaign built around radio. Ghana's Institute of Journalism in Accra was begun by KWAME NKRUMAH in the late 1950s; it was succeeded by an Institute of Communication in the University of Ghana. Nigeria established an Institute of Mass Communications at the University of Lagos. Senegal was the first country in French-speaking Africa to organize university-level training for journalism and mass communication. The Centre d'Études des Sciences et Techniques de l'Information (CESTI) was founded in 1965 at the University of Dakar, but it closed in 1968 because of student unrest. It reopened in 1970 and made a cooperative agreement with the International Advanced School of Journalism at Yaoundé and the Center for Information Sciences at Antananarivo, Madagascar, for a common course of study. Senegal's three-year program leads to a diploma, equivalent to a university *license*, from the University of Dakar. The National University of Zaire, in Kinshasa, established in 1970 a Department of Social Communication within its Faculty of Economic and Social Sciences. This department's mission is to undertake teaching, research, and documentation and to provide training for cultural change and community development.

Despite these developments, a UNESCO-supported survey in 1987 found that 60 percent of the textbooks in journalism and communication were published in the United States and 20 percent in Great Britain and that there were few copies of any text to go around. In most classes the only TEXTBOOK belonged to the teacher, who distributed mimeographed handouts to students. Many of the basic needs of communication study are still not being met in most countries of Africa and the Third World. UNESCO's efforts to help meet these needs received little support from its wealthiest members. Hope for the future seemed to rest with the revival of international and regional cooperation and emphasis on cultural policy in the development effort. *See also* AFRICA, TWENTIETH CENTURY; ISLAMIC WORLD, TWENTIETH CENTURY.

Bibliography. Asian Mass Communication Research and Information Centre, *Asian Mass Communication Institutions: Teaching, Training, and Research—A Directory,* Singapore, 1973, 1975; Charles Berger and Steven Chaffee, *Handbook of Communication Science,* Beverly Hills, Calif., 1987; Garland C. Elmore, *Communication Media in Higher Education,* Annandale, Va., 1987; May Katzen, *Mass Communication: Teaching and Studies at Universities,* Paris, 1975.

GEORGE GERBNER AND WILBUR SCHRAMM

COMMUNICATIONS RESEARCH: ORIGINS AND DEVELOPMENT

The historical roots of modern communications research reach back into the nineteenth century, when scholars began their systematic inquiry into the changes in the pattern of life brought about by the Industrial Revolution. The spread of LITERACY and the development of a popular literature (see LITERATURE, POPULAR), which were part of this transformation, received attention as did the daily newspaper, judged by many to be the most powerful organ in the formation and expression of PUBLIC OPINION (see NEWSPAPER: HISTORY). As French historian and political theorist Alexis de Tocqueville observed in 1835, when people are no longer united by firm and lasting ties they cannot combine until a "newspaper takes up the notion or the feeling which had occurred simultaneously, but singly to each of them."

Role of the Press

Tocqueville's and other pioneering attempts to analyze the role of the press were usually based on the writers' impressions of the political scene gathered through travel and journalistic experience, which were presented together with historical vignettes. All subscribed to the view that public opinion (in the modern sense) had developed in conjunction with the press, and they agreed, more or less, that its organs (newspapers) were highly effective in articulating certain dominant viewpoints but were not necessarily able to create them. That political leaders should fasten on newspapers as one of the important levers of influence was understandable, because with the help of newspapers one could make public opinion, if only for a day. As Albert Schäffle, an early sociologist, put it, "falsified" opinion often overshadowed native-grown opinion that one could not so easily grasp or measure, at least not with the methods then available. Schäffle was also very much aware, as were contemporaries such as economist Karl Knies, of the role of the press as a mediator between political parties and other interest groups.

Knies, in a book published in 1857 on how the telegraph affected the economics of information (see TELEGRAPHY), went a step farther and concluded that editors had the power to "set the agenda" (in contemporary parlance; see AGENDA-SETTING) but were constrained by their economic interest. Despite ample experience with one-sided reporting in his earlier career as a journalist, Knies insisted that the pressure to increase sales meant that editors had to appeal to the readers whom their paper purported or aspired to represent. This reciprocal influence of journalists on their readership and, indirectly, of readers on what appeared in the newspaper was seen as another kind of mediation by the press.

That the power of the press was not the same in every country was fully recognized. Tocqueville had gone out of his way to set forth the reasons why this power was greater in France than in the United States, where three-quarters of the newspaper space was devoted to ADVERTISING. It is not often that one finds much space devoted to the kind of passionate discussion with which French journalists are wont to indulge their readers. Because the influence of the press increases to the degree that it is centrally directed, it is important to note that there were far fewer newspapers in France than in the United States and that the most powerful were concentrated in a single metropolitan center under like-minded control. In the United States, however, almost every hamlet had its own newspaper. Consequently the U.S. press was influential only when a great number of papers took the same position on an issue and assailed public opinion from one viewpoint.

European scholars focused especially on the "anonymity" of the press. They reasoned that the absence of a byline and the frequent omission of any source of attribution—common practice at the time—gave all items the same claim to reliability and credibility. Even if some readers were uncritical enough to accept at face value whatever newspapers printed, knowledge of AUTHORSHIP would enable others to weigh more critically these impersonal, official-looking, and hence supposedly unbiased reports. The infamous Dreyfus affair, which so polarized France for several years in the late 1890s over the guilt or innocence of an alleged spy, had driven home more than any other event prior to World War I the ability of the press to fan emotion to a point at which—in the words of JEAN-GABRIEL DE TARDE, a student of collective psychology—the French public was exhibiting the characteristics of an irrational crowd (see CROWD BEHAVIOR).

In spite of this, most of these writers, including Tarde, remained aware that public reactions to sensational stories reported by a highly partisan press often fell short of alarmist expectations. Having examined in some detail six cases of war scare prior to 1914, English economist F. W. Hirst concluded that in these instances the yellow press had influenced the minds and policies of ministers without having any proportionate effect on the citizenry. To evoke a real national panic, as opposed to the semblance of such a panic, is very difficult.

None of the work mentioned so far involved the kind of systematic data collection that has come to be identified as communication research in the narrower sense. The first steps in this direction involved compilations of historical statistics on newspaper production and circulation. With the publication between 1859 and 1864 of Eugène Hatin's eight-volume tome on the political and literary history of the French press, followed two years later by a bibliographical essay to which he attached a compendium of statistics, a major milestone was passed. Other noteworthy studies were those by German historians Heinrich Wuttke, *Die deutschen Zeitschriften und die Entstehung der öffentlichen Meinung* (1875), and Ludwig Salomon, *Geschichte des deutschen Zeitungswesens*, whose three volumes (1900–1906) treat the history of the press up to 1850.

Karl Bücher, economist, historian, sociologist, statistician, and founder of the Institut für Zeitungskunde at the University of Leipzig during World War I, helped routinize the systematic collection of all kinds of newspaper statistics in Germany. He is still better known as one of the first to treat the modern newspaper as primarily a commercial contrivance for the exchange of intellectual and material goods. His synthesis foreshadows in many ways writings on the immigrant press in the United States and on the nature of news by ROBERT PARK, who had studied in Germany and must have been aware of at least some of this work but never acknowledged a direct debt. Bücher investigated every aspect of newspaper production, including advertising, by which he meant not only sales promotion but every kind of PUBLIC RELATIONS and self-promotion. He recognized that advertising worked best in the promotion of new products, believing that it was most effective when improvements in industrial technology (*Betriebstechnik*) no longer made much difference to consumers. He saw all advertising as subject to the law of diminishing returns, concluding that once a product had found its market additional effort could bring no more than a few gleanings from people not previously reached.

About this same time other researchers were taking a closer look at the news carried in newspapers. Rudimentary forms of CONTENT ANALYSIS began to appear around the turn of the century. An early U.S. study by Delos F. Wilcox (1900) classified the allocation of space in a single issue of each of 240 newspapers; in 1902 Henri de Noussance presented even more detailed statistical tabulations of the contents of 20 Parisian and 7 French provincial newspapers for a single day. Drawing on the findings of the French study, Paul Stoklossa collected data about one week's output in 13 metropolitan and 17 German provincial papers over a full week as a basis for comparing the metropolitan and the provincial press in the two countries. These investigations were essentially evaluative, to see if the press was measuring up to what he deemed its moral obligations.

Content analysis was also singled out as the starting point for the large cooperative study of the press proposed by MAX WEBER to the first meeting of the German Sociological Association in 1910. Weber was not interested in moral evaluations; he wanted a value-free inquiry aimed at discovering the historical and social causes that explained why things were as they were. The questions he wanted addressed are still germane: What gets into the papers, and what does not? How have views changed on what should get into the papers, and with what social and ideological variables do these views correlate? How do the policies and practices on what is privileged and what is legitimately in the public domain affect the distribution of power in society? What are the causes and consequences of the tension between the press as a source of information—especially of political information—and the press as an advertising medium? Do large papers with high capital investments become more (or less) sensitive about alienating their readership? What are the implications of chain ownership and MONOPOLY for the development of public opinion? Still other questions focused on journalistic traditions as affected by relations of the press to news sources, by a paper's dependence on newsstand sales, by the leeway a paper gives to individual journalists, by a paper's use of free-lance writers, by the trend toward factual reporting, and more generally by the existence of press associations and of corporations representing what in the 1980s would be called the "consciousness industry."

Weber believed that the answers to some of these questions were to be found in the papers themselves. To find them one had to proceed "in the most pedestrian manner, by measuring with compass and scissors" the relevant aspects of their content, and then, on the basis of these quantitative findings, to address the more qualitative ones. The content analysis was to be followed by an empirical study of journalists (their social origins, educational backgrounds, career patterns, and relation to politics) and of the social, political, and cultural effects newspapers have on readers (*see* MASS MEDIA EFFECTS).

Propaganda

Weber's comprehensive proposal, which never got off the ground, moved closer to implementation some three decades later, largely as an outgrowth of the interest in PROPAGANDA, an interest directly traceable to the all-too-apparent excesses of both sides during World War I and to the growing totalitarian threat of the following years. The prime mover was HAROLD D. LASSWELL, a University of Chicago political scientist, who led his contemporaries in focusing on the role of symbols in politics (*see* POLITICAL SYMBOLS). Working from the postulate that political power rests as much on symbol manipulation as on physical force, Lasswell sought to document how private deprivations and internalized conflict become attached to public (i.e., secondary) symbols. He showed how quantitative content analysis could be used not only to detect hidden propaganda themes but also to make inferences about communicators and how communicators played on the susceptibility of audiences. One had to rely on communication output to study an otherwise inaccessible political unit, as during World War II when the United States devoted significant amounts of social science resources to the analysis of Nazi propaganda.

That research effort, in which many German refugee scholars participated, led to the elaboration of a number of social science propositions about propaganda in general and the conditions for its effectiveness. The idea that propaganda could not create facts but only reinterpret existing ones received firmer underpinning. Ernst Kris and Nathan Leites found that there was in much World War II propaganda a more factual tone than had prevailed in World War I, with less extreme divergence from the facts. They interpreted this trend as a sophisticated strategy for countering two pervasive tendencies in target populations: a generalized distrust of authority, including the fear of being manipulated, and a tendency on the part of many people to withdraw into their private worlds when confronted with global issues they found hard to understand and whose outcomes they did not believe they could influence.

In a synthesis of studies on morale in the German army during World War II, Edward A. Shils and Morris Janowitz noted the basic imperviousness of ordinary German soldiers to Allied propaganda even after a series of reverses should have made them recognize the inevitability of defeat. As long as primary groups retained their cohesiveness and continued to minister to these soldiers' essential need for survival, Allied leaflets offering safe conduct to deserters were found to have had little effect. All but a few misfits preferred to stick it out with their units. The effectiveness of primary groups as transmitters of organizational norms was further enhanced by repressive measures that prevented the open assertion of ideologically deviant tendencies. Most notable was the remarkable resiliency of faith in Adolf Hitler against all evidence of an impending catastrophe.

Group Interaction and Persuasion

The relative efficacy of face-to-face communication versus the more impersonal forms of public communication had already been a central topic for KURT LEWIN, another German expatriate, who had begun to test the utility of constructs derived from his topological psychology for problems of group interaction and attitude change (see ATTITUDES; GROUP COMMUNICATION). Experiments were conducted as part of the war effort on how best to persuade families in the United States to change their food buying and eating habits and to stop discarding as inedible certain nutritious meats still in ample supply during the general meat shortage. These experiments showed that discussion among shoppers when followed by a group decision was a better strategy for producing change than lectures by experts. In conceptualizing these findings Lewin developed the notion of a gatekeeper able to control the flow of information. Gatekeeper functions can be performed by an informal OPINION LEADER, as in the group experiments, or by persons formally appointed to managerial or editorial positions. The latter play a crucial role in the determination of what gets into print or on the air and, as communicators, are as deserving of researchers' attention as the more feared propagandists.

Other achievements came from studies on PERSUASION by cognitive psychologists working under CARL HOVLAND as part of the U.S. Army Research Branch. The group systematically investigated the persuasive power of different versions of orientation films prepared by the army for new recruits. To what extent did new information change attitudes? Who was most affected? Did these changes persist, and under what conditions? After the war members of the research group continued this line of investigation using new variables and refining the ones used previously, but the effectiveness achieved in a contrived, simplified laboratory situation did not always carry over into the more complex situations encountered in real life.

Motion Pictures

The ENTERTAINMENT film, along with comic books (see COMICS), loomed large in the public mind (as television does in the 1980s) as a possible and probable cause of antisocial behavior among the young (see CHILDREN—MEDIA EFFECTS; VIOLENCE). In fact, the landmark studies underwritten by the Payne Fund at the behest of the Motion Picture Council of America are strikingly similar in focus, though less sophisticated in method and more overtly moralistic in tone, to more recent studies on television and social behavior. Produced in the early 1930s by psychologists, sociologists, and educators from several universities, these monographs fall into two groups. One was aimed at measuring the effect of MOTION PICTURES as such on children and youths in five areas: information, attitudes, emotions, health, and conduct. The other was directed at current motion picture content and children's actual movie attendance in order to assess the overall effect of current commercial movie fare. The series included results of experiments and surveys, summaries of evidence gleaned from autobiographical essays by high school students, and reports from detailed follow-up interviews with some of the students.

The general conclusions drawn from all these studies, as set forth in the official summary by W. W. Charters, were that motion pictures as such were a "potent medium of education," inasmuch as even a single exposure could produce "measurable" attitude change. This effect may recede over time but is apt to be magnified by cumulative exposure to a large number of pictures. The movie fare, with its scenes of emotion-stirring drama, was judged to contain "too much sex and crime and love," the inference being that it could result in "much more harm than help" to children. With this conclusion goes the reminder that motion pictures are only "one of many influences which mould the experience of children," such as the home (see FAMILY), the SCHOOL, the church, street life, and community customs, none of which was surveyed by any of the studies.

In a volume entitled *Art and Prudence* philosopher Mortimer J. Adler was extremely critical of the methods and assumptions underlying these studies. Correlations between moviegoing and socially undesirable behavior, he pointed out, fall short of establishing a causal link. However, evidence that movies determine many of the games children play was at least suggestive, especially considering that movie portrayals are apt to have their greatest influence on those aspects of life about which people have not yet formed "definitely shaped images." At least some of the characters, objects, and modes of living that receive dramatic and unambiguous realization in movies will be new to the experience of some viewers (especially the younger ones) and can lead them to redefine their rights and ideas about what they are entitled to enjoy. The possibility was raised, but by no means demonstrated, that those experiencing the greatest discrepancy between their own drab lives and the pleasures of freedoms portrayed on the screen may indeed become dissatisfied or discontented to the point of rebellion.

Radio and Audience Research

That even purely auditory imagery can carry conviction was documented during the transmission of "The War of the Worlds," a RADIO production by ORSON WELLES based on the futuristic novel by H. G. Wells. It was aired about the time of heightened tensions in Europe generated by Hitler's territorial demands on Czechoslovakia. A significant number of listeners were persuaded that invading Martians were wreaking destruction on the New York metropolitan area. HADLEY CANTRIL seized the occasion to do field interviews, which produced lively accounts. Analysis turned on only two points: how "news" of invading Martians fit into people's frames of reference, and how, given this fit, "suggestibility" to the broadcast message hinged on an individual's critical ability. Panic reactions were confined to those who mistook the fictional presentation for a live report because they had neither consulted their program logs nor paid attention to announcements within

the program and had failed to check the impressions received against other reliable sources of information. The study documents what scholars in earlier periods had already surmised, namely, that critical ability can greatly reduce the influence of false reporting.

The advent of radio and the commercial interests tied to it were an obvious boost to audience research, in the development of which Vienna-born PAUL F. LAZARSFELD had a major hand. The methodological orientation he brought to the early work on radio listening and program evaluation—much of it in collaboration with psychologist Frank Stanton, research director (later president) of the Columbia Broadcasting System (CBS)—has been extremely fruitful for programmatic research by broadcasting organizations in the United States and around the world. In his insistence that radio be looked at in the context of other communication activities Lazarsfeld went well beyond mere measurement. Studies by him and his students revealed an all-or-none pattern in the use of media. Heavy consumers of one medium tended to be heavy consumers of other media. Audience overlap—a measure of how many attending one medium, source, or program are also attentive to some other—turned out to be a useful concept for probing the way audiences were stratified into clusters. The stratification of the audience was replicated in the stratification of other activities. Thus low media consumers were also less active in politics, and their participation in the thought life of the larger community was severely restricted.

Media Effects

Lazarsfeld, notwithstanding his heavy involvement in research for limited practical purposes (administrative research), was in no sense oblivious to larger issues. For a good part of his career he was preoccupied with the design and analysis of a survey to pinpoint media effects of every kind: on how people voted, on what they purchased, on their attitudes toward minority groups, and so forth. Studies of the 1940 and 1948 presidential elections in the United States sought to track through repeat interviews with the same persons how voting preferences crystallized. With this innovation, the panel survey, as it came to be called, emerged as the favorite technique for explaining voting behavior as it related to communication exposure. These two studies and others that followed revealed that the correlations between how people vote and measures of exposure, usually based on self-reports, were greatly exceeded by correlations with other nonmedia influences. Many who followed in Lazarsfeld's footsteps were apt to generalize from these findings to media effects without noting the limitations of this technique. For one thing, such a survey was better suited for explaining variations that are related to personality, social background, social status, and other attributes of individuals than for uncovering how the mass media collectively intrude into everyone's thinking. For another, the specific effects observed during these electoral campaigns were limited by the fact that neither of the contending parties enjoyed anything even approaching a media monopoly, by the awareness of people during such a campaign that they were being propagandized, by the relatively short time span of a political campaign, and by the ignoring of other media-related aspects of the political situation. The tracking of attitudes by polls, which had begun by World War II, should probably have alerted the research community to how responsive people were to world events they could know only through the media. *See also* GAL-LUP, GEORGE; POLL; ROPER, ELMO.

The Critical Approach and Culture Studies

Concerns of a more basic kind were most clearly articulated by the group that had coalesced in Frankfurt around Max Horkheimer and THEODOR ADORNO in the years before Hitler. Nearly all its members later emigrated to the United States, resulting in some cross-fertilization between an empirical approach, more typical of U.S. research, and a "critical" European tradition. These émigré scholars were less preoccupied with specific measurable effects than with the values and ideological images reflected in the media content, particularly as these values and images were being modified by marketing strategies aimed at the popularization of knowledge, literature, and other elements of CULTURE through the same techniques developed in the United States for selling goods. To the exponents of the critical viewpoint, communications research should address the more subtle and long-term implications of the underlying structure and the implicit themes in the media content rather than specific effects directly traceable to some overt message content.

The mass media entertainment fare provided a rich archive of material for this kind of research. LEO LOWENTHAL's content analysis of biographies in popular magazines (*see* MAGAZINE) revealed that a decisive shift had occurred between the first and fourth decades of the twentieth century in the occupation and achievements of persons selected as appropriate subjects. In the latter period, the heroes of consumption prevailed over the previously dominant heroes of production. The shift indexed a more fundamental change in the character of U.S. society. In roughly similar fashion, Patricke Johns-Heine and Hans H. Gerth used magazine FICTION, Martha Wolfenstein and Nathan Leites used the movies, and Rudolf Arnheim used the daytime radio SERIAL as windows on prevailing values or, at least, on values presumed to hold the allegiance of audiences.

What made these offerings so appealing could be studied empirically. For example, conventional audience research had indicated that only a minority of women, albeit a sizable one, were attracted to the radio drama serials known as SOAP OPERA. Herta Herzog, another European closely associated with Lazarsfeld, found differences between listeners and nonlisteners to be related to the greater dependence of the former on radio, a difference that remained even after the effect of education had been eliminated. Her line of inquiry was later pursued by U.S. scholars W. Lloyd Warner and William E. Henry. From intensive interviews and projective psychological tests of regular listeners they inferred the gratifications these women derived from a serial whose plot revolved around "family-type" problems. An interesting outcome of this study was the difference between listeners' responses to the Thematic Apperception Test (TAT) pictures (which reflected their own difficulties in coping with life) and their responses to the Verbal Projective test (which tested their expectations about future plot directions in the serial). The projected outcomes for future plots were much more positive than the responses to the TAT pictures. Hence the program seemed to be a positive influence: it made women experiencing difficulties in coping with life feel similar to important people (the main characters in the serial), thereby directing their hopes into confident and optimistic channels.

The process resembles what Lowenthal in another context had dubbed "psychoanalysis in reverse." Its hypothesized effects run counter to the inference of rising dissatisfaction based on observations of youthful moviegoers in the Payne Fund studies. On a more general level, however, the two inferences are consistent; each implies that the popular fare, although catering to the dispositions and concerns of target audiences, helps shape rather than merely reflects their values.

Other evidence of hegemonic influence comes from studies of radio music conducted with some input from Adorno, who made this subject his sociological specialty. Research had been able to demonstrate empirically that "plugging" a song did indeed increase its popularity. The effect on musical taste remained within a specifiable musical GENRE. Could a radio symphony series create an audience for music different from what listeners were used to? According to one study, such a program served primarily to "reactivate" interest among persons with previous acquaintance but little subsequent opportunity to hear serious music performed live. The billing of the program as "symphonic" rather than "popular" music may have frightened away an undetermined number of potential listeners leery of anything with such a label. In an ingeniously designed study conducted in Denmark in the late 1940s, German-born sociologist Theodor Geiger was able to show that an identical repertoire of by no means "ear-pleasing" serious musical selections attracted many more listeners when advertised as popular rather than classical and that very few of the listeners to the so-called popular program tuned out. Although Danish listeners had fewer stations to choose from than listeners in the United States, the study provides a compelling argument for the importance of labels in supporting an established hierarchy among TASTE CULTURES, an observation consistent with at least some tenets of the Frankfurt school.

Repeated exposure over time may indeed channel musical taste and increase the popularity of serious music. But Adorno in particular had remonstrated against the efficacy of this use of radio on the ground that dimensions mattered. On radio, he argued, the sound is no longer larger than the individual; the surrounding function of music disappears. Instead of hearing the musical piece, listeners merely pick up bits and pieces of information about it. The appropriation of the opening in Beethoven's Fifth Symphony as the victory theme in World War II is an example of this process, as are people who walk around whistling these "melodies." When the elements of the musical composition become detached from the action, they acquire the character of quotations for listeners eager to demonstrate their ability to recognize great music in order to qualify as small cultural owners within a big ownership culture.

This transformation of the music was seen by Adorno as more significant than any report by listeners of what they may have come to like. The music itself has ceased to be thought provoking, and their listening has degenerated into a merely pleasurable pastime. Whether such a transformation has actually taken place is an intriguing and researchable question, and some studies did indeed touch on it. Edward A. Suchman found the radio-initiated listeners to symphonic music were less appreciative of the more difficult classical composers than those who supplemented a well-developed prior interest by listening to the radio. The preference of the former for romantic as opposed to classical composers could be an empirical confirmation of Adorno's more esoteric speculations. It would have been worthwhile to find out whether radio listeners develop their taste to a point at which they seek out live performances. Of equal interest, of course, are the possible effects of mechanical reproduction, and electronic transmission affects not only the type of music produced but also other literary and visual genres. The pursuit of these questions could have led to a potentially highly productive fusion of communications research with cultural studies.

All too often empirical communications research has been mistakenly seen as a rather recent U.S. invention spurred by economic interests. Its deeper roots in the intellectual, social, and cultural concerns that agitated European scholars as well tend to be overlooked. In fact, nearly all the empirical methods attributed to U.S. research were pioneered in the Old World and then were exported to the United States, many by refugee scholars. The other false notion is that the modern media were once considered to be all-powerful. On the contrary, most of the earlier writers revealed a sensitivity to the political and cultural context of communication that seems lacking in the more recent technically proficient but narrowly focused research.

See also MASS COMMUNICATIONS RESEARCH; MODELS OF COMMUNICATION.

Bibliography. Bernard Berelson, "The State of Communication Research," *Public Opinion Quarterly* 23 (1959): 1–6; W. W. Charters, *Motion Pictures and Youth*, New York, 1933; Donald Fleming and Bernard Bailyn, eds., *The Intellectual Migration: Europe and America, 1930–1960*, Cambridge, Mass., 1969; Hanno Hardt, *Social Theories of the Press*, Beverly Hills, Calif., 1979; Carl I. Hovland, Arthur A. Lumsdaine, and Fred D. Sheffield, *Experiments on Mass Communication*, Princeton, N.J., 1949; Kurt Lang, "The Critical Functions of Empirical Communication Research: Observations on German-American Influences," *Media Culture and Society* 1 (1979): 83–96; Anthony Oberschall, *Empirical Social Research in Germany 1848–1914*, Paris and The Hague, 1965.

KURT LANG

COMPUTER: HISTORY

The history of the computer is the story of a search for tools to help with laborious calculations and sorting through long lists. Early computer innovators sought both a saving in time and reduction in errors.

Early history. The first innovation that was developed to assist in calculations was the mechanical calculating machine, the equivalent of the modern four-function electronic pocket calculator. The first successful machine capable of adding and subtracting was built by French mathematician Blaise Pascal in 1642 (see Figure 1). Gottfried Wilhelm Leibniz, another mathematician, made a mechanical four-function calculator in 1694, and his design formed the basis for many later machines of this type. Neither Pascal nor Leibniz had adequate technology available to them to make commercially useful machines, but their machines did function and led the way to later commercial machines, such as the nineteenth-century comptometer.

The digital computer, or programmed calculator, was invented in the nineteenth century by English mathematician CHARLES BABBAGE as a way of computing tables of polynomials. Babbage conceived of a programmable calculator with a memory, an arithmetic unit, and punched-card input and output. One invention that influenced Babbage was the Jacquard

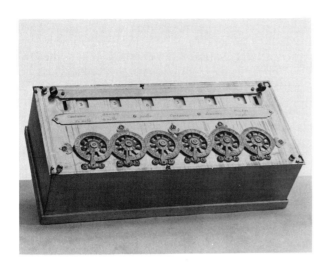

Figure 1. *(Computer: History)* Replica of the calculating machine of Blaise Pascal, 1642. Exterior. Trustees of the Science Museum, London.

neering than Babbage was able to command were necessary to bring his idea to a practical realization.

The path to an effective digital computer led first through the development of a punched-card tabulating system by U.S. inventor Herman Höllerith. In the Jacquard loom the information coded on cards was sensed mechanically. Höllerith, however, used a combined electrical and mechanical sensing method in which movable conducting rods made electrical contact through the holes in the cards with mercury contacts underneath them. Höllerith's machine was used successfully in compiling the 1890 census, and this success led to his forming the Tabulating Machine Company in 1896 (see Figure 2). Improved versions of his machine incorporated new capabilities such as addition and subtraction, automatic card handling, and a decimal keypunch. He sold his company in 1911; it was merged with two other companies, and the merged company became the International Business Machines Corporation (IBM) in 1924.

These punched-card tabulating machines became essential tools for business accounting, and complex accounting jobs were performed with sets of interconnected punched-card machines. Scientific use of these machines developed after L. J. Comrie demonstrated their capability for astronomical computations in England in 1929. Wallace J. Eckert assembled a set of machines under centralized control at Columbia University in 1934, with the assistance of IBM, and used them for scientific computation.

The two remaining steps to the modern computer were the use of electronic technology to speed up the

loom (invented in 1801), which facilitated the weaving of intricately designed fabrics. The Jacquard loom's use of punched cards for input and sequence control was an essential and original step that made Babbage's "analytical engine" possible. Another key concept used by Babbage in his design was the algebra of binary arithmetic developed by the Englishman George Boole; the punched card uses a binary representation of numbers or characters. Conceptually, everything needed to make a digital computer was present in the device Babbage described at a scientific meeting in 1840. But better technology and engi-

Figure 2. *(Computer: History)* Engraving of the sorting counting machine of Herman Höllerith, 1890. Trustees of the Science Museum, London.

computations and the implementations of the stored-program concept. A major advance toward the use of electronic technology was made by John Mauchly and J. Presper Eckert at the University of Pennsylvania during World War II in response to the needs of the U.S. Army for improved ballistic trajectory computations. They completed the first operational electronic digital computer, the ENIAC, in 1946 (see Figure 3). The ENIAC group included JOHN VON NEUMANN from 1944 to 1946, and out of this group also came the stored-program concept and a means for implementing it. A memo from von Neumann is the first recorded description of the concept.

The ENIAC required that the instructions to the machine be entered by throwing a large number of switches, one by one. A new machine conceived by the group, the EDVAC, was designed to accept its instructions on punched cards, along with its input data, and to store the program internally. The EDVAC was described in a series of lectures at the University of Pennsylvania in 1946 and became operational in 1951. Also in 1951 the first UNIVAC computer was delivered. The UNIVAC, the first electronic digital computer built for commercial use, was made by the Eckert-Mauchly Computer Corporation, which was sold to the Remington Rand Corporation in 1950. The UNIVAC was the first computer to catch the public eye, and it did so by predicting the results of the 1952 U.S. presidential election. With less than 7 percent of the vote tallied, UNIVAC gave 438 electoral votes to Dwight D. Eisenhower and 93 to Adlai Stevenson. The final tally was 442 for Eisenhower and 89 for Stevenson.

Commercial development in the 1950s and 1960s. The UNIVAC, like the ENIAC, was a giant machine using thousands of unreliable vacuum tubes. It was usable, but vacuum-tube technology was clearly not suited to the task it was being asked to perform. Each computer circuit needed less than one-thousandth of one watt of power to carry out its operations, which were similar in principle to the stepping of the relays in mechanical adding machines. But each computer circuit included a vacuum tube requiring a heater that consumed more than a thousand times this amount of power in order to operate at all. The requirement of a heater for each electronic switch not only created a need for cooling but also made the early computers bulky and unreliable. Although individual electron tubes could be made to last thousands of hours, when eighteen thousand were connected together the probability of at least one failure in any given hour was very high. It was evident in the early 1950s that the vacuum tube would soon be replaced by some form of solid-state device that did not require a heater. Reliable semiconductor diodes (two-element devices) were available in 1950, and many of the essential computer circuits could be built with diodes. The three-element solid-state device (the *transistor*) was invented in 1948 by John Bardeen, Walter Brattain, and William Shockley, and this device made the electronic computer a practical reality because it permitted all the computer circuits to be built with reliable electronic switches that consumed little power beyond that required to send signals to other circuits in the system. To a considerable extent, the story of the computer since 1950 has been the story of the *semiconductor*, and the computer industry has been the best customer of the semiconductor industry.

Remington Rand failed to make the necessary investments to maintain the leadership position it held in 1951 when the UNIVAC was introduced. IBM did make the necessary investments and developed a number of new computers in the 1950s in order to meet demand in both accounting and scientific applications. One of the most successful of these early computers was the IBM 650, first delivered in 1954. It used a magnetic-drum memory, which limited its speed but made it reliable and relatively cheap. About eighteen hundred were produced and delivered. Most major U.S. universities had one or more IBM 650s available in the late 1950s for scientific computation, and the machine was widely used in accounting as well. This machine was one of the first to allow the use of *assembly language,* as contrasted with *machine language.*

In machine language, the programmer, in effect, specifies the internal switches that are to be thrown in order to make the computation proceed as desired in terms of ones and zeros. In assembly language, programming is done through a symbolic language that does the same job as machine language but is easier to use. Still easier to use are *high-level languages* such as FORTRAN or BASIC. A high-level language is more like English than assembly language, but it cannot be executed directly by the computer. It is translated into machine language by a special program called a *compiler.* FORTRAN was introduced by IBM in 1957 as a scientific language for use with the IBM 704. FORTRAN offered computer programmers a significant time saving compared to assembly language and opened up computer programming to a large number of new users because it was so much easier to learn.

The IBM 704, first delivered in 1955, was an important early large machine. It used a magnetic-core main memory, which was much faster than drums or disks and more reliable than any available alternatives. The magnetic-core memory was invented at the Massachusetts Institute of Technology by Jay Forrester in 1949. The 704 made many scientific applications feasible for the first time because of its speed and the size of its main memory. The first *operating system* was developed to go with the

Figure 3. *(Computer: History)*   ENIAC, the first general-purpose electronic calculator, which was dedicated at the Moore School of Electrical Engineering, University of Pennsylvania, in February 1946. In the foreground are the coinventors, J. Presper Eckert, Jr. *(left)*, and John W. Mauchly. UPI/ Bettmann Newsphotos.

704, and it quadrupled the 704's output capability. Before operating systems, the computer was given to users one at a time. Each user entered a program and input data through a card reader, printed out the results, and made way for the next user. The operating system provided an automatic mechanism within the computer for executing one job after another without operator intervention, so a backlog of jobs could be entered and maintained ready for execution. The input and output devices no longer limited the speed of the system. A related development was time-sharing, in which a number of user terminals are connected to the computer simultaneously. Time-sharing works by allocating each user a small amount of computer time every few seconds. Because users act so slowly relative to machine speed, each user seems to be able to communicate with the computer and receive results from the computer as if there were no other users sharing the machine.

By 1961 IBM was marketing fifteen different central processors and seven separate lines of computers with very little software compatibility. Even the peripheral equipment was not compatible from one line to another. The IBM System/360 was the next major step in computer development (see Figure 4). The

System/360 line of computers consisted of a number of models, each with a different price and performance. Both hardware and software compatibility were maintained throughout the line so that users could upgrade their systems and still use their old

Figure 4. *(Computer: History)*   The IBM System/360, 1964. Courtesy of International Business Machines Corporation.

programs and peripherals. The System/360 set the pattern for all future large computer systems. The decision to develop the System/360 was an unusual business decision in that it replaced IBM's entire product line almost all at once. The number of IBM systems installed in the United States in 1964, when the System/360 was announced, was eleven thousand; in 1970 the number was thirty-five thousand, and IBM sales were twice as great as in 1964. The IBM System/360 can be viewed as the culmination of the early development of the computer. It did everything Babbage could have asked for, did it cheaply and well, and offered the capability in a wide range of packages to fit the needs of users with different applications.

Innovations and specialization. The System/360 and almost all computers before it were general-purpose computers. After 1965, however, the history of the computer moved in two directions: (1) toward continued improvements and cost reductions in general-purpose machines, and (2) toward the development of specialized machines for particular applications.

At the time the IBM System/360 was introduced the semiconductor industry had developed *integrated circuits*, but they were not yet reliable enough to be used in the System/360. Five years later, however, almost all new machines were built around integrated circuits. The appearance of a large general-purpose computer did not change much when integrated circuits were used, although the cost, size, and cooling requirements decreased.

Some users did not need the full-service package offered by IBM and wanted the hardware by itself, at the lowest price possible. Such users found that the *minicomputer* introduced in 1963 by the Digital Equipment Corporation fit their needs for low-cost computers that operated with the same program for years at a time. One example of a minicomputer application is process control in a chemical plant, in which a number of quantities, such as temperature or concentration, are monitored and a programmed response from a minicomputer adjusts settings of valves, heat sources, and so on. In a sense, the first robots were factory and plant automation systems of this sort, based on minicomputers. The minicomputer is thus a general-purpose computer that can be made into a specialized, single-purpose device by programming it to do a specialized job. The modern version of this application of the minicomputer is the *microcomputer,* or computer-on-a-chip, that is being built into a variety of machines to make their operation simpler, more precise, or more controllable. For example, the modern oscilloscope includes a small computer that allows the operator a wide range of options with respect to the display and analysis of signals being monitored.

The Tandem Computer Company introduced another type of specialized computer, which serves businesses such as airlines, banks, and telephone companies that make on-line transactions and are willing to pay a substantial premium for a computer that does not have any "downtime." It uses two parallel processors and software that allows the processors to work simultaneously (and also to work around any unit that fails) in order to increase reliability.

Computers and communications. A modern general-purpose computer consists of a central processing unit connected by means of cables that provide communication links to its input and output devices and to its data storage systems. In most systems the input devices are data terminals similar to personal computers. It is not difficult to design such systems to use communication links that allow the data terminals to be thousands of miles from the computer instead of a few feet. Airline reservation systems, credit card verification systems, and other transaction systems use this basic arrangement to permit users to communicate with a central computer that maintains a single, continuously updated file of airline seats or charges to particular accounts. Such systems allow users throughout the world to communicate with the computer through the existing worldwide TELEPHONE network. Specialized computer networks that use packet switching perform a similar function for substantially less than the cost of using a voice circuit. Packet switching, invented by Paul Baran in 1964, uses minicomputers to switch the data traffic, which is initially created in standardized packets. Each packet contains the address to which it is to be delivered and, typically, a thousand bits of information. Packet switching reduces costs by time-sharing a data channel among many users, each of whom typically uses the channel only a small part of the time.

This same type of computer system, with extended links to data terminals through the telephone network, can also be used to send personal messages from one user to another. Such systems provide electronic message service to their users by storing the message in the central computer and making it available to its intended recipient whenever the recipient logs onto the system. Modern private branch exchanges (PBXs) offer electronic message service to local users who have the proper data terminals as well as telephone service. In the future it appears that most business users will have both voice and data terminals on their desks and will be able to exchange messages in both forms.

To create a print message for an electronic message service, the user must have a system capable of some form of word processing. The user needs to be able to delete characters or words and to rearrange and insert characters, words, or paragraphs into existing text. But this same set of word-processing functions is also needed if a user is preparing a printed text on paper for transmission through the mail. And a variety of extensions of word processing exist that permit users to create graphic displays of various sorts, to manipulate the graphics in ways that are similar conceptually to the insertion and deletion of text, and to print the resulting figures on paper, using multicolor inks if desired. The use of computers in word processing and in the creation of graphic displays makes possible print-on-paper communication of high quality at a much lower cost than has been possible in the past.

An electronic message service can include maintaining a file of the messages sent and received, thus creating a user file of personal correspondence. Office automation is usually conceived of as including electronic message service, word processing, personal files, and access to other data bases, such as an up-to-date company telephone directory. Computers are also widely used to provide access to large data bases maintained for use by the general public, such as bibliographic search files and census data.

Computers have played an important role in the development of the telephone network. Telephone switching is itself a form of computing in which the input data, the number called, is transformed into the closing of a specific set of switches that establishes a connection between the caller's telephone instrument and the receiver's instrument. The path between the two telephone instruments may be thousands of miles long and may involve closing hundreds of individual switches. The path chosen depends on what other calls are in progress at the time a call is made. The telephone switching computer must be able to seek out alternative routings automatically when the simplest route is busy (see Figure 5).

In the early switching systems one or more switches were closed mechanically somewhere in the system each time the caller dialed a number, until all the numbers were dialed and the final switch needed to establish the connection was closed. But switches can operate at speeds thousands or millions of times faster than callers can dial. Quite early in the development of the network this fact was realized and a device called a sender was used to store the dialed number and operate the actual switches at a much higher rate. In modern systems the number dialed is first stored in a computer. Then a signal is sent from the computer to the appropriate telephone switches, causing them to close. If the call is completed, the computer records the number called, the number to be charged, the duration of the call, and the charge, and it stores this information for use in preparing the subscriber's bill.

The modern electronic computer is conceptually

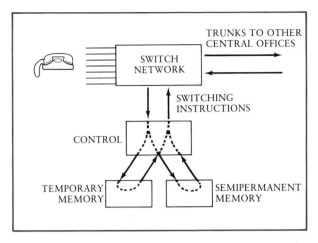

Figure 5. *(Computer: History)* A simplified diagram of the telephone switching system used in the 1960s. Adaptation of illustration by James Egleson in H. S. Feder and A. E. Spencer, "Telephone Switching," *Scientific American* 207 (July 1962): 141 (top).

remarkably similar to the machine conceived by Babbage in 1840. Its powerful central processing unit is now a compact, efficient set of integrated circuits. Its input/output devices and peripherals can be linked through the telephone network, allowing a wide range of personal message and transaction services to be provided on a worldwide basis. The cost of a basic machine dropped from a few hundred thousand dollars in the 1950s to a few hundred dollars in the 1980s. The applications of computers include factory automation, office automation, transaction services, message services, scientific uses, and personal computing (see Figure 6). The scope and intensity of these applications continue to increase as users and providers of software become more aware of the possibilities.

During the initial decades of the postwar period, IBM and other U.S. firms, universities, and research institutes led the field internationally in computer research and innovation. IBM maintained a major market share in the world computer market through the 1980s, but competition among North American, western European, and Japanese firms extended increasingly to many facets of computer system development. For example, improvements in quality control by Japanese firms gained them a market share in the market for semiconductor chips. Economic rivalries in the information technology sector can only be expected to intensify in the years ahead.

See also COMPUTER: IMPACT; DATA BASE; FIBER OPTICS; MICROELECTRONICS; TELECOMMUNICATIONS POLICY.

Bibliography. Stan Augarten, *Bit by Bit: An Illustrated History of Computers and Their Inventors*, New York, 1984; Donald A. Dunn, *Models of Particles and Moving Media*, New York, 1971; H. S. Feder and A. E. Spencer,

Figure 6. *(Computer: History)* A student at Marist High School, Atlanta, Georgia, masters a computer game on a school computer. UPI/ Bettmann Newsphotos.

"Telephone Switching," *Scientific American* 207 (1962): 133–143; Herman H. Goldstine, *The Computer from Pascal to von Neumann*, Princeton, N.J., 1972; René Moreau, *The Computer Comes of Age: The People, the Hardware, and the Software* (Ainsi naquit l'informatique), trans. by J. Howlett, Cambridge, Mass., 1984; Abbe Mowshowitz, *The Conquest of Will: Information Processing in Human Affairs*, Reading, Mass., 1984; Montgomery Phister, Jr., *Data Processing Technology and Economics*, 2d ed., Bedford, Mass., 1979; Joseph Weizenbaum, *Computer Power and Human Reason*, San Francisco, 1976.

DONALD A. DUNN

COMPUTER: IMPACT

This entry examines the social ramifications of the computer in a series of seven articles:
1. Overview
2. Impact on Military Affairs
3. Impact on Government
4. Impact on Education
5. Impact on Commerce
6. Impact on the Work Force
7. Impact on the World Economy

1. OVERVIEW

Following an initial period of military-sponsored innovation around World War II, computerized data processing rapidly penetrated the industrial and financial base of the economy. By 1960 an estimated nine thousand computers were in use worldwide. In the United States, which accounted for nearly two-thirds of the total, computers had appeared in airlines, communications, utilities, banks, real estate, EDUCATION, government, and especially manufacturing. Computer use was concentrated heavily in urban economic centers.

It soon became clear that the interrelationships between computers and telecommunications systems would increase. Large corporate computer users increasingly sought to transmit data to and from distant sites; numerous business applications, from centralized inventory control to production scheduling and credit card verification, demanded the kinds of data functions that computers could provide. TELEPHONE switching began to be performed by instruments displaying a marked similarity to programmable computers. Data-transmission techniques and capabilities expanded. Experimentation focused on higher-capacity communications channels such as microwave RADIO, satellites (*see* SATELLITE), and processes based on FIBER OPTICS; development of sophisticated equipment for carrying data over conventional analog telephone lines (modems and multiplexers); and variants of digital switching. Regulatory policies devised to support basic voice telephone service were abandoned in favor of policies designed to accommodate specialized, and disparate, data-transmission needs—with profound implications for the structure and terms of access to public switched telephone networks. Computer applications burst through barriers set down by centralized batch processing, and by the mid-1960s networks using terminals to interact with host computers had grown more common. The number of on-line terminals in the United States mushroomed from 520 in 1955 to almost 46,000 a decade later. By the 1980s a single gigantic computer network—the AT&T telephone system—reportedly connected 100,000 terminals.

Social impact. At the same time, there was a growing concern to understand the social impact of large-scale computerization. Some early observers were concerned about the consequences for labor of this "second industrial revolution," and the term *automation* was coined, some years before the first commercial computer was installed in 1954. This concept served to focus thinking about computerization on the consequences for work and employment. A succession of broader theories developed, stemming from the manifold changes in U.S. economic and occupational trends but at least partly inspired by an explicit concern with the computer's social impact. These theories gave rise to the concepts of the services economy, the knowledge society, and the postindustrial society. Borrowing heavily from these approaches was a new synthesis, called the information society.

Information society analysts referred to several related shifts. First, computerized information systems were cited as constituting an unprecedented "intellectual technology," radically discontinuous from past systems of information processing and control. Second, they claimed that a new class of white-collar information or knowledge professionals was coming to compose the vital portion of the work force in advanced market economies. Finally, they argued that information itself had supplanted capital and labor as the decisive factor of production. As a consequence, information services were said to be replacing manufacturing industry as the springboard to economic growth.

In fact, information society theorists tended to overstate their distance from the recent past. Some quite fundamental changes did indeed occur during the computer revolution. However, as noted by Krishan Kumar, a leading critic of the postindustrialists, the trends singled out by these theorists were often just "extrapolations, intensifications, and clarifications of tendencies which were apparent from the very birth of industrialism." In this sense Alvin Toffler's onetime neologism, the "superindustrial society," captured more of what was truly new than Daniel Bell's "postindustrial society" or Marc Porat's "information economy."

After all, the new information technology built directly on earlier innovations such as TELEGRAPHY,

telephony, punched-card electromechanical data processing, the typewriter, and vertical files. These developments in turn were intimately related to the growth of big business around 1900 and, especially, with business's need to centralize control over production and marketing in expanding national markets. Later technological innovations, such as advances in MICROELECTRONICS, were stimulated by the needs of businesses and military agencies, which directed that investments be made in the new technologies. Each historical enlargement of the scale of business enterprise relied upon essential innovations in message transport and information processing.

Impact on work. The existence of a purported new class of knowledge workers was also often overstated. At issue were not the millions of white-collar workers pouring into the labor markets of advanced nations, even as farm and manufacturing labor categories shrank. In fact, the white-collar phenomenon originated in the late nineteenth century, when growing business enterprises replaced male clerks with legions of lower-paid women. According to information society theorists, however, the burgeoning white-collar sector differed in crucial ways from the older industrial working class. In marked contrast to the factory proletariat of previous decades, postwar knowledge workers were supposed to be highly skilled and to exercise considerable control over their work. In reality, empirical studies have shown that the vast majority of white-collar workers were not professionals but clerks, whose work was rigorously organized and supervised. Even in ostensibly professional refuges like medicine, architecture, and university teaching, the pace and substance of work were increasingly determined not by individual decision but by bureaucratized routine. The new class, in short, shared many of the characteristics of its pre-computer-age counterparts.

Global impact. Did knowledge replace capital and labor as the decisive factor of production? There can be no question that information was applied more and more systematically to all manner of productive and administrative processes. Econometric models, equations, and flow charts became the common coin of the business realm, along with computer-assisted prediction, projection, and modeling. The functions of research universities were also profoundly affected by the role of information in the business world. Universities were a growing market for computer and telecommunications companies and textbook publishers hawking information systems, networks, and software. Far from transcending the profit motive, as postindustrial analysts would wish, the university itself became subordinated to it. In sum, the character and quality of information of every kind were broadly restructured by market imperatives.

In this regard the information society theorists

were correct in claiming that information had become the key to economic growth. In the early 1980s U.S. annual exports of communication and information services were valued at an astonishing $40 billion. Global markets for information showed unparalleled economic concentration across a wide range of enterprises. Investment in information systems by the U.S. services sector correspondingly increased rapidly. What *Business Week* called "the rapid industrialization of the service sector" impinged on everything from the organization and control of work to overall business strategy in fields as diverse as airline transport, data-base publishing, and international banking.

A global grid of TELECOMMUNICATIONS NETWORKS, permitting integration of once separate systems and services such as voice, data, and video, made possible the flexible distribution of computerized information services in a world market. Capacious digital networks became a chief object of telecommunications engineering, policy making, and planning in all the wealthy nations as well as multilateral organizations like the International Telecommunication Union. The evolution of these wideband, multipurpose digital networks, however, raised critical issues of access and control. Considerable disparities emerged in the control exerted over information resources by rich and poor nations and by private as opposed to public authorities. As a result, the next generation of information systems may well determine fundamental political and economic relationships.

By the early 1980s, as international economic competition intensified, information technology had been identified as essential to national prosperity in nations as diverse as France, Brazil, Canada, Great Britain, Japan, and the United States. National information policies correspondingly came to command increasing attention. An early exponent of deliberate national policy to shape and channel information technology development was Japan.

Earlier, Japan had reconstructed its industrial and manufacturing infrastructure and had begun to fashion a major role for itself as an exporter of manufactures. By the 1970s this role was decisively enlarged as Japanese companies and government agencies worked together to forge a place in information technology and electronics markets as well. Strong Japanese competitors emerged across an expanding range of technology industries, including producers of microelectronic circuits, telecommunications and computer equipment, and advanced instrumentation. With considerable consequences for U.S. and European firms, Japanese information technology companies such as Fujitsu, NEC, and Hitachi made major inroads into world markets.

Three exceptions to this trend should be noted. First, U.S. companies retained their lead in information services, including data bases, software, and related services. This was in part owing to the continuing dominance of the English language, not only in business and commerce but also in international science and popular culture. Second, major funding of computer and electronics companies by the U.S. Department of Defense continued to stimulate work on the cutting edge of the field, frequently at a level far surpassing that of Japan. Finally, both in mainframe computing and in many related markets, U.S.-based IBM remained a determining force. When coupled with growing recognition of the strategic, economic, and military importance of information technology, the extent of IBM's market power prompted reciprocal government initiatives in the information sector.

In western Europe these national efforts to defend domestic information companies and other interests had begun to falter by the 1980s. The costs of research and development for emerging generations of digital equipment such as telephone switches could no longer be recovered within any single national market. Yet coordination across national boundaries within the European Economic Community—the essential prerequisite for any concerted European initiative in information technology—proved difficult to achieve. Although some joint research and development efforts were launched, most of the activity occurred in a series of joint ventures between European- and U.S.-based telecommunications and computer firms, which created new intercorporate links and interests at the expense of national cooperation between states. The problems of competition and policy in the field of information technology were even more serious for smaller and poorer countries.

Increased role of business. One of the main sweeping results of the changes that occurred in the information technologies since World War II was the consistent extension of the market into wholly new areas: education, medicine, libraries, and even government. Like land and labor before it, information was transformed into a commodity—something produced solely for profitable exchange.

To serve global markets, a few thousand transnational business enterprises demanded substantial outlays for performance of information-based work in research, marketing, sales, and so forth. This inspired them to search for ways of making information work—like other types of work—continuously more productive and cost-efficient. Expenditures on information systems at such companies often became the third- or even the second-largest operating expense, amounting to hundreds of millions of dollars annually.

Computerized information systems also became essential to the competition for markets. One widely cited example was the manipulation of computerized airline reservation systems to favor carriers in a position to sponsor and diffuse the new technology; administration of invaluable intellectual property through licensing of patents, trademarks, and copyrights is another. Information and information technology were used as weapons of economic competition in everything from corporate planning to manufacturing processes to product design.

As information about markets, inventions, products, and new production processes was recognized as a major source of competitive advantage, the whole field of information resource management—treating information as a budgetable commodity with assignable production and distribution costs—became established in the corporate world. Increasingly, some of the largest corporations staked claims, not just to information technology but to information markets themselves. Each from its unique market sector, ranging from heavy manufacturing to consumer travel, attempted to capitalize on corporate knowledge.

Important though these market changes are—for instance, for relationships between countries—they also indicate a far broader social transformation. As information technology facilitates extension of the market economy into a vast new field, what features will come to characterize relations between business and the rest of society? Over what span of social and political life will business enterprises obtain direct dominion? Which of the functions such as child rearing and education, health care, and governance will remain outside the market? Will hierarchical forms of work organization and control come to define every form of social labor? The answers to such questions will be of profound import in the evolution of the social context for the computerization process.

Bibliography. Daniel Bell, *The Coming of Post-Industrial Society: A Venture in Social Forecasting*, New York, 1973; Ernest Braun and Stuart MacDonald, *Revolution in Miniature: The History and Impact of Semiconductor Electronics Re-Explored*, 2d ed., Cambridge, 1982; Harry Braverman, *Labor and Monopoly Capital*, New York, 1974; Irving D. Canton, "Learning to Love the Service Economy," *Harvard Business Review* 62 (May–June 1984): 89–97; David Dickson, *The New Politics of Science*, New York, 1984; Krishan Kumar, *Prophecy and Progress*, New York, 1978; Fritz Machlup, *The Production and Distribution of Knowledge in the United States*, Princeton, N.J., 1962; Dan Schiller, *Telematics and Government*, Norwood, N.J., 1982; Herbert I. Schiller, *Who Knows: Information in the Age of the Fortune 500*, Norwood, N.J., 1981; Norbert Wiener, *Cybernetics: Or, Control and Communication in the Animal and the Machine*, 2d ed., Cambridge, Mass., 1961; Raymond Williams, *The Year 2000*, New York, 1983.

DAN SCHILLER

2. IMPACT ON MILITARY AFFAIRS

The computer and the military have had a long association. The military has made pioneering innovations in the computer field, and military technologies and strategies have become almost entirely dependent on computers. The consequences of this reciprocal relationship raise several new and troubling questions.

Military role in computer development. In the 1930s the U.S. Army and Navy used machines that employed high-speed digital circuits and a punch-card format for analyzing and deciphering CODE. However, these forerunners of the modern computer were highly specialized for a particular task (*see* COMPUTER: HISTORY). In the 1940s the military advanced the construction of general-purpose computers. In 1943 scientists at the University of Pennsylvania built the Electronic Numerical Integrator and Calculator (ENIAC) to compute artillery firing tables automatically for the U.S. Army. At about the same time IBM built the Mark 1 at Harvard University to process information about shell trajectories for the U.S. Navy, and a British team developed Colossus to decipher the codes in which the Germans sent military messages. By using computers to enhance weapons accuracy and gather intelligence, scientists developed the technique of stored program control. This allowed computers to carry out a number of different tasks simultaneously from instructions contained within the computer.

After World War II the military continued to shape the development of computer hardware and software. Stimulated by the development of the SAGE air-defense system, the United States maintained its lead in computer development. Great Britain remained second throughout the 1950s, although by the end of the decade the Federal Republic of Germany, France, Sweden, and the USSR had built workable electronic digital computers. The USSR was in fact the first nation in continental Europe to build a stored-program electronic digital computer. It began work on the project in 1948 and completed the MESM in 1951.

The United States maintained this lead through the 1960s and 1970s with a system of military investment and commercial development, principally through IBM. The Department of Defense provided much of the funding for the transition from large, unreliable vacuum tubes to transistors and eventually to semiconductor integrated circuits. Between 1958 and 1974 the U.S. military provided about $1 billion for semiconductor research and purchased between one-third and one-half of the chips produced. The U.S. military is largely responsible for underwriting the development of computer software, including the widely used computer languages COBOL (Common Business-Oriented Language) and, in the 1980s, Ada. In 1958 the United States established DARPA (Defense Advanced Research Projects Agency) to organize its research and development efforts in computers and to respond to Soviet developments culminating in Sputnik. DARPA worked with the Massachusetts Institute of Technology (MIT) to build time-sharing computers and with MIT, Stanford University, and the University of California, Los Angeles (UCLA), to create packet switching, a system that packages bits of information for distribution over a communication network. These developments led to the creation of Arpanet, a prototype computer communications network. The military used these evolving computer communications systems in a wide range of applications, including development of the intercontinental ballistic missile (ICBM), worldwide intelligence gathering led by the National Security Agency, and battlefield sensing and "automated battlefield" systems in Vietnam.

Computer applications in the military. Computers are used in a variety of administrative and battlefield applications. The former include such standard business functions as financial accounting, personnel management, supply, and stock control. In addition to these standard management functions, there are operations that require adaptations of commercial computer hardware and software. Among these are systems for training personnel, maintaining systems, and, of growing significance, operations analysis, or war gaming.

Computers are used extensively in weaponry and in command and control systems. Indeed, according to a U.S. Army deputy chief of staff, "Literally every weapons system that we are planning and bringing into development in some way employs minicomputers and microelectronics." Studies report that about 40 percent of all U.S. military hardware is electronic. Battlefield computers are used primarily for remote sensing of enemy troop movements, precise targeting and firing, and damage assessment. Miniaturization has spread the portable computer throughout the modern battlefield. GRiDSE.T, a briefcase-sized computer with a built-in mechanism for telecommunications, has been tested in action in Lebanon and Grenada, on the Space Shuttle, and in a nuclear weapon retargeting exercise aboard an airborne command post.

Computers are also widely used in naval forces. A typical guided-missile cruiser carrying nuclear warheads, antisubmarine rocket torpedos, and attack helicopters is managed by multiple on-board computers. These computer banks are organized into a system such as Aegis, which is driven by tactical software programs that provide instructions on what weapons to fire, at what targets, and when.

Military computers are integrated into systems of command, control, communication, and intelligence (C^3I). Computers have given weapons greater range, speed, and accuracy. Linked to communication technologies, particularly satellites, computers have expanded intelligence, surveillance, and reconnaissance by providing more information over greater distances. As the real size of the battlefield increases over the earth and into space, C^3I systems to acquire, process, and communicate information and issue commands grow more vital. C^3I systems for local application, such as assessing troop maneuvers, are themselves integrated into global networks, such as the U.S. Worldwide Military Command and Control System (WWMCCS).

The growth of computerized weaponry and C^3I systems has prompted creation of a specific field of military action called electronic warfare (EW). This refers to the battle for control of the electromagnetic SPECTRUM, including efforts to promote effective use of electronic communication and to resist efforts to obstruct it. The U.S. military spent $3.4 billion on electronic warfare in 1984.

Owing to its slow start in computer development, the Soviet Union has lacked a command and control system as sophisticated as that of the United States. Though a leader in theoretical computer science and CYBERNETICS, the USSR has not kept pace in applications, particularly in the development of computer software. Until the late 1970s Soviet software existed primarily in isolated pockets of machine language programs. Nevertheless, the USSR has compensated for this deficiency by creating highly redundant military systems. For example, the Soviets have built about three hundred underground command posts for launching their ICBM force, three times the number in the United States. The United States has three very-low-frequency transmitters and six backup ones for communicating with its submarine fleet; the Soviet Union has built twenty-six. The U.S. military is very dependent on its land-based telecommunications network; the Soviet Union has a more extensive communications SATELLITE system that uses a large number of much simpler satellites to relay messages to and from its forces. In essence the United States relies on more sophisticated technology to provide military systems that the Soviets lack, such as instantaneous photoreconnaissance, early warning or elec-

Figure 1. *(Computer: Impact—Impact on Military Affairs)* Fire control computer of the Multiple Launch Rocket System (MLRS), containing the computer that integrates the vehicle and the rocket launching operations. Courtesy of the U.S. Army, Public Information Division, Washington, D.C.

tronic-intelligence satellites in geosynchronous orbits, or advanced computers. The Soviet Union chooses simpler, more redundant, and more durable systems.

Computers have their widest and most critical application in strategic weapons. Computers are essential for the amount and speed of information processing required for sensing, warning, launching, or responding to a nuclear attack. Moreover, as military weaponry enters outer space in the form of satellite, laser, particle beam, and other weapons, computer capabilities must expand.

Just as the military pioneered the development of computers in the 1940s, military projects continue to propel advances in computer technology. These include research on Very High Speed Integrated Circuits (VHSIC), Very Large-Scale Integration (VLSI), and alternative semiconductor materials such as gallium arsenide to decrease the size and increase the speed of computers.

One major goal is to develop computers with an ARTIFICIAL INTELLIGENCE capability. In 1984 the United States embarked on a five-year, $600 million project, the Strategic Computing Initiative, to build such so-called expert systems. Major research areas include pattern and SPEECH recognition that could make drone aircraft and remote-controlled submarines commonplace, as well as increase the autonomy of land and space vehicles. Research in this area has strengthened the ties among the military; the computer, semiconductor, and communication industries; and major research universities. The only more ambitious artificial intelligence project is Japan's government-industry effort to develop commercial applications for expert systems.

Questions about military use. A number of issues have arisen about the use of computers in the mili-

tary, particularly in the area of nuclear weapons. Military policy officials wonder about the ability to achieve interoperability, or integration of the global network of military computers; similarly, nuclear planners work on strategic connectivity, or the ability to command and control nuclear forces. Ironically, technical advances that replaced electromechanical with completely electronic switching in computer communications systems make these systems more vulnerable to the high-energy charge, or electromagnetic pulse (EMP), released by a nuclear detonation. Moreover, greater integration increases the potential for security problems. Expenditures of more than $100 million a year have not maintained complete security for the Pentagon's large computers. Other groups raise the specter of a war triggered by one or a series of computer malfunctions. The likelihood grows as the speed and power of weapons make for greater reliance on computers for detection and response. The computerized technology, it is widely held, has strengthened society's dependence on military applications for technological innovation and led to a greater reliance on military solutions to global problems.

See also DIPLOMACY.

Bibliography. Paul Bracken, *The Command and Control of Nuclear Forces*, New Haven, Conn., 1983; Daniel F. Ford, *The Button*, New York, 1985; N. Metropolis, J. Howlett, and Gian-Carlo Rota, eds., *A History of Computing in the Twentieth Century* (International Research Conference on the History of Computing, Los Alamos Scientific Laboratory, 1976), New York, 1980.

VINCENT MOSCO

3. IMPACT ON GOVERNMENT

Government use of computers for civilian data began in 1951, only five years after the first electronic computer was constructed, when the U.S. Census Bureau acquired Sperry Rand's UNIVAC I, the first electronic digital computer delivered on a commercial basis. In just over three decades, the U.S. government was spending more than $10 billion annually on computing and telecommunications services. Throughout this time, federal agencies in the United States took a leading role in the governmental application of computer technology to both international matters and other jurisdictions within the federal system. Although U.S. federal agencies were the real pioneers in the government use of computers, state and local governments rapidly adopted computer technology in the 1960s and 1970s. By the mid-1970s more than 90 percent of U.S. cities with populations greater than fifty thousand were using computers.

Most advanced industrialized nations depended heavily on U.S. computing equipment manufacturers, particularly International Business Machines, through the 1970s, and they lagged behind the United States in both the application and the study of government information systems. Despite this lag, patterns of adoption and use of government information technology were similar cross-nationally, with the exception of the Soviet Union and several eastern European nations, which placed higher priorities on such uses of computing as planning and decision-oriented applications. Moreover, during the 1980s, the gap between the United States and other advanced industrialized nations narrowed as the computer industry developed in Canada, the Federal Republic of Germany, and Japan as well as in France, Great Britain, and other wealthy countries.

Organizational context. Early predictions about the implications of computing seldom recognized the flexibility of the technology and the degree to which its effects would be limited by its social and organizational setting. In government settings, the gap between expectations and performance was shaped less by the technology of computing than by the way public officials, administrators, and other personnel applied the technology.

During the 1950s and 1960s, digital computers were adopted primarily to replace electrical accounting machines used for large-volume data-processing operations such as accounting and billing. Governments continued to use computers for electronic data-processing through the 1980s, primarily for routine data-processing tasks. Public officials placed lower priority on the application of computing to management-oriented tasks such as record restructuring and sophisticated analysis (e.g., property tax assessment,

simulation, budget forecasting). Lagging still further behind were applications of computing to communication support tasks such as graphic and visual arts and communications.

In general, then, rather than using computer technology to provide public information services, governments automated revenue-producing and expenditure-controlling activities such as accounting, finance, budgeting, treasury, personnel, purchasing, inventory, and billing. In this respect, computing enhanced the prevailing priorities of governments, reinforcing public attitudes stressing government efficiency and law enforcement rather than social services or amenities.

Computer technology was managed conservatively by most government agencies, which had limited budgetary support for computing (about 1 percent of their operating budgets). The few agencies that approached the state of the art in the technology budgeted four to five times that allocation for computing and actually spent as much as double the amount budgeted. As a result, few governments have been highly computerized. Most U.S. local governments, for example, even by the late 1970s were using the equivalent of about one medium-sized business computer. Taxing and spending limitation measures permitted only incremental expansions of computing during the 1970s. Thus, governmental computing systems are often based on older technology than that available in industries of comparable scale. The fact that governmental computing is seldom state of the art has been important because advanced technology is a major determinant of the impact of computing on government operations.

Implications. The implications of computing in government affect several broad areas that cover most of the ways in which government institutions function. The areas that have been most affected by the introduction of computer technology are (1) responsiveness to the public, (2) decision-making resources and methods, (3) efficiency, and (4) degree of management control.

Responsiveness in this context has come to refer to the willingness of government institutions to supply information in response to public requests. In the 1960s, some U.S. academics felt that since new technologies made it possible for individuals to participate in public affairs from both home and office, computing and telecommunications could enhance public access to information and, in turn, to the democratic process. However, the reality rarely approached this ideal. For the most part, public officials did not use computing to provide public services, information, or opportunities for participation to citizens. In fact, computing has actually threatened public access in some ways. By making it more profitable to repackage and disseminate public information, the new technologies tended to undermine the traditional role of the government in providing information to the public. This poses the risk that more information will migrate from the individual, home, and public agency into private and public files, where it will be treated as a marketable commodity.

Management and decision scientists expected that computer-based information systems, such as models, simulations, and data banks, would facilitate the rationalization of decision making by providing easier access to more accurate, wide-ranging, and up-to-date information. And there is evidence that computing did lead to qualitative improvements in the information available for planning and management decision making. However, in contrast to early expectations, the most valuable applications of computing for decision making have often been simple listings and ad hoc reports rather than more sophisticated decision-oriented analyses.

Computing improved the efficiency of many government operations, particularly routine and high-volume information tasks such as the processing of traffic tickets or social security checks. However, despite the expectation that office automation would cut costs, there has been little evidence in the public sector that computing has reduced clerical, management, or operational staff. Computing did make it possible for some agencies to handle increased work loads without hiring additional staff. However, computing also created the new challenges of "information technology management" as the problems of storing, searching, transmitting, and disseminating information without compromising efficiency, accuracy, or confidentiality were recognized. In the United States, such concerns led to the Paperwork Reduction Act of 1980, which established an Office of Information and Regulatory Affairs to oversee the use of computing, telecommunications, and information practices in federal agencies. While aimed at reducing paperwork burdens on the public and lowering the costs of information processing within the federal government, the establishment of a central coordinating office had implications for the relative autonomy of various agencies and departments of the federal government.

The introduction of computers also had implications for the degree of management control over government agencies. Public officials and managers believed that computing improved management control by providing information to management about the performance of subordinates. However, computing also created the potential for power shifts within these agencies, since the introduction of computing increases the likelihood that technocrats (the experts who understand how to use computing) will become more effective within organizations. While computing has generally been adopted and used in ways that

tend to consolidate rather than redistribute power in government organizations, the importance of the technocrats has tended to reinforce the general shift of power from legislative and judicial branches of the government to the executive departments and agencies, particularly top managers and their staffs.

Privacy and civil liberties. Since the 1960s, PRIVACY concerns have been the major public issue raised by the governmental use of computing technologies. Most nations of western Europe and North America have established privacy and data protection laws. In the United States rights to privacy derive from the First, Fourth, and Fifth Amendments to the Constitution and were incorporated in such federal legislation as the Privacy Act of 1974 and the Cable Telecommunications Act of 1984, and in hundreds of state and local privacy laws. Several European nations created independent privacy and data protection boards to oversee governmental uses of personal information. In the United States this protection has been more decentralized, although it is the formal responsibility of the Office of Management and Budget, a federal agency. Canada, Great Britain, Sweden, and the United States have sponsored major studies of the implications of computers for privacy.

While the underlying issue of privacy is independent of computing, the new technologies have increased the scale on which abuses of privacy can occur. Computers expand the possibilities for monitoring telephone conversations, analyzing transactional data bases (such as those created by electronic banking), searching large files, matching (e.g., comparing social security numbers within different files so that they can be merged), profiling (e.g., using information about an individual to estimate the likelihood of a particular kind of behavior, such as tax evasion), and other forms of electronic surveillance. Early privacy studies directed by Alan Westin concluded that in many cases computing improved the handling of information without jeopardizing privacy. Later studies—of automated criminal justice information systems—have presented a more negative assessment by identifying problems with the accuracy, accountability, and comprehensibility of large-scale data banks. Moreover, in the mid-1980s several accounts of military and political surveillance by major U.S. government agencies such as the National Security Agency renewed fears about actual invasions of privacy.

As computers become increasingly essential for communication within government and between the government and the public, the applications of computers will have a growing influence on such issues as freedom of speech, press, and assembly, and the right to petition the government. As more government records and communications are computer-based, issues of freedom to publish and obtain access to government officials and records—the right to know—inevitably become tied to computer technology.

Bibliography. James N. Danziger, William H. Dutton, Rob Kling, and Kenneth L. Kraemer, *Computers and Politics: High Technology in American Local Governments,* New York, 1982; William H. Dutton and Kenneth L. Kraemer, *Modeling as Negotiating: The Political Dynamics of Computer Models in the Policy Process,* Norwood, N.J., 1985; Stephen E. Frantzich, *Computers in Congress,* Beverly Hills, Calif., 1982; Kenneth L. Kraemer, William H. Dutton, and Alana Northrop, *The Management of Information Systems,* New York, 1981; Kenneth C. Laudon, *Computers and Bureaucratic Reform,* New York, 1974; Alan F. Westin and Michael A. Baker, *Data Banks in a Free Society: Computers, Record-Keeping, and Privacy,* New York, 1972.

WILLIAM H. DUTTON

4. IMPACT ON EDUCATION

The role of the computer in EDUCATION has been the subject of educational research and development for decades. The introduction of the microcomputer made computer technology widely accessible to teachers, students, and parents and ushered in a new era of discussion about the appropriate design and use of software and hardware (see Figure 1).

As microcomputers entered homes, schools, and offices, children and adolescents were among their primary users (*see* SCHOOL). Computer-assisted instruction, games and simulations, word processing, data bases (*see* DATA BASE), and electronic mail are contributing to a changing media environment for learners of all ages. Often compared with television in its attractiveness to young people, the computer offers new opportunities for flexibility and interactivity between student and subject matter and ultimately for improving the processes of learning (*see* INTERACTIVE MEDIA). By combining features of print and visual media as well as mass and INTERPERSONAL COMMUNICATION, the computer is redefining the boundaries of communications media (*see* MASS COMMUNICATIONS RESEARCH).

The increasing use of computers in education has also amplified debates about the virtues and vices of educational technology. Decisions to implement computers in the CLASSROOM raise fundamental questions about the philosophy of education in the selection of subject matter, curriculum goals, and instructional style. Should computers be used to convey traditional school subject matter or to prepare students for living and working in a computerized society? Given a school's limited financial resources, should computers be used mainly to bring lower-achieving students up to a par with their classmates or to accelerate the progress of more talented students? Should computer software emphasize the transmission of knowledge directed from teacher to student or stress a child's own discovery of knowledge? These and other questions will be asked frequently as the technology advances and educational experience accumulates.

Technological Features

Two basic types of computer systems in use in education can be distinguished. The first and older sys-

Figure 1. *(Computer: Impact—Impact on Education)* Children at the Tri-Cities Children's Center, Fremont, California, learning to use Qume's electronic graphics tablet, 1982. Words and pictures are reproduced on both a computer screen and a printer terminal. UPI/Bettmann Newsphotos.

tems involve groups of computer terminals attached via cable to large mainframe computers. "Courseware," ranging from individual lessons to entire courses, resides in the mainframe computer, with students able to work through the material according to individual aptitude and pace. The computer keeps a record of each student's progress and, in more sophisticated systems, provides individualized guidance for skill improvement. The second configuration, made possible through microprocessors, involves stand-alone microcomputers—also known as personal computers—each with its own memory, processing unit, and software loaded from a storage medium, most commonly diskette.

Historical Development

Use of computer technology for instructional purposes dates back to the 1950s. Since the 1960s large mainframe computers have provided courseware based on principles of programmed instruction. This style of software, known as computer-assisted instruction (CAI), encompasses several types of programs. CAI can include drill-and-practice programs in which students receive training in discrete skill areas, such as arithmetic or foreign languages; tutorials, in which the computer poses questions and can interpret a limited range of student responses; and demonstrations, in which the computer's GRAPHICS, color, and sound are used to depict concepts and relationships, typically in the sciences or MATHEMATICS. CAI systems of various kinds have been developed in the United States, Great Britain, Canada, Japan, and other countries.

The microcomputer brought computer ownership within the reach of individual schools and families. Microcomputer adoption by schools in the United States has outpaced other educational innovations (see DIFFUSION), increasing dramatically from around thirty thousand in 1981 to more than one million by 1985. By the mid-1980s over 90 percent of elementary and secondary schools had at least one computer, and one-fourth of the nation's teachers were using computers. Adoption rates were higher in high schools than in elementary schools and in schools with larger student populations (see Figure 2).

Estimates of home ownership of microcomputers in the United States during the mid-1980s ranged between 20 and 25 percent, increasing for wealthier urban and suburban communities. School systems in other countries, notably Great Britain and France, also made acquisition of microcomputers a priority, often through the sponsorship of centralized educational authorities. Home and school purchases of computers continue at a steady pace, aided by falling prices in computer hardware.

During the second half of the 1980s computers

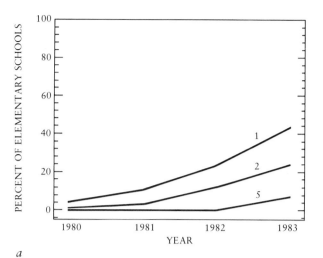

1 = 1 micro in school
2 = 2 or more micros
5 = 5 or more micros

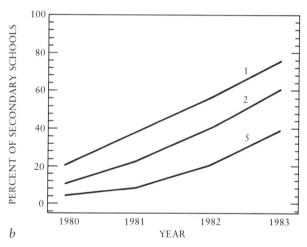

Figure 2. *(Computer: Impact—Impact on Education)* Microcomputers in *(a)* U.S. elementary schools and *(b)* U.S. secondary schools. Redrawn after H. J. Becker, "How Schools Use Microcomputers," *Classroom Computer Learning* 12 (1983): 41–44.

entered a more mature phase of utilization characterized by a developing professionalism among teachers, principals, software designers, computer manufacturers, researchers, and education officials. Software continued to diversify and improve, accompanied by a more stable market in computer hardware. A growing corps of teachers at both the elementary and secondary levels is acquiring greater sophistication in the uses of computers in classrooms. Several national and INTERNATIONAL ORGANIZATIONS, such as Computer-Using Educators (CUE), and conferences, such as the National Educational Computing Conference, provide ongoing forums for exchanging knowledge about the role of computers in educational practice, a process additionally supported by numerous publications, including trade magazines, academic journals, and newsletters (*see* MAGAZINE; NEWSLETTER).

Research Issues

Research on computers in education brings together work at the forefront of several social sciences, including communication, education, cognitive psychology, and computer science. As with older print and broadcast media, the research can be divided into two broad domains of inquiry: effects and utilization. The first class examines types of educational effects that occur from exposure to computers and can include changes in academic achievement, cognitive skills, or ATTITUDES. The second domain studies patterns of utilization within educational environments, including formal instruction in schools as well as informal education in homes, museums, computer camps, or other settings. Both types of research can help shape educational policies to promote patterns of use related to positive learning outcomes.

Computer literacy and computer programming. The research agenda for computers in education has been evolving with uses of the technology. In the 1970s and 1980s studies of educational effects focused on traditional computer LITERACY and computer programming courses. Instruction in computer literacy emphasizes basic computer concepts, such as the components of computer systems, the history and social role of computers, and elementary programming. Computer programming has been studied as a possible aid to COGNITION. Programming languages commonly taught in schools include BASIC, Pascal, FORTRAN, and LOGO. LOGO, developed by Seymour Papert and others at the Massachusetts Institute of Technology in the 1970s, has attracted much attention as a powerful language designed especially for use by young children. Since programming requires detailed specification of procedures and their interrelationships, it has been hypothesized that acquisition of programming concepts might foster higher-order cognitive skills related to problem solving, planning, and systematic thinking.

Nonprogramming applications. With proliferation of other instructional uses of computers besides programming, and anticipation that future uses of computers will not require programming skills, research has shifted to include learning from educational computer games, simulations, word processors, and other "applications" software. Some of this software is designed to convey content knowledge or skills in specific subject matter, such as language arts, mathematics, or history, often in a gamelike format.

Other types of software commonly in use are designed to facilitate performance of information tasks, such as word processors for WRITING, data bases and spreadsheets for data organization and handling, and graphics for data presentation. Questions about the educational potential of these types of software involve not only mastery of their features but also longer-term transfer of learning to higher-order intellectual skills. Will word processors improve the quality of students' writing by simplifying the process of revision, providing checks on GRAMMAR and spelling, and encouraging planning and organization? Will data bases provide students with powerful models for categorizing and manipulating information? These questions exemplify a developing research agenda for computers in education.

Computers also offer an alternative channel to face-to-face communication between teachers and students (*see* INTERACTION, FACE-TO-FACE). Computer networks make it possible for students and teachers to exchange information through electronic mail and conferencing, within classrooms and across schools. Since there are typically fewer computers than students in a classroom, computer usage can lead to new methods of classroom organization and teacher-student interaction. For instance, computers can be used in ways that encourage peer collaboration and reciprocal tutoring. The technology can also help ease teachers' administrative burdens. Software for generating student grades, lesson plans, and handouts has provided teachers with a tool for minimizing paperwork.

The computer can also operate as a terminal for receiving information and software "downloaded" over phone or cable lines or through broadcast transmission. This use of the computer, generically termed VIDEOTEX, also holds educational potential. Students and teachers can tie into computer networks for communication with other students, teachers, professionals in various fields, and special-interest groups, or access data bases of subject matter or reference materials (e.g., on-line encyclopedias, newspapers, and bibliographic collections). *See also* ELECTRONIC PUBLISHING.

Computers and social equity. The diffusion of educational computing raises issues of social equity as well. Computers may contribute to "knowledge gaps" between social groups. Most obviously the financial investment required for computers threatens to create gaps in their availability and use among more and less economically advantaged families and schools.

Studies of microcomputer adoption have indicated a predictable pattern of early purchase by wealthier families and schools. Initial studies also found inequities in school use, with some evidence that, for instance, CAI was more frequently used with lower-achieving, inner-city, or minority students. Whether ownership of computers will continue to divide the computer "haves" from the "have-nots" is not clear.

Local- and state-funded initiatives, as well as donations and discounts from computer manufacturers, may serve to narrow such gaps in computer ownership.

Other equity issues involve psychological, cultural, and attitudinal factors in computer use. GENDER differences in computer use, from childhood through adulthood, have emerged as another significant equity issue. The computer sciences, like other fields of science and engineering, have historically attracted greater participation from males than from females. Studies of microcomputers have often documented more frequent use and positive attitudes among male students than among female students, especially during the adolescent years. Just as gender gaps in mathematics, science, and engineering decreased through the 1970s and 1980s, the gender gap in computing may be ameliorated by the entry of more young women into those related fields and by the rise of numerous applications for computers in business, the humanities, and the arts.

A further equity issue concerns the use of computers in special education. For students with physical or mental disabilities the computer can help promote equality of educational opportunity, serving as a powerful "prosthetic device" offering access to educational materials. New devices for user interfaces (e.g., special keyboards for the physically handicapped, the Kurzweil Reading Machine for the blind) and engaging software may help students to overcome barriers posed by impairments to movement, hearing, speech, or sight.

Research on educational and social effects of computers can profit from the legacy of communications research on earlier media, most notably the extensive body of television research (see MASS MEDIA EFFECTS). Foremost among those lessons is the need to look beyond simplistic, mechanistic conceptions of direct "effects" of computers on students to more detailed study of specific attributes of the educational stimulus, variation in learner aptitude and motivation, and differences in educational settings and instructional styles of teachers.

Future Directions

Advances in computer technology will offer newer, faster, and "friendlier" computers with improved options for text, graphics, and user interfaces. Research on ARTIFICIAL INTELLIGENCE may enable computers to utilize complex mental models of learners in the course of computer-assisted instruction. Such systems have been developed, for instance, for diagnosing patterns of student errors in arithmetic problems. This genre of software, termed "intelligent computer-assisted instruction" (ICAI), may place impressive new tools in the hands of teachers and educators. At the same time, ICAI confronts difficult challenges in attempting to model the complexities of the human mind.

New computer-based systems merge the computer with other developing technologies, such as the videodisc, combining the power of computers with the full audio and visual features of television and film. The first generation of interactive videodiscs has been used primarily in training and simulation for corporations and the military, although intriguing experiments have been conducted, for instance, in science and art education. New storage media, such as compact discs, may overcome current memory limitations of microcomputers. Farther into the future, computers may communicate by accepting human speech input and responding through synthesized speech.

These new learning machines again pose a familiar dilemma for communications media: technological progress advances more swiftly than human progress in understanding. In 1948, three decades before the age of the microcomputer, HAROLD D. LASSWELL posed the classic question for communication research: "Who says what to whom through which channel and with what effects?" That question can be restated for computers in education: "Who learns what from which attributes of a computer-based system and with what effects on other learning and behavior?"

Bibliography. Milton Chen and William Paisley, eds., *Children and Microcomputers: Research on the Newest Medium*, Beverly Hills, Calif., 1985; Jack Culbertson and Luvern L. Cunningham, eds., *Microcomputers and Education*, Chicago, 1986; Seymour Papert, *Mindstorms: Children, Computers, and Powerful Ideas*, New York, 1980; Gavriel Salomon, *Interaction of Media, Cognition, and Learning*, San Francisco, 1979; Robert Taylor, ed., *The Computer in the School: Tutor, Tutee, Tool*, New York, 1980; Sherry Turkle, *The Second Self: Computers and the Human Spirit*, New York, 1984; Decker F. Walker and Robert D. Hess, eds., *Instructional Software: Principles and Perspectives for Design and Use*, Belmont, Calif., 1984.

MILTON CHEN

5. IMPACT ON COMMERCE

Commerce includes both the large-scale exchange or buying and selling of goods and a wide variety of supporting functions necessary to facilitate these transactions. It encompasses not only wholesale and retail operations but also banking, insurance, commodity and other exchanges, warehousing, transportation, and business communications. Human efforts devoted to commerce are enormous; in the United

States, for example, more than a third of the labor force was engaged in commerce in 1980, and the sector had been growing rapidly for decades.

All components of commerce depend heavily on information. Many of the advances in information technology, starting with the development of WRIT-ING, have been made in response to commercial needs. In particular, the computer has had and will continue to have a major impact on how commercial activities are conducted. To understand the impact of the computer on commerce, it is useful to consider three characteristics of commerce: standardization, regulation, and intermediaries.

Standardization. The need for agreement among related businesses and for the development of standards has an important influence on the use of technology; in fact, it almost always delays the introduction of new technologies until long after the technologies have become available in practical form. A good example of the issue of standardization in commerce is the commonly used service offered by banks—the checking account. Checks became a widespread and reliable means for making and receiving payments only after agreements were reached, and supported by law and regulation, concerning obligations and liabilities with regard to checks for which inadequate payer funds were available and concerning procedures for prompt processing of checks from the bank of deposit to the payer's bank. Modern check processing by computer required still further agreements, this time in order to establish STANDARDS for Magnetic Ink Character Recognition (MICR) machine-readable codes. (These codes were to be imprinted on all checks to identify the account on which the check was drawn and the bank at which this account was located.) The overall process took almost fifteen years. However, the development of the standard code for MICR also provided a basis for automating all demand deposit (e.g., checking) accounts and offered a starting point for the introduction of computerized teller support systems and automatic teller machines. Later, similar codes were used with a different code system imprinted on debit cards. Through terminals located at retail stores, these cards permitted payments for goods to be made by instantaneous transfer of funds from a purchaser's bank account to the store's. The same codes were again employed as a nationwide bank-at-home system was evolving.

Similar needs for standardization can be found in many other areas of commerce. One example is the development of Universal Product Code (UPC) bar coding on food items to permit use of automatic checkout equipment. Its adoption required cooperation among a number of different industry associations. More complicated was the introduction of large-scale containerization in maritime operations.

This required the development of physical standards for the containers themselves and a host of agreements among the many parties involved (shippers, freight forwarders, overland carriers, insurance companies, longshoremen, customs brokers, shipping lines, and various regulatory agencies), as well as the availability of modern computers, before the innovation could become practical.

A somewhat different approach to establishing compatibility among participants is to focus on the communications link. In 1980 the U.S. grocery industry followed this path by adopting Electronic Data Interchange (EDI) standards for industrywide ordering and shipment advisory activities. Individual participants then either implemented the same standards for internal use or built computer software interfaces between their internal systems and the communications standards. The Transportation Data Coordinating Committee (TDCC) has been active in this field for many years, and the approach is likely to be followed by other industry groups.

Regulation. Throughout history governments have both regulated commerce and facilitated its development. The regulation of commerce has had a significant impact on decisions to implement new, computer-assisted technologies. These effects are particularly pronounced when regulation is combined with government subsidies or when tax benefits are granted. An example of the influence subsidies can exert is illustrated in U.S. maritime operations. For many years subsidies were provided to balance the relative costs of U.S. and foreign crews. This subsidy removed the incentives for introducing more automated ship control and handling equipment, which would have been a more farsighted economic path to have followed. *See* GOVERNMENT REGULATION.

Price regulation also has implications for the introduction of new technologies. For example, it will favor use of technology for cost reduction purposes, since the financial returns from cost savings can be made very rapidly in a price-regulated industry. Regulator attitudes toward depreciation policy also affect the ability of technologically based industries to install improved versions of equipment rapidly, and tax treatment of depreciation can have similar results. At the same time, the deregulation of both banks and telecommunications in the United States arose in part because the growth of new, largely computer-based technologies permitted businesses to bypass and render ineffective the government regulation of these activities.

Intermediaries. Commerce is replete with intermediaries engaged in providing information services and other types of interaction between participants. The entire investment community, and much of the operations of banking and insurance, are devoted to providing highly structured intermediaries for those

Figure 1. *(Computer: Impact—Impact on Commerce)* Examples of Universal Product Code (UPC) bar coding.

who wish to exchange properties and money. Computer technology is a powerful factor in changing the role of these intermediaries and in some cases bypassing them entirely. Large investors make use of computer-based systems for trading blocks of stocks, which reduces the role of brokerage firms. Individuals and corporate travel offices bypass travel agents by using computer systems to order air travel tickets directly from airlines. More and more, the two parties involved in commercial transactions deal directly with each other, rather than operating through a series of intermediaries. And most of these changes have been made practical by the introduction of computers and improved communications. At the same time, the need for increased information to support the ability of parties to deal directly with one another has grown dramatically; here again, the computer provides solutions. As a result, information services and information brokerage have expanded rapidly.

Evolution of computer uses. Commercial organizations were often the pioneers in adopting the new computer technology. Four overlapping phases characterized the process:

1. *Batch record storage and manipulation.* These systems were installed in the mid-1950s and dealt primarily with bookkeeping operations and the production of transaction records such as bills and invoices. Usually the operations were not unlike the early punched-card systems, although key-to-tape input was adopted rapidly once it became available. In large installations the batch operations acquired many of the characteristics of continuous-flow operations. By the early 1980s, batch recordkeeping and transaction systems were in use in essentially all medium-size and larger businesses. Very small businesses, employing fewer than twenty people, were dependent on service bureaus or continued to use manual systems until the introduction of low-cost microcomputers. With microcomputers, even the smallest companies could conduct their own computing operations, although penetration was slow until appropriate software became available.

2. *Real-time transaction systems.* Far more relevant to the needs of commercial enterprises was the introduction of real-time transaction systems, which started in 1963 with the first commercial airline reservation system. Computer technology facilitated the rapid growth of airline operations during the 1960s and 1970s, since the earlier semiautomatic reservation systems simply could not have handled the massive increase in passengers. Automated airline reservations led in due course to automated ticketing and seat selection. The availability of reservation systems was expanded from airlines to hotels, theatrical and sporting events, automobile rental, and a host of other activities. The on-line techniques also moved into the financial industries and mail-order organizations, making on-line inquiry and automated ordering services easier and quicker to conduct. This phase of computer applications was largely completed early in the mid-1980s. More importantly, it laid the groundwork for the third phase—user-input transaction processing.

3. *Direct user transaction systems.* This activity was still in an early growth period in the 1980s. For businesses a typical application was the cash management system provided by banks that permitted business customers to enter directly instructions for the movement of funds from one account to another. For consumers debit cards provided a related type of service. Numerous information service companies offered individuals opportunities to inquire about prices and then order a wide variety of goods and information services, and to make airline and other reservations directly through their own computers. Bank-at-home systems began to make it practical to eliminate check writing and directly enter instructions for the conduct of a large number of household financial transactions. Existing direct user transaction systems bypassed numerous intermediaries. Some of these were independent operators, such as travel agents; others were members of the labor force of, for example, financial institutions, such as bank personnel who previously processed checks.

4. *Advanced decision support processes.* This development phase, which emerged in the mid-1980s, was based on the application of ARTIFICIAL INTELLIGENCE techniques to the problems of commercial organizations. While not the first pri-

vate-sector users of artificial intelligence, financial institutions were leaders in the development or purchase of early applications. Attention initially was focused on financial planning, portfolio management, loan analysis, and some types of trading operations. Not far behind were applications in the communications and transportation sectors, such as diagnosis of pending equipment failures or causes of actual failures, support of complex scheduling problems, and design of complex equipment configurations.

In contrast to many of the applications described earlier, the advanced decision support phase was limited more by technology than by the constraints of standardization or regulation. Artificial intelligence efforts were devoted mainly to systems that could be used within a single company, as tools of competition, rather than to those requiring some form of industrywide adoption. In the long run, the major limitations of these systems are likely to be technological—until new types of computer and software architectures can deal with greater complexity and with many more subject areas—and management-related, since management structures will require changes to employ effectively more of the available total corporate knowledge.

The computer has come a long way in commerce. Its capabilities have been used to lower costs, improve quality, increase capacity, speed transactions, and contribute to the development of a global economy. As its capabilities grow and are spread more widely, computer technology will continue to exert a major influence on this key economic area.

See also COMPUTER: HISTORY; COMPUTER: IMPACT—OVERVIEW; COMPUTER: IMPACT—IMPACT ON GOVERNMENT; COMPUTER: IMPACT—IMPACT ON THE WORLD ECONOMY; DATA BASE; ORGANIZATIONAL COMMUNICATION.

Bibliography. James L. Heskett, "Sweeping Changes in Distribution," *Harvard Business Review* 51 (1973): 123–132; Arthur D. Little, Inc., *The Consequences of Electronic Funds Transfer: A Technology Assessment of Movement toward a Less Cash/Less Check Society*, prep. for the National Science Foundation, Research Applied to National Needs (RANN), Washington, D.C., 1975; idem, *The Relationship between Market Structure and the Innovation Process*, prep. for American Telephone and Telegraph Co., under the direction of Gordon Raisbeck with the assistance of Mark Schupack, Cambridge, Mass., 1976 (filed April 8, 1976, FCC Docket 20003, Bell exhibit 52); John H. Mahoney, *Intermodal Freight Transportation*, Westport, Conn., 1985; James Martin, *The Wired Society*, Englewood Cliffs, N.J., 1978; National Transportation Policy Study Commission, *National Transportation Policies through the Year 2000*, Washington, D.C., 1979.

MARTIN L. ERNST

6. IMPACT ON THE WORK FORCE

Computerization differs in several ways from earlier phases of automation. In the first place, it involves the substitution of machinery for human mental as well as physical labor. Second, before the development of computers, machines could normally perform only one fixed sequence of operations. Computers and computerized equipment, on the other hand, can be programmed to perform a variety of tasks. During the nineteenth and early twentieth centuries the mechanization of work usually meant that jobs had to be broken down into a number of separate tasks, each performed by a different group of workers using a different machine. With computer-based automation, and particularly with the growing use of integrated computer-communications networks, this process is reversed, and a single computerized system can be used to control a complex series of diverse activities. *See* COMPUTER: HISTORY.

The role of computers in the workplace. Computers have transformed many types of work. In the first stage of computer applications beginning in the 1950s, factory computerization took three main forms: process automation, numerical control (NC), and the use of robots. In process automation, computers were used to monitor crucial variables in the production process, such as the volume and flow of raw materials and temperature changes. Numerical control refers to methods of controlling the operations of machine tools by means of numerical programs, which developed in the early 1950s. The 1970s saw the rapid diffusion of a more sophisticated version of this system, computer numerical control (CNC), whereby the machine tools are directly connected to a computer that stores several programs. Robots were introduced into industry in the first half of the 1960s. They are widely used in tasks such as welding and spray painting. Although earlier versions were sometimes programmed in other ways, by the late 1970s virtually all robots were computer-controlled.

The second stage of factory automation began in the mid-1970s and emphasized the use of computer and communications technology to create integrated productive systems. One example is the flexible manufacturing system (FMS), in which various types of computer-controlled machinery are linked together into a hierarchy whose apex is a central computer, which communicates to and receives information from all parts of the factory.

In the office, as in the factory, there has been a trend from the computerization of individual activities toward the creation of integrated computer-communications networks serving many needs. In the 1950s and early 1960s the use of computers was most widespread in areas such as scientific research and the processing of large amounts of standardized data (payrolls, censuses, etc.). The growing use in

Figure 1. *(Computer: Impact—Impact on the Work Force)* At a refinery in Rotterdam, ST 3000 smart transmitters accurately measure and control process flow, liquid level, and pressure. Courtesy of Honeywell, Inc.

the 1970s of mini- and microcomputers and the development of new applications (e.g., word processing) led to the increasing computerization of routine office work. Technical and managerial work was also affected by the introduction of applications such as computer-aided design (CAD) and management information systems (MIS). At the same time there was growing interest in the development of total computerized office systems. By the first half of the 1980s communications developments such as the local area network (LAN) were making it possible for a small but increasing number of offices to introduce such systems, in which many forms of information could be both processed and communicated from one part of the office to another.

Integrated computer-communications systems have not only appeared within the factory and the office. By the 1980s they were also beginning to link factory and office together. In a U.S. communications equipment company, for example, new designs from the research laboratory were transmitted directly to a computer in the factory, which calculated manufacturing specifications and conveyed them to minicomputers controlling the factory's automated machine tools. This type of system is called computer-integrated manufacturing (CIM).

Since computers connect workplaces with one another, they have the potential to change the spatial distribution of employment. They even make it possible for some employees to work at home using terminals linked to a central computer. In 1984 one British firm employed 850 computer-service workers, 80 percent of whom worked from home.

Computers and the quality of work. There can be no doubt that these developments have radically altered the nature of many occupations. There is debate, however, about whether computerization improved or degraded the quality of work. Computers can have both positive and negative effects on work. For example, they may make old skills redundant but may also make new skills necessary. The impact of computers also varies according to the nature of the job and even according to the organizational structure of the factory or office concerned. Surveys in Japan have shown that the use of computerized equipment has both advantages and disadvantages in the eyes of the workers but that the costs and benefits differ depending on the type of equipment used. Electrical-assembly workers and machinists in highly automated plants were found to be more likely than their counterparts in unautomated plants to feel that their work in a computerized setting was important and that it helped them develop new skills, but they were also more likely to feel "used by the machine." In welding, however, the introduction of robots appeared to have a predominantly negative effect on the quality of work. Welders in robotized factories were more likely than others to feel that their work was unimportant, low-skilled, and machine-controlled.

As a general rule, factory automation seems to reduce the depth of skill but increase its breadth: demand for specialized manual skills in occupations such as welding, painting, and machining decreases, while the amount of nonmanual supervisory work such as checking machines and reading dials expands. When integrated computer-control systems are introduced, the workers responsible for operating the systems are usually able to obtain a broader overview of the operations of their factory than nonautomated-factory workers, who are more often involved in only one part of the productive process.

In the office the impact of computerization is rather different. Secretarial and clerical work has traditionally been more varied than factory work. One U.S. study suggests that as little as 2 percent of the average working day of general secretarial staff may be devoted to typing. The remainder is spent photocopying, carrying messages, filing, taking dictation, and so on. With the emergence of integrated office information systems, several of these functions (typing, communicating messages, filing, copying documents) can be transferred onto the computer. As a result, while efficiency increases, variety is likely to decrease. The amount of general office work is reduced, and the amount of keyboard work expands.

For managerial and technical workers computerization offers easier access to data and may reduce dependence on the help of secretarial and clerical staff. The trend is likely to increase with the development of computers that are capable of effective voice recognition. As much as 85 percent of the working time of managers and administrators is spent communicating written and spoken information. Computer networks and teleconferencing systems, which speed flows of information between offices and reduce the need for travel to meetings, have great potential to enhance managerial productivity. As communication flows improve and management-related software standardizes various administrative tasks, patterns of decision making within the managerial hierarchy will also change. Some studies suggest that higher-level planning functions will become increasingly centralized, and certain lower-level routine decision-making tasks will be decentralized.

The changing structure of employment. Computerization has resulted in the disappearance of some jobs and the creation of others. Because computers can store human knowledge about methods of performing particular tasks and can use this information to control machinery, their introduction tends to reduce the need for direct manufacturing labor and to increase the amount of labor directed to the creation of knowledge (research, planning, design, engineering, programming, etc.). An analysis of the cost of a typical U.S. batch-manufactured product in the early 1980s showed that direct manufacturing labor costs accounted for a mere 5 percent, while engineering costs accounted for 15 percent, of the total sales price. Computer-integrated manufacturing makes it possible for companies to change the design of their products more rapidly. As a result, the share of the work force engaged in research, design, and planning is likely to increase still more in the future.

Many of the occupations whose decline can be directly attributed to the computer are skilled manual jobs, and the occupations created by computerization are mostly in the area of knowledge production. Both trends can be seen in the Japanese machine tool industry. In this industry between 1977 and 1980 production expanded and planning and research staff increased, but the number of manufacturing jobs fell by an estimated 4.8 percent. The assembly of computerized equipment often requires less labor than the production of older types of mechanical equipment. In the Federal Republic of Germany the manufacture of office and data-processing machinery grew rapidly from 1970 to 1977, but employment in the industry fell by more than twenty thousand. Although the production of computer hardware did not create much employment, software production was a major source of job creation. Between 1960 and 1985 the number of computer-programming jobs in the United States increased by about three hundred thousand.

Many people believe, therefore, that computerization is a reason for the proportional decline of manufacturing employment and the increase of information-sector employment in developed countries. By 1980 it was estimated that almost half of the U.S. work force was employed in information-related occupations and that the figure in most developed nations was more than one-third.

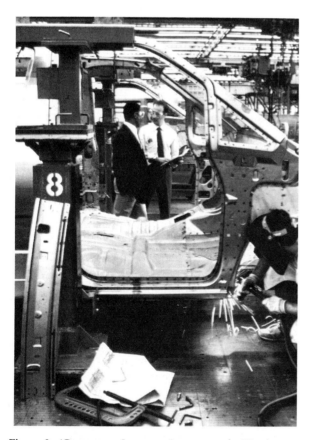

Figure 2. *(Computer: Impact—Impact on the Work Force)* At a large automobile plant in the United States, a computer system simplifies the engineering process. Courtesy of Honeywell, Inc.

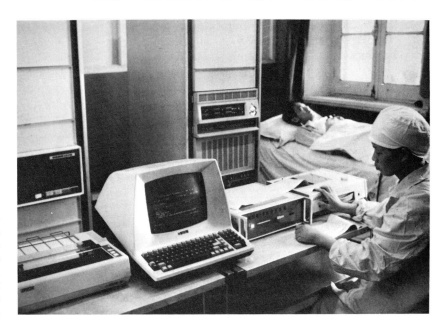

Figure 3. *(Computer: Impact—Impact on the Work Force)* The "XZY-1 Computerized Diagnosis System of Electrocardiogram," developed at Wuhan City, Hubei Province, People's Republic of China, being put to clinical use in 1983. The Bettmann Archive, Inc.

But computers have not encouraged the growth of all types of information work. The development of simpler programming methods and more effective computer-communications networks reduces the amount of human labor involved in the transmission and routine processing of data. In banking, for example, the introduction of computer networks has been associated in many countries with a decline in the number of bank tellers. The spread of computerized office information systems is also likely to reduce demand for secretarial and clerical skills.

Some analysts predict that if the automation of relatively routine information-related jobs continues, the work force could become polarized between well-paid, highly educated information producers on the one hand and, on the other, people employed in the lower-paid personal service jobs that have not yet been greatly affected by automation.

Computers and unemployment. Do computers destroy more jobs than they create? In 1950 NORBERT WIENER, the originator of CYBERNETICS, prophesied that computerization would have effects far more serious than those of the Great Depression, and ever since then the idea of computer-generated unemployment has been a source of widespread concern. In the late 1970s, when computer usage multiplied manyfold, most developed countries experienced unusually high levels of unemployment, but it is not possible to trace a simple or direct connection between the two phenomena. Attempts to balance the job losses and job gains directly connected with computerization have failed to show that computers are a major source of unemployment. A study conducted in Great Britain in the first half of the 1980s suggested that only about 5 percent of job losses in

manufacturing were directly attributable to new technologies. In Japan a similar survey estimated that between 1977 and 1982 about 180,000 jobs had been lost through the introduction of robots and NC equipment, while some 176,000 new jobs had been generated in the production of computerized equipment and software.

The employment implications of computerization cannot be precisely measured because there are many indirect effects to be taken into consideration. For example, if the new computer-related jobs were well paid, the workers in these occupations would help to create new employment by spending their incomes on various goods and services. On the other hand, information-related jobs generally require skills that redundant blue-collar workers do not possess. In the absence of suitable EDUCATION policies there is a danger of a mismatch of skills, with redundant workers existing side by side with unfilled vacancies in expanding occupations. Furthermore, the impact of computers is not confined by national borders. When one country adapts to a new technology more successfully than others, it may reap the employment benefits of computerization while its trading rivals suffer job losses. This problem is of great concern to many less developed countries whose industries rely heavily on labor-intensive production techniques and who are vulnerable to competition from the highly computerized corporations of the developed world. Efficient computer communications also mean that information used in one country can be processed overseas. This again is likely to result in a concentration of job creation in information-rich countries (*see* NEW INTERNATIONAL INFORMATION ORDER).

Dire predictions of computer-generated unemployment have proved incorrect. However, computers do reduce the amount of labor needed to produce a given quantity of goods or information. In the future, unless high rates of growth prevail, this may cause a reduction in demand for human labor. Whether the result is increased LEISURE or increased unemployment will depend on the economic and social choices of individuals and societies.

See also AGENDA-SETTING.

Bibliography. Robert Blauner, *Alienation and Freedom,* Chicago and London, 1964; Harry Braverman, *Labor and Monopoly Capital,* New York and London, 1974; Tom Forester, ed., *The Information Technology Revolution,* Cambridge, Mass., 1985; Barry O. Jones, *Sleepers, Wake! Technology and the Future of Work,* New York and Melbourne, 1982; Koyō Sokushin Jigyōdan Shokugyō Kunren Kenkyū Sentā, *Mekatoronikusu Jidai no Jinzai Kaihatsu* (The Development of Human Resources in the Mechatronics Age), Tokyo, 1983; Mitchell L. Moss, ed., *Telecommunications and Productivity,* Reading, Mass., 1981; Simon Nora and Alain Minc, *L'informatisation de la société,* Paris, 1978 (The Computerization of Society, Cambridge, Mass., 1980); Organisation for Economic Co-operation and Development, *Information Activities, Electronics and Telecommunications Technologies: Impact on Employment, Growth and Trade,* Paris, 1981; Diane Werneke, *Microelectronics and Office Jobs,* Geneva, 1983.

TESSA MORRIS-SUZUKI

7. IMPACT ON THE WORLD ECONOMY

After World War II the world economy moved rapidly into increasingly dense electronic relationships in which the computer, linked with television, cable, SATELLITE, VIDEO, and other new technologies, played an increasingly prominent role. The effects of computerization and the new information technologies on the world economy were complex and uneven. Important questions raised by these effects concern the degree to which the introduction of these technologies helped bring about a more equitable balance among nations and peoples or reinforced earlier inequitable relationships. *See* CABLE TELEVISION; TELEVISION HISTORY.

Structure of the world economy. The introduction of computer technology occurred unevenly across the globe. An important cause of these regional variations was the complex and contradictory organization of the world economy—that is, its division into organizational and decision-making systems that affect the introduction of any new product or technology on a global scale. On the one hand there is the very visible system of nation-states. On the other there is the world business system, composed of several thousand transnational corporations, each located in more than one country and engaged in billions of global economic transactions. This world business system has been responsible for a large and growing share of world economic activity.

In addition to the major division of the world economy into more or less sovereign political states and powerful private economic units, there are innumerable other entities, all of which affect developments in the world economy. Among these—and perhaps the most influential—are the intergovernmental agencies such as the United Nations, UNESCO, the World Health Organization, the Law of the Sea Conference, and the International Telecommunications Union (*see* INTERNATIONAL ORGANIZATIONS). There are also nongovernmental groups representing professional organizations and special interests such as consumers, women, labor, lawyers, and librarians. Finally, there are millions of individuals who enter into international activities such as TOURISM; these individuals constitute a diffuse but by no means negligible force in the world economy.

Since the early 1960s, when the new instrumentation began to be available on a large scale, the initiative in promoting the new equipment and processes was exercised by the transnational corporate system and, more precisely, by individual companies within that order. With the considerable assistance and encouragement of government in matters of funding research and development and promulgating supportive legal arrangements, national and international networks and communication infrastructures were created as the transnational firms installed and applied the new instrumentation and processes to their daily business on a truly global scale. As a result a huge and growing volume of data in electronic form flowed through intercontinental and national circuits, constituting the so-called transborder data flow. Its major components are records of financial transactions, production and resource information, tax and fiscal data, and personnel and individual records.

Complementing the private networks of data transmission were the global electronic connections that enabled national military systems to maintain a worldwide presence. A high-technology information industry came to be viewed not only as a basis for major industrial growth but at the same time as an essential component of military power and influence (see section 2, above).

Deregulation. A related and key development from the end of World War II on—largely an outcome of the enormously strengthened transnational business system evolving during this period—was the movement toward deregulation. Originating in the United States and extending rapidly to western Europe and elsewhere, deregulation meant the comprehensive reduction of the size and scope of publicly administered functions such as the POSTAL SERVICE, transport, communication, health, EDUCATION, and an ever-widening number of economic activities. This process was accompanied by privatization, in which vital activities were transferred from the public sphere to private ownership and direction. Public and state-managed enterprises—PTTs (government agencies administering postal, telegraph, and TELEPHONE services), broadcasting systems, and communication facilities—were thus reduced while private electronic networks were established and strengthened. The main users of these new private networks and the information they supplied were the transnational companies and the military.

International division of labor. All of these related developments—the greatly expanded power of the transnational corporations, the development of advanced information technology, and the spread of deregulation—had important consequences for the structure of the world economy and particularly for the labor force in various countries. The economic importance and implications of the new information industries led to a long-term global rearrangement, a worldwide redistribution of industrial manufacturing, which placed serious burdens on many workers, including job loss and dislocation as a result of these larger developments. The resulting shifts constituted a new international division of labor.

It is important to note that while the new division of labor clearly resulted from many independent decisions by a large number of people, it was not a random or accidental process. It reflected the widely held view that optimal benefits occur when each nation exchanges what it produces most advantageously. Thus the most developed countries were producing electronic technology and developing processed information goods and services while the rest of the world was turning to older forms of industrialization.

Techniques such as remote sensing by satellites and complex information processing of the secured data have afforded new kinds of power on a global scale. Older mechanisms of global influence—control of capital flows, deployment of armed forces, political PERSUASION and coercion—hardly disappeared. But they were significantly supplemented by the new powers of information organization and control.

The less industrialized nations were by no means denied the new technologies. On the contrary, the installation of advanced communication technology in as many places as possible, as rapidly as possible, seemed to serve the purposes of developed and developing societies alike. But these were served differently. As exports of information hardware and information-processing services flowed out of the centers of high technology, data flowed in, were processed, and returned to the international information current as U.S. or other Western products.

In the 1980s the United States was the world's leading importer and exporter of information technology and data.

To a large extent the drives stemming from developing societies for a new economic order and a new information order were successfully diverted by the transnational corporate system. Production in conventional goods and services was transferred worldwide to sites with impoverished workers, tax exemptions, and cooperative governments, creating new centers of industrial activity in far-flung locations. At the same time information industries became central bases of economic activity in the regions that had been the first to industrialize. That a new economic order and a new information order were unfolding was clear. But the rise and diffusion of the new technologies, in ways that involved new inequities, compounded existing inequalities and generated resistance. The resistance seemed certain to persist, manifesting itself in diverse arenas (*see* NEW INTERNATIONAL INFORMATION ORDER; SPECTRUM).

The use of computers in the world economy has been and will continue to be affected by the major social movements of the times. These remain the global quest for meaningful national independence and, equally, a near-universal striving for both material improvement and greater social equity within national boundaries. The extent to which computerization is applied to the implementation of these aspirations will depend on the shape of evolving structures, national and international, in the world economy.

Future issues. The transcendent issue revolves around priorities to be assigned to the usage of the new technologies. For example, it has been taken for granted that the densest communication networks should be those between the most advanced market economies. However, another approach might be based on social need. This could lead to a very different global disposition of computerization and telecommunications facilities. The conflict is also one between private and international decision making, a conflict involving many intractable issues.

Bibliography. *Communications, Computing and Global Development* (special issue), *InterMedia* 12, nos. 4–5, 1984; Wilson P. Dizard, *The Coming Information Age*, New York, 1982; Oswald H. Ganley and Gladys D. Ganley, *To Inform or to Control: The New Communications Network*, New York, 1982; George Gerbner and Marsha Siefert, eds., *World Communications: A Handbook*, New York, 1984; Robert W. Haigh, George Gerbner, and Richard B. Byrne, eds., *Communications in the Twenty-first Century*, New York, 1981; Cees J. Hamelink, *Finance and Information*, Norwood, N.J., 1983; Intergovernmental Bureau for Informatics (IBI), publications and proceedings, Rome, 1961–; Armand Mattelart, *Multinational Corpora-*

400 / CONFUCIUS

tions and the Control of Culture: The Ideological Apparatuses of Imperialism, Sussex, Eng., 1979; Dan Schiller,
Telematics and Government, Norwood, N.J., 1982; Herbert I. Schiller, Information and the Crisis Economy, Norwood, N.J., 1984; idem, Who Knows: Information in the
Age of the Fortune 500, Norwood, N.J., 1981; Anthony
Smith, The Geopolitics of Information: How Western Culture Dominates the World, New York, 1980; Transnational Data Report (TDR), Vols. 1–7, Amsterdam, 1978–;
United Nations Centre on Transnational Corporations,
publications, New York, 1977–.

HERBERT I. SCHILLER

CONFUCIUS (ca. 551–479 B.C.E.)

Chinese philosopher whose name and ideas (or supposed ideas) have been a constant presence in Chinese
communications since ancient times. His prestige has
been such that his name was constantly invoked as
an accepted point of reference for correct action in
such diverse fields as governing, EDUCATION, the arts,
and DIPLOMACY. It served as a kind of ideological
continuum, a powerful unifying factor. His status
has been under attack at various times but remains
an extraordinary phenomenon of Chinese life. See
EAST ASIA, ANCIENT.

His real name was Kong Qiu. The name Confucius
is the latinized form of Kong Fuzi ("Master Kong").
He was born in the state of Lu (now Shandong
Province) at a time when China was a congeries of
contending feudal states. Member of a noble but
impoverished clan, he received a good education and
became an itinerant teacher. His fame spread as a
man of learning and upright character, and disciples
recorded his teachings. In response to the incessant
strife and lawlessness of his time Confucius developed the concept of ren, the righteous way in personal conduct and social relations. He taught not a
religious but an ethical code of conduct as a way to
overcome the evils of society.

Confucius had a chance to put his theories into
practice when at the age of fifty he was appointed
the state of Lu's minister for crime. His administration apparently helped to restore order, and Lu became strong and prosperous. Later enemies brought
about his dismissal, and in 496 B.C.E. Confucius
again became a traveling teacher seeking a ruler who
would share his ideas. Returning to Lu in retirement,
he wrote commentaries on the classics until his death.

Confucianism as we know it today is the product
of the development of his ideas by notable disciples
such as Mencius (Meng Zi, ca. 390–ca. 305 B.C.E.)
and Xun Zi (ca. 298–ca. 230 B.C.E.) and the neo-
Confucianist Zhu Xi (1130–1200 C.E.). The basic
texts of Confucianism are known as the Five Classics:
Yi jing (Book of Changes), Shu jing (Book of History), Shi jing (Book of Poetry), Li ji (Book of Rites),

Figure 1. *(Confucius)* Confucius. Stone rubbing from a
relief after a painting by Tang Dynasty artist Wu Tao-
tzu. Courtesy, Museum of Fine Arts, Boston.

and Chun qiu (Spring and Autumn Annals), edited
by Confucius; and the Four Books: the Lun yu
(Analects); the Da xue (Great Learning); the Zhong
yong (Doctrine of the Mean), collections of his say-
ings with commentaries by his disciples; and the
Meng Zi (Book of Mencius), an exposition of Confucius's teachings by his most illustrious follower.
These volumes present Confucius's philosophical, so-

cial, political, and ethical precepts. He believed the turmoil of his time could be checked if rulers provided compelling examples of worthy living and people followed the path of righteous conduct; that if right relations were not established among the basic elements of society—in families and between people and government—the basic structure of society would not be sound. The ethical teachings of Confucius stress the virtues of *ren* (benevolence, love of humankind), *yi* (integrity), *xiao* (filial piety), *li* (decorum, proper behavior), *shu* (charity), and *chung* (loyalty) and include his version of the Golden Rule: "Do not do unto others what you do not wish to be done to yourself." Mencius underscored the duty of a ruler to care for the people or risk being deposed. The facility of the immediate and later followers of Confucius in adapting his basic ideas to current needs helped to assure their long-lasting influence.

The Confucian classics were the basic texts in education in the centralized Chinese feudal empires from the third century B.C.E. to the republican revolution of 1911. Success in the imperial civil service examinations was the gateway to an official career, and success demanded proficiency in the Confucian classics. But the teachings of Confucianism proved inadequate when China was invaded by the modern, industrialized world in the mid-nineteenth century. Progressive intellectuals of the twentieth century (*see* ASIA, TWENTIETH CENTURY) saw exclusive reliance on the Confucian classics as a cause of the nation's decline and opened modern schools to teach science and democratic ideals.

During Mao Zedong's Cultural Revolution, Confucius was vilified as never before as a proponent of slavery, but later his statues and memorial temples were restored. While the quasi-religious veneration once accorded him has ended, the influence of his ethical teachings remains pervasive in Chinese life.

Bibliography. William T. De Bary, Wing-tsit Chan, and Burton Watson, *Sources of Chinese Tradition*, New York, 1960; Jack Chen, *Inside the Cultural Revolution*, New York, 1975; Confucius, *The Analects*, ed. by William Edward Soothill, New York (reprint of 1910 ed., Shansi), 1968; Yang Jung-kuo, ed., *Selected Articles: Criticizing Lin Piao and Confucius*, Beijing, 1974.

JACK CHEN

CONSUMER RESEARCH

Advertisers study the consumer in four ways, starting with (1) introspection, and proceeding to analysis of observed consumer behavior with (2) segmentation, (3) analysis of attitude structures, and (4) analysis of decision processes. Campaign planners do this research to assess the soundness of alternative communication strategies.

Introspection. ADVERTISING planners start with introspection because they realize that they themselves are consumers. Studies have shown that advertising executives' introspections about their own consumer behavior are more accurate predictors of actual consumer behavior than are those same executives' guesses about consumer behavior. This does not mean that introspection can be used as a total research program. It does mean, however, that introspection can provide a realistic beginning to a program of research on consumers.

Planners and researchers invoke introspection by using the product themselves and asking themselves a series of questions about their personal relationship to the product. Over and over again, creative people in advertising talk about how their own experiences trigger ideas. These kinds of experiences come from the introspection stage.

Segmentation. Effective advertising campaigns are targeted at specific population segments. Researchers look for those segments that are most likely to respond to advertising. A segment is a grouping of people defined by certain socioeconomic, demographic, psychological, or usage characteristics. Such groups may be highly homogeneous internally and quite different from other groups or segments.

Advertisers need to identify segments carefully because this allows them to allocate resources efficiently to particular campaign strategies and media. The resource allocation involves assigning particular messages to media vehicles that are known to reach certain groups or segments of consumers efficiently. It is never possible to direct a campaign to a particular audience segment with complete efficiency (i.e., reaching only people in the segment). Therefore, knowledge about the characteristics of a segment allows construction of messages that will attract that particular segment, which will then self-select the campaign's message.

It is important to distinguish between consumer segments and publics on the one hand and marketing segments on the other. Publics are large groups of people who may or may not actually buy or use the marketing offering but may affect and be affected by the communicating organization. Public sector marketing organizations and advertisers doing corporate campaigns are most concerned with publics (*see* PUBLIC RELATIONS).

Marketing segments are groupings of distribution organizations, such as retailers or wholesalers, that demand different types of marketing and advertising programs. Marketing segmentation almost always follows a concern with segmentation of the consumer population.

There is a wide variety of segment descriptors. Researchers segment on the basis of geographic, socioeconomic, personality, benefits, product usage, and brand loyalty descriptors. The dilemma is that while brand loyalty segmenting is the most useful and sensitive, data relating to it are the least accessible and applicable, particularly in terms of resource allocation. On the other hand, geographic and socioeconomic data are quite accessible for campaign resource allocation purposes but less useful and sensitive in terms of actual consumer response.

There are several solutions to this dilemma. First, there are research services that give product usage and brand loyalty data by media exposure. Second, advertisers can use psychographics, a combined use of all the types of descriptors, to get a detailed insight about the type of person in the target segment (*see* MOTIVATION RESEARCH). Psychographics concentrates on the personality and benefit segment descriptors, and begins with long questionnaires asking about psychological variables such as ATTITUDES, interests, and opinions. Other types of variables are also measured to give accurate and lifelike pictures of people for communication planning. A third solution to the segmentation problem is attitude structure analysis (described below), which is used for various usage and loyalty segments.

Advertising researchers have found that segment response to advertising is critically related to three factors: motivation, ability, and opportunity. Motivation is the degree to which a consumer segment considers it important to make the right choice in the product category. This is sometimes called product category involvement. Ability is the amount of awareness and experience the consumer has with the product or service to be advertised. Opportunity relates to where consumers get their information. Print media, for instance, give more opportunity for deep processing of messages than do broadcast media such as television. When motivation, ability, and opportunity are high, consumers are likely to experience each individual advertising exposure at a deeper level.

While there are as many segmenting strategies as there are advertising campaigns, the most typical situation is characterized by three segment types: those favorable to the advertiser's message, those opposed to the message, and those who are neutral. Planners usually attempt to maintain the favorable segments, avoid those opposed, and concentrate on those with potential for favorable shift.

Attitude structure analysis. Once segments are discovered and understood in an intimate and significant way, it is important to understand how people in each segment think specifically about the problems and market offerings. At this stage advertisers want to know what is in their key prospects' minds.

Attitude structure analysis requires data on four consumer factors: (1) the product characteristics or attributes considered by the key segment to be sig-

nificant, (2) the relative importance attached to each attribute by consumer prospects, (3) perceptions of the advertised brand on each attribute, and (4) perceptions of each competitive brand on each attribute. Once these four factors are determined, it is possible to develop a matrix showing consumer perceptions.

These data can be developed first by introspection and then in an exploratory way by using focus groups of individuals from the target segment, brought together to interact and discuss the market offering. Once salient product characteristics are determined in a provisional way by focus groups, it is possible to determine perceptions more precisely by other techniques such as interview and questionnaire research, in which consumers' perceptions are determined by their ratings of the relative characteristics of various market offerings.

This research allows the advertiser at least six positioning strategies. The first strategy would be to attempt to change consumer goals and events related to the whole product class (e.g., the "frequent flyer" bonus programs offered by many airlines). With the second strategy, advertisers would attempt to make salient a product characteristic or attribute that previously was not considered by consumers (e.g., new television sets that are cable-ready or can also be used as computer monitors). The third strategy involves altering the perception of product characteristics already considered by consumers. This could be done either by increasing the importance or salience of attributes or by changing the range of acceptable product attributes (e.g., pharmaceutical products packaged in more than one way for greater consumer convenience, such as pain relievers available in various forms). The fourth strategy is the one most often used in advertising. With it, advertisers attempt to change perceptions of their market offering—usually trying to improve the perception of one or more attributes, sometimes attempting to improve perceptions of the brand in general without regard to particular attributes (often called image advertising; e.g., a brand of toothpaste that claims endorsement from a majority of dentists). The fifth possible strategy recognizes that no brand or market offering is an island unto itself. Therefore, this strategy is an attempt to change perceptions of competing brands. Although all strategies are formed in relation to competition, this one most specifically addresses that issue (e.g., by including tables comparing products and their features, companies and the services they offer, etc.). Finally, when advertisers use the sixth possible strategy they attempt to change the way consumers use their perceptions to make decisions about products and brands. For instance, if the advertiser finds that the product is strong on one important attribute but relatively weak on others, the advertising could suggest that consumers make decisions on only that attribute rather than considering all attributes (e.g., trying to sell a car on engine power alone, without mention of cost, safety, energy efficiency, and other features).

Consumer decision process analysis. Once advertisers know their target segments and the perceptions and preferences held by those segments, they can begin to look at the steps consumers go through to make purchase and use decisions for the product, service, or social issue of concern.

The consumer decision process for any advertising situation can be determined by any combination of introspection, archival searches of secondary data (*see* DATA BASE), exploratory research with focus groups, questionnaire research, and computer simulation. Advertisers usually do not have to do extensive research on decision processes, because virtually all consumers go through four steps in a typical decision process; all occur at some time in a consumer's experience with each product, service, or social issue in question. The four common steps are developing need, searching for and comparing alternatives, purchasing, and the postpurchase stage. Advertising is done differently depending on how consumers go through these stages. In some situations—such as buying a home or electronic equipment or making an industrial purchase—consumers consider all four stages quite thoroughly. In other situations, when consumers are making an infrequent but economically unimportant decision, they go through all four stages but not with great intensity. In still other situations the need-development, search, and postpurchase activities are almost nonexistent, and repeated purchases are made almost automatically.

It is possible for the entire target segment to be at a particular stage in the decision process. For new products or products that are new to a segment, for instance, the need-development part of the decision process is most important, and advertising to consumers is done accordingly. For more mature products and consumers with more experience, the stage of searching for and comparing alternatives is most important, and advertising that positions market offerings among competition on the basis of attributes is indicated. When the product battle is in the store or at the sales call, the act of purchasing is most important, and advertising can emphasize prices, specific alternatives, places where the brand can be purchased, and the act of purchasing itself. For many advertising situations the postpurchase stage, in which consumer satisfaction and communication to other consumers about the product are determined, is extremely important. The nature of advertising for this type of situation is to support and augment consumer-use experiences or to suggest ways in which consumers can communicate brand benefits to other consumers—thereby extending the effectiveness of the advertising campaign.

See also COMMERCIALS; MASS MEDIA EFFECTS; OPINION MEASUREMENT.

Bibliography. Leo Bogart, *Strategy in Advertising*, 2d ed., Chicago, 1985; Harold H. Kassarjian and Thomas S. Robertson, *Perspectives in Consumer Behavior*, 3d ed., Glenview, Ill., 1981; Charles Ramond, *Advertising Research: The State of the Art*, New York, 1976; Michael L. Ray, *Advertising and Communication Management*, Englewood Cliffs, N.J., 1982; Leon G. Shiffman and Leslie Lazar Kanuk, *Consumer Behavior*, 2d ed., Englewood Cliffs, N.J., 1983.

MICHAEL L. RAY

CONTENT ANALYSIS

Content analysis is indigenous to communication research and is potentially one of the most important research techniques in the social sciences. It seeks to analyze data within a specific context in view of the meanings someone—a group or a culture—attributes to them. Communications, messages, and symbols differ from observable events, things, properties, or people in that they inform about something other than themselves; they reveal some properties of their distant producers or carriers, and they have cognitive consequences for their senders, their receivers, and the institutions in which their exchange is embedded. Whereas most social research techniques are concerned with observing stimuli and responses, describing manifest behaviors, differentiating individual characteristics, quantifying social conditions and testing hypotheses relating these, content analysis goes outside the immediately observable physical vehicles of communication and relies on their symbolic qualities to trace the antecedents, correlates, or consequences of communications, thus rendering the (unobserved) context of data analyzable. The methodologically critical requirement of any content analysis is to justify the inferential step this involves.

Definition. Formally, content analysis is a research technique for making replicable and valid inferences from data to their context. This definition encompasses those of Bernard Berelson, which equates content analysis with the scientific "description of the . . . content of communication," and of HAROLD D. LASSWELL, which emphasizes the quantification of the "what" that messages communicate. Ole R. Holsti adds such antecedents as the "who" (the source), the "why" (the encoding process), the "how" (the channel), and the consequences or "effects" they have "on whom." Although conventional conceptions of content (what) and communication contexts (who says it to whom) are common in content analysis, the formal definition encompasses other communicative circumstances and contexts, such as psychoanalytical (psychological conditions that explain a particular statement), institutional (socioeconomic interests that underlie a particular television program), and cultural (functions that particular rituals serve).

Data for content analysis. The most obvious sources of data appropriate for content analysis are texts to which meanings are conventionally attributed: verbal discourse, written documents, and visual representations (*see* MEANING). The mass media have been the most prominent source, and the literature is dominated by content analyses of newspapers, magazines, books, RADIO broadcasts, films, comics, and television programming. However, the technique is increasingly applied to data that are less public: personal letters, children's talk, disarmament negotiations, witness accounts in courts, audiovisual records of therapeutic sessions, answers to open-ended interview questions, and computer conferences. Data that are meaningful only to small groups of experts are also considered: postage STAMPS, motifs on ancient pottery, speech disturbances, the wear and tear of books, and dreams. Anything that occurs in sufficient numbers and has reasonably stable meanings for a specific group of people may be subjected to content analysis.

Uses of Content Analysis

Content analysis rarely aims at a literal description of communications content. Examples of exceptions are efforts to determine whether a radio station used obscene language in its broadcasts or to establish the exact phrasing of a politician's campaign commitments. The ability to support inferences that go beyond the unaided understanding of a text is largely due to the systematic treatment of content analysis data. Ordinary readers (including literary scholars) tend to change their perspective as they read through large volumes of material and to be selective in support of their favored hypotheses. Content analysis assures not only that all units of analysis receive equal treatment, whether they are entered at the beginning or at the end of an analysis but also that the process is objective in that it does not matter who performs the analysis or where and when. Moreover, content analysis allows researchers to establish their own context for inquiry, thus opening the door to a rich repertoire of social-scientific constructs by which texts may become meaningful in ways that a culture may not be aware of. Both features enable the content analyst to provide aggregate accounts of inferences from large bodies of data that reveal trends, patterns, and differences no longer obvious to the untrained individual.

Studies of media content. Probably the most widespread use of content analysis is to infer the importance writers, producers, media, or even whole cultures assign to particular subject-matter categories from the frequency or volumes with which such subject matter is mentioned. Early examples are analyses of how the attention by newspapers to particular news categories has changed over time, how advertisements intrude into the coverage of religious matters, and how SPORTS and crime have taken over space from the cultural sphere. Others sought to explain differences among newspapers' attention in terms of ethnicity, readership characteristics, economics, and so on. Many of these studies are motivated by the feeling that journalistic standards are inadequately applied. For example, concerns for fairness are implied in numerous content analyses that aim to show the inequality of the coverage of the two (or more) sides of a public controversy, the imbalance in the favorable and unfavorable treatment of an issue, public figure, or foreign country.

The attention paid to particular phenomena, ideas, or ATTITUDES is the target of many social research efforts. An early content analysis showed how the image of popular heroes in MAGAZINE fiction had changed over a forty-year period from merchant-entrepreneurs to entertainers. Similarly, the images of teachers, scientists, police officers, and important politicians have been studied comparatively, in different media, and over time. A worldwide content analysis of the POLITICAL SYMBOLS in the prestige papers of several countries attempted to discern structural changes in governments and to predict revolutions. Analyses of the demographic, socioeconomic, ethnic, and professional characteristics of the population of television characters yielded considerable biases when compared with corresponding audience characteristics. Longitudinal studies of the kind, magnitude, and frequency of television VIOLENCE, attitudes toward war, the role women assume in popular serials, and arguments used to sell products or services have provided a basis for cultural criticism and have made the public aware of how the mass media may create particular beliefs or reinforce existing prejudices. Content analyses of news sources and references to foreign countries in various national media have demonstrated considerable imbalances in international news flow and attention. Systems for monitoring a corporation's symbolic environment by content analyzing newspaper clippings on issues and public attitudes of interest to that corporation have aided experiments in public relations and signaled significant changes in product perception, corporate image, state of the competition, and so forth.

Evidence provided by content analysis has been presented in U.S. courts in cases of plagiarism and COPYRIGHT violations and in a famous case involving the identity of foreign news bureaus operating in the U.S. Inferences regarding the latter were based on various tests revealing privileged access to information, consistency with stated (foreign) PROPAGANDA aims, and deviations from neutral news sources.

Intelligence gathering and political studies. A government's knowledge about political developments in foreign countries often relies on communications in the form of diplomatic correspondence, foreign broadcasts, journalistic accounts in the domestic press, or speeches made by political leaders not necessarily intended to reveal these developments. Although political analysts typically do not take the time to codify their methods of drawing inferences from such data, there are several examples in which content analysis has provided important insights. Speeches by Soviet Politburo members delivered on the occasion of Joseph Stalin's birthday revealed the power structure within the Politburo and shed light on the anticipated succession to power (substantiated after Stalin's death). During World War II inferences about the war mood in Germany and changes in the relationships between Axis countries were based on systematically monitored domestic broadcasts. Similarly, the speeches of JOSEPH GOEBBELS, intended to boost German morale and prepare the population for forthcoming events, were successfully used to extract military intelligence. Content analyses to monitor a country's compliance with strategic arms limitation agreements have been proposed. Content analyses of communications exchanged on the eve of World War I, during the Cuban Missile Crisis (1962), and in the Sino-Soviet conflict (late 1950s) have employed interactional constructs, viewing the diplomatic and public statements made by leaders of countries in conflict as stimulus-response sequences.

Beyond these uses in politics, content analyses have shed light on the kind of values expressed and attitudes held on particular issues by candidates for political offices, and how these change in response to particular circumstances and with the kind of audiences addressed. Cross-national comparative analyses revealed differences in leadership values and elite aspirations, and studies of party platforms, British crown speeches, and Soviet May Day slogans established trends of interest to political scientists. Early efforts to detect propaganda techniques and to identify the "propagandists" thought to use these techniques to undermine rational judgments might be mentioned here as well.

Social sciences and literature. Much of the determination of individual psychology rests on verbal responses to interview questions, taped psychoanalytic sessions, diaries, essays, and letters (*see* DIARY; LETTER). The search for patterns of speech that would indicate particular psychopathologies is widespread. Content analysis is virtually built into projective tests, in which subjects give verbal responses to standardized stimuli that are then categorized and counted. Content analysis is also used to infer various psychological states of a speaker, such as the level of anxiety from the frequency of a speaker's speech disturbances (*see* SPEECH ANXIETY), or a speaker's idiosyncratic worldview from the kind of logical errors made during arguments. The kind of construct underlying the latter inferences has been applied to suicide notes, talk by alcoholics, and speeches by historical figures. Personal letters are similarly analyzed to reconstruct the individual dynamics and personality of the writer. Verbal records of dreams are a similar source of insights that content analysis opens to systematic inquiry.

In EDUCATION content analysis has been used to analyze textbooks for the sexual, racial, and national prejudices they contain, including how the depiction of wars differs in the history books of former enemies. An important educational use of content analysis is to infer the readability and reading interest of a text from the kinds of words, grammatical constructions, punctuation, and so on used. *See* READING; TEXTBOOK.

A natural candidate for content analysis is literature. The construction of concordances and the analysis of literary metaphors, symbols, themes, figures of expression, styles, GENRE differences, and intended audiences all fall into the domain of content analysis but are rarely so called. An interesting exception is the statistical identification of the unknown author of a literary work, successfully accomplished in the case of the medieval text *De Imitatione Christi*, several unsigned *Federalist* papers, and the differentiation of sections of a text written by different authors. The establishment of literary influences might be mentioned here as well as efforts to date documents by an analysis of WRITING styles and contents, attempts to infer achievement imagery in Greek literary works, and searches for themes that differentiate best-sellers from other novels (*see* STYLE, LITERARY).

Content analysis may be an integral part of a larger social research effort. For example, to minimize interviewer biases, open-ended answers to interview questions are often subjected to content analysis in order to obtain frequency distributions, scales, indexes, or variables that can then be correlated with directly measurable interviewee characteristics. Experiments with small (problem-solving, conflict simulation, or therapeutic) groups employ content analyses to differentiate among kinds of verbal interactions, to quantify the contributions made by members, and to conceptualize the role they assume in directing the emergence of social structures that may become explainable in these terms. MASS MEDIA EFFECTS have been studied by correlating content analysis measures of fictional television violence with estimates of actual violence obtained from heavy and light viewers.

Content analysis may also parallel other research techniques and check or shed light on the validity of either's findings. For example, a comparison of the actual crime statistics in a U.S. city, a poll of residents' concern about violence in that city, and a content analysis of the crime coverage in the local newspapers showed significant correlations only between the latter two, suggesting that they both indicate similar phenomena that are only marginally related to the "facts." A content analysis of essays written by students yielded findings substantially similar to those obtained from attitudinal questionnaires filled out by the same students. Such parallelisms enhance the analysts' confidence in the validity of their findings and justify their substitutability. On the other hand, an effort to find a strong correlation between various ways of counting references to U.S. presidents in a political science text, commonly accepted as a measure of attention or importance, and rank orders of the significance of these presidents provided by the author of that text failed to reach acceptable levels. This speaks against the unreflected use of frequency measures and points to the importance of establishing the validity of any content analysis.

Procedures and Their Criteria

Content analyses commonly contain six steps that define the technique procedurally.

Design. A conceptual phase during which analysts define their *context,* what they wish to know and are unable to observe directly; explore the source of relevant data that either are or may become avail-

able; and adopt an analytical construct that formalizes the knowledge available about the data-context relationship, thereby justifying the inferential step involved in going from one to the other. These three principal features constitute the framework for analysis (see Figure 1). Besides delineating the empirical procedures to be employed, the design should also spell out the observational conditions under which the inferences made could be considered valid, in the sense of representing what they claim to represent.

Unitizing. The phase of defining and ultimately identifying units of analysis in the volume of available data. *Sampling units* make possible the drawing of a statistically representative sample from a population of potentially available data: issues of a newspaper, whole books, television episodes, fictional characters, essays, advertisements. *Recording units* are regarded as having meanings independent of one another: references to events, individuals, or countries; evaluative assertions; propositions; themes.

Sampling. While the process of drawing representative samples is not indigenous to content analysis, there is the need (1) to undo the statistical biases inherent in much of the symbolic material analyzed (e.g., the attitudes of important people are expressed more frequently in the mass media than are those of the larger population) and (2) to ensure that the often conditional hierarchy of chosen sampling units (e.g., publications–newspaper dates–page numbers–articles–paragraphs–words) becomes representative of the organization of the symbolic phenomena under investigation.

Coding. The step of describing the recording units or classifying them in terms of the categories of the

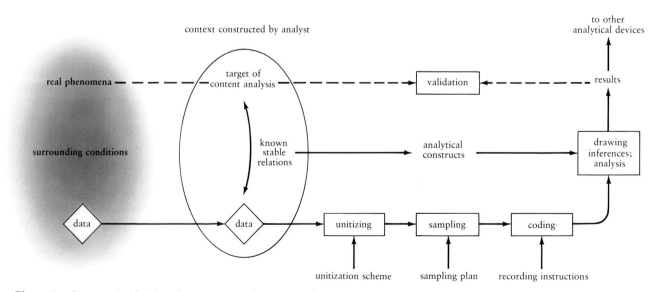

Figure 1. *(Content Analysis)* The content analysis research process. Diagram by Klaus Krippendorff.

analytical constructs chosen. This step replicates an elementary notion of meaning and can be accomplished either by explicit instructions to trained human coders or by computer coding. The two evaluative criteria, reliability as measured by intercoder agreement and relevance or meaningfulness, are often at odds. Human coders tend to be unreliable but good at interpreting semantically complex texts (*see* INTERPRETATION). Computers have no problems with reliability but must be programmed to simulate much of a native speaker's linguistic competence. Notwithstanding major advances in the use of computers, their application usually sacrifices the criterion of meaningfulness in favor of reliability and speed.

Drawing inferences. The most important phase in a content analysis. It applies the stable knowledge about how the variable accounts of coded data are related to the phenomena the researcher wants to know about. The inferential step involved is rarely obvious. How the frequency of references indicates the attention a source pays to what it refers to, which distinct literary style uniquely identifies a particular author, and the way preferences for certain verbal attributions manifest speaker or listener attitudes need to be established by independent means. Analytical constructs of this kind need not be so simple either. In extracting military intelligence from enemy broadcasts, analysts employ elaborate "maps" of known relationships involving the role of and conflicts within the national leadership and among the population addressed. Similarly, inferences about individuals' worldviews from their idiosyncratic styles of reasoning involve several levels, each employing elaborate psychological constructs of their cognition.

Validation. The desideratum of any research effort. However, validation of content analysis results is limited by the intention of the technique to infer what cannot be observed directly and for which validating evidence is not readily available. For example, why would one want to extract military intelligence from enemy propaganda if the adversary's planned activities were already known, why would one want to infer media attention if attention were measurable directly, or why would one want to infer Kennedy's changing attitudes during the Cuban Missile Crisis from his communications if it were possible to interview him? Nevertheless, content analysis should not be undertaken without at least the possibility of bringing validating evidence to bear on its findings.

Limitations

Despite its claim to generality, content analysis has some inherent limitations. The first stems from its commitment to scientific decision making. Statistically significant findings require many units of analysis, and seeking such findings amounts to a commitment to be quantitative. This discourages the

analysis of unique communications or connected (nondecomposable) discourses characteristic of literary, historical, or psychoanalytic inquiries.

The second limitation stems from the replicability requirement. This implies fixed and observer-independent categories and procedures that must be codified without reference to the analyst and the material being analyzed. Computer content analysis is one of its results. It favors the use of data in contexts that entail stable and unambiguous interpretations and leaves little room for those whose meanings evolve in the process of communication and in ways characteristic of the different communicators or social groups involved. Such ambiguities are frequent in political and private discourses.

The expectation to contribute to social theory leads to the third limitation. If categories are obtained from the very material being analyzed, findings are not generalizable much beyond the given data. If they are derived from a general theory, findings tend to ignore much of the symbolic richness and uniqueness of the data in hand. The compromises content analysis must seek are rarely easy ones.

See also AGENDA-SETTING; COMMUNICATIONS RESEARCH: ORIGINS AND DEVELOPMENT; MASS COMMUNICATIONS RESEARCH.

Bibliography. Bernard Berelson, *Content Analysis in Communication Research*, Glencoe, Ill., 1952, reprint New York, 1971; George Gerbner, Ole R. Holsti, Klaus Krippendorff, William J. Paisley, and Philip J. Stone, *The Analysis of Communication Content: Developments in Scientific Theories and Computer Techniques*, New York, 1969; Ole R. Holsti, *Content Analysis for the Social Sciences and Humanities*, Reading, Mass., 1969; Klaus Krippendorff, *Content Analysis: An Introduction to Its Methodology*, Beverly Hills, Calif., 1980; Harold D. Lasswell, Nathan Leites et al., eds., *Language of Politics*, Cambridge, Mass., 1949; Harold D. Lasswell, Daniel Lerner, and Ithiel de Sola Pool, *The Comparative Study of Symbols*, Stanford, Calif., 1952; Klaus Merten, *Inhaltsanalyse*, Opladen, FRG, 1983.

KLAUS KRIPPENDORFF

CONVERSATION

Most human communication takes place in face-to-face informal settings in what may be described loosely as conversational exchanges. In these exchanges the linguistic, paralinguistic, and kinesic (*see* KINESICS) channels are all involved and interlinked simultaneously. This form of human communication is quite obviously basic. It is the context in which children acquire their first languages (*see* LANGUAGE; LANGUAGE ACQUISITION), and until the comparatively recent developments of widespread LITERACY and electronic communications it was almost the only fundamental kind of human verbal communication found in all societies.

Despite this self-evident primacy, conversation has been studied intensively only in very recent years, this study having been facilitated by advances in recording equipment. This research has revealed that, in contrast to earlier views, conversation is not a relatively unstructured form of human interaction. Conversational exchanges are subject to extremely complex procedures that regulate when and how speaking is done and how particular contributions—verbal or nonverbal—will be understood (which depends on their placement with respect to earlier contributions).

Organization of conversation. We owe our knowledge of the structural properties of conversation largely to a group of sociologists—Harvey Sacks, Emanuel Schegloff, Gail Jefferson, and others—who have undertaken intensive qualitative study of taped natural talk. Some of their basic findings can be briefly summarized.

A crucial property of conversation is that it is fundamentally interactional: how a conversation develops is determined jointly rather than by any one party to it, and this holds at almost every level. For example, a pause is something that can only be produced if all parties to a conversation desist from speaking; it is not the product of a single speaker. By the same token, an utterance that is produced without overlap (i.e., simultaneous SPEECH from another) is to that extent jointly arranged.

This coordination is achieved through the use of procedures that regulate verbal interaction as it unfolds. An obvious but fundamental characteristic of conversation is rapid turn taking, that is, speech by one party accompanied by silence from others, with frequent transition of parties between speaking and nonspeaking roles. This repetitive transition is often achieved with split-second timing and little overlap; typically no greater pauses occur between speakers than are found within a single speaker's utterance. Such transitions might be effected in a number of ways, for example, by a speaker producing as long an utterance as desired followed by an "over and out" signal, as on a field radio. Although some investigators have claimed to discover subtle verbal or nonverbal signals with this function, such signals do not seem to be essential to coordinated turn transitions. Rather, turn taking seems to be organized on the following rule-governed basis: the current speaker has the right to finish a minimal linguistic unit (clause or other prosodically defined unit), at the end of which any party may choose to speak, first speaker winning rights to that next unit, which in turn is subject at its completion to competitive turns by others. This predicts, correctly, that overlap will occur typically at transition points and will be caused by competitive first starts. Or overlap can occur just before the intended transition point at which a speaker has appended a tag question, name, or other unpredictable addition. When, because of competitive simultaneous starts, two speakers find themselves speaking simultaneously, there seem to be methods for resolving who should continue to speak. These methods largely involve indicating a degree of determination to continue, signaled, for example, by amplitude increase and syllable lengthening.

Despite ethnographic reports to the contrary, such a system of turn taking in informal talk appears to be universal. Claims that in other cultures people generally speak simultaneously, and thus do not abide by any turn-taking arrangements, seem to be based on impression rather than on careful analysis. For example, quarrels typically involve simultaneous speech, but this is produced more by competitive starts at turn-transition points (as allowed by the hypothesized rules) than by sheer disrespect for the current speaker's right to a turn.

A speaker may use his or her turn to constrain the possibilities of the next speaker's turn by, for example, selecting the next speaker by name or using one of a set of paired turn types, like greetings or question-answer pairs. Known as "adjacency pairs" because each part is normally (but not invariably) produced one after the other, these turn types produce a minimal conversational "sequence" of (at least) two turns, in which the first is so produced to elicit the second and the second so designed to address the first. However, they can also serve to structure considerable portions of conversation, as in the following:

A:	Where's the nearest post office?	(Question 1)
B:	Well, you know the town hall?	(Question 2)
A:	Yes.	(Answer 2)
B:	Just down from there.	(Answer 1)

Note that although the answer to the first question is not adjacent to it, the second question is interpreted as preparatory to the still relevant answer. Adjacency pairs are also utilized to coordinate joint actions, as in the exchange of greetings and partings that achieve orderly initiation and termination of conversations.

Responses to adjacency pairs may be delayed (as in the above example), but they are nevertheless due. Nor are all possible responses equal in kind. For example, an invitation acceptance is usually immediate, brief, and simple ("Sure, we'd love to come"), whereas a rejection is likely to be hesitant and hedged with excuses ("We'd love to, but . . ."). Responses that are simple and direct have been termed "preferred," in the sense that the asymmetry of response types favors that kind of response. A small pause (or other sign of hesitation) after an invitation, offer, or request will be interpreted as a preface to the "dispreferred" or rejecting action, providing a powerful SEMIOTICS of pauses.

There are other kinds of recurrent sequences. For example, requests or invitations (themselves first parts of adjacency pairs) are often preceded by "pre-sequences":

A: Are you busy?   (Pre-request)
B: Not too bad, why?   ("Go ahead")
A: Could you possibly help me move this filing cabinet?
B: Sure.

Pre-sequences typically check whether the forthcoming request or invitation is likely to meet with success, a motivation apparently being to avoid the dispreferred response (a refusal). One kind of sequence is basic to the maintenance of effective communication, namely, a procedure for indicating problems of hearing and understanding and for effecting resolution of those problems. Known as the system for "repair," it often engenders sequences such as:

A: John's got an Amstrad.
B: He's got a what?
A: An Amstrad computer.

Here a specific syntactic pattern ("echo-question") is used by a puzzled recipient to indicate the word causing the communication problem and to request an amplification or correction. In this example B has initiated (requested) repair of the preceding turn in the following turn, requiring the speaker of the problem word to explain. Often, however, the speaker may detect (e.g., from the recipient's pause) that what he or she has said so far is unclear, so that the speaker may continue the turn and without explicit prompting deliver a correction or amplification. This "self-initiated self-repair" is in fact the preferred option; the recipient may delay a response specifically to invite such a self-correction.

These kinds of procedures, which operate across a few turns at a time and which may be invoked at almost any point, are the essential characteristics of conversational exchanges. But such procedures occur selectively outside conversations proper—even, for example, in courtroom interrogation (but not in sermons, lectures, or other forms of monologue). Mostly these other kinds of exchanges are characterized partly by a selection from the wide range of procedures available in conversation; British or U.S. courtroom testimony, for example, is restricted almost entirely to question-answer adjacency pairs. They may, however, involve systems of turn taking alien to conversation, as when speakers' turns are allocated in advance by an agenda or selected by a chairperson in a committee. In either case our understanding of these other kinds of talk exchange is greatly enhanced by attending to the selection or alteration of conversational procedures.

In addition to these conversational procedures (which appear to have considerable cross-cultural generality) conversations, as opposed to other kinds of speech exchange, have recognizable (and here culture-specific) overall structures. Conversations have conventional opening sequences (of the "Hello, how are you" sort) and closing sequences and, at least in the case of telephone calls, an expectation that the overt reason for engaging in talk will be produced immediately after the opening sequence in what is recognizably "first topic" position. Thus we can say that a conversation is characterized not only by employing conversational procedures (most forms of talk use at least some of those) but also by conforming to certain expectations about how the whole exchange will be structured.

Inferential basis for conversational coherence. In addition to the organizational procedures that may be seen to guide conversational interaction there are other ways of analyzing conversational process. One mode of analysis, derived from speech act theory (*see* SEMANTICS), seeks to explain the sense of cohesion in conversation in terms of an underlying level of action: each utterance, or turn, performs an action (e.g., the utterance of an interrogative sentence performs the act of requesting the addressee to supply the indicated information), to which the next utterance responds by performing the relevant next action (e.g., the utterance of an assertion, which performs the action of supplying the questioner with the requested information). Thus cohesion lies in the rule-governed sequence of interlocking actions, each expressed linguistically or nonlinguistically. Such an approach has been promoted by both sociolinguists and workers in ARTIFICIAL INTELLIGENCE, but it has numerous difficulties. It is hard to specify by invariant rule which utterances perform which actions and which action sequences are allowable.

Another related approach seeks the cohesion in conversation in unstated inferential links. English philosopher H. Paul Grice has proposed that conversation is governed by the presumption of cooperation, which gives rise to numerous unstated, nonlogical, but nevertheless reasonable inferences. For example, if A asks, "What time is it?" and B responds, "Well, the newspaper has just been delivered," we interpret the response as a connected answer to the question even though superficially it appears unrelated; what transforms the response into an answer is the inference that "the time is just after whenever the newspaper is normally delivered," but this inference is only warranted on the assumption that B is being cooperative and not, for example, introducing another topic.

Grice's ideas have stimulated much work on inference in conversation, and this has shown the great extent to which our understanding of discourse is based on inferential principles. Meanwhile in LINGUISTICS and artificial intelligence other ideas are being explored about how these inferences are made and how, for example, pronouns are linked to the nouns for which they do duty. It is to be hoped that future work will be able to synthesize the best in these various traditions.

See also INTERACTION, FACE-TO-FACE.

Bibliography. J. Maxwell Atkinson and John Heritage, eds., *Structures of Social Action: Studies in Conversation Analysis*, Cambridge, 1984; Geoffrey Beattie, *Talk: An Analysis of Speech and Non-verbal Behaviour in Conversation*, Milton Keynes, Eng., 1983; Michael Brady and Robert C. Berwick, eds., *Computational Models of Discourse*, Cambridge, Mass., 1983; Teun A. van Dijk, ed., *Handbook of Discourse Analysis*, 4 vols., New York, 1985; Charles Goodwin, *Conversational Organization: Interaction between Speakers and Hearers*, New York, 1981; John Gumperz, *Discourse Strategies*, Cambridge, 1982; William Labov and David Fanshel, *Therapeutic Discourse: Psychotherapy as Conversation*, New York, 1977; Stephen C. Levinson, *Pragmatics*, Cambridge, 1983; George Psathas, ed., *Everyday Language: Studies in Ethnomethodology*, New York, 1979; Jim Schenkein, ed., *Studies in the Organization of Conversational Interaction*, New York, 1978; Dan Sperber and Deirdre Wilson, *Relevance: Communication and Cognition*, Cambridge, Mass., 1986.

STEPHEN C. LEVINSON

COOLEY, CHARLES HORTON (1864–1929)

U.S. sociologist whose work has significantly influenced the study of communications. Born in Ann Arbor, Michigan, Charles Horton Cooley spent his entire academic career at the University of Michigan in the Department of Economics but early on shifted his research and teaching interests to sociology.

Some authors, like Edward Jandy and Robert Cooley Angell (the latter Cooley's relative and disciple), stress the intimate relationship between Cooley's early years and the nature of his later scholarly work. Apparently ill of digestive maladies for long periods while growing up, Cooley came to appreciate his mind as his most important possession. He treasured the mental abilities of the human species and gave the mind a central place in his work. There are two fundamental propositions of Cooley's thought: the mind is social, and society is a construct of individual minds. The first proposition is now taken almost for granted, especially by sociologists and social psychologists, in the explanation of individual human development. Nevertheless, it should be stressed that Cooley's work, together with that of WILLIAM JAMES, JOHN DEWEY, and GEORGE HERBERT MEAD, laid the foundations for such an explanation. On the other hand, the proposition that society is a collective mental construct was controversial from the beginning. Mead, for instance, disagreed with Cooley. According to Cooley, the ideas we develop about others are the real fabric of society. But Mead affirmed the objective existence of the social self independent of the individual's perception or idea of it.

The originality of Cooley's work is evident in his studies of the self and the group, especially his coinage of the terms *looking-glass self* and *primary group*. He built his theory of self-development by observing his own three children, but he was greatly influenced by James's explanation of the social self in *Principles of Psychology* (1890). Cooley was also in debt to Dewey's activism and James Mark Baldwin's dialectics of personal growth in developing his own explanation of the group as an organic whole that behaves in a tentative fashion. Cooley's concepts of the self and the group have repeatedly contributed to the study of human communication. The first concept, the self, has been instrumental to our understanding of LANGUAGE ACQUISITION and use and the emergence of consciousness, reflective mental skills, and empathy. Cooley's discovery of the primary group has influenced the study of how information flows through society. For instance, the concept of the primary group helped communication scholars to eliminate the notion—or, for some authors, the myth—of the mass media as all-powerful. The "sociological argument," as Elihu Katz has named it, explains that the information originating from the media passes through different steps and gets filtered and reinterpreted before it reaches the target audience. The information passes through the social milieu that surrounds the individual receiver: the group.

This explanation helped bring about the conception of the mass media's limited effects (*see* MASS MEDIA EFFECTS), based on the work of KURT LEWIN regarding the DIFFUSION of new habits. Another important theoretical development in mass communication studies grounded in the notion of primary groups is the anchoring of people's ATTITUDES (political and otherwise) in their respective reference groups. This research tradition originated in social psychology with the Bennington studies carried out by Theodore Newcomb and later evolved into MASS COMMUNICATIONS RESEARCH, especially in the study of the effects of persuasive messages (*see* PERSUASION).

Cooley was also directly interested in communication as a process of both personal and social development. In the second part of his *Social Organization* (1909) he devoted five chapters to the analysis of the nature and importance of communication in society. For Cooley communication was "the mechanism through which human relations exist and develop—

all the symbols of the mind, together with the means of conveying them through space and preserving them in time." The study of communication was to a very large extent the study of the integration of society and its development, which paralleled the integration and development of the individual. At the societal level the integration of the social whole occurred in terms of WRITING, PRINTING, TELEGRAPHY, the TELEPHONE, and "whatever else may be the latest achievement in the conquest of space and time." At the individual level attitudes, FACIAL EXPRESSION, GESTURE, and voice provided the means to come into contact with others and to develop oneself.

Cooley's work can be viewed as the mirror image of Mead's. Cooley tried to demonstrate that the explanation of the emergence of the self—that is, the point at which the individual and society meet— leads us to the conception of society as the larger mind; Mead concluded that the emergence of the self bears witness to the fact that the nature of the human mind incorporates what society is, transforming the individual into a social whole. As a U.S. scholar writing at the end of the nineteenth century and the beginning of the twentieth, Cooley also continued the pragmatic interest in MEANING started by CHARLES S. PEIRCE and joined in the optimistic belief that society is a vital means to attaining progress and democracy.

See also DURKHEIM, ÉMILE; FOUCAULT, MICHEL; PIAGET, JEAN; VYGOTSKY, LEV.

Bibliography. Charles Horton Cooley, *Human Nature and the Social Order* (1902), rev. ed., New York and Chicago, 1922; idem, *Social Organization: A Study of the Larger Mind*, New York, 1909, reprint 1962; idem, *Social Process*, New York, 1918.

ABRAHAM NOSNIK

COPYRIGHT

This entry, tracing the development of copyright from ancient to modern times, comprises three articles:
1. **The Evolution of Authorship Rights**
2. **International Arena**
3. **Challenge of the Communications Revolution**

1. THE EVOLUTION OF AUTHORSHIP RIGHTS

Copyright is the term used in English-speaking countries to denote the legal protection of rights in creative works of AUTHORSHIP. *Copyright law* usually refers to the body of statutes, regulations, and jurisprudence defining the beneficiaries, subject matter, scope, conditions, and duration of protection for works of authorship within a particular country; a copyright is the aggregate of rights that the owner of a work enjoys under the country's copyright law.

Historically copyright in this sense can be dated from enactment in England of the first copyright statute in the early eighteenth century.

But copyright is much more than a statute or a body of positive law. The concept of copyright is better expressed by the terms used in some other languages (*le droit d'auteur, Urheberrecht, el derecho del autor,* etc.): the rights that authors can rely on to control the exploitation of their works, to be remunerated fairly for the uses to which their works are put, and to be protected against piracy and plagiarism. An important adjunct to copyright in some countries is the so-called moral right, a personal right of authors to be identified with their works and to prevent distortion or mutilation of the works. Considered in its broadest sense—as the various means societies employ for encouraging and rewarding creative expression—copyright can be traced back to the beginnings of human history.

Ancient Beginnings

Long before the invention of alphabets (*see* ALPHABET) and written records, something resembling a copyright system existed in primitive societies. Individuals in patriarchal or tribal communities were encouraged to give expression to their creative thoughts for the benefit or glorification of their leaders or social units and were honored and perhaps rewarded for their contributions. A form of proprietary control over the use of creative works was exercised. The cultural expressions of a particular society—folktales and songs, magical teachings, tribal myths and legends, carvings, paintings, ceremonial dances and other rituals—were tightly controlled by the rulers of the tribal unit and were divulged only under strict conditions.

The discovery of WRITING and the evolution of WRITING MATERIALS made it possible to give material form to creative expression, to preserve and duplicate it, and to disseminate it to others outside one's presence. These developments gradually changed the nature and conditions of authorship. Classes of authors and scribes emerged; authors' works began to be collected and consulted in libraries, and in a few cases they were even reproduced and distributed in copies. For the most part authors did their work under tight authoritarian control and were remunerated as in any other master-servant relationship of the time. There were, however, some examples of a patronage system. During the reign of Ramses II (1304–1237 B.C.E.) in Egypt a number of philosophers, poets, and scholars were assembled at the royal court and were handsomely honored and rewarded by the patron for their best efforts. In ancient China authorship was one of the most honored of professions. It attracted a large number of scholars and creative writers who were compensated directly from the state treasury and were given honors, preferments, official appointments, and apparently a good deal of influence and intellectual freedom. *See* EAST ASIA, ANCIENT.

It appears that the masterpieces of Greek literature were created by their authors mainly in hope of receiving the honor of the laurel crown from their fellow citizens and without much thought of material compensation. Distribution of books was extremely limited, and works of authorship reached the public mainly through PERFORMANCE, recitations, orations, and lectures (*see* ORATORY; PUBLIC SPEAKING). In some cases authors apparently shared in the receipts from paying audiences, and many authors enjoyed royal patronage, but it is hard to find any evidence of systematic compensation. Later on, when the growth of an educated class of scribes and copyists enabled BOOK production and distribution to exist in Athens on a larger scale, most of the works being copied were by authors long dead. Although Greek literature is generally silent on how authors managed to subsist, it is full of controversies about plagiarism. Uncredited borrowings and outright appropriations were not uncommon and were widely deplored; but, except in a few extreme cases, the injured author could do nothing but complain. *See* HELLENIC WORLD.

Following the Roman conquest of Greece, Alexandria became the greatest center of literary activity in the world. The publishers of Alexandria and their armies of expert scribes acquired a virtual monopoly on book production that lasted for nearly three centuries. Scholars and authors from throughout the Hellenic world were attracted to Alexandria and were given salaried appointments to support their research and writing. There is also evidence to suggest that in Alexandria, for the first time, authors began to share in the profits from publication of their works.

At first the books that reached the Roman public were written in Greek by Greek authors. Later, Roman authors writing in Latin simply appropriated as their own the whole body of Greek literature, translating and adapting as they saw fit and in most cases making no reference to the original authors. In the early days of the Roman republic plagiarism was far more common than original authorship.

As Rome expanded its borders and influence the remarkable network of military outposts and colonial settlements, connected by excellent roads, made possible the widespread distribution of Roman goods. Roman publishers emerged and developed their own book manufacturing and distribution machinery. An enthusiastic and wealthy reading public evolved. Authors and scholars were attracted to Rome as a cultural center. Some found rich patrons; one of these, Maecenas, gave his name to all bountiful supporters of literature and the arts. *See* ROMAN EMPIRE.

During the century following the establishment of the empire, Caesars from Augustus through Hadrian strongly encouraged all sorts of cultural pursuits and creative endeavors. Roman publishers supplanted those of Alexandria, and Roman authors were able to break away from Greek models and write original works in Latin for a large audience of readers, playgoers, and listeners. For the first time in history a large class of contemporary authors were not only encouraged to write original works but were also able to see their own works reproduced in multiple copies and efficiently distributed to widely separated readers. And in some cases at least, authors were able to share in the profits of the PUBLISHING enterprise.

A major factor contributing to this outpouring of cultural activity was the existence of a large class of educated slaves who were trained as scribes and copyists and were remarkably skillful in the fast and accurate reproduction of manifold copies. Editions of between five hundred and one thousand copies of a book were common. One way of producing multiple copies was to have a reader dictate the work to a group of *notarii*, who transcribed identical copies simultaneously.

Writings from the centuries of the Roman Empire are full of references to the business dealings between authors and publishers, the financial difficulties facing authors, and the continuing problems of plagiarism. Roman law gave no recognition whatsoever to authors' rights. Nevertheless, CICERO's letters to his publisher show that he was compensated for the sale of his published works and that the amount of payment was related to the number of copies sold; and after his death the rights in his works were transferred from one publisher to another. Other authors received one-time lump-sum payments for their works, and some complained that the amounts were too low. Martial and Horace, among others, often inveighed against plagiarism; Martial, in fact, was the first to apply the term *plagiarius* (the kidnapping of slaves and children) to literary theft.

Authors and Rights in the Middle Ages

It is hard to overestimate the importance of the role played during the MIDDLE AGES by Benedictine monasteries in preserving and reproducing ancient manuscripts and in providing centers for learning and scholarship. But the culture that was being preserved, analyzed, studied, and taught was based on writings of earlier times; there is little evidence to suggest that contemporary authors or their rights received consideration. At the same time, the creative work of the copyists themselves came to represent a magnificent ART form. Illuminated manuscripts were treated as precious literary property. Manuscripts were hidden, folios were chained to desks, anathema was called down upon anyone who stole or mutilated them, and the right to make copies was sometimes transferred for a fee or other remuneration.

A famous dispute of this sort, which arose in Ireland in 567 C.E., resulted in the first reported copyright decision. Columba of Iona (then known as Columba or Columcille) paid a visit to his former teacher, Finian of Moville, and asked to be allowed to copy a psalmbook that Finian had shown him. On being refused permission, Columba worked during several nights and finished his own copy, only to be caught red-handed. Finian demanded surrender of the copy, Columba refused, and the dispute was referred to the high king, Diarmit, who was holding court at Tara. The king ruled in favor of Finian, declaring: "To every cow her young cow, that is her calf, and to every book its transcript. And therefore to Finian belongeth the book thou has written, O Columcille."

The monasteries not only preserved the works of the past in their libraries and duplicated them in their scriptoria; they also distributed copies to other monasteries and established schools (see SCHOOL) in which READING and the heritage of the past were taught. In some cases such a school evolved into a UNIVERSITY, and, beginning in the thirteenth century, universities developed into centers of learning and intellectual activity outside the direct control of the church. The teaching methods employed at those universities relied heavily on the written textbook, and a new class of publishers and scribes emerged to supply this need. For a long time these *stationarii* were licensed and their activities closely regulated by the university authorities. By the beginning of the fifteenth century, however, there was enough popular demand for literature outside the universities to create a regular trade in manuscripts in some cities. The scene was thus set for the arrival of the PRINTING press, with a structure of professional publishers and booksellers already in place and a reading public eager for cheap books.

The Renaissance, the Printing Press, and Privileges

The explosive revival of learning and creativity known as the RENAISSANCE brought with it a new class of independent authors, some of them writing in the vernacular, and added to the pressure to discover a manufacturing method capable of reproducing multiple copies of books at low cost. JOHANNES GUTENBERG's technological breakthrough in 1450 not only revolutionized book production and distribution; it also vastly increased the demand for works of authorship and led directly to the legal recognition of literary property, authors' rights, and what we now call copyright.

Within twenty years after publication of Gutenberg's first book, printing presses sprang up in mercantile centers in Germany, Italy, and France. It did not take long for the printers to discover that, easy as it was to reproduce one's own edition from a manuscript, it was even easier to issue a piratical edition of someone else's printed book. An instance of book piracy was recorded as early as 1466, and a dispute between two publishers over the literary property rights in a series of books was decided by a court in Basel in 1480.

Before the end of the fifteenth century, Venice emerged as a world leader in printed book production, as well as a pioneer in the protection of literary property. Venice's greatest printer-publisher, Aldo Mannucci (Aldus Manutius), founder of the Aldine Press, operated his press for some twenty years beginning in 1495; the high quality, prestige, and educational value of his work attracted printers and scholars from east and west and made Venice a center of learning and a latter-day Alexandria in the production of books.

It was in Venice that the pattern of granting a "privilege" for the exclusive production of certain printed books or types of printed books originated. The Doge of Venice in 1469 granted such a privilege to Johann of Speyer, giving him a monopoly for five years on the printing of books in Venice and prohibiting the importation of books printed elsewhere. By giving government-protected rights of this kind for written material, this privilege combined elements of copyright protection and trade monopoly. In 1486 the Venetian senate created something much closer to a modern copyright: it granted to the historian Antonio Sabellico the exclusive right to publish his *Decade of Venetian Affairs* for an indefinite period of time and prescribed a fine of five hundred ducats for infringement of this right. It appears that Sabellico was not only the first copyright owner in the modern sense but also the first individual author in history to be accorded state-recognized rights in his own work.

By the last decade of the fifteenth century the system of privileges had started to gain momentum. Although the earliest privileges were granted to authors and were unlimited in time, the large majority of later privileges were accorded to printer-publishers for works of both classical and contemporary authors and were subject to time limits and other conditions. In 1496 the Aldine Press received a twenty-year privilege for all works it might print and publish in the Greek language, and there are other examples of privileges covering whole bodies of literature of one sort or another. Most privileges, however, were granted upon receipt of a formal petition or application covering a particular work.

Since it was generally assumed during the pre-Reformation era that ownership of a copy gave a right to reproduce it freely, piracy and the need of protection existed wherever there was a printing press. The Venetian system of granting privileges was adopted in other Italian cities and gradually spread throughout Europe. In Germany the earliest privilege was granted in 1501; privileges in France date from 1503, and in England from 1518.

But the system of privileges was complicated and haphazard, hard to enforce, territorially limited, and subject to abuse. To afford themselves better protection, some printer-publishers began banding together in associations, guilds, and "book fairs," whose members undertook not to poach on one another.

It did not take authorities long to realize that the granting of privileges could be combined, conveniently and effectively, with CENSORSHIP. Publishers, to obtain privileges protecting themselves against piracy, were required to submit their works for government approval and to receive an official imprimatur or license attesting that the works were free of heresy and authorizing publication. The granting of privileges became a widespread and standardized procedure involving applications, deposit of copies, and in some cases payment of fees. In addition, authorities balanced suppression of writings they found objectionable with encouragement of unobjectionable writings through increasingly liberal privileges and patronage.

Combining privileges with censorship therefore had mixed results. It turned the evolution of copyright toward a system in which government approval and permission were the price for protection against piracy. In the long run, however, the combining of privileges and censorship fostered the development of copyright. The granting of exclusive rights in works of authorship was greatly accelerated, and the whole system of privileges was beginning to fall into patterns approaching standardized legal norms. In the public mind piracy was beginning to be regarded as morally reprehensible if not legally wrong.

The Situation of the Individual Author

By seeking privileges from those in authority and by banding together to protect their own mutual interests, publishers had at least some possibility of combating piracy and realizing a profit on their investment. But individual authors, the real creators of the economic good, had no equivalent bargaining power or political influence.

In the sixteenth century, however, there is some evidence to suggest that, underlying the privilege system and despite the rampant piracy, authors retained inherent rights in their works. Certainly this was true with respect to works in advance of their publication. Authors were regularly compensated for the sale of their manuscripts—an act that, in effect, conveyed first publication rights. In this connection a decree of the Venetian Council of Ten in 1545 represented a landmark of sorts. It forbade the printing or selling of a work without first presenting documentary proof of the author's consent.

The granting of privileges always started on a one-to-one, personal, ad hoc basis and without any governing standards. At some point this arbitrary arrangement would begin to break down in complexities and uncertainties, disputes between rival privilege holders, onerous formalities, and abuses by unscrupulous publishers. The ruler or government authority would then step in to lay down the law in some definite terms, in some cases abolishing old privileges and starting from scratch with new ordinances, statutes, or decrees. Examples of this progression can be found in Venice, Germany, France, and elsewhere, but perhaps the clearest and most significant example occurred in England.

The early history of English publishing and authorship is one of diminishing freedom and gradually increasing crown control over every aspect of the press. The first step was the appointment in 1504 of a "royal stationer," or official printer to the king. Through this office Henry VIII proceeded to assume complete monopoly rights in several important bodies of printed literature, including statutes and other government publications, Bibles, testaments, and the Book of Common Prayer.

As in other countries the spread of English printing was accompanied by a proliferation of piracy and, before long, by urgent petitions from printers and publishers seeking government protection. In England the earliest documented privileges, sometimes called patents, were granted by Henry VIII in 1518. After that date great numbers of privileges, usually of seven years' duration, were granted to publishers and an occasional author. A kind of early copyright notice, including the phrase *cum privilegio a rege*, began to appear commonly in English books. English printers were also protected from foreign competition by an act of Parliament in 1534 that prohibited the sale and importation of books manufactured abroad.

Privileges gave protection against piracy but not against competition from other publications in the same field. As part of their move toward absolute control over the press in England, Henry VIII and his Tudor successors, notably Elizabeth I, began to grant "patents of monopoly," which gave publishers

COPYRIGHT—THE EVOLUTION OF AUTHORSHIP RIGHTS / 415

exclusive dominion over specified bodies of literature (e.g., law books, schoolbooks, and almanacs) in which the crown claimed a royal prerogative.

Finally, having assumed control over who could print books in England, Henry VIII tried to take control over what could be printed. To censor every book published in England involved a great deal of complicated administrative machinery. The crown, which was already granting privileges and patent monopolies to publishers, found an ingenious way to combine this with the licensing system. In effect, the London publishers agreed to operate the crown's licensing system in exchange for suppression of competition and the recognition and protection of their "copies" (i.e., their copyrights).

The Stationers Company, the corporate association of ninety-seven publishers formed for this purpose, was chartered by Mary Tudor (and her husband King Philip of Spain) in 1557. The charter prohibited all printing except by members of the company or by printers who held a special license from the queen. Over the next century and more, the powers of the Stationers Company were further confirmed and expanded by successive acts of the crown, the Star Chamber (the judicial arm of the Privy Council), and Parliament. The control of the Stationers Company over publishing in England was nearly complete.

There is little evidence that any consideration was given to the legal rights of authors. The regular granting of privileges under Henry VIII was soon superseded by entry on the Stationers Company Register, and only member-publishers could make registration. Unless they contrived to find another source of income, authors had to subsist on patronage and outright sale of their manuscripts. Some, including Shakespeare, possibly shared in the profits from performance of their dramatic works, but the notion of authors' royalties from sale of printed copies was virtually unknown during this era.

Yet the rights of authors to their unpublished writings were certainly recognized, even before the seventeenth century, and the justice of protecting authors' rights after publication was beginning to be argued. A unique and apparently ineffective order issued by the House of Commons in 1642 required the Stationers Company "to take especial Order that the printers do neither print nor reprint anything without the name and consent of the Author." The voices of well-known authors were also beginning to be heard on the subject. In his great 1644 tract, *Areopagitica,* one of the landmarks in the struggle for freedom of the press, JOHN MILTON referred to "the just retaining of every man his several copy [i.e., copyright] (which God forbid should be gainsaid)," and in his 1649 book, *Eikonoklastes,* Milton declared: "Every author should have the property of his work reserved to him after his death, as well as

living." In 1667 Milton negotiated a contract with the publisher of *Paradise Lost* that, although the amounts were pitifully small, may be the first royalty agreement in the history of English publishing.

The Statute of Anne

The history of English copyright during the seventeenth century shows four trends. One was the establishment and repeated confirmation of the existence of the "copy" (copyright) as a property right in published works, presumably without time limit, and recognition of a government obligation to offer effective protection against piracy to the owner of the copyright, if the work had been entered on the Stationers Company Register. A second trend was a general revulsion against censorship and repressive control through the licensing of printing and publishing, with a corresponding increase of support for complete freedom of the press. A third was dissatisfaction with the monopolistic practices of some London publishers, accompanied by strong sentiment for breaking up the Stationers Company monopoly, allowing freer competition among publishers in Britain and giving readers more books at lower prices. And fourth, there was increasing concern for the rights of authors, with recognition that by giving a printing monopoly to publishers rather than authors under the old system, the government had done an injustice to the individuals who actually created the works being monopolized by others.

These trends led to profound changes in political, social, and intellectual attitudes. One result was that, despite objections from the crown, the last of the printing acts was allowed to expire in 1694. With it went organized government censorship, control over the press, and publishers' monopolies. But this also meant the loss of government-sanctioned copyright protection and an almost immediate surge of piracy. For the next fifteen years there was increasing pressure on Parliament by members of the Stationers Company to save their copyrights. Their petitions were based on the assumption that they already had common-law protection but that they needed a statute giving them more. They claimed that, by virtue of their purchases of the rights of authors and their successors, they still had perpetual rights for their works under English common law but that the remedies for infringement of common-law copyrights were insufficient to deter piracy. What they needed, the publishers said, was the restoration of perpetual statutory protection with strong enforcement provisions and ample monetary remedies.

These petitions and what led to them brought copyright history to its great watershed, the Statute of Anne. Enacted by Parliament in 1709 with an effective date of April 10, 1710, the new law turned out to be quite different from what the publishers had been seeking. Under the Statute of Anne the beneficiary of protection was the author or the author's successors; the copyright consisted of "the sole right of printing"; and the subject matter of protection was limited to "books." Two terms of copyright were provided: (1) for books already printed, twenty-one years from April 10, 1710; (2) for new books, a first term of fourteen years from date of publication, plus another term of fourteen years to be returned to the author if he or she were still alive at the end of the first term. After each of the terms the statute added the phrase "and no longer." Statutory penalties for infringement were specified, and there were provisions aimed at keeping the price of books reasonable. Entry in the Stationers Company Register was required as a condition of protection, but the opportunity to register a copyright was no longer confined to members of the Stationers Company; it was now open to all copyright owners, including authors.

As interpreted by the English courts during the eighteenth century, the Statute of Anne had truly revolutionary results. It broke the Stationers Company copyright monopoly and therefore the monopoly over English publishing, in effect reducing the company to a registry office. By granting copyright protection in the first instance to the individual author rather than the publisher, the statute enhanced the legal position of authorship and made it possible for future generations of authors to own their own copyrights and exploit their works to their best advantage. It laid the groundwork for royalty arrangements whereby authors could enjoy a continuing share in the benefits from use of their works.

The Statute of Anne based the copyright term on the date of publication, but it also made the length of the term dependent on the length of an individual author's life. It thus paved the way for later statutes giving copyright to authors for their lifetimes and beyond. By superseding and cutting off common-law copyright in published works and substituting definite terms of duration, the statute brought an end to the publishers' claims to own exclusive rights in old works in perpetuity. And it set the pattern for copyright statutes enacted during the next two centuries in countries throughout the world.

Bibliography. Lyman Ray Patterson, *Copyright in Historical Perspective*, Nashville, Tenn., 1968; H. L. Pinner, *The World of Books in Classical Antiquity*, Leiden, 1948; George Haven Putnam, *Authors and Their Public in Ancient Times*, 3d ed., New York, 1896, reprint 1967; idem, *Books and Their Makers in the Middle Ages*, 2 vols., New York, 1896–1897, reprint (1906–1907 ed.) 1962; Fredrick S. Siebert, *Freedom of the Press in England, 1476– 1776: The Rise and Fall of Government Controls*, Urbana, Ill., 1952.

BARBARA RINGER

2. INTERNATIONAL ARENA

In the mid-eighteenth century dramatic changes in the rights and interrelationships of authors and publishers were brought about by the Statute of Anne (see section 1, above), the first national copyright statute. As the copyrights granted under the statute began to expire, English publishers were again faced with competition from unauthorized editions and found that their only recourse was to the courts, reiterating their claim to perpetual common-law protection underlying the expired statutory rights. It is noteworthy that in bringing their cases to court the publishers no longer argued for protection in their own right but based their claim on the purchase of the rights of individual authors.

A series of cases on this question produced decades of intense public debate and ultimately resulted in a landmark decision of the House of Lords in *Donaldson v. Becket* (1767). The Donaldson case, which established the fundamental framework for copyright jurisprudence in English-speaking countries, confirmed the individual author as the fountainhead of copyright protection and recognized the author's inherent rights in unpublished works. At the same time it denied the possibility of natural or inherent rights in published works subject to statutory protection; once a work is published its protection is governed entirely by the terms of the statute. This supremacy of statutory or positive law over natural rights has distinguished Anglo-Saxon copyright systems from those of civil-law countries throughout their history.

The Era of National Copyright Legislation

On the Continent, as in England, authors were becoming their own most effective advocates and helped bring about an outpouring of copyright statutes throughout Europe and the rest of the world. To Denmark belongs the honor of enacting the second national copyright statute, a 1741 act giving liberal protection to authors and publishers. But the French republican decree on copyright of 1793 was the most influential of the early acts. It remained the foundation of the French copyright system for 150 years and during the Napoleonic conquests was extended to Belgium, the Netherlands, Italy, and Switzerland; it eventually became the model for copyright protection in other civil-law countries.

In France the 1793 decree was the most generous offered by an enactment up to that time. It covered "writings of all kinds" and provided protection to authors during their lifetimes and to their heirs and assigns for ten years thereafter. The term of ten years *post mortem auctoris* was extended in 1810 to life plus twenty years, in 1854 to life plus thirty years, and in 1866 to life plus fifty years. After well over a century the life-plus-fifty term remains the international norm for copyright duration.

By 1886 sixteen European countries and eight countries in the Western Hemisphere had adopted full-fledged copyright statutes, and nine other countries had laws of some sort protecting authors' rights. Spain enacted copyright statutes in 1834, 1847, and 1879, and these were the models for statutes in Latin America. In czarist Russia the earliest statutory copyright provisions appeared in an 1828 CENSORSHIP law, and with minor amendments and a transfer to the law on property these remained in effect throughout the rest of the century.

As might be expected, the two centuries after the Statute of Anne saw a great deal of further English copyright legislation. Subject matter, duration of protection, and rights of copyright owners were all substantially expanded, but by a patchwork of separate acts and amendments that by the end of the nineteenth century cried out for codification.

The first of many laws enacted expressly for the protection of graphic artists was the Engravers' Copyright Act of 1735, known as Hogarth's Act after the great artist whose problems with piracy led him to initiate the legislation and lobby for it. This provided protection for the work of engravers and certain other graphic artists for fourteen years. This term was doubled in 1767. The act was expanded in 1852 to cover all kinds of prints, including lithographs. Beginning with protection for fabric designs, other acts were passed to protect other kinds of creative ART, culminating in the Fine Arts Copyright Act of 1862, which covered paintings, drawings, and photographs and gave the creators of these works control over the making and sale of reproductions. Although the Statute of Anne was held to cover printed dramatic and musical works as "books" and to protect them against reprinting, it offered no protection against unauthorized performances. Bulwer-Lytton's Act, the Dramatic Copyright Act of 1833 named after its chief sponsor, took a step toward filling this gap. The authors of lectures were given statutory protection in 1835 against unauthorized printing and publication of their works. Another act, in 1842, extended performing rights for the full copyright term to both dramatic and musical composition.

Length of copyright in Great Britain was also extended substantially in the nineteenth century. In 1814 Parliament lengthened copyright to twenty-eight years from publication or the life of the author,

whichever was longer. After a famous debate in which Thomas Babington Macaulay, the historian, was a chief participant, the term of protection was further extended in 1842 to forty-two years from publication or life plus seven years, whichever was longer. This remained the basic English copyright statute until 1911.

In the United States all federal copyright legislation is based on Article I, section 8 of the U.S. Constitution, which empowers Congress "To promote the Progress of Science and useful Arts by securing for limited times, to Authors . . . the exclusive Right to their . . . Writings. . . ." The first federal copyright statute was enacted on May 31, 1790, during the second session of the first Congress. Like earlier state laws enacted under the Articles of Confederation, it paralleled the Statute of Anne but with certain differences. Protection was given to "charts, maps and books" but was available only to citizens and residents of the United States; compliance with additional formalities, including a copyright notice in newspapers and renewal registration for the author's second fourteen-year term, was required.

The early development of U.S. copyright law followed somewhat the same course as that in England. The subject matter of copyright protection was gradually enlarged. The term of protection was extended to forty-two years (first term of twenty-eight years plus renewal term of fourteen). The scope of copyright was gradually broadened to include (in addition to the exclusive right to print, reprint, copy, and vend) the rights to perform a dramatic work (1856, 1897), to dramatize or translate a work (1870), and to perform musical compositions in public (1897). But there were still some major differences.

Most obvious was the duration of copyright: by 1900 most countries had adopted terms based on the life of the author, but U.S. copyright was still based firmly on the date of first publication and was destined to remain so for many more generations. Another major difference lay in the insistence of U.S. courts and lawmakers on punctilious observance of formal requirements as a condition of copyright protection. A notice of copyright appearing on published copies of the work, registration of the copyright, and deposit of copies were all mandatory, and for a long time the courts were extraordinarily finicky in their demands for exact formal compliance. By far the most controversial feature of U.S. copyright law between 1790 and 1891, however, was its failure to offer any protection to works by foreign authors. By limiting its beneficiaries in this way, the U.S. law sanctioned the unrestrained reprinting of works by popular English authors, to the disastrous competitive disadvantage of the very national U.S. literature it was supposed to encourage. Rampant piracy in the

United States produced fierce resentment and agitation on both sides of the Atlantic, and the names of some of the greatest literary figures of the time—Charles Dickens, Anthony Trollope, Thomas Carlyle, William Cullen Bryant, and Mark Twain, to name only a few—figured prominently in the struggle for reform. Although the International Copyright Act of 1891 made U.S. copyright protection possible for foreign works, it also introduced the so-called manufacturing clause making U.S. manufacture a condition of copyright. The requirements of this clause were so rigid that they made the extension of copyright protection to foreigners illusory. Although the manufacturing clause was liberalized a number of times between 1904 and 1986, it remained throughout most of the twentieth century as a discriminatory affront to authors and publishers of English-language books.

The Berne International Copyright Convention

The problems of international copyright piracy in western Europe during the latter half of the nineteenth century induced a number of countries to negotiate bilateral treaties, but these proved ineffective. A movement was started among authors and artists aimed at establishing a worldwide union of countries pledged to the uniform protection of authors' rights, and this ultimately produced the first worldwide multilateral copyright treaty in history, the Convention for the Protection of Literary and Artistic Works adopted at Berne (Bern), Switzerland, on September 9, 1886. Although a modest beginning, the original Berne Convention established some fundamental international copyright principles. Instead of adopting the concept of reciprocity, which obliges a country to protect foreign works only to the extent that its own works are protected in return, the Berne Convention is based on the principle of national treatment or assimilation, under which a country agrees to give foreign authors the same protection it accords its own authors. The Berne Convention established an International Copyright Union of all member states, still known as the Berne Union. It required that, among union members, the right to translation be protected for a minimum of ten years. The 1886 text established no other specific requirements, but its later revisions have so expanded the minimum requirements that Berne members must now offer a relatively high level of copyright protection. The original Berne Union membership consisted of only fourteen countries but grew to more than seventy countries, not including the United States or the Soviet Union.

Building on the added minimum requirements incorporated into the texts of the Berne Convention adopted in Berlin in 1900 and in Rome in 1928, the 1948 Brussels revision probably represents a high-water mark in international copyright protection. It was adopted at a time when the impact of new communications technology and the challenge of the developing countries had not yet been felt in international copyright. The prevailing philosophy was one of broadening the international protection of authors, and the only real challenge to this concept came from broadcasting interests, which did achieve some concessions.

Under the Brussels text, protection is required for "every production in the literary, scientific and artistic domain, whatever may be the mode or the form of its expression." Member states were obliged to accord a wide range of exclusive rights to these works, including public PERFORMANCE, broadcasting, wire diffusion, adaptation, arrangement, translation, recording (see SOUND RECORDING—INDUSTRY), and motion picture adaptation (see MOTION PICTURES). Each and every one of these rights had to be granted, though some of them could be limited in certain ways.

An important innovation at Brussels was the provision recognizing the author's "moral right" as a mandatory requirement: regardless of the ownership of copyright in authors' works, the authors themselves had to be given rights to claim authorship and prevent distortion throughout their lifetimes. Even more important was the establishment of a mandatory minimum term of protection set at the life of the author plus fifty years. The Brussels text retained the provision, introduced in Berlin in 1908, prohibiting member countries from copyright protection conditional on the performance of any formality.

The Universal Copyright Convention

By the time of the Brussels conference there was general recognition that the international copyright situation had become unsatisfactory and that some way had to be found to bring the United States and other non-Berne countries, mainly in Latin America, into a global copyright system. It was clear that the Berne Union would not permit the level of protection achieved in the Brussels revision of 1948 to be lowered to accommodate nonunion countries. But it was equally apparent that the United States in particular would continue to insist on maintaining certain principles of its law—notably, compliance with formalities as a precondition of copyright and a term of protection based on first publication—and that any further effort to gain U.S. adherence to the Berne Convention would be futile.

Under the leadership of forces within the United States, the Berne Union, and the newly formed UNESCO (United Nations Educational, Scientific and Cultural Organization), a compromise solution was found. The approach adopted was a new "common denominator" convention intended to establish a minimum level of international copyright relations throughout the world without weakening or supplanting the Berne Convention. In a remarkably short time after it was first proposed, the Universal Copyright Convention (UCC) was adopted in Geneva on September 6, 1952.

Like the original Berne Convention of 1886, which it resembled in many ways, the UCC was based on the principle of national treatment and contained very few minimum requirements. UCC countries were required to give works originating in other countries protection at least equivalent to that given their own works; this protection had to be "adequate and effective"; there was an obligation to recognize translation rights for at least seven years, after which compulsory licensing would be established; and, with some qualifications, the minimum term of protection had to be twenty-five years from either the death of the author or the date of publication. Unlike the Berne Convention, the UCC did not require adherents to give retroactive protection to works previously considered to be in the public domain in their own countries.

The greatest compromise of the UCC involved formalities. Article III provides that the formal requirements of a country's copyright law would be satisfied for foreign UCC works if all published works bore a special UCC notice: the symbol © with the name of the copyright owner and the year of publication printed in a reasonably prominent position. In exchange for this single formality the United States agreed to forgo, for works by foreign UCC authors, the other formalities of its law: the special notice requirements, deposit and registration, and the manufacturing clause.

For their part the members of the Berne Union agreed to accept a convention with a lower level of protection and a notice requirement in exchange for new multipartite copyright relations with the United States and other countries. To ensure that the Berne Convention was not weakened in the process, however, they prudently insisted on something called the Berne safeguard clause. This intricate provision established two principles: (1) between states that are members of the Berne Convention as well as parties to the UCC, it is the Berne Convention that governs their copyright relations; and (2) no country may leave the Berne Union and thereafter receive protection in any Berne country under either the Berne Union or the UCC. The second part of this safeguard clause constitutes a sanction against any country denouncing the Berne Convention.

The United States was one of the first nations to ratify the UCC, which came into effect on September 19, 1955. Between 1955 and 1971 the membership of the UCC grew to include roughly the same number of countries as that of the Berne Convention, and there was a large overlap in membership between the two conventions. The UCC vastly simplified copyright relations between the United States and other countries, and it brought other countries into the international copyright community on terms they found acceptable. The basic aim of the UCC—to form a bridge between the Berne Union and the rest of the world—seemed to have been achieved.

The Stockholm Conference and the Paris Conventions, 1967–1971

Beginning in the mid-1950s more and more countries were gaining independence from colonial authority. By 1967 some thirty-seven out of fifty-eight members of the Berne Union were developing countries (*see* DEVELOPMENT COMMUNICATION). As these new countries came to grips with their problems they began to feel the pinch of copyright obligations. They urgently wanted access to printed materials from developed countries but were inhibited by the high level of protection imposed on them by the Berne Convention. And they found they could not denounce the Berne Convention and rely on the UCC because of the Berne safeguard clause.

Rumblings about the need for concessions to developing countries became a roar in the 1960s. The first line of attack was aimed at revising the UCC to remove the safeguard clause, but this was deflected pending the outcome of the scheduled conference for revision of the Berne Convention, held in Stockholm in 1967.

The Stockholm Conference turned out to be an epochal event in the history of copyright. The developing Berne Union countries, under the leadership of India, went to Stockholm with a well-organized and aggressive program aimed at special concessions in their favor. The developed nations were caught off guard; they were not yet prepared for the difficult problem of balancing, on an international level, the rights of authors with the needs of the Third World. *See* NEW INTERNATIONAL INFORMATION ORDER.

Aside from the question of concessions in developing countries, the Stockholm Conference had some other accomplishments to its credit. It created the World Intellectual Property Organization (WIPO) as the secretariat of the Berne Union; WIPO later became a specialized agency of the United Nations. The Stockholm Conference also adopted a number of relatively minor changes in the Brussels text of the Berne Convention. It added reproduction to the exclusive rights a union country must protect and broadened somewhat the exemptions dealing with news reporting and instructional uses. It included provisions to facilitate the international exchange of motion pictures and television programs (*see* TELE-VISION HISTORY), to strengthen the author's "moral right," and to create special minimum terms for the duration of copyright in motion pictures, photographs, and works of applied art.

But the most significant product of the Stockholm Conference appeared to be the Protocol Regarding Developing Countries (the Stockholm Protocol). This consisted of extremely sweeping concessions to developing countries, allowing them to make unauthorized use of works of other union countries under broad and loosely defined compulsory licensing systems. As it turned out, the concessions were so broad that the developed countries refused to accept the new text as long as the Stockholm Protocol was part of it. The developing countries threatened to denounce both the Berne Convention and (because of the safeguard clause) the UCC.

As the impasse deepened into a crisis, urgent if belated efforts were undertaken to save the structure of international copyright and to find a way to meet the needs of developing countries without damaging the legitimate copyright interests of developed countries.

These efforts proved successful. International conferences for the revision of both the Berne Convention and the UCC were held in Paris in 1971. The coordinated program of these conferences resulted in revised texts of both conventions. The Paris text of the Berne Convention retained the revisions already adopted at Stockholm but dropped the protocol in favor of an "additional act" that made more realistic concessions to developing countries with respect to reproduction and translation of materials having educational value. Equivalent changes were made in the UCC, which was also amended to require member countries to accord at least some minimum level of protection to the rights of reproduction, public performance, and broadcasting. The Paris text made it possible for developing countries to leave the Berne Union without forfeiting rights under the UCC, but since the concessions to developing countries were the same in the two conventions there would be less incentive for them to do so.

The 1971 revisions of both the Berne and the Universal Copyright Conventions came into effect in 1974. At least for the immediate future they seemed to have restored stability in international copyright and to have left the two conventions—complemented by multilateral treaties adopted in the 1960s and 1970s to protect performers, record producers, and broadcasters and to prohibit piracy of sound recordings and SATELLITE signals—relatively harmonious. But the world of media was experiencing a communications revolution, which would have an impact on human life and culture comparable to that of the printing press five centuries earlier—and perhaps be

even more sweeping. Its effect on AUTHORSHIP, the dissemination of works of the intellect, and the protection of authors' rights would be profound and would involve challenges that seemed to defy solution.

Bibliography. American Bar Association, *Two Hundred Years of English and American Patent, Trademark, and Copyright Law*, Chicago, 1977; Augustine Birrell, *Seven Lectures on the Law and History of Copyright in Books*, London and New York, 1899; Richard R. Bowker, *Copyright, Its Law and Its Literature*, New York and Boston, 1886; P. F. Carter-Ruck and F. E. Skone James, *Copyright: Modern Law and Practice*, London, 1965; Richard C. De Wolf, *An Outline of Copyright Law*, Boston, 1925; Eaton S. Drone, *A Treatise on the Law of Property in Intellectual Productions in Great Britain and the United States*, Boston, 1879; F. E. Skone James, ed., *Copinger and Skone James on the Law of Copyright*, 8th ed., London, 1948; Benjamin Kaplan, *An Unhurried View of Copyright*, New York, 1967; Stephen P. Ladas, *The International Protection of Literary and Artistic Property*, 2 vols., New York, 1938; T. E. Scrutton, *The Law of Copyright*, 4th ed., London, 1903.

BARBARA RINGER

3. CHALLENGE OF THE COMMUNICATIONS REVOLUTION

In the closing decades of the twentieth century the principles of copyright appeared to face an uncertain future. Copyright, as it had come to exist between 1750 and 1950 (see section 2, above), guaranteed exclusive control over the market for a work, enabled authors to share in the returns from that market, and offered effective legal sanctions when the market was invaded. But new communication devices were making it impossible for existing copyright laws to perform these functions.

The earliest of the new communication devices—SOUND RECORDING, silent and sound MOTION PICTURES, RADIO and television broadcasting (*see* TELEVISION HISTORY)—resulted in widespread piracy and enormous copyright controversies. Yet there was still the possibility of a link between the copyright owner and the user, and copyright law was able to function. Exclusive rights could still be licensed, and unlicensed uses could still be suppressed; when the link became too weak, it was still possible to reinforce it by setting up collective arrangements and compulsory licensing schemes under copyright law.

But with the next wave of communications technology—including magnetic audio and VIDEO recordings, photocopying and microreproduction, computers (*see* COMPUTER: IMPACT), and SATELLITE transmissions—the potential link between copyright owner and user was broken. When every individual had immediate, unrestricted access to a work and the unlimited technological capability of storing, displaying, reproducing, performing, and transmitting it, there seemed no way for traditional copyright principles to operate. The author's old markets were being lost because they could not compete with unauthorized uses that were incredibly cheap and easy; and the new uses could not be controlled because they were pandemic.

For the most part the national copyright laws enacted in the 1950s, 1960s, and 1970s showed little recognition of the fundamental change in the condition of AUTHORSHIP and the new problems of protecting authors' rights. Even in countries in which the new devices were already in people's homes, the copyright statutes largely followed old models and the Berne Convention.

This was the case with the British Copyright Act of 1956; although its provisions are detailed and elaborate, they did not go much beyond the 1948 Brussels text or the Berne Convention. Similarly, the United States did not break much new ground with its Copyright Act of 1976, although the statute was revolutionary in a different way: it finally severed ties with eighteenth-century English law and went at least partway toward adopting the standards of the Berne Convention. The 1976 act abolished common-law copyright and established a system of automatic federal statutory copyright from creation, to last for the life of the author plus fifty years. Unlike earlier U.S. laws, which had emphasized publishers' rights, the 1976 act was directed much more toward the rights of individual authors and included a number of provisions aimed at protecting authors in their dealings with publishers, producers, and other entrepreneurs. It expanded the copyright owner's exclusive rights and for the first time created rights to royalties, under compulsory licensing systems, for jukebox performances, nonprofit broadcasting, and CABLE TELEVISION transmissions. Notice, registration, deposit, and manufacturing formalities were retained, but their requirements were greatly liberalized.

Compared with concurrent copyright enactments in other countries, the U.S. Copyright Act of 1976 offered a fairly high level of protection. Like the other enactments, however, it largely failed to protect copyright owners from the onslaught of the new communication devices.

Nonetheless, there were indications that copyright experts were awakening to the changed situation and that legislators were beginning to undertake the difficult task of adapting copyright law to meet the challenge of the new technology. Provisions in a few statutes (such as the 1965 copyright law of the Federal Republic of Germany), some amendments to existing copyright laws, and a variety of separate enactments for specific purposes suggest directions that copyright law may be on the verge of taking. The following trends are discernible:

- *Increased compulsory licensing.* In some cases in which users can be identified but their uses are so great in number, variety, or unpredictability as to make one-on-one licensing impracticable, blanket licensing or, more often, compulsory licensing schemes are being established under government control and supervision.

- *Unified collection agencies.* To save certain types of users from an impossible task of seeking out and negotiating copyright licenses with an indeterminate number of copyright owners or organizations, unified collection agencies may very probably be recognized or established. Users will pay a total amount of specified royalties into a single pool, and to receive their share of the royalties authors and copyright owners will have to either belong to the agencies or at least deal with them.

- *Government tribunals.* Government bodies have been or will be set up to ensure that compulsory licensing royalty rates are adjusted to economic conditions, to regulate the activities of collecting agencies and their members, and in some cases for purposes of CENSORSHIP. As copyright law changes to include more collective activities and rate-making requirements, these official bodies will assume greater authority. They will inevitably begin contributing to or making government copyright policy.

- *Abandonment of the "first sale" doctrine.* Under traditional copyright principles the buyer of a copy or record embodying a copyrighted work was free to exhibit or dispose of the artifact without copyright restrictions. Changes in technology have begun to break down this once-sacred doctrine. Exclusive rights with respect to the display of copies owned by someone else are beginning to be recognized. Provisions giving copyright owners rights to control or obtain royalties from rentals of copies and records are being enacted. "Lending right" statutes providing royalties from libraries to authors under a variety of royalty arrangements have been adopted in quite a few countries.

- *Surcharges on reproducing equipment.* Governments are beginning to recognize that there are cases in which it is impossible to identify or restrain a user but in which authors are entitled to be remunerated for the use. Individual users with reproducing equipment cannot be prevented from using that equipment to capture, store, copy, and perform copyrighted works, and no direct payment from user to copyright owner can be expected or demanded in this situation. Traditional copyright markets are being devastated by these practices, and alternative methods to recompense copyright owners are urgently being sought. In some countries that already have the necessary structure of a single collecting organization and a regulatory government tribunal, a method being tried is to place a surcharge on the purchase of "software" for reproduction (e.g., audio- and videotape), on "hardware" for reproduction (e.g., recording and photocopying machines), or on both. This surcharge is paid by the buyer through the retailer to the collecting organization.

• *"Fair use" or "fair dealing" provisions.* The doctrine of fair use has grown up alongside copyright statutes to excuse small noncompetitive uses of copyrighted material. In recent decades there has been a trend toward broadening the concept of fair use from a privilege to an outright exemption to the exclusive rights of copyright owners. Fair use came to be a justification for widespread and systematic photocopying, microreproduction, audio and video recording, and computer uses—not only by libraries, educational institutions, and research organizations but also by their suppliers and by individuals using the institutions' equipment for personal use. At least in developed countries there seems to be a trend away from recognizing these broad exemptions.

• *The rights of individual authors.* In an era when technology appears to be forcing more and more collectivization upon the operation of the copyright law, the pecuniary and personal situation of individual authors once more becomes a major issue. The age-old problems recur in a new setting: freedom of expression versus censorship; freedom to publish versus state-controlled MONOPOLY; independent creation versus creation as an employee for hire or as a member of a collective group; moral rights versus the power of entrepreneurs or governments to distort the author's work, to suppress the author's name, or to suppress the work itself.

The long struggle for authors' rights represents too important a chapter in human history to be lost to new technology. In altering the course of copyright law to meet the challenge of technology, governments would do well to study copyright history and to learn from the lessons it has to teach.

Bibliography. Lyman Ray Patterson, *Copyright in Historical Perspective,* Nashville, Tenn., 1968.

BARBARA RINGER

CRITICAL THEORY. *See* COMMUNICATION, PHILOSOPHIES OF; COMMUNICATIONS RESEARCH: ORIGINS AND DEVELOPMENT; FEMINIST THEORIES OF COMMUNICATION; IDEOLOGY; MARXIST THEORIES OF COMMUNICATION; POETICS.

CROWD BEHAVIOR

Crowds have been analyzed and studied at different levels and by different disciplines, the most prominent of which include psychology, sociology, and history. In the late nineteenth and early twentieth centuries French sociologist Gustave Le Bon endeavored to adapt the theory and practice of government to the challenges of mass society, while his colleague and contemporary JEAN-GABRIEL DE TARDE moved toward a psychology of mass communications when he examined the notions of *public* and *opinion* (*see* PUBLIC OPINION).

Background. The French Revolution was the first event of modern history in which crowds played a pivotal role. The framework for understanding social movements of this sort includes the Industrial Revolution and increased urbanization, which attracted to the cities multitudes of individuals predisposed by the rupture of traditional bonds to other forms of association. The crowd was the most spectacular of the new forms.

Le Bon's celebrated and influential study, *Psychologie des foules* (Psychology of Crowds, 1895), which appeared in English as *The Crowd: A Study of the Popular Mind* (1896), has continued to dominate most thinking on the subject. His work was organized around the opposition individual/crowd. Such corresponding polarities as conscious/unconscious, rational/irrational, and moderate/extremist reflect the general feeling that individuals should be guided by intelligence, not dominated by emotion. That is why crowds tend to seem menacing, dangerous, indeed criminal, even if one does not deny them courage, heroism, and sometimes generosity.

In the late nineteenth century hypnosis was cited in attempts to explain in a coherent way both the suggestibility that leads to the fusion of individuals into a crowd and the ascendancy of the leader—for, in Le Bon's words, "the leader has most often been first a follower hypnotized by an idea of which he has subsequently become the apostle." To this conception of natural or spontaneous crowds, Tarde and SIGMUND FREUD added that of artificial or organized crowds, thereafter called *masses.* Church and army are prototypes, but political parties, unions, and government institutions are obviously other examples. The theory thus enriched encompasses all aspects of social and political life, from its temporary and egalitarian forms to other more permanent, hierarchical ones.

The public. In *L'opinion et la foule* (On Communication and Social Influence, 1901) Tarde announced the appearance of a new type of social group

Figure 1. *(Crowd Behavior)* Jean-Louis Prieur, *The Taking of the Bastille*, July 14, 1789. Musée Carnavalet, Paris. Giraudon/Art Resource, New York.

defined as a "dispersed crowd, where the influence of minds on each other operates . . . at greater and greater distances": the public. From the crowd the public derives the simultaneity of experience and from the mass the permanence of a spiritual community, but it is distinguished from both by an inclination to ignore traditional borders, whether local or national. The distinctive role of a public is to generate opinion. In past eras PUBLIC SPEAKING played an important part in this, largely supplanted in modern times by mass media. In all eras an especially crucial role is played by private talk.

Tarde's approach can be seen as an early version of the "two-step flow of communication" promulgated decades later by PAUL F. LAZARSFELD and Elihu Katz, which again emphasized the role of interpersonal relations. The opinion leaders of modern theory (*see* OPINION LEADER) are not far distant from Tarde's *élites*. The close kinship between old and new approaches may be seen further in the common perception that communication is interrelated with all sorts of social phenomena worldwide. An important example is the spectacular development of ADVERTISING (*publicité*), which links consumers (publics) and producers (as sources of influence) in complex systems of markets, prices, and far-flung wholesale and retail transactions.

As a factor in the growing role of crowd psychol-ogy, Tarde noted the amplification made possible by mass media when he wrote, "A pen is sufficient to set millions of tongues in motion." If updated, such a statement would have to take note of television and its impact in all societies in which it has been introduced. Its effectiveness in enacting the first step in the two-step flow of communication may perhaps be explained in part by the hypnotism model. As Tarde put it, with regard to the press, "every newspaper has its *star*, and this star—highlighted every now and then—captures the attention of all readers, hypnotized by its brilliance."

Outlook. Studies of crowd behavior have had an influence on sociology and political thought (e.g., in the work of ÉMILE DURKHEIM and Hannah Arendt) and echoes in philosophy (e.g., in José Ortega y Gasset, Henri Bergson, and Karl Jaspers) as well as in literary works by Hermann Broch and Elias Canetti, among others. Yet crowd behavior studies have gone through a period of decline. Experimental psychology, little represented because the subject does not lend itself readily to experimentation, has nevertheless contributed ingenious tests of hypotheses. For example, the "crowd crystals" evoked by Canetti to describe the genesis of a crowd became, in a field experiment by Stanley Milgram and Hans Toch, "precipitating groups" in a New York City street crowd.

The decline, however, could only be temporary, given the importance of the issues involved in the study of crowds. Tarde's call for a shift from the study of crowds to the study of publics has, in fact, been heeded—as evidenced, for example, in the multitude of public opinion polls (see POLL) and in analyses of the audiences for the mass media (see RATING SYSTEMS: RADIO AND TELEVISION). The media's dispersed publics, constituted of isolated individuals, find themselves unable to "talk back" to the media effectively, subjected to a one-way process that has reduced the importance of conversation and, in general, of all interpersonal channels. Thus a new kind of crowd has been created: mass society, a primary concern of the Frankfurt school (see ADORNO, THEODOR) for which the central questions—never fully answered—of crowd behavior become relevant: What is a mass? How can it have so much influence on the individual? What is the nature of the transformation undergone by individuals as they become part of this mass? These questions have drawn new interest in the 1980s (e.g., Serge Moscovici's *The Age of the Crowd*, 1985) because prominent contemporary events—modern social upheavals and the governments that emerge from them—can scarcely be understood unless such questions are successfully confronted. To do so would seem to be of crucial importance, with implications for the future of civilization itself.

See also DEMONSTRATION; MASS COMMUNICATIONS RESEARCH; MASS MEDIA EFFECTS; MASS OBSERVATION; POLITICAL COMMUNICATION.

Bibliography. Sigmund Freud, "Group Psychology and the Analysis of the Ego" (1921), in *The Standard Edition of the Complete Psychological Works of Sigmund Freud*, Vol. 18, ed. by James Strachey, London, 1953; Carl F. Graumann and Serge Moscovici, eds., *Changing Conceptions of Crowd Mind and Behavior*, New York, 1985; Elihu Katz and Paul F. Lazarsfeld, *Personal Influence*, Glencoe, Ill., 1955; Gustave Le Bon, *The Crowd: A Study of the Popular Mind* (Psychologie des foules), 1896, reprint New York (with a new intro. by Robert K. Merton), 1960; Stanley Milgram and Hans Toch, "Collective Behavior: Crowds and Social Movements," in *Group Psychology and Phenomena of Interaction*, Vol. 4, *The Handbook of Social Psychology*, 2d ed., ed. by Gardner Lindzey and Elliott Aronson, Reading, Mass., 1969; Serge Moscovici, *The Age of the Crowd* (L'âge des foules), trans. by J. C. Whitehouse, Cambridge and New York, 1985; Jean-Gabriel de Tarde, *L'opinion et la foule* (On Communication and Social Influence), Paris, 1901.

MARTIN GORIN AND SERGE MOSCOVICI

CRUSADES, THE

The modern name given to a number of military expeditions instigated by the papacy between the end of the eleventh and the fifteenth centuries. These expeditions were launched in the interests of the Christian community that used the Latin rite and looked to the pope as its head, not in the interests of any particular secular government. Appeals to take part in a crusade were addressed by the popes, bishops, and priests to Christians in many parts of western Europe.

The Crusades can be seen in retrospect as a major chapter in the evolution of international communication, with complex and often contradictory effects. They extended Western civilization and control into areas hitherto under Muslim or other domination. They were among the phenomena that contributed to the growth and consolidation of papal authority in the Western church and, subsequently, to the exposure of the papacy to criticism; to development of new forms of the religious life; to the devising of new forms of taxation, both of clergy and of laity; to the increased use of indulgences, both as an inducement to give support to a crusade and as a financial device; to the extension of trading activity by Italian merchants; to European penetration of Asia; and to changed Western attitudes toward Muslims and wider acceptance of the idea of converting them to Christianity. This promoted the study of Arabic and other oriental languages as part of the training of missionaries. The effects reverberated through later centuries.

The best-known crusades were the successive expeditions directed by popes to the eastern Mediterranean. The main purpose of these was ensuring that the Holy Land in general and the Christian holy places in Jerusalem in particular were either conquered from the Muslims or defended against them. The original undertaking of this kind was preached by Pope Urban II in 1095 (Figure 1). This First Crusade conquered Jerusalem by force in 1099, the only crusade ever to do so (Figure 2).

As a result of this success, a minority of those who had taken part in the First Crusade settled in Palestine and Syria and took their places as a ruling group among the indigenous Christian and Muslim population. Some of the leaders of the crusade established governments in Jerusalem, Antioch (now Antakiya in Turkey), Edessa (now Urfa in Turkey), and Tripoli (now in Lebanon). Such were the so-called crusader states, which in the latter stages of their history maintained themselves only with difficulty in the face of mounting Muslim pressure. In 1291 they were finally extinguished on the Asian mainland.

The crusader states were always in need of reinforcement from western Europe, and in time of crisis that reinforcement sometimes arrived in the form of a major crusade. Thus the loss of Edessa to the Turkish atabeg (governor) Zangī in 1144 provoked the Second Crusade, while the loss of Jerusalem to the Muslim sultan Saladin (Figure 3) in 1187 brought

Figure 1. *(Crusades, The)* Pope Urban II arrives in France and preaches his call for a crusade at the Council of Clermont in 1095. From Roman de Godefroi de Bouillon, 1337. Giraudon/Art Resource, New York.

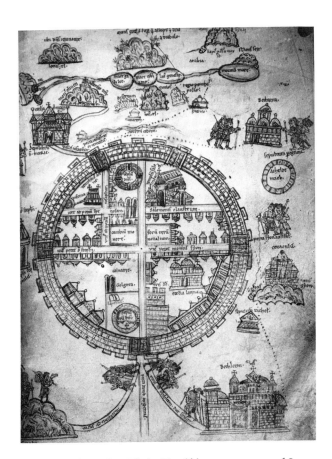

Figure 2. *(Crusades, The)* Twelfth-century map of Jerusalem. The Bettmann Archive/BBC Hulton.

Figure 3. *(Crusades, The)* Portrait of Saladin (?), Persian miniature, Fatimid school, ca. 1180 C.E. Giraudon/Art Resource, New York.

the Third, in which England's Richard I (Lion-Hearted) played so prominent a part. His efforts to regain Jerusalem in 1191–1192 failed, but further attempts were made during the thirteenth century. Some failed while far from their objective. The Fourth Crusade (1202–1204) was diverted to Constantinople; the Fifth (1217–1221) and the Seventh (1248–1250) tried to break Muslim power in the Nile delta and got no farther. The Eighth in 1270 did no more than besiege Tunis. As a result of the Sixth (1228–1229), Jerusalem was regained by the negotiating skill of the Western emperor Frederick II, but it was lost again in 1244. These eight are the expeditions that have been traditionally regarded as the Crusades. There were other important expeditions to the Holy Land (for example, in 1124, 1129, 1177, 1239, and 1271) that were not included in the traditional numbered sequence.

The medieval papacy promoted episodes of warfare other than those intended to deliver or defend the Holy Land. The Muslims who held the land in which the human Christ had lived and the city in which he had died were seen as damaging the interests of Western Christians as a whole. There were those who believed that similar damage was done by groups both inside and outside Europe who deprived Christians of lands they considered rightfully theirs, or who threatened the security or unity of the church of which they were members, or the ability of the papacy to govern it. Such government was widely seen as necessary to preserve the unity and faith of the Roman church. Muslims in Spain, Slavs in the Baltic lands, Greek Christians in Byzantium, or groups of heretics in Europe who rejected the authority of the Roman see—even secular rulers in the Christian West who threatened the temporal rule of the popes in parts of Italy—all these were seen by some as no less dangerous to Christian interests than the Muslims of the Levant. They too needed to be removed by force. The popes took the lead in organizing warfare against them, and the means employed were the same as those used to send crusades to Jerusalem. From this point of view they were in all respects crusades.

Among present-day historians, therefore, there are two ways of regarding the Crusades. Traditionalists reserve the name for the expeditions planned against the Muslims in the eastern Mediterranean, especially in the Holy Land. A growing number, however, extend the term to the whole range of military undertakings set on foot by the medieval papacy, in which the participants wore the sign of the cross and received the material and spiritual privileges first devised for the crusade to Jerusalem. This was the view taken by the U.S. historians who planned the great cooperative *History of the Crusades,* with volumes published at the University of Pennsylvania and later at the University of Wisconsin.

Organization of the Crusades

These crusades, numbered and unnumbered, not only had the common objectives already described, but also came to have common features in recruitment and organization. They were initiated and publicized by various popes. In order to finance them, novel measures of taxation came to be devised, some by secular rulers and some by the popes, who levied mandatory taxes on the entire Western clergy. Individuals joined a crusade by making a solemn vow to take part in it and displayed their commitment visibly by stitching a cross to their clothing. When they had thus formally become Crusaders, the church made it easier for them to leave home for what might be a lengthy period by guaranteeing the protection of their lands, goods, and families. If they were involved in litigation, proceedings were stayed until their return, and so was the repayment of interest on their debts. The most powerful inducement of all was the indulgence. The advantages this bestowed were differently understood at different times by different people. They certainly included the remission of the penance due for the commission of sin, both during life on earth and in purgatory after death; but many came to believe that indulgences removed all guilt and all punishment for sin.

The promotion and organization of a crusade depended on oral and written communication throughout western Europe. The original appeal to Christians to take part was normally initiated in the papal curia or at a council over which the pope presided. It was carried further by preaching tours undertaken sometimes by the pope himself and sometimes by other designated clerical agents. The pope also sent encyclical letters to a wide variety of addressees, many of them archbishops of Western Christendom. In them the pope urged, often quite eloquently, the need for a new crusade. It was intended that these letters should be read aloud in provincial and diocesan synods, as well as in churches, and should be made the basis of preaching there. *See also* HOMILETICS.

Influence of the Crusades

The extent to which the Crusades affected the transmission of information, ideas, and attitudes is not easily determinable. Crusading activity contributed in some degree to a number of developments that would have occurred even if there had been no Crusades. For example, papal initiatives in launching and sustaining the crusading movement helped to build up the authority of the Roman see in the Western church, just as the growing volume of criticism of the Crusades in the later MIDDLE AGES included the papacy in the criticism; but the growth of papal government, like its subsequent difficulties, stemmed from many causes, of which the Crusades were only one. The same is true of the ever more extensive trading carried on in the Levant (and subsequently still farther east) by Italian merchants, especially those from Venice, Genoa, and Pisa. The naval help they gave to crusading expeditions and to the establishment of the crusader states in Palestine and Syria assisted these developments but did not create them. Nonetheless, the contribution made by the Crusades was important, extending in some degree to further changes to which the growth of Mediterranean trading gave rise. These included a greater volume of interregional trading within Europe itself, a multiplication of the fairs and markets in which goods were exchanged, and the greater importance of merchants in medieval society and of the towns in which they lived.

Other changes arose mainly and more directly from the Crusades. The need to protect and care for pilgrims in the Holy Land as well as the pressure for campaigns against Muslims there and in Spain brought into being a new form of the religious life. These were the military orders, the most famous of which were the Templars and Hospitalers, whose members took the normal monastic vows of poverty, chastity, and obedience, but who also pledged themselves to fight mounted and armored against the Saracen enemy.

The use of indulgences involved another change. At first a device for rewarding those who went on crusades, it came to be offered to those who made only financial contributions. By the end of the Middle Ages this development had made indulgences a subject of criticism and even of scandal, which played their part in bringing about the Lutheran Reformation (Figure 4).

There came to be a close connection between crusading and missionary work. The earliest crusades were sent against Muslims, not with the object of converting them to Christianity, but with that of driving them by force from formerly Christian territory and of wresting from Muslim control Jerusalem and its holy places. There were always a few Crusaders, however, who expressed the hope that some Muslims might be converted, and a few such conversions were recorded during the course of each crusade. The coming of the friars gave further encouragement to the advocates of missions to non-Christians. The preaching of St. Francis of Assisi before the sultan of Egypt during the Fifth Crusade set an example to members of his rapidly growing Franciscan order. The Dominicans followed the same path and before 1300 had taken the lead in setting up schools in which friars could learn the languages of the peoples among whom they would preach. This initiative received official approval from the Roman church when authority was given at the Council of Vienne in 1311 for the establishment of schools in certain Western universities at which the Arabic and Tartar languages would be taught.

During the thirteenth and fourteenth centuries the connection between crusades and missions was often discussed. There were those who rejected crusades altogether, partly on the grounds that their repeated failure showed them to be displeasing to God. Relations with non-Christians, it was argued, should be founded on discussion and peaceful persuasion. At the other extreme were those who believed that the only arguments non-Christians understood were those of force. The strongest support was given to a position midway between the two extremes, which was stated most effectively by Pope Innocent IV (1243–1254). He believed that a crusade could be used legitimately to compel a non-Christian ruler to admit Christian missionaries into his lands.

There were occasions in the thirteenth century when missionaries were sent far into Asia to seek out the Mongol khans. These missionaries hoped that if the khans could be converted to Christianity the purposes of the Crusades could be achieved by the forging of an irresistible alliance against Islam.

Figure 4. *(Crusades, The)* Hans Holbein the Younger, *The Traffic in Indulgences* (detail), early sixteenth century. The Metropolitan Museum of Art, New York, Harris Brisbane Dick Fund, 1936. (36.77)

Italian merchants, whom crusading had helped to bring into Asia, undertook similar journeys. As a direct result of crusading, then, missionaries and merchants discovered more about Asia than medieval Europeans had ever known and provided a powerful incentive to further international communication.

Throughout the Middle Ages and even into early modern times crusading never entirely lost its appeal. The movement declined, however, as mounting costs, divisions within the Western church, and the preoccupations of secular rulers nearer home progressively increased the difficulties of launching an expedition, especially against distant objectives.

See also ISLAM, CLASSICAL AND MEDIEVAL ERAS; RELIGION.

Bibliography. A. S. Atiya, *The Crusade in the Later Middle Ages*, 2d ed., London, 1938, reprint New York, 1970; Eric Christiansen, *The Northern Crusades*, London, 1980; Norman Housely, *The Italian Crusades*, Oxford, 1982; B. Z. Kedar, *Crusade and Mission*, Princeton, N.J., 1984; Derek W. Lomax, *The Reconquest of Spain*, London, 1978; Hans Eberhard Mayer, *The Crusades* (in German), trans. by J. Gillingham, Oxford, 1972; Jonathan Riley-Smith, *What Were the Crusades?* London, 1977; idem, and Louise Riley-Smith, *The Crusades: Idea and Reality, 1095–1274*, London, 1981; Sir Steven Runciman, *A History of the Crusades*, 3 vols., Cambridge, 1951–1954; Kenneth M. Setton, ed., *A History of the Crusades*, 2d ed., 4 vols., Madison, Wis., 1969–.

R. C. SMAIL

CRYPTOLOGY

The technology of secret communication. SECRECY distinguishes cryptology from the rest of communication. Cryptological communications are not public communications. Cryptology includes the mechanisms that, on the one hand, produce private communications and, on the other, illegitimately penetrate them. Thus it incorporates the scientific study of both *cryptography* (the transformation of messages into secret form by codes and ciphers) and *cryptanalysis* (the solution of secret messages). Cryptology has changed as communications technology has changed, and major advances in technology, such as the invention of the RADIO, have significantly affected it. *See also* CODE.

Communications Intelligence and Communication Security

Cryptology here is used in its narrow sense to refer only to people-to-people communications; it will not deal with electronic intelligence, which includes active and passive sensors, such as radar and infrared detectors.

The means of penetrating secret communications are called collectively *communications intelligence.* They fall into three categories:

1. *Interception.* Begins with simple eavesdropping and mail opening and includes monitoring radio transmissions, wiretapping, bugging, and gaining unauthorized access to a computer's data bank. In addition, technological advances now allow the acquisition of acoustic or electromagnetic emanations of office equipment. For example, the display on a computer terminal screen gives off voltages that can be picked up from many feet away and used to reproduce the display.
2. *Traffic analysis.* Maps communication networks (on the basis of radio direction finding, call signs, message receipts, common frequencies, message serial numbers) to infer underlying organization and determines volume on different links to predict forthcoming actions.
3. *Cryptanalysis.* Solves codes or ciphers to reveal the text of the messages encrypted in them and analyzes recordings of acoustic and electromagnetic emanations to determine the letters or symbols they represent. For example, the sound of a typewriter striking an *a* will differ slightly from the sound of it striking a *b*, and the sounds, or their graphic representations, can be treated as a cryptogram and solved like one.

The means of protection, called *communication security,* fall into three corresponding categories:

1. *Steganography and transmission security, emanation security, and computer-system security.* Steganography hides the presence of a message by means of, for example, invisible ink, microdots, open codes, or messages concealed in pictures. Transmission security consists of such methods as whispering, sealing letters, and transmitting a long radio message in a spurt. Emanation and computer-system security utilize metal shielding and other techniques to prevent or minimize electrical leaks, electrical sweeps of rooms to detect bugs, passwords, and restrictions on levels of access.
2. *Traffic security.* Changes radio frequencies, varies call signs, imposes radio silence, transmits dummy messages.
3. *Cryptography, cryptophony, and cryptoeidography.* Cryptography puts messages, whether from humans, computers, or sensors (such as telemetered data from missiles or spacecraft), into secret form using codes or ciphers. The word *attack* may become BUUBDL in a substitution cipher; *do not yield* might become ODONYTEIDL in a transposition cipher. Cryptophony encompasses such varied forms of secret oral communication

as criminals' argot, pig latin, and scrambled telephony. Cryptoeidography includes a third-base coach's secret hit-and-run sign (*see also* SIGN LANGUAGE—ALTERNATE SIGN LANGUAGES), a collusive glance between friends, encrypted facsimile sent over long-distance telephone wires, and the coded broadcasts of subscription television (*see also* CABLE TELEVISION).

The Development of Cryptology

The development of cryptology has been affected significantly by advances in communications technology. The historical record suggests that secret WRITING arises in any culture as soon as writing becomes widely enough used to be more than a secret communication itself. This happened, for example, in Egypt, Mesopotamia, and India—though not in China, perhaps because of its ideographic writing system or because LITERACY was uncommon. The Greeks Homer and Herodotus mention uses of cryptography, and other reports come from Nigeria, Thailand, Scandinavia, Armenia, Persia, and ancient Ireland. The Arabs discovered cryptanalysis by letter frequency no later than the fourteenth century, but their discoveries were subsequently lost.

Cryptanalysis was apparently reinvented in the West when permanent embassies emerged during the RENAISSANCE. Cipher secretaries prepared elaborate nomenclators (lists of letters, syllables, and names with secret equivalents) for confidential communications between the Italian city-states and their ambassadors. And cryptanalysts sought, often with success, to solve the enciphered missives of rivals. By the 1700s their efforts had expanded into full-fledged black chambers—curtained, candlelit rooms where letters were unsealed and ciphers broken.

The telegraph reshaped cryptography. For flexible signal communications, armies developed the field cipher—cryptographic systems on a sheet or two of paper with keys that could be changed easily. For secrecy and economy, foreign offices evolved thick codebooks, in which words and whole phrases were represented by code groups like MIRASOL and 07181.

Half a century after the development of TELEGRAPHY, radio, whose transmissions are easily intercepted, made cryptanalysis into a significant intelligence force. During World War I the German army's readings of Russian military messages helped it defeat the czarist forces; French solutions of German army messages opened the way to one tactical victory after another. The British cracking of the Zimmermann telegram, in which the German foreign minister was revealed offering Mexico her "lost territories" of Texas, Arizona, and New Mexico in return for engaging in hostilities against the United States, helped bring the United States into the war.

The enormous burden of encrypting so many radiograms stimulated inventors to mechanize the work. In 1917 a U.S. engineer, Gilbert S. Vernam, automated cryptography. He joined an electromechanical ciphering device to a teletypewriter to make a mechanism that, once fed its key of punched tape, encrypted the plaintext (the message to be sent in secret form) and transmitted the result without human intervention to the receiving cipher teletypewriter. This teletypewriter automatically decrypted the ciphertext (the enciphered or encoded plaintext) and printed the plaintext. U.S. Army major Joseph O. Mauborgne, basing his work on Vernam's key tape, combined the concept of a key that was random with that of a key that was endless into the one-time system, the only theoretically and practically unbreakable cipher. At about the same time, a U.S. entrepreneur, Edward H. Hebern, and a German engineer, Arthur Scherbius, independently invented the rotor, or wired code wheel.

The armed forces of various nations adopted rotor machines of their own design in the 1920s and 1930s, but brilliant, mathematically oriented cryptanalysts solved them. U.S. cryptanalyst William F. Friedman solved Hebern's mechanism, and Polish mathematician Marian Rejewski broke Scherbius's Enigma machine.

During World War II code breaking—sometimes aided by protocomputers—led to the victories of Midway and the battle of the Atlantic, to the cutting of Japan's lifelines by U.S. submarines and the midair assassination of Admiral Isoroku Yamamoto, and to scores of tactical victories on the battlefields of Europe. It shortened the war by months.

In the decades following the war, computers played a major role in helping both to solve and to design cryptosystems (*see* COMPUTER: IMPACT—IMPACT ON MILITARY AFFAIRS). The transistor and the integrated circuit permitted the development of systems far more complex than electromechanical devices were capable of. Nonlinear shift registers, for example, can generate streams of binary digits for keys that are electronically added, modulo 2, to the plaintext binary digits; the sum constitutes the cryptogram. Even if a part of the key stream is known to an enemy, what is known cannot be extended forward to read further cryptograms. Many modern cryptosystems are unbreakable in practice. Moreover, microprocessors have made good encryption so cheap and easy to use that more and more communications systems are utilizing it. For example, the messages between bank cash-dispensing machines and the bank's central computer are encrypted.

In all these "classic" cryptosystems both sender and receiver must have been given in advance and in a secure way the cryptosystem's key. Recently, cryptosystems have been developed in which encrypting keys differ from decrypting ones. If encrypting ones are made public (as in a telephone directory) and decrypting keys kept private, anyone may, without prearrangement, send a secret message to another that only the recipient can read. This public-key or asymmetric cryptography is most useful in distributing cryptographic keys in complex communication networks.

The fear of interception of communications transmitted over microwave or SATELLITE links, concern about the security of electronic funds transfers, and anxiety about the PRIVACY of personal information in large data banks have led more businesses to use and more researchers to study secret communications. The growth of communications technology continues to foster the growth of cryptology.

See also ESPIONAGE.

Bibliography. James Bamford, *The Puzzle Palace,* Boston, 1982; Henry J. Beker and Fred C. Piper, *Cipher Systems,* New York, 1982; Donald W. Davies and Wyn L. Price, *Security for Computer Networks,* Chichester, Eng., and New York, 1984; Cipher A. Deavours and Louis Kruh, *Machine Cryptography and Modern Cryptanalysis,* Dedham, Mass., 1985; Whitfield Diffie and Martin E. Hellman, "Privacy and Authentication," *Proceedings of the IEEE* (Institute of Electrical and Electronics Engineers) 67 (1979): 397–427; David Kahn, *The Codebreakers,* New York, 1967; idem, *Kahn on Codes,* New York, 1984; David Shulman, *An Annotated Bibliography of Cryptography,* New York, 1976.

DAVID KAHN

CULTIVATION ANALYSIS

A set of theoretical and methodological assumptions and procedures designed to assess the contributions of television viewing to people's conceptions of social reality. An influential and sometimes controversial research approach, it is the third "prong" of the CULTURAL INDICATORS research program developed by George Gerbner and his colleagues to investigate (1) the institutional processes underlying the production of media content, (2) the message systems themselves, and (3) relationships between exposure to television messages and audience beliefs and behaviors.

Much research and debate on the impact of television has tended to focus on individual messages, programs, episodes, series, or genres (*see* GENRE), usually in terms of their ability to produce immediate changes in audience ATTITUDES and behavior (*see* MASS MEDIA EFFECTS). Cultivation analysis is concerned with more general and pervasive consequences of cumulative exposure to cultural media. Although its underlying theoretical framework could be applied to any dominant form of communication, most cultivation analysis has focused on television

because of that medium's uniquely repetitive and pervasive message characteristics. In its simplest form cultivation analysis has been utilized to determine whether people who spend more time watching television are more likely to perceive the *real* world in ways that reflect the most common messages and "lessons" of the television world than people who watch less television but are otherwise comparable in terms of, for example, important demographic characteristics. *See* LEISURE; MASS COMMUNICATIONS RESEARCH.

Conceptual Assumptions

The messages of a CULTURE are produced and comprehended through complex, shared symbol systems and give rise to the symbolic environment of that culture. Human thought and behavior derive a large part of their definitions and significance, potentials and limitations, associations and relationships, from this environment. Stories, myths, images, and representations of "facts" express, define, and help maintain a culture's dominant assumptions, expectations, and interpretations of social reality. This process is a distinctly human—and humanizing—phenomenon. *See* FOLKTALE; ORAL HISTORY.

Mass communication represents a historical transformation in the sources of cultural consciousness and the context of social behavior. Mass communication creates mass publics and bridges publics separated by barriers of time, space, and social class. Television's mass-produced messages and images have come to form the mainstream of the common symbolic environment in which people live and die, define themselves and others, and develop and maintain beliefs and assumptions about social reality. *See* TELEVISION HISTORY.

Particularly in advanced industrial societies that have had it for many years, television has become a centralized system of storytelling. Its DRAMA, COMMERCIALS, news, and other programs bring a relatively coherent world of common images and messages into every home. Dramatic stories need not present credible accounts of how things *are* in order to perform the more critical function of demonstrating how things really *work*. Cultivation analysis assumes that television images represent the dominant IDEOLOGY of contemporary cultures and attempts to explain the process by which underlying assumptions, values, and worldviews are nourished and sustained (i.e., "cultivated") by television. The concern is with cumulative correlates and consequences of television exposure and *not* with short-term responses to or individual interpretations of television content. It also emphasizes aggregate patterns over *all* messages and programs, not specific genres, episodes, and least of all individual messages.

The cultivation perspective does not take too seriously the presumed differences among the various categories of media messages—particularly in the case of television. TELEVISION NEWS, drama, quiz and game shows (*see* QUIZ SHOW), SPORTS, and commercials share underlying similarities of casting, theme, emphasis, and value. Even the most widely accepted distinctions (i.e., news versus ENTERTAINMENT programs versus commercials) are easily blurred. Decisions about which events are newsworthy and how to present them are heavily influenced by considerations of dramatic form and content (e.g., conflict and resolution) that are drawn from fictional archetypes; and the polished minidramas of many commercials reveal a sophisticated mastery of fictional conventions, just as dramatic programs promote a style of consumption and living that is quite in tune with their neighboring commercial messages. More important, the blending of stylistic conventions allows for greater efficacy and mutual support in packaging and diffusing common values.

Cultivation theory assumes dynamic, reciprocal relationships between television messages and people's beliefs about them. It argues that the amount of viewing is an indicator of relative immersion in the cultural mainstream partially shaped and maintained by television. People with certain dispositions or lifestyles are more drawn to television, and their continued exposure to television's dominant messages in turn cultivates those dispositions. At the same time, television fosters greater homogeneity among those of otherwise diverse social and cultural groups who are more heavily exposed to its messages.

Some findings. In the world of U.S. television, as it has evolved over several decades, young people make up one-third and older people one-fifth of their true proportion in the population. Blacks on television represent three-fourths and Hispanics one-third of their share of the U.S. population, and a disproportionate number are minor rather than major characters (*see* MINORITIES IN THE MEDIA). The prominent and stable overrepresentation of well-off white males in the prime of life pervades prime time. Women are outnumbered by men at a rate of three to one and are allowed a narrower range of activities and opportunities. The dominant white males are more likely to commit violence, whereas old, young, female, and minority characters are more likely to be victims. Crime in prime time is at least ten times as rampant as in the real world, and an average of five to six acts of overt physical violence per hour involve well over half of all major characters. *See* CONTENT ANALYSIS; VIOLENCE.

Researchers have argued that these messages of power, dominance, segregation, and victimization instill relatively restrictive and intolerant views regarding personal morality and freedoms, women's roles, and minority rights. Cultivation theory contends that heavy exposure to television violence is less likely to stimulate aggression than to cultivate insecurity, mistrust, apprehension, alienation, and a willingness to accept potentially repressive measures in the name of security, all of which strengthen and help maintain the prevailing hierarchy of social powers. Furthermore, it is argued that television contributes to a blurring of cultural, political, social, regional, and other distinctions; to the blending of social attitudes into the television mainstream; and to the bending of that mainstream in the direction of the political and economic tasks of the medium and its client institutions.

Procedures

Cultivation analysis begins by identifying and assessing the most recurrent and stable patterns of television content, including images, portrayals, and values that cut across most "types" of programs (as determined through content analysis of prime-time, weekend, and daytime network television). Its main goal, however, is to determine whether differences in the attitudes, beliefs, and actions of light and heavy viewers reflect differences in their viewing patterns and habits that are independent of—or that interact with—other social, cultural, and personal factors that differentiate lighter and heavier viewers.

There are many significant discrepancies between "the world" and "the world as portrayed on television." The shape and contours of the television world rarely match "objective reality" (though they often do match dominant ideologies and values). Findings from systematic analyses of television's content are used to formulate questions about people's conceptions of social reality. Some of the questions are semiprojective, some use forced-error choices, and others simply measure beliefs, opinions, attitudes, or behaviors.

Using standard techniques of survey research, questions are posed to samples of children, adolescents, or adults. Secondary analyses of national surveys have often been used when they include questions relating to identifiable aspects of the television world, and respondents have been asked about their media habits. The determination of what constitutes light, medium, and heavy viewing is generally made on the basis of hours of self-reported daily television viewing within a particular sample. The questions do not mention television, and the respondents' awareness of the source of their information is considered irrelevant. Most of the questions have a television answer (the way things appear in the world of television) and a real-world answer that more closely reflects reality. The relationship, if any, between amount of viewing and the tendency to respond to these questions by giving the television answer is an indication of television's contribution to viewers' conceptions of social reality.

Instances of clear-cut divergence between symbolic and "objective" reality provide convenient tests of the extent to which television versions of the "facts" are incorporated or absorbed into what heavy viewers take for granted about the world. For example, television drama in the United States tends sharply to underrepresent older people, the fastest-growing segment of the U.S. population. Heavy viewers are more likely than light viewers to believe that the elderly are in worse health, that they do not live as long, and that there are fewer of them compared to twenty years ago.

Violence profiles. Much cultivation analysis has focused on the implications of exposure to television violence. Year after year, well over half of all major characters on prime-time U.S. television are involved in some kind of violent action, and violence is overwhelmingly more prevalent on television than in real life. The research has generally found that heavy exposure to the world of television cultivates exaggerated perceptions of the number of people involved in violence, as well as numerous other inaccurate beliefs about crime and law enforcement. But cultivation analysis is not limited to the comparison of television "facts" with real-world statistics. The "facts" of the world of television can become the basis for a broader, more general worldview, thus making television a subtle but significant source of general values, ideologies, and perspectives as well as specific assumptions, beliefs, and images.

The "mean world" syndrome. One example of this has been called the "mean world" syndrome of interpersonal mistrust. Studies of television content say little explicitly about people's selfishness or altruism, and there are no real-world statistics about the extent to which people can be trusted. Yet the research suggests that one "lesson" viewers derive from regular heavy exposure to the overly violent television world is that most people cannot be trusted and that most people are just looking out for themselves.

Similarly, cultivation researchers have argued that since television's messages are designed to disturb as few viewers as possible (in order to attract as many viewers as possible), they tend to avoid potentially controversial extremes, attempt to balance opposing perspectives, and steer a middle course along a safe and supposedly nonideological mainstream. This has been used to explain the finding that heavy viewers are significantly and substantially more likely to label themselves politically "moderate" rather than either "liberal" or "conservative."

Thus cultivation analysis explores specific assumptions about facts and extrapolations from those facts

to more general perspectives and orientations. Overall, cross-sectional and longitudinal results consistently demonstrate television's ability to cultivate beliefs and assumptions in a wide variety of areas, such as images of violence, sex- and age-role stereotypes, conceptions of occupations, science, EDUCATION, health, FAMILY life, minorities, political self-designations and orientations, RELIGION, and other issues.

Specifying the Process

Demographic, social, family, and personal contexts influence the precise shape, scope, and degree of the contribution of television to viewer conceptions. Therefore cultivation is not a unidirectional flow of influence from television to audiences but part of a dynamic process of interaction among messages and contexts.

In some cases those who watch more television are more likely—in all or most subgroups—to give the television answers. But in many cases the patterns are more complex. Television viewing usually relates in different ways to different groups' life situations and worldviews.

Cultivation is both dependent on and a manifestation of the extent to which television's imagery dominates viewers' sources of information. Cultivation research has found that factors such as personal interaction make a difference. Adolescents whose parents are more involved in their use of television show smaller relationships between amount of viewing and perceiving the world in terms of television's portrayals, and children who are more integrated into cohesive peer or family groups are less vulnerable to cultivation (*see* CHILDREN—USE OF MEDIA).

Direct experience also plays a role. The relationship between amount of viewing and fear of crime is strongest among those who live in high-crime urban areas—a phenomenon called *resonance,* because reality and television provide a "double dose" of messages that "resonate" and amplify cultivation. Further, relationships between amount of viewing and the tendency to hold exaggerated perceptions of violence are more pronounced within those real-world demographic subgroups (usually minorities) whose fictional counterparts are more frequently victimized on television.

In sum, a wide variety of demographic, individual, social, and family factors and processes produce systematic and theoretically meaningful variations in cultivation patterns. "Mainstreaming," a particular pattern of differential vulnerability, has received greater research attention.

Mainstreaming. Transcending historic barriers of LITERACY and mobility, television has become a primary source of everyday culture for otherwise heterogeneous populations. Television provides, perhaps for the first time since preindustrial religion, a strong cultural link between the elites and all other publics. It provides a shared daily RITUAL of highly compelling and informative content for millions of otherwise diverse people in all regions, ethnic groups, social classes, and walks of life. From the perspective of cultivation analysis, television provides a relatively restricted set of choices for a virtually unrestricted variety of interests and publics.

The mainstream is a relative commonality of outlooks and values that heavy exposure to the features and dynamics of the television world tends to cultivate. Mainstreaming implies that heavy television viewing may absorb or override individual differences in perspectives and behavior stemming from other factors and influences. In other words, differences in the responses of different groups of viewers or differences that can be associated with varied cultural, social, and political characteristics of these groups are diminished or even absent from the responses of heavy viewers. Mainstreaming thus represents a relative homogenization and absorption of divergent views held by otherwise disparate viewers.

Perspective

Cultivation analysis has been criticized on theoretical, methodological, and epistemological grounds. Lively (and occasionally acrimonious) debates have led to refinements and enhancements in the approach. Some researchers have examined additional intervening variables and processes (e.g., perceived reality, active versus passive viewing), some have questioned the assumptions of stability in program content over time and across genres, and others have studied cultivation in countries such as England, the Netherlands, Korea, Sweden, the Federal Republic of Germany, and elsewhere. The literature contains numerous failures to replicate its findings as well as many independent confirmations of its conclusions. This debate suggests that the theory of cultivation and its associated methodology will continue to play an important role in communication research.

Bibliography. George Gerbner, "Cultural Indicators: The Third Voice," in *Communication Technology and Social Policy,* ed. by George Gerbner, Larry Gross, and William H. Melody, New York, 1973; George Gerbner and Larry Gross, "Living with Television: The Violence Profile," *Journal of Communication* 26 (1976): 173–199; George Gerbner, Larry Gross, Michael Morgan, and Nancy Signorielli, "The 'Mainstreaming' of America: Violence Profile No. 11," *Journal of Communication* 30 (1980): 10–29; idem, "Living with Television: The Dynamics of the Cultivation Process," in *Perspectives on Media Effects,* ed. by Jennings Bryant and Dolf Zillmann, Hillsdale, N.J., 1986; Robert P. Hawkins and Suzanne Pingree, "Television's Influence on Social Reality," in *Television and Behavior: Ten Years of Scientific Progress and Implications for the 80's,* Vol. 2, ed. by David Pearl, Lorraine Bouthilet, and Joyce B. Lazar, Washington, D.C., 1982; Gabriele Melischek, Karl Erik Rosengren, and James Stappers, eds., *Cultural Indicators: An International Symposium,* Vienna, 1984.

MICHAEL MORGAN

CULTURAL INDICATORS

A standardized instrument of measurement by means of which it is possible to assess quantitatively some relevant aspect of a society's CULTURE. Such measurements are necessary for relating culture to other large societal systems, such as the economy. The systematic juxtaposition of economic, social, and cultural indicators allows a quantitative study of these relationships, about which until recently only verbal speculation has been possible.

The term *cultural indicators* was coined by U.S. social scientist George Gerbner in 1969 and was then taken to cover three different approaches: (1) *institutional process analysis* inquiring into mass media decision making and policy formation; (2) *message system analysis* studying large aggregates of media content, especially on television, as a reflection of the mainstream of modern cultures (see TELEVISION HISTORY); and (3) *cultivation analysis* based on controlled comparisons of groups of light and heavy users of the medium being studied.

The systematic study of culture by means of indicators has proceeded at least since the 1930s in the United States, when sociologist William F. Ogburn included quantitative measurements of mass media content in his *Recent Social Trends in the United States* (1933) and when sociologist Pitirim Sorokin wrote his four-volume landmark work, *Social and Cultural Dynamics* (1937–1941). Other pioneers of cultural indicators research include the political scientists HAROLD D. LASSWELL and Ronald Inglehart and the psychologists David McClelland and Milton Rokeach.

Cultural indicators may be used to measure specific subsystems of high culture, such as ART and literature, but in general they are used to tap culture in the sense of the word used in social science and communication studies: patterns of shared ideas manifesting themselves in regularities of actions and artifacts characterizing whole societies or relevant subsystems thereof. In modern societies culture in this sense is to a large extent produced and reproduced, distributed, consumed, and gradually changed by means of the mass media. Cultural indicators research therefore falls to a considerable extent within the field of MASS COMMUNICATIONS RESEARCH.

Types. Theoretically there are two main types of cultural indicators: one tapping the *structure* of culture (as well as changes of that structure), the other the *processes* occurring within that structure. The former is system oriented, measuring macrophenomena; the latter is individual oriented, measuring microphenomena.

Methodologically there are three main types of cultural indicators, based on (1) quantitative CONTENT ANALYSIS, (2) survey analysis, and (3) statistical analysis of behavioral data (often secondary analyses of data collected originally for other purposes).

A close relationship exists between theoretical and methodological aspects of cultural indicators. Thus cultural indicators based on content analysis have been used primarily to measure culture as structure: patterns of societal values appearing in the mass media. Gerbner's VIOLENCE profile based on content analysis of U.S. television output exemplifies this type of indicator. Cultural indicators based on secondary analysis of statistical data have been used primarily to measure the individual behavioral processes occurring within a given cultural structure. Various types of time-budget data, consumption statistics, and the like may be used to this end. Survey analysis measuring values and cognitions held by individuals in the population may be said to tap culture either as a process (societal values and cognitions as flowing into the individuals) or as a structure (cognitions and values held by groups of individuals sharing this or that social characteristic). Gerbner's CULTIVATION ANALYSIS exemplifies the former type of individual-oriented indicators; Rokeach's and Inglehart's value scales exemplify the latter.

Since cultural indicators may be related to economic and social indicators, it is important that the theoretical relationships among these three types of societal indicators be clarified. Economic indicators tap the production and accumulation of goods in society. Social indicators tap the distribution and consumption of goods (and ills) in society. Cultural indicators tap the state of culture (as well as its reproduction and gradual change): the patterns of ideas, beliefs, and values that govern and are governed by the other large societal systems.

Being functionally rather than substantively defined, economic, social, and cultural indicators are not bound to any specific substantive sector of society. For instance, economic and social indicators may be, and actually have been, applied in the cultural sector of society (see, for instance, the UNESCO Statistical Yearbook), while cultural indicators could be used to evaluate important aspects of the economic and political culture of a given society.

Approaches. In the late 1970s cultural indicators research had two main centers: the Cultural Indicators group at the University of Pennsylvania in Phil-

adelphia and the Swedish Cultural Indicators Research Program. While the Philadelphia group to a large extent is utilitarian and empiricist in its approach, Swedish cultural indicators research has been more interested in theoretical and methodological problems, trying to establish connections with the precursors of cultural indicators research mentioned above.

At the Vienna Symposium on Cultural Indicators Research in 1982 it became clear, however, that the notion of cultural indicators was used in much wider circles than these two groups. For instance, in the U.S.-European Namenwirth-Weber-Klingemann group, economic indicators were related with some success to cultural indicators based on computerized content analysis. Thus the time-honored problem expressed in Marxist theory as the relationship between base and superstructure has become amenable to sophisticated quantitative analysis (*see* MARXIST THEORIES OF COMMUNICATION). The two techniques of multivariate statistical analysis, LISREL and PLS, working with causal relations between latent and manifest variables, are eminently suited to these and similar problems.

The flow of information, beliefs, opinions, ATTITUDES, and values from the mass media to their audiences represents a special case of the general process by which a society's culture—a macrostructure—is transferred to and internalized by the individuals in it, especially the young. The process is multifaceted and goes under a host of terms, such as enculturation, socialization (primary and secondary), and EDUCATION. In mass communications research such phenomena have been conceptualized in two ways: either the use made by the individual of a given mass media content or the effects of the mass media on their audiences (*see* MASS MEDIA EFFECTS).

Over the decades, effects research has gradually turned from the study of specific, short-term effects to more general, long-term effects. These developments have brought both uses-and-gratifications research and effects research closer to socialization research. Indeed, the term *cultivation*, as used by the Philadelphia group for the specific, long-term type of effect exercised by television on its audience, is very appropriate in that it highlights this phenomenon. Cultivation is a specific type of effects process: enculturation and socialization by means of individuals' use of television.

No doubt cultural indicators research will continue to draw on the heritage of the classical scholars of social science who have dealt with the problem of culture and society—KARL MARX, MAX WEBER, Talcott Parsons, and others—as well as on the methodological and theoretical advances made by the modern precursors of cultural indicators research. Indeed, if cultural indicators research succeeds in combining the heritage from its past with the possibilities offered by modern multivariate statistical analysis, it is likely that gradually it will be able to provide answers to such basic problems as

- the relationship between a society's technoeconomical base and its mental superstructure;
- the relationship between a society's social system and its cultural system;
- the way in which a society (1) produces, reproduces, and develops its culture; and (2) distributes it among its members.

See also COMMUNICATIONS RESEARCH: ORIGINS AND DEVELOPMENT; EVALUATION RESEARCH; SELECTIVE RECEPTION.

Bibliography. Teun van Dijk, ed., *Discourse and Communication: New Approaches to the Analyses of Mass Media Discourse and Communication*, Berlin, 1985; George Gerbner, Ole R. Holsti, Klaus Krippendorff, William J. Paisley, and Phillip J. Stone, eds., *The Analysis of Communication Content: Developments in Scientific Theories and Computer Techniques*, New York, 1969; Ronald Inglehart, *The Silent Revolution: Changing Values and Political Styles among Western Publics*, Princeton, N.J., 1977; K. G. Jöreskog and Herman Wold, eds., *Systems under Indirect Observation: Causality, Structure, Prediction*, Amsterdam, 1982; Hans-Dieter Klingemann, ed., *Computerunterstützte Inhaltsanalyse in der empirischen Sozialforschung*, Kronberg/TS, 1982; David C. McClelland, *The Achieving Society*, Princeton, N.J., 1961; Gabriele Melischek, Karl Erik Rosengren, and James Stappers, eds., *Cultural Indicators: An International Symposium*, Vienna, 1984; J. Zvi Namenwirth and Harold D. Lasswell, *The Changing Language of American Values*, Beverly Hills, Calif., 1970; Milton Rokeach, ed., *Understanding Human Values*, New York, 1979; Karl Erik Rosengren, *The Climate of Literature*, Lund, Sweden, 1983; Pitirim A. Sorokin, *Social and Cultural Dynamics*, 4 vols., London, 1937–1941.

KARL ERIK ROSENGREN

CULTURE

The concept of culture has an agricultural origin: it first referred to the tending or "cultivation" of crops. In the later stages of its history the concept has retained within it the sense of process. The "culture of the mind" is not acquired at once, nor does a person become "cultivated" at once. Many attempted definitions of the word *culture* have been inspired by the sense that it was being misused. One reason is that during the eighteenth and nineteenth centuries it acquired new meanings far removed from its humble origins. For some people it became a thing in itself, a state rather than a process, or perhaps an achievement or veneer, something that persons or societies either had or did not have. Pride in a specific national culture was a buttress of nationalism, and both developing educational and communications systems were geared to enhancing it.

For Matthew Arnold (1822–1888), self-proclaimed bearer of "sweetness and light" to mid-Victorian Britain, culture was "the pursuit of our total perfection by means of getting to know, on all the matters which most concern us, the best which has been thought and said in the world." In referring to the world and not to the nation, Arnold was insisting that the best was universal. He objected to parochialism in both space and time and insisted that the pursuit of culture should be "disinterested," a "mode of enquiry." Thus he was also one of the first critics of media manipulation. His influence has remained considerable in the twentieth century, since one of the ways into cultural studies (and related communications studies) has been through literature. Arnold had less to say about other aspects of culture, and what he said about the need for literary discrimination has provoked charges of social bias.

For less idealistic social critics who wished to distinguish among different cultures, sometimes in the name of evolution, culture was the creative expression of a particular society through its symbols, literature, ART, and music and, for some, its institutions and the values and experiences that shaped them. Such creative expression was thought of as constituting a cultural heritage transmitted from one generation to the next. It had to be safeguarded, however, as well as communicated. Such a sense of culture could encourage either cultural relativism or the placing of cultures in an order that could be conceived of as evolutionary or aesthetic. In any case it was deemed essential to appreciate cultures and "to get inside them" rather than simply to observe or describe them.

On the basis of this second approach to culture it was also possible to classify and to analyze. "High culture" was distinguished from "peasant culture," "folk culture," "popular culture," "mass culture," and "midculture," and each of the variants was distinguished from and related to the rest. Subcultures were identified also, variants of a main culture shared by limited segments of a population identified by, for example, age, economic level, or social class. Such distinctions were related both to other social indicators and to modes of communication. Thus the origins of high culture were traced back through cities—with a debate about whether there was a significant difference between "culture" and "civilization"—or through monasteries, universities, academies, and societies. Peasant cultures were compared with one another. Preindustrial folk culture was contrasted with postindustrial popular culture. The roles of technology and of travel were examined.

Mass Culture

As the conceptual vocabulary expanded, clusters of new meanings were introduced into the ascription of forms and styles of culture. New issues were also opened up. One of the most controversial issues has been the assessment of mass culture, which drew concern about the erosion of quality as soon as it appeared. In the twentieth century this concern has focused especially on the effects of technology via postprint media. For Bernard Rosenberg modern technology was "the necessary and sufficient cause of mass culture," and the products of that technology were "broadened and thickened and coarsened characters." The "cultivated person" was in danger of being contaminated. For Dwight Macdonald, writing in 1952 before the growth of the television audience, "masscult," as he called it, was "bad in a new way; it doesn't even have the theoretical possibility of being good." Such an approach to mass culture, which was sometimes but not always distinguished from popular culture—some held that the one had destroyed the other—was attacked from the start. One line of attack was that it rested on a false view of "mass" and "masses." Another was that it was elitist. A third was that it stifled curiosity—and fun.

Sociologists attempted to sort out the issues. Edward Shils distinguished in 1960 between "superior or refined culture"; "mediocre culture," less original than "superior" culture but more reproductive; and "brutal culture," in which "the depth of penetration" was almost negligible, "subtlety" was almost entirely lacking, and "a general grossness" of PERCEPTION was a common feature. Such sorting out became increasingly difficult during the 1960s and has remained so since.

Cultural myths. There had always been a danger that argument about culture could become highly abstract and that philosophical or even prophetic strains would become dissociated from empirical fact. The history of culture as written in the twentieth century was shot through with myth long before World War II. Theories of "massification," like those of José Ortega y Gasset, whose *La deshumanización del arte* appeared as early as 1925, four years before his *La rebelión de las masas,* often rested on massive generalization. Theories of discrimination, like those of British critic F. R. Leavis, made too much of organic village community before the Industrial Revolution. Folk culture, it was often claimed, rested on the base of personal face-to-face communication, and the culture grew directly from the people who enjoyed it (*see* FOLKLORE). By contrast mass culture was a commodity marketed by profit-seeking providers who claimed misleadingly that they were giving the people what they wanted. The contrast was too sharp, as historians of the development of popular culture have shown, but they in turn have been accused of "culturalism," neglecting economy and technology.

Whatever the standpoint of the writer, the history of culture in the twentieth century has always been directly related to the history of communications. All historians have noted the strategic importance of converging economic and technological change in the late nineteenth century, with the development of the telegraph (*see* TELEGRAPHY), the TELEPHONE, electricity, RADIO, MOTION PICTURES, the automobile, ADVERTISING, and the popular press. These developments gave a new sense to both space and time and elicited many prophetic pronouncements, as diverse as they were numerous.

Prophets and liberators. The implications of a continuing communications revolution did not begin to be fully discussed until the 1950s and 1960s, and then there was no shortage of prophets. MARSHALL MCLUHAN followed up his *The Mechanical Bride: Folklore of Industrial Man* (1951) with *The Gutenberg Galaxy* (1962) and *Understanding Media: The Extensions of Man* (1964). A later title was *Culture Is Our Business* (1970). Macdonald reserved his main critique not for "masscult" but for "midcult," Shils's "mediocre culture," the merging of high and low culture in a swampy middle ground. There was also excitement in the feeling that the artist was "smashing open the doors of perception." Some subcultures—intellectual, literary, musical, or artistic—had always been AVANT-GARDE or, in different terms, "adversary cultures." Now there was talk of a "counterculture" or "bomb culture." Far from pursuing "the best," cultural rebels spurned all aspects of the authority that seemed to them to determine the criteria by which the best was chosen. They chose instead to liberate themselves from all authority and to subvert it or ridicule it in public. There were strong critical reactions. Daniel Bell wrote of a "radical disjunction" between the social structure and the culture. George Steiner coined the term *postculture* to cover "disarray, regress into violence, moral obtuseness." Meanwhile, in China—a very different culture with strong traditions—there was a self-proclaimed "cultural revolution" during which the cultural heritage of the past was deliberately and violently jettisoned. The contest seemed to be as universal as Arnold's quest for perfection. *See also* REVOLUTION; VIOLENCE.

Culture and Government

The radical attitudes toward culture during the 1960s eventually became dated. Some of them influenced the development of "mainstream culture." Others were themselves jettisoned, not least in China. Cultural discontents have not disappeared. Meanwhile culture itself has increasingly come to be thought of as a sector of government. The word itself has followed the word *industry* in being used with reference not to a particular human quality but to a range of institutionalized activities sponsored respectively by business and government. The origins of both business and governmental institutions go back before the 1960s. There were ministers of culture before World War II, and cultural committees and delegations. Since the 1960s their numbers have increased. In Third World countries fears of "cultural penetration" and loss of cultural identity have been a potent force in encouraging explicit "cultural policies." These may have a developmental or a protectionist character. *See* DEVELOPMENT COMMUNICATION.

There has also been international debate on such issues, much of it centered in UNESCO, just as there has been debate inside developed countries on the implications of mass culture (*see* INTERNATIONAL ORGANIZATIONS; NEW INTERNATIONAL INFORMATION ORDER). The fact that the United States from the rise of the film industry onward has been a major exporter of cultural products has colored the debate. In the longer-term perspective there have been many other influences. The colonial empires created their own networks of cultural communication that have not completely snapped in the postcolonial era (*see* COLONIZATION). They work through LANGUAGE and customs, leaving intact, for instance, a great cultural divide between the English-speaking and the French-speaking former colonial territories. Thus there can be stronger cultural links with the distant former metropolis than with neighboring countries. Each country also has its own cultural geography, which is influenced by MIGRATION as much as by former political association. One of the most interesting situations is in Canada, where there is not only a strong cultural difference between English-speaking and French-speaking provinces but also a strong sense of the presence of the United States as a neighbor with a very different cultural history from both.

The Anthropological Approach

A third approach to culture, the anthropological, necessarily moves within a world context. The origin of the view that culture is a "whole way of life" can be traced back to German writers on ethnology a generation before E. B. Tylor published his *Primitive Culture* in 1871. It has been Tylor's definition of culture, however, that has been most often quoted, a proof of the selective nature of intellectual and cultural transmission over time. For Tylor culture was that "complex whole which includes knowledge, belief, art, morals, customs and many other capabilities and habits acquired by man as a member of society."

Religionists and Marxists. Many nineteenth- and twentieth-century anthropologists held that RELIGION, through myth, was the key to the understanding of "primitive culture," a view congenial to T. S. Eliot, who in his *Notes towards the Definition of Culture* (1948) called culture "the incarnation of religion." It did not require a direct Marxist influence to establish the importance within a "whole way of life" of "material culture"—culture as revealed in materials and artifacts (*see* ARTIFACT). But this view characterizes the Marxist influence derived from KARL MARX's specifically materialist interpretation. For Marx the material base along with the modes of production determined systems of meanings and values. Culture was "superstructure." There was room for a great variety of Marxist interpretations of the relationship between base and superstructure, and there has been ample debate on competing versions since the 1950s, some of it directly related to the debate on cultural revolution. No Marxist version, of course, would be compatible with an interpretation that the springs of culture are religious in character. *See also* MARXIST THEORIES OF COMMUNICATION.

All anthropological approaches to culture center, however, on regularities within cultural patterns, explicit or implicit. Culture is seen as being transmitted from one generation to the next through symbols and through artifacts, through records and through living traditions. There can be breaks in transmission, as in twentieth-century Europe, the United States, and China. Yet a "whole way of life" can be upset either from within, through atrophy or conflict, or from without, through contact with other cultures, including contact through trade, technology, war, invasion, or empire. The result can be cultural disintegration. In twentieth-century postcolonial circumstances the invasion could be conceived of as a communications invasion through imported communications technology or programs or through TOURISM. Migration outside and return could have similar consequences.

While it became a tradition in British anthropology to start with social structures and to refer to anthropology itself as social anthropology, most U.S. anthropologists started with culture traits, culture patterns, personality and culture, and comparative cultures and called their subject cultural anthropology. In the light of the latter tradition A. L. Kroeber and Clyde Kluckhohn reviewed concepts and definitions of culture in 1952 on the eve of some of the biggest changes in cultural sensibilities. More recently Clifford Geertz, collecting evidence from many societies, has conceived of culture as everything that is produced by and capable of sustaining shared symbolic experience, including, for example, cooking and sport (*see* FOOD; SPORTS). CLAUDE LÉVI-STRAUSS, outside both U.S. and British traditions of anthropology, has treated culture as comprehensive and universal, and society as derivative: "Man reaches his essence, his universality only in culture." Behind a multiplicity of forms, old and new, there are underlying configurations of meanings, which have to be decoded (*see* CODE; MEANING).

Structuralist influence. It is via the anthropology of Lévi-Strauss and French LINGUISTICS and semiology that structuralist approaches to culture have come to influence the whole development of cultural studies (including communications studies), particularly, though not exclusively, in Europe since the 1950s (*see* SEMIOTICS; STRUCTURALISM). Structuralist approaches have converged with explicitly Marxist influences, too, especially through the work of ANTONIO GRAMSCI and Lucien Goldmann, and have reshaped attitudes toward both cultural history and contemporary culture and subcultures. Their influence can be discerned, for instance, in the writings of Raymond Williams, whose first important book, *Culture and Society* (1958), was within as distinctive an English tradition as the work of the social anthropologists. The influence of Gramsci's theories of cultural hegemony has been particularly apparent in the publications of the Center of Cultural Studies at Birmingham University. There is still a gulf, however, between the different approaches to culture and the terms used, and fashion as well as science or politics determines the outcomes.

Bibliography. Matthew Arnold, *Culture and Anarchy*, London, 1869, reprint Cambridge, 1960; Daniel Bell, *The Cultural Contradictions of Capitalism*, New York and London, 1976; Tony Bennett, Graham Martin, Colin Mercer, and Janet Woollacott, eds., *Culture, Ideology, and Social Process*, London, 1981; T. S. Eliot, *Notes towards the Definition of Culture*, London, 1948; Herbert J. Gans, *Popular Culture and High Culture: An Analysis and Evaluation of Taste*, New York, 1974; A. L. Kroeber and Clyde Kluckhohn, *Culture: A Critical Review of Concepts and Definitions*, Cambridge, Mass., 1952; Bernard Rosenberg and David Manning White, eds., *Mass Culture*, Glencoe, Ill., 1957; Bernard Waites, Tony Bennett, and Graham Martin, eds., *Popular Culture: Past and Present*, London, 1982; Raymond Williams, *Culture and Society*, London, 1958.

ASA BRIGGS

CUNEIFORM

Writing systems in which signs were made by the impression of a sharpened reed stylus on clay tablets. The term comes from the Latin for "wedge-shaped." The first and principal cuneiform system was invented to write the Sumerian LANGUAGE in southern Mesopotamia just before 3000 B.C.E. and persisted into the first centuries of this era (see Figure 1). The earliest cuneiform tablets, excavated at the site of the ancient city of Uruk, evolved from a preexisting numerical notation system of CLAY TOKENS and token-inspired impressed tablets. Cuneiform, a system of more than one thousand signs that could represent not only numbers and measures but words and personal names, vastly increased the possibilities for information storage and communication. This is the earliest example of a durable, nonspoken representation of language. *See* SIGN; WRITING.

The speed and efficiency of cuneiform writing depended on impressing the wedge-shaped stylus onto a soft surface, and 99 percent of all surviving cuneiform documents are clay tablets ranging in size from 2 by 2 centimeters to 30 by 30 centimeters. The only other suitable medium for accepting the stroke of the stylus was wax; wax-covered writing boards were used extensively in the first millennium, though only one has survived. For purposes of commemoration or identification, cuneiform could be chiseled into stone, engraved in metal, and painted or scratched on wood or ceramics. *See* WRITING MATERIALS.

The invention of cuneiform writing is the subject of an episode in the Sumerian epic tale Enmerkar and the Lord of Aratta. Enmerkar, mythical ruler of the Sumerian city of Uruk whose historical prototype would have ruled about 2700 B.C.E., demands submission and tribute from the ruler of the distant Iranian city of Aratta, rich in the natural resources that Sumer lacked. Enmerkar's demands are communicated in a series of long messages delivered by a courier. When one message is too long for the courier to remember, Enmerkar invents "writing on clay tablets" as an aide-mémoire. This native etiology is scarcely plausible, and documentary evidence indicates that the earliest use of writing was for administrative recordkeeping, not diplomatic exchange—that is, cuneiform was used for information storage for several centuries before its full communicative potential was realized.

Development and evolution. Each sign stood for a Sumerian word of one or two syllables. In the earliest cuneiform repertory there were some abstract signs, such as a cross inscribed in a circle for "sheep." However, the great majority of signs were originally pictographic (see Figure 2), although modern scholars frequently cannot determine exactly what a given sign depicts. Whereas pictograms can adequately represent concrete objects, a variety of devices were employed to represent abstract notions. Signs could be juxtaposed, as in "woman" + "foreign land" = "slavegirl" (see Figure 2*f*), or "mouth" + "food" = "to eat" (see Figure 2*j*). In addition, a pictograph might be used to suggest an action accomplished by means of the pictured object, as in "foot" = "to go, stand" (see Figure 2*m*). But the potential to express

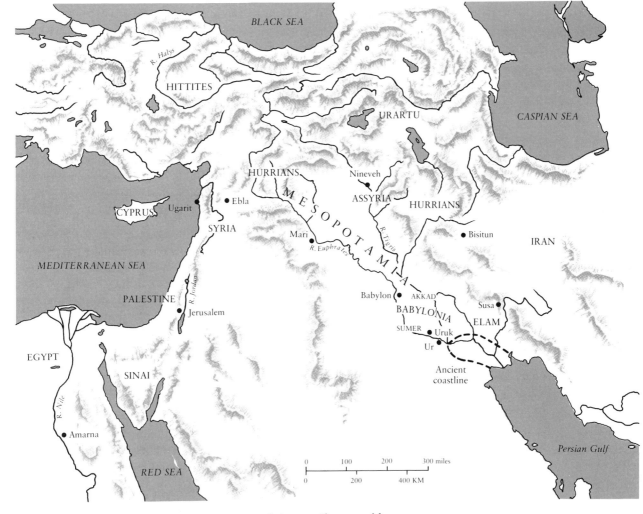

Figure 1. *(Cuneiform)* Ancient Mesopotamia and the cuneiform world.

the complete lexical and grammatical possibilities of language depended on the development of purely phonetic representation, which was accomplished through use of the rebus principle, by which the sign for one word came also to represent a homophone (a word that sounded the same but had a different meaning). Rebus writing allowed the use of the pictogram for the Sumerian word *ti* ("arrow") to be used to write its near homophone *ti(l)* ("to live"), or the pictogram *ga* ("[jar of] milk") to be used to write the verbal prefix *ga-* ("let me . . .").

The small number of rebus writings present in the earliest tablets proves that phoneticism was incipient at writing's beginning, but it was far more fully developed in later centuries. The rebus principle not only made the writing of many abstract words and grammatical particles possible but also enabled cuneiform signs to be used as purely phonetic representations in the writing of languages other than Sumerian.

Spread—linguistic and geographical. Speakers of the Semitic language ancestral to Akkadian (Assyro-Babylonian) were present in southern Mesopotamia early in the third millennium. Another Semitic lan-

guage, known from the Italian excavations at Ebla, was spoken in northern Syria. The early use of cuneiform to write Semitic languages in both these areas was confined to proper names, and at Ebla, lists of Semitic words and their Sumerian equivalents. Otherwise, documents from these regions use Sumerian elements, which may have been read as Semitic, with only a few phonetically written Semitic prepositions and pronouns.

The first continuous texts written completely in Semitic are attested in Mesopotamia proper in the Old Akkadian, or Sargonic, period (beginning ca. 2350 B.C.E.). Akkadian cuneiform persisted in Mesopotamia into the early years of the current era, although Akkadian as a spoken language began to be replaced by Aramaic (*see* ALPHABET) early in the first millennium B.C.E. In all periods, the paradigm for writing Akkadian established in the Old Akkadian period remained valid: phonetic representation using a restricted corpus of monosyllabic signs, supplemented by a limited number of Sumerian logograms, that is, words written in Sumerian but read as Akkadian. These usually represented very com-

439

CHRONOLOGICAL PERIODS

I Protoliterate (3000 B.C.E.)
II Early Dynastic (2700 B.C.E.)
III Early Dynastic II/III (2500 B.C.E.)
IV Third Dynasty of Ur (2000 B.C.E.)
V Neo-Assyrian (900–700 B.C.E.)

READING AND MEANING OF THE SIGNS

a *dingir* (god); *an* (heaven)
b *ki* (earth, place)
c *lu* (man)
d *munus* (woman); *sal* (thin, fine)
e *kur* (mountain, foreign land)
f *geme* (female slave)
g *sag* (head)
h *ka* (mouth); *inim* (word); *dug* (to speak)
i *ninda* (food, bread); *gar* (to place)
j *ku* (to eat)
k *a* (water)
l *nag* (to drink)
m *du* (to go); *gub* (to stand)
n *mushen* (bird)
o *ku* (fish)
p *gud* (bull)
q *ab* (cow)
r *she* (grain, barley)

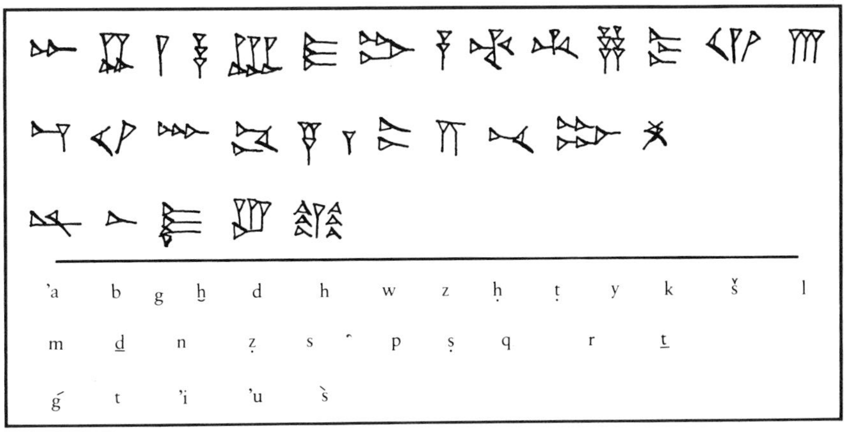

Figure 3. *(Cuneiform)* The Ugaritic alphabet as written on an exercise tablet excavated at Ugarit. From David Diringer, *Writing*, London: Thames and Hudson, 1962, pp. 115, 116. Transliteration updated by Jo Ann Hackett, The Johns Hopkins University.

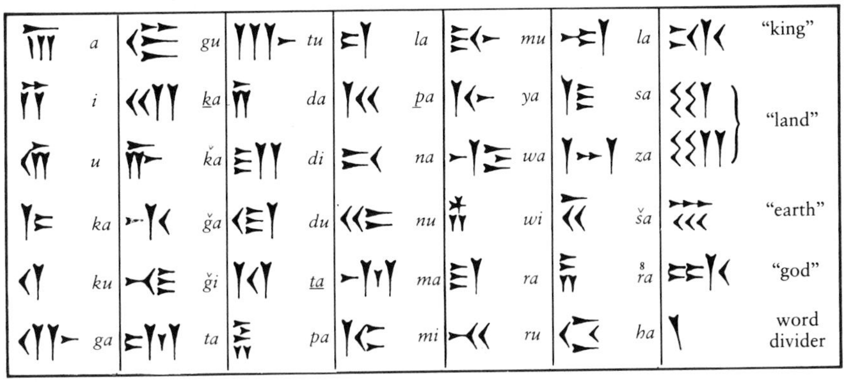

Figure 4. *(Cuneiform)* The Old Persian syllabary. From G. R. Driver, *Semitic Writing from Pictograph to Alphabet*, London: Oxford University Press, 1948, p. 132.

mon terms, such as "king" or "earth"; legal formulas; or technical terms, such as the names of items of furniture, semiprecious stones, or parts of the sheep's liver.

By the middle of the second millennium B.C.E., several of Mesopotamia's neighbors had adapted the Akkadian syllabary together with Sumerian logograms to write their own languages. These include the Elamites of southwestern Iran; the Hurrians, who were spread in an arc stretching from the Zagros Mountains in the east to the Taurus ranges in the west; and the Hittites, who controlled a large empire from their capital in central Anatolia. During this same period (ca. 1500–1200 B.C.E.), Akkadian became the lingua franca of the Near East and was used regularly in diplomatic communications between capitals. A large archive of Akkadian tablets unearthed at Amarna, in Egypt, contains the correspondence to pharaohs from Assyrian, Babylonian, Hurrian, and Hittite rulers as well as from Egypt's vassals in Syria and Palestine.

In the first millennium, Sumero-Akkadian cuneiform was used to write other languages only in the east (Elam) and the far north, where it was adapted to write Urartian, a language akin to Hurrian spoken

◁ Figure 2. *(Cuneiform)* The development of cuneiform signs. From Samuel N. Kramer, *The Sumerians*, Chicago: The University of Chicago Press, 1963, pp. 304, 305.

in the area that would later become Armenia. In Syria and Palestine cuneiform and clay tablets were replaced by the easier-to-learn alphabet and papyrus or parchment, a process that was occurring in Mesopotamia as well.

Sumero-Akkadian cuneiform inspired two completely new and radically simplified writing systems utilizing configurations of wedges impressed on clay tablets. At Ugarit, on the Syrian coast, archives from the late second millennium containing both Akkadian records and records written in the local Canaanite language, Ugaritic, have been excavated. Ugaritic was written in a cuneiform alphabet of thirty signs, which suggests that the Semitic cursive alphabet had been developed already (see Figure 3). In the middle of the first millennium, the Achaemenid Persians developed a cuneiform syllabary of thirty-six signs and five logograms (see Figure 4) for writing Old Persian, which they used for commemorative purposes only; their administrative records are in cuneiform Elamite or alphabetic Aramaic.

Content. An enormous variety of texts were written in Sumerian and Akkadian, the languages of the vast majority of all cuneiform texts. As in modern civilization, the most common are records—administrative, legal, and economic—the "laundry lists" recording the daily transactions of large bureaucratic organizations (temple and palace) as well as individual families and firms. Many letters were exchanged in the course of these transactions as well as for personal reasons between individuals (*see* LETTER). Affairs of state are recorded in diplomatic correspondence and international treaties. Commemorative inscriptions of rulers identify donations to the gods or building activities and often contain records of military accomplishments. Assyrian annals and Babylonian chronicles were dedicated to recording events of historical importance, the former in the name of the king and hence never less than flattering, the latter seemingly disinterested and objective. A small number of collections of laws, including the famous Code of Hammurabi (ca. 1800 B.C.E.), attest to a long tradition of legal conceptualization and formalization. There was a large body of scientific and technical texts, often arranged in long, multitablet series. Their subjects include divination, rituals, astronomy, mathematics, medicine, glassmaking, and lexicography.

Literature represents the smallest textual category, although there are many thousands of tablets containing literary compositions. These include hymns and incantations; epic and myth, including the justly celebrated Gilgamesh Epic and the Enuma Elish (Creation Epic); wisdom literature, such as the Poem of the Righteous Sufferer, proverbs, and fables; and historiographic compositions, which provided tendentious literary interpretations of events and great figures of the past (*see* HISTORIOGRAPHY). Both the number of copies of an individual composition and catalogs of literary texts in single holdings reflecting the scribal curriculum suggest that there was a sort of canon of literary texts, which were copied and transmitted by scribes in the course of their education and beyond. However, this canon was not at all rigid, and there is certainly no evidence for a category of forbidden texts. *See also* LITERARY CANON.

Literacy. It is assumed that, as in most traditional societies, LITERACY was restricted. This assumption is reinforced by the comparative complexity of cuneiform, the mastery of which required a rather long period of education. But there is no way of knowing whether it was restricted to scribes, scientists, and technicians or whether there was a wider literate public. In some periods, at least, there is evidence to suggest that businessmen could have mastered a repertory of signs large enough to understand their business records and letters.

The initial steps toward cuneiform literacy were copying individual signs and short excerpts from sign lists. Extant tablets preserve the instructor's copy in the left-hand column and the awkward student's imitation on the right; often the student's attempt has been wiped away many times. After learning how to write, the student copied more advanced lexical lists, compendiums of legal phrases, sample documents, and literary and technical compositions. The only detailed information available on the or-

ganization of schools and the curriculum is for the period around 1800 B.C.E., when education seemed to be provided by private academies rather than the large religious or secular institutions. A whole GENRE of literature, predominantly humorous and ironical, takes the scribal academy as its topic.

Decipherment. Cuneiform first drew the attention of Europeans through artifacts and reports brought back by visitors to the Near East, especially Persepolis, the ancient Persian capital, in the seventeenth and eighteenth centuries. Copies of Achaemenid royal inscriptions on stone were circulated, and it was soon established that some were trilingual, although none of the three languages—Old Persian, Elamite, and Akkadian—had been deciphered at that time. One of the three languages was written in a much simpler writing system, which by the early nineteenth century was correctly assumed to be Old Persian, the language of the Achaemenids (see Figure 4). The first steps toward decipherment were taken by the Göttingen scholar Georg Friedrich Grotefend (1775–1853). His work was continued by other scholars, but substantial progress could be made only when a sufficiently long inscription was found and copied. This was accomplished by the Englishman Henry Rawlinson (1810–1895), who at great personal risk copied the inscription of Darius I on the cliffside at Bisitun. In 1848 he published his decipherment of the Old Persian version, and by the mid-1850s the third language of the inscriptions, Akkadian, had been deciphered through the efforts of Rawlinson, the Irishman Edward Hincks (1792–1866), and the Frenchman Jules Oppert (1825–1905). This was possible only when it was realized that Akkadian was written both syllabically and logographically and that syllabic Akkadian writing was both polyphonic and homophonic (i.e., a given sign could have more than one reading, and a given sound might be expressed by any one of several signs). Because Akkadian was clearly related to other, better-known Semitic languages, this initial breakthrough led to rapid progress in decipherment, in turn facilitating the decipherment of cuneiform texts in a variety of languages during the following decades.

The second language of the Achaemenid inscriptions, Elamite, is without any known relation and is still only imperfectly understood. Sumerian, whose existence was established only after study of the tablets excavated by the British at NINEVEH, also has no known cognate languages, and its decipherment proceeded more slowly than that of Akkadian. Cuneiform Hittite was deciphered in 1915—less than a decade after the first lot of tablets was excavated—by the Czech scholar Bedřich Hrozný (1879–1952). The decipherment of Ugaritic (see Figure 3) was even more rapid. Soon after the first tablets were discovered by French excavators in 1929, independent decipherments were offered by the French scholars

Charles Virolleaud (1879–1968) and Édouard Dhorme (1881–1966) and the German Theo Bauer (1896–1957). The first Eblaite tablets were published by the Italian scholar Giovanni Pettinato after their discovery in 1974, and work on them has been continued by him and other scholars.

Divine patrons. The Sumerian god of wisdom was Enki (Ea in Akkadian), but writing proper was the domain of the goddess Nisaba, patron of scribes and the scribal academy. By the first millennium, this role had been transferred to the god Nabu. Nabu's emblems were the scribe's stylus and tablet.

See also ARTIFACT; EGYPTIAN HIEROGLYPHS; INDUS SCRIPT.

Bibliography. D. O. Edzard, "Keilschrift," *Reallexikon der Assyriologie*, Vol. 5, Berlin (1928 ed.), 1980; Samuel N. Kramer, *The Sumerians*, Chicago, 1963; Ministry of Culture, *Naissance de l'écriture: Cunéiformes et hiéroglyphes*, Paris, 1982; A. Leo Oppenheim, *Ancient Mesopotamia*, 2d ed., rev., Chicago, 1977.

JERROLD S. COOPER

CYBERNETICS

The word *cybernetics* was derived by mathematician and social philosopher NORBERT WIENER from the Greek word for the art of steering, *kybernētēs*. He defined it as "the science of control and communication," and to emphasize that the material embodiments of these processes were not central to its concern he added "in the animal and the machine." Before its modern meaning, André-Marie Ampère had used the word in 1838 and 1843, and ideas of cybernetics have been traced to Hero of Alexandria, who lived in the first century C.E.

Cybernetics is fundamentally concerned with organization, how organization emerges and becomes constituted by networks of communication processes, and how wholes behave as a consequence of the interaction among the parts. Cybernetics surfaced in a series of interdisciplinary meetings that began in the 1940s at a time when machines were envisioned that could do intellectual work; when communication and control became an increasingly important feature of society; when organizational challenges, especially during World War II, revealed scientific limitations; and when overarching organizing principles such as religion, IDEOLOGY, and imperialism seemed to give way to notions of autonomy, self-government, and, last but not least, information.

Wiener's book *Cybernetics*, first published in 1948, summarized the interdisciplinary collaboration and set forth the accomplishments and visions of the new field. In 1956 British psychiatrist W. Ross Ashby wrote an influential introduction to the field and suggested that cybernetics be concerned with systems that contain and process their own information or are informationally closed. For management consultant Stafford Beer, cybernetics became the science of effective organization. U.S. neurophysiologist Warren S. McCulloch saw in cybernetics an experimental epistemology that enabled him to study communication within the brain and between observers and their environments. Late in his life JEAN PIAGET recognized cybernetics as an approach to modeling the cognitive processes underlying the human mind (*see* COGNITION). And GREGORY BATESON stressed that whereas the subject matter of science previously had been matter and energy, cybernetics, as a branch of MATHEMATICS dealing with problems of control, recursiveness, and information, focuses on forms and "the patterns that connect."

Circularity and Purpose

Probably the single most fertile idea in cybernetics is that of circularity. When A causes B and B causes C but C causes A, then A essentially causes itself, and the whole—consisting of A, B, and C—somewhat defies external manipulation. The cybernetic notion of circular reasoning has expanded scientific explanation and has yielded extraordinarily important constructions.

Traditional machines, culminating in the Industrial Revolution of the nineteenth century, replaced human physical labor in many areas, but humans still had to control the machines. For example, cars contain engines for locomotion, but drivers have to keep them on course. Early control theory aimed at the design of servomechanisms, that is, machines that could control other machines. Thermostats for temperature regulation, automatic pilots, industrial robots, wholly automated chemical plants, and, unfortunately, goal-seeking missiles are the results. In all of these examples the purpose is imposed from the outside by a human user or designer. When this theory is applied to human behavior, the negative feedback implied requires internal representations of desired states of affairs against which perceived deviations are measured and counteracted. For example, William T. Powers linked actions to perceptions and developed a psychology from the insight that all human behavior controls PERCEPTION.

During the seminal Macy Foundation conferences on cybernetics between 1946 and 1953 the multidisciplinary participants came to realize that circular causalities—such as a steersman who acts on the observed consequences of his actions, a speaker who continuously modifies her presentation while monitoring audience reactions to what she says, or the homeostatic mechanisms by which a living organism keeps important physiological variables in balance—underlie all purposive actions and that systems that embody them are fundamentally different from those that do not. As a consequence of circular causalities within their organization the initial conditions and actual trajectories of behavior of such systems are insignificant in view of the final state to which they converge or the goal that they maintain in spite of outside disturbances. This recognition gave rise to a new teleology in which circular forms of organization (processes) and final conditions (states or structures) mutually define each other without reference to an origin or external purpose. Finding such circularities everywhere in the human nervous system suggested scientific research into questions of mind, consciousness, the notion of self (as in self-organization, self-identification, self-awareness), and an approach to human behavior without recourse to inside representations of outside events, controllers, or values. Such research is distinct from a search for linear causalities that either remains incomplete or ends in ultimate causes (theology). The early study of circular causalities helped to identify pathologies of the nervous system and aided the design of artificial organs. To social scientists it meant that purpose and mind may be seen as distributed (not centralized) and imminent in the way people interact or communicate with one another regardless of whether participants are fully aware of them. Examples of applications of this principle range from the maintenance of homeostasis in families to the working of checks and balances in an economy. Here cybernetics shifted attention from control *of* to control *within*.

Stability and Morphogenesis

Control theory is conservative in the double sense of motivating systems capable of stabilizing some of its variables and of requiring that such systems remain organizationally invariant during the process (morphostasis). Consequently, the modeling of social phenomena in terms of negative feedback control theory tends to promote the status quo. But circular causalities also can lead to runaways, such as arms races, explosions, meltdowns, or cancerous growths. These appear "uncontrolled" for fear of the unknown destruction they may cause. However, Japanese anthropologist Magoroh Maruyama has shown that deviation-amplifying circular causalities need not always be destructive. They may lead, through temporary instabilities, to new forms (morphogenesis), and in fact may account for many processes of social change. For example, above a certain threshold, organizational success breeds more success and initiates growth until new constraints are encountered; or an originally insignificant dissatisfaction may mushroom into widespread dissent until the whole social system is ready to undergo structural changes, reorganize itself, or assume a new identity. Managers, politicians, and therapists do not hesitate to initiate such "vicious cycles" for creating new systems. Ash-

by's concept of ultrastability, French mathematician René Thom's catastrophe theory, and Belgian physicist and Nobel laureate Ilya Prigogine's work on dissipative structures all concern such forms of morphogenesis.

Communication

Modern communication theory arose out of the cybernetic marriage of statistics and control theory. The idea that messages could be distorted by unpredictable perturbations ("noise") and recovered within limits by a receiver led to a concept of communication as the variation that senders and receivers share, or of information as the pattern that is invariant throughout the noisy transmission of messages from one place or medium to another. CLAUDE SHANNON's 1948 monograph "A Mathematical Theory of Communication" was a milestone for understanding communication quantitatively (*see* INFORMATION THEORY). Since its publication, explanations in terms of information processing, encoding-decoding functions, channels of communication, pattern recognition, uncertainty, redundancy, noise, equivocation, entropy, and the like have come to be used in nearly all fields of science. The theory reflects a shift in emphasis from isolated objects to organized wholes or from the separate study of senders, receivers, and messages to an inquiry into how they are related dynamically and quantitatively. Ashby's extension of the originally bivariate notion of communication to one embracing many variables renders information theory a statistical tool for tracing information flows in complex systems. The theory also provides measures of diversity, memory capacity, intelligence, and organization, plus a new way of conceptualizing cultural functions of art.

Computation and Algorithms

The development in cybernetics of an algorithmic logic that incorporates circularities in the form of recursive functions (functions that contain themselves in their arguments, like the square root of the square root of the square root . . .) and time profoundly changed scientific thinking. Against the background of Kurt Gödel's famous incompleteness theorem, whose proof involved recursive functions, British mathematician Alan M. Turing's work on a theory of computation, McCulloch and Walter H. Pitts's logic of neuronal networks containing loops, and, after experiences with ENIAC (the first operational vacuum-tube-based "ultra-rapid calculating machine"), JOHN VON NEUMANN presented a landmark proposal to an international symposium on Cerebral Mechanisms of Behavior (the 1948 Hixon Symposium) that became the foundation of the theory of finite-state automata and a blueprint for modern programmable digital computers (*see* COMPUTER:

HISTORY). These ideas not only gave birth to computer science, the field of ARTIFICIAL INTELLIGENCE, and the computerization of society but also shifted scientific attention from existing structures (ontology) to the operations that bring about particular phenomena (ontogenesis). In addition, they challenged the verification theory of truth, on which traditional science could heretofore rely, by positing instead a computability/decidability criterion. The notion of computation has since been generalized to a great many processes—technological, mental, and social—and theory constructions in the form of algorithms, which are a prerequisite of computer and mathematical modeling, are increasingly common. *See also* COMPUTER: IMPACT.

Contributions to Biology

Research in biology, by U.S. physiologist Walter B. Cannon on homeostasis and continued by Ashby on adaptation, ultrastability, information, and intelligence, revealed the enormous "wisdom" in the human nervous system. Work by McCulloch on neuronal communication nets, by von Neumann on self-reproduction, and by Austrian-born biophysicist Heinz von Foerster on learning and self-organization led to a view of the human brain as a model of sophisticated computing machinery and expanded greatly the conception of computers as an aid to human intelligence. (In the field of artificial intelligence this relationship is often reversed, taking computers as models of human cognition.)

Chilean biologists Humberto R. Maturana and Francisco G. Varela, along with others, suggested autopoiesis, a recursive process of self-production, as the fundamental process characterizing all living systems. Varela proposed various principles of biology, based on the autopoietic organization of living systems, relating especially to the concepts of autonomy and closure, that aim to overcome the previous preoccupation with control. In Maturana's work on the biology of cognition he challenged the epistemological foundations of all sciences that claim to study nature without acknowledging that all scientists are constitutionally tied to their own biology of cognition and that their universe is thus confined to computations in their own nervous systems. These ideas originated in biology, but the theories and computational models they inform are generalizable to other disciplines.

Contributions to the Social Sciences

Wiener, quoting Bateson and MARGARET MEAD, recognized that the social sciences are fundamentally concerned with organization, that communication systems and circular flows of messages in particular are the "glue" that holds social organizations together, and that cybernetics therefore is essential for

understanding the ontogenesis of society. Von Neumann and Oskar Morgenstern's game theory was an early cybernetic contribution to social interaction. It formalizes the coordination of action by players who have to consider their own behavior and the behavior of others. Extended to many players—so-called *n*-person game theory—to longer strategic commitments—so-called meta-game theory—and to different levels of information available, the theory is now a standard approach in economics and political decision making.

The idea that purpose could be structurally manifest in social organization proved attractive to anthropologists, sociologists, political scientists, and management scientists. With its emphasis on organization, variety, teleology, autonomy, and epistemology, cybernetics offered attractive alternatives to the usual theological, hierarchical, and linear causal constructions of social reality. Beer derived cybernetic principles of decision making, social learning, and adaptation and successfully applied them to business organizations and governments. Political scientist Karl W. Deutsch explored teleological models in the social sciences and developed a cybernetic approach to government. For some sociologists, cybernetics has lent mathematical substance to KARL MARX's idea of "structural purpose." Polish economist Oskar Lange used cybernetics to model the economics of production. Bateson suggested "messages in circuit" as a unit of analysis and applied cybernetics in his explorations of art as communication, of human reasoning, and later of family therapy. Taking seriously the fundamental circularity in human interactive communication, Bateson saw the therapist as a participant in a system in which the family could develop its own autonomy, much as British educational theorist Gordon Pask viewed education as a mutual process in which teachers and learners adapt to and learn from each other. U.S. anthropologist Roy A. Rappaport employed cybernetics to demonstrate the regulative function of RITUAL and sanctity in human ecology. And in a related analysis Bateson showed convincingly how planning, as a supreme manifestation of human conscious purpose, will destroy the environment and thereby humans as well unless this received mode of action is replaced by a cybernetic understanding of the human role in an ecology of mind.

Contributions to Epistemology

Since Mead suggested in 1968 that cybernetics apply its insights about circular communication and organization to itself, the cybernetics of cybernetics, or second-order cybernetics as von Foerster called it, has become an increasingly fascinating subject. In this pursuit cybernetics not only relativizes itself but also challenges the traditional paradigm of scientific inquiry at its base. Whereas the latter insists that scientific observers not enter their domain of observation, the cybernetics of cybernetics suggests instead that observers cannot escape participation in the very phenomena they observe. This necessarily self-referential involvement converges to world constructions that reflect more the recursivity of observing than the (unknowable) perturbations that may enter the process from outside. Austrian-born psychologist and philosopher Ernst von Glasersfeld, who calls himself a radical constructivist, therefore insists that all realities are, within experiential constraints, cognitively constructed. Von Foerster worked on the role of LANGUAGE and logic in such constructions. Austrian-born family therapist Paul Watzlawick points to the interactional grounding of such constructions. With this shift in ground, cybernetics leaves ontology (the branch of philosophy concerned with the nature of reality or what exists independent of its observation) in favor of an epistemology (the branch of philosophy concerned with processes by which we come to know) and lays the foundation for a new approach to human social cognition and self-understanding.

For the scientific study of communication the methodological consequences of this development are enormous. Theories of communication in systems that include their observers must be constructed within the very object they claim to describe, and the act of formulating such theories is also an act of changing the object while it is being described. Knowledge so obtained can no longer be evaluated as representative of an independently existing reality but as recursively embedded in actions that realize (construct or compute) its claims. Scientists—or any cognitively involved being, for that matter—can then no longer blame an objective reality for their "findings" but must assume responsibility for their own constructions. This responsibility has become the basis for ethical considerations of a cybernetic epistemology.

Cybernetics is not a mere collection of facts but a scientific approach to communication, knowledge, and reality construction with all of its cognitive and social consequences. True to its interdisciplinary origin, it provides a language for scientists to talk to one another across disciplinary boundaries. Cybernetics has been a continuous source of revolutionary ideas, has given rise to numerous specialized disciplines, and is providing a theoretical foundation for understanding the paths toward an information society. Its implicitly humanistic aim is wholly emancipatory.

See also MODELS OF COMMUNICATION.

Bibliography. W. Ross Ashby, *An Introduction to Cybernetics*, London, 1956, reprint New York, 1961; Gregory Bateson, "Cybernetic Explanation," in *Steps to an Ecology of Mind*, New York, 1972; Gregory Bateson and Mary Catherine Bateson, *Angels Fear*, New York, 1987; Mary Catherine Bateson, *Our Own Metaphor*, New York, 1972; Stafford Beer, *Cybernetics and Management*, London and New York, 1959, reprint 1964; Walter F. Buckley, ed., *Modern Systems Research for the Behavioral Scientist*, Chicago, 1968; Walter B. Cannon, *The Wisdom of the Body*, rev. and enl. ed., New York, 1939; Roger Conant, ed., *Mechanisms of Intelligence: Ross Ashby's Writings on Cybernetics*, Seaside, Calif., 1981; Karl W. Deutsch, *The Nerves of Government: Models of Political Communication and Control*, New York, 1963; Oskar Lange, *Wholes and Parts* (Całość i rozwój w świetle cybernetyki), trans. by E. Lepa, Oxford, 1965; Warren S. McCulloch, *Embodiments of Mind*, Cambridge, Mass., 1965; Warren S. McCulloch and Walter H. Pitts, "A Logical Calculus of the Ideas Immanent in Nervous Activity," *Bulletin of Mathematical Biophysics* 5 (1943): 115–133; Magoroh Maruyama, "The Second Cybernetics: Deviation-Amplifying Mutual Causal Processes," *American Scientist* 51 (1963): 164–179, 250A–256A; Humberto R. Maturana and Francisco J. Varela, *Autopoiesis and Cognition*, Boston, 1980; Otto Mayr, *The Origins of Feedback Control* (Zur Frühgeschichte der technischen Regelungen), Cambridge, Mass., 1970; William T. Powers, *Behavior: The Control of Perception*, Chicago, 1973; Ilya Prigogine and Isabelle Stengers, *Order Out of Chaos* (La nouvelle alliance), New York, 1984; Roy A. Rappaport, *Pigs for the Ancestors*, new enl. ed., New Haven, Conn., 1984; Arturo Rosenblueth and Norbert Wiener, "Purposeful and Non-purposeful Behavior," *Philosophy of Science* 17 (1950): 318–326; Arturo Rosenblueth, Norbert Wiener, and Julian Bigelow, "Behavior, Purpose, and Teleology," *Philosophy of Science* 10 (1943): 18–24; Francisco J. Varela, *Principles of Biological Autonomy*, New York, 1979; Heinz von Foerster, ed., *Cybernetics of Cybernetics*, San Jose, Calif., 1985; Heinz von Foerster et al., eds., *Cybernetics: Circular Causal and Feedback Mechanisms in Biological and Social Systems*, 5 vols., New York, 1950–1955; John von Neumann, "The General and Logical Theory of Automata," in *Cerebral Mechanisms in Behavior*, ed. by Lloyd A. Jeffress, New York, 1951, reprint 1967; John von Neumann and Oskar Morgenstern, *Theory of Games and Economic Behavior*, 3d ed., Princeton, N.J., 1944, reprint 1980; Norbert Wiener, *Cybernetics: Or Control and Communication in the Animal and the Machine*, 2d ed., Cambridge, Mass., 1961; idem, *The Human Use of Human Beings: Cybernetics and Society*, 2d ed., rev., Garden City, N.Y., 1954, reprint 1967; Marshall C. Yovits, G. T. Jacobi, and G. D. Goldstein, eds., *Self-Organizing Systems*, Washington, D.C., 1962.

KLAUS KRIPPENDORFF

(dī), the fourth letter of the Roman alphabet, corresponding in position and power to the Phœnician and Hebrew *daleth* and Greek *delta*, Δ, whence also its form was derived by rounding one angle of the triangular form. It represents the sonant dental mute, or point-voice stop consonant, which in English is alveolar rather than dental. The plural has been written D's, *D*s, de's.

DAGUERRE, LOUIS (1789–1851)

French artist and inventor of the first successful photographic process. Louis-Jacques-Mandé Daguerre dedicated himself to capturing and communicating to large audiences the visible world. His first achievement—the diorama—created the illusion of nature through a combination of exact draftsmanship and imaginative lighting effects. When enthusiasm for such illusions waned, Daguerre turned to the exploitation of light itself. Building on the discoveries of JOSEPH-NICÉPHORE NIEPCE, he perfected a process using silver iodide and mercury vapor that revolutionized the way people looked at the world around them and at one another: the daguerreotype.

Daguerre was initially trained as a painter of stage designs, in which the goal was to display a scene with such impact that the audience almost accepted the illusion as a reality. In 1822 he opened a diorama whose scenes were so realistic that viewers claimed to have seen figures in them move. By manipulating ceiling and wall panels Daguerre was even able to vary the light and create a sense of passing time and changing events (e.g., avalanches, volcanic eruptions).

Daguerre soon began a long series of experiments aimed at using light to create images of real objects, not just to illuminate the artist's designs. In 1829 he became the partner of Niepce, who by about 1826 had created the first permanent photograph using bitumen on a pewter plate. Daguerre rightly insisted that iodine on silver would yield better results, and in 1835 he found that a relatively short exposure to light (as little as five minutes) created a latent image, which could then be brought out by the action of mercury vapor. This photographic chain of events, in which a latent image is developed after exposure of the picture, remains the basis of film processes today.

The last major obstacle was the need to fix the

Figure 1. *(Daguerre, Louis)* Honoré Daumier, "Pose considered the most suitable for obtaining an attractive Daguerreotype portrait." Lithograph, 1844. Gernsheim Collection, Harry Ransom Humanities Research Center, The University of Texas at Austin.

LES BONS BOURGEOIS.

Position réputée la plus commode pour avoir un joli portrait au Daguerréotype

image permanently. In 1837 Daguerre found that common salt would perform the duty; two years later English scientist Sir John Herschel found a superior fixative, hyposulfite of soda, and Daguerre eagerly adopted it. The French government agreed to buy all rights to the process, and Daguerre's procedure was triumphantly announced to the world at a meeting of the French Academy of Sciences on August 19, 1839. The result was a craze for PHO-TOGRAPHY that has never abated. Although the wet collodion process soon superseded Daguerre's process, the daguerreotype remained unequaled for sharpness until the development of fine-grained films in the twentieth century.

HARTLEY S. SPATT

DANCE

A complex form of communication that combines the visual, kinesthetic, and aesthetic aspects of human movement with (usually) the aural dimension of musical sounds and sometimes POETRY. Dance is created out of culturally understood symbols within social and religious contexts, and it conveys information and MEANING as RITUAL, ceremony, and en-

tertainment. For dance to communicate, its audience must understand the cultural conventions that deal with human movement in time and space.

Many definitions of dance have been proposed, but none has focused on its communicative aspects. With few exceptions writers simply assert without further elaboration that dance communicates, or else they focus on the NARRATIVE or mimetic potential of dance movement. From such assertions one can conclude only that the rigorous formulation and investigation of the communicative aspects of dance are still in their infancy.

Dance in a Cultural Context

Dance is a cultural form that results from creative processes that manipulate (that is, handle with skill) human bodies in time and space so that the formalization of movement is intensified in much the same manner as poetry intensifies the formalization of LANGUAGE. The cultural form produced, though transient, has structured content that conveys meaning, is a visual manifestation of social relations, and may be the subject of an elaborate aesthetic system. Often the process of performing is as important as the cultural form produced (see PERFORMANCE). Dance may be considered ART, work, ritual, ceremony, en-

Figure 1. *(Dance)* O bon festival dance *(bon odori)* performed in mid-August, Japan. Courtesy of Japan National Tourist Organization.

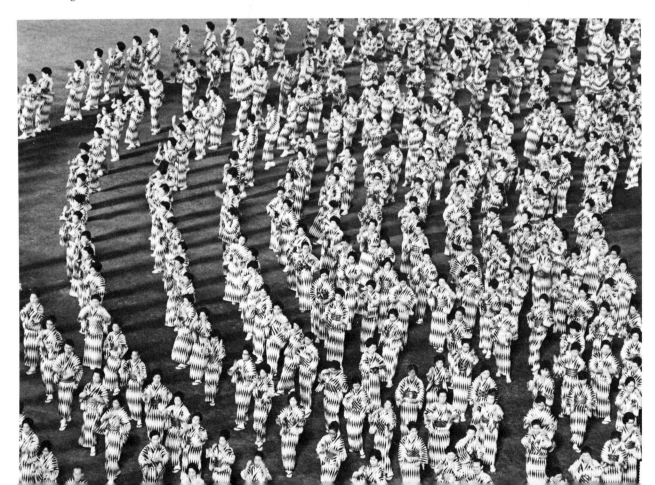

tertainment, or any combination of these, depending on the culture or society that produces it. It is misleading to assume that dance is a universal language, as many have done in the past. Except on a most superficial level, dance cannot be understood (i.e., communicate) cross-culturally unless individual dance traditions are understood in terms of the culture in which each tradition is embedded.

Dance consists of structured movement that is usually part of some larger activity or activity system. Many societies do not have a cultural category comparable to what Westerners call dance, and it could be argued that dance is not a valid cross-cultural category. Structured human movement that has the characteristics mentioned above is found in most societies. Indigenous categories can best define dance in any particular society, but a larger view that takes other performances into consideration is more appropriate for studying dance as communication. In some societies cultural forms based on human movement performed for the gods may be considered ritual instead of dance, but essentially the same movement sequences may be considered dance if performed for a human audience. The movement dimension of a Balinese religious FESTIVAL communicates to specific supernatural beings that the ritual is being carried out in order to obtain specific ends. The same group of movement sequences performed on a secular stage will communicate different information to a human audience, and this information will vary depending on whether the viewer is from the dancer's own village, a Balinese from a different village, an Indonesian who is not Balinese, a non-Indonesian who understands the specific cultural form through study or participation, or a non-Indonesian who knows little or nothing about this cultural form.

Different "dance" forms within a culture may communicate different information to different audiences. In Japan, for example, *mikagura*, a movement activity performed by specific individuals for the gods in Shinto shrines, communicates primarily to gods, priests, and believers that the proper ritual is being carried out. The movement product is an elegant, basically bilaterally symmetrical form. The movement form known as *buyo*, performed within or separate from a Kabuki DRAMA, communicates to a knowledgeable audience a story or part of one as a dramatic incident with moral, social, or religious implications. The movements are often diagonally focused and asymmetrical, recalling the AESTHETICS of flower arranging and the "floating world" of another time and place through sumptuous costumes and elaborate staging. The movement activity that accompanies the O bon festival known as *bon odori* comprises dances of participation performed to honor the dead. In a circular pattern around a structure that usually holds the musicians, the movements are

Figure 2. *(Dance)* Masked dancers (Aruava), Kayapo, Central Brazil. Joan Bamberger/Anthro-Photo.

choreographed in a simple way so that everyone may join in. Primarily a social/religious activity, performing *bon odori* helps one remember the dead in a less emotional context and in addition communicates to oneself as well as to others that one is Japanese or is appreciative of Japanese culture. *Mikagura, buyo,* and *bon odori* use quite different movements, in different contexts, and with different intent. What these movement sequences communicate and to whom is also vastly different both in Japan and elsewhere, such as in Hawaii, where numerous O bon festivals are held throughout the summer.

Structure and Meaning

In order to communicate, dance must be grammatical. Dance GRAMMAR, like the grammar of any lan-

Figure 3. *(Dance)* British Morris dancing. Copyright British Tourist Authority.

guage, includes both structure and meaning, and one must learn the movements and syntax. From a cross-cultural perspective several types of movement can be identified. Movement may communicate mimetically. Australian Aborigines use mimetic movements of kangaroos, snakes, and other animals as part of rituals dealing with the conservation and fertility of their land, as well as its human and nonhuman inhabitants. Dance may communicate through RE-ALISM and drama. The many forms of the Indian Ramayana usually tell a segment of the story through realistic and dramatic means in which the storytellers are actors who use movements of their whole bodies

to illustrate specific incidents. Communication will have taken place if the spectator knows where the incident fits into the Ramayana epic as a whole and understands its portrayal.

Dance also may communicate in a more abstract way akin to poetry. In Polynesia, for example, although it is said that "the hands tell the story," if one does not know the abstract conventions that the hands and arms are projecting as movement, the story cannot be understood. And even if one understands the movement conventions in one Polynesian society, it does not follow that one will understand the movement conventions in other Polynesian societies. In Hawaiian dance, for example, a flower may be suggested by shaping the hands to look like a flower, essentially illustrating the flower as a noun. In Tonga a flower may be suggested by moving the hands around each other, alluding to the agitation of air that carries the smell of flowers. In both dances the movements enhance the text they accompany, which in some way makes reference to flowers. In both cases, however, the referent is probably a chief who is referred to metaphorically as a flower. The movement is an abstraction of the essence of a flower (in Hawaii the way a flower looks, in Tonga the way a flower smells), which is a METAPHOR for a high-status person.

A further abstraction includes movements that never had and never were meant to have referential meaning. This probably includes most movements in any dance tradition. Thus, relating movement to communication theory, dance movements may be signs or symbols in any combination that convey various kinds of information in many contexts. The observers—participants, human audience, or gods—must know or look for a familiar pattern of structure or patterned sets (i.e., not isolated movements) in order to decode the message.

Figure 4. *(Dance)* Traditional Chinese "ribbon dance." Courtesy of the Information and Communication Division in New York, Coordination Council for North American Affairs.

In addition to MIME, dramatic realism, or abstraction, movement may communicate as a kind of decorative cultural ARTIFACT conveying the primary message that these movements belong to a specific culture or subculture or that a specific GENRE of movement is being activated for a particular purpose. Such movements may be participatory, movements to empathize with, or movements to admire as art or work. Such movements may have been given by the gods or ancestors and retained and perpetuated as cultural artifacts and aesthetic performances. These movements are important, even if their meanings have been changed or forgotten, as reference points for ethnic or cultural identity that nurtures itself through forms of cultural expression.

In order to understand movement as a cultural artifact the performer and observer must have communicative competence in the medium, socially as well as cognitively constituted. This is acquired in much the same way as competence in a language. Only after one has competence in this enlarged sense is it possible to improvise in a culturally appropriate manner. The movement and choreographic dimensions often are only components in a larger social activity that must be understood as a whole in order to understand what or how dance communicates in a particular instance.

Dance movement, syntax, and meaning are learned by watching and participating, the knowledge passing from teacher to student in a more or less formal manner. The teacher communicates to the student not only the movement tradition, choreography, style, and context but also information about the culture in which the movement tradition is embedded, such as male and female roles in movement (see GENDER), social status, and social structure. Learning about dancing varies from watching at a distance to some Balinese styles in which the teacher actually moves the student's body and limbs.

Theories of Dance

We understand the meaning of what is being communicated if we understand the rules or grammar of a cultural form. It remains, then, to discuss what dance grammar is and how the moving body is a mechanism by which meaning is produced; how dance communicates as syntax, SEMANTICS, and pragmatics.

Adapting linguistic analogies to the study of dance, some scholars have used the emic/etic distinction to derive emic units or kinemes by observing movement behavior and questioning which etic behaviors are cognitively grouped or separated into emes (that is, are they the same or different—do they contrast). They then derive the movement system by observing and questioning how the emic units are structured into morphokines and motifs and what the relationships are between them. With this syntactic knowledge—which dancers of a specific tradition and those

Figure 5. *(Dance)* Grand battement jeté. From Lincoln Kirstein and Muriel Stuart, *The Classic Ballet: Basic Technique and Terminology*, New York: Alfred A. Knopf, 1952, plate 10.

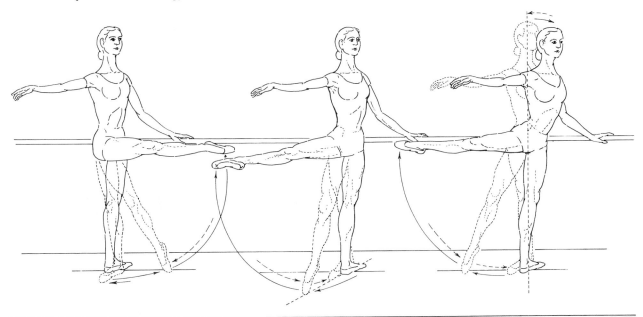

with competence in it already know "intuitively"—an observer or participant will be able to tell whether movement sequences are grammatical. In Western ballet, for example, a dance (pas de deux, etc.) can convey meaning as "pure dance," that is, through its form and structure; it can also convey emotion, such as a male-female pas de deux as part of *Swan Lake.* In other dance traditions such as Indian Bharata Natyam, the smallest hand gesture of the *hasta mudra* system may convey specific narrative meaning.

Other theories using linguistic analogies are concerned primarily with the semantics of body languages and focus on meaning as "linguistically tied, mathematically structured and empirically based" human actions. In this system one or more kinemes make up a kineseme, which is analogous to a word or lexeme. Kinesemes are independent units of movement that involve the whole body, include the element of time, and convey meaning.

Both of these systems emphasize that communication involves both structure and meaning—syntax and semantics—tied to specific cultural traditions. Pragmatically dance (or the movement dimension of activities) conveys or communicates information as a symbolic medium that is quite different from language and thereby is a significant part of uniquely human social and cultural systems. Dance as a symbolic system that operates through conventionalization creates meanings that can be undone or revised with relative ease and thereby can respond to changing contexts or circumstances. As biologically undetermined, arbitrary forms, dances convey conventionalized information only to those who understand the cultural and social constructs of which they are a part. Personal, social, and cultural, dance communicates as form and feeling in context.

See also ACTING; BODY MOVEMENT NOTATION; CHOREOMETRICS.

Bibliography. Jack Anderson, *Dance,* New York, 1974; Judith Lynne Hanna, *To Dance Is Human: A Theory of Nonverbal Communication,* Austin, Tex., 1979; Adrienne L. Kaeppler, "Structured Movement Systems in Tonga," in *Society and the Dance: The Social Anthropology of Process and Performance,* ed. by Paul Spencer, Cambridge and New York, 1985; Joann W. Kealiinohomoku, "A Comparative Study of Dance as a Constellation of Motor Behaviors among African and United States Negroes," *CORD Dance Research Annual* 7 (Dance Research Monograph No. 2), ed. by Adrienne L. Kaeppler, New York, 1976; Mary M. Smyth, "Kinesthetic Communication in Dance," *Dance Research Journal* 16 (1984): 19–22; Drid Williams, "Introduction to Special Issue on Semasiology," *Journal for the Anthropological Study of Human Movement* 1 (1981): 207–225.

ADRIENNE L. KAEPPLER

Figure 1. *(Darwin, Charles)* Julia Margaret Cameron, *Portrait of Charles Darwin,* 1868–1869. Photograph, albumen print. National Portrait Gallery, London.

DARWIN, CHARLES (1809–1882)

English naturalist whose writings—especially *The Origin of Species, The Descent of Man,* and *The Expression of the Emotions in Man and Animals*—profoundly altered humanity's view of itself and its institutions and relationships, including ways of communicating. In particular, his observations on animal signaling and human facial expressions and gestures sparked an interest in the study of NONVERBAL COMMUNICATION.

Charles Robert Darwin was born and raised in Shrewsbury, England. He studied medicine at Edinburgh and then theology at Cambridge. But his major preoccupation was natural history, and this led to his being appointed ship's naturalist on what he later wrote of as "The Voyage of the *Beagle.*" During this five-year expedition, Darwin made observations that caused him to question the immutability of species.

In South America and the Galápagos Islands, Darwin found, for example, a correlation between species affinity and geographical proximity and a similarity between extinct and extant forms from the same localities that seemed to him to be inconsistent with the creation doctrine. Back in England he became persuaded by his evidence that evolution had occurred. He then read, in 1838, Thomas Malthus's *An Essay on the Principle of Population*, which argued that since food production cannot keep up with human population growth, people are forced into a struggle for existence. Darwin saw that the same principle applied in nature but also that individual variation must bias the chances of success. Individuals whose characteristics best suit them to the circumstances will live longer and leave more progeny than their competitors; assuming such characteristics to be hereditary, the representation of the most fit in the population will increase as generation follows generation. This process of "natural selection" gave evolution the transforming agency that Darwin needed to parallel that of artificial selection in the production of domestic strains of plants and animals.

Darwin wrote preliminary drafts of his theory but shrank from the prospect of publication. Then, in 1858, he received from Alfred Russel Wallace a statement of a theory essentially like his own, which put his priority in jeopardy. To solve the problem, Darwin's and Wallace's versions were made public together. They caused little stir. The following year (1859) Darwin published *The Origin of Species*. Reaction was immediate, sensational, and divided. The work represented a challenge to basic principles of biology and to many Western assumptions about humankind.

Darwin continued to work on biological problems for the rest of his life. *The Origin of Species*, in addition to its theory of evolution, provided a framework for consideration of aspects of communication, such as how signaling evolves. However, its chapter on instinct can be viewed as a mixed blessing. While it demonstrated that there is evidence for behavioral evolution comparable to that for the evolution of structure, it used the term *instinct* in several different senses and fostered confusions that have confounded much subsequent discussion, such as that of heredity versus experience in behavioral development.

The Descent of Man is important mainly for its theory of sexual selection, an attempt to account for instances of differences between the sexes that seemed maladaptive, such as bright coloration in males of many fish and bird species that increases their conspicuousness to predators, and courtship displays that take time and energy away from supposedly more pressing activities like foraging. According to Darwin, the selective pressures in such cases are competition among members of the same sex for access to resources necessary for breeding—for example, territory; or mate choice, in which sexual advertisement affects an individual's chances of being picked as a breeding partner. Signals have been elaborated for use in both intrasexual and intersexual

Figure 2. *(Darwin, Charles)* Caricature of Darwin, from the *London Sketch Book*, 1870s. The Bettmann Archive/BBC Hulton.

competition in ways that ETHOLOGY and sociobiology continue to elucidate. *See also* ANIMAL SIGNALS.

In *The Expression of the Emotions in Man and Animals*, Darwin anticipated ethology in showing how signals can evolve from behavior serving other functions and be interpreted in motivational terms. His observations on human facial expressions, postures, and gestures also pioneered the study of nonverbal communication and KINESICS.

See also ANIMAL COMMUNICATION; BODY MOVEMENT; FACIAL EXPRESSION; GESTURE.

Bibliography. Gavin de Beer, *Charles Darwin: Evolution by Natural Selection*, Garden City, N.Y., 1964; Michael T. Ghiselin, *The Triumph of the Darwinian Method*, Berkeley, Calif., 1969; Howard Gruber, *Darwin on Man: A Psychological Study of Scientific Creativity*, 2d ed., Chicago, 1981.

COLIN G. BEER

DATA BASE

An ordered collection of information in computer-readable form. Data bases vary by type, subject matter, and content and may be word-oriented or number-oriented. There are data bases covering virtually all types of information, ranging from such major subject areas as chemistry, finance, law, physics, and medicine to more specialized topics such as automobile recalls and solid-waste disposal. Some contain complete information including textual material and are sometimes called source data bases; others contain pointers to information or data and may be called reference data bases.

Development. The earliest data bases were created in the 1950s, when computers first came into prominent use, to take advantage of their capacity for storing and searching large amounts of data. The data-base industry grew continuously in the following decades. The number of data bases available to the public grew to about three hundred by the mid-1970s and to more than thirty-five hundred by the late 1980s. *See* COMPUTER: HISTORY; COMPUTER: IMPACT.

The first generation of data bases was funded mainly by the U.S. government and included those of the National Aeronautics and Space Administration (NASA) and the Atomic Energy Commission (AEC); these were mission-oriented and contained bibliographic information and references to published literature, mainly government reports. In the 1960s several professional societies and other not-for-profit enterprises like the American Institute of Physics and Engineering Index (later Engineering Information, Inc.) and the Chemical Abstract Service of the American Chemical Society created their own data bases; these were largely subject-oriented and contained bibliographic information. Some began as experiments supported by government funding. The originators of these data bases were quick to adopt techniques that were facilitating the computerization of the printing industry, recognizing that the magnetic tapes used as part of the photocomposition process could also be used for information storage and retrieval. It was not long before data bases began to be designed with search and retrieval as primary objectives, not merely as secondary benefits. Most of the not-for-profit data bases became available to the public, but in the 1960s data bases especially designed for public use were started by a number of commercial organizations.

By the late 1970s the majority of publicly available data bases stemmed from the private sector, even though in many cases the basic information came from government sources; government data were often repackaged, embellished, and sold by private-sector entrepreneurs. Significant among them were data bases that were also known as data banks, containing numeric data, especially business and economic information essential to the business world; and data bases in the legal field, providing full texts of cases and statutes. The 1980s saw further important developments in full-text data bases as a number of encyclopedias, journals, and major reference works were put on-line for public use. By this time data bases were in operation in a number of countries, and the industry had an increasingly international aspect. *See* ENCYCLOPEDIA; LANGUAGE REFERENCE BOOK.

Availability and use. Both public- and private-sector organizations charge for the use of their data bases and search services. Government data bases generally focus on defense, social services, and biomedicine; commercial data bases lean toward business and economic information.

A number of developments and innovations have made data bases increasingly accessible and "user-friendly." In the 1950s and 1960s data-base use was primarily through so-called batch systems. These permitted multiple users to submit their queries to a central location so that all the queries could be matched against a data base at one time, after which the results were printed out and distributed. In the 1960s interactive on-line systems, providing nearly instantaneous response to user queries, were introduced in the United States. An example was the ELHILL system developed for the National Library of Medicine. A number of on-line search services such as DIALOG of Lockheed, ORBIT of System Development Corporation, and LEXIS of Mead Data Central came into general use, later joined by Bibliographic Retrieval Services, Inc., Westlaw, and others. These systems used a mainframe at a central location with network access from virtually any location in the world. Users needed a terminal or microcomputer and a modem at their local site to connect first to the communications network and then to the host computer.

Outlook. Because a great diversity of on-line systems had come into being, each with its own distinct command language and system of responses and procedures, a movement developed in the 1970s and 1980s to create a system of common command languages and gateways so that users would be able to consult numerous data bases without learning a separate language for each. The problem was seen as a major challenge but one that would remove what might become an obstacle to maximum growth. The development of increasingly sophisticated equipment, including terminals with some memory and processing capacity (called intelligent terminals), and the fast adoption and spread of personal computers led to the belief that more individuals would do their own searching if the search systems were easy enough to use.

See also ARCHIVES; LIBRARY.

Bibliography. *Annual Review of Information Sciences and Technology* (published for the American Society for Information Science, Washington, D.C.), 1966–; Cuadra Associates, *Directory of Online Databases*, Santa Monica, Calif., 1979–; *Database*, Weston, Conn., 1978–; *Electronic Publishing Review*, Oxford and Marlton, N.J., 1981–; Carol Fenichel and Thomas H. Hogan, *Online Searching: A Primer*, 2d ed., Medford, N.J., 1984; Donald T. Hawkins, *On-line Information Retrieval Bibliography, 1964–1979*, Oxford and Marlton, N.J., 1980 (supplements appear in the April issues of *Online Review*, 1977–); *International Online Meeting, Proceedings*, Oxford and New York, 1977–; *Journal of the American Society for Information Science*, New York, 1974–; *National Online Meeting, Proceedings*, Medford, N.J., 1981–; *Online*, Weston, Conn., 1977–; *Online Review*, Oxford and New York, 1977–; Martha E. Williams, Laurence Lannom, and Carolyn G. Robins, eds., *Computer-Readable Data Bases: A Directory and Data Sourcebook*, 2 vols., Chicago and Amsterdam, 1985.

MARTHA E. WILLIAMS

DAY, BENJAMIN H. (1810–1889)

U.S. journalist and publisher, called "the father of the penny press." At age twenty-three, working alone as a job printer, Benjamin Henry Day launched the New York *Sun*, priced at one cent per copy although other dailies generally sold for six cents or more. The idea had been tried before in Philadelphia, Boston, and New York but had failed. Succeeding this time, it set off an explosion of journalistic enterprise that revolutionized the U.S. press, brought new thousands into the newspaper-reading population, attracted rising volumes of ADVERTISING, and shifted much of newspaper publishing costs from reader to advertiser—with long-range social and economic implications.

Day had learned PRINTING as apprentice to a Springfield, Massachusetts, printer and publisher. A seasoned craftsman at twenty, he left for New York, and after working as a compositor for several New York newspapers, he used his savings to set up a small printing shop. A cholera epidemic and bank

Figure 1. *(Day, Benjamin H.)* Newsboy selling papers. Woodcut, ca. 1869. The Bettmann Archive, Inc.

failures drove him close to bankruptcy but brought the turning point that made his career. To keep his idle press busy he started a four-page newspaper, the *Sun*, which made its first appearance on September 3, 1833. He did everything himself except hawk his paper in the streets, which was done for the first time by newsboys (Figure 1). They bought their copies from Day for resale; Day charged them sixty-seven cents per hundred copies if they paid cash, seventy-five cents if they purchased them on a credit basis. Thus Day set in motion a new occupation that would become a part of big-city folklore.

The newsboys had quick success. In six months the *Sun* had a circulation of eight thousand—a response to jaunty content as well as street promotion. Flippantly reported police-court items—domestic quarrels, robberies, brouhahas involving drunkards—became the *Sun*'s feature attractions. When an out-of-work printer, George W. Wisner, joined Day to provide these items, at four dollars a week, he was the *Sun*'s only reporter. The style was strongly assailed (but also emulated) by other newspapers. In 1835 writer Richard Adams Locke replaced Wisner and fashioned a series of reports that became known as the Moon Hoax. This story so excited the public that the *Sun*'s circulation soared, reaching a level claimed as the world's highest. Locke, who received twelve dollars a week, offered a straight-faced account of astonishing astronomical discoveries made through an immense telescope built in South Africa by a British astronomer. In a series that went on for days Locke described life on the moon, including a "glimpse of a strange amphibious creature of a spherical form, which rolled with great velocity across the pebbly beach." The story was soon exposed as a fake, but this in no way dimmed the popularity of the *Sun*. Its circulation grew to thirty thousand, its pages increased in number and size, and advertising occupied three-quarters of the space. Its success paved the way for other penny papers. Some, like JAMES GORDON BENNETT's *New York Herald* (1835), combined elements of Day's style with journalism of broader scope. HORACE GREELEY's *New York Tribune* (1841) likewise supplied a more solid leadership.

The rise of the penny press did much to change and expand the readership of U.S. newspapers. In earlier periods newspapers had been read mainly by a propertied elite and sold by subscription rather than on city streets. The penny press attracted new segments of the population, including such groups as artisans and mechanics.

Day sold the *Sun* in 1837 and later published *Brother Jonathan*, a story paper considered one of the forerunners of the paperback BOOK. He lived to see the *Sun* rise to new prominence after the Civil War under Charles Anderson Dana's editorship. Day's son Benjamin invented the engraving process known as benday.

See also NEWSPAPER: HISTORY; PUBLISHING—HISTORY OF PUBLISHING.

JOHN TEBBEL

DE FOREST, LEE (1873–1961)

U.S. inventor and broadcasting pioneer. Son of a minister, Lee De Forest was expected to follow him into religious work but veered instead toward science, finding his own life mission in the advent of wireless. At the Sheffield Scientific School of Yale University he earned a Ph.D. in wireless TELEGRAPHY, then plunged into constant research. GUGLIELMO MARCONI had given the world wireless transmission of dots and dashes; De Forest made the wireless transmission of SOUND—voice and music—his special concern. In 1906, building on the work of John Ambrose Fleming of England and the Canadian-born REGINALD FESSENDEN, De Forest reached a dramatic new level of clarity with his triode vacuum tube, the Audion. It ultimately became the basis for the electronics industry and, more immediately, stirred excitement over what some were calling the wireless telephone, although others called it RADIO. De Forest became known as the "father of radio." He formed the De Forest Radio Telephone Company and began to make and sell his Audion tubes (for detection and amplification of radio waves) and other radio components to experimenters of all sorts—military, academic, and amateur.

The U.S. Navy, the most important early backer of radio, looked on it as a means for point-to-point (ship-to-ship, ship-to-shore) communication. De Forest preached a different message: broadcasting. He felt that there should be stations continually sending music and information to whoever might listen, and he demonstrated the idea with constant transmissions—from the Eiffel Tower in Paris, from the Metropolitan Opera stage in New York, and from his New York laboratory. In 1907 De Forest, in a prose style that seemed to echo his evangelical upbringing, wrote in his diary:

My present task (happy one) is to distribute sweet melody broadcast over the city and sea so that in time even the mariner far out across the silent waves may hear the music of his homeland.

This seemed to most people a quixotic notion. How could it be made to pay? Not until the 1920s was this question answered in ways that set off the broadcasting boom of that decade (*see* SPONSOR).

De Forest made a number of sales to the U.S. Navy, but such sales were seldom profitable, and he was constantly in financial difficulties. For a time he became associated with a promoter, Abraham White, who persuaded him to stage dramatic demonstrations at fairs and amusement parks for the sale of stock. Providing De Forest with sufficient funds to keep the research going, White himself quickly grew rich—until he went to jail for stock fraud. The messy affair cast a cloud over De Forest's company. During 1913–1915, in dire financial distress, he sold most of his patent rights (in tubes, circuits, and other components) to AT&T for what many considered a pittance. But it saved De Forest from bankruptcy and enabled him to keep his research laboratory going. For AT&T the Audion, used as a line amplifier, proved invaluable in the company's efforts to extend its long-distance operation into a coast-to-coast service, which it achieved in time for the 1915 San Francisco World's Fair.

With the start of World War I lone experimenters like De Forest were ruled off the air, and radio became an activity reserved for the military, which placed huge electronic equipment orders with Western Electric (an AT&T subsidiary), General Electric, and Westinghouse. Serving numerous war needs, this production also created the infrastructure that made possible the postwar broadcasting boom. De Forest had meanwhile moved toward a new challenge: talking pictures. By 1922 he was ready to demonstrate his "phonofilm" process and began producing two-reel sound films featuring musicians, popular entertainers, and public figures like President Calvin Coolidge and playwright George Bernard Shaw. The films were well received at several dozen test theaters, but HOLLYWOOD, enjoying boom times with silent films, had no wish to take a plunge into sound. When the sound transition finally came in 1927–1929 (*see* MOTION PICTURES—SOUND FILM) the system adopted

Figure 1. *(De Forest, Lee)* Lee De Forest in his laboratory, 1907. State Historical Society of Wisconsin, Erik Barnouw Collection/Smithsonian Institution, Washington, D.C.

was similar to De Forest's. *See* SOUND RECORDING—HISTORY.

In 1950 De Forest published an autobiography titled *Father of Radio*. But he had become deeply distressed by radio's commercial trends in the United States. Addressing a protest to the 1946 meeting of the National Association of Broadcasters (NAB), he asked:

What have you gentlemen done with my child? . . . You have made of him a laughing stock to intelligence, surely a stench in the nostrils of the gods of the ionosphere; you have cut time into tiny segments called spots (more rightly stains) wherewith the occasional fine program is periodically smeared with impudent insistence to buy and try.

De Forest, always a solitary figure, had become a stranger in a media world he had done much to create.

Bibliography. Lee De Forest, *Father of Radio: The Autobiography of Lee De Forest*, Chicago, 1950.

HARTLEY S. SPATT

DEBATE. *See* FORENSICS; POLITICAL COMMUNICATION—BROADCAST DEBATES.

DECEPTION

Any action or series of actions intended to manipulate an appearance so that the manipulator—whether individual, group, class, or state—can control what the audience takes to be immutable, real, or truthful. As Alexander Klein says, "Every deception, every imposture is an assumption of power; the person deceived is reduced in stature, symbolically nullified, while the imposter is temporarily powerful. . . ."

Uses and Users

Deception has long been the staple of spies, subversives, and saboteurs and is traditionally associated with hoaxers, tricksters, cheaters, swindlers, and a variety of other double-dealers, but it is in fact used by almost everyone. Its use may be motivated by a desire for money, power, status, prestige, protection, or fun. Deception to conceal nefarious money-making or to perpetrate some subterfuge is paralleled by its use to counter crime and treachery, where it may range from unmarked police cars to covert businesses and "sting" operations. No less deceptive are the masquerades of investigative journalists or the false or exaggerated claims of advertisers and manufacturers (*see* ADVERTISING; CHILDREN—MEDIA EFFECTS; COMMERCIALS).

More generally, individuals may mislead hostile questioners to preserve their self-identities from moral attack, social stigma, or the exposure of some physical flaw (such as the loss of limbs, teeth, or hair). Governments may protect citizens by lying to an enemy about their defensive capabilities. Also in the interests of protection, parents misinform children, professionals conceal information about clients, and medics deceive the seriously ill about their conditions. Medical experimenters use placebos, and the purpose of many psychological investigations is deliberately misrepresented to the subjects. From Venus's-flytrap, stick insects, and the opossum's faking dead (*see* ANIMAL COMMUNICATION; ANIMAL SIGNALS) to the tales of liars' clubs and ruling-class IDEOLOGY, deceptive communication is a pervasive feature of life.

Approaches

Deception has been studied by scholars from disciplines with different orientations to the topic. Anthropologists are interested in cultural variations in deception, whereas psychologists study the minutiae of verbal and nonverbal modes of communication (*see* NONVERBAL COMMUNICATION). Microsociologists document the different strategies and motives for bringing off deceptive performances; macrosociologists are interested in the functions and disfunctions of deception for maintaining or changing the social structure and deception's ideological role in institutional and class power. Finally, philosophers consider the principles for evaluating whether and on what occasions deceptive communication is ethically justified.

Definitions and Kinds of Deception

Some agreement exists that there are two primary forms of deception. Passive deception—concealment or secrecy—is the omission of information in order to communicate a partial or misleading impression. Active deception—falsification or lying—is the presentation of false information with some claim that it is true. U.S. psychologist Paul Ekman restricts the use of these two types to occasions when "one person intends to mislead another, doing so deliberately, without prior notification of this purpose and without having been explicitly asked to do so by the target." But this limitation excludes occasions in which control over the decision to deceive is lost, as in pathological lying or self-deception—the paradoxical situation in which a manipulator is taken in by his or her own PERFORMANCE, forfeiting control to the appearance. It also excludes occasions in which people knowingly accept deception and, in ERVING GOFFMAN's terms, conspire to "save the show."

For Goffman, deception encompasses all face-to-face encounters in which performers "engage in concealed practices which are incompatible with fostered impressions." He documents the strategies used in everyday interaction for managing impressions of the self as a performed character or dramatic effect. But Goffman's micro focus does not consider the knowing or unknowing acceptance of deception as a result of power differences between the manipulator and the audience. An ideologically sensitive definition of deception such as that of Jürgen Habermas discusses systematically distorted communication or pseudo-communication that "produces a system of misunderstandings which, due to the false assumption of consensus, are not recognized as such." Habermas considers that the knowledge produced within an economically rational society permeates all interaction and thereby suppresses the communicative prerequisites for self-reflective consciousness.

Strategies

Active or passive deception involves manipulating up to five modes of communication: (1) LANGUAGE, oral or written, (2) images or pictures, (3) FACIAL EXPRESSION, (4) body language (see BODY MOVEMENT; KINESICS; PROXEMICS), and (5) dress or outward appearance (see CLOTHING). Goffman uses the theatrical METAPHOR to explain how individuals perform "routines" designed to maximize impressions

of the self. He identifies a "front region," which defines the situation for an audience in terms of a "setting"—such as a doctor's office—and a "personal front." The latter conveys a performer's social statuses, whereas the "manner" in which the performer appears is the cue for the oncoming role performance. During the routine "a performer tends to conceal or underplay those activities, facts and motives which are incompatible with an idealized version of himself and his products." Performers can also distance themselves from a structured role in order to leave the audience with the impression that the performer is something other than that which is being performed. In addition, a different impression of the self is conveyed "backstage," when, for example, the performer is with a team of cooperating coconspirators (such as a doctor with other doctors). Goffman says performers also provide ways to help the audience preserve the false impression created.

Language and accounts as deceptive strategies. Ekman argues that language as a communicative medium is more practiced than the other modes because people are held more accountable for their words than for their facial expressions or body movements. Concealing and falsifying what is said can be practiced in advance through thought experiments, and words can be monitored as they are spoken, managing the effects in the light of responses. In giving accounts people may use language as rationalization to protect themselves against recriminations for past acts. Such "remedial work," says Goffman, functions "to alter the meaning that otherwise might be given to an act, transforming what could be seen as offensive into what could be seen as acceptable."

Individuals who engage in questionable conduct protect themselves through "normalization" or "deviancy disavowal," in which their present identity is claimed to be different from the one that committed the act in question. Child molesters, for example, excuse their behavior by saying they were drunk at the time and not able to control their sexual urges. U.S. sociologist David Matza identifies five such excuses and justifications, which he calls "techniques of neutralization." These either deny responsibility for the act, deny it caused injury, deny the right or existence of the victim, condemn those questioning, or appeal to higher loyalties as influences, such as best friends or God.

When the possibility of using defensive accounts successfully is considered before committing an act, it can allow the act to be committed. An embezzler's internal CONVERSATION about "borrowing" and "paying back" bridges any moral inhibition against trust violation, permitting the embezzlement. If neutralizing moral inhibition occurs through the unwitting duplication, distortion, and extension of customary beliefs, such as the right of self-defense, and if this occurs before the act is even contemplated, the perpetrator is sent on a "moral holiday" and deceives unintentionally.

Ideology as a deceptive strategy. Ideology as deception can range from selective and presentational bias in news media reports that systematically distort events in favor of class interests to the molding of sexist and racist attitudes during socialization (*see* MINORITIES IN THE MEDIA; SEXISM). Some Marxists call deceptive ideology "false consciousness" and examine the production and legitimating role of images, such as the view that capitalism in the United States has produced a classless society, that differential incomes are needed to attract top people to top jobs, and that through social mobility anyone can make it to the top. They are concerned with the ways these images mystify and mask the inherent class, sexual, and ethnic divisions that otherwise would result in conflict and radical social change. MICHEL FOUCAULT examines how what becomes accepted as knowledge is managed as truth and is used to exercise power and control. *See also* FEMINIST THEORIES OF COMMUNICATION; GENDER; MARXIST THEORIES OF COMMUNICATION.

Detecting and Controlling Deception

Catching deceivers has been a major preoccupation of psychologists and crime controllers such as employers, police, and counterintelligence agents. The three principal ways to reveal deception are by systematic questioning, objective measurement, and reading behavioral clues.

Systematic questioning is used to control subjects' responses to questions and to eliminate biased answers. A "lie scale" that includes both relevant and irrelevant questions and a "guilty knowledge test" involving questions referring to past misdeeds are incorporated into surveys. It is assumed that the innocent are able to answer relevant questions truthfully but are disturbed by control questions, whereas the guilty react most strongly to relevant questions, being unperturbed by control questions.

An arguably more objective method of detection is to measure changes in the body's autonomic responses, which are generated involuntarily by emotion. To do this a lie detector, or polygraph, is used, which simultaneously traces changes in pulse, respiration, blood flow, blood pressure, brain waves, and the electrical resistance of the skin (Galvanic Skin Response). A voice stress analyzer can also measure warble. These devices have come under much criticism because scientific studies reveal that polygraphs are only about 80 percent accurate.

Reading behavioral clues rests on the idea that emotions produced during deception are more likely to be revealed through facial expressions and body language than through the analysis of written language. These emotions are harder to control, conceal, or falsify.

Such devices are of little use in exposing more macrolevel ideological deception. For this the concept of *critique* is used. It involves revealing inconsistencies between what is claimed to be and what is; subverting an existing ideology by substituting another that allegedly does not falsify reality; and, for Foucault, interrupting the smooth passage of "regimes of truth," disrupting forms of knowledge that have assumed a self-evident quality, and engendering uncertainty among those servicing the network of power-knowledge relations.

The Ethics of Deception

The German philosopher Immanuel Kant took the moral-absolutist view that general moral rules must be followed to avoid deception because deception compromises respect for rationality and the integrity of the deceived. Philosopher Sissela Bok, from a more Aristotelian perspective, believes that deception may be justified under special conditions, depending on whether it is of the active or passive kind. She says that any intentionally deceptive message is a prima facie wrong; undiscovered lies have a negative effect on the choices and autonomy of both the liar and those duped, and discovered lies taint the institutions of trust and cooperation. Lying requires justification and explanation, but the justifications generally given—such as avoiding harm, producing benefits, correcting injustices, and concern for ultimate truth—are unacceptable. For example, lying to an enemy may seem fair, but it is not always certain who the enemies are, and friends may also be taken in inadvertently. Stanley Milgram's psychological experiments on authority might be justified by the utility of learning that 60 percent of ordinary citizens will harm others if told to do so by an authority figure. But does this finding warrant the distress felt by the unknowing subjects who were recruited to assist in a scientific experiment and asked to administer electric shocks to apparent subjects who were actually actors faking pain? According to Bok a lie is justified only if (1) an alternative course of action will not resolve the difficulty, (2) the lie will accomplish a higher moral outcome, and (3) these considerations are subject to a public of reasonable people.

Passive deception may be more easily justified. Bok argues that secrecy that protects intimacy and PRIVACY is virtuous, whereas public secrecy allied with power, as in the professions or government, is wrong. Critics argue that deception can have positive effects and that ethical judgments do not consider the negative effects of truth.

The End of Deception

Deception of any audience ceases only when its members impose some view of reality on the appearance and no longer respond to further attempts at manipulation. Self-deception ends only when a person stops constructing and investing in images.

See also CRYPTOLOGY; ESPIONAGE.

Bibliography. Sissela Bok, *Lying: Moral Choice in Public and Private Life*, New York, 1978; idem, *Secrets: On the Ethics of Concealment and Revelation*, New York, 1982; Paul Ekman, *Telling Lies: Clues to Deceit in the Marketplace, Politics, and Marriage*, New York, 1985; Michel Foucault, *Power/Knowledge: Selected Interviews and Other Writings, 1972–1977* (in French), ed. and trans. by Colin Gordon, Brighton, Eng., and New York, 1980; Erving Goffman, *The Presentation of Self in Everyday Life*, New York, 1959, reprint Woodstock, N.Y., 1973; Jürgen Habermas, *Knowledge and Human Interests* (Erkenntnis und Interesse), trans. by Jeremy J. Shapiro, Boston, 1971; idem, *Legitimation Crisis* (Legitimationsprobleme im Spätkapitalismus), trans. by Thomas McCarthy, Boston, 1975; Alexander Klein, ed., *Grand Deception*, New York, 1955; Arnold M. Ludwig, *The Importance of Lying*, Springfield, Ill., 1965; David Matza, *Delinquency and Drift*, New York, 1964.

STUART HENRY

DECONSTRUCTION. *See* AUTHORSHIP.

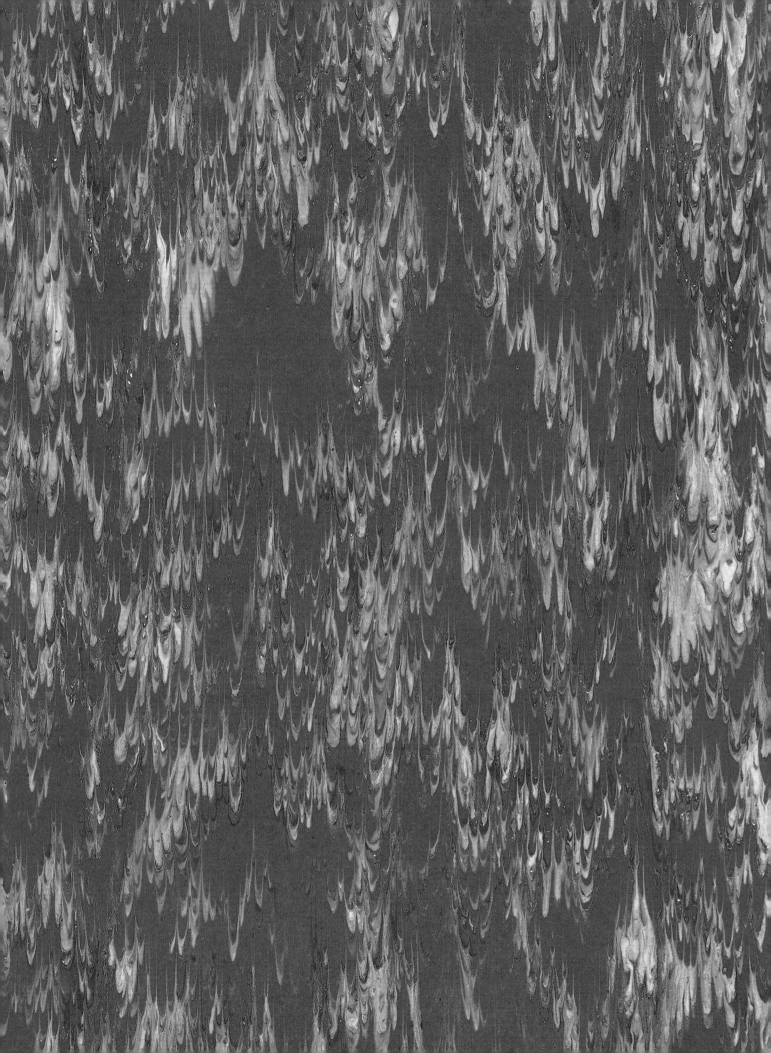